Readings in Planning Theory

Readings in Planning Theory

Third Edition

Edited by

Susan S. Fainstein and
Scott Campbell

A John Wiley & Sons, Ltd., Publication

Library of Congress Cataloging-in-Publication Data

Fainstein, Susan S.
    Readings in planning theory / edited by Susan S. Fainstein, Scott Campbell. – 3rd ed.
        p.   cm.
    Includes bibliographical references and index.
    ISBN 978-1-4443-3080-9 (pbk.)
1. City planning.   I. Fainstein, Susan S.   II. Campbell, Scott, 1958–   III. Title.
    HT165.5.R43 2011
    307.1'216–dc22

                                                                    2011014939

A catalogue record for this book is available from the British Library.

Set in 10.5/13pt Minion by SPi Publisher Services, Pondicherry, India
Printed and bound in Singapore by Ho Printing Singapore Pte Ltd

4   2013

Contents

Part III   Planning Types/Normative Frameworks   153

Part IV   Planning in Action: Successes, Failures, and Strategies   235

Part V   Social Justice: Race, Gender, Class   315

Introduction

The Structure and Debates of Planning Theory

Susan S. Fainstein and Scott Campbell

Planning theory is an elusive subject of study. It draws on a variety of disciplines and has no widely accepted canon. The purpose of this reader is twofold: (1) to define the boundaries of this area of inquiry and the works that constitute its central focus; and (2) to confront the principal issues that face planners as theorists and practitioners. It is organized by the questions that its editors raise, rather than by the chronological development of the field.

Compiling a reader in planning theory presents a dilemma. One can reprint the early postwar classics – thereby duplicating several other anthologies and providing little space for contemporary debates – or else risk over-representing transient contemporary ideas.[1] We have chosen a somewhat different path. Rather than trying to cover the whole field, whether historically or at the present moment, we have selected a set of readings – both "classic" and recent – that effectively address the pressing and enduring questions in planning theory.

We see the central question of planning theory as the following: *What role can planning play in developing the good city and region within the constraints of a capitalist political economy and varying political systems? A further question is whether planners should focus on the desired objects of their efforts – the city and region – or whether they should concern themselves primarily with the process by which planning decisions are made and assume that a good process will produce a good outcome.* In addressing these questions, we look for explanations and guides to planning practice based both on abstract reasoning and also on analyses of planning experiences in different parts of the world. Our effort is designed to determine the historical and contextual influences and strategic opportunities that shape the capacity of planners to affect the urban and regional environment.

Readings in Planning Theory, Third Edition. Edited by Susan S. Fainstein and Scott Campbell.
Editorial material and organization © 2012 Blackwell Publishing Ltd.
Published 2012 by Blackwell Publishing Ltd.

What Is Planning Theory?

It is not easy to define planning theory: the subject is slippery, and explanations are often frustratingly tautological or disappointingly pedestrian. There are four principal reasons for this difficulty. First, many of the fundamental questions concerning planning belong to a much broader inquiry concerning the roles of the state, the market, and civil society in social and spatial transformation. Consequently, planning theory appears to overlap with theory in all the social science disciplines, and it becomes hard to limit its scope or to stake out a turf specific to planning.

Second, the boundary between planners and related professionals (such as real estate developers, architects, city council members) is not sharp: planners do not just plan, and non-planners also plan. Failure to distinguish adequately the specific influence of planning from the broader effects of urbanization makes it hard to recognize what is actually accomplished by planners. The most basic of questions too often remains unanswered: who exactly designs, builds, manages, and finally tears down cities? Ambitious, omnipotent planning theories often collide with the modest, constrained powers of actual planning practice.

Third, the field of planning is divided among those who define it according to its object (producing and regulating the relations of people and structures in space) and those who do so by its method (the process of decision making as it relates to spatial development). The result is two largely separate sets of theoretical questions and priorities that undermine a singular definition of planning. As noted above, whether to emphasize one or the other of these definitions is a problematic issue within planning theory and constitutes, as will be discussed later in this introduction, one of the principal debates in the field.

Finally, many fields (such as economics) are defined by a specific set of methodologies. Yet planning commonly borrows diverse methodologies from many different fields, and so its theoretical base cannot be easily defined by its tools of analysis. It is determined more by a shared interest in space and place, a commitment to civic community, and a pragmatic orientation toward professional practice. The theoretical and practical questions dealt with by planning theory reflect its somewhat ungainly straddling of both academic and professional concerns.

Taken together, these considerable disagreements over the scope and function of planning and the problems of distinguishing who is actually a planner make difficult the specification of an appropriate body of theory. Whereas most scholars can agree on what constitutes the economy and the polity – and thus what is economic or political theory – they differ as to the content of planning theory. The difficulty has increased as post-modernist theorizing has deconstructed earlier propositions regarding rationality, so that a simple definition of planning as identifying the most efficient means to reach agreed-upon ends no longer suffices.

Most planning practitioners largely disregard planning theory. In this respect, planning resembles other academic disciplines. Most politicians do not bother with political theory; business persons generally do not familiarize themselves with econometrics; and community organizers do not regularly concern themselves with social theory. Planning as a practical field of endeavor, however, differs from other activities in its claim to be able to predict the consequences of its actions. Planners need to generalize from prior experience if they are to practice their craft. In their day-to-day work, they may rely more on intuition than explicit theory; yet this intuition may in fact be assimilated theory. In this light, theory represents cumulative professional knowledge. Though many practicing planners may look upon the planning theory of their graduate education as inert and irrelevant – and see in their professional work a kind of homespun, in-the-trenches pragmatism – theory allows one to see the conditions of this "pragmatism." Just as John Maynard Keynes warned of being an unwitting slave to the ideas of a defunct economist, we believe that it is also possible to be a slave to the ideas of a defunct planning theorist.

Why Do Planning Theory?

One of our prime motives in selecting the readings for this book is to enable practitioners to achieve a deeper understanding of the processes in which they are engaged than can be attained through simple intuition and common sense. Although many in the field have decried the gap between theory and practice, we do not envision eliminating it completely. It is both unrealistic and inadvisable that planning practice and education become identical. We should no more expect practicing land use planners to implement the unadulterated arguments of the German philosopher Jürgen Habermas (who provides the conceptual foundations for communicative planning) in their jobs than expect graduate students to accept uncritically existing land use practice. True, if the gap is *too big*, then planning education is irrelevant, but if there is *no* gap, then planning education is redundant. The role of planning theory should be to generate a creative tension that is both critical and constructive and that provokes reflection on both sides. In other words, its role is to create both the reflective practitioner and the practical scholar. These two need not think alike, but they should at least be able to talk to each other.

We therefore believe that theory can inform practice. Planning theory is not just some idle chattering at the margins of the field. If done poorly, it discourages and stifles, but if done well, it defines the field and drives it forward. We have consequently identified a set of readings that address themselves to the questions that planners must ask if they are to be effective and to improve the urban condition, and we include case studies of planning in action with this purpose in mind.

Beyond this intention, we aim to establish a theoretical foundation that provides the field not only with a common structure for scientific inquiry but also with a means for defining what planning is – especially in the intimidating company of more established academic disciplines. Theory allows for both professional and intellectual self-reflection. It tries to make sense of the seemingly unrelated, contradictory aspects of urban development and to create a framework within which to compare and evaluate the merits of different planning ideas and strategies. It seeks the underlying conceptual elements that tie together the disparate planning areas, from housing and community development to transportation policy and urban design. Providing a common language is an important function of introductory theory and history courses for master's students, who gain a shared identity as planners with other students during their first year before veering into their sub-specialties in the second year. It can be both comforting and encouraging, when encountering the challenges of contemporary urban poverty, shortages of public space, the greed and shortsightedness of urban developers, the enormous informal settlements within the developing world, to know the ways in which earlier reform movements have addressed similar problems. We not only know that we have been here before, but we also remind ourselves that in many ways urban life *has* improved, and planners can take some credit for this.

As a result of this common language, planning theory becomes the arena where the field of planning reassesses itself. Though too often this reflection degenerates into self-doubt (such as "if planning is everything, perhaps it is nothing"), it is not an exaggeration to say that planning theory is the philosophical conscience of the discipline. This self-critical function of planning theory therefore cuts both ways: one can use it to both scrutinize the mistakes of the past and to propose normative principles to guide the profession in the future.

The language of planning theory also encourages planners to translate their specific issues into more general social-scientific theoretical language. It allows ideas and values from planning to find a broader audience, and it gives planning greater intellectual scope. As planning touches on so many other disciplines, it is useful for theorists to translate arguments drawn from other social sciences into their discussion. At the same time, planning's action orientation requires scholars to go beyond analyses of social, economic, and political structures to spell out their implications for policy. Public policy is the academic subject to which planning is most closely akin, but policy analysis does not have the concern with space and the built environment that is one of the defining characteristics of urban and regional planning. So, planning theory should borrow, but with caution and rigor, avoiding formulaic application of ideas intended for others contexts.

A well-developed theoretical foundation serves as a declaration of scholarly autonomy, often institutionalized in the form of a planning theory requirement for master's degree programs and professional certification in city planning. The growth of planning PhD programs goes hand in hand with the rise of planning theory. Such programs not only support research within planning departments; they also encourage the development of the discipline's theoretical foundations. PhD programs also use more abstract theory to distinguish and elevate themselves above master's programs and professional training.

Though theory helps planning assert its distinctiveness as an autonomous field, that field remains a diminutive newcomer surrounded by larger, more established disciplines. The result is that planning must define (and defend) itself by differentiating itself from its larger neighbors: if next to architecture, planning will emphasize the socio-economic city; in relation to geography, planning stresses the field's policy orientation; if adjacent to public policy, planners focus on space and local communities;

and in contrast to most economists, planners attend to issues of social justice. These institutional boundary lines become crucial when planning shifts its academic location, such as from a school of design to a school of public policy, business, or social welfare. This relational identity of planning shapes the debate regarding the "natural" institutional home of planning: should we go back to our architectural/land-use roots, push further ahead into social science, be subsumed into public policy, or strategically ally ourselves more closely with business and real estate? As a consequence of these issues, planning theory becomes an arbiter of the field's changing boundaries.

Our Approach to Planning Theory

Our approach in this book is to place planning theory at the intersection of political economy, history, and philosophy. We do not see it as mechanistically determined by its historical path or by structural forces. Those who interpret structural theory as implying that outcomes are preordained will inevitably fall victim to a sense of helplessness. Instead, we consider that the planners should use theory to view how the local and national political economy, in addition to the field's own history, influences the collective imagination of planning's possibilities, limitations, and professional identity. The challenge for this professional – and sometimes activist – discipline is to find the negotiating room within the larger social structure to pursue the good city.

We also place planning theory at a second intersection: that of the *city and region* as a phenomenon and *planning* as a human activity. Planning adapts to changes in the city and region, which in turn are transformed by planning and politics. This interaction is not a closed system. Planners not only plan places; they also negotiate, forecast, research, survey, and organize financing. Nor do planners have an exclusive influence over territories; developers, business groups, politicians, and other actors also shape urban and regional development. The result is that the discipline of planning is influenced by a wide variety of procedural and substantive ideas beyond its own disciplinary boundaries. Studies of planning refer to works in political science, public policy, philosophy, and sociology that examine how decisions are made and who benefits from them. Writings about cities and regions draw upon traditions primarily in urban history, urban sociology, anthropology, geography, and economics. Though not always consistently, we use the practical distinction of decision making regarding the built environment versus analysis of the character of cities and regions to distinguish *Readings in Planning Theory* from its companion volume, *Readings in Urban Theory* (Fainstein and Campbell 2011).

Debates Define Theory: Six Questions of Planning Theory

The teaching of planning theory requires that we should explicitly explore the roots and implications of long-standing disputes in the field. In fact, it is the conflict between approaches rather than a single outlook that permits characterization of the field. Planning, because it involves the distribution of benefits and the relations among social groups, is messy and contentious; theory provides the means to spell out and address differences over the methods and objects of planning and understand their deeper roots.

In this light, we view planning theory as a series of debates. Here are six questions at issue.

What are the historical roots of planning?

The first question of theory is one of identity, which in turn leads to history. The traditional story told of modern city planning is that it arose from several separate movements at the turn of the twentieth century: the Garden City, the City Beautiful, and public health reforms (Krueckeberg 1983; Hall 2002). Four basic eras characterized its history: (1) the formative years during which the pioneers (Ebenezer Howard, Patrick Geddes, Daniel Burnham, etc.) did not yet identify themselves as planners (late 1800s to *ca.* 1915); (2) the period of institutionalization, professionalization, and self-recognition of planning, together with the rise of regional and national planning efforts (*ca.* 1920–1945); (3) the postwar era of standardization, crisis, and diversification of planning (1945–1975); (4) the redefinition of planning in relation to the private sector, with emphasis on public–private partnerships and the planner as mediator, strategist, and advocate.

This story, often repeated in introductory courses and texts, is useful in several ways. The multiplicity of technical, social, and aesthetic origins explains planning's eclectic blend of design, civil engineering, local politics, community organization, and social justice. Its status as either a quasi- or secondary profession is explained by its development as a twentieth-century, public-sector, bureaucratic profession, rather than as a late-nineteenth-century, private-sector one like medicine (Hoffman 1989).

At the most basic level, this framework gives the story of planning (at least modern professional planning) a starting point. Planning emerges as the twentieth-century response to the nineteenth-century industrial city (Hall 2002). It also provides several foundational texts: Howard and Osborn's *Garden Cities of Tomorrow: A Peaceful Path to Real Reform* (1945 [1898]), Charles Robinson's *The Improvement of Towns and Cities; or the Practical Basis of Civic Aesthetics* (1901), and Daniel Burnham's plan for Chicago (Commercial Club of Chicago et al. 1909), as well as several defining events: Baron Georges-Eugène Haussmann's redevelopment of Paris during the 1850s and 1860s; the Columbia Exposition in Chicago (1893), which launched the City Beautiful Movement in the United States; the construction of Letchworth, the first English Garden City (1903); and the first national conference on city planning, held in Washington, DC in 1909.

Yet this tale of planning's birth is also problematic. As the years go by and the planning pioneers fade from memory, the story is simplified and unconditionally repeated. Contingent or coincidental events and texts are elevated to necessary steps in the inevitable progressive development of modern planning. Even the best of tellers can succumb to repeating this tale of the "great men of planning history." The result is an essentialistic life-cycle model of planning's birth, growth, maturation, mid-life crisis, and eventual accommodation – a model that largely excludes the political, economic, and cultural forces that continually transform planning in both ideology and practice and to which planning always stands in a dialectical relationship.

One path out of a simplistic view of planning history told as heroic stories of the great men is through a critical examination of the past. Richard Foglesong's *Planning the Capitalist City* (1986; an excerpt is Chapter 6), David Harvey's *Paris: Capital of Modernity* (2003), Robert Fishman's *Bourgeois Utopias: The Rise and Fall of Suburbia* (1987), and Robert Self's *American Babylon* (2003) are some of the better examples. The challenge is to write a planning history that encourages not only an accurate, but also a critical, subtle, and reflective understanding of contemporary planning practice and the forces acting upon it. An effective planning history helps the contemporary planner shape his or her complex professional identity.

What is the justification for planning? When should one intervene?

Planning is intervention with an intention to alter the existing course of events. The timing and legitimacy of planned intervention therefore become questions central to planning theory: Why and in what situations should planners intervene? Implicit here is an understanding of the alternative to planning by the public sector. Though it is most commonly assumed that the alternative is the free market, it could equally be chaos or domination by powerful private interests. Proponents of relying on the market regard planning as producing sub-optimal results and, at an extreme, consider that it is antithetical to freedom (Hayek 1944). Supporters of planning argue that it can replace the uncertainty and cruelties of the market with the logic of the plan and thereby produce a more rational arrangement of the environment. Whereas the collapse of Eastern European state socialism is frequently cited in support of the former view, the Great Depression seems to vindicate the latter.

The duality between planning and the market is a defining framework in planning theory, and is the leitmotiv of classic readings in the field (such as Mannheim 1949; Meyerson and Banfield 1964; Dahrendorf 1968; Galbraith 1971). Evaluations of planning reflect assumptions about the relationships between the private and public sectors – and how much the government should "intrude." The safe stance in planning has been to see its role as making up for the periodic shortcomings of the private market (Klosterman, 1985; Moore 1978). In this interpretation planning acts as the patient understudy, filling in when the market fails or even helping the market along (Frieden and Sagalyn 1989). Accordingly planning should never presume to replace the market permanently or change the script of economic efficiency. This way of legitimizing planning significantly limits creative or redistributive planning efforts, but it does make a scaled-down version of planning palatable to all but the most conservative economists.

Nevertheless, not everyone prefers the role of planning to be minimal. For some, the function of planning is to confront the private market directly and focus on remedying disadvantage (Krumholz and Forester 1990; Fainstein 2010). In this view privileging the market reinforces unjust outcomes, while empowering planning has the potential for enhancing equity. As framed in terms of state versus market, the debate assumes a neat and tidy division between the public and private worlds, each with its unique advantages. One can, however, challenge this dualism. Public and private sectors no longer, if they ever did, represent mutually exclusive sets of actors, interests, or planning tools. The rise of public–private partnerships in the wake of urban renewal efforts reflects this blurring of sectoral boundaries (Squires 1989). The growing number of planners working in the private sector further upsets the traditional professional role that planners play in the battles between public and private interests. Public-sector planners borrow tools developed in the private sector, such as strategic planning and place marketing (Levy 1990). The emergence of autonomous public authorities to manage marine ports, airports, and other infrastructures has created hybrid organizations that act like both a public agency and a private firm (Doig 1987; Walsh 1978). In addition, the growing non-profit or "third sector," embodied in community development corporations within the United States and housing associations in Europe, demonstrates the inadequacies of viewing the world in a purely dichotomous framework of the government versus the market (Rubin 2000; Harloe 1995).

Arguably more troublesome than this public–private blur, however, is critique that sees the appropriation of the public domain by the logic of privatization. Privatization of traditionally public services raises the question of whether the public sector can serve the public interest or whether democratic citizenship – and all its rights and responsibilities – is being reduced to consumerism and consumer freedom. This critique in one formulation regards the public sector as wholly captured by capitalist interests, engaging in activities imitative of ruthless corporations, and generally incapable of planning for the benefit of the mass of people (Harvey 1985, 1989). In more temperate presentations the outcome of the tug of war between capitalist and community interests is regarded as dependent on conflict, bargaining, and the mobilization of political resources, the results of which are not predetermined (Stone 1993; Purcell 2008; Clavel 2010).

"Rules of the game": What values are incorporated within planning? What ethical dilemmas do planners face?

This growing complexity and uncertainty in the planner's stance between the public and private sectors also renders problematic traditional ethical assumptions. As planners increasingly work in the private and quasi-private sectors, do they still owe loyalty to the public at large? Planners are torn between serving clients, the general public, and specific groups within the population (Marcuse 1976, 2011). In this terrain of contested loyalties, what remains of the once accepted cornerstone of planning – serving the public interest – especially when the very idea of the existence of a unitary public interest is problematic (Beauregard 1989)?

This dilemma is further complicated when the scope of planning extends beyond technical activities to larger social, economic, and environmental challenges. Within society at large the values of democracy, equality, diversity, and efficiency often clash (Fainstein 2010). These conflicts are reflected in the choices that planners must make as they try to reconcile the goals of economic development, social justice, and environmental protection. Despite the long-term promises of sustainable development, this triad of goals has created deep-seated tensions not only between planners and the outside world but also within planning itself (Campbell, Chapter 20, this volume).

Another ethical dimension arises from the difficulties surrounding the planner's role as expert. Questions concerning the proper balance between expertise and citizen input arise in issues like the siting of highways and waste disposal facilities, when particular social groups must bear the costs of more widespread social benefits. They are played out when experts seek to quantify risk, placing a monetary value on human life (Fischer 1991). They show up, as Martin Wachs argues, in the assumptions used by model builders when they forecast the future impacts of public facilities (Wachs 1982). Critics of those relying on expertise to justify policy doubt the legitimacy of ostensibly scientific methods, arguing that technical language disguises the values being interjected and obscures who wins and who loses (Fischer, Chapter 22, this volume). Nevertheless, the development of technical forecasting methods is necessary if planners are to fulfill their responsibility of designing policies for the long term.

The constraints on planning power – how can planning be effective within a mixed economy?

Even if we decide that planners should routinely intervene in the private market, we have no assurance that their intervention would be effective. Unlike some other professionals, planners do not have a monopoly on power or expertise over their object of work. They operate within the constraints of the capitalist political economy, and their urban visions compete with those of developers, consumers, politicians, and other more powerful groups. When they call for a type of development to occur, they do not command the resources to make it happen. Instead, they must rely on either private investment or a commitment from political leaders. They also work within the constraints of democracy and bureaucratic procedures (Foglesong, Chapter 6, this volume). Moreover their concerns may have low priority within the overall political agenda. Thus, despite the planning ideal of a holistic, proactive vision, planners are often restricted to playing frustratingly reactive, regulatory roles, especially in the United States.

The most powerful American planners are those who can marshal the resources to effect change and get projects built (Doig 1987; Ballon and Jackson 2007). They bend the role of the planner and alter the traditional separation between the public and private sectors. The resulting public–private partnerships make the planner more activist (Squires 1989); yet they also strain the traditional identity of the public planner and make many idealistic planners squirm (Siemiatycki, Chapter 13 this volume). How else can one explain the uncomfortable mixture of disgust and envy that a lot of planners felt towards Robert Moses, who as the head of various New York City agencies had far more projects built than did all the traditional city planners he disparaged (Caro 1974)?

Style of planning: What do planners do?

The justification for planning is often comprehensiveness. Yet the ideal of comprehensiveness has suffered serious criticism. Standard accounts of planning theories explained comprehensive planning as the attempt to coordinate the multiple development and regulatory initiatives undertaken in a region or city. Success depended on a high level of knowledge and the technological capability to use it. It was ostensibly a worthy attempt, but failed on two accounts. First, it required a level of knowledge, analysis, and organizational coordination that was impossibly complex, causing critics to ask whether planners had any special capacity for coordinating all the specialists (Altshuler 1965). This critique led to the endorsement of incremental planning (Lindblom, Chapter 9, this volume). Second, it presumed a common public interest but often gave voice only to powerful interests and ignored the needs of the poor and the weak. This critique led to the call for advocacy planning (Davidoff, Chapter 10, this volume).

The assault on comprehensive planning continued into the 1970s and 1980s. Strategic planning rejected comprehensive planning's impossibly general goals and instead embraced the "lean and mean" strategies from the business and military sectors (Kaufman and Jacobs 1987; Swanstrom 1987). By contrast, equity planning emerged as a less combative form of advocacy planning that allowed planners to serve the interests of the poor from within the system (Krumholz 1996).

There are problems with writing a tidy obituary for comprehensive planning, however. First, many planners continue to use the comprehensive approach as the model of their work, both because they continue to believe in it, and because they dislike the alternatives (Dalton 1986). Second, the primary task for many planners continues to be the writing and revising of comprehensive plans for their communities.

In writing the history of planning, chroniclers may misunderstand the real influence of the comprehensive model. Theorists at times presume a dominance of comprehensive rational planning during the early postwar years that may never have actually occurred in practice. In retelling the history of planning, planners arguably are guilty of after-the-fact revisionism in their creation of a straw man out of comprehensive planning. Commentators on the comprehensive model remember a once united field when what did actually exist was a young, diverse field seeking to define itself during a turbulent era. Even in the early postwar days of urban renewal and public housing construction, there were voices of skepticism and dissent in the planning community, long before Jane Jacobs's 1961 diatribe against mod ernist planning from her Greenwich Village stoop (Chapter 3, this volume). Arguably planning achieved greater comprehensiveness in European metropoles than in the United States, but even in European cities deviations were multiple, and different urban bureaucracies followed varying paths.

Much of the debate over comprehensiveness took place within very limited bounds. Planners often argued about the proper role of planning based simply on the merits of the concepts themselves (e.g., large- versus small-scale; top-down versus bottom-up), while ignoring the vaster political and economic forces that shaped and constrained planning.

Process v. outcome

In its early days planning concerned itself primarily with outcomes. Baron Haussmann in Paris, Daniel Burnham in Chicago, among those who saw their vision translated into reality, pictured modern cities with efficient transportation systems, attractive public spaces, and imposing buildings. Their methods consisted primarily of influencing developers and government officials to achieve these ends. While they assumed technical expertise on the part of those doing the actual designing, their orientation was toward the results of their efforts, not the process by which they were achieved.

Throughout the twentieth century, however, planners increasingly focused on procedures. Rules for creating master plans and zoning maps, regulations that would insure adherence to plans, and methodologies for calculating transport impacts became more and more prominent. During the years after World War II, approaches pioneered by the military and the private sector gave rise to the use of the "rational model" and cost-benefit analysis for decision making. These strategies relied on quantification and involved figuring out the least-cost alternative to achieving desired goals. The underlying assumption was that adhering to proper procedures would insure beneficial outcomes. The goals would be developed external to the planning function, and the job of planners was to figure out the means.

Criticisms of these approaches questioned the subjectivity disguised by numerical exactitude. Reaction to the depredations caused by top-down decision making justified by an apparently scientific methodology led to the development of the communicative model. In this approach planners would no longer prescribe either ends or means, but instead would act as negotiators or mediators among the various stakeholders, working out a consensus on what to do. The resulting compromise would constitute a plus game in which all participants would receive some benefit. Although communicative rationality represented a sharp break from earlier methods-based approaches, it resembled them in focusing on process rather than outcomes.

The model of the "just city" arose in response to the emphasis on communication. The argument of just city theorists is that inequalities of resources and power lead to unjust planning decisions (Marcuse et al. 2009; Fainstein 2010). Countering inequity requires pressing for a contrary vision. Although planners alone cannot overcome inequity, they can avoid contributing to it by always pressing for more just outcomes and spelling out policies that can improve the situation of the relatively disadvantaged. This becomes especially crucial as, under neo-liberal regimes,[2] income distributions have become more unequal and public benefits reduced within many metropolitan areas. Justice planning requires sensitivity to differences among social groups and to democratic expression, but most importantly to economic structure. It also calls for a greater emphasis within planning theory on the object of planning – that is, the metropolis –instead of a focus on the activities of planners (Fainstein, Chapter 8 this volume; Beauregard 1990).

The Continuing Evolution of Planning Theory

This contemporary revisionism of planning reflects a new period of critical re-examination. Planning theorists debate not only the relative merits of competing approaches to planning, but also question the selection of stories which the field uses to define itself. Challenges to the accepted standard list of iconic planners (including Haussmann, Burnham, Howard, Mumford, Moses, and Le Corbusier) and their projects (City Beautiful, Garden Cities, regionalism, and so forth) have opened up planning history to new voices and new iconic places; we are in the midst of a rethinking of the legitimate boundaries of planning history.

Over a generation, the most significant advances in planning theory are a changing understanding of power (Brindley, Rydin, and Stoker 1996; Flyvbjerg 1998), of communicative action and the planner's role in mediating interactions among stakeholders (Healey, Chapter 12 this volume; Booher and Innes 2010), of modernization/modernism (Scott, Chapter 2 this volume), and of the complex links between diversity, equity, democracy and community (deFilippis, Chapter 14; Young, Chapter 16; and Thomas, Chapter 17, this volume), and of the relations between processes and outcomes (Fainstein, Chapter 8 this volume).

Even since the publication of the first edition of this reader (in 1996), the field has continued to shift. While postmodernism has faded as a central subject in the field, its influence endures in an increased emphasis on discourse, on varied ways of knowing, and on pluralism of interpretation. It has contributed the idea of a historical break with the past, allowing the planning field to distance itself from the more unsavory aspects of twentieth-century planning by deeming them as by-products of a now-abandoned modernism: disruptive urban renewal, dysfunctional high-rise public housing, the rejection of rich historical forms of reference, and an excessive zeal towards a universal norm of planning and design at the expense of local traditions and conditions. This engagement with the broader ideas of postmodernism can be seen in the assumption that we have entered a new historical period of post-industrialism, globalization, post-Fordism, and the "New Economy."[3]

Communicative planning – the mediation of community discourse rather than the creation of a technically rational plan – has arguably also entered a new phase: it is simultaneously more accepted, differentiated, and criticized. Perhaps some of its early thunder is gone; despite the best efforts of its advocates, communicative action has not gained mass appeal as a totalizing new planning paradigm (Innes 1995). Paradoxically, we have both internalized it as an accepted role for planning – "Haven't planners *always* communicated?" – but also seen its operation as just one of many roles for planners. And despite the best intentions of communicative planners to construct beautiful narratives of a community's envisioned future from the "stories" of local residents, the graphs and financial reports from the rational, technocratic engineers, accountants, and developers still typically trump community vision.

A separate movement, called the "New Urbanism," promotes a revitalized vision of high-density, transit-and pedestrian-friendly neighborhoods as an antidote to faceless suburban sprawl. This movement has arguably influenced planning practice more than communicative or just city theories because of its more direct engagement with land use, design, real estate development, and environmentalism. Indeed, the revitalized interest in innovative land-use planning (once seen as a central but somewhat routinized area of planning) can in part be traced to a more sophisticated environmentalism, vocal growth-containment movements, regional planning, and other elements of the new urbanism.

Like communicative action, New Urbanism has both proponents of its paradigm-shifting potential and vocal critics. Often the debate is a battle between two extreme camps: those who would run a narrow fence around New Urbanism and then proceed to demolish it for being too narrow, and those who would claim that *any* innovation in urban development (having to do with in-fill, preservation, transit orientation, neighborhood design, or ecology) is a victory for New Urbanism (Burns et al. 1997 presents a variety of viewpoints on the merits of the approach). Some planning theorists initially dismissed the movement as preoccupied with architectural design, possessing both a Disney-like unreality and a narrow, rose-colored nostalgia for small-town America. It also evokes an image of communitarianism that some find claustrophobic and intolerant (see, for example, Harvey 1997). However, if New Urbanism continues to head in the direction of being a big, tolerant movement that embraces ideas of regionalism, sustainable development, affordable housing, environmental justice, communitarianism, and anti-sprawl – and thus builds alliances with environmental, community, and social justice groups – then it could emerge as a flexible, dynamic planning idea of substance and endurance.[4]

If we assume that planning theory will evolve in response to changes in planning practice, the development of cities, and the rise of social movements, then we can speculate on future directions for planning theory. Planners urgently need a larger conceptual world view to understand the ramifications of the digital revolution of the Internet, massive data storage and retrieval, and geographic information systems (GIS). Theories of communicative action provide but an initial entrée to the shift from old school statistics and mechanistic optimization modeling to multimedia, web-based, interactive, participatory visualization modeling built upon theories of complex systems. If communicative action theory envisions planners as the facilitators of community self-definition, then in the age of the Internet this places planners not just at evening planning board meetings, but also as managers of local network-based interest groups, as webmasters, and as virtual chat room monitors. Planning methodologies, once built upon the assumption of scarce, incomplete data, need to be revised to deal with the coming flood of data. The real-time tracking of flows in time–space coordinates (e.g., microchips and bar codes creating a world of geo-coded products, resources, and even people) creates new opportunities for planners to understand dynamic spatial processes, such as time–space-based user fees, development impact fees, and GIS-based performance zoning. However, this data revolution will also thrust the field into the tricky ethical world of data privacy issues.

These prospects raise new dilemmas for planning: the field has traditionally focused on the design and management of physical, land-based networks (roads, sidewalks, rail, shipping routes) and nodes (zoning of residential, commercial, industrial, and public space). Does the rise of non-place-specific virtual networks threaten the traditional foundation of planning by bypassing the old planning infrastructure? If planning is traditionally tied to place, how might planning transform itself to remain relevant within the "space of flows" (Castells 2000)? Should planners claim "cyberspace" as a legitimate terrain for their tools of spatial analysis, coordination, and zoning?

Increasing globalization will force planning theory to incorporate different types of cities into what had been Euro-American models of urbanization; Shanghai, Tokyo, Mexico City, Mumbai, and so forth will provide the basis for concepts of planning's role and aims. However, this will likely come with a growing tension between the preservation of local communities and the acceleration of global networks, and will sharpen the divide between the priorities of place-based versus flow-based planning and between equity and competitiveness. In a paradoxical world that is simultaneously fragmenting and globalizing, local space is both so segregated, yet so highly permeable by the outside world, that traditional notions of an autonomous, self-determined local community do not easily endure (Graham and Marvin 2001). Nevertheless, we may cling to this notion of attachment to place for both good normative and empirical reasons (see, for example, Clavel 2010). How might planning theory help us understand the relation between the global and the local?

All these examples suggest that the interaction between theory, urban change, and planning practice is symbiotic and often asynchronous. We would like to think that planning theory acts primarily as a kind of intellectual vanguard, pushing the professional field to rethink its outdated practices and the assumptions that underlie them. However, much of planning theory is instead an attempt to bring our thinking of planning up to date and in line with either urban phenomena (sprawl, globalization, etc.) or social theories from other fields (such as deliberative democracy or critical theory). In addition, the theory–practice time lag may run the other way round: the task of planning theory is often to catch up with planning practice itself, codifying and restating approaches to planning that practitioners have long since used (such as disjointed incrementalism or dispute mediation). Planning theory can therefore alternately be a running commentary, parallel and at arm's length to the profession; a prescriptive avant-garde; or instead a trailing, reflective echo of planning practice.

If there is a persistent gap between grand theory and modest accomplishment, it may also be overly simplistic to attribute it to the distance between theory and practice. It may instead reflect the discrepancy between what the theorist rightfully envisions as the ideal social–spatial arrangement of the world (i.e. the good, just city) and the more modest contributions that planners can make towards this ideal (given the political-economic constraints posed on the profession). Planning scholars frequently conflate the two, imagining an ideal urban society and then making all its characteristics the goals of the planning agenda. However, should the discipline be faulted for its lofty (and overreaching) ambitions?

The Enduring Question of the Public Interest

The most enduring question in planning theory revolves around the definition of the public interest (Campbell and Marshall, Chapter 5 this volume). Planning continues to face the central controversy of whether there is indeed a single public interest and of whether planners recognize and serve it. Incremental planners claim that the excessive complexity of discovering the comprehensive public interest prevents the planner from serving it directly, while advocate planners argue that what is portrayed as the public interest in fact represents merely the interests of the privileged. More recently, postmodernists and poststructuralists have challenged the universal master narrative that gives voice to the public interest, seeing instead a heterogeneous public with many voices and interests.

Nevertheless, planners have not abandoned the idea of serving the public interest, and rightly so. Postmodernists provided planning with a needed break from its preoccupation with a monolithic "public" (epitomized by Le Corbusier's and Robert Moses' love of the public but disdain for people); yet, a rejection of Enlightenment rationality, shared values, and generally applicable standards leaves the planner without adequate methods for serving a fragmented population. Some have touted strategic planning and other borrowed private-sector approaches as the appropriate path for planning, but these approaches neglect the "public" in the public interest. A belief in the public interest is the foundation for a set of values that planners hold dear: equal protection and equal opportunity, public space, and a sense of civic community and social responsibility.

The challenge is to reconcile these elements of a common public interest with the diversity that comes from many communities living side by side. David Harvey looked to generally held ideas of social justice and rationality as a bridge to overcome this dilemma (Harvey 2001); similarly, Susan Fainstein (2010; Chapter 8 this volume) presents the model of the just city. The recent interest in communicative action – planners as communicators rather than as autonomous, systematic thinkers – also reflects an effort to renew the focus of planning theory on the public interest (Healey, Chapter 12, this volume; Forester 1989; Innes 1998). Within this approach planners accept the multiplicity of interests, combined with an enduring common interest in finding viable, politically legitimate solutions. Planners serve the public interest by negotiating a kind of multicultural, technically informed pluralism.

In the end, the question of the public interest is the leitmotiv that holds together the defining debates of planning theory. The central task of planners is serving the public interest in cities, suburbs, and the countryside. Questions of when, why, and how planners should intervene – and the constraints they face in the process – all lead back to defining and serving the public interest, even while it is not static or fixed. The restructured urban economy, the shifting boundaries between the public and private sectors, the effects of telecommunications and information technology, and the changing tools and available resources constantly force planners to rethink the public interest. This constant rethinking is the task of planning theory.

The Readings

We have selected the readings for this volume to represent what we think are the central issues in planning theory. In particular, they address the challenges and dilemmas of planning as defined at the beginning of this introduction: *What role can planning play in developing the good city and region within the constraints of a capitalist global economy and varying political systems? Should planners focus on the desired objects of their efforts – the city and region – or should they concern themselves primarily with the process by which development decisions are made and assume that a good process will produce a good outcome*. We approach this question primarily through texts that address specific theoretical issues. However, we have also included several case studies that provide vivid and concrete illustrations of these questions.

Planning theory is a relatively young field; yet one can already speak of "classic readings." Our guide has been to choose readings – both old and new – that still speak directly to contemporary issues. Most have been written in the past ten years, though some articles from the 1960s are still the best articulation of specific debates. Most draw upon experiences in North America and Europe, but this edition differs from earlier ones in including a section on the developing world. The selections compiled here represent a substantial revision of the second edition of *Readings in Planning Theory* (2003). Over half the selections are new, reflecting more recent or more accessible statements of planning theories, or newly emerging themes. We have retained those readings from earlier editions that students and teachers of planning theory continue to find useful and exciting.

The readings are organized into seven parts, each prefaced with a short introduction to the main themes. We begin with the foundations of modern planning, including both traditional and critical views of planning history. We then turn to two interrelated questions: *What is the justification for planning intervention?* and *How should planners intervene?* Addressing the political and economic justifications for planning, we have selected readings that examine institutional, Marxist, and pluralist arguments. They place planners in the larger context of the relationship between the private market and government (both local and national). Regarding the style of planning, the readings examine dominant planning approaches: equity, incrementalism, advocacy, and communicative rationality. The case studies presented in the fourth part illustrate the opportunities for, and constraints on, planners in developed, democratic countries.

Racial and gender politics have emerged as powerful, transformative, and conflictual forces in urban planning. The readings in the fifth part explore the themes of difference, discrimination, and inequality. These theories challenge planning to be more inclusive, to accept the city as home to divergent populations with radically different experiences and needs, to see how the existing city fabric perpetuates antiquated social and gender relations, and to pursue social justice more aggressively. The next part deals with planning ethics, professionalism, communication, and the environment. Each piece addresses a shortcoming of the traditional, rational-comprehensive model of planning, whether it is its simplistic conception of the public interest, its lack of subtlety about ethical conflicts, its presumption of privileged expert knowledge, or its inability to handle the politically charged issue of environmental sustainability. The emerging stance for planners involves a greater savvy about political conflicts, a proactive role in the communication of choices and risks, and an understanding of complex social and ecological systems.

Finally the book concludes with a short selection of readings that examine issues for planners in developing countries. The principal question raised here is whether the theories that have arisen in the West are applicable in parts of the world with vastly different economic circumstances, political frameworks, and social divisions.

Notes

1　Faludi (1973) contains a classic set of readings. Hillier and Healey's (2008) three-volume collection attempts to be inclusive.
2　Neo-liberalism refers to the body of ideas that argues for the efficiency of markets and against state interference in social and economic processes. It is incorporated in policies for privatization, deregulation, and decentralization.
3　See the companion volume to this collection of readings, Fainstein and Campbell, *Readings in Urban Theory* (2011) for discussions of the contemporary global economy.
4　See Emily Talen, "Connecting New Urbanism and American Planning: An Historical Interpretation," in the companion volume, *Readings in Urban Theory* (2011).

References

Altshuler, Alan. 1965. The Goals of Comprehensive Planning. *Journal of the American Institute of Planning*, 31: 186–94.
Ballon, Hilary, and Kenneth T. Jackson, eds. 2007. *Robert Moses and the Modern City: The Transformation of New York*. New York: W.W. Norton.

Beauregard, Robert. 1989. Between Modernity and Postmodernity: The Ambiguous Position of US Planning. *Environment and Planning D: Society and Space*, 7: 381–95.

Beauregard, Robert. 1990. Bringing the City Back In. *Journal of the American Planning Association*, 56(2): 210–15.

Booher, David E., and Judith E. Innes. 2010. Governance for Resilience: CALFED as a Complex Adaptive Network for Resource Management. *Ecology and Society*, 15 (3): 337.

Brindley, Tim, Yvonne Rydin, and Gerry Stoker. 1996. *Remaking Planning: The Politics of Urban Change*. 2nd edn. New York: Routledge.

Burns, Carol, Robert Campbell, Andres Duany, Jerold Kayden, and Alex Krieger. 1997. Urban or Suburban? A Roundtable Discussion. *Harvard Design Magazine*, 1, Winter/Spring: 47–61.

Caro, Robert. 1974. *The Power Broker: Robert Moses and the Fall of New York*. New York: Alfred Knopf.

Castells, Manuel. 2000. *The Rise of the Network Society*, rev. edn. Oxford: Blackwell.

Clavel, Pierre. 2010. *Activists in City Hall*. Ithaca: Cornell University Press.

Commercial Club of Chicago, David Hudson Burnham, Edward H. Bennett, and Charles Moore. 1909. *Plan of Chicago*. Chicago: The Commercial Club.

Dahrendorf, Ralf. 1968. *Essays in the Theory of Society*. Stanford, CA: Stanford University Press.

Dalton, Linda. 1986. Why the Rational Paradigm Persists: The Resistance of Professional Education and Practice to Alternative Forms of Planning. *Journal of Planning Education and Research*, 5(3): 147–53.

Doig, Jameson. 1987. Coalition Building by a Regional Agency: Austin Tobin and the Port of New York Authority. In Clarence Stone and Heywood Sanders, eds., *The Politics of Urban Development*. Lawrence: University Press of Kansas, pp. 73–104.

Fainstein, Susan S. 2010. *The Just City*. Ithaca, NY: Cornell University Press.

Fainstein, Susan S., and Scott Campbell (eds.). 2011. *Readings in Urban Theory*, 3rd edn. Malden, MA: Wiley-Blackwell.

Faludi, Andreas (ed.). 1973. *A Reader in Planning Theory*. New York: Pergamon Press.

Fischer, Frank. 1991. Risk Assessment and Environmental Crisis: Toward an Integration of Science and Participation, *Industrial Crisis Quarterly*, 5(2): 113–32.

Fishman, Robert. 1987. *Bourgeois Utopias: The Rise and Fall of Suburbia*. New York: Basic Books.

Flyvbjerg, Bent. 1998. *Rationality and Power: Democracy in Practice*. Chicago: University of Chicago Press.

Foglesong, Richard E. 1986. *Planning the Capitalist City*. Princeton: Princeton University Press.

Forester, John. 1989. *Planning in the Face of Power*. Berkeley: University of California Press.

Frieden, Bernard, and Lynn Sagalyn. 1989. *Downtown Inc. How America Rebuilds Cities*. Cambridge, MA: MIT Press.

Galbraith, John K. 1971. *The New Industrial State*. New York: New American Library.

Graham, Stephen, and Simon Marvin. 2001. *Splintering Urbanism*. London: Routledge.

Hall, Peter. 2002. *Cities of Tomorrow: An Intellectual History of Urban Planning and Design in the Twentieth Century*, 3rd edn. Oxford: Blackwell.

Harloe, Michael. 1995. *The People's Home*. Oxford: Blackwell.

Harvey, David. 1985. On Planning the Ideology of Planning. In *The Urbanization of Capital*, Baltimore: Johns Hopkins University Press, pp. 165–84.

Harvey, David. 1989. From Managerialism to Entrepreneurialsim: The Transformation in Urban Governance in Late Capitalism. *Geografiska Annaler: Series B, Human Geography*, 71(1): 3–17.

Harvey, David. 1997. The New Urbanism and the Communitarian Trap. *Harvard Design Magazine*, 1, Winter/Spring: 1–3.

Harvey, David. 2001. Social Justice, Postmodernism and the City. In *Readings in Urban Theory*, ed. S. S. Fainstein and S. Campbell, 2nd edn. Cambridge, MA: Blackwell.

Harvey, David. 2003. *Paris: Capital of Modernity*. New York: Routledge.

Hayek, Friedrich A. 1944. *The Road to Serfdom*. Chicago: University of Chicago Press.

Hillier, Jean, and Patsy Healey. 2008. *Critical Essays in Planning Theory* (3 vols). Burlington, VT: Ashgate.

Hoffman, Lily. 1989. *The Politics of Knowledge: Activist Movements in Medicine and Planning*. Albany: SUNY Press.

Howard, Ebenezer, and Frederic James Osborn. 1945 [1898]. *Garden Cities of Tomorrow*. London: Faber & Faber.

Innes, Judith E. 1995. Planning Theory's Emerging Paradigm: Communicative Action and Interactive Practice. *Journal of Planning Education and Research*, 14(3): 183–9.

Innes, Judith E. 1998. Information in Communicative Planning. *Journal of the American Planning Association*, 64(Winter): 52–63.

Kaufman, Jerome L., and Harvey M. Jacobs. 1987. A Public Planning Perspective on Strategic Planning. *Journal of the American Planning Association*, 53: 23–33.

Klosterman, Richard E. 1985. Arguments for and against Planning. *Town Planning Review*, 56(1): 5–20.

Krueckeberg, Donald A. (ed.). 1983. The Culture of Planning. In D. A. Krueckeberg, ed., *Introduction to Planning History in the United States*, New Brunswick, NJ: Center for Urban Policy Research, pp. 1–12.

Krumholz, Norman. 1996. A Retrospective View of Equity Planning: Cleveland, 1969–1979. In S. Campbell and S. S. Fainstein, eds., *Readings in Planning Theory*, Cambridge, MA and Oxford, UK: Blackwell, pp. 344–62.

Krumholz, Norman and John Forester. 1990. *Making Equity Planning Work*. Philadelphia: Temple University Press.

Levy, John M. 1990. What Local Economic Developers Actually Do: Location Quotients versus Press Releases. *Journal of the American Planning Association*, 56(2): 153–60.

Mannheim, Karl. 1949. *Man and Society in an Age of Reconstruction*. New York: Harcourt, Brace.

Marcuse, Peter. 1976. Professional Ethics and Beyond: Values in Planning. *Journal of the American Institute of Planning*, 42(3): 264–74.

Marcuse, Peter. 2011. Social Justice and Power in Planning History and Theory. In Naomi Carmon and Susan S. Fainstein, eds. *Urban Planning as if People Mattered*. Philadelphia: Penn Press.

Marcuse, Peter, James Connolly, Ingrid Olivo Magana, Johannes Novy, Cuz Potter, and Justin Steil, eds. 2009. *Searching for the Just City*. New York: Routledge.

Meyerson, Martin, and Edward C. Banfield. 1964. *Politics, Planning and the Public Interest*. New York: Free Press.

Moore, Terry. 1978. Why Allow Planners to Do What They Do? A Justification from Economic Theory. *Journal of the American Institute of Planning*, 44(4): 387–98.

Purcell, Mark. 2008. *Recapturing Democracy*. New York: Routledge.

Robinson, Charles Mulford. 1901. *The Improvement of Towns and Cities; or the Practical Basis of Civic Aesthetics*. New York: G. P. Putnam.

Rubin, Herbert J. 2000. *Renewing Hope within Neighborhoods of Despair*. Albany: SUNY Press.

Self, Robert O. 2003. *American Babylon*. Princeton: Princeton University Press.

Squires, Gregory D., ed. 1989. *Unequal Partnerships: The Political Economy of Urban Redevelopment in Postwar America*. New Brunswick, NJ: Rutgers University Press.

Stone, Clarence N. 1993. Urban Regimes and the Capacity to Govern: A Political Economy Approach. *Journal of Urban Affairs*, 15(1): 1–28.

Swanstrom, Todd. 1987. The Limits of Strategic Planning for Cities. *Journal of Urban Affairs*, 9(2): 139–57.

Wachs, Martin. 1982. Ethical Dilemmas in Forecasting Public Policy. *Public Administration Review*, 29 (Nov/Dec): 562–7.

Walsh, Annmarie Hauck. 1978. *The Public's Business: The Politics and Practices of Government Corporations*. Cambridge, MA: MIT Press.

I
Foundations of Twentieth-Century Planning Theory

Introduction

Influential Visions of Planning

The readings in this first part examine influential visions of modern planning. They offer both established and critical views of planning history. We begin with Robert Fishman's examination of two foundational figures in planning's intellectual history: Ebenezer Howard and Le Corbusier. (Fishman's larger book on *Urban Utopias*, from which this chapter is excerpted, also looks at a third visionary of twentieth century urbanism: Frank Lloyd Wright.) Fishman goes beyond the standard account of Howard and Le Corbusier to examine the social history behind their distinctive utopias. Although all were reacting to the grimy reality of industrial cities, each took a fundamentally different path towards planning their ideal urban society. Corbusier's Radiant City was mass-scaled, dense, vertical, hierarchical – the social extension of modern architecture. Wright went to the other extreme: his Broadacre City was a mixture of Jeffersonian agrarian individualism and prairie suburbanism, linked by superhighways. Howard's Garden Cities were scaled somewhere in between: self-contained villages of 35,000 residents held together by a cooperative spirit, private industrial employers, and a communal greenbelt. The three utopias symbolize fundamental choices in the scale of human settlements: Corbusier's mass *Gesellschaft*, Howard's village-like *Gemeinschaft*, or Wright's American individualism. (Dolores Hayden will invoke this settlement triad later in this volume.)

To complete the traditional foundation of city planning, one needs to include also the City Beautiful Movement at the turn of the previous century. With its origins in civic improvement, the Columbian Exposition of 1893 in Chicago,

Readings in Planning Theory, Third Edition. Edited by Susan S. Fainstein and Scott Campbell.
Editorial material and organization © 2012 Blackwell Publishing Ltd.
Published 2012 by Blackwell Publishing Ltd.

and Daniel Burnham's 1909 Chicago Plan, the City Beautiful Movement was an important catalyst for the rise of planning commissions, public–private partnerships, and civic aesthetic awareness. Yet the City Beautiful Movement also became an easy target of criticism: it was elitist if not totalitarian, advocating the beautification of the city surface while ignoring the poverty and inequality inherent in the political-economic structure of the city. (For further readings on the movement, see Foglesong 1986; Wilson 1989.)

The political scientist James Scott traces the roots of modernist planning's effort to impose order on the messiness of humans and their environment – particularly focusing on what he calls "authoritarian high modernism." In an excerpt from his book, *Seeing Like a State: How Certain Schemes to Improve the Human Condition Have Failed*, Scott traces the link between modernism and the modern nation-state's efforts to simplify and standardize, while rejecting local context and initiative, to make the nation legible, measurable, and counted. This is how the modern state "sees." Scott identifies three elements common to disastrous abuses of modern state development: administrative ordering of nature and society through simplification and standardization ("high modernism"); the unrestrained use of the power of the modern state to implement these rational designs; and a civil society too weak to resist effectively. "Social engineering" becomes the consequence of high modernism and nation-state power, and the authoritarian tendencies of the single modernist voice of rationality displace all other forms of judgment.

Scott sees three effective strategies to counter authoritarian high modernism: the belief in a private sphere of activity outside the interference of the state (the idea of the private realm); liberal political economy (e.g., the ideas of Hayek); and, most importantly, civil society and democratic political institutions. What are the implications for planning? Plans should not be so ambitious and meticulous that they are closed systems. Smaller and reversible steps, flexibly open to both surprises and human inventiveness, will break with the hubris of modernist planning. In Scott's call for local initiative ("Metis"), as an alternative to state-level technocratic planning, one hears echoes of arguments also made by Jane Jacobs, Charles Lindblom, and others.

Though these various foundations of intellectual planning history might represent distinctly different choices in imagining the ideal city, Jane Jacobs argues that they all suffer from a similar, dangerous misconception of how real cities actually operate. She summarily discredits these classic planning prototypes together under the label of the "Radiant Garden City Beautiful." She sees in Howard, Burnham, and Le Corbusier a shared uneasiness with actual cities, each of them seeking to replace the rich complexity of a real metropolis with the abstract logic of an idealized planned city. We include here the introductory chapter to her landmark 1961 critique of postwar American urban renewal, *The Death and Life of Great American Cities*. This book makes unfortunate oversimplifications about the evils of planning, while both neglecting the destructive role of the private sector in urban renewal and romanticizing the capabilities of small, competitive, neighborhood businesses. Yet the book remains one of the most compelling and well-written arguments for encouraging diversity and innovation in big, dense, messy cities. (That said, Jacobs' "diversity" is primarily about creating a wide range of building types and land uses, rather than a more contemporary focus of "diversity" as including a multicultural array of racial and ethnic urban residents.) Jacobs' ideas also signal the long transition of planning theory from an early faith in science and comprehensiveness to a more self-critical, incremental approach. It thereby anticipates a later interest in complexity and emergence. Jacobs demonstrates that the simple process of daily, intimate observation can lead to an understanding of the complexity of cities. (By contrast, many of the elaborate, mathematically minded urban models built by regional scientists and others led to a frustratingly simplistic view of cities in the 1960s.)

This Part concludes with an essay by John Friedmann, long an influential and provocative voice in planning theory. Like Fishman, Friedmann employs the term "utopia," though Fishman used it to characterize a range of urban visions at the beginning of the twentieth century, while Friedmann instead revives the term as a legitimate and indeed fundamental task for planning's future.

Friedmann begins his essay unconventionally: he pens a lengthy open letter to Manual Castells, expressing both intellectual admiration but also unease with Castells' concluding thoughts in his *End of Millennium* (2000) book. Specifically, Friedmann takes exception to what he interprets as Castells' retreat from ideology-inspired visions of the future. Friedmann embraces the utopian vision as a vital tool to both critique the present and imagine an alternative (and better) future. For Friedmann, utopian thinking is not pie-in-the-sky idealism but instead has productive effects on the ground, linking material and civil aspirations. Nor does Friedmann fall into the rigid Marxian dichotomy of scientific vs. utopian socialism. His vision of the good urban future is not just a material one; he instead views material well-being as a means to achieve an autonomous, vibrant civil life. Jane Jacobs rejected utopian models of urban form as static, closed, undemocratic, and authoritarian. In contrast, Friedmann's utopian thinking is ongoing, discursive, open-ended and emergent: it informs the search for the good city, rather than dictating its physical attributes. It also is built upon an enduring belief in a common good of a city – a belief that Friedmann see as necessary in the face of critics who reject the idea as "either propaganda or an act of self-deception."

References

Castells, Manuel. 2000. *The End of Millennium*, 2nd edn. Oxford: Blackwell.

Foglesong, Richard E. 1986. *Planning the Capitalist City*. Princeton: Princeton University Press.

Wilson, William H. 1989. *The City Beautiful Movement*. Baltimore: Johns Hopkins University Press.

1

Urban Utopias in the Twentieth Century
Ebenezer Howard, Frank Lloyd Wright, and Le Corbusier

Robert Fishman

Introduction

What is the ideal city for the twentieth century, the city that best expresses the power and beauty of modern technology and the most enlightened ideas of social justice? Between 1890 and 1930 three planners, Ebenezer Howard, Frank Lloyd Wright, and Le Corbusier, tried to answer that question. Each began his work alone, devoting long hours to preparing literally hundreds of models and drawings specifying every aspect of the new city, from its general ground plan to the layout of the typical living room. There were detailed plans for factories, office buildings, schools, parks, transportation systems – all innovative designs in themselves and all integrated into a revolutionary restructuring of urban form. The economic and political organization of the city, which could not be easily shown in drawings, was worked out in the voluminous writings that each planner appended to his designs. Finally, each man devoted himself to passionate and unremitting efforts to make his ideal city a reality.

Many people dream of a better world; Howard, Wright, and Le Corbusier each went a step further and planned one. Their social consciences took this rare and remarkable step because they believed that, more than any other goal, their societies needed new kinds of cities. They were deeply fearful of the consequences for civilization if the old cities, with all the social conflicts and miseries they embodied, were allowed to persist. They were also inspired by the prospect that a radical reconstruction of the cities would solve not only the urban crisis of their time, but the social crisis as well. The very completeness of their ideal cities expressed their convictions that the moment had come for comprehensive programs, and for a total rethinking of the principles of urban planning. They

Readings in Planning Theory, Third Edition. Edited by Susan S. Fainstein and Scott Campbell.
Editorial material and organization © 2012 Blackwell Publishing Ltd.
Published 2012 by Blackwell Publishing Ltd.

rejected the possibility of gradual improvement. They did not seek the amelioration of the old cities, but a wholly transformed urban environment.

This transformation meant the extensive rebuilding and even partial abandonment of the cities of their time. Howard, Wright, and Le Corbusier did not shrink from this prospect; they welcomed it. As Howard put it, the old cities had "done their work." They were the best that the old economic and social order could have been expected to produce, but they had to be superseded if mankind were to attain a higher level of civilization. The three ideal cities were put forward to establish the basic theoretical framework for this radical reconstruction. They were the manifestoes for an urban revolution.

These ideal cities are perhaps the most ambitious and complex statements of the belief that reforming the physical environment can revolutionize the total life of a society. Howard, Wright, and Le Corbusier saw design as an active force, distributing the benefits of the Machine Age to all and directing the community onto the paths of social harmony. Yet they never subscribed to the narrow simplicities of the "doctrine of salvation by bricks alone" – the idea that physical facilities could *by themselves* solve social problems. To be sure, they believed – and who can doubt this? – that the values of family life could be better maintained in a house or apartment that gave each member the light and air and room he needed, rather than in the cramped and fetid slums that were still the fate of too many families. They thought that social solidarity would be better promoted in cities that brought people together, rather than in those whose layout segregated the inhabitants by race or class.

At the same time the three planners understood that these and other well-intended designs would be worse than useless if their benevolent humanitarianism merely covered up basic inequalities in the social system. The most magnificent and innovative housing project would fail if its inhabitants were too poor and oppressed to lead decent lives. There was little point in constructing new centers of community life if the economics of exploitation and class conflict kept the citizens as divided as they had been in their old environment. Good planning was indeed efficacious in creating social harmony, but only if it embodied a genuine rationality and justice in the structure of society. It was impossible in a society still immured in what Le Corbusier called "the Age of Greed." The three planners realized that they had to join their programs of urban reconstruction with programs of political and economic reconstruction. They concluded (to paraphrase one of Marx's famous *Theses on Feuerbach*) that designers had hitherto merely *ornamented* the world in various ways; the point was to *change* it.

The ideal cities were therefore accompanied by detailed programs for radical changes in the distribution of wealth and power, changes that Howard, Wright, and Le Corbusier regarded as the necessary complements to their revolutions in design. The planners also played prominent roles in the movements that shared their aims. Howard was an ardent cooperative socialist who utilized planning as part of his search for the cooperative commonwealth; Wright, a Jeffersonian democrat and an admirer of Henry George, was a spokesman for the American decentrist movement; and Le Corbusier had many of his most famous designs published for the first time in the pages of the revolutionary syndicalist journals he edited. All three brought a revolutionary fervor to the practice of urban design.

And, while the old order endured, Howard, Wright, and Le Corbusier refused to adapt themselves to what planning commissions, bankers, politicians, and all the other authorities of their time believed to be desirable and attainable. They consistently rejected the idea that a planner's imagination must work within the system. Instead, they regarded the physical structure of the cities in which they lived, and the economic structure of the society in which they worked, as temporary aberrations which mankind would soon overcome. The three planners looked beyond their own troubled time to a new age each believed was imminent, a new age each labored to define and to build.

Their concerns thus ranged widely over architecture, urbanism, economics, and politics, but their thinking found a focus and an adequate means of expression only in their plans for ideal cities. The cities were never conceived of as blueprints for any actual project. They were "ideal types" of cities for the future, elaborate models rigorously designed to illustrate the general principles that each man advocated. They were convenient and attractive intellectual tools that enabled each planner to bring together his many innovations in design, and to show them as part of a coherent whole, a total redefinition of the idea of the city. The setting of these ideal cities was never any actual location, but an empty, abstract plane where no contingencies existed. The time was the present, not any calender day or year, but that revolutionary "here and now" when the hopes of the present are finally realized.

These hopes, moreover, were both architectural and social. In the three ideal cities, the transformation of the physical environment is the outward sign of an inner transformation in the social structure. Howard, Wright, and Le Corbusier used their ideal cities to depict a world in which their political and economic goals had already been achieved. Each planner wanted to show that the urban designs he advocated were not only rational and beautiful in themselves, but that they embodied the social goals he believed in. In the context of the ideal city, each proposal for new housing, new factories, and other structures could be seen to further the broader aims. And, in general, the ideal cities enabled the three planners to show modern design in what they believed was its true context – as an integral part of a culture from which poverty and exploitation had disappeared. These cities, therefore, were complete alternative societies, intended as a revolution in politics and economics as well as in architecture. They were utopian visions of a total environment in which man would live in peace with his fellow man and in harmony with nature. They were social thought in three dimensions.

As theorists of urbanism, Howard, Wright, and Le Corbusier attempted to define the ideal form of any industrial society. They shared a common assumption that this form could be both defined and attained, but each viewed the ideal through the perspective of his own social theory, his own national tradition, and his own personality. Their plans, when compared, disagree profoundly, and the divergences are often just as significant as the agreements. They offer us not a single blueprint for the future, but three sets of choices – the great metropolis, moderate decentralization, or extreme decentralization – each with its corresponding political and social implications. Like the classical political triad of monarchy–aristocracy–democracy, the three ideal cities represent a vocabulary of basic forms that can be used to define the whole range of choices available to the planner.

Seventeen years older than Wright and thirty-seven years older than Le Corbusier, Ebenezer Howard started first. His life resembles a story by Horatio Alger, except that Alger never conceived a hero at once so ambitious and so self-effacing. He began his career as a stenographer and ended as the elder statesman of a worldwide planning movement, yet he remained throughout his life the embodiment of the "little man." He was wholly without pretension, an earnest man with a round, bald head, spectacles, and a bushy mustache, unselfconscious in his baggy pants and worn jackets, beloved by neighbors and children.

Yet Howard, like the inventors, enlighteners, self-taught theorists, and self-proclaimed prophets of the "age of improvement" in which he lived, was one of those little men with munificent hopes. His contribution was "the Garden City," a plan for moderate decentralization and cooperative socialism. He wanted to build wholly new cities in the midst of unspoiled countryside on land that would remain the property of the community as a whole. Limited in size to 30,000 inhabitants and surrounded by a perpetual "greenbelt," the Garden City would be compact, efficient, healthful, and beautiful. It would lure people away from swollen cities like London and their dangerous concentrations of wealth and power; at the same time, the countryside would be dotted with hundreds of new communities where small-scale cooperation and direct democracy could flourish.

Howard never met either Frank Lloyd Wright or Le Corbusier. One suspects those two architects of genius and forceful personalities would have considered themselves worlds apart from the modest stenographer. Yet it is notable that Wright and Le Corbusier, like Howard, began their work in urban planning as outsiders, learning their profession not in architectural schools but through apprenticeships with older architects and through their own studies. This self-education was the source of their initiation into both urban design and social theory, and it continued even after Wright and Le Corbusier had become masters of their own profession. Their interests and readings flowed naturally from architecture and design to city planning, economics, politics, and the widest questions of social thought. No one ever told them they could not know everything.

Frank Lloyd Wright stands between Howard and Le Corbusier, at least in age. If Howard's dominant value was cooperation, Wright's was individualism. And no one can deny that he practiced what he preached. With the handsome profile and proud bearing of a frontier patriarch, carefully brushed long hair, well-tailored suits and flowing cape, Wright was his own special creation. His character was an inextricable mix of arrogance and honesty, vanity and genius. He was autocratic, impolitic, and spendthrift; yet he maintained a magnificent faith in his own ideal of "organic" architecture.

Wright wanted the whole United States to become a nation of individuals. His planned city, which he called "Broadacres," took decentralization beyond the small community (Howard's ideal) to the individual family home. In Broadacres all cities larger than a county seat have disappeared. The center of society has moved to the thousands of homesteads that cover the countryside. Everyone has the right to as much land as he can use, a minimum of an acre per person. Most people work part-time on their farms and part-time in the small factories, offices, or shops that are nestled among the farms. A network of superhighways joins together the scattered elements of society. Wright believed that individuality must be founded on individual ownership. Decentralization would make it possible for everyone to live his chosen lifestyle on his own land.

Le Corbusier, our third planner, could claim with perhaps even more justification than Wright to be his own creation. He was born Charles-Édouard Jeanneret and grew up in the Swiss city of La Chaux-de-Fonds, where he was apprenticed to be a watchcase engraver. He was saved from that dying trade by a sympathetic teacher and by his own determination. Settling in Paris in 1916, he won for himself a place at the head of the avant-garde, first with his painting, then with his brilliant architectural criticism, and most profoundly with his own contributions to architecture. The Swiss artisan Jeanneret no longer existed. He had recreated himself as "Le Corbusier," the Parisian leader of the revolution in modern architecture.

Like other "men from the provinces" who settled in Paris, Le Corbusier identified himself completely with the capital and its values. Wright had hoped that decentralization would preserve the social value he prized most highly – individuality. Le Corbusier placed a corresponding faith in organization, and he foresaw a very different fate for modern society. For him, industrialization meant great cities where large bureaucracies could coordinate production. Whereas Wright thought that existing cities were at least a hundred times too dense, Le Corbusier thought they were not dense enough. He proposed that large tracts in the center of Paris and other major cities be leveled. In place of the old buildings, geometrically arrayed skyscrapers of glass and steel would rise out of parks, gardens, and superhighways. These towers would be the command posts for their region. They would house a technocratic elite of planners, engineers, and intellectuals who would bring beauty and prosperity to the whole society. In his first version of the ideal city, Le Corbusier had the elite live in luxurious high-rise apartments close to the center; their subordinates were relegated to satellite cities at the outskirts. (In a later version everyone was to live in the high-rises.) Le Corbusier called his plan "'the Radiant City,' a city worthy of our time."

The plans of Howard, Wright, and Le Corbusier can be summarized briefly, but the energy and resources necessary to carry them out can hardly be conceived. One might expect that the three ideal cities were destined to remain on paper. Yet, as we shall see, their proposals have already reshaped many of the cities we now live in, and may prove to be even more influential in the future.

The plans were effective because they spoke directly to hopes and fears that were widely shared. In particular, they reflected (1) the pervasive fear of and revulsion from the nineteenth-century metropolis; (2) the sense that modern technology had made possible exciting new urban forms; and (3) the great expectation that a revolutionary age of brotherhood and freedom was at hand.

Caught in our own urban crisis, we tend to romanticize the teeming cities of the turn of the century. To many of their inhabitants, however, they were frightening and unnatural phenomena. Their unprecedented size and vast, uprooted populations seemed to suggest the uncontrollable forces unleashed by the Industrial Revolution, and the chaos that occupied the center of modern life. Joseph Conrad eloquently expressed this feeling when he confessed to being haunted by the vision of a "monstrous town more populous than some continents and in its man-made might as if indifferent to heaven's frowns and smiles; a cruel devourer of the world's light. There was room enough there to place any story, depth enough there for any passion, variety enough for any setting, darkness enough to bury five millions of lives."[1]

The monstrous proportions of the big city were relatively new, and thus all the more unsettling. In the first half of the nineteenth century the great European cities had overflowed their historic walls and fortifications. (The American cities, of course, never knew such limits.) Now boundless, the great cities expanded into the surrounding countryside with reckless speed, losing the coherent structure of a healthy organism. London grew in the nineteenth century from 900,000 to 4.5 million inhabitants; Paris in the same period quintupled its population, from 500,000 to 2.5 million residents. Berlin went from 190,000 to over 2 million, New York from 60,000 to 3.4 million. Chicago, a village in 1840, reached 1.7 million by the turn of the century.[2]

This explosive growth, which would have been difficult to accommodate under any circumstances, took place in an era of laissez-faire and feverish speculation. The cities lost the power to control their own growth. Instead, speculation – the blind force of chance and profit – determined urban structure. The cities were segregated by class, their traditional unifying centers first overwhelmed by the increase in population and then abandoned. Toward the end of the nineteenth century the residential balance between urban and rural areas began tipping, in an unprecedented degree, towards the great cities. When Howard, Wright, and Le Corbusier began their work, they saw around them stagnation in the countryside, the depopulation of rural villages, and a crisis in even the old regional centers. First trade and then the most skilled and ambitious young people moved to the metropolis.

Some of these newcomers found the good life they had been seeking in attractive new middle-class neighborhoods, but most were caught in the endless rows of tenements that stretched for miles, interrupted only by factories or railroad yards. Whole families were crowded into one or two airless rooms fronting on narrow streets or filthy courtyards where sunlight never penetrated. In Berlin in 1900, for example, almost 50 percent of all families lived in tenement dwellings with only one small room and an even smaller kitchen. Most of the rest lived in apartments with two tiny rooms and a kitchen, but to pay their rent, some of these had to take in boarders who slept in the corners.[3] "Look at the cities of the nineteenth century," wrote Le Corbusier, "at the vast stretches covered with the crust of houses without heart and furrowed with streets without soul. Look, judge. These are the signs of a tragic denaturalization of human labor."[4]

Howard, Wright, and Le Corbusier hated the cities of their time with an overwhelming passion. The metropolis was the counter-image of their ideal cities, the hell that inspired their heavens. They saw precious resources, material and human, squandered in the urban disorder. They were especially fearful that the metropolis would attract and then consume all the healthful forces in society. All three visualized the great city as a cancer, an uncontrolled, malignant growth that was poisoning the modern world. Wright remarked that the plan of a large city resembled "the cross-section of a fibrous tumor"; Howard compared it to an enlarged ulcer. Le Corbusier was fond of picturing Paris as a body in the last stages of a fatal disease – its circulation clogged, its tissues dying of their own noxious wastes.

The three planners, moreover, used their insight into technology to go beyond a merely negative critique of the nineteenth-century metropolis. They showed how modern techniques of construction had created a new mastery of space from which innovative urban forms could be built. The great city, they argued, was no longer modern. Its chaotic concentration was not only inefficient and inhumane, it was unnecessary as well.

Howard, Wright, and Le Corbusier based their ideas on the technological innovations that inspired their age: the express train, the automobile, the telephone and radio, and the skyscraper. Howard realized that the railroad system that had contributed to the growth of the great cities could serve the planned decentraliza-tion of society equally well. Wright understood that the personal automobile and an elaborate network of roads could create the conditions for an even more radical decentralization. Le Corbusier looked to technology to promote an opposite trend. He made use of the skyscraper as a kind of vertical street, a "street in the air" as he called it, which would permit intensive urban densities while eliminating the "soulless streets" of the old city.

The three planners' fascination with technology was deep but highly selective. They acknowledged only what served their own social values. Modern technology, they believed, had outstripped the antiquated social order, and the result was chaos and strife. In their ideal cities, however, technology would fulfill its proper role. Howard, Wright, and Le Corbusier believed that industrial society was inherently harmonious. It had an inherent structure, an ideal form, which, when achieved, would banish conflict and bring order and freedom, prosperity and beauty.

This belief went far beyond what could be deduced from the order and power of technology itself. It reflected instead the revolutionary hopes of the nineteenth century. For the three planners, as for so many of their contemporaries, the conflicts of the early Industrial Revolution were only a time of troubles which would lead inevitably to the new era of harmony. History for them was still the history of pro-gress; indeed, as Howard put it, there was a "grand purpose behind nature." These great expectations, so difficult for us to comprehend, pervaded nineteenth-century radical and even liberal thought. There were many prophets of progress who contributed to creating the optimistic climate of opinion in which Howard, Wright, and Le Corbusier formed their own beliefs. Perhaps the most relevant for our pur-poses were the "utopian socialists" of the early nineteenth century.

These reformers, most notably Charles Fourier, Robert Owen, and Henri de Saint-Simon, drew upon the tradition of Thomas More's *Utopia* and Plato's *Republic* to create detailed depictions of communities untainted by the class struggles of the Industrial Revolution. Unlike More or Plato, however, the utopian socialists looked forward to the immediate realization of their ideal commonwealths. Owen and Fourier produced detailed plans for building utopian communities, plans for social and architectural revolution which anticipated some of the work of Howard, Wright, and Le Corbusier. Two themes dominated utopian socialist planning: first, a desire to overcome the distinction between city and country; and second, a desire to overcome the physical isolation of individuals and families by grouping the community into one large "family" structure. Most of the designs envisioned not ideal cities but ideal communes, small rural establishments for less than 2,000 people. Owen put forward a plan for brick quadrangles which he called "moral quadrilaterals." One side was a model factory, while the other three were taken up with a communal dining room, meeting rooms for recreation, and apartments.[5] His French rival Fourier advanced a far more elaborate design for a communal palace or "phalanstery" which boasted theaters, fashionable promenades, gardens, and gourmet cuisine for everyone.[6]

The utopian socialists were largely forgotten by the time Howard, Wright, and Le Corbusier began their own work, so there was little direct influence from them. As we shall see, however, the search of each planner for a city whose design expressed the ideals of cooperation and social justice led him to revive many of the themes of his utopian socialist (and even earlier) predecessors. But one crucial element sharply separates the three planners' designs from all previous efforts. Even the most fantastic inventions of an Owen or a Fourier could not anticipate the new forms that twentieth-century technology would bring to urban design. The utopian socialists' prophecies of the future had to be expressed in the traditional architectural vocabulary. Fourier, for example, housed his cooperative community in a "phalanstery" that looked like the château of Versailles. Howard, Wright, and Le Corbusier were able to incorporate the scale and pace of the modern world into their designs. They worked at the dawn of the twentieth-century industrial era, but before the coming of twentieth-century disillusionment. Their imaginations were wholly modern; yet the coming era of cooperation was as real to them as it had been for Robert Owen. Their ideal cities thus stand at the intersection of nineteenth-century hopes and twentieth-century technology.

The three ideal cities, therefore, possessed a unique scope and fervor, but this uniqueness had its dangers. It effectively isolated the three planners from almost all the social movements and institutions of their time. In particular, it separated them from the members of two groups who might have been their natural allies, the Marxian socialists and the professional planners. The three ideal cities were at once too technical for the Marxists and too revolutionary for the growing corps of professional planners. The latter was especially intent on discouraging any suggestion that urban planning might serve the cause of social change. These architect–administrators confined themselves to "technical" problems, which meant, in practice, serving the needs of society – as society's rulers defined them. Baron Haussmann, that model of an administrative planner, had ignored and sometimes worsened the plight of the poor in his massive reconstructions of Paris undertaken for Louis Napoleon. But the plight of the poor was not his administrative responsibility. He wanted to unite the isolated sectors of the city and thus quicken the pace of commerce. The wide avenues he cut through Paris were also designed to contribute to the prestige of the regime and, if necessary, to serve as efficient conduits for troops to put down urban disorders. Haussmann's physically impressive and socially reactionary plans inspired worldwide imitation and further increased the gap between urban design and social purpose.[7]

Even the middle-class reformers who specifically dedicated themselves to housing and urban improvement were unable to close this gap. Men like Sir Edwin Chadwick in London bravely faced official indifference and corruption to bring clean air, adequate sanitation, and minimal standards of housing to the industrial cities. Yet these philanthropists were also deeply conservative in their social beliefs. Their rare attempts at innovation almost always assumed the continued poverty of the poor and the privileges of the rich. The model tenements, "cheap cottages," and factory towns that were commissioned in the second half of the nineteenth century were filled with good intentions and sound planning, but they never failed to reflect the inequities of the society that built them. When, for example, the English housing reformer Octavia Hill built her model tenements, she kept accommodations to a minimum so that her indigent tenants could pay rents sufficient not only to cover the complete cost of construction, but also to yield her wealthy backers 5 percent annual interest on the money they had advanced her.[8] (This kind of charitable enterprise was known as "philanthropy at 5 percent.") Not surprisingly, designs put forward under these conditions were almost as bleak as the slums they replaced.

Howard, Wright, and Le Corbusier were not interested in making existing cities more profitable or in building "model" tenements to replace the old ones. These views might have been expected to have attracted the sympathetic attention of the Marxian socialists who then controlled the most powerful European movements for social change. Indeed, the *Communist Manifesto* had already recognized the necessity for radical structural change in the industrial cities by putting the "gradual abolition of the distinction between town and country" among its demands. Nevertheless, the socialist movement in the second half of the nineteenth century turned away from what its leaders regarded as unprofitable speculation. In an important series of articles collected under the title *The Housing Question* (1872), Friedrich Engels maintained that urban design was part of the "superstructure" of capitalist society and would necessarily reflect that society's inhumanities, at least until after the socialist revolution had succeeded in transforming the economic base. He concluded that any attempt to envision an ideal city without waiting for the revolution was futile and, indeed, that any attempt to improve the cities significantly was doomed so long as capitalism endured. The working class must forget attractive visions of the future and concentrate on immediate revolution after which the dictatorship of the proletariat would redistribute housing in the old industrial cities according to need. Then and only then could planners begin to think about a better kind of city.[9]

Howard, Wright, and Le Corbusier could therefore look neither to the socialists nor to the professional planners for support. Initially, at least, they were forced back upon themselves. Instead of developing their ideas through collaboration with others and through practical experience, they worked in isolation on more and more elaborate models of their basic ideas. Their ideal cities thus acquired a wealth of brilliant detail and a single-minded theoretical rigor that made them unique. This isolation was no doubt the necessary precondition for the three planners' highly individual styles of social thought. Certainly their mercurial and independent careers showed a very different pattern from the solid institutional connections of, for example, Ludwig Mies van der Rohe or Walter Gropius. Mies, Gropius, and the other Bauhaus architects were also deeply concerned with the question of design and society; yet none of them produced an ideal city. They had more practical but also more limited projects to occupy them.[10] The ideal city is the genre of the outsider who travels at one leap from complete powerlessness to imaginary omnipotence.

This isolation encouraged Howard, Wright, and Le Corbusier to extend their intellectual and imaginative capacities to their limits, but it also burdened their plans with almost insurmountable problems of both thought and action. They had created plans that were works of art, but the city, in Claude Lévi-Strauss' phrase, is a "*social* work of art." Its densely interwoven structure is the product of thousands of minds and thousands of individual decisions. Its variety derives from the unexpected juxtapositions and the unpredictable interactions. How can a single individual, even a man of genius, hope to comprehend this structure? And how can he devise a new plan with the same satisfying complexities? For his design, whatever its logic and merits, is necessarily his alone. In imposing a single point of view, he inevitably simplifies the parts which make up the whole. Howard, Wright, and Le Corbusier each filled his ideal city with *his* buildings; *his* sense of proportion and color; and, most profoundly, with *his* social values. Would there ever be room for anyone else? The three ideal cities raise what is perhaps the most perplexing question for any planner: in attempting to create a new urban order, must he repress precisely that complexity, diversity, and individuality which are the city's highest achievements?

The problem of action was equally obvious and pressing. Deprived of outside support, the three planners came to believe that their ideas were inherently powerful. As technical solutions to urban problems and embodiments of justice and beauty, the three ideal cities could properly claim everyone's support. By holding up a ready-made plan for a new order, Howard, Wright, and Le Corbusier hoped to create their own movements. This strategy, however, led directly to the classic utopian dilemma. To appeal to everyone on the basis of universal principles is to appeal to no one in particular. The more glorious the plans are in theory, the more remote they are from the concrete issues that actually motivate action. With each elaboration and clarification, the ideal cities move closer to pure fantasy. Can imagination alone change the world? Or, as Friedrich Engels phrased the question: how can the isolated individual hope to *impose his idea* on history?

These two related problems of thought and action confronted Howard, Wright, and Le Corbusier throughout their careers; yet they never doubted that ultimately they could solve both. Each believed that if a planner based his work on the structure inherent in industrial society and on the deepest values of his culture, there could be no real conflict between his plan and individual liberty. Patiently, each searched for that harmonious balance between control and freedom: the order that does not repress but liberates the individual.

With equal determination, they sought a valid strategy for action. Their ideal cities, they knew, could never be constructed all at once. But at least a "working model" could be begun, even in the midst of the old society. This model would demonstrate both the superiority of their architectural principles and also serve as a symbol of the new society about to be born. Its success would inspire emulation. A movement of reconstruction would take on momentum and become a revolutionary force in itself. Rebuilding the cities could thus become, in a metaphor all three favored, the "Master Key" that would unlock the way to a just society.

The three planners, therefore, looked to the new century with confidence and hope. Against the overwhelming power of the great cities and the old order that built them, Howard, Wright, and Le Corbusier advanced their designs for planned growth, for the reassertion of the common interest and higher values, for a healthy balance between man's creation and the natural environment. It would seem to be an uneven contest. Nevertheless, the three planners still believed that an individual and his imagination could change history. The revolution they were seeking was precisely an assertion of human rationality over vast impersonal forces. They resolved that in the coming era of reconciliation and construction, the man of imagination must play a crucial role. He would embody the values of his society in a workable plan, and thus direct social change with his prophetic leadership. For Howard, Wright, and Le Corbusier, this next revolution would finally bring imagination to power. "What gives our dreams their daring," Le Corbusier proclaimed, "is that they can be achieved."[11]

Ebenezer Howard: The Ideal City Made Practicable

Town and country *must be married*, and out of this joyous union will spring a new hope, a new life, a new civilization. (Ebenezer Howard 1898)

Of the three planners discussed here, Ebenezer Howard is the least known and the most influential. His *To-morrow: A Peaceful Path to Real Reform* (1898, now known under the title of the 1902 edition, *Garden Cities of To-Morrow*) has, as Lewis Mumford acknowledged, "done more than any other single book to guide the modern town planning movement and to alter its objectives."[12] And Howard was more than a theoretician. He and his supporters founded two English cities, Letchworth (1903) and Welwyn (1920), which still serve as models for his ideas.

More important, he was able to organize a city planning movement which continues to keep his theories alive. The postwar program of New Towns in Great Britain, perhaps the most ambitious of all attempts at national planning, was inspired by his works and planned by his followers.

In the United States the "Greenbelt Cities" undertaken by the Resettlement Administration in the 1930s owed their form to the example of the Garden City. The best recent example of an American New Town is Columbia, Maryland, built in the 1960s as a wholly independent community with houses and industry. In 1969 the National Committee on Urban Growth Policy urged that the United States undertake to build 110 New Towns to accommodate 20 million citizens.[13] The following year, Congress created a New Town Corporation in the Department of Housing and Urban Development to begin this vast task.[14] [At the time of writing], sixteen American New Towns have either been planned or are under construction. The most fruitful period of Ebenezer Howard's influence is perhaps only beginning.

If Howard's achievements continue to grow in importance, Howard the man remains virtually unknown. The present-day New Town planners are perhaps a little embarrassed by him. They are highly skilled professional bureaucrats or architects; Howard's formal education ended at fourteen, and he had no special training in architecture or urban design. The modern planners are self-proclaimed "technicians" who have attempted to adapt the New Town concept to any established social order. Howard was, in his quiet way, a revolutionary who originally conceived the Garden City as a means of superseding capitalism and creating a civilization based on coop-eration. Howard's successors have neglected this aspect of his thought, and without it the founder of the Garden City movement becomes an elusive figure indeed. He shrank from the personal publicity which Frank Lloyd Wright and Le Corbusier so eagerly and so skillfully sought. Throughout his life he maintained the habits and the appearance of a minor clerk. He once said that he enjoyed his chosen profession, stenography, because it enabled him to be an almost invisible observer at the notable events he recorded. Even at the meetings of the association he headed, he preferred to sit in an inconspicuous position behind the podium, where he could take down the exact words of the other speakers. Frederic J. Osborn, one of his closest associates, remembered him as "the sort of man who could easily pass unnoticed in a crowd."[15] He was, Osborn added, "the mildest and most unassuming of men … universally liked, and notably by children."[16]

Nonetheless, Howard succeeded where more charismatic figures failed. In 1898 he had to borrow £50 to print *To-morrow* at his own expense. Five years later his sup-porters were advancing more than £100,000 to begin the construction of the first Garden City. The rapidity of this turn of events surprised Howard and is still diffi-cult to explain. The root of the mystery is Howard himself. He had reached middle age before beginning his work on city planning and had never given any indication that he was capable of originality or leadership. His book, however, was a remarkable intellectual achievement. He concisely and rigorously outlined a new direction for the development of cities and advanced practical solutions that covered the whole range of city planning problems: land use, design, transportation, housing, and finance. At the same time, he incorporated these ideas into a large synthesis: a plan for a complete alternative society and a program for attaining it.

Howard, moreover, proved to be a surprisingly effective organizer. He was an indefatigable worker who bent with slavelike devotion to the task of promoting his own ideas. At cooperative societies, Labour Churches, settlement houses, temperance unions, debating clubs – at any group that would pay his railroad fares and provide a night's hospitality – he preached the "Gospel of the Garden City" under the title "The Ideal City Made Practicable, A Lecture Illustrated with Lantern Slides." He possessed a powerful speaking voice, and, more important, he was able to communicate an overwhelming sense of earnestness, an absolute conviction that he had discovered "the peaceful path to real reform." Mankind, he proclaimed, was moving inevitably toward a new era of brotherhood, and the Garden City would be the only fitting environment for the humanity of the future. His original supporters were not planners or architects but social reformers whose own dreams he promised would be realized in the Garden City. Patiently, he assembled a broad coalition of backers that ranged from "Back to the Land" agrarians to George Bernard Shaw. Working constantly himself, he felt free to draw upon the resources and talents of others. He thus made his ideas the basis of a movement which, fifty years after his death, continues to grow. As one of Shaw's characters in *Major Barbara* observes, absolute unselfishness is capable of anything.

[…]

Ebenezer Howard: Design for Cooperation

Between 1889 and 1892 Howard created the basic plan for his ideal community. He envisaged his Garden City as a tightly organized urban center for 30,000 inhabitants, surrounded by a perpetual "green belt" of farms and parks. Within the city there would be both quiet residential neighborhoods and facilities for a full range of commercial, industrial, and cultural activities. For Howard did not conceive the Garden City as a specialized "satellite town" or "bedroom town" perpetually serving some great metropolis. Rather, he foresaw the great cities of his time shrinking to insignificance as their people desert them for a new way of life in a decentralized society. No longer would a single metropolis dominate a whole region or even a whole nation. Nor would the palatial edifices and giant organizations of the big city continue to rule modern society. Instead, the urban population would be distributed among hundreds of Garden Cities whose small scale and diversity of functions embody a world in which the little person has finally won out.

Howard does not seem to have been familiar with the designs for geometric cities that utopian socialists had put forward earlier in the nineteenth century. Nonetheless the perfectly circular, perfectly symmetrical plan he devised for the Garden City bears a distinct resemblance to some of these, notably James Silk Buckingham's cast-iron Victoria (1849).[17] The explanation, however, lies not in direct influence but in shared values. For Howard had inherited that tradition in English utopian thought in which it was assumed that society could be improved just as a machine could – through the appropriate adjustments. A properly functioning society would thus take on the precise and well-calculated look of a good machine.

For Howard, therefore, there was nothing merely "mechanical" in the relentless symmetry of the Garden City. He wanted to make the design the physical embodiment of his ideal of cooperation, and he believed that his perfectly circular plan would best meet the needs of the citizens. He promised that every building would be "so placed to secure maximum utility and convenience."[18] This "unity of design and purpose" had been impossible in old cities formed, in Howard's view, by "an infinite number of small, narrow, and selfish decisions."[19] In the Garden City, however, an active common interest would make possible a uniform, comprehensive plan. With selfish obstructions removed, the city could assume that geometric form which Howard believed was the most efficient and the most beautiful. The symmetry of the Garden City would be the symbol and product of cooperation, the sign of a harmonious society.

The only relevant book he remembered reading was written by a physician, Dr Benjamin Richardson, and entitled *Hygeia, A City of Health*.[20] It was an imaginative presentation of the principles of public sanitation in which Dr Richardson depicted a city whose design would be the healthiest for its inhabitants. He prescribed a population density of twenty-five people per acre, a series of wide, tree-shaded avenues, and homes and public gardens surrounded by greenery. "Instead of the gutter the poorest child has the garden; for the foul sight and smell of unwholesome garbage, he has flowers and green sward."[21] Howard was happy to follow this prescription. The public health movement, of which Dr Richardson was a prominent representative, was a vital force for civic action; it had persuaded the public that there was a strong correlation between the health of a community and its political and moral soundness. Howard maintained that the Garden Cities would be the healthiest in the nation. He incorporated the low population density, the wide avenues, and other features of *Hygeia* into the geometry of his own city.

The problem of health was especially important because Howard planned the Garden City to be a manufacturing center in which the factories would necessarily be close to the homes. In order to separate the residential areas and also to ensure that everyone would be within walking distance of his place of work, Howard put the factories at the periphery of the city, adjacent to the circular railroad that surrounds the town and connects it to the main line. Here one can find the enterprises appropriate to a decentralized society: the small machine shop, or the cooperative printing works, or the jam factory where the rural cooperative processes its members' fruits. As usual in the plan, physical location has a symbolic aspect. Industry has its place and its function, but these are at the outskirts of the community. Howard had little faith in the role of work – even if cooperatively organized – to provide the unifying force in society. This he left to leisure and civic enterprise.

There are two kinds of centers in the Garden City: the neighborhood centers and the (one) civic center. The neighborhoods, or "wards" as Howard called them, are slices in the circular pie. Each ward comprises one-sixth of the town, 5,000 people or about 1,000 families. Each, said Howard, "should in some sense be a complete town by itself" (he imagined the Garden City being built ward by ward).[22] The basic unit in the neighborhood is the family living in its own home surrounded by a garden. Howard hoped to be able to provide houses with gardens to all classes. Most residents would be able to afford a lot 20 by 130 feet; the most substantial homes would be arranged in crescents bordering Grand Avenue, a park and promenade that forms the center of the ward. In the middle of Grand Avenue is the most important neighborhood institution, the school. This, Howard commented, should be the first building constructed in each ward and will serve as a library, a meeting hall, and even as a site for religious worship. Churches, when they are built, also occupy sites in Grand Avenue.[23]

There are two cohesive forces that bring the residents out of their neighborhoods and unite the city. The first is leisure. The center of the town is a Central Park, which provides "ample recreation grounds within very easy access of all the people."[24] Surrounding the park is a glassed-in arcade, which Howard calls the "Crystal Palace": "Here manufactured goods are exposed for sale, and here most of that class of shopping which requires the joy of deliberation and selection is done."[25]

The Crystal Palace, in addition to providing an attractive setting for consumption, also permits the town, by granting or withholding leases, to exercise some control over distribution. Howard, as always, recommended a balance between individualism and central organization. He rejected the idea of one great cooperative department store run by the community, like the one in *Looking Backward*. Instead, he advocated that there be many small shops, but only one for each category of goods. If customers complain that a merchant is abusing his monopoly, the town rents space in the Crystal Palace to another shopkeeper in the same field, whose competition then restores adequate service. Whatever the merits of this solution, it aptly reflects the Radical ambivalence toward the trades that supported so many of them, the desire for economic independence without the self-destructive competition that accompanied it.

Important as consumption and leisure were in his system, Howard nonetheless reserved the very center of the Central Park to the second cohesive force, "civil spirit." He wanted an impressive and meaningful setting for the "large public buildings": town hall, library, museum, concert and lecture hall, and the hospital. Here the highest values of the community are brought together – culture, philanthropy, health, and mutual cooperation.

We might wonder what kind of cultural life a Garden City of 30,000 could enjoy, but this question did not bother Howard. He never felt the need of that intensification of experience – the extremes of diversity and excellence – that only a metropolis can offer. We must also remember, however, that Howard lived in a milieu that did not look to others to provide entertainment or enlightenment. The English middle class and a sizable part of the working class created its own culture in thousands of voluntary groups: lecture societies, choral groups, drama guilds, chamber symphonies. Here, as elsewhere, Howard disdained the kind of centralization that focused the life of a nation on a few powerful metropolitan institutions. He looked to small-scale voluntary cooperation not only for the economic base of the community but also for its highest cultural attainments.

The Garden City occupies 1,000 acres in the middle of a tract of 5,000 acres reserved for farms and forests.[26] This "Agricultural Belt" plays an integral role in the economy of the Garden City; the 2,000 farmers who live there supply the town with the bulk of its food. Because transportation costs are almost nonexistent, the farmer receives a good price for his produce, and the consumer gets fresh vegetables and dairy products at a reduced price. The Agricultural Belt, moreover, prevents the town from sprawling out into the countryside and ensures that the citizens enjoy both a compact urban center and ample open countryside. "One of the first essential needs of Society and of the individual," wrote Howard, "is that every man, every woman, every child should have ample space in which to live, to move, and to develop."[27] He added a new element to the rights of man — the right to space.

The Garden City in all its aspects expressed Howard's ideal of a cooperative commonwealth. It was the Zion in which he and his fellow Radicals could be at ease, the environment in which all the Radical hopes could be realized. Yet the Garden City was more than an image of felicity for Howard had carefully wedded his vision of the ideal city to a concrete plan for action. Indeed, he devoted relatively little attention to the details of the new city and a great deal to the means of achieving it. He wanted to show that there was no need to wait for a revolution to build the Garden City: it could be undertaken immediately by a coalition of Radical groups working within the capitalist system. The first successful Garden City would be a working model of a better society, and those that succeeded it would decisively alter English society. Building the Garden City was itself the revolution. The planned transformation of the environment was the nonviolent but effective strategy that the Radical movement had been seeking. The Garden City was, as Howard put it, "the peaceful path to real reform."

Howard wanted the building of the first Garden City to be an example of voluntary cooperation, and he devoted most of his book to outlining and defending his method. The key to Howard's strategy was his contention that building a new city could be *practical*, i.e., that money advanced for its construction could be paid back with interest. Funds could thus be solicited from high-minded and thrifty Radicals with the assurance that they would be both helping the cause and earning a modest return for themselves. The germ of Howard's scheme could be found in an article written in 1884 by the distinguished economist Alfred Marshall.[28] Marshall had pointed out that the rail networks that covered Great Britain rendered the concentration of so many businesses in London economically irrational. Many businesses could be carried out far more cheaply, efficiently, and pleasantly where land was inexpensive and abundant. Marshall proposed that committees be established to buy up suitable land outside London and coordinate the movement of factories and working people. The value of the land in these new industrial parks would rise sharply, and the committees that owned them would reap a handsome profit.

Howard, who knew both the proposal and its author,[29] took up this suggestion and transformed it to suit his own ends. He began by asking the reader to assume that a group of his supporters – "gentlemen of responsible position and undoubted probity and honor," as he hopefully described them – had banded together to form a nonprofit company. They would raise money by issuing bonds yielding a fixed rate (4 or 5 percent), purchase 6,000 acres of agricultural land, and lay out a city according to Howard's plans. They would build roads, power and water plants, and all other necessities, and then seek to attract industry and residents. The company would continue to own all the land; as the population rose, the rents too would rise from the low rate per acre for agricultural land to the more substantial rate of a city with 30,000 residents. All rent would go to the company and would be used to repay the original investors. Any surplus that remained after the financial obligations had been discharged would provide additional services to the community.[30]

Howard proposed, in other words, that the Garden City be founded and financed by philanthropic land speculation. The scheme was speculative because it was a gamble on the rise in values that would result from attracting 30,000 people to a plot of empty farmland, and philanthropic because the speculators agreed in advance to forgo all but a fixed portion of the expected profits. The concept was not original with Howard. "Philanthropy at 5 percent" was a familiar feature in English reform circles, and activists from the Owenites to the Christian Socialists made use of fixed-dividend corporations to raise money for cooperative stores and workshops. The Reverend Charles Kingsley, a Christian Socialist, aptly illustrated the spirit of this reconciliation of God and Mammon when he exhorted his followers to "seek first the Kingdom of God and his Righteousness with this money of yours and see if all things – profits and suchlike – are not added unto you."[31]

Howard did add a new emphasis to this method. He stipulated that part of the rental income each year be placed in a sinking fund and used to purchase the bonds of the original investors. As the number of bondholders decreased, the amount that the company had to pay each year to the ones remaining would also decrease. Meanwhile, income from rents would be constantly growing as the town grew; the surplus, as we have seen, was earmarked for community services. Eventually the Garden City would buy out all the original investors, and the entire income from rents could be used to benefit the citizens. Taxes would be unnecessary; rents alone would generously support schools, hospitals, cultural institutions, and charities.[32]

The residents of the Garden City would thus continue to pay rent, but landlords would be eliminated. The private ownership of land for the benefit of individuals would be replaced by collective ownership for the benefit of the community. Howard placed tremendous emphasis on this change. He, like almost every other Radical, believed that the "land question" – the concentration of the ownership of land in Great Britain in the hands of a few – was, as he put it, the "root of all our problems."[33] As late as 1873 an official survey had shown that 80 percent of the land in the United Kingdom was owned by less than 7,000 persons.[34] The spread of Garden Cities would transfer land ownership on a large scale from individuals to the community, thus inaugurating an economic and social revolution.

Howard's analysis of the crucial importance of the "land question" derived from the writings of the American reformer Henry George, a hero of English

Radicals in the 1880s. George was probably the most influential man of one idea in nineteenth-century Anglo-American history. His panacea, the Single Tax (the appropriation of all rent by taxation) was based on his view that there was no real conflict between capital and labor. The "antagonism of interests," he argued, "is in reality between labor and capital on the one side and land ownership on the other."[35] The great landowners used their natural monopoly to demand exorbitant rents and thus appropriate without compensation the lion's share of the increased wealth from material progress that ought to go to the workmen and entrepreneurs who actually produced it. This perversion of the economic order impoverished the proletariat, imperiled the manufacturer, and upset the natural balance of supply and demand. It was the real cause of depression, class conflict, and the spreading poverty that seemed an inevitable companion to progress.

Characteristically, Howard accepted everything in George's theory that pointed toward reconciliation and rejected everything that promised conflict. He rejected the Single Tax because he saw that it meant the expropriation of a whole class. He accepted, however, George's view that the solution to the land question would restore the economy to a healthy balance and create the conditions for a reconciliation of capital and labor. He believed he had found the solution to the land question himself. The Garden City, he wrote, "will, by a purely natural process, make it gradually impossible for any landlord class to exist at all." Private landholding "will die a natural but not too sudden death."[36] Building Garden Cities would accomplish all of George's aims "in a manner which need cause no ill-will, strife or bitterness; is constitutional; requires no revolutionary legislation; and involves no direct attack on vested interest."[37] The Garden City company would, in fact, enjoy all the privileges of a profit-making concern. The legal forms that landlords had designed to protect their own interests would now foster the creation of a higher form of society.

The powers extended to the Garden City company as sole landlord would be greater than the legal authority possessed by any nineteenth-century English municipality. Through its control of all leases it could effectively enforce the ground plan and zone the community without special legal authority. Howard was a firm believer in "gas and water socialism," and he stipulated that the town's board of management should provide all utilities on a nonprofit basis. He also thought the town might well establish municipal bakeries and laundries.[38]

Although the Garden City company would have the legal right to own and operate all the industry in the Garden City, Howard favored a balance of public and private control. The large factories on the periphery were clearly to be established by private industry, though Howard hoped that through profit sharing they would eventually take on a cooperative character. They still would be subject to the authority that the town as sole landlord could impose: No polluters or employers of "sweated" labor would be allowed.[39] The board of management would also share responsibility for public services with private citizens. Howard hoped that individuals would establish a large group of what he called "pro-municipal enterprises." These were public services whose necessity was not yet recognized by the majority of the citizens, but "those who have the welfare of society at heart [would], in the free air of the city, be always able to experiment on their own responsibility, ... and enlarge the public understanding."[40] In addition to the more conventional charitable and philanthropic activities, "pro-municipal enterprises" included cooperative building and pension societies.

As income from rents grew, the municipality would gradually take over the services that voluntary cooperation had initiated. In industry, too, Howard believed the evolutionary trend was toward greater public ownership and control. The most important principle, however, was that no one have the right to impose a degree of socialism for which the citizens were not ready. The elimination of landlord's rents would remove, in Howard's view, any immediate conflict of capital with labor and permit the peaceful coexistence of capitalist and socialist industry. The balance between the public and private sectors must shift slowly with the increasing capacity of the citizens for cooperation.

Howard had the patience to begin with imperfect forms because he had the capacity to see his ideal society evolving in time. He realized that a single Garden City of 30,000 was too small to provide the full measure of diversity that a genuine city must have. A Garden City could not, however, increase its size or density; that would spoil its plan. He proposed that it grow by establishing a new sister city beyond the Agricultural Belt. Howard believed that the cities should eventually organize themselves into "town clusters, each town in the cluster being of different design from the others, yet the whole forming one large and well-thought-out plan."[41] A diagram that appeared in *To-morrow* showed six Garden Cities arranged in a circle around a larger Center City. The plan had the cities connected by a circular canal which provided power, water, and transportation. In the 1902 edition the canal was replaced by a more sober rapid-transit system.[42]

The Social City, as Howard called each cluster of towns, represented his most advanced conception of the marriage of town and country; here "each inhabitant of the whole group, though in one sense living in a town of small size, would be in reality living in, and would enjoy all the advantages of, a great and most beautiful city; and yet all the fresh delights of the country ... would be within a very few minutes' ride or walk."[43] With small communities already established as the basic units in society, these units could be arranged in planned federations to secure the benefits of larger size as well. Rapid communications between the towns meant greater convenience for trade, and, "because the people, in their collective capacity own the land on which this beautiful group of cities is built, the public buildings, the churches, the schools and universities, the libraries, picture galleries, theatres, would be on a scale of magnificence which no city in the world whose land is in pawn to private individuals can afford."[44] Once established, the Social City would become the base for still higher stages of evolution that Howard never ventured to describe.

Howard's reluctance to prescribe every detail or to foresee every contingency is one of the most important aspects of his method. The visionary planner can easily become a despot of the imagination. Working alone, deprived of the checks and balances of other minds, he is tempted to become the *roi soleil* of his realm and to order every detail of life of his ideal society. If Howard's geometric plans resemble a Baroque *Residenzstadt*, Howard himself was singularly free of the pretensions of a Baroque monarch. His plans, as he pointed out, were merely diagrams to be modified when put into practice.

The same may be said for his plans for social organization. In Howard's time the advocates of Socialism and Individualism (both usually capitalized) confronted each other like Matthew Arnold's ignorant armies. Bellamy, as we have seen, believed that the entire economy of the United States could be centrally directed by a few men of "fair ability." Herbert Spencer in his individualist phase held that the use of tax money to support public libraries was a step toward collectivist slavery.[45] Howard did not presume to judge this momentous debate. He made the spatial reorganization of society his fundamental demand because he believed that a new environment would open possibilities for the reconciliation of freedom and order that neither Bellamy nor Spencer could imagine. Howard sought to discover the minimum of organization that would secure the benefits of planning while leaving to individuals the greatest possible control over their own lives. He was a collectivist who hated bureaucratic paternalism and an apostle of organization who realized that planning must stay within self-imposed limits.

[...]

Le Corbusier: The Radiant City

The Radiant City retained the most important principle of the Contemporary City: the juxtaposition of a collective realm of order and administration with an individualistic realm of family life and participation. This juxtaposition became the key to Le Corbusier's attempt to resolve the syndicalist dilemma of authority and participation. Both elements of the doctrine receive intense expression in their respective spheres. Harmony is in the structure of the whole city and in the complete life of its citizens.

The Radiant City was a more daring and difficult synthesis than the Contemporary City. In his effort to realize the contradictory elements of syndicalism, Le Corbusier made the Radiant City at once more authoritarian and more libertarian than its predecessor. Within the sphere of collective life, authority has become absolute. The Contemporary City had lacked any single power to regulate all the separate private corporations that accomplished the essential work of society; Le Corbusier had then believed that the invisible hand of free competition would create the most efficient coordination. The Great Depression robbed him of his faith. He now held that organization must extend beyond the large corporations. They had rationalized their own organizations, but the economy as a whole remained wasteful, anarchic, irrational. The planned allocation of manpower and resources which had taken place within each corporation must now be accomplished for society. In the Radiant City every aspect of productive life is administered from above according to one plan. This plan replaces the marketplace with total administration; experts match society's needs to its productive capacities.

The preordained harmony which Le Corbusier had called for in urban reconstruction would now be imposed on all productive life. The great works of construction would become only one element in the plan. This was a crucial extension of the concept of planning. Ebenezer Howard and Frank Lloyd Wright had believed that once the environment had been designed, the sources of disorder in society would be minimized and individuals could be left to pursue their own initiatives. This belief rested on a faith in a "natural economic order," a faith which Le Corbusier no longer shared. He confronted a world threatened by chaos and collapse. It seemed that only discipline could create the order he sought so ardently. Coordination must become conscious and total. Above all, society needed authority and a plan.

Syndicalism, Le Corbusier believed, would provide a "pyramid of natural hierarchies" on which order and planning could be based. The bottom of this pyramid is the *syndicat*, the group of workers, white-collar employees, and engineers who run their own factory. The workers have the responsibility of choosing their most able colleague to be their manager and to represent them at the regional trade council. Le Corbusier believed that although citizens would usually find it impossible to identify the most able man among a host of politicians, each worker is normally able to choose his natural leader. "Every man is capable of judging the facts of his trade," he observed.[46]

The regional council of plant managers represents the first step in the hierarchy. Each level corresponds to a level of administrative responsibility. The manager runs his factory; the regional leaders administer the plants in their region. The regional council sends its most able members to a national council, which is responsible for the overall control of the trade. The leader of this council meets with his fellow leaders to administer the national plan. This highest group is responsible for coordinating the entire production of the country. If, for example, the national plan calls for mass housing, they allot the capital needed for each region and set the goals for production. The order is passed down to the regional council, which assigns tasks to individual factories and contractors. The elected representatives of the *syndicat* return from the regional council with instructions that determine his factory's role in the national productive effort.

This hierarchy of administration has replaced the state. As Saint-Simon had urged, a man's power corresponds exactly to his responsibilities in the structure of production. He issues the orders necessary for fulfilling his quotas, and these orders provide the direction that society needs. The divisive issues of parliamentary politics cannot arise, for everyone shares a common concern that the resources of society be administered as efficiently as possible. Even the tasks of the national council are administrative rather than political. The members do not apportion wealth and power among competing interests groups. Their task, like that of all the other functionaries, is a "technical" one: they carry out the plan.

"Plans are not political," Le Corbusier wrote.[47] The plan's complex provisions, covering every aspect of production, distribution, and construction, represent a necessary and objective ordering of society. The plan is necessary because the

Machine Age requires conscious control. It is objective because the Machine Age imposes essentially the same discipline on all societies. Planning involves the rational mastery of industrial process and the application of that mastery to the specific conditions of each nation. The plan is a "rational and lyric monument" to man's capacity to organize.

The plan is formulated by an elite of experts detached from all social pressure. They work "outside the fevers of mayors' and prefects' offices," away from the "cries of electors and the cries of victims." Their plans are "established serenely, lucidly. They take account only of human truths."[48] In the planner's formulations, "the motive forces of a civilization pass from the subjective realm of consciousness to the objective realm of facts." Plans are "just, long-term, established on the realities of the century, imagined by a creative passion."[49]

This plan for Le Corbusier was more than a collection of statistics and instructions; it was a social work of art. It brought to consciousness the complex yet satisfying harmonies of an orderly productive world. It was the score for the great industrial orchestra. The plan summed up the unity that underlay the division of labor in society; it expressed the full range of exchange and cooperation that is necessary to an advanced economy.

Le Corbusier used the vocabulary and structures of syndicalism to advance his own vision of a beautifully organized world. His "pyramid of natural hierarchies" was intended to give the human structure of organization the same clarity and order as the great skyscrapers of the business center. The beauty of the organization was the product of the perfect cooperation of everyone in the hierarchy. It was the expression of human solidarity in creating a civilization in the midst of the hostile forces of nature. The natural hierarchy was one means of attaining the sublime.

Man at work create a world that is truly human. But that world, once created, is a realm of freedom where man lives in accord with nature, not in opposition to it. Like the Contemporary City, the Radiant City identifies the realm of freedom with the residential district. As if in recognition of the need to counterbalance the industrial realm's increased emphasis on organization, Le Corbusier has displaced the towers of administration from the central position they occupied in the earlier plan. The residential district stands in the place of honor in the Radiant City.

It is, moreover, a transformed residential district. Le Corbusier had lost the enthusiasm for capitalism which had led him originally to segregate housing in the Contemporary City according to class – elite in the center, proletariat at the outskirts. Now he was a revolutionary syndicalist, with a new appreciation of workers' rights. When he visited the United States in 1935, he found much to admire in the luxury apartment houses that lined Central Park and Lake Shore Drive, but he added, "My own thinking is directed towards the crowds in the subway who come home at night to dismal dwellings. The millions of beings sacrificed to a life without hope, without rest – without sky, sun, greenery."[50] Housing in the Radiant City is designed for them. The residential district embodies Le Corbusier's new conviction that the world of freedom must be egalitarian. "If the city were to become a human city," he proclaimed, "it would be a city without classes."[51]

No longer does the residential district simply mirror the inequalities in the realm of production. Instead, the relation between the two is more complex, reflecting Le Corbusier's resolve to make the Radiant City a city of organization *and* freedom. The realm of production in the Radiant City is even more tightly organized, its hierarchies of command and subordination even stricter than in the Contemporary City. At the same time, the residential district – the realm of leisure and self-fulfillment – is radically libertarian, its principles of equality and cooperation standing in stark opposition to the hierarchy of the industrial world. The citizen in Le Corbusier's syndicalist society thus experiences both organization and freedom as part of his daily life.

The centers of life in the Radiant City are the great high-rise apartment blocks, which Le Corbusier calls "Unités" These structures, each of which is a neighborhood with 2,700 residents, mark the culmination of the principles of housing that he had been expounding since the Dom-Inos of 1914. Like the Dom-Ino house, the Unité represents the application of mass-production techniques; but where the Dom-Ino represents the principle in its most basic form, the Unité is a masterful expression of scale, complexity, and sophistication. The disappointments of the 1920s and the upheavals of the 1930s had only strengthened Le Corbusier in his faith that a great new age of the machine was about to dawn. In the plans for the Unité he realized that promise of a *collective* beauty that had been his aim in the Dom-Ino design; he achieved a collective grandeur, which the Dom-Ino houses had only hinted at; and finally, he foresaw for all the residents of the Unité a freedom and abundance beyond even that which he had planned for the elite of the Contemporary City. The apartments in the Unité are not assigned on the basis of a worker's position in the industrial hierarchy but according to the size of his family and their needs. In designing these apartments, Le Corbusier remarked that he "thought neither of rich nor of poor but of man."[52] He wanted to get away both from the concept of luxury housing, in which the wasteful consumption of space becomes a sign of status, and from the concept of *Existenzminimum*, the design of workers' housing based on the absolute hygienic minimums. He believed that housing could be made to the "human scale," right in its proportions for everyone, neither cramped nor wasteful. No one would want anything larger nor get anything smaller.

The emphasis in the Unité, however, is not on the individual apartment but on the collective services provided to all the residents. As in the Villa-Apartment Blocks of the Contemporary City, Le Corbusier followed the principle that the cooperative sharing of leisure facilities could give to each family a far more varied and beautiful environment than even the richest individual could afford in a single-family house. These facilities, moreover, take on a clear social function as the reward and recompense for the eight hours of disciplined labor in a factory or office that are required of all citizens in a syndicalist society. The Unité, for example, has a full range of workshops for traditional handicrafts whose techniques can no longer be practiced in industries devoted to mass production. Here are meeting rooms of all sizes for participatory activities that have no place in the hierarchical sphere of production. There are cafes, restaurants, and shops where sociability can be cultivated for its own sake. Most important, in Le Corbusier's own estimation, the Unité provides the opportunity for a full range of physical activities that are severely curtailed during working hours in an industrial society. Within each Unité there is a full-scale gymnasium; on the roof are tennis courts, swimming pools, and even sand beaches. Once again, the high-rise buildings cover only 15 percent of the land, and the open space around them is elaborately landscaped into playing fields, gardens, and parkland.

The most basic services which the Unité provides are those that make possible a new concept of the family. Le Corbusier envisioned a society in which men and women would work full-time as equals. He therefore presumed the end of the family as an economic unit in which women were responsible for domestic services while men worked for wages. In the Unité, cooking, cleaning, and child raising are services provided by society. Each building has its day-care center, nursery and primary school, cooperative laundry, cleaning service, and food store. In the Radiant City the family no longer has an economic function to perform. It exists as an end in itself.

Le Corbusier and Frank Lloyd Wright were both intensely concerned with the preservation of the family in an industrial society, but here as elsewhere they adopted diametrically opposite strategies. Wright wished to revive and strengthen the traditional economic role of the family, to ensure its survival by making it the center both of the society's work and of its leisure. Wright believed in a life in which labor and leisure would be one, whereas Le Corbusier subjected even the family to the stark division between work and play that marks the Radiant City. The family belongs to the realm of play. Indeed, it virtually ceases to exist during the working day. When mother and father leave their apartment in the morning for their jobs, their children accompany them down on the elevator. The parents drop them off at the floor where the school or day-care center is located and pick them up after work. The family reassembles in the afternoon, perhaps around the pool or at the gym, and when the family members return to their apartment they find it already cleaned, the laundry done and returned, the food ordered in the morning already delivered and prepared for serving. Individual families might still choose to cook their own food, do their own laundry, raise vegetables on their balconies, or even raise their own children. In the Radiant City, however, these activities have become leisure-time hobbies like woodworking or weaving, quaint relics of the pre-mechanical age.

The Unité is thus high-rise architecture for a new civilization, and Le Corbusier was careful to emphasize that its design could only be truly realized after society had been revolutionized. He therefore never concerned himself with such problems as muggings in the parks or vandalism in the elevators. In the Radiant City, crime and poverty no longer exist.

But if the Unité looks to the future, its roots are in the nineteenth-century utopian hopes for a perfect cooperative society, the same hopes that inspired Ebenezer Howard's cooperative quadrangles. Peter Serenyi has aptly compared the Unité to that French utopian palace of communal pleasures, the phalanstery of Charles

Fourier.[53] An early nineteenth-century rival of Saint-Simon, Fourier envisioned a structure resembling the château of Versailles to house the 1,600 members of his "phalanx" or rural utopian community. "We have no conception of the compound or collective forms of luxury," Fourier complained, and the phalanstery was designed to make up that lack.[54] He believed that in a properly run society all man's desires could find their appropriate gratification. The phalanstery, therefore, contains an elaborate series of lavish public rooms: theaters, libraries, ballrooms, and Fourier's special pride, the dining rooms where "exquisite food and a piquant selection of dining companions" can always be found.

The phalanstery can be seen as the nineteenth-century anticipation and the Unité as the twentieth-century realization of architecture in the service of collective pleasure. Both designs represent what Le Corbusier termed "the architecture of happiness," architecture created to deliver what he was fond of calling "the essential joys." Fourier, however, could only express his vision in the anachronistic image of the baroque palace. Le Corbusier finds the forms of collective pleasure in the most advanced techniques of mass production. For him, the architecture of happiness is also the architecture for the industrial era.

The comparison of the phalanstery and the Unité suggests, finally, the complexity of Le Corbusier's ideal city. For Fourier was the bitter antagonist of Saint-Simon, whose philosophy is so central to Le Corbusier's social thought. The rivalry of the two nineteenth-century prophets was more than personal. Since their time, French utopian thought has been divided into two distinct traditions. The Saint-Simonian tradition is the dream of society as the perfect industrial hierarchy. Its setting is urban, its thought technological, its goal production, and its highest value organization. Fourier and his followers have envisioned society as the perfect community: rural, small-scaled, egalitarian, dedicated to pleasure and self-fulfillment. In the Radiant City, Le Corbusier combines these two traditions into an original synthesis. He places a Fourierist phalanstery in the center of a Saint-Simonian industrial society. Community and organization thus find intense and appropriate expression: both are integral parts of Le Corbusier's ideal city for the Machine Age.

Notes

1   Joseph Conrad, *The Secret Agent* (New York, 1953), p. 11. The quotation is drawn from the Preface, first published in 1921.
2   For statistics of urban growth, see Adna Ferrin Weber, *The Growth of Cities in the Nineteenth Century* (Ithaca, NY, 1899).
3   Hsi-Huey Liang, "Lower-class Immigrants in Wilhelmine Berlin," in *The Urbanization of European Society in the Nineteenth Century*, eds. Andrew Lees and Lynn Lees (Lexington, Mass. 1976), p. 223.
4   Le Corbusier, *La Ville radieuse* (Boulogne-Seine, 1935), p. 181.
5   For Owen, see J. F. C. Harrison, *Quest for the New Moral World* (New York, 1969).
6   For Fourier, see Jonathan Beecher and Richard Bienvenu, eds., *The Utopian Vision of Charles Fourier* (Boston, 1971).

7   For Haussmann and his influence see David H. Pinkney, *Napoleon III and the Rebuilding of Paris* (Princeton, NJ, 1958); Howard Saalman, *Haussmann: Paris Transformed* (New York, 1971); and Anthony Sutcliffe, *The Autumn of Central Paris* (London, 1970).

8   Peter H. Mann, "Octavia Hill: An Appraisal," *Town Planning Review* 23, no. 3 (Oct. 1953): 223–37.

9   Friedrich Engels, *Zur Wohnungsfrage*, 2d edn. (Leipzig, 1887).

10 See Barbara Miller Lane, *Architecture and Politics in Germany, 1918–1945* (Cambridge, Mass., 1968).

11 Le Corbusier, *Urbanisme* (Paris, 1925), p. 135.

12 Lewis Mumford, "The Garden City Idea and Modern Planning," introductory essay to F. J. Osborn's edition of *Garden Cities of To-morrow* (Cambridge, Mass., 1965), p. 29. Although Osborn's edition bears the title of the 1902 edition, his text restores portions of the 1898 text that were cut in 1902. Osborn's is therefore a "definitive" text and I follow his usage in always referring to Howard's book as *Garden Cities of To-morrow*. All further references will come from Osborn's edition, abbreviated *GCT*.

13 See Donald Canty, ed., *The New City* (New York, 1969) for the details of this recommendation.

14 The New Towns, however, have had their problems. See "'New Towns' Face Growing Pains," *New York Times*, June 13, 1976, p. 26.

15 F. J. Osborn, Preface to *GCT*, p. 22.

16 Ibid., pp. 22–3.

17 James Silk Buckingham, *National Evils and Practical Remedies, with the Plan of a Model Town* (London, 1849). Although Howard mentions the utopian city of Buckingham in the text of *GCT* as one of the proposals he combined into the Garden City, he states in a footnote that in fact he had not seen Buckingham's plan until he had "got far on" with his project.

18 E. Howard, Papers, Early draft of *GCT*, Folio 3.

19 Ibid.

20 E. Howard, "Spiritual Influences Toward Social Progress," *Light*, April 30, 1910, p. 196. *Hygeia* was published in London in 1876.

21 Benjamin Ward Richardson, *Hygeia, A City of Health* (London, 1876), p. 21.

22 *GCT*, p. 76.

23 Ibid., pp. 50–6 and 71. Placing the churches along Grand Avenue means that no single church occupies the center of town. Howard's religious upbringing was Non-conformist.

24 *GCT*, p. 53.

25 Ibid., p. 54.

26 *GCT*, diagram #2. The diagram also shows such institutions as "convalescent homes" and the "asylums for blind and deaf" in the green belt. In an earlier version of his plan, Howard wanted the Agricultural Belt to cover 8,000 acres. See his "Summary of E. Howard's proposals for a Home Colony," *The Nationalisation News* 3, no. 29 (Feb. 1893): 20.

27 Howard Papers, Common Sense Socialism, Folio 10.

28 Alfred Marshall, "The Housing of the London Poor," *Contemporary Review* 45, no. 2 (Feb. 1884): 224–31.

29 Howard Papers, Folio 10. Howard recalled meeting Marshall in connection with stenography work he did for parliamentary commissions and discussing the Garden City idea with him. In a note added to *GCT* he claimed that he had not seen Marshall's article when he first formulated his ideas: *GCT*, p. 119.

30   *GCT*, pp. 58–88.

31   Howard Papers, quoted by Howard in an early draft of *GCT*, Folio 3.

32   *GCT*, pp. 89–111.

33   Ibid., p. 136.

34   "Return of Owners of Land Survey," analyzed in F. M. L. Thompson, *English Landed Society in the Nineteenth Century* (London, 1963), pp. 317–19.

35   Henry George, *Progress and Poverty* (New York, 1911), p. 201.

36   Howard, quoted in W. H. Brown's interview with him, "Ebenezer Howard, A Modern Influence," *Garden Cities and Town Planning* 7, no. 30 (Sept. 1908): 116.

37   *GCT*, p. 131.

38   Ibid., pp. 96–111.

39   Howard Papers, Lecture to a Fabian Society, January 11, 1901, Folio 3.

40   *GCT*, p. 104.

41   Ibid., p. 139.

42   I suspect the population of the Central City was put at 58,000 so that the whole complex would attain a population of exactly 250,000.

43   *GCT*, p. 142.

44   Ibid.

45   Ibid. Spencer held that public libraries in themselves were only "mildly communistic." See his "The New Toryism," *Contemporary Review*, 45, no. 2 (Feb. 1884): 153–67. These of course were Spencer's later views. A younger Spencer in *Social Statics* had called for the nationalization of the land. This permitted Howard to refer to Spencer as one of his influences: *GCT*, pp. 123–5.

46   Le Corbusier, *La ville radieuse* (Boulogne Seine, 1935), p. 192.

47   Ibid., title page.

48   Ibid., p. 154.

49   Ibid., p. 153.

50   Le Corbusier, *Quand les cathédrales étaient blanches* (Paris, 1937), pp. 280–1.

51   Le Corbusier, *La ville radieuse*, p. 167.

52   Ibid., p. 146.

53   Peter Serenyi, "Le Corbusier, Fourier, and the Monastery at Ema," cited footnote 15, chapter 21.

54   Charles Fourier, "An Architectural Innovation: The Street Gallery," in Jonathan Beecher and Richard Bienvenu, eds. and trans., *The Utopian Vision of Charles Fourier* (Boston, 1971), p. 243.

2

Authoritarian High Modernism

James C. Scott

> Then, as this morning on the dock, again I saw, as if for the first time in my life, the impeccably straight streets, the glistening glass of the pavement, the divine parallelepipeds of the transparent dwellings, the square harmony of the grayish blue rows of Numbers. And it seemed to me that not past generations, but I myself, had won a victory over the old god and the old life.
>
> Eugene Zamiatin, *We*

> Modern science, which displaced and replaced God, removed that obstacle [limits on freedom]. It also created a vacancy: the office of the supreme legislator-cum-manager, of the designer and administrator of the world order, was now horrifyingly empty. It had to be filled or else.... The emptiness of the throne was throughout the modern era a standing and tempting invitation to visionaries and adventurers. The dream of an all-embracing order and harmony remained as vivid as ever, and it seemed now closer than ever, more than ever within human reach. It was now up to mortal earthlings to bring it about and to secure its ascendancy.
>
> Zygmunt Bauman, *Modernity and the Holocaust*

...[S]tate simplifications...have the character of maps. That is, they are designed to summarize precisely those aspects of a complex world that are of immediate interest to the mapmaker and to ignore the rest. To complain that a map lacks nuance and detail makes no sense unless it omits information necessary to its function. A city map that aspired to represent every traffic light, every pothole, every building, and every bush and tree in every park would threaten to become as large and as complex as the city that it depicted.[1] And it certainly would defeat the purpose of mapping,

Readings in Planning Theory, Third Edition. Edited by Susan S. Fainstein and Scott Campbell.
Editorial material and organization © 2012 Blackwell Publishing Ltd.
Published 2012 by Blackwell Publishing Ltd.

which is to abstract and summarize. A map is an instrument designed for a purpose. We may judge that purpose noble or morally offensive, but the map itself either serves or fails to serve its intended use.

In case after case, however, we ... [see] the apparent power of maps to transform as well as merely to summarize the facts that they portray. This transformative power resides not in the map, of course, but rather in the power possessed by those who deploy the perspective of that particular map.[2] A private corporation aiming to maximize sustainable timber yields, profit, or production will map its world according to this logic and will use what power it has to ensure that the logic of its map prevails. The state has no monopoly on utilitarian simplifications. What the state does at least aspire to, though, is a monopoly on the legitimate use of force. That is surely why, from the seventeenth century until now, the most transformative maps have been those invented and applied by the most powerful institution in society: the state.

Until recently, the ability of the state to impose its schemes on society was limited by the state's modest ambitions and its limited capacity. Although utopian aspirations to a finely tuned social control can be traced back to Enlightenment thought and to monastic and military practices, the eighteenth-century European state was still largely a machine for extraction. It is true that state officials, particularly under absolutism, had mapped much more of their kingdoms' populations, land tenures, production, and trade than their predecessors had and that they had become increasingly efficient in pumping revenue, grain, and conscripts from the countryside. But there was more than a little irony in their claim to absolute rule. They lacked the consistent coercive power, the fine-grained administrative grid, or the detailed knowledge that would have permitted them to undertake more intrusive experiments in social engineering. To give their growing ambitions full rein, they required a far greater hubris, a state machinery that was equal to the task, and a society they could master. By the mid-nineteenth century in the West and by the early twentieth century elsewhere, these conditions were being met.

I believe that many of the most tragic episodes of state development in the late nineteenth and twentieth centuries originate in a particularly pernicious combination of three elements. The first is the aspiration to the administrative ordering of nature and society, an aspiration ... at work in scientific forestry, but one raised to a far more comprehensive and ambitious level. "High modernism" seems an appropriate term for this aspiration.[3] As a faith, it was shared by many across a wide spectrum of political ideologies. Its main carriers and exponents were the avant-garde among engineers, planners, technocrats, high-level administrators, architects, scientists, and visionaries. If one were to imagine a pantheon or Hall of Fame of high-modernist figures, it would almost certainly include such names as Henri Comte de Saint-Simon, Le Corbusier, Walther Rathenau, Robert McNamara, Robert Moses, Jean Monnet, the Shah of Iran, David Lilienthal, Vladimir I. Lenin, Leon Trotsky, and Julius Nyerere.[4] They envisioned a sweeping, rational engineering of all aspects of social life in order to improve the human condition. As a conviction, high modernism was not the exclusive property of any political tendency; it had both right- and left-wing variants, as we shall see. The second element is the unrestrained use of the power of the modern state as an instrument for achieving these designs. The third element is a weakened or prostrate civil society that lacks the capacity to resist these plans. The ideology of high modernism provides, as it were, the desire; the modern state provides the means of acting on that desire; and the incapacitated civil society provides the leveled terrain on which to build (dis)utopias.

We shall return shortly to the premises of high modernism. But here it is important to note that many of the great state-sponsored calamities of the twentieth century have been the work of rulers with grandiose and utopian plans for their society. One can identify a high-modernist utopianism of the right, of which Nazism is surely the diagnostic example.[5] The massive social engineering under apartheid in South Africa, the modernization plans of the Shah of Iran, villagization in Vietnam, and huge late-colonial development schemes (for example, the Gezira scheme in the Sudan) could be considered under this rubric.[6] And yet there is no denying that much of the massive, state-enforced social engineering of the twentieth century has been the work of progressive, often revolutionary elites. Why?

The answer, I believe, lies in the fact that it is typically progressives who have come to power with a comprehensive critique of existing society and a popular mandate (at least initially) to transform it. These progressives have wanted to use that power to bring about enormous changes in people's habits, work, living patterns, moral conduct, and world view.[7] They have deployed what Václav Havel has called "the armory of holistic social engineering."[8] Utopian aspirations per se are not dangerous. As Oscar Wilde remarked, "A map of the world which does not include Utopia is not worth even glancing at, for it leaves out the one country at which Humanity is always landing."[9] Where the utopian vision goes wrong is when it is held by ruling elites with no commitment to democracy or civil rights and who are therefore likely to use unbridled state power for its achievement. Where it goes brutally wrong is when the society subjected to such utopian experiments lacks the capacity to mount a determined resistance.

What is high modernism, then? It is best conceived as a strong (one might even say muscle-bound) version of the beliefs in scientific and technical progress that were associated with industrialization in Western Europe and in North America from roughly 1830 until World War I. At its center was a supreme self-confidence about continued linear progress, the development of scientific and technical knowledge, the expansion of production, the rational design of social order, the growing satisfaction of human needs, and, not least, an increasing control over nature (including human nature) commensurate with scientific understanding of natural laws.[10] *High modernism* is thus a particularly sweeping vision of how the benefits of technical and scientific progress might be applied – usually through the state – in every field of human activity.[11] If, as we have seen, the simplified, utilitarian *descriptions* of state officials had a tendency, through the exercise of state power, to bring the facts into line with their representations, then one might say that the high-modern state began with extensive *prescriptions* for a new society, and it intended to impose them.

It would have been hard not to have been a modernist of some stripe at the end of the nineteenth century in the West. How could one fail to be impressed – even awed – by the vast transformation wrought by science and industry?[12] Anyone who was, say, sixty years old in Manchester, England, would have witnessed in his or her lifetime a revolution in the manufacturing of cotton and wool textiles, the growth of the factory system, the application of steam power and other astounding new mechanical devices to production, remarkable breakthroughs in metallurgy and transportation (especially railroads), and the appearance of cheap mass-produced commodities. Given the stunning advances in chemistry, physics, medicine, math, and engineering, anyone even slightly attentive to the world of science would have almost come to expect a continuing stream of new marvels (such as the internal combustion engine and electricity). The unprecedented transformations of the nineteenth century may have impoverished and marginalized many, but even the victims recognized that something revolutionary was afoot. All this sounds rather naive today, when we are far more sober about the limits and costs of technological progress and have acquired a postmodern skepticism about any totalizing discourse. Still, this new sensibility ignores both the degree to which modernist assumptions prevail in our lives and, especially, the great enthusiasm and revolutionary hubris that were part and parcel of high modernism.

The Discovery of Society

The path from description to presecription was not so much an inadvertent result of a deep psychological tendency as a deliberate move. The point of the Enlightenment view of legal codes was less to mirror the distinctive customs and practices of a people than to create a cultural community by codifying and generalizing the most rational of those customs and suppressing the more obscure and barbaric ones.[13] Establishing uniform standards of weight and measurement across a kingdom had a greater purpose than just making trade easier; the new standards were intended both to express and to promote a new cultural unity. Well before the tools existed to make good on this cultural revolution, Enlightenment thinkers such as Condorcet were looking ahead to the day when the tools would be in place. He wrote in 1782: "Those sciences, created almost in our own days, the object of which is man himself, the direct goal of which is the happiness of man, will enjoy a progress no less sure than that of the physical sciences, and this idea so sweet, that our descendants will surpass us in wisdom as in enlightenment, is no longer an illusion. In meditating on the nature of the moral sciences, one cannot help seeing that, as they are based like physical sciences on the observation of fact, they must follow the same method, acquire a language equally exact and precise, attaining the same degree of certainty."[14] The gleam in Condorcet's eye became, by the mid-nineteenth century, an active utopian project. Simplification and rationalization previously applied to forests, weights and measures, taxation, and factories were now applied to the design of society as a whole.[15] Industrial-strength social engineering was born. While factories and forests might be planned by private entrepreneurs, the ambition of engineering whole societies was almost exclusively a project of the nation-state.

This new conception of the state's role represented a fundamental transformation. Before then, the state's activities had been largely confined to those that contributed to the wealth and power of the sovereign, as the example of scientific forestry and cameral science illustrated. The idea that one of the central purposes of the state was the improvement of all the members of society – their health, skills and education, longevity, productivity, morals, and family life – was quite novel.[16] There was, of course, a direct connection between the old conception of the state and this new one. A state that improved its population's skills, vigor, civic morals, and work habits would increase its tax base and field better armies; it was a policy that any enlightened sovereign might pursue. And yet, in the nineteenth century, the welfare of the population came increasingly to be seen, not merely as a means to national strength, but as an end in itself.

One essential precondition of this transformation was the discovery of society as a reified object that was separate from the state and that could be scientifically described. In this respect, the production of statistical knowledge about the population – its age profiles, occupations, fertility, literacy, property ownership, law-abidingness (as demonstrated by crime statistics) – allowed state officials to characterize the population in elaborate new ways, much as scientific forestry permitted the forester to carefully describe the forest. Ian Hacking explains how a suicide or homicide rate, for example, came to be seen as a characteristic of a people, so that one could speak of a "budget" of homicides that would be "spent" each year, like routine debits from an account, although the particular murderers and their victims were unknown.[17] Statistical facts were elaborated into social laws. It was but a small step from a simplified description of society to a design and manipulation of society, with its improvement in mind. If one could reshape nature to design a more suitable forest, why not reshape society to create a more suitable population?

The scope of intervention was potentially endless. Society became an object that the state might manage and transform with a view toward perfecting it. A progressive nation-state would set about engineering its society according to the most advanced technical standards of the new moral sciences. The existing social order, which had been more or less taken by earlier states as a given, reproducing itself under the watchful eye of the state, was for the first time the subject of active management. It was possible to conceive of an artificial, engineered society designed, not by custom and historical accident, but according to conscious, rational, scientific criteria. Every nook and cranny of the social order might be improved upon: personal hygiene, diet, child rearing, housing, posture, recreation, family structure, and, most infamously, the genetic inheritance of the population.[18] The working poor were often the first subjects of scientific social planning.[19] Schemes for improving their daily lives were promulgated by progressive urban and public-health policies and instituted in model factory towns and newly founded welfare agencies. Subpopulations found wanting in ways that were potentially threatening – such as indigents, vagabonds, the mentally ill, and criminals – might be made the objects of the most intensive social engineering.[20]

The metaphor of gardening, Zygmunt Bauman suggests, captures much of this new spirit. The gardener – perhaps a landscape architect specializing in formal gardens is the most appropriate parallel – takes a natural site and creates an entirely designed space of botanical order. Although the organic character of the flora limits what can be achieved, the gardener has enormous discretion in the overall arrangement and in training, pruning, planting, and weeding out selected plants. As an untended forest is to a long-managed scientific forest, so untended nature is to the garden. The garden is one of man's attempts to impose his own principles of order, utility, and beauty on nature.[21] What grows in the garden is always a small, consciously selected sample of what *might* be grown there. Similarly, social engineers consciously set out to design and maintain a more perfect social order. An Enlightenment belief in the self-improvement of man became, by degrees, a belief in the perfectibility of social order.

One of the great paradoxes of social engineering is that it seems at odds with the experience of modernity generally. Trying to jell a social world, the most striking characteristic of which appears to be flux, seems rather like trying to manage a whirlwind. Marx was hardly alone in claiming that the "constant revolutionizing of production, uninterrupted disturbance of all social relations, everlasting uncertainty and agitation, distinguish the bourgeois epoch from all earlier times."[22] The experience of modernity (in literature, art, industry, transportation, and popular culture) was, above all, the experience of disorienting speed, movement, and change, which self-proclaimed modernists found exhilarating and liberating.[23] Perhaps the most charitable way of resolving this paradox is to imagine that what these designers of society had in mind was roughly what designers of locomotives had in mind with "streamlining." Rather than arresting social change, they hoped to design a shape to social life that would minimize the friction of progress. The difficulty with this resolution is that state social engineering was inherently authoritarian. In place of multiple sources of invention and change, there was a single planning authority; in place of the plasticity and autonomy of existing social life, there was a fixed social order in which positions were designated. The tendency toward various forms of "social taxidermy" was unavoidable.

The Radical Authority of High Modernism

> The real thing is that this time we're going to get science applied to social problems and backed by the whole force of the state, just as war has been backed by the whole force of the state in the past. (C. S. Lewis, *That Hideous Strength*)

The troubling features of high modernism derive, for the most part, from its claim to speak about the improvement of the human condition with the authority of scientific knowledge and its tendency to disallow other competing sources of judgment.

First and foremost, high modernism implies a truly radical break with history and tradition. Insofar as rational thought and scientific laws could provide a single answer to every empirical question, nothing ought to be taken for granted. All human habits and practices that were inherited and hence not based on scientific reasoning – from the structure of the family and patterns of residence to moral values and forms of production – would have to be reexamined and redesigned. The structures of the past were typically the products of myth, superstition, and religious prejudice. It followed that scientifically designed schemes for production and social life would be superior to received tradition.

The sources of this view are deeply authoritarian. If a planned social order is better than the accidental, irrational deposit of historical practice, two conclusions follow. Only those who have the scientific knowledge to discern and create this superior social order are fit to rule in the new age. Further, those who through retrograde ignorance refuse to yield to the scientific plan need to be educated to its benefits or else swept aside. Strong versions of high modernism, such as those held by Lenin and Le Corbusier, cultivated an Olympian ruthlessness toward the subjects of their interventions. At its most radical, high modernism imagined wiping the slate utterly clean and beginning from zero.[24]

High-modernist ideology thus tends to devalue or banish politics. Political interests can only frustrate the social solutions devised by specialists with scientific tools adequate to their analysis. As individuals, high modernists might well hold democratic views about popular sovereignty or classical liberal views about the inviolability of a private sphere that restrained them, but such convictions are external to, and often at war with, their high-modernist convictions.

Although high modernists came to imagine the refashioning of social habits and of human nature itself, they began with a nearly limitless ambition to transform nature to suit man's purposes – an ambition that remained central to their faith. How completely the utopian possibilities gripped intellectuals of almost every political persuasion is captured in the paean to technical progress of the *Communist Manifesto*, where Marx and Engels write of the "subjection of nature's forces to man, machinery, and the application of chemistry to agriculture and industry, steam navigation, railways, electric telegraphs, clearing of whole continents for cultivation, canalization of rivers, whole populations conjured out of the ground."[25] In fact, this promise, made plausible by capitalist development, was for Marx the point of departure for socialism, which would place the fruits of capitalism at the service of the working class for the first time. The intellectual air in the late nineteenth century was filled with proposals for such vast engineering projects as the Suez Canal, which was completed in 1869 with enormous consequences for trade between Asia and Europe. The pages of *Le Globe*, the organ of utopian socialists of Saint-Simon's persuasion, featured an endless stream of discussions about massive projects: the construction of the Panama Canal, the development of the United States, far-reaching schemes for energy and transportation. This belief that it was man's destiny to tame nature to suit his interests and preserve his safety is perhaps the keystone of high modernism, partly because the success of so many grand ventures was already manifest.[26]

Once again the authoritarian and statist implications of this vision are clear. The very scale of such projects meant that, with few exceptions (such as the early canals), they demanded large infusions of monies raised through taxes or credit. Even if one could imagine them being financed privately in a capitalist economy, they typically required a vast public authority empowered to condemn private property, relocate people against their will, guarantee the loans or bonds required, and coordinate the work of the many state agencies involved. In a statist society, be it Louis Napoleon's France or Lenin's Soviet Union, such power was already built into the political system. In a nonstatist society, such tasks have required new public authorities or "super-agencies" having quasi-governmental powers for sending men to the moon or for constructing dams, irrigation works, highways, and public transportation systems.

The temporal emphasis of high modernism is almost exclusively on the future. Although any ideology with a large altar dedicated to progress is bound to privilege the future, high modernism carries this to great lengths. The past is an impediment, a history that must be transcended; the present is the platform for launching plans for a better future. A key characteristic of discourses of high modernism and of the public pronouncements of those states that have embraced it is a heavy reliance on visual images of heroic progress toward a totally transformed future.[27] The strategic choice of the future is freighted with consequences. To the degree that the future is known and achievable – a belief that the faith in progress encourages – the less future benefits are discounted for uncertainty. The practical effect is to convince most high modernists that the certainty of a better future justifies the many short-term sacrifices required to get there.[28] The ubiquity of five-year plans in socialist states is an example of that conviction. Progress is objectified by a series of preconceived goals – largely material and quantifiable – which are to be achieved through savings, labor, and investments in the interim. There may, of course, be no alternative to planning, especially when the urgency of a single goal, such as winning a war, seems to require the subordination of every other goal. The immanent logic of such an exercise, however, implies a degree of certainty about the future, about means–ends calculations, and about the meaning of human welfare that is truly heroic. That such plans have often had to be adjusted or abandoned is an indication of just how heroic are the assumptions behind them.

In this reading, high modernism ought to appeal greatly to the classes and strata who have most to gain – in status, power, and wealth – from its world view. And indeed it is the ideology par excellence of the bureaucratic intelligentsia, technicians, planners, and engineers.[29] The position accorded to them is not just one of rule and privilege but also one of responsibility for the great works of nation building and social transformation. Where this intelligentsia conceives of its mission as the dragging of a technically backward, unschooled, subsistence-oriented population into the twentieth century, its self-assigned cultural role as educator of its people becomes doubly grandiose. Having a historic mission of such breadth may provide a ruling intelligentsia with high morale, solidarity, and the willingness to make (and impose) sacrifices. This vision of a great future is often in sharp contrast to the disorder, misery, and unseemly scramble for petty advantage that the elites very likely see in their daily foreground. One might in fact speculate that the more intractable and resistant the real world faced by the planner, the greater the need for utopian plans to fill, as it were, the void that would otherwise invite despair. The elites who elaborate such plans implicitly represent themselves as exemplars of the learning and progressive views to which their compatriots might aspire. Given the ideological advantages of high modernism as a discourse, it is hardly surprising that so many postcolonial elites have marched under its banner.[30]

Aided by hindsight as it is, this unsympathetic account of high-modernist audacity is, in one important respect, grossly unfair. If we put the development of high-modernist beliefs in their historical context, if we ask who the enemies of high modernism actually were, a far more sympathetic picture emerges. Doctors and public-health engineers who did possess new knowledge that could save millions of lives were often thwarted by popular prejudices and entrenched political interests. Urban planners who could in fact redesign urban housing to be cheaper, more healthful, and more convenient were blocked by real-estate interests and existing tastes. Inventors and engineers who had devised revolutionary new modes of power and transportation faced opposition from industrialists and laborers whose profits and jobs the new technology would almost certainly displace.

For nineteenth-century high modernists, the scientific domination of nature (including human nature) was emancipatory. It "promised freedom from scarcity, want and the arbitrariness of natural calamity," David Harvey observes. "The development of rational forms of social organization and rational modes of thought promised liberation from the irrationalities of myth, religion, superstition, release from the arbitrary use of power as well as from the dark side of our human natures."[31] Before we turn to later versions of high modernism, we should recall two important facts about their nineteenth-century forebears: first, that virtually every high-modernist intervention was undertaken in the name of and with the support of citizens seeking help and protection, and, second, that we are all beneficiaries, in countless ways, of these various high-modernist schemes.

Twentieth-Century High Modernism

The idea of a root-and-branch, rational engineering of entire social orders in creating realizable utopias is a largely twentieth-century phenomenon. And a range of historical soils have seemed particularly favorable for the flourishing of high-modernist ideology. Those soils include crises of state power, such as wars and economic depressions, and circumstances in which a state's capacity for relatively unimpeded planning is greatly enhanced, such as the revolutionary conquest of power and colonial rule.

The industrial warfare of the twentieth century has required unprecedented steps toward the total mobilization of the society and the economy.[32] Even quite liberal societies like the United States and Britain became, in the context of war mobilization, directly administered societies. The worldwide depression of the 1930s similarly propelled liberal states into extensive experiments in social and economic planning in an effort to relieve economic distress and to retain popular legitimacy. In the cases of war and depression, the rush toward an administered society has an aspect of *force majeure* to it. The postwar rebuilding of a war-torn nation may well fall in the same category.

Revolution and colonialism, however, are hospitable to high modernism for different reasons. A revolutionary regime and a colonial regime each disposes of an unusual degree of power. The revolutionary state has defeated the *ancien régime*, often has its partisans' mandate to remake the society after its image, *and* faces a prostrate civil society whose capacity for active resistance is limited.[33] The millennial expectations commonly associated with revolutionary movements give further impetus to high-modernist ambitions. Colonial regimes, particularly late colonial regimes, have often been sites of extensive experiments in social engineering.[34] An ideology of "welfare colonialism" combined with the authoritarian power inherent in colonial rule have encouraged ambitious schemes to remake native societies.

If one were required to pinpoint the "birth" of twentieth-century high modernism, specifying a particular time, place, and individual – in what is admittedly a rather arbitrary exercise, given high modernism's many intellectual wellsprings – a strong case can be made for German mobilization during World War I and the figure most closely associated with it, Walther Rathenau. German economic mobilization was the technocratic wonder of the war. That Germany kept its armies in the field and adequately supplied long after most observers had predicted its collapse was largely due to Rathenau's planning.[35] An industrial engineer and head of the great electrical firm A.E.G. (Allgemeine Elektricitäts-Gesellschaft), which had been founded by his father, Rathenau was placed in charge of the Office of War Raw Materials (Kriegsrohstoffabteilung).[36] He realized that the planned rationing of raw materials and transport was the key to sustaining the war effort. Inventing a planned economy step by step, as it were, Germany achieved feats – in industrial production, munitions and armament supply, transportation and traffic control, price controls, and civilian rationing – that had never before been attempted. The scope of planning and coordination necessitated an unprecedented mobilization of conscripts, soldiers, and war-related industrial labor. Such mobilization fostered the idea of creating "administered mass organizations" that would encompass the entire society.[37]

Rathenau's faith in pervasive planning and in rationalizing production had deep roots in the intellectual connection being forged between the physical laws of thermodynamics on one hand and the new applied sciences of work on the other. For many specialists, a narrow and materialist "productivism" treated human labor as a mechanical system which could be decomposed into energy transfers, motion, and the physics of work. The simplification of labor into isolated problems of mechanical efficiencies led directly to the aspiration for a scientific control of the entire labor process. Late nineteenth-century materialism, as Anson Rabinbach emphasizes, had an equivalence between technology and physiology at its metaphysical core.[38]

This productivism had at least two distinct lineages, one of them North American and the other European. An American contribution came from the influential work of Frederick Taylor, whose minute decomposition of factory labor into isolable, precise, repetitive motions had begun to revolutionize the organization of factory work.[39] For the factory manager or engineer, the newly invented assembly lines permitted the use of unskilled labor and control over not only the pace of production but the whole labor process. The European tradition of "energetics," which focused on questions of motion, fatigue, measured rest, rational hygiene, and nutrition, also treated the worker notionally as a machine, albeit a machine that must be well fed and kept in good working order. In place of workers, there was an abstract, standardized worker with uniform physical capacities and needs. Seen initially as a way of increasing wartime efficiency at the front and in industry, the Kaiser Wilhelm Institut für Arbeitsphysiologie, like Taylorism, was based on a scheme to rationalize the body.[40]

What is most remarkable about both traditions is, once again, how widely they were believed by educated elites who were otherwise poles apart politically. "Taylorism and technocracy were the watchwords of a three-pronged idealism: the elimination of economic and social crisis, the expansion of productivity through science, and the reenchantment of technology. The vision of society in which social conflict was eliminated in favor of technological and scientific imperatives could embrace liberal, socialist, authoritarian, and even communist and fascist solutions. Productivism, in short, was politically promiscuous."[41]

The appeal of one or another form of productivism across much of the right and center of the political spectrum was largely due to its promise as a technological "fix" for class struggle. If, as its advocates claimed, it could vastly increase worker output, then the politics of redistribution could be replaced by class collaboration, in which both profits and wages could grow at once. For much of the left, productivism promised the replacement of the capitalist by the engineer or by the state expert or official. It also proposed a single optimum solution, or "best practice," for any problem in the organization of work. The logical outcome was some form of slide-rule authoritarianism in the interest, presumably, of all.[42]

A combination of Rathenau's broad training in philosophy and economics, his wartime experience with planning, and the social conclusions that he thought were inherent in the precision, reach, and transforming potential of electric power allowed him to draw the broadest lessons for social organization. In the war, private industry had given way to a kind of state socialism; "gigantic industrial enterprises had transcended their ostensibly private owners and all the laws of property."[43] The decisions required had nothing to do with ideology; they were driven by purely technical and economic necessities. The rule of specialists and the new technological possibilities, particularly huge electric power grids, made possible a new social-industrial order that was both centralized and locally autonomous. During the time when war made necessary a coalition among industrial firms, technocrats, and the state, Rathenau discerned the shape of a progressive peacetime society. Inasmuch as the technical and economic requirements for reconstruction were obvious and required the same sort of collaboration in all countries, Rathenau's rationalist faith in planning had an internationalist flavor. He characterized the modern era as a "new machine order … [and] a consolidation of the world into an unconscious association of constraint, into an uninterrupted community of production and harmony."[44]

The world war was the high-water mark for the political influence of engineers and planners. Having seen what could be accomplished in extremis, they imagined what they could achieve if the identical energy and planning were devoted to popular welfare rather than mass destruction. Together with many political leaders, industrialists, labor leaders, and prominent intellectuals (such as Philip Gibbs in England, Ernst Jünger in Germany, and Gustave Le Bon in France), they concluded that only a renewed and comprehensive dedication to technical innovation and the planning it made possible could rebuild the European economies and bring social peace.[45]

Lenin himself was deeply impressed by the achievements of German industrial mobilization and believed that it had shown how production might be socialized. Just as Lenin believed that Marx had discovered immutable social laws akin to Darwin's laws of evolution, so he believed that the new technologies of mass production were scientific laws and not social constructions. Barely a month before the October 1917 revolution, he wrote that the war had "accelerated the development of capitalism to such a tremendous degree, converting monopoly capitalism into *state*-monopoly capitalism, that *neither* the proletariat *nor* the revolutionary petty-bourgeois democrats *can* keep within the limits of capitalism."[46] He and his economic advisers drew directly on the work of Rathenau and Mollendorf in their plans for the Soviet economy. The German war economy was for Lenin "the ultimate in modern, large-scale capitalist techniques, planning and organization"; he took it to be the prototype of a socialized economy.[47] Presumably, if the state in question were in the hands of representatives of the working class, the basis of a socialist system would exist. Lenin's vision of the future looked much like Rathenau's, providing, of course, we ignore the not so small matter of a revolutionary seizure of power.

Lenin was not slow to appreciate how Taylorism on the factory floor offered advantages for the socialist control of production. Although he had earlier denounced such techniques, calling them the "scientific extortion of sweat," by the time of the revolution he had become an enthusiastic advocate of systematic control as practiced in Germany. He extolled "the principle of discipline, organization, and harmonious cooperation based upon the most modern, mechanized industry, the most rigid system of accountability and control."[48]

> The Taylor system, the last word of capitalism in this respect, like all capitalist progress, is a combination of the subtle brutality of bourgeois exploitation and a number of its great scientific achievements in the fields of analysing mechanical motions during work, the elimination of superfluous and awkward motions, the working out of correct methods of work, the introduction of the best system of accounting and control, etc. The Soviet Republic must at all costs adopt all that is valuable in the achievements of science and technology in this field.… We must organize in Russia the study and teaching of the Taylor system and systematically try it out and adapt it to our purposes.[49]

By 1918, with production falling, he was calling for rigid work norms and, if necessary, the reintroduction of hated piecework. The first All-Russian Congress for Initiatives in Scientific Management was convened in 1921 and featured disputes between advocates of Taylorism and those of energetics (also called ergonomics). At least twenty institutes and as many journals were by then devoted to scientific management in the Soviet Union. A command economy at the macrolevel and Taylorist principles of central coordination at the microlevel of the factory floor provided an attractive and symbiotic package for an authoritarian, high-modernist revolutionary like Lenin.

Despite the authoritarian temptations of twentieth-century high modernism, they have often been resisted. The reasons are not only complex; they are different from case to case. While it is not my intention to examine in detail all the potential obstacles to high-modernist planning, the particular barrier posed by liberal democratic ideas and institutions deserves emphasis. Three factors seem decisive. The first is the existence and belief in a private sphere of activity in which the state and its agencies may not legitimately interfere. To be sure, this zone of autonomy has had a beleaguered existence as, following Mannheim, more heretofore private spheres have been made the object of official intervention. Much of the work of Michel Foucault was an attempt to map these incursions into health, sexuality, mental illness, vagrancy, or sanitation and the strategies behind them. Nevertheless, the idea of a private realm has served to limit the ambitions of many high modernists, through either their own political values or their healthy respect for the political storm that such incursions would provoke.

The second, closely related factor is the private sector in liberal political economy. As Foucault put it: unlike absolutism and mercantilism, "political economy announces the unknowability for the sovereign of the totality of economic processes and, as a consequence, the *impossibility of an economic sovereignty*."[50] The point of liberal political economy was not only that a free market protected property and created wealth but also that the economy was far too complex for it ever to be managed in detail by a hierarchical administration.[51]

The third and by far most important barrier to thoroughgoing high-modernist schemes has been the existence of working, representative institutions through which a resistant society could make its influence felt. Such institutions have thwarted the most draconian features of high-modernist schemes in roughly the same way that publicity and mobilized opposition in open societies, as Amartya Sen has argued, have prevented famines. Rulers, he notes, do not go hungry, and they are unlikely to learn about and respond readily to curb famine unless their institutional position provides strong incentives. The freedoms of speech, of assembly, and of the press ensure that widespread hunger will be publicized, while the freedoms of assembly and elections in representative institutions ensure that it is in the interest of elected officials' self-preservation to prevent famine when they can. In the same fashion, high-modernist schemes in liberal democratic settings must accommodate themselves sufficiently to local opinion in order to avoid being undone at the polls.

Notes

1 My colleague Paul Landau recalls the story by Borges in which a king, unhappy at maps that do not do justice to his kingdom, finally insists on a map with a scale of one-to-one. When complete, the new map exactly covers the existing kingdom, submerging the real one beneath its representation.

2 A commonplace example may help. One of the ordinary frustrations of the modern citizen, even in liberal democracies, is the difficulty of representing his unique case to a powerful agent of a bureaucratic institution. But the functionary operates with a simplified grid designed to cover all the cases that she confronts. Once a decision has been made as to which "bin" or "pigeonhole" the case falls into, the action to be taken or the protocol to be followed is largely cut-and-dried. The functionary endeavors to sort the case into the appropriate category, while the citizen resists being treated as an instance of a category and tries to insist, often unsuccessfully, that his unique case be examined on its singular merits.

3 I have borrowed the term "high modernism" from David Harvey, *The Condition of Post Modernity: An Enquiry into the Origins of Social Change* (Oxford: Basil Blackwell, 1989). Harvey locates the high-water mark of this sort of modernism in the post-World War II period, and his concern is particularly with capitalism and the organization of production. But his description of high modernism also works well here: "The belief 'in linear progress, absolute truths, and rational planning of ideal social orders' under standardized conditions of knowledge and production was particularly strong. The modernism that resulted was, as a result, 'positivistic, technocratic, and rationalistic' at the same time as it was imposed as the work of an elite avant-garde of planners, artists, architects, critics, and other guardians of high taste. The 'modernization' of European economies proceeded apace, while the whole thrust of international politics and trade was justified as bringing a benevolent and progressive 'modernization process' to a backward Third World" (p. 35).

4 For case studies of "public entrepreneurs" in the United States, see Eugene Lewis's study of Hyman Rickover, J. Edgar Hoover, and Robert Moses, *Public Entrepreneurs: Toward a Theory of Bureaucratic Political Power: The Organizational Lives of Hyman Rickover, J. Edgar Hoover, and Robert Moses* (Bloomington: Indiana University Press, 1980). Monnet, like Rathenau, had experience in economic mobilization during World War I, when he helped organize the transatlantic supply of war material for Britain and France, a role that he resumed during World War II. By the time he helped plan the postwar integration of French and German coal and steel production, he had already had several decades of experience in supranational management. See François Duchene, *Jean Monnet: The First Statesman of Interdependence* (New York: Norton, 1995).

5 I will not pursue the argument here, but I think Nazism is best understood as a reactionary form of modernism. Like the progressive left, the Nazi elites had grandiose visions of state-enforced social engineering, which included, of course, extermination, expulsion, forced sterilization, and selective breeding and which aimed at "improving" genetically on human nature. The case for Nazism as a virulent form of modernism is made brilliantly and convincingly by Zygmunt Bauman in *Modernity and the Holocaust* (Oxford: Oxford University Press, 1989). See also, along the same lines, Jeffery Herf, *Reactionary Modernism: Technology, Culture, and Politics in Weimar and the Third Reich*

(Cambridge: Cambridge University Press, 1984), and Norbert Frei, *National Socialist Rule in Germany: The Führer State, 1933–1945*, trans. Simon B. Steyne (Oxford: Oxford University Press, 1993).

6 I am grateful to James Ferguson for reminding me that reactionary high-modernist schemes are about as ubiquitous as progressive variants.

7 This is not by any means meant to be a brief for conservatism. Conservatives of many stripes may care little for civil liberties and may resort to whatever brutalities seem necessary to remain in power. But their ambitions and hubris are much more limited; their plans (in contrast to those of reactionary modernists) do not necessitate turning society upside down to create new collectivities, new family and group loyalties, and new people.

8 Václav Havel, address given at Victoria University, Wellington, New Zealand, on March 31, 1995, reprinted in the *New York Review of Books* 42, no. 11 (June 22, 1995): 36.

9 Quoted in Zygmunt Bauman, *Socialism: The Active Utopia* (New York: Holmes and Meier, 1976), p. 11.

10 For an enlightening discussion of the intellectual lineage of authoritarian environmentalism, see Douglas R. Weiner, "Demythologizing Environmentalism," *Journal of the History of Biology* 25, no. 3 (Fall 1992): 385–411.

11 See Michael Adas's *Machines as the Measure of Men: Science, Technology, and Ideologies of Western Dominance* (Ithaca: Cornell University Press, 1989) and Marshall Berman's *All That Is Solid Melts into Air: The Experience of Modernity* (New York: Penguin, 1988). What is new in high modernism, I believe, is not so much the aspiration for comprehensive planning. Many imperial and absolutist states have had similar aspirations. What are new are the administrative technology and social knowledge that make it plausible to imagine organizing an entire society in ways that only the barracks or the monastery had been organized before. In this respect, Michel Foucault's argument, in *Discipline and Punish: The Birth of the Prison*, trans. Alan Sheridan (New York: Vintage Books, 1977), is persuasive.

12 Here I want to distinguish between advances in scientific knowledge and inventions (many of which occurred in the eighteenth century or earlier) and the massive transformations that scientific inventions wrought in daily material life (which came generally in the nineteenth century).

13 Witold Kula, *Measures and Men*, trans. R. Szreter (Princeton: Princeton University Press, 1986), p. 211.

14 Quoted in Ian Hacking, *The Taming of Chance* (Cambridge: Cambridge University Press, 1990), p. 38. A few years later, the Jacobins were, one could argue, the first to attempt to actually engineer happiness by transforming the social order. As Saint-Just wrote, "The idea of happiness is new in Europe." See Albert O. Hirschman, "Rival Interpretations of Market Society: Civilizing, Destructive, or Feeble," *Journal of Economic Literature* 20 (December 1982): 1463–84.

15 I am greatly indebted to James Ferguson, whose perceptive comments on an early draft of the book pointed me in this direction.

16 See, for example, Graham Buschell, Colin Gordon, and Peter Miller, eds., *The Foucault Effect: Studies in Governmentality* (London: Harvester Wheatsheaf, 1991), chap. 4.

17 Hacking, *The Taming of Chance*, p. 105. Hacking shows brilliantly how a statistical "average" metamorphosed into the category "normal," and "normal," in turn, into a "normative" standard to be achieved by social engineering.

18 By now, a great deal of historical research has made crystal clear how widespread throughout the West was the support for eugenic engineering. The belief that the state must intervene to protect the races' physical and mental characteristics was common among progressives and animated a well-nigh international social movement. By 1926, twenty-three of the forty-eight U.S. states had laws permitting sterilization.

19 See Gareth Stedman-Jones, *Languages of Class: Studies in English Working-Class History, 1832–1982* (Cambridge: Cambridge University Press, 1983). It is important to recognize that, among Western powers, virtually all the initiatives associated with the "civilizing missions" of colonialism were preceded by comparable programs to assimilate and civilize their own lower-class populations, both rural and urban. The difference, perhaps, is that in the colonial setting officials had greater coercive power over an objectified and alien population, thus allowing for greater feats of social engineering.

20 For a science-fiction account of the attempt to create a "technocratic and objective man" who would be free of "nature," see C. S. Lewis, *That Hideous Strength: A Modern Fairy Tale for Grown-Ups* (New York: Macmillan, 1946).

21 There is the interesting and problematic case of the "wild" garden, in which the precise shape of "disorder" is minutely planned. Here it is a matter of an aesthetic plan, designed to have a certain effect on the eye – an attempt to copy untended nature. The paradox is just as intractable as that of a zoo designed to mimic nature – intractable, that is, until one realizes that the design does not extend to allowing the critters to eat one another!

22 Karl Marx, from the *Communist Manifesto*, quoted in Berman, *All That Is Solid Melts into Air*, p. 95.

23 The airplane, having replaced the locomotive, was in many respects the defining image of modernity in the early twentieth century. In 1913, the futurist artist and playwright Kazimir Malevich created the sets for an opera entitled *Victory over the Sun*. In the last scene, the audience heard from offstage a propeller's roar and shouts announcing that gravity had been overcome in futurist countries. Le Corbusier, Malevich's near contemporary, thought the airplane was the reigning symbol of the new age. For the influence of flight, see Robert Wohl, *A Passion for Wings: Aviation and the Western Imagination, 1908–1918* (New Haven: Yale University Press, 1996).

24 The Jacobins intended just such a fresh start, starting the calendar again at "year one" and renaming the days and months according to a new, secular system. To signal its intention to create a wholly new Cambodian nation, the Pol Pot regime began with "year zero."

25 Quoted in Harvey, *The Condition of Post-Modernity*, p. 99.

26 In this section, the masculine personal pronoun is less a convention than a choice made with some deliberation. See Carolyn Merchant, *The Death of Nature: Women, Ecology, and the Scientific Revolution* (San Francisco: Harper, 1980).

27 See, for example, Margaret M. Bullitt, "Toward a Marxist Theory of Aesthetics: The Development of Socialist Realism in the Soviet Union," *Russian Review* 35, no. 1 (January 1976): 53–76.

28 Baruch Knei-Paz, "Can Historical Consequences Falsify Ideas? Or, Karl Marx after the Collapse of the Soviet Union," paper presented to Political Theory Workshop, Department of Political Science, Yale University, New Haven, November 1994.

29 Raymond Aron's prophetic dissent, *The Opium of the Intellectual*, trans. Terence Kilmartin (London: Secker & Warburg, 1957), is a key document in this context.

30 The larger, the more capital-intensive, and the more centralized the schemes, the greater their appeal in terms of power and patronage. For a critique of flood-control projects and World Bank projects in this context, see James K. Boyce, "Birth of a Megaproject: Political Economy of Flood Control in Bangladesh," *Environmental Management* 14, no. 4 (1990): 419–28.

31 Harvey, *The Condition of Post-Modernity*, p. 12.

32 See Charles Tilly's important theoretical contribution in *Coercion, Capital, and European States*, A.D. 990–1992 (Oxford: Blackwell, 1990).

33 A civil war, as in the Bolshevik case, may be the price of consolidating the revolutionaries' power.

34 White-settler colonies (e.g., South Africa, Algeria) and anti-insurgency campaigns (e.g., Vietnam, Algeria, Afghanistan) have carried out huge population removals and forced resettlements. In most such cases, however, even the pretense that the comprehensive social planning was for the welfare of the affected populations has been paper-thin.

35 Here I am particularly indebted to the discussion of George Yaney, *The Urge to Mobilize: Agrarian Reform in Russia* (Urbana: University of Illinois Press, 1982), pp. 448–62.

36 Anson Rabinbach, *The Human Motor: Energy, Fatigue, and the Origins of Modernity* (Berkeley: University of California Press, 1992), pp. 260–71. In 1907, long before the war, Rathenau and a number of architects and political leaders had founded Deutsche Werkbund, which was devoted to fostering technical innovation in industry and the arts.

37 See Gregory J. Kasza, *The Conscription Society: Administered Mass Organizations* (New Haven: Yale University Press, 1995), especially chap. 1, pp. 7–25.

38 Rabinbach, *The Human Motor*, p. 290.

39 For recent assessments of the evolution of technology and production in the United States, see Nathan Rosenberg, *Perspectives on Technology* (Cambridge: Cambridge University Press, 1976); Rosenberg, *Inside the Black Box: Technology and Economics* (New York: Cambridge University Press, 1982); and Philip Scranton, *Figured Tapestry: Production, Markets, and Power in Philadelphia, 1885–1942* (New York: Cambridge University Press, 1989).

40 See the inventive article by Ernest J. Yanorella and Herbert Reid, "From 'Trained Gorilla' to 'Humanware': Repoliticizing the Body-Machine Complex between Fordism and Post-Fordism," in Theodore R. Schatzki and Wolfgang Natter, eds., *The Social and Political Body* (New York: Guildford Press, 1996), pp. 181–219.

41 Rabinbach, *The Human Motor*, p. 272. Rabinbach is here paraphrasing the conclusions of a seminal article by Charles S. Maier, "Between Taylorism and Technocracy: European Ideologies and the Vision of Industrial Productivity in the 1920s," *Journal of Contemporary History* 5, no. 2 (1970): 27–63.

42 Thorstein Veblen was the best-known social scientist expounding this view in the United States. Literary versions of this ideology are apparent in Sinclair Lewis's *Arrowsmith* and Ayn Rand's *Fountainhead*, works from very different quadrants of the political spectrum.

43 Rabinbach, *The Human Motor*, p. 452. For Rathenau's writings, see, for example, *Von kommenden Dingen* (Things to come) and *Die Neue Wirtschaft* (The new economy), the latter written after the war.

44   Walther Rathenau, *Von kommenden Dingen* (1916), quoted in Maier, "Between Taylorism and Technocracy," p. 47. Maier notes that the apparent harmony of capital and labor in wartime Germany was achieved at the cost of an eventually ruinous policy of inflation (p. 46).

45   Michael Adas, *Machines as the Measure of Men: Science, Technology, and Ideologies of Western Dominance* (Ithaca: Cornell University Press, 1989), p. 380. Sheldon Wolin, in *Politics and Vision: Continuity and Innovation in Western Political Thought* (Boston: Little, Brown, 1960), provides an extensive list of like-minded thinkers spanning the political spectrum, from fascists and nationalists at one end to liberals, social democrats, and communists at the other, and hailing from France, Germany, Austria-Prussia (the Prussian Richard von Moellendorf, a close associate of Rathenau and a publicist for a managed postwar economy), Italy (Antonio Gramsci on the left and fascists Masimo Rocca and Benito Mussolini on the right), and Russia (Alexej Kapitonovik Gastev, the "Soviet Taylor").

46   V. I. Lenin, *The Agrarian Programme of Social-Democracy in the First Russian Revolution, 1905–1907*, 2nd rev. ed. (Moscow: Progress Publishers, 1954), p. 195, written September 28, 1917 (first emphasis only added).

47   Leon Smolinski, "Lenin and Economic Planning," *Studies in Comparative Communism* 2, no. 1 (January 1969): 99. Lenin and Trotsky were explicit, Smolinski claims, about how electric centrals would create a farm population dependent on the center and thus make state control of agricultural production possible (pp. 106–7).

48   Lenin, *Works* (Moscow, 1972), 27: 163, quoted in Ranier Traub, "Lenin and Taylor: The Fate of 'Scientific Management' in the (Early) Soviet Union," trans. Judy Joseph, *Telos* 34 (Fall 1978): 82–92 (originally published in *Kursbuch* 43 (1976). The "bard" of Taylorism in the Soviet Union was Alexej Kapitonovik Gastev, whose poetry and essays waxed lyrical about the possibilities of a "union" between man and machine: "Many find it repugnant that we want to deal with human beings as a screw, a nut, a machine. But we must undertake this as fearlessly as we accept the growth of trees and the expansion of the railway network" (quoted in ibid., p. 88). Most of the labor institutes were closed and their experts deported or shot in the Stalinist purges of the 1930s.

49   Lenin, "The Immediate Tasks of the Soviet Government," *Izvestia*, April 28, 1918, cited in Maier, "Between Taylorism and Technocracy," p. 51 n. 58.

50   Graham Burchell, Colin Gordon, and Peter Miller, *The Foucault Effect: Studies in Governmentality*, with two lectures by and an interview with Michel Foucault (London: Wheatsheaf, 1991), p. 106.

51   This point has been made forcefully and polemically in the twentieth century by Friedrich Hayek, the darling of those opposed to postwar planning and the welfare state. See, especially, *The Road to Serfdom* (Chicago: University of Chicago Press, 1976).

James C. Scott, "Authoritarian High Modernism," from *Seeing Like a State: How Certain Schemes to Improve the Human Condition Have Failed*, pp. 87–102, 376–81, Yale University Press, 1998. © Yale University Press.

3

The Death and Life of Great American Cities

Jane Jacobs

This chapter is an attack on current city planning and rebuilding. It is also, and mostly, an attempt to introduce new principles of city planning and rebuilding, different and even opposite from those now taught in everything from schools of architecture and planning to the Sunday supplements and women's magazines. My attack is not based on quibbles about rebuilding methods or hairsplitting about fashions in design. It is an attack, rather, on the principles and aims that have shaped modern, orthodox city planning and rebuilding.

In setting forth different principles, I shall mainly be writing about common, ordinary things: for instance, what kinds of city streets are safe and what kinds are not; why some city parks are marvelous and others are vice traps and death traps; why some slums stay slums and other slums regenerate themselves even against financial and official opposition; what makes downtowns shift their centers; what, if anything, is a city neighborhood, and what jobs, if any, neighborhoods in great cities do. In short, I shall be writing about how cities work in real life, because this is the only way to learn what principles of planning and what practices in rebuilding can promote social and economic vitality in cities, and what practices and principles will deaden these attributes.

There is a wistful myth that if only we had enough money to spend – the figure is usually put at $100 billion – we could wipe out all our slums in ten years, reverse decay in the great, dull, gray belts that were yesterday's and day-before-yesterday's suburbs, anchor the wandering middle class and its wandering tax money, and perhaps even solve the traffic problem.

But look what we have built with the first several billions: low-income projects that become worse centers of delinquency, vandalism, and general social hopelessness than the slums they were supposed to replace. Middle-income housing projects that

Readings in Planning Theory, Third Edition. Edited by Susan S. Fainstein and Scott Campbell.
Editorial material and organization © 2012 Blackwell Publishing Ltd.
Published 2012 by Blackwell Publishing Ltd.

are truly marvels of dullness and regimentation, sealed against any buoyancy or vitality of city life. Luxury housing projects that mitigate their inanity, or try to, with a vapid vulgarity. Cultural centers that are unable to support a good bookstore. Civic centers that are avoided by everyone but bums, who have fewer choices of loitering place than others. Commercial centers that are lackluster imitations of standardized suburban chain-store shopping. Promenades that go from no place to nowhere and have no promenaders. Expressways that eviscerate great cities. This is not the rebuilding of cities. This is the sacking of cities.

Under the surface, these accomplishments prove even poorer than their poor pretenses. They seldom aid the city areas around them, as in theory they are supposed to. These amputated areas typically develop galloping gangrene. To house people in this planned fashion, price tags are fastened on the population, and each sorted-out chunk of price-tagged populace lives in growing suspicion and tension against the surrounding city. When two or more such hostile islands are juxtaposed the result is called "a balanced neighborhood." Monopolistic shopping centers and monumental cultural centers cloak, under the public relations hoo-ha, the subtraction of commerce, and of culture too, from the intimate and casual life of cities.

That such wonders may be accomplished, people who get marked with the planners' hex signs are pushed about, expropriated, and uprooted much as if they were the subjects of a conquering power. Thousands upon thousands of small businesses are destroyed, and their proprietors ruined, with hardly a gesture at compensation. Whole communities are torn apart and sown to the winds, with a reaping of cynicism, resentment, and despair that must be heard and seen to be believed. A group of clergymen in Chicago, appalled at the fruits of planned city rebuilding there, asked,

> Could Job have been thinking of Chicago when he wrote:
> Here are men that alter their neighbor's landmark ...
> shoulder the poor aside, conspire to oppress the friendless.
> Reap they the field that is none of theirs, strip they the vine-yard wrongfully seized from
>   its owner ...
> A cry goes up from the city streets, where wounded men lie groaning ...

If so, he was thinking of New York, Philadelphia, Boston, Washington, St Louis, San Francisco, and a number of other places. The economic rationale of current city rebuilding is a hoax. The economics of city rebuilding do not rest soundly on reasoned investment of public tax subsidies, as urban renewal theory proclaims, but also on vast, involuntary subsidies wrung out of helpless site victims. And the increased tax returns from such sites, accruing to the cities as a result of this "investment," are a mirage, a pitiful gesture against the ever-increasing sums of public money needed to combat disintegration and instability that flow from the cruelly shaken-up city. The means to planned city rebuilding are as deplorable as the ends.

Meantime, all the art and science of city planning are helpless to stem decay – and the spiritlessness that precedes decay – in ever more massive swatches of cities. Nor can this decay be laid, reassuringly, to lack of opportunity to apply the arts of planning. It seems to matter little whether they are applied or not. Consider the Morningside Heights area in New York City. According to planning theory it should not be in trouble at all, for it enjoys a great abundance of parkland, campus, playground, and other open spaces. It has plenty of grass. It occupies high and pleasant ground with magnificent river views. It is a famous educational center with splendid institutions – Columbia University, Union Theological Seminary, the Juilliard School of Music, and half a dozen others of eminent respectability. It is the beneficiary of good hospitals and churches. It has no industries. Its streets are zoned in the main against "incompatible uses" intruding into the preserves for solidly constructed, roomy, middle-and upper-class apartments. Yet by the early 1950s Morningside Heights was becoming a slum so swiftly, the surly kind of slum in which people fear to walk the streets, that the situation posed a crisis for the institutions. They and the planning arms of the city government got together, applied more planning theory, wiped out the most run-down part of the area and built in its stead a middle-income cooperative project complete with shopping center and a public housing project – all interspersed with air, light, sunshine, and landscaping. This was hailed as a great demonstration in city saving.

After that Morningside Heights went downhill even faster.

Nor is this an unfair or irrelevant example. In city after city, precisely the wrong areas, in the light of planning theory, are decaying. Less noticed, but equally significant, in city after city the wrong areas, in the light of planning theory, are refusing to decay.

Cities are an immense laboratory of trial and error, failure and success, in city building and city design. This is the laboratory in which city planning should have been learning and forming and testing its theories. Instead the practitioners and teachers of this discipline (if such it can be called) have ignored the study of success and failure in real life, have been incurious about the reasons for unexpected success, and are guided instead by principles derived from the behavior and appearance of towns, suburbs, tuberculosis sanatoria, fairs, and imaginary dream cities – from anything but cities themselves.

If it appears that the rebuilt portions of cities and the endless new developments spreading beyond the cities are reducing city and countryside alike to a monotonous, unnourishing gruel, this is not strange. It all comes, first-, second-, third-, or fourth-hand, out of the same intellectual dish of mush, a mush in which the qualities, necessities, advantages, and behavior of great cities have been utterly confused with the qualities, necessities, advantages, and behavior of other and more inert types of settlements.

There is nothing economically or socially inevitable about either the decay of old cities or the fresh-minted decadence of the new unurban urbanization. On the contrary, no other aspect of our economy and society has been more purposefully manipulated for a full quarter of a century to achieve precisely what we are getting. Extraordinary governmental financial incentives have been required to achieve this degree of monotony, sterility, and vulgarity. Decades of preaching, writing, and exhorting by experts have gone into convincing us and our legislators that mush like this must be good for us, as long as it comes bedded with grass.

Automobiles are often conveniently tagged as the villains responsible for the ills of cities and the disappointments and futilities of city planning. But the destructive effects of automobiles are much less a cause than a symptom of our incompetence at city building. Of course planners, including the highwaymen with fabulous sums of money and enormous powers at their disposal, are at a loss to make automobiles and cities compatible with one another. They do not know what to do with automobiles in cities because they do not know how to plan for workable and vital cities anyhow – with or without automobiles.

The simple needs of automobiles are more easily understood and satisfied than the complex needs of cities, and a growing number of planners and designers have come to believe that if they can only solve the problems of traffic, they will thereby have solved the major problem of cities. Cities have much more intricate economic and social concerns than automobile traffic. How can you know what to try with traffic until you know how the city itself works and what else it needs to do with its streets? You can't.

It may be that we have become so feckless as a people that we no longer care how things do work but only what kind of quick, easy outer impression they give. If so, there is little hope for our cities or probably for much else in our society. But I do not think this is so.

Specifically, in the case of planning for cities, it is clear that a large number of good and earnest people do care deeply about building and renewing. Despite some corruption, and considerable greed for the other man's vineyard, the intentions going into the messes we make are, on the whole, exemplary. Planners, architects of city design, and those they have led along with them in their beliefs are not consciously disdainful of the importance of knowing how things work. On the contrary, they have gone to great pains to learn what the saints and sages of modern orthodox planning have said about how cities *ought* to work and what *ought* to be good for people and businesses in them. They take this with such devotion that when contradictory reality intrudes, threatening to shatter their dearly won learning, they must shrug reality aside.

Consider, for example, the orthodox planning reaction to a district called the North End in Boston. This is an old, low-rent area merging into the heavy industry of the waterfront, and it is officially considered Boston's worst slum and civic shame. It embodies attributes that all enlightened people know are evil, because so many wise men have said they are evil. Not only is the North End bumped right up against industry, but worse still it has all kinds of working places and commerce mingled in the greatest complexity with its residences. It has the highest concentration of dwelling units, on the land that is used for dwelling units, of any part of Boston, and indeed one of the highest concentrations to be found in any American city. It has little parkland. Children play in the streets. Instead of superblocks, or even decently large blocks, it has very small blocks; in planning parlance it is "badly cut up with wasteful streets." Its buildings are old. Everything conceivable is presumably wrong with the North End. In orthodox planning terms, it is a three-dimensional textbook of "megalopolis" in the last stages of depravity. The North End is thus a recurring assignment for MIT and Harvard planning and architectural students, who now and again pursue, under the guidance of their teachers, the paper exercise of converting it into superblocks and park promenades, wiping away its nonconforming uses, transforming it to an ideal of order and gentility so simple it could be engraved on the head of a pin.

Twenty years ago, when I first happened to see the North End, its buildings – town houses of different kinds and sizes converted to flats, and four- or five-story tenements built to house the flood of immigrants first from Ireland, then from Eastern Europe, and finally from Sicily – were badly overcrowded, and the general effect was of a district taking a terrible physical beating and certainly desperately poor.

When I saw the North End again in 1959, I was amazed at the change. Dozens and dozens of buildings had been rehabilitated. Instead of mattresses against the windows, there were Venetian blinds and glimpses of fresh paint. Many of the small, converted houses now had only one or two families in them instead of the old crowded three or four. Some of the families in the tenements (as I learned later, visiting inside) had uncrowded themselves by throwing two older apartments together, and had equipped these with bathrooms, new kitchens, and the like. I looked down a narrow alley, thinking to find at least here the old, squalid North End, but no: more neatly repointed brickwork, new blinds, and a burst of music as a door opened. Indeed, this was the only city district I have ever seen – or have seen to this day – in which the sides of buildings around parking lots had not been left raw and amputated, but repaired and painted as neatly as if they were intended to be seen. Mingled all among the buildings for living were an incredible number of splendid food stores, as well as such enterprises as upholstery making, metalworking, carpentry, food processing. The streets were alive with children playing, people shopping, people strolling, people talking. Had it not been a cold January day, there would surely have been people sitting.

The general street atmosphere of buoyancy, friendliness, and good health was so infectious that I began asking directions of people just for the fun of getting in on some talk. I had seen a lot of Boston in the past couple of days, most of it sorely distressing, and this struck me, with relief, as the healthiest place in the city. But I could not imagine where the money had come from for the rehabilitation, because it is almost impossible today to get any appreciable mortgage money in districts of American cities that are not either high-rent, or else imitations of suburbs. To find out, I went into a bar and restaurant (where an animated conversation about fishing was in progress) and called a Boston planner I know.

"Why in the world are you down in the North End?" he said. "Money? Why, no money or work has gone into the North End. Nothing's going on down there. Eventually, yes, but not yet. That's a slum!"

"It doesn't seem like a slum to me," I said.

"Why, that's the worst slum in the city. It has 275 dwelling units to the net acre! I hate to admit we have anything like that in Boston, but it's a fact."

"Do you have any other figures on it?" I asked.

"Yes, funny thing. It has among the lowest delinquency, disease, and infant mortality rates in the city. It also has the lowest ratio of rent to income in the city. Boy, are those people getting bargains. Let's see ... the child population is just above average for the city, on the nose. The death rate is low, 8.8 per thousand, against the average city rate of 11.2. The TB death rate is very low, less than 1 per ten thousand, can't understand it, it's lower even than Brookline's. In the old days the North End used to be the city's worst spot for tuberculosis, but all that has changed. Well, they must be strong people. Of course it's a terrible slum."

"You should have more slums like this," I said. "Don't tell me there are plans to wipe this out. You ought to be down here learning as much as you can from it."

"I know how you feel," he said. "I often go down there myself just to walk around the streets and feel that wonderful, cheerful street life. Say, what you ought to do, you ought to come back and go down in the summer if you think it's fun now. You'd be crazy about it in summer. But of course we have to rebuild it eventually. We've got to get those people off the streets."

Here was a curious thing. My friend's instincts told him the North End was a good place, and his social statistics confirmed it. But everything he had learned as a physical planner about what is good for people and good for city neighborhoods, everything that made him an expert, told him the North End had to be a bad place.

The leading Boston savings banker, "a man way up there in the power structure," to whom my friend referred me for my inquiry about the money, confirmed what I learned, in the meantime, from people in the North End. The money had not come through the grace of the great American banking system, which now knows enough about planning to know a slum as well as the planners do. "No sense in lending money into the North End," the banker said. "It's a slum! It's still getting some immigrants! Furthermore, back in the Depression it had a very large number of foreclosures; bad record." (I had heard about this too, in the meantime, and how families had worked and pooled their resources to buy back some of those foreclosed buildings.)

The largest mortgage loans that had been fed into this district of some 15,000 people in the quarter-century since the Great Depression were for $3,000, the banker told me, "and very, very few of those." There had been some others for $1,000 and for $2,000. The rehabilitation work had been almost entirely financed by business and housing earnings within the district, plowed back in, and by skilled work bartered among residents and relatives of residents.

By this time I knew that this inability to borrow for improvement was a galling worry to North Enders, and that furthermore some North Enders were worried because it seemed impossible to get new building in the area except at a price of seeing themselves and their community wiped out in the fashion of the students' dreams of a city Eden, a fate that they knew was not academic because it had already smashed completely a socially similar – although physically more spacious – nearby district called the West End. They were worried because they were aware also that patch and fix with nothing else could not do forever. "Any chance of loans for new construction in the North End?" I asked the banker.

"No, absolutely not!" he said, sounding impatient at my denseness. "That's a slum!"

Bankers, like planners, have theories about cities on which they act. They have gotten their theories from the same intellectual sources as the planners. Bankers and government administrative officials who guarantee mortgages do not invent planning theories nor, surprisingly, even economic doctrine about cities. They are enlightened nowadays, and they pick up their ideas from idealists, a generation later. Since theoretical city planning has embraced no major new ideas for considerably more than a generation, theoretical planners, financiers, and bureaucrats are all just about even today.

And to put it bluntly, they are all in the same stage of elaborately learned superstition as medical science was early in the last century, when physicians put their faith in bloodletting, to draw out the evil humors that were believed to cause disease. With bloodletting, it took years of learning to know precisely which veins, by what rituals, were to be opened for what symptoms. A superstructure of technical complication was erected in such deadpan detail that the literature still sounds almost plausible. However, because people, even when they are thoroughly enmeshed in descriptions of reality that are at variance with reality, are still seldom devoid of the powers of observation and independent thought, the science of bloodletting, over most of its long sway, appears usually to have been tempered with a certain amount of common sense. Or it was tempered until it reached its highest peaks of technique in, of all places, the young United States. Bloodletting went wild here. It had an enormously influential proponent in Dr Benjamin Rush, still revered as the greatest statesman-physician of our revolutionary and federal periods, and a genius of medical administration. Dr Rush Got Things Done. Among the things he got done, some of them good and useful, were to develop, practice, teach, and spread the custom of bloodletting in cases where prudence or mercy had heretofore restrained its use. He and his students drained the blood of very young children, of consumptives, of the greatly aged, of almost anyone unfortunate enough to be sick in his realms of influence. His extreme practices aroused the alarm and horror of European bloodletting physicians. And yet as late as 1851, a committee appointed by the State Legislature of New York solemnly defended the thoroughgoing use of bloodletting. It scathingly ridiculed and censured a physician, William Turner, who had the temerity to write a pamphlet criticizing Dr Rush's doctrines and calling "the practice of taking blood in diseases contrary to common sense, to general experience, to enlightened reason, and to the manifest laws of the divine Providence." Sick people needed fortifying, not draining, said Dr Turner, and he was squelched.

Medical analogies, applied to social organisms, are apt to be farfetched, and there is no point in mistaking mammalian chemistry for what occurs in a city. But analogies as to what goes on in the brains of earnest and learned men, dealing with complex phenomena they do not understand at all and trying to make do with a pseudoscience, do have a point. As in the pseudoscience of bloodletting, just so in the pseudoscience of city rebuilding and planning, years of learning and a plethora of subtle and complicated dogma have arisen on a foundation of nonsense. The tools of technique have steadily been perfected. Naturally, in time, forceful and able men, admired administrators, having swallowed the initial fallacies and having been provisioned with tools and with public confidence, go on logically to the greatest destructive excesses, which prudence or mercy might previously have forbade. Bloodletting could heal only by accident or insofar as it broke the rules, until the time when it was abandoned in favor of the hard, complex business of assembling, using, and testing, bit by bit, true descriptions of reality drawn not from how it ought to be but from how it is. The pseudoscience of city planning and its companion, the art of city design, have not yet broken with the specious comfort of wishes, familiar superstitions, oversimplifications, and symbols – and have not yet embarked upon the adventure of probing the real world.

So in this chapter we shall start, if only in a small way, adventuring in the real world, ourselves. The way to get at what goes on in the seemingly mysterious and perverse behavior of cities is, I think, to look closely, and with as little previous expectation as is possible, at the most ordinary scenes and events and attempt to see what they mean and whether any threads of principle emerge among them ....

One principle emerges so ubiquitously, and in so many and such complex different forms, ... [that it] becomes the heart of my argument. This ubiquitous principle is the need of cities for a most intricate and close-grained diversity of uses that give each other constant mutual support, both economically and socially. The components of this diversity can differ enormously, but they must supplement each other in certain concrete ways.

I think that unsuccessful city areas are areas that lack this kind of intricate mutual support, and that the science of city planning and the art of city design, in real life for real cities, must become the science and art of catalyzing and nourishing these close-grained working relationships. I think, from the evidence I can find, that there are four primary conditions required for generating useful great city diversity, and that by deliberately inducing these four conditions, planning can induce city vitality (something that the plans of planners alone, and the designs of designers alone, can never achieve)....

Cities are fantastically dynamic places, and this is strikingly true of their successful parts, which offer a fertile ground for the plans of thousands of people....

The look of things and the way they work are inextricably bound together, and in no place more so than cities. But people who are interested only in how a city "ought" to look and uninterested in how it works will be disappointed. ... It is futile to plan a city's appearance, or speculate on how to endow it with a pleasing appearance of order, without knowing what sort of innate, functioning order it has. To seek for the look of things as a primary purpose or as the main drama is apt to make nothing but trouble.

In New York's East Harlem, there is a housing project with a conspicuous rectangular lawn that became an object of hatred to the project tenants. A social worker frequently at the project was astonished by how often the subject of the lawn came up, usually gratuitously as far as she could see, and how much the tenants despised it and urged that it be done away with. When she asked why, the usual answer was,

"What good is it?" or "Who wants it?" Finally one day, a tenant more articulate than the others made this pronouncement: "Nobody cared what we wanted when they built this place. They threw our houses down and pushed us here and pushed our friends somewhere else. We don't have a place around here to get a cup of coffee or a newspaper even, or borrow fifty cents. Nobody cared what we need. But the big men come and look at that grass and say, 'Isn't it wonderful! Now the poor have everything!'"

This tenant was saying what moralists have said for thousands of years: Handsome is as handsome does. All that glitters is not gold.

She was saying more: There is a quality even meaner than outright ugliness or disorder, and this meaner quality is the dishonest mask of pretended order, achieved by ignoring or suppressing the real order that is struggling to exist and to be served.

In trying to explain the underlying order of cities, I use a preponderance of examples from New York because that is where I live. But most of my basic ideas come from things I first noticed or was told in other cities. For example, my first inkling about the powerful effects of certain kinds of functional mixtures in the city came from Pittsburgh, my first speculations about street safety from Philadelphia and Baltimore, my first notions about the meanderings of downtown from Boston, my first clues to the unmaking of slums from Chicago. Most of the material for these musings was at my own front door, but perhaps it is easiest to see things first where you don't take them for granted. The basic idea, to try to begin understanding the intricate social and economic order under the seeming disorder of cities, was not my idea at all, but that of William Kirk, head worker of Union Settlement in East Harlem, New York, who, by showing me East Harlem, showed me a way of seeing other neighborhoods, and downtowns too. In every case, I have tried to test out what I saw or heard in one city or neighborhood against others, to find how relevant each city's or each place's lessons might be outside its own special case.

I have concentrated on great cities, and on their inner areas, because this is the problem that has been most consistently evaded in planning theory. I think this may also have somewhat wider usefulness as time passes, because many of the parts of today's cities in the worst, and apparently most baffling, trouble were suburbs or dignified, quiet residential areas not too long ago; eventually many of today's brand-new suburbs or semisuburbs are going to be engulfed in cities and will succeed or fail in that condition depending on whether they can adapt to functioning successfully as city districts. Also, to be frank, I like dense cities best and care about them most.

But I hope no reader will try to transfer my observations into guides as to what goes on in towns, or little cities, or in suburbs that still are suburban. Towns, suburbs, and even little cities are totally different organisms from great cities. We are in enough trouble already from trying to understand big cities in terms of the behavior, and the imagined behavior, of towns. To try to understand towns in terms of big cities will only compound confusion.

I hope any reader will constantly and skeptically test what I say against his or her own knowledge of cities and their behavior. If I have been inaccurate in observations or mistaken in inferences and conclusions, I hope these faults will be quickly corrected. The point is, we need desperately to learn and to apply as much knowledge that is true and useful about cities as fast as possible.

I have been making unkind remarks about orthodox city planning theory, and shall make more as occasion arises to do so. By now, these orthodox ideas are part of our folklore. They harm us because we take them for granted. To show how we got them, and how little they are to the point, I shall give a quick outline here of the most influential ideas that have contributed to the verities of orthodox modern city planning and city architectural design.[1]

The most important thread of influence starts, more or less, with Ebenezer Howard, an English court reporter for whom planning was an avocation. Howard looked at the living conditions of the poor in late-nineteenth-century London and justifiably did not like what he smelled or saw or heard. He not only hated the wrongs and mistakes of the city, he hated the city and thought it an outright evil and an affront to nature that so many people should get themselves into an agglomeration. His prescription for saving the people was to do the city in.

The program he proposed, in 1898, was to halt the growth of London and also repopulate the countryside, where villages were declining, by building a new kind of town – the Garden City, where the city poor might again live close to nature. So that they might earn their livings, industry was to be set up in the Garden City; for while Howard was not planning cities, he was not planning dormitory suburbs either. His aim was the creation of self-sufficient small towns, really very nice towns if you were docile and had no plans of your own and did not mind spending your life among others with no plans of their own. As in all utopias, the right to have plans of any significance belonged only to the planners in charge. The Garden City was to be encircled with a belt of agriculture. Industry was to be in its planned preserves; schools, housing, and greens in planned living preserves; and in the center were to be commercial, club, and cultural places, held in common. The town and green belt, in their totality, were to be permanently controlled by the public authority under which the town was developed, to prevent speculation or supposedly irrational changes in land use and also to do away with temptations to increase its density – in brief, to prevent it from ever becoming a city. The maximum population was to be held to thirty thousand people.

Nathan Glazer has summed up the vision well in *Architectural Forum*: "The image was the English country town – with the manor house and its park replaced by a community center, and with some factories hidden behind a screen of trees, to supply work."

The closest American equivalent would probably be the model company town, with profit sharing, and with the parent-teacher associations in charge of the routine, custodial political life. For Howard was envisioning not simply a new physical environment and social life but a paternalistic political and economic society.

Nevertheless, as Glazer has pointed out, the Garden City was "conceived as an alternative to the city, and as a solution to city problems; this was, and is still, the foundation of its immense power as a planning idea." Howard managed to get two garden cities built, Letchworth and Welwyn, and of course Great Britain and Sweden have, since World War II, built a number of satellite towns based on Garden City principles. In the United States, the suburb of Radburn, New Jersey, and the depression-built, government-sponsored Green Belt towns (actually suburbs) were all incomplete modifications of the idea. But Howard's influence in the literal, or reasonably literal, acceptance of his program was as nothing compared to his influence on conceptions underlying all American city planning today. City planners and designers with no interest in the Garden City as such are still thoroughly governed intellectually by its underlying principles.

Howard set spinning powerful and city-destroying ideas: He conceived that the way to deal with the city's functions was to sort and sift out of the whole certain simple uses, and to arrange each of these in relative self-containment. He focused on the provision of wholesome housing as the central problem, to which everything else was subsidiary; furthermore he defined wholesome housing in terms only of suburban physical qualities and small-town social qualities. He conceived of commerce in terms of routine, standardized supply of goods, and as serving a self-limited market. He conceived of good planning as a series of static acts; in each case the plan must anticipate all that is needed and be protected, after it is built, against any but the most minor subsequent changes. He conceived of planning also as essentially paternalistic, if not authoritarian. He was uninterested in the aspects of the city that could not be abstracted to serve his utopia. In particular, he simply wrote off the intricate, many faceted, cultural life of the metropolis. He was uninterested in such problems as the way the great cities police themselves, or exchange ideas, or operate politically, or invent new economic arrangements, and he was oblivious to devising ways to strengthen these functions because, after all, he was not designing for this kind of life in any case.

Both in his preoccupations and in his omissions, Howard made sense in his own terms but none in terms of city planning. Yet virtually all modern city planning has been adapted from, and embroidered on, this silly substance.

Howard's influence on American city planning converged on the city from two directions: from town and regional planners on the one hand, and from architects on the other. Along the avenue of planning, Sir Patrick Geddes, a Scots biologist and philosopher, saw the Garden City idea not as a fortuitous way to absorb population growth otherwise destined for a great city but as the starting point of a much grander and more encompassing pattern. He thought of the planning of cities in terms of the planning of whole regions. Under regional planning, garden cities would be rationally distributed throughout large territories, dovetailing into natural resources, balanced against agriculture and woodland, forming one far-flung logical whole.

Howard's and Geddes's ideas were enthusiastically adopted in America during the 1920s, and developed further by a group of extraordinarily effective and dedicated people – among them Lewis Mumford, Clarence Stein, the late Henry Wright, and Catherine Bauer. While they thought of themselves as regional planners, Catherine Bauer has more recently called this group the "Decentrists," and this name is more apt, for the primary result of regional planning, as they saw it, would be to decentralize great cities, thin them out, and disperse their enterprises and populations into smaller, separated cities or, better yet, towns. At the time, it appeared that the American population was both aging and leveling off in numbers, and the problem appeared to be not one of accommodating a rapidly growing population but simply of redistributing a static population.

As with Howard himself, this group's influence was less in getting literal acceptance of its program – that got nowhere – than in influencing city planning and legislation affecting housing and housing finance. Model housing schemes by Stein and Wright, built mainly in suburban settings or at the fringes of cities, together with the writings and the diagrams, sketches, and photographs presented by Mumford and Bauer, demonstrated and popularized ideas such as these, which are now taken for granted in orthodox planning: The street is bad as an environment for humans; houses should be turned away from it and faced inward, toward sheltered greens. Frequent streets are wasteful, of advantage only to real estate speculators who measure value by the front foot. The basic unit of city design is not the street but the block and, more particularly, the superblock. Commerce should be segregated from residences and greens. A neighborhood's demand for goods should be calculated "scientifically," and this much and no more commercial space allocated. The presence of many other people is, at best, a necessary evil, and good city planning must aim for at least an illusion of isolation and suburban privacy. The Decentrists also pounded in Howard's premises that the planned community must be islanded off as a self-contained unit, that it must resist future change, and that every significant detail must be controlled by the planners from the start and then stuck to. In short, good planning was project planning.

To reinforce and dramatize the necessity for the new order of things, the Decentrists hammered away at the bad old city. They were incurious about successes in great cities. They were interested only in failures. All was failure. A book like Mumford's *The Culture of Cities* was largely a morbid and biased catalog of ills. The great city was Megalopolis, Tyrannopolis, Nekropolis, a monstrosity, a tyranny, a living death. It must go. New York's midtown was "solidified chaos" (Mumford). The shape and appearance of cities was nothing but "a chaotic accident ... the summation of the haphazard, antagonistic whims of many self-centered, ill-advised individuals" (Stein). The centers of cities amounted to "a foreground of noise, dirt, beggars, souvenirs, and shrill competitive advertising" (Bauer).

How could anything so bad be worth the attempt to understand it? The Decentrists' analyses, the architectural and housing designs that were companions and offshoots of these analyses, the national housing and home financing legislation so directly influenced by the new vision – none of these had anything to do with understanding cities or fostering successful large cities, nor were they intended to. They were reasons and means for jettisoning cities, and the Decentrists were frank about this.

But in the schools of planning and architecture – and in Congress, state legislatures, and city halls too – the Decentrists' ideas were gradually accepted as basic guides for dealing constructively with big cities themselves. This is the most amazing event in the whole sorry tale: that finally people who sincerely wanted to strengthen great cities should adopt recipes frankly devised for undermining their economies and killing them.

The man with the most dramatic idea of how to get all this anticity planning right into the citadels of iniquity themselves was the European architect Le Corbusier. He devised in the 1920s a dream city, which he called the Radiant City, composed not of the low buildings beloved of the Decentrists but instead mainly of skyscrapers within a park. "Suppose we are entering the city by way of the Great Park," Le Corbusier wrote. "Our fast car takes the special elevated motor track between the majestic skyscrapers: as we approach nearer, there is seen the repetition against the sky of the twenty-four skyscrapers; to our left and right on the outskirts of each particular area are the municipal and administrative buildings; and enclosing the space are the museums and university buildings. The whole city is a Park." In Le Corbusier's vertical city the common run of mankind was to be housed at 1,200 inhabitants to the acre, a fantastically high city density indeed, but because of building up so high, 95 percent of the ground could remain open. The skyscrapers would occupy only 5 percent of the ground. The high-income people would be in lower, luxury housing around courts, with 85 percent of their ground left open. Here and there would be restaurants and theaters.

Le Corbusier was planning not only a physical environment. He was planning for a social utopia too. Le Corbusier's utopia was a condition of what he called maximum individual liberty, by which he seems to have meant not liberty to do anything much, but liberty from ordinary responsibility. In his Radiant City nobody, presumably, was going to have to be his brother's keeper any more. Nobody was going to have to struggle with plans of his own. Nobody was going to be tied down.

The Decentrists and other loyal advocates of the Garden City were aghast at Le Corbusier's city of towers in the park, and still are. Their reaction to it was, and remains, much like that of progressive nursery school teachers confronting an utterly institutional orphanage. And yet, ironically, the Radiant City comes directly out of the Garden City. Le Corbusier accepted the Garden City's fundamental image, superficially at least, and worked to make it practical for high densities. He described his creation as the Garden City made attainable. "The garden city is a will-o'-the-wisp," he wrote. "Nature melts under the invasion of roads and houses and the promised seclusion becomes a crowded settlement…The solution will be found in the 'vertical garden city.'"

In another sense too, in its relatively easy public reception, Le Corbusier's Radiant City depended upon the Garden City. The Garden City planners and their ever-increasing following among housing reformers, students, and architects were indefatigably popularizing the ideas of the superblock; the project neighborhood; the unchangeable plan; and grass, grass, grass. What is more, they were successfully establishing such attributes as the hallmarks of humane, socially responsible, functional, high-minded planning. Le Corbusier really did not have to justify his vision in either humane or city-functional terms. If the great object of city planning was that Christopher Robin might go hoppety-hoppety on the grass, what was wrong with Le Corbusier? The Decentrists' cries of institutionalization, mechanization, depersonalization seemed to others foolishly sectarian.

Le Corbusier's dream city has had an immense impact on our cities. It was hailed deliriously by architects and has gradually been embodied in scores of projects, ranging from low-income public housing to office-building projects. Aside from making at least the superficial Garden City principles superficially practical in a dense city, Le Corbusier's dream contained other marvels. He attempted to make planning for the automobile an integral part of his scheme, and this was, in the 1920s and early 1930s, a new, exciting idea. He included great arterial roads for express one-way traffic. He cut the number of streets because "cross-roads are an enemy to traffic." He proposed underground streets for heavy vehicles and deliveries, and of course like the Garden City planners he kept the pedestrians off the streets and in the parks. His city was like a wonderful mechanical toy. Furthermore, his conception, as an architectural work, had a dazzling clarity, simplicity, and harmony. It was so orderly, so visible, so easy to understand. It said everything in a flash, like a good advertisement. This vision and its bold symbolism have been all but irresistible to planners, housers, designers – and to developers, lenders, and mayors too. It exerts a great pull on "progressive" zoners, who write rules calculated to encourage nonproject builders to reflect, if only a little, the dream. No matter how vulgarized or clumsy the design, how dreary and useless the open space, how dull the close-up view, an imitation of Le Corbusier shouts, "Look what I made!" Like a great, visible ego it tells of someone's achievement. But as to how the city works, it tells, like the Garden City, nothing but lies.

Although the Decentrists, with their devotion to the ideal of a cozy town life, have never made peace with the Le Corbusier vision, most of their disciples have. Virtually all sophisticated city designers today combine the two conceptions in various permutations. The rebuilding technique variously known as "selective removal" or "spot renewal" or "renewal planning" or "planned conservation" – meaning that total clearance of a run-down area is avoided – is largely the trick of seeing how many old buildings can be left standing and the area still converted into a passable version of Radiant Garden City. Zoners, highway planners, legislators, land-use planners, and parks and playground planners – none of whom live in an ideological vacuum – constantly use, as fixed points of reference, these two powerful visions and the more sophisticated merged vision. They may wander from the visions, they may compromise, they may vulgarize, but these are the points of departure.

We shall look briefly at one other, less important, line of ancestry in orthodox planning. This one begins more or less with the great Columbian Exposition in Chicago in 1893, just about the same time that Howard was formulating his Garden City ideas. The Chicago fair snubbed the exciting modern architecture that had begun to emerge in Chicago and instead dramatized a retrogressive imitation Renaissance style. One heavy, grandiose monument after another was arrayed in the exposition park, like frosted pastries on a tray, in a sort of squat, decorated forecast of Le Corbusier's later repetitive ranks of towers in a park. This orgiastic assemblage of the rich and monumental captured the imagination of both planners and public. It gave impetus to a movement called the City Beautiful, and indeed the planning of the exposition was dominated by the man who became the leading City Beautiful planner, Daniel Burnham of Chicago.

The aim of the City Beautiful was the City Monumental. Great schemes were drawn up for systems of baroque boulevards, which mainly came to nothing. What did come out of the movement was the Center Monumental, modeled on the fair. City after city

built its civic center or its cultural center. These buildings were arranged along a boule-
vard as at Benjamin Franklin Parkway in Philadelphia, or along a mall like the
Government Center in Cleveland, or were bordered by park, like the Civic Center at
St Louis, or were interspersed with park, like the Civic Center at San Francisco.
However they were arranged, the important point was that the monuments had been
sorted out from the rest of the city and assembled into the grandest effect thought possible, the whole being treated as a complete unit, in a separate and well-defined way.

People were proud of them, but the centers were not a success. For one thing,
invariably the ordinary city around them ran down instead of being uplifted, and
they always acquired an incongruous rim of ratty tattoo parlors and secondhand-
clothing stores, or else just nondescript, dispirited decay. For another, people stayed
away from them to a remarkable degree. Somehow, when the fair became part of the
city, it did not work like the fair.

The architecture of the City Beautiful centers went out of style. But the idea
behind the centers was not questioned, and it has never had more force than it does
today. The idea of sorting out certain cultural or public functions and decontami-
nating their relationship with the workaday city dovetailed nicely with the Garden
City teachings. The conceptions have harmoniously merged, much as the Garden
City and the Radiant City merged, into a sort of Radiant Garden City Beautiful, such
as the immense Lincoln Square project for New York, in which a monumental City
Beautiful cultural center is one among a series of adjoining Radiant City and Radiant
Garden City housing, shopping, and campus centers.

And by analogy, the principles of sorting out – and of bringing order by repression of all plans but the planners' – have been easily extended to all manner of city
functions, until today a land-use master plan for a big city is largely a matter of
proposed placement, often in relation to transportation, of many series of decon-
taminated sortings.

From beginning to end, from Howard and Burnham to the latest amendment on
urban renewal law, the entire concoction is irrelevant to the workings of cities.
Unstudied, unrespected, cities have served as sacrificial victims.

Note

1   Readers who would like a fuller account, and a sympathetic account, which mine is not,
    should go to the sources, which are very interesting, especially *Garden Cities of Tomorrow*,
    by Ebenezer Howard; *The Culture of Cities*, by Lewis Mumford; *Cities in Evolution*, by Sir
    Patrick Geddes; *Modern Housing*, by Catherine Bauer; *Toward New Towns for America*, by
    Clarence Stein; *Nothing Gained by Overcrowding*, by Sir Raymond Unwin; and *The City of
    Tomorrow and Its Planning*, by Le Corbusier. The best short survey I know of is the group
    of excerpts under the title "Assumptions and Goals of City Planning," contained in *Land-
    Use Planning, A Casebook on the Use, Misuse and Re-use of Urban Land*, by Charles M. Haar.

4

The Good City
In Defense of Utopian Thinking

John Friedmann

An Open Letter to Manuel Castells

I consider social action and political projects to be essential in the betterment of a society that clearly needs change and hope. And I do hope that this book, by raising some questions and providing empirical and theoretical elements to treat them, may contribute to informed social action in the pursuit of social change. In this sense, I am not, and do not want to be, a neutral, detached observer of the human drama.

However, I have seen so much misled sacrifice, so many dead ends induced by ideology, and such horrors provoked by artificial paradises of dogmatic politics that I want to convey a salutary reaction against trying to frame political practice in accordance with social theory, or, for that matter, with ideology. Theory and research, in general as well as in this book, should be considered as a means for understanding our world, and should be judged exclusively on their accuracy, rigor, and relevance. How these tools are used, and for what purpose, should be the exclusive prerogative of social actors themselves, in specific social contexts, and on behalf of their values and interests. No more meta-politics, no more "*maitres a penser*", and no more intellectuals pretending to be so (Castells, 1998: 359).

Dear Manuel,

Reading these closing paragraphs of volume three of your great trilogy took me back to my university days in Chicago. It was the early 1950s, and we eagerly debated the possibilities and merits of a "value-free" social science. I won't bore you with arguments that, as a sociologist, you know far better than I. But I had thought that, in the end, the resolution of those arguments was that the social sciences are

Readings in Planning Theory, Third Edition. Edited by Susan S. Fainstein and Scott Campbell.
Editorial material and organization © 2012 Blackwell Publishing Ltd.
Published 2012 by Blackwell Publishing Ltd.

inevitably imprinted with the values and interests of the author, and that, having torn the "veil of ignorance" from our scientific persona, we could get on with our work. Until I came to your sentence about how theory and research "should be judged exclusively on their accuracy, rigor, and relevance". Until I read: "How these tools are used, and for what purpose, should be the exclusive prerogative of social actors themselves ..."

I think I understand, and even have some sympathy for, your position at the end of this over-ideologized century. But we cannot escape ideology. In a recent essay, Janet Abu-Lughod defines ideology as "deep sets of beliefs about how the world works" (Abu-Lughod, 1998: 77). And so I could as readily call the "empirical and theoretical elements" we bring together in our books a form of ideology, that is, a set of elementary beliefs about the far-reaching changes that are perturbing our lives in what you call the "information age". That is the heart of their message. The question is, to whom is the message addressed?

You seem to want to draw a line between the authorial self and those whom you call social actors, who, embedded in their specific contexts, have their own "values and interests". But who are these actors? And aren't we all social actors, even as we sit in front of our computers, drafting chapters that, in one way or another, are likely to create a stir among our readers? Or are we simply "speaking truth to power" as Aaron Wildavsky claimed? Is there really this determinate boundary you want to draw between the academy, with its austere values of "accuracy, rigor, and relevance", and the world of political passions? Doesn't any narrative have its own rhetoric of persuasion that is so clearly pitched at intellectuals like yourself and at members of certain power elites, all of whom, you quite rightly assume, will have agendas of their own and make such use of our work as they see fit. Of one thing I am certain: the stories we tell are unlikely to be read by social activists in the trenches of the many struggles for the better world for which we both hope. They don't have the leisure to read "The information age" with its more than 1400 pages of text, footnotes and scholarly references.

But there is one particular group of readers that, I think, you and I would both like to reach – for otherwise, why choose to be an academic? – a group that will be deeply disappointed by your act of self-renunciation. I refer to students and other intelligent young people everywhere. I want to quote from a speech given by Tan Le, age 21, and nominated as the 1998 Young Australian of the Year. Tan Le is a lawyer now, and this is what she said:

> *I have just completed a law degree. One of the reasons I chose law – and many other young people also include this reason for choosing it – was because I believed that a law degree would enable me to contribute in a special way, to do what I could to make a better world.*
>
> *Of course I can do this as a lawyer, but nothing in the entire law curriculum addressed this issue in a serious and engaging way. And other tertiary courses are the same ...*

Young people are not being educated to take their place in society. They are being trained – trained in a narrow body of knowledge and skills that is taught in isolation from larger and vital questions about who we are and what we might become.

There is, in other words, a complete absence of a larger vision, and many young people who enter university in the hope that what they learn will help them make a better world soon find out that this is not a consideration.

And it is not just in tertiary education courses that this lack of vision prevails. We lack it as a society. We have replaced it with what might be called a rationale. To my mind, this is not the same thing as a vision. It is more pragmatic, smaller in scope, less daring, and it does not fire the heart or capture the imagination. It does not inspire.

Vision carries the connotation of value, meaning and purpose – and of something beyond our reach that is nevertheless worth striving for and aspiring to. A rationale, on the other hand, is limited and attainable, and the tighter and more compact the rationale is, the more attainable it is.

And we do have a tight and compact rationale for our lives and for what we do. It is an economic rationale, and economic in a very narrow sense. It is solely interested in a certain type of efficiency and profit – efficiency and profit to the exclusion of, and in isolation from, everything else, particularly the future (Le, 1999: 17).

Tan Le's plea is for a utopian vision, and by renouncing an alternative to the present, you deprive her of what is most important to her life and give her a prepackaged "rationale" instead.

There are no inevitabilities in this world, not even the apparent inevitability of globalization and the new power structures that are emerging alongside. There are always responses, resistances, attempts at shaping and reshaping the historical forces that impinge on our lives. Like yourself, I believe that the future is open-ended, even though not infinitely malleable, and that in order to bring about a world that is fit to live in, we need new and solid ideas for living, persuasive images of the good society. And I also believe that, by virtue of our intellectual understanding of what is happening around us, we – you and I – have a special responsibility to try and come up with some images of this sort. There is very little danger that our images of the good society, or the good city, will be abused by leaders mad for power, by turning them into yet another tyranny, or that our words will send waves of good society warriors to their ignoble death, as they try to scale the impossible walls of utopia. If indeed I thought that was the case, I would stop writing now.

You do know that I have always admired your work, even when I did not agree with it, and your present trilogy is an impressive achievement. But you and I are also social actors by virtue of what we write, and this imposes certain obligations, if only to help fill the terrible void in the soul of young people like Tan Le.

As ever, your colleague and friend, etc. etc.

The Utopian Impulse

Utopian thinking: the capacity to imagine a future that departs significantly from what we know to be a general condition in the present. It is a way of breaking through the barriers of convention into a sphere of the imagination where many things beyond our everyday experience become feasible. All of us have this ability, which is inherent in human nature, because human beings are insufficiently programmed for the future. We need a constructive imagination that we can variously use for creating fictive worlds. Some of these worlds can be placed in the past, others in the future, and some, like Dante's *Divina comedia*, even in afterlife.

There are other ways of deploying this capacity than in the imagining of utopias. Religion is one of them, and for many people religious faith satisfies their thirst for meaning. Belief in hegemonic ideologies is a secular counterpart to religion. American ideology, repeated *ad nauseam* by our leaders and reinforced by the media, incorporates the idea of bliss in a consumer society, so that a better world is seen to be chiefly one of greater material affluence for individuals. This is the ideology we are selling around the world. Along with belief in a never-ending abundance of material goods, it includes the rhetoric of representative democracy, and blind trust in the powers of technology to overcome whatever problems that might be encountered along the way to a "free society"[1] Intensely nationalistic feelings may also satisfy the need for ordinary lives to have a transcendent meaning.[2] The question of "why are we here" arises precisely because the human condition is to be open to the future, and it requires a response on our part.

Beyond the alternative constructions of religion, ideology and nationalism, there are many good reasons why we might wish to engage utopian thinking. For some of us, it is merely an amusing pastime. For others it serves as a veiled critique of present-day evils. For still others it may be, in the phrase of Sir Philip Sidney's comment on Thomas More's *Utopia* in 1595, a persuasive means of "leading men to virtue" (Manuel and Manuel, 1979: 2). In the peculiar form of dystopias, it may alert us to certain tendencies in the present which, if allowed to continue unchecked and carried to a logical extreme, would result in a world we find abhorrent. The twentieth century has produced many literary dystopias (not to mention the many actual dystopias in the real world), from Aldous Huxley's *Brave New World* to the cyberpunk novels of William Gibson and others (Warren *et al.*, 1998). But most important of all, utopian thinking can help us choose a path into the future that we believe is justified, because its concrete imagery is informed by values which are precious to us.

Utopian thinking has two moments that are inextricably connected: critique and constructive vision. The critique is of certain aspects of our present condition: injustices, oppression, ecological devastation. It is precisely an enumeration of these "evils", however, that implies a code of moral values that is being violated. The code may not be written out, or it may merely be suggested symbolically by invoking slogans such as "freedom", "equality", "solidarity". But it is there nonetheless. The moral outrage over an injustice implies that we have a sense, however inarticulate, of justice. And so on, for each of our terms of condemnation.

Now it is true that negative and positive images are not necessarily symmetrical with respect to each other. Most of us might agree that great material inequalities are unjust, yet differ vehemently about what might constitute a "just" distribution of incomes or other material good. But differences about social justice are ultimately political, not philosophical arguments. In any event, they are unavoidable, because if injustice is to be corrected (or, for that matter, any other "evil"), we will need the concrete imagination of utopian thinking to propose steps that would bring us closer to a world we would consider "just".

It is this concrete vision – the second moment of utopian thinking – which Tan Le was calling for to give her a sense of a meaningful deployment of her own powers in the public sphere.

Such visionings are always debatable, both in their own terms and when measured against alternative proposals. That is why I call them political. Where the uncensored public expression of opinions is allowed, they should become the substance of political argument. Utopian thinking is thus not at all about fairytales but about genuine futures around which political coalitions may be built.

There are always limitations on purposive action – of leadership, power, resources, knowledge. But if we begin with these limitations rather than with images of the desirable future, we may never arrive at utopian constructs with the power to generate the passion necessary for a social movement that might bring us a few steps closer to the vision they embody.

The Utopian Tradition in Planning

With considerations of this sort, we find ourselves back on the familiar ground of planning. City and regional planning (or spatial planning) has an enduring tradition of utopian thought (Friedmann and Weaver, 1979; Weaver, 1984; Friedmann, 1987). The evocation of the classics requires no references: Robert Owen, Charles Fourier, Pierre Joseph Proudhon, William Morris, Peter Kropotkin, Ebenezer Howard, Lewis Mumford, Frank Lloyd Wright, Percival and Paul Goodman are all names in common currency among the tribe. In more recent decades, we can mention the illustrious names of Kevin Lynch and, for some of us also E.F. Schumacher and Ivan Illich. Still closer to our time and, indeed, contemporary with us, I could mention Jane Jacobs (1961), Dolores Hayden (1984) and Leonie Sandercock (1997). Given this chain of utopian writings stretching over 200 years that have influenced the education of planners and, to a greater or lesser degree, have also shaped their practice, it would be hard to argue that even the mainstream of the planning profession has kept itself aloof from utopian thinking.

In a recent essay, Susan Fainstein poses the question of whether we can make the cities we want (Fainstein, 1999). In her account, the important values that should inform our thinking about cities include material equality, cultural diversity, democratic participation and ecological sustainability in a metropolitan milieu. Fainstein's background is in political economy, and so it is not surprising that she should give pride of place to the question of material equality (or rather inequality) and follow, if not uncritically, David Harvey's lead in *Justice, nature and the geography of difference* (1996). I will come back to this particular prioritization of social values when I present my own answer to Fainstein's challenging question.

But before I do this, I would like to recall an argument I made in *Planning in the public domain* (Friedmann, 1987). The second and third parts of this volume attempt to sketch an intellectual history of planning, but, at the same time, to go beyond this history in advocating a transformative planning that, because it is based on the mobilization of the disempowered groups in society, I called radical. The central focus of radical planning in this sense is political action by organized groups within civil society (which is the more familiar "community" of planning discourse but situated in a different theoretical setting). Its radicalism derives from actions that, with or without and even against the state, are aimed at universal emancipation. "A key principle in radical, transformative practice", I wrote, "is that *no group can be completely free until freedom* [from oppression] *has been achieved for every group*. Thus, the struggle for emancipation leads to results that will always be partial and contradictory, until the final and possibly utopian goal of a free humanity is reached" (*ibid*, 1987: 301).[3] I then went on to examine what planners, who opt for emancipatory struggles, do. Among the many things I considered are elaborating a hard-hitting critical analysis of existing conditions; assisting in the mobilization of communities to rectify these conditions; assisting in devising appropriate strategies of struggle; refining the technical aspects of transformative solutions; facilitating social learning from radical practice; mediating between the mobilized community and the state; helping to ensure the widest possible participation of community members in all phases of the struggle; helping to rethink the group's course of action in the light of new understandings; and becoming personally involved in transformative practice (*ibid*, 303–7). I wanted it to be understood that utopian thinking, at least so far as planners are concerned, is historically grounded in specific emancipatory struggles. Planning of this sort stands in the grand utopian tradition. In her most recent work, Leonie Sandercock calls it an insurgent planning (Sandercock, 1999).

In the present essay, my intention is somewhat different. Rather than talk about political struggles to resist specific forms of oppression, my aim is to delineate some elements for a positive vision of the "good city". And I want to do so in the manner of an achievable utopia rather than paint a scenario set in a distant, indeterminate future.

A century during which the vast majority of the world's population will have to live in urban environments cries out for images of the good city. I have purposely phrased this need in the plural. Taking the world as a whole, the diversity of starting conditions is so great that no single version of the city will suffice. Fifty years from now, the world's urban population will be roughly double the existing numbers of

2.9 billion. We can thus look ahead to a historically unprecedented age of city-building. And city-builders need not only blueprints for their work, but *guiding, normative images*. The following remarks are addressed to planners and to anyone else who wishes to confront the multiple challenges of the age.[4]

Imagining the Good City I: Theoretical Considerations

Before proceeding, however, some preliminaries must be considered. First, in setting out an account of the good city, whose city are we talking about? Can we legitimately assume the possibility of a "common good" for the city? Second, are we concerned only with process or only with outcomes, or should outcome and process be considered jointly? And finally, how is a normative framework such as we are considering to be thought of in relation to professional practice?

Whose city?

We have been bludgeoned into accepting as gospel that to speak of a common good in a given polity is either propaganda or an act of self-deception. The attacks on the common weal have come from all ideological directions. Pluralists see only group interests that strike temporary bargains in the political arena. Marxists argue on roughly similar grounds that the "common good" is a phrase used by the hegemonic class, i.e. the bourgeoisie, to hide purposes that are simply an expression of class interest. Postmodern critics who see only a world of fleeting kaleidoscopic images, dissolve the "common good" into a thousand discursive fragments, dismissing any attempt to raise one of them above any of the others as an unjustifiable attempt to establish a new "metanarrative" in an age from which metanarratives have been banned.

Against all of these intellectually dismissive critics, I would argue for the necessity of continuing to search for the "common good" of a city if only because, without such a conception, there can be neither a sense of local identity nor a political community. In democratic polities, there has to be minimal agreement on the structure of the community and on the possibility of discovering a "common good" through political discourse. An administered city is not a political community and might as well be a hotel managed by some multinational concern. In that case, the answer to the question of "whose city" is very clear. But in a putative democracy, the city is ultimately "the people", and the cliché notwithstanding, it is the people who must find a way among themselves to define, time after time, in what specific action agendas the "common good" of the city may be found. It seems to me that it makes a world of difference whether we seek to justify an action by grounding it in a conception of the "common good", a conception that always remains open to political challenge, or merely to assert it without voices of dissent, or omit any reference to it altogether.

Process vs. outcomes

This opposition of terms has a long pedigree. Democratic proceduralists believe in process, partly because they assume that the differences among the parties in contention are relatively minor, and because today's majority will become tomorrow's minority, and vice versa. Everybody, so to speak, gets their turn in the long run. Opposed to them are Kantian idealists for whom good intentions are sufficient to define the good. A third position is held by those who are so persuaded of the rightness of their own ethical position that they lack patience with democratic procedure, pursuing their ends by whatever means are at hand. Among them are many who believe in the theory of the "big revolutionary bang". Transformative change, according to this theory, requires a sharp break with the past, a break that is often connected with some violence, because the *ancien régime* must be "smashed" before the revolutionary age can dawn.

My own position is to deny this separation of ends and means, outcomes and process. Process, by which I specifically mean democratic procedures, is no less important than desirable outcomes. But democratic procedures are likely to be abandoned if they do not lead, in the longer term, to broadly acceptable outcomes. Moreover, process in a liberal democracy, also includes the non-violent struggles for social justice and other concerns that take place outside the formal institutional framework. So, on the one hand, we need an inclusive democratic framework that allows for the active pursuit of political objectives even when these are contrary to the dominant interests. On the other hand, we need to be clear about the objectives to be pursued. The imaginary of the good city has to embrace both these terms.

Intention and practice

The good city requires a committed form of political practice which I call transformative. It was Hannah Arendt who formed my concept of action or political praxis (she used the terms interchangeably). She writes: "To act, in its most general sense, means to take an initiative, to begin … to set something into motion … It is in the nature of beginning that something new is started which cannot be expected from whatever may have happened before. The character of startling unexpected-ness is inherent in all beginnings and in all origins" (Arendt, 1958: 177–8). To act, in other words, is to set something new into the world. And this requires an actor, or rather a number of such, because political action of the transformative kind always involves a collective entity or group. There are certain conditions of action. The group must first be brought together and mobilized. This means leadership. It must also have the material, symbolic and moral power sufficient to overcome resistance to its projects. In the longer term, the group's actions, and the counter-actions to its initiatives, lead to results that are boundless and therefore require continuous social learning. The group must be passionately committed to its practice or it will be defeated in the first rounds of struggle (Friedmann, 1987: 44–7).

The Good City II: Human Flourishing as a Fundamental Human Right

If they are not to be seen as arbitrary, principles of the good city must be drawn from somewhere, they must be logically connected to some foundational value. Such a founding principle should be clearly and explicitly formulated, so that it can be communicated even to those among us who are not philosophically inclined but make their living as carpenters, domestic workers or on construction jobs. I would formulate this principle as follows:

- *Every human being has the right, by nature, to the full development of their innate intellectual, physical and spiritual potentials in the context of wider communities.*

I call this the right to human flourishing, and regard it as the most fundamental of human rights. Despite this, it has never been universally acknowledged as a right inherent to being human. Slave societies knew nothing of it; nor did caste societies, tribal societies, corporate village societies or totalitarian states. And in no society have women ever enjoyed the same right to human flourishing as men. But as the fundamental, inalienable right of every person, human flourishing is ingrained in the liberal democratic ethos.

Human flourishing underlies the strongly held belief in contemporary western societies, and particularly in America, that privilege should be earned rather than inherited. Accordingly, human beings should have an equal start in life. Over a lifetime, individual and group outcomes will, of course, vary a good deal because of differences in inborn abilities, family upbringing, entrenched class privilege and social oppression. Still, the idea of a basic equality among all citizens underlies the mild socialism of western countries with their systems of public education, public health, the graduated income tax, anti-discriminatory legislation and so forth, all of which seek some sort of leveling of life chances among individuals and groups.

As this reference to political institutions makes evident, the potential of human flourishing can only be realized in the context of wider communities, so that right from the start, we posit humans, not as Leibnizian monads but as social beings. It is unconscionable, therefore, as Margaret Thatcher is reported to have done, to dismiss the concept of society as a mere fiction. Alone, we cannot survive without the unmediated support of others, from intimate family on up to larger structures and emotional bonds to individuals and groups. Without them, nothing can be accomplished.

The social sphere imposes certain requirements of its own, and these may appear as constraints on willful action. Although as individuals we are ultimately responsible for what we do, we are always constrained (1) by our social relations with family, friends, workmates, and neighbors, in short, by a culturally specific ethics of mutual obligation within civil society and (2) by the wider sociopolitical settings of our lives that inhibit human flourishing. The two are intertwined in many ways,[5] it would require a separate essay, however, to even begin to disentangle them and to do justice to the powerful constraints we, and especially women, encounter in the sphere of relations I call civil. Instead, I will turn to the sociopolitical sphere which is my primary focus.

Briefly, my argument is that local citizens do not merely use the city to advance their personal interests – some will do so more successfully than others – but, as citizens of a political community, which is the city in its political aspect, also contribute to establishing those minimal conditions – political, economic, social, physical and ecological – which are necessary for human flourishing. I refer to these conditions – and please remember that I call them minimal conditions – as the common good of the polity, or the good city, because human flourishing is inconceivable without them. In this understanding, the "common good" of the city appears as something akin to citizen rights, that is, to the claims that local citizens can legitimately make on their political community as a basis for the flourishing of all its citizens. Making these claims, and at the same time to contribute to their realization in practice, is one of the deep obligations of local citizenship.

The Good City III: Multipli/city as a Primary Good

Human flourishing serves us as a template for judging the performance of cities. But to assist us in this detailed, critical work of assessing the extent to which a city provides an adequate setting for human flourishing, further guidelines are needed. I propose to do this by suggesting a primary good – multipli/city – together with certain conditions that would allow multipli/city to be realized in practice.

By multipli/city, I mean an autonomous civil life relatively free from direct supervision and control by the state. So considered, a vibrant civil life is the necessary social context for human flourishing. Multipli/city acknowledges the priority of civil society, which is the sphere of freedom and social reproduction – and it is for its sake that the city can be said to exist. Political economists might disagree with this ordering. They tend to describe the city in terms of capital accumulation, external economies, market exchange, administrative control, and the like, and urban populations in terms of their incorporation into labor markets and social classes. From an analytical perspective, I don't object to these characterizations. But if our project is the good city, a different, explicitly normative approach is needed.

In its political aspect, civil society comprises the political community of the city. But there are other aspects of a richly articulated civil life, including religious, social, cultural and economic life, all of which can be subsumed under the concept of a self-organizing civil society.[6] Michael Walzer calls civil society "a project of projects", foreshadowing my characterization of multipli/city. The relevant passage is worth quoting in full:

> Civil society is sustained by groups much smaller than the *demos* or the working class or the mass consumers or the nation. All these are necessarily pluralized as they are incorporated. They become part of the world of family, friends, comrades and

colleagues, where people are connected to one another and made responsible for one another. Connected and responsible: without that, "free and equal" is less attractive than we once thought it would be. I have no magic formula for making connections or strengthening the sense of responsibility. These are not aims that can be underwritten with historical guarantees or achieved through a single unified struggle. Civil society is a project of projects; it requires many organizing strategies and new forms of state action. It requires a new sensitivity for what is local, specific, contingent – and, above all, a new recognition (to paraphrase a famous sentence) that the good life is in the details (Walzer, 1992: 107).

Throughout history, city populations have grown primarily through migration, and migrants come from many parts. Some don't speak the dominant language of the city; others practice different religions; still others follow folkways that are strange to the city. They come to the city for its promise of a more liberated, fulfilling life, and also perhaps, as refugees, escaping from the danger of physical harm. They do not come to the city to be regimented, to be molded according to a single concept of correct living. Nor do they seek diversity as such. Rather, they want to live by their own lights as undisturbed as possible, so that diversity appears as simply a by-product of the "project of projects". But cities are not always hospitable, and mutual tolerance of difference must be safeguarded by the state so long as certain conditions are fulfilled: respect for human rights and the assumption of the rights and obligations of local citizenship. In a broadly tolerant society, one may perhaps hope for a step beyond tolerance, which is to say, for mutual acceptance and even the affirmation of difference.

Reflected in a thickly quilted mosaic of voluntary associations, multipli/city requires a solid material base. A destitute people can only think about survival, which absorbs nearly all the time and energies at their disposal. A substantial material base, therefore, must provide for the time, energy and space needed for active citizenship. Four pillars support the material foundations for the good city. First in importance is socially *adequate housing* together with complementary public services and community facilities. As innumerable struggles in cities throughout the world have shown, housing needs, along with water and affordable urban transit, are viewed as a first priority of individual households. By common consent, the greatest social disaster (in peacetime) is to be homeless. *Affordable healthcare* comes second, particularly for women, infants, the physically and mentally challenged, the chronically ill and the elderly, as a prime condition for human flourishing. *Adequately remunerated work* for all who seek it is the third pillar. In urban market societies, a well-paying job is a nearly universal aspiration not only for the income it brings but for the social regard that attaches to regular work in capitalist society. Finally, *adequate social provision* in housing, medical care, human services and income must be made for the weakest citizens, if their own efforts are insufficient to provide for what is regarded as the social minimum.

Each of these four pillars has given rise to a vast literature, both technical and philosophical, and it is not my intention here to review it. I do want to take up a point of difference, however, that I have with the old socialist Left which has consistently argued that justice – social justice – demands "equal access to material well-being". The Left has always given priority to material inequalities as their rallying cry. And though it is undoubtedly true that unconstrained capitalist accumulation leads to greater material inequalities, gross differences in income and wealth are, in fact, found in all social formations since the beginnings of urban society seven millennia ago. My disagreement is, therefore, with a vision that regards material questions as primary and thus as the appropriate focus of popular struggle. All large-scale attempts to level inequalities, as in Maoist China, have had to employ barbaric methods to suppress what appears to me to be precisely a primary good, which is a flourishing civil life. It is certainly true that since the neutralization of the so-called Gang of Four, major inequalities have again surfaced in urban China, but alongside this are also the beginnings of a civil society reborn (Brook and Frolic, 1997). As much as I welcome the second, I have no wish to justify the first, which brings about its own evils of exploitation and corruption. Still, the two phenomena are not independent of each other, as they point to a general relaxation of government control over social and economic life. And even though I argue here for "four pillars" to provide the material foundations of the good city, I regard them as chiefly a means to a more transcendent end, which is a vibrant civil life. Genuine material equality, Maoist-style, is neither achievable nor desirable. Whereas we will always have to live with material inequalities, what we must never tolerate is a contemptuous disregard for the qualities of social and political life, which is the sphere of freedom. A good city is a city that cares for its freedom, even as it makes adequate social provision for its weakest members.

The Good City IV: Good Governance

If process is as important as outcome, as I argued at the beginning of this essay, we will have to consider the processes of governance in the good city. Governance refers to the ways by which binding decisions for cities and city-regions are made and carried out. It is thus a concept considerably more inclusive than traditional government and administration and reflects the fact that increasingly there is a much wider range of participants in these processes than was traditionally the case.

Three sets of potential actors can be identified. First, there are the politicians and bureaucrats, representing the institutions of the local state. It is because of them that decisions concerning city-building are made "binding". The state stands at the apex of a pyramid whose base is defined, respectively, by corporate capital and civil society. The role of corporate capital in city-building has become more pronounced in recent years, encouraged by privatization and the growing emphasis on mega-projects in city-building, from apartment blocks, new towns, office developments and technology parks to toll roads, bridges, harbor reclamation schemes and airports. The role of civil society has been a more contested issue. Beyond rituals of "citizen participation" in planning, civil society's major role, in most cities, has taken the form of protest and resistance to precisely the mega-projects dear to state and capital.[7] Civil society has also put pressure on the state for more sustainable cities, for environmental justice and for more inclusive visions of the city.

It is tempting, in a utopian exercise, to invert the order of things and, as in this case, to place local citizens at the top of the governance pyramid. This would be broadly in accord with democracy theory as well as with my earlier claim that the city exists for the sake of its citizens, who are bound to each other by mutual agreement, thus forming a political community. But I hesitate, because I am not convinced that city-regions on the scale of multiple millions can be organized like town meetings or the Athenian *agora*. Nor do I believe in the vaunted capacity of the Internet – even supposing universal access – to overcome the problem of scale. Democratic governance requires something more than a "thumbs up" and "thumbs down" to public intervention on any given issue, which would be no more meaningful than a telephone survey at the end of a public debate which asks the question: "Who won?"

An alternative would be simply to scale down city-regional governance until governance becomes coextensive with what I have elsewhere called "the city of everyday life". Thomas Jefferson had a name for it: "the republic of the wards" (for a summary, see Friedmann, 1973: 220–2). More recently, there have been calls (in the United States) for "neighborhood governments" (Kotler, 1969: Morris and Hess, 1975; King and Stivers, 1998). And there is even a Chinese-Taiwanese version of this idea, citing the writings of Lao Zi (Lao Tzu) (Cheng and Hsia, 1999), as well as a striking example from southern Brazil (Abers, 1998). Evidently, there is something very attractive about this devolution of powers to the most local of local levels – the neighborhood, the street. But a city-region is more than the sum of its neighborhoods, and each level of spatial integration must be slotted into a larger whole, which is the prevailing system of governance. The question, then, is how to articulate this whole so as to further the idea of multipli/city and the four pillars of a good city.

I do not claim great originality for my criteria of good governance. But I would like to think that they have some cross-cultural validity, because they address what are ultimately very practical issues that must be dealt with in cities East and West, North and South. Still, in any attempt to apply them, differences in political culture must be borne in mind. I would propose, then, the following six criteria for assessing the performance of a system of city-regional governance:

- *Inspired political leadership*: leaders capable of articulating a common vision for the polity, building a strong consensus around this vision and mobilizing resources towards its realization.
- *Public accountability*: (1) the uncoerced, periodic election of political representatives and (2) the right of citizens to be adequately informed about those who stand for elections, the standing government's performance record and the overall outcomes for the city.
- *Transparency and the right to information*: governance should be transparent in its manner of operation and, as much as possible, be carried out in full view of citizen observers. Citizens should have the right to information, particularly about contracts between the city and private corporations.

- *Inclusiveness*: the right of all citizens to be directly involved in the formulation of policies, programs and projects whenever their consequences can be expected to significantly affect their life and livelihood.
- *Responsiveness*: the primordial right of citizens is to claim rights and express grievances; to have access to appropriate channels for this purpose; to have a government that is accessible to them in the districts of their "everyday life"; and to timely, attentive and appropriate responses to their claims and grievances.
- *Non-violent conflict management*: institutionalized ways of resolving conflicts between state and citizens without resort to physical violence.

The "utopian" character of these criteria becomes immediately apparent as soon as we invert the terms and picture a form of governance that displays a bungling leadership without vision, deems it unnecessary to render public accounts of its actions, transacts the state's business in secrecy, directs resources to groups favored by the state without consulting with affected local citizens, responds to expression of grievance with a mailed fist, and resolves conflicts with the arrest of opposition leaders and the brutal suppression of citizen protest.

This litany may no longer apply to North American or West European forms of city-regional governance, except perhaps in times of extreme tension – I am thinking of Paris and Chicago in 1968. But in much of the rest of the world, and especially in Asia where urbanization is now in full swing, the dystopia of governance still prevails, and criteria of good governance, especially at local levels, are a considerable novelty. And in any event, good governance always hangs on slender threads. The last State of Victoria's Minister of Planning in Australia, responsible for planning and development in the City of Melbourne, suspended public consultation and declared public information on major city projects as no longer a requirement. This was the same Minister who, a few years earlier, suspended elected local councils and replaced them with city managers appointed by the state. He then proceeded to redraw council boundaries and issue administrative instructions on the privatization of council responsibilities. In the Australian State of Victoria, at least, good governance was, until recently, in jeopardy, and so perhaps it is not irrelevant, after all, even in a putative democracy, to be reminded of what some criteria of good governance might be.

A Summing Up

As human beings, we are cursed with a consciousness of our own death. This same consciousness places us in a stream of irreversible time. Minute by minute, lifetime by lifetime, we move through a continuing present – like the Roman god, Janus, forever facing in two directions – reading and re-reading the past and imagining possible futures even as we deal with the practicalities of the day. Shrouded in both darkness and light, as Gerda Lerner reminds us, history as memory helps us to locate ourselves in the continuing present while imagining alternative futures that are meant to serve us as beacons of warning and inspiration (Lerner, 1997: Chapter 4).

In our two-faced gaze, we are a time-binding species whose inescapable task in a fundamentally urbanized world is to forge pathways towards a future that is worth struggling for.

In this essay, I have set down my own utopian thinking about the good city. It is a revisiting of a problem terrain on which I worked, on and off, during the 1970s (Friedmann, 1979). At the time, I was thinking through what I called a transactive model of social planning to which the practice of dialogue would be central. These concerns subsequently expanded into my interest in social learning and the traditions of radical/insurgent planning. My investigations then led me further to examine the micro-structures of civil action, such as the household economy, culminating in a theory of empowerment and disempowerment (Friedmann, 1992). Today's communicative turn in planning (Innes, 1995) is a more mainstream version of some of these ideas.

The good city, as I imagine it, has its foundations in human flourishing and multipli/city. Four pillars provide for its material foundations: housing, affordable health care, adequately remunerated work and adequate social provision. And because process cannot be separated from outcome, I also delved into the question of what a system of good governance might look like, attempting a thumbnail description of such a system. The protagonist of my visioning is an autonomous, self-organizing civil society, active in making claims, resisting and struggling on behalf of the good city within a framework of democratic institutions.

Physical planners and urban designers will miss a discussion of the three dimensional city, but this is not my domain, and I refer them to the well-known "urban design manifesto" by Allan Jacobs and Donald Appleyard (1987), where these matters are taken up in a context not very different from the value premises that underlie the present essay. Also missing from my account is any reference to the "sustainable" city, which I am prepared to leave to the experts who will want to talk, more knowledgeably than I, about resource-conserving cities, blue skies and clear water.

So my image of the city remains incomplete, and I think that is proper, because no one should have a final say about the good city. Utopian thinking is an ongoing, time-binding discourse intended to inform our striving. It is no more than that, but also nothing less.

Notes

1 According to the distinguished Israeli sociologist, S.N. Eisenstadt (1998: 123), America forged a civil religion out of disparate elements including "a strongly egalitarian, achievement-oriented individualism, republican liberties, with the almost total denial of the symbolic validity of hierarchy; disestablishment of official religion beginning with the federal government; basically anti-statist premises; and a quasi-sanctification of the economic sphere".

2 Utopian thinking may also be denied altogether. In destitution and other situations *in extremis*, survival has priority and leaves no room for utopian thinking,

despite wish-dreams of cornucopia. Finally, there are those who make a virtue of problem-solving via "muddling through" in Charles Lindblom's (1959) provocative formulation, where our choices are guided by nothing more than a simple pleasure-pain calculus. Market fundamentalists are similarly averse to charting the long-term future.

3   I would like here to quote from a recent essay by Gerda Lerner (1997: 197), which expresses a similar conviction:

> As long as we regard class, race, and gender dominance as separate though overlapping systems, we fail to understand their actual integration. We also fail to see that they cannot be abolished sequentially, for like the many-headed hydra, they continuously spawn new heads. Vertical theories of separate systems inevitably marginalize the subordination of women and fail to place it in the central relationship it has to the other aspects of the system. The system of hierarchies is interwoven, interpenetrating, interdependent. It is one system, with a variety of aspects. Race, class and gender oppression are inseparable; they construct, support and reinforce one another.

4   Some other notable attempts to imagine normative frameworks for city-building include Allan Jacobs and Donald Appleyard's *Toward an urban design manifesto* (1987), Richard Rogers' *Cities for a small planet* (1997), and an interesting utopian experiment in Germany, involving four cities (Stadt Münster, 1997). Called an "*Agreement concerning the quality [of life] for a league of cities of the future*", this program includes specific discussions under five headings: (1) economizing land management practices; (2) forward-looking environmental protection; (3) socially responsible housing programs; (4) transportation policy guidance for a sustainable urban future; (5) promoting an economy that will ensure a firm foundation for the city's future within a sustainable and resource-conserving framework.

5   For a devastating look at the entanglement of political and civil spheres in twentieth century China, see Chang (1991).

6   For a discussion of civil society, see Keane (1988), Seligman (1992) and Walzer (1992). Friedmann (1998) has attempted to introduce the concept into the discourse on planning.

7   But see the case studies of "deliberative democracy" which are cited in Fung and Wright (1998).

Editor's note [in the original publication]: Manuel Castells declined to respond to this article. Readers are invited to provide their reactions.

References

Abers, R. (1998) Learning democratic practice: distributing government resources through popular participation in Porto Alegre, Brazil. In M. Douglass and J. Friedmann (eds.), *Cities for citizens: planning and the rise of civil society in a global age*, John Wiley & Sons, Chichester.

Abu-Lughod, J. (1998) The world system perspective in the construction of economic history. In P. Pomper, R.H. Elphick and R.T. Vann (eds.), *World history: ideologies, structures and identities*, Blackwell, Oxford.

Arendt, H. (1958) *The human condition*. The University of Chicago Press, Chicago.

Brook, T. and B.M. Frolic (eds.) (1997) *Civil society in China*. M.E. Sharpe, Armonk, NY.

Castells, M. (1998) *End of the millennium. Vol. III of The information age: economy, society and culture*. Blackwell Publishers, Oxford.

Chang, J. (1991) *Wild swans: three daughters of China*. Anchor Books, New York.

Cheng, L. and C-J. Hsia (1999) Exploring territorial governance and transterritorial society: alternative visions of 21st-century Taiwan. In J. Friedmann (ed.), *Urban and regional governance in the Asia Pacific*, University of British Columbia, Institute of Asian Research, Vancouver.

Eisenstadt, S.N. (1998) World histories and the construction of collective identities. In P. Pomper, R.H. Elphick and R.T. Vann (eds.), *World history: ideologies, structures, and identities*, Blackwell, Oxford.

Fainstein, S.S. (1999) Can we makes the cities we want? In S. Body-Gendrot and R.A. Beauregard (eds.), *The urban moment*, Sage, Thousand Oaks, CA.

Friedmann, J. (1973) *Retracking America: a theory of transactive planning*. Anchor Press/ Doubleday, Garden City, NY.

Friedmann, J. (1979) *The good society*. The MIT Press, Cambridge, MA.

Friedmann, J. (1987) *Planning in the public domain: from knowledge to action*. Princeton University Press, Princeton, NJ.

Friedmann, J. (1992) *Empowerment: the politics of alternative development*. Blackwell, Oxford.

Friedmann, J. (1998) The new political economy of planning: the rise of civil society. In M. Douglass and J. Friedmann (eds.), *Cities for citizens: planning and the rise of civil society in a global age*, John Wiley & Sons, Chichester.

Friedmann, J. and C. Weaver (1979) *Territory and function: the evolution of regional planning*. University of California Press, Berkeley.

Fung, A. and E.O. Wright (1998) *Experiments in deliberative democracy: introduction*. <http:// www.ssc.wisc.edu/~wright/experiments6-1.html>

Harvey, D. (1996) *Justice, nature and the geography of difference*. Blackwell, Oxford.

Hayden, D. (1984) *Redesigning the American dream: the future of housing, work, and family life*. W.W. Norton, New York.

Inncs, J. (1995) Planning theory's emerging paradigm: communicative action and interactive practice. *Journal of Planning Education and Research* 14.3, 183–9.

Jacobs, A. and D. Appleyard (1987) [1996 edn.] Toward an urban design manifesto. In R.T.L. Gates and F. Stout (eds.), *The city reader*, Routledge, New York.

Jacobs, J. (1961) *The death and life of great American cities*. Random House, New York.

Keane, J. (1988) *Democracy and civil society*. Verso, London.

King, C.S. and C. Stivers (1998) *Government is us: public administration in an anti-government era*. Sage, Thousand Oaks, CA.

Kotler, M. (1969) *Neighborhood government*. Bobbs-Merril, Indianapolis.

Le, T. (1999) A nation without vision. *The Age* 3 March, 17.

Lerner, G. (1997) *Why history matters: life and thought*. Oxford University Press, New York.

Lindblom, C. (1959) The science of muddling through. *Public Administration Review* 19.2, 79–99.

Manuel, F.E. and F.P. Manuel (1979) *Utopian thought in the western world*. The Belknap Press of Harvard University Press, Cambridge, MA.

Morris, D. and K. Hess (1975) *Neighborhood power*. Beacon Press, Boston.

Rogers, R. (1997) *Cities for a small planet*. Faber and Faber, London.

Sandercock, L. (1997) *Towards cosmopolis: planning for multicultural cities*. John Wiley & Sons, London.

Sandercock, L. (ed.) (1999) Knowledge practices: Towards an epistemology of multiplicity of insurgent planning. *Plurimondi* 1.2: 169–79.

Seligman, A.B. (1992) *The idea of civil society*. Princeton University Press, Princeton, NJ.

Stadt Münster (1997) Experimenteller Wohnungs- und Städtebau: Qualitätsvereinbarung für ein Bündnis Städte der Zukunft.

Walzer, M. (1992) The civil society argument. In C. Mouffe (ed.), *Dimensions of radical democracy: pluralism, citizenship, community*, Verso, London.

Warren, R., S. Nun and C. Warren (1998) The future of the future in planning: appropriating cyberpunk visions of the city. *Journal of Planning Education and Research* 18.3, 49–60.

Weaver, C. (1984) *Anarchy, planning, and regional development*. John Wiley & Sons, London.

John Friedmann, "The Good City: In Defense of Utopian Thinking," *International Journal for Urban and Regional Research*, 24, 2 (2000), pp. 460–72.

II

Planning
Justifications and Critiques

Introduction

This part addresses a perennial question of planning theory: What is the justification for planning intervention? Rather than offering an abstract, ideological answer, the readings emphasize planning's larger institutional environment: what are the comparative advantages of planning intervention – and when should planning step aside and yield to other logics and forces shaping the built environment? Underlying these questions is the boundary mapping of planning thought and action given the limits of knowledge, human rationality, coordination, and authority. A core task of planning theory has long been to examine arguments for and against planning, alternately using neo-classical economic, institutional, and structuralist perspectives and placing the profession in the political-economic context of the relationship between the private market and government (both the local and national states). We begin with Heather Campbell and Robert Marshall's re-evaluation of the public interest justification for planning. Foglesong then deftly identifies the contradictory nature of planning's support and opposition: private economic interests both resist government intrusion but also insist on it to provide the larger order and infra-structure for an effective marketplace. The final reading (by Tim Love) examines the complex relationship between public planning and private development in the world of large-scale urban development projects, and offers alternative public–private urban design strategies to create more vibrant, multifaceted cityscapes.

In their discussion of the public interest, Heather Campbell and Robert Marshall ask whether this traditional rationale for planning intervention remains relevant in our contemporary, fragmented society. If one starts with the ostensibly straight-forward notion that some restriction of private property rights is necessary to protect the public interest, and yet one cannot clearly define or measure the public

Readings in Planning Theory, Third Edition. Edited by Susan S. Fainstein and Scott Campbell.
Editorial material and organization © 2012 Blackwell Publishing Ltd.
Published 2012 by Blackwell Publishing Ltd.

interest, then what becomes of this foundational validation of planning? The lack of a consensual, unitary public interest was at the center of Davidoff's 1965 rejection of the comprehensive planning model (Chapter 10). In today's intellectual climate of fragmented, diverse, postmodern relativism, the claim for a shared public interest may seem antiquated or even deceitful. However, Campbell and Marshall do not simply echo this torrent of anti-public interest criticism; they instead present a careful, nuanced analysis of the way that the "public interest" has evolved in the modern period and argue for the enduring centrality of the public interest to give planning its role and purpose.

Campbell and Marshall begin by revisiting the historical roots of the idea, ranging from Burke and Madison to Bentham. They subsequently examine how the notion of the public interest regarding the best use of land shaped mid-twentieth-century British and American planning. However, this mid-century planning/public interest alliance was later threatened by two larger developments: the critiques flowing from the intellectual attacks and popular protests against what James Scott (Chapter 2) terms high modernism; and the market liberalism of the Reagan and Thatcher eras with its accompanying shift towards entrepreneurial local planning. The "public interest" was arguably no longer uniform, identifiable or even in the best interest of the public. Campbell and Marshall develop a theoretical path out of this conundrum through careful normative interpretation of the public interest, differentiating between outcome- and processed-focused frameworks, including rights-based, utilitarian and dialogical approaches. The authors do not bluntly side with one approach over all others. They instead delineate the benefits and shortcomings of two public interest frameworks: communicative-based and substantive, outcome-based. One without the other will not lead planning to the common well-being.

In a brief excerpt from his book, *Planning the Capitalist City*, Richard Foglesong provides his own perspective on the justification for planning, based on a Marxist view of the role of the state (and thus public planning) in not only restraining economic activity, but also maintaining the built environment as a support system for private enterprise. He departs from the market failure model's tidy and benign division of labor between the public and private sectors and instead sees a conflicted, contradictory relationship between government and business. The key dynamic to understanding the ambivalent role of planning in capitalist society is the "property contradiction": the contradiction between the social character of land and its private ownership and control. This conflict does not invariably lead to collapse or social upheaval, but it does create political conflict. The private sector naturally resists government intrusion into its affairs, yet at the same time needs government to socialize the control of land. For example, the private sector needs government to cope with externality problems, to help provide housing for the working poor, and to build and coordinate infrastructure. As a result, resistance to planning should not be misinterpreted as a simple rejection of planning as unnecessary. For Foglesong, this property contradiction is related to another contradiction: that between capitalism and democracy. Development interests have a particular agenda that is at odds with the needs of the broad public for land, and it is the role of planning to reconcile the two. In other words, planners act to legitimize policies contrary to the interests of the public.

The dichotomy between regulation and laissez-faire has been a staple of planning theory debates. More recently, it has been joined by the modernist/postmodernist divide. Planning theorists were drawn to the emerging ideas of postmodernism during the 1980s; these ideas were novel enough to promote a burst of theoretical creativity and vague enough to tolerate imprecise planning polemics. The appeal was understandable: the transition from modernism to postmodernism provided an overall framework in which to critique the whole era of modernist planning. It thus allowed postmodernist analysts to distance themselves from modernism's monolithic obsession with the grid, the box, and the comprehensive plan (and led to much broad-brushed scapegoating of modernist icons such as Le Corbusier, Robert Moses, and Walter Gropius). Postmodernism's rejection of the master narrative in place of multiple discourses also provided theoretical support for the emerging interest in multiculturalism and collaboration.

In "Urban Design after *Battery Park City*," Tim Love takes an ostensibly architectural/design question – what causes monotonous urban landscapes? – and links it to this part's leitmotiv: the underlying relationship between planning and the market, or more precisely, between land use planners, architects, large-scale developers and public space advocates. Confronting contemporary mega-projects devoid of vitality or diversity, the tendency is to blame the architecture – and the architects. However, this blame is often misplaced. The culprit instead is the underlying urban design framework: the street patterns, zoning, block and parcel sizes, and the integration of existing and new buildings. Both developers and public officials too often take this underlying city format as a given, neutral, even universal template. These urban frameworks, however, are often relics of antiquated urban design ideology; in place, they constrain and thwart the emergence of rich, heterogeneous landscapes. In addition, large-scale, private projects, managed by sophisticated real estate companies, constitute the new reality of urban development, and old planning strategies to guide urban development are no longer up to the task required of them.

Love advocates for moving away from the solo-architect approach (that usually creates only a veneer of variety) towards a multi-actor urban design process, phased over time, which creates true variety and diversity of scale, design, cost and use. Planners should use urban design to leverage the power and logic of real estate development. In this model of city building, innovation arises from the creative interaction – rather than the merger – of urban design and architecture. Urban design guidelines are not the answer: they are insufficient to create vibrant cityscapes. Revising streetscapes through zoning should be linked to a savvy understanding of the real estate market and parcel configurations; this is not an abstract task of space syntax. Love effectively illustrates these divergent approaches through case studies of large-scale projects in New York, Toronto, Boston and Cambridge, MA.

5

Utilitarianism's Bad Breath?
A Re-evaluation of the Public Interest Justification for Planning

Heather Campbell and Robert Marshall

Introduction

The legitimization of planning as an activity which intervenes in land and property markets has long rested on the notion that some restrictions of individual property rights are necessary if the public interest is to be upheld. This idea of a determinative public interest or public good was central to the deliberations which produced the great 1947 Town and Country Planning Act in Britain and it has continued to underpin attempts to place explicitly value on the land use planning activity. Despite this, there are a number of writers (commenting often from very different ideological positions) who have questioned the value of the "public interest" as a legitimizing concept because it cannot be given meaning either by those who make policy or by those who evaluate it. It is merely, some would argue, an expression of preference or commendation which provides no standard against which decisions or policies can be judged or evaluated (Flathman, 1966). Reade (1987, 1997), for example, has argued that the public interest is a smokescreen or facade which prohibits any real evaluation of what effects the planning system actually has in practice. Within the arena of theoretical debate postmodernist critiques have rendered universalizing concepts, such as the public interest, problematic in a world of difference. Sandercock (1998: 197), for example, asserts that "class, gender, and race-based critiques have left this particular notion of 'the public interest' in tatters, as have the lived realities of late twentieth century existence."

While we accept the problematic and contested nature of the concept, we nevertheless contend that the discourse central to the idea of the public interest

Readings in Planning Theory, Third Edition. Edited by Susan S. Fainstein and Scott Campbell.
Editorial material and organization © 2012 Blackwell Publishing Ltd.
Published 2012 by Blackwell Publishing Ltd.

remains the pivot around which discussions concerning the purpose and role of planning must turn. As Flathman (1966: 13) has said:

> Determining justifiable government policy in the face of conflict and diversity is central to the political order…. The much discussed difficulties with the concept [of the public interest] are difficulties with morals and politics. We are free to abandon the *concept* but if we do so we simply have to wrestle with the *problems* under some other heading.

In its most limited sense "public interest" is used to express approval, approbation or commendation of public policy (Flathman, 1966) and, as noted above, some would argue that this is all that the public interest represents which renders it useless as a standard against which to judge public actions. However, governments are expected to justify their actions and it is in this descriptive sense of defining what is "good" that it provides a normative standard against which decisions or policies can be evaluated. Public interest functions to justify action in situations in which there is disagreement. It relates to the problem of the "one and the many" (Pennock, 1962).

It is in this spirit that we explore the problems of the concept in relation to contemporary reflections on the role and purpose of planning. We begin by briefly examining the origins of the concept. This is followed by a consideration of the way in which "public interest" has been regarded in the planning literature in the period since the Second World War. The third section is devoted to an evaluation of alternative conceptions of "public interest". This is premised upon a typology which distinguishes both procedural (deontological) as well as outcome focused (consequentialist) conceptualizations of the public interest. It is argued that while deontological theories have become dominant, planning practice cannot evade the responsibility for making determinative and ethical choices in public policy-making.

Interests and Politics in the Modern Period

The word "interest" is used in two different senses (Pitkin, 1967). The first, which in the context of this article need not detain us long, is concerned with having an interest *in* something. It relates to a *concern with* or *attention to* something. Thus we might have an interest in historic buildings or 20th-century music. The concept in this mode of use is entirely subjective. The second sense in which it is used is particularly relevant to consideration of "public interest" and it implies "having something at stake" (Pitkin, 1967) and is associated with welfare, gain or advantage (or, in utilitarian terms, with happiness or utility). Although interest in this sense may be attached to an individual or to a group, it can also occur "unattached" so that we can speak, for example, of something being in the interests of amenity or the environment. Even attached interests, however, can be conceived as being independent of anyone's particular wishes or feelings. Pitkin (1967) gives the example of class interests in Marxist theory. Within the concept of interest as "having something at stake" there is the possibility of both objective and subjective uses of the word. This objective/subjective polarity has been important, as we shall see, in the way public interest has been variously defined but, possibly, the dominant view within the western liberal tradition since the 19th century has been the notion that only the individual affected can determine whether she or he has something at stake and this view was central to utilitarianism (although not unambiguously so as we shall see later) as it took shape in the writings of Bentham and his followers.

Although politics has always recognized the importance of individual interest, it was not until the Enlightenment that the idea of *satisfying* individual subjective interests came to be an important objective of political action (Flathman, 1966). The idea of "interest" in the realm of politics has, however, in the period since the 18th century been seen in a variety of different ways. Following Pitkin (1967) we identify three contrasted interpretations exemplified in: first, Burke's concept of virtual representation; second, Madisonian conceptions of liberalism in the United States; and, third, the utilitarian tradition as it developed in Britain.

Edmund Burke was a conservative political theorist who placed emphasis on tradition and stability (MacIntyre, 1985). He took an elitist view of government identifying a "natural aristocracy" and limited franchise as integral to any well-founded state. Despite this conservatism, Burke's concept of representation still resonates with contemporary ideas of representative government and how it should operate (Benn and Peters, 1959). Burke's conception of interest was essentially objective – unattached from the particular views of those being represented (Pitkin, 1967).

Burke took the view that political deliberation was the means by which government would arrive at right decisions. For him, Members of Parliament represented interests and not people and, since he also believed that there were good reasons to suppose that people might well be mistaken about their interests, Members of Parliament were under no obligation to follow the wishes or opinions of their constituents. Interests for Burke were broad and objective and not specific and particularistic. "Parliament", he argued, "is a *deliberative* assembly of *one* nation, with *one* interest, that of the whole – where not local purposes, not local prejudices, ought to guide, but the general good, resulting from the general reason of the whole" (Burke, 1774: 158).

For Burke, therefore, the public interest was a unitary concept based not upon the adding together of the subjective preferences of electors but representing "the sum of the objective interests that comprise the nation when these are correctly determined through rational deliberation" (Pitkin, 1967: 186). In this process of deliberation, account would be taken of people's feelings, opinions and needs but decisions would not be determined by them. If correctly carried out, reason would prevail in the deliberative process which would result in consensus and agreement (Pitkin, 1967).

At the same time as Burke in England was setting out his ideas on government and representation, alternative ideas were being developed in America where liberalism entailed quite different ideas of "interests". For Madison, interests were always plural, attached and subjective. Only the individual can know what his or her interests are. The problem for those drawing up the United States Constitution was to seek to ensure that a governing faction would not use its power and authority to exploit other (minority) groups in the population. Interests, indeed, were viewed negatively rather than positively (Pitkin, 1967) because they could become factions which might tyrannize other groups. For Madison, a representative was mandated to follow his constituent's wishes. If this were the case, he argued, the various interests or factions in the nation would balance each other out such that harmful interests would be held in check and stability would prevail. The efficacy of the checks and balances would be enhanced, moreover, the larger the state and the greater the diversity of interests within it. Already, therefore, in the late 18th century, America was anticipating the idea of a plural society in which the government would balance and adjust sectional interests rather than responding directly to a majoritarian preference (Benn and Peters, 1959) or seeing its role as one of taking an objective deliberative view of the public interest.

English utilitarianism also developed a subjective view of interest but in a significantly different way from that which was emerging in the US. Utilitarianism was premised on the assumption that only the individual can know her or his interests and that the only consistent test of the consequences of an action is the pleasure or pain that is experienced by the person(s) affected. Moreover, in the realm of public choice a *good* policy is one which in aggregate terms maximizes individual pleasure or utility and in the felicific calculus each person is to count as one and only one.

As Pitkin (1967) points out, the assertion that only the individual is truly able to know his or her interest might lead logically to the conclusion that a government cannot act effectively in the interests of its citizens and that a minimalist state would be the preferred mode of governance. In fact, of course, Bentham was interested in parliamentary, legal and social reform and utilitarianism came to play a major role in the social reform movement of 19th-century Britain. Utilitarianism was no libertarian creed.

Bentham, in fact, recognized that each individual has a social or other-regarding interest as well as a self-regarding interest. But since the majority of individuals prefer to pursue their private interest rather than their public interest it was, he argued, the task of government (if need be) through wise legislation to persuade or coerce citizens to act in the interests of the common good (Pitkin, 1967). A system of rewards and punishments would be the means by which behaviour would be influenced. Bentham believed that institutional reform would ensure that "the controlling part of government shall be in the hands of those whose interest it is that good government shall take the place of misrule" (Bentham, quoted by Pitkin, 1967: 200). He was, as were his supporters, advocates of representative government and of virtual universal suffrage (Rosen, 1983). John Stuart Mill was even less equivocal than Bentham. Government, he argued, could take what Sugden (1989) refers to as a synoptic view of interest and could discern the "real" interests of individuals better than they could themselves (Pitkin, 1967). This "synoptic" or "spectator" view of interest was a long-range and often remote perspective which individuals could not easily perceive. Clearly, in respect of these kinds of views of interest one moves away from the subjective viewpoint and the question inevitably arises as to how those ideas can be compatible with the axiom that each person knows his or her interest better than anyone else. Pitkin (1967) adduces Ayer's interpretation as a means of resolving the apparent contradiction. Ayer (1954) argued that, while the individual is the best judge of how his/her interest is affected at the point at which the consequences of an action are experienced, it is not necessarily the case that the individual will know *in advance* what his/her best interests are. Pitkin (1967: 204) draws an analogy to make the point: "[o]nly the wearer can tell if the shoe pinches. But this does not mean that the wearer knows in advance which shoe will pinch him; in fact, it is much more likely that a shoe specialist will know this better than he."[1]

Although the subjective/objective distinction provides the most common way of categorizing interpretations of the public interest, in practice the distinction is not always easy to uphold. Utilitarianism especially has spawned a number of different approaches some of which imply objective or, possibly, trans-subjective interpretations of interests. We return to some of these ambiguities in the penultimate section of the article. First, however, we look more specifically at the treatment of the public interest in the planning literature.

The Public Interest and Planning

We see in this brief examination of the origins of the idea of the public interest that different interpretations have held sway at different times and in different places. Within the domain of the public planning activity, it has also occupied a shifting position and has always given rise to contestation and argument. In this section we consider some of the ambiguities of the concept in relation to planning in the period since the Second World War. In doing so, we draw on the literature relating principally to the UK and the US.

The creation of an effective land use planning system in Britain in the 1940s struck at the heart of private interests in land and property. Planning was conceived as the means by which the *best* use of land could be secured irrespective of market conditions and this required unreserved acceptance of the need to subordinate private interests to the public interest (Expert Committee on Compensation and Betterment, 1942). Determination of the "best" use of land was not itself seen to be problematic and was frequently conceived as the application of predetermined prescriptive standards to local situations in the interests of securing amenity, convenience and efficiency. That there might be significant disagreement over what constitutes the "best" use of land did not appear to be an issue which vexed the minds of members of the Uthwatt Committee (the Expert Committee on Compensation and Betterment). The unanimity of the nation and its preparedness to accept collectivist provision and state intervention in the market were matters which astonished American observers of the British scene (see Haar, 1961).

The unanimity suggests that there was a unitary concept of the public interest shaping conceptions of land use planning and what it might accomplish. In practice, other reasons were being proposed by observers by the 1950s to explain the *apparent* consensus and while analysis did not necessarily undermine the public interest foundation of legitimacy, it did call into question the basis upon which the claim to unitary public interest was built. The sociologist, Ruth Glass, commented upon the lack of self-awareness in the British planning system: "… there is comparatively little scepticism or even curiosity about the system because it has been established by common consent, in recognition of the public interest" (Glass, 1959: 397). This lack of critical reflection she attributed not only to the stability and strength of the planning machinery established in the 1940s but also to the effects of the professionalism of the activity. Those involved in the activity had vested interests to maintain the status quo and were resistant to change.

Glass also commented upon the ambiguity and ambivalence of the ideas concerning social change implied in contemporary planning ideology which, in turn, contributed to its ability to maintain support from different sections of society. Interestingly, Glass was not seeking to undermine the idea of the public interest as the determinative value guiding planning processes. Quite the reverse because she saw in the profession's too ready acceptance of established ideas and its lack of clear focus about aims and purpose "a growing indifference to the public interest" which she juxtaposed with the growing "Americanization of British planning" (Glass, 1959: 406).

Transatlantic comparisons were frequently made in the 1950s and 1960s underlining the perceived differences between the emerging systems of regulation in Britain and the US. In particular, Americans were keen observers of the British scene (Foley, 1960; Haar, 1961; Mandelker, 1962; Altshuler, 1965). Foley, for example, in a celebrated article, took up the ideas of Glass and argued that in Britain ideology built upon "seemingly self-evident truths and values" provided an "operating rationale" which bestowed "a self-justifying tone to its main propositions and chains of reasoning" (Foley, 1960: 212). Ambiguity and ambivalence enhanced its role to win support not only from the public at large but from politicians and officials. "[P]hrases like 'the public interest'", he argued, "may take the place of fuller substantive reasoning which is implicit in the ideology(ies)" (Foley, 1960: 213).

In fact, the immediate post-war years in America were also characterized by a strong belief on the part of the emerging profession that the public interest stood at the heart of their professional concerns (Howe, 1992). The significant influence in the 1940s came from the progressive movement which exerted a strong belief in the role of professional expertise in ameliorating social ills. The role model was the professional expert providing apolitical advice to elected representatives (Howe, 1992). There were, however, major studies published in the 1950s and 1960s, based on case study investigations, which appeared to belie this faith in a public interest conception of professional competence. Meyerson and Banfield's (1955) study of the provision of public housing in Chicago revealed a policy process far removed from a rational model of decision-making and Altshuler (1965) found in his studies of Minneapolis and St Paul a lack of political realism and the absence of a clear rationale for professional practice. A serious challenge to the rational comprehensive model of decision-making was also mounted by Lindblom (Lindblom, 1959; Braybrooke and Lindblom, 1963). The plurality of interests, with each interest or value having its own watchdog, had, he argued important implications for public policy-making. First, it made any ordering of goals impossible. Second, "mutual adjustment" between competing claims to value led to incremental change which served a broader range of interests than could be achieved through comprehensive centralized approaches to policy-making.

Lindblom's analysis undermined the idea of the public interest and, indeed, other political scientists in the 1950s and 1960s were mostly hostile to the idea of the public interest either because they held it had no value as an explanatory device or because it could not be used as an operational norm (Schubert, 1957, 1960, 1967; Sorauf, 1957, 1967; Downs, 1962). Running somewhat against mainstream opinion were Barry (1964), Flathman (1966) and Held (1970) who argued, from different premises, in its defence. Despite criticism of the concept, Howe (1992) argues that planners in the US continued to place faith in some idea of the public interest although there was no dominant conception of its meaning and role. In the 1950s and 1960s planning thought was very much influenced by positivism and technical rationality. Professional value-neutrality was upheld in the sense that rational decision-making models emphasized a separation between ends and means. Determination of ends (value orientations) was the province of politicians whereas professional expertise had a major part to play in the generation and evaluation of the means by which aspirations might be met (Howe, 1992). By the late 1960s, however, the faith in technocratic conceptions of planning and in a consensus-based idea of the public interest was being increasingly challenged. Not only was it apparent that planning endeavours were not having much impact on the problems they were seeking to remedy but, worse than that, the prescriptions of planners were creating their own unanticipated problems. As Schön (1983: 207) observes, "[p]lanning 'problems' came to seem more like dilemmas made up of conflicts of values, interests, and ideologies unresolvable by recourse to the facts."

In the face of the plurality of competing interest groups the idea of an overarching public interest receded and planners searched for new roles given that centralized comprehensive conceptions of planning could no longer be sustained (Schön, 1983). A splintered society of special interest groups competing for attention and resources implied new strategies and modified conceptions of professional responsibility. Either, it seemed, planners must become overtly partisan and align themselves as advocates to particular interest groups especially the poor and dispossessed (Davidoff, 1965) or should seek process forms appropriate to the particularities of the contexts which they encountered in their work.

The story in Britain was similar although there were important differences both because the planning system and its profession had a securer foundation within a very different system of government than was the case in the US and because disenchantment with the consequences of intervention in a period of rapid change emerged somewhat later. The 1960s, in general, were a period in which planning was held in relatively high esteem (although public disaffection began to manifest itself towards the end of the decade). The criticisms of Glass and Foley were addressed in so far as the profession became more reflective and self-critically aware, a process which was assisted by the widening of the basis of its membership as social scientists were attracted into it in increasing numbers and eventually ended the domination of the profession by those initially trained as architects, engineers and surveyors. The period was one of both economic and population growth and the planning system had a particular role to play in controlling and managing the physical demands arising from growth. Moreover, "growth" had normative connotations not just for planners but in the wider sphere of political debate. Economic growth was seen as the key not only for material progress but also to social justice and even environmental well-being. The good life would emerge through enlarged prosperity and maximizing opportunities for individual choice. The post-war consensus on the need for planning was maintained and so was the underlying (and largely implicit) belief in the public interest basis of its legitimacy.

There was recognition that planning involved conflicting claims over values and could not escape the inherently political nature of the task of adjudicating between these claims. In defining their own role and purpose, however, planners embraced technical managerialist conceptions of their function. They saw themselves standing either above or below politics (Low, 1991). Although in theory this meant that their professional task was to proffer expert advice on the best means of achieving externally generated ends, in practice not only were ends and means inextricably intertwined but professionalism was so ingrained into the structure of local government, that practitioners played a significant role in shaping preferred values and ends in so far as discretion was possible within the statutory powers exercised by local councils and within the constraints imposed by central government policy.

Any lingering attachment to positivism and rational comprehensive models of the planning process was dissipated during the 1970s and by the 1980s the modernist planning project appeared to be in tatters. Two influences were particularly important. The first was the triumph of market liberalism in the 1980s (the vestiges of which are still very much apparent) and the associated restructuring of economic institutions and the relationships between state and society, The second was the intellectual assault on the Enlightenment project by postmodernism. Both of these challenges raised questions not only about current planning practices but about the very enterprise of planning (Healey, 1997).

In market liberalism the public interest becomes consumer or customer interest and Adam Smith's hidden hand is invoked to illustrate the way in which individual self-interest is converted into the interests of society (Douglas, 1992). Writing at the end of the 1980s, Beauregard (1989: 387) observed in relation to the US, "[n]o longer is the idea to improve society ... Economic development, not reform is the political aim of the 1980s, and it sacrifices regulation and the welfare state to the lure of new investment and jobs."

Planners, argued Beauregard, had become dealmakers rather than regulators and it was no longer possible to maintain a conflict-free public interest. Beauregard's observations concerning the American scene in the 1980s could equally apply to the UK over the same period. Thatcherism, indeed, became emblematic of the doctrines of market liberalism the effects of which on the planning system have been well-documented elsewhere (Thornley, 1993; Allmendinger and Thomas, 1998).

Postmodernism also struck at the heart of the modernist planning project. Two related themes are particularly important in this respect. These are, first, the recognition of difference, otherness and the dynamic nature of situations and, second, the rejection of universalism and the supremacy of scientific reasoning. A key issue for postmodernism and for feminist and postcolonial critiques of modernist thinking is the recognition of the fragmented nature of communities and the variety of lived experiences. In order to understand the individual or the community of which they are a part it is necessary, the argument goes, to engage with the heterogeneity of individual lived experiences – experiences which are themselves constituted through language and discourse and, in turn, are contingent and historically specific. As a consequence all forms of knowledge are perceived to be situated within heterogeneous worlds of difference. This conception of knowledge provides a link to the second key theme within the postmodern debate, namely the rejection of foundationalism and universalism. Metaphysical claims concerning truth, objectivity and validity in epistemology or to higher order moral values are regarded as misguided and potentially dangerous. Notions of universality are condemned because of their totalizing, homogenizing and elitist qualities. The public interest, so the argument goes, is such a universalizing, homogenizing concept which carries with it the danger that difference and heterogeneity will be masked and representing, therefore, a potentially oppressive idea. While, from the 1960s through to the 1980s, planning gave recognition to the existence of plural interests and searched for ways of reconciling them, postmodernist and feminist thinking does not look for reconciliation but seeks instead to encourage and celebrate plurality and difference (Milroy, 1991). A politics of difference "is the struggle for the right to difference, as well as the right to a voice in decisions affecting a wide range of groups, including indigenous peoples, migrants and refugees, women, and gays and lesbians" (Sandercock, 2000: 15). The challenge posed to planning as a consequence of epistemological relativism and the politics of difference has preoccupied the planning academy in the period since the late 1980s (see, for example, Milroy, 1989, 1991; Beauregard, 1989, 1991; Harper and Stein, 1995; Healey, 1997; Sandercock, 1998, 2000).

Public interest conceptions of planning have, therefore, been undermined by the critical debates of the recent past. Nevertheless, some writers have sought to resuscitate the idea (Howe, 1992, 1994; Klosterman, 1980; Fainstein, 2000; Campbell and Marshall, 2000a). Howe, in particular, has identified a continuing place for the notion both in theory and in practice. Indeed, she argues that the critique of positivism in the 1970s and 1980s, in releasing planners from the straitjacket of neutrality and impartiality, gave planners a new moral mandate. As a result there was recognition of the view "that planners do exercise discretion, that their personal values do influence their work, and that they are called upon to make moral choices in their activities" (Howe, 1992: 232). And, certainly, a very influential voice has persistently argued in the last decade in support of similar contentions. John Forester (1989, 1993, 1999a, 1999b) has put the case for a transformative role for planning and planners and has argued that ethical judgments are central to the day-to-day work of practitioners. However, the idea of the public interest as something definable and knowable he casts as a chimera. The dominant contemporary view within the planning academy is therefore dismissive of the public interest either because it is too vague to be useful or because it is an elitist and potentially anti-democratic idea. Despite this ambivalence or rejection on the part of planning theorists there is some evidence that it still holds sway with the practice community (Howe, 1994; Campbell and Marshall, 1998, 2000a).

Normative Interpretations of the Public Interest

In the preceding review of the public interest in relation to planning thought it is apparent that, although a contentious concept, the idea of the public interest has never entirely been abandoned and it is evident too that rather different conceptions have held sway at different times. In this section of the article we seek to categorize some of these alternative conceptualizations in an effort to pin down some of their distinguishing characteristics.

A number of attempts have been made to categorize public interest conceptualizations (Banfield, 1955; Sorauf, 1957; Held, 1970; Cochran, 1974; Howe, 1992). In the construction of their typologies important distinctions are the point of view (whether subjective or objective) and the interest base (whether individual or collective). In general, the subjective categorizations involve variants of utitilitarianism and are individualistic in the sense that they assume that judgments in the end are dependent on individual evaluations of good or bad, better or worse. In contrast, objective categories emphasize collective values either in the sense of interests generally shared by everyone or in terms of a normative standard against which judgments are made concerning collective interests or the common good.

In addition to the distinctions concerning the "point of view" and the "interest base" we would introduce a third which relates to whether the conception of the public interest is outcome focused (consequentialist) or procedurally focused (deontological). To identify deontological categories of the public interest is possibly contentious but we argue that communicative planning theorists are not dispensing with the idea of the public interest but are placing their faith in the future of the planning project in procedural norms and rules by which the public interest can somehow be discovered discursively through participatory practice. Dryzek (1990: 54), for example, asks us to think of communicative rationality "as a procedural standard, dictating no substantive resolution about the values to be pursued". And Healey (1997: 297) writes "… the 'public interest' has to reflect the diversity of our interests and be discovered discursively." In the typology which we offer below we have therefore made the distinction between outcome and procedurally focused approaches a primary one. In the case of consequentialist conceptions we distinguish three contrasted perspectives – utilitarianism, modified utilitarianism and the unitary approach. Procedurally focused conceptions include rights-based and dialogical approaches. The categorization, which provides an integrative framework for the discussion which follows, is summarized in Table 5.1.

Utilitarianism

The problems of utilitarianism are many and most were acknowledged and attempts made to address them within its mainstream 19th-century tradition especially in the writings of John Stuart Mill. A basic objection is the use of "happiness" or "pleasure"

Table 5.1   Concepts of the public interest

Focus	Approach	Interest base	Objective/subjective
Outcome focused	Utilitarianism	Individualistic	Subjective
	Modified utilitarianism	Individualistic	Objective
	Unitary	Collective	Objective
Procedurally focused	Rights-based	Individualistic	Objective
	Dialogical	Group/stakeholders	Inter-subjective

as the measure of value. Apart from quantity, there is the quality, intensity, and duration of pleasure and pain to be considered. How is it possible to equate the many different conditions of happiness or the many varieties of pleasure (MacIntyre, 1985; Bobbio, 2000)? The reductionism entailed through a unitary principle of valuing, especially in circumstances where the hedonistic calculation is based on monetary value, is also a source of concern (Hampshire, 1978, 1983; Smith, 1988; Harvey, 1996). "Quality of pleasure being equal, pushpin is as good as poetry" asserted Bentham and many recoil from such an absurd equation. This was a problem which Mill sought to address in his essay on *Utilitarianism*, where he rejected the unitary scale of valuation, introducing instead a qualitative distinction between what he called the higher and lower pleasures (Mill, 1861). For Mill, the higher pleasures are to be preferred to the lower and the distinction between them is to made by those who have experienced both. But, as MacIntyre (1998) shows, the distinction between higher and lower pleasures does not help in practical terms. Pleasure for Mill, as for Bentham, retains its unitary status because it embraces anything which an individual might desire or aim for. It loses through this process of extenuation any evaluative moral purchase (MacIntyre, 1998). Utilitarianism has also been criticized because its mechanistic calculation can condone exploitation or other horrific ends if they are compatible with the general happiness principle (Hampshire, 1978, 1983; MacIntyre, 1998; Campbell and Marshall, 1999; Bobbio, 2000).

Despite the criticisms of utilitarianism, its impact upon public policy-making has been enormous. Undoubtedly, it was a major influence on the social and administrative reform movement in 19th-century Britain. Bentham, it must be noted, was not centrally concerned with moral philosophy but with jurisprudence (Warnock, 1962) and, for his followers, the practical issues with which they were concerned including prisons, hospitals, public health and so on were, in the crudest sense, amenable to a calculation concerning the effects of reform on general welfare (MacIntyre, 1998).

In theory, the individual stands at the centre of utilitarianism. It is the sentient human being who experiences pain or pleasure. In practice, as we noted earlier, the utilitarian principle, at least as a means of determining public choice questions, recognizes the conflict between public and private interests and that the state has a necessary role in ensuring that the individual's pursuit of private pleasure is consonant with the collective good as represented by general welfare.

It falls to the enlightened "expert" to determine what constitutes the best nexus of private utility and public interest.

Consequently, although utilitarianism, as originally formulated, is based on a subjective view of interest, in practice trading off one person's utility against another's is an ethical judgment made by someone who is assigned the role of defining the common good. The stance, therefore, becomes objective and it is for this reason that we have distinguished *modified utilitarianism* as a separate category. Sugden's (1989) synoptic view of interest falls into this category as does welfarism as it emerged in the 20th century. Welfarism, as Samuelson and Bergson first formulated it, arose when economists began to doubt whether it was possible to compare one person's utility with another's because utility merely represents an expression of subjective preference. The Bergson-Samuelson approach accepted the impossibility of an inter-subjective comparison of utility but argued that it was still permissible for someone to make judgments about the common good provided it was made clear that the determination is made on the basis of value judgments (Sugden, 1989). Sen, as Sugden notes, took this line of reasoning further by stressing the normative aspects of interpersonal comparisons of utility and arguing that it may also be necessary to take into account "non-utility information" such as overriding ethical principles including rights (Sen, 1979; Sen and Williams, 1982).

Despite these modifications to utilitarian theories, it was the economic-analytical methods of quantifying the predicted consequences of policies particularly through cost-benefit analysis which offered widespread appeal to planners in the 1960s and 1970s. Howe (1992) argues that one of the problems of this approach is its failure to take account of the distributive aspects of choices in that it is the balance of total benefits over costs which is determinative. Lichfield (Lichfield et al., 1975) attempted to overcome this weakness through his planning balance sheet in which the differential impacts on groups affected by a proposal or policy are taken into account and, subsequently, through his community impact evaluation approach (Lichfield, 1992). The saga of the third London airport in the 1960s and early 1970s represented in Britain at least the apotheosis of cost-benefit analysis and with it of rational comprehensive planning.

The utilitarian ethic still has its ardent proponents. Singer (1993), for example, has developed a utilitarianism based on interests. Instead of judging consequences in relation to the balance of pleasure over pain, Singer argues that they should be assessed on the basis of what fosters the interests of those affected. As he observes, given the ambiguity concerning the way in which pleasure and pain were defined in classical utilitarianism, the difference between it and his version may not, indeed, be significant.

Unitary public interest

This conceptualization differs from the utilitarian concept in that, while individual interests are seen to be an important part of determining the public interest, it also gives emphasis to an "outsider" perspective or an "objective" evaluation. The necessity for this is based upon three important considerations. First, there is the existence of inequalities of various kinds (status, resources and other personal attributes) which requires someone (authority/government) to compensate for the differences. The second consideration is the notion that individuals may be mistaken in their interests. We return here to the shoe-pinching analogy referred to earlier. Third, it acknowledges the existence of collective values and principles which transcend private interests and their summation.

Flathman (1966) puts the case for what he calls the "trans-subjective view of the public interest". The public interest, he argues, is not to be equated with the sum of self-defined interests (the utilitarian concept) but is a *moral* concept the consequences of which require that citizens are obliged to obey particular laws, commands, policies even when they are contrary to their personal interest. Flathman (1966: 38) writes: "It is true that self-interest has a legitimate place in the public interest, but deciding whose self-interest and to what extent requires the utilization of values and principles which transcend such interests." An important principle for Flathman is universalization by which he means that when a policy or decision is made or put into effect by the state it must apply to *all* members of the society in question.

Although for Flathman universalization is a necessary pre-condition, it is not the only principle entailed by the concept of the public interest. Those in authority, he argues, must give good reasons why they have chosen one course of action as against others. Of course, in the final analysis people will judge whether a policy is right or wrong, good or bad and their judgment will be based upon their assessment of the substantive consequences of the policy as it affects themselves and others. At the end of the day, it is the ballot box which gives citizens the opportunity to express approval or disapproval of the choices made on their behalf by their elected leaders.

Some would see in the principles described above positivistic and/or elitist ideas but we would argue that this is not necessarily the case. The approach does not preclude deliberative and participatory practices. Nor does it necessarily privilege expert over other forms of knowledge. What it does recognize is that claims to values conflict and that politics is the means by which we settle those claims and in that process we recognize collective values and interests which individuals cannot achieve by themselves and which sometimes require the active promotion of some interests as against others.

Deontological interpretations of the public interest

Deontological views of morality focus not on substantive outcomes but on rights, fairness of approach and justice. Chambers (1996) identifies the following characteristics of deontological theories of morality. First, the right is prior to the good – the basis of morality is independent of the goals or ends for which human beings strive. Second, the principles or procedures entailed have a formal and fixed quality. Third, these principles do not tell us what to do but are a "testing" mechanism for helping us decide what we ought to do.

Conceptualizations of the public interest have, for the most part, eschewed a deontological frame of reference. An exception is Cochran's (1974) typology in which a proceduralist approach is identified. Although Howe's (1992) typology focused on consequentialist conceptions of the public interest her subsequent book did find an important place for deontological views of the public interest influenced by the ways in which practising planners themselves identified the public interest which included both consequentialist and procedural interpretations (Howe, 1994). Broadly, Howe identified two deontological versions of the public interest. The first is focused on rights and especially the right of everyone to be considered fairly and equally in the planning or policy-making process. The second concerns the transparency of the process by which planning decisions are arrived at with the implication that where a participatory approach is adopted then the result will be in the public interest whatever the actual outcome is. There is, of course, an important link between these two views because the second implies an entitlement by members of the public to a right to be heard – to have an opportunity to influence outcomes. In our typology we make a similar distinction to Howe's except that we give emphasis in our second category to current preoccupations within the planning academy to dialogical processes of deliberative debate as a way of achieving consensus and agreement.

Rights-based approaches

The deontological emphasis on rules is premised on the assumption that this is the best means of achieving consistent, universal and impartial decisions and therefore of protecting individual rights. Concern with the protection of rights is a central plank of liberal thinking. As Anderson (1987: 27) states, "[t]he persistent aim of liberal philosophy has been to devise principles of individual rights and legitimate public purpose from a basic agnosticism concerning conceptions of the good or ultimate human purpose." We return, therefore, to the view that values are subjective and that individuals should be free to pursue their own conceptions of the good life constrained only to the extent that in doing so they do not prevent others from doing likewise.

Rawls's (1971) theory of justice stands within this liberal tradition. It is premised on the assumption that in a society composed of free and autonomous individuals, there are "many conflicting and incommensurable conceptions of the good" (Rawls, 1982: 160). The role of the state is to facilitate citizens in their individual pursuit of the good whilst ensuring that the principles of justice are upheld. In his later work, Rawls (1982, 1993) has addressed more centrally the political implications of his theory and, in particular, how it is that citizens continue to acknowledge shared understanding of the claims of justice when they remain deeply divided over conceptions of the good. This similarity of interests rests on two higher-order conceptions of the good. The first is "moral personality" and the second is the agreement of citizens to advance the same primary goods, these being "the same rights, liberties and opportunities as well as certain all-purpose means such as income and wealth" (Rawls, 1982: 161).

Rawls's theory is not purely deontological because distributional justice is acknowledged in the second of his principles. Acceptance of his rules of justice is accounted for by the original position by which we are asked to imagine the principles by which people would choose to be governed if they were making the choice before they knew what endowments or talents they would possess or what privileges they might enjoy by virtue of birth or social standing. This process of arriving at principles of justice is conducted monologically and not by real social agents, a source of criticism and an important point of difference with Habermas's theory of communicative action (Moon, 1995). It is interesting that Rawlsian-type principles of justice were acknowledged by some of Howe's planners who broadened out a concept of rights as fairness into a principle of social justice (Howe, 1994).

To be sure, rights are a crucial buttress in ensuring that the dignity and equality of minorities will be respected by the majority (Dworkin, 1978). In this regard, therefore, they have social value in that they are good for society as a whole (Sen, 1979). Nevertheless, as Dworkin (1978) is at pains to point out rights are principles of individual duty or entitlement and not policy instruments for achieving some collective goal. Dworkin also emphasizes that there is a difference between "having a right" and "doing right". Crucial though rights are we contend that a rights-based theory of the public interest presents some problems. It is, for example, one thing for formal rights to be recognized in law but quite another for *all* citizens to make use of them (Benton, 1993). The opportunity or ability to exercise rights is not distributed equally. It can be argued, indeed, that rights solidify and perpetuate inequalities (Benton, 1993).

Since rights are assigned to individuals it would be surprising if they were not used in certain contexts to buttress self-interest against the claims of collective values and the needs of others. This is particularly pertinent to planning where rights to property are crucially affected by the decisions being made. Our findings from empirical work carried out in the Bay Area of California in the US exemplified some of the problems stemming from a rights-based approach (Campbell and Marshall, 2000b). The focus on the right of individuals or communities to articulate their self-interests virtually paralysed the decision-making process. When the right to defend one's interests becomes agonistic, collective values are likely to be squeezed out and local democracy reduced to confusion and noise.

Dialogical approaches

In this conception of the public interest the focus is on deliberation as a means of arriving at consensus and agreement. The emphasis is on procedural norms and rules. It is commonly associated with participatory forms of democracy but in the context of institutional structures which seek to avoid agonistic clashes of self-interest and the development of *open dialogue* encouraging the emergence of *shared solutions* through the uncovering of *new forms of knowledge and understanding* (Gutmann and Thompson, 1996). The notion of communicative rationality has been based upon Habermas's theory of communicative action. Habermas's theory is deontological through and through. It is a theory of justice but one which does not, as in Rawls's case, depend upon individuals making their own self-centred contracts behind a veil of ignorance. Instead, Habermas's practical discourse requires all participants to imagine themselves in others' places in the process of deciding whether a proposed norm is fair. It is a process which must be carried out by real social agents and, moreover, it is essential that agreement is reached uncoerced and willingly by all those who will be subject to the norms. Argumentation is the only process allowed and there should be no forced closure of debate in order to secure agreement or a decision.

What for Habermas was a theory of *moral* discourse concerning a process of argumentation focusing on the overlap of generalizable interests[2] has in the hands of his supporters been transformed into a more general theory of democratic will formation. Habermas's aspirations have, we would contend, been rather less ambitious than some of his critics and, it must be said, some of his supporters would have us believe. Communicative rationality, nevertheless, has had enormous impact and has come to occupy a dominant place in the current debates on planning theory. This is not the place to examine in detail the arguments in that debate but we would like to discuss some of the more general criticisms concerning the problems of operationalizing deliberative democracy.

First, the stringent requirements established by Habermas for effective communicative discourse are inevitably relaxed in the real world. Dryzek (1990), for example, argues that universal participation is unnecessary and, indeed, he stresses the need for "communicatively competent" people to be involved in the process of debate. More generally, communicative planning theorists propose that participants should represent the major interests or stakeholders involved. Selectivity inevitably raises questions concerning who should be involved and who should set the agenda. As with all participatory processes there is the evident difficulty of ensuring inclusiveness so that all relevant interests are given voice.

Second, the emphasis is solely on process. Even if agreement is not reached, the process of debate is seen to have value in its own right. Thus Innes and Booher (1999), in their analysis of actual consensus-building exercises, stress the beneficial consequences which arise even when agreements are not reached because participants' ways of knowing and understanding are changed. Healey (1997) also stresses the transformative nature of the "reflexive process of intersubjective communication". In Healey's terms collaborative planning is "future seeking" and not "future defining". It can have no prior conception of the ends to be sought. Such planning, she writes, may enable us "to agree on what to do next, on how to "start out" and "travel along" for a while. We cannot know where this will take us" (Healey, 1992: 156).

Third, participants in communicative discourse are expected to shed important aspects of their personalities so that the cognitive rather than the affective dimensions of the self come into play (Warren, 1995) but it seems most unlikely that individuals will be dissuaded from using strategic argumentation or distorted communication as a means of resolving conflict. As we have noted elsewhere (Campbell and Marshall, 2002):

> … the distinguishing hallmark of planning is its concern for strategically linking multiple policy arenas and decision fields across space and through time…. Given the unequal distribution of rights, resources of all kinds and, hence power, negotiation, bargaining, trade-offs, strategic argumentation and other competitive practices, which do not meet the requirements of discursive argumentation, are an intrinsic part of the process.

Fourth, models of deliberative democracy are too optimistic in confronting the pluralism of modern societies. Given the deep divisions of interest within society, the persistence of disagreement and the prevalence of discord and conflict it seems unlikely that a consensus can be discursively constructed. The corollary of this is that if communicative discourse is to work at all it is likely to be most effective in small homogeneous groups. Localism is, we suspect, likely to favour conservatism and exclusivity. As Fainstein (2000) observes, communicative planning theory evades the problem of what to do when democratic processes produce unjust results.

Conclusions

Although the idea of the public interest is often scorned by contemporary planning theorists this article has argued that it nevertheless remains the pivot around which debates about the nature of planning and its purposes turn. Those who are dismissive of the value of the concept as conventionally conceived are, we have argued, putting their faith in a procedural interpretation of the public interest. In framing our own categorization we have consequently proposed a typology which makes a distinction between consequentialist and deontological versions of the public interest. To offer a categorization of the public interest in deontological terms is possibly contentious but the article has argued that the communicative turn in planning theory is based upon the assumption (whether explicitly or implicitly stated) that the public interest is best discovered discursively through participatory processes.

Although we have included deontological conceptions of the public interest in our typology, the article has been critical of them. Communicative planning theory, in placing emphasis on difference, diversity and democracy, has made a positive contribution to the debate about the future of the planning enterprise. However, although we do not dissent from the idea that public deliberation and debate are essential for a responsible and responsive planning system, we nevertheless argue that choices cannot be left endlessly open. Planning cannot evade what Harvey (2000) refers to as the dialectic of the either/or. Closure must occur when one design or alternative is materialized as opposed to others and as Harvey (2000: 188) states "closure is in itself a material statement that carries its own authority in human affairs." Modernist planning emerged as a state activity precisely because of recognition that there are important goods which are manifestly in everyone's interest to have but in no one's interest to provide. An open agenda for public deliberation seems unlikely to provide the means by which important collective values can be upheld and maintained. To paraphrase Pitkin (1981), no account of planning, politics and the public can be of value if it is empty of all substantive content, of what is at stake.

Notes

The title of this article we owe to E.P. Thompson (1978: 368).

1   John Dewey drew a similar analogy in *The Public and its Problem* when he wrote:

[Popular government] forces a recognition that there are common interests, even though the recognition of *what* they are is confused; and the need it enforces of discussion and publicity brings about some clarification of what they are. The man who wears the shoe knows best that it pinches and where it pinches, even if the expert shoemaker is the best judge of how the trouble is to be remedied. (Dewey, 1927: 364)

See also Barry (1964: 5):

Whether his opportunities are increased or narrowed by being unemployed is some-thing each man may judge for himself; but it is surely only sensible to recognise that most people's opinions about the most effective policies for securing given ends are likely to be worthless.

2   Generalizable interests are those interests which are of concern to everyone. Habermas's discourse ethics are concerned with questions concerning how we ought to act and not with particularistic interests and needs. Habermas (1990) argues that as pluralism has increased in the modern world society has become more differentiated with the result that morally justified norms have become even more generalized and abstract.

References

Allmendinger, P. and Thomas, H. (eds.) (1998) *Urban Planning and the New Right*. London: Routledge.

Altshuler, A. (1965) *The City Planning Process: A Political Analysis*. Ithaca, NY: Cornell University Press.

Anderson, C.W. (1987) "Political Philosophy, Practical Reason and Policy Analysis'", in F. Fischer and J. Forester (eds) *Confronting Values in Policy Analysis*, pp. 22–44. London: Sage.

Ayer, A.J. (1954) *Philosophical Essays*. London: Macmillan.

Banfield, E.G. (1955) 'Note on a Conceptual Scheme', in M. Meyerson and E.G. Banfield *Politics, Planning and the Public Interest: The Case of Public Housing in Chicago*, pp. 303–29. New York: Free Press.

Barry, B.M. (1964) "The Public Interest", *Proceedings of the Aristotelian Society* Supplementary Volume 38: 1–18.

Beauregard, R.A. (1989) 'Between Modernity and Postmodernity: The Ambiguous Position of US Planning', *Environment and Planning D* 7(4): 381–95.

Beauregard, R.A. (1991) "Without a Net: Modernist Planning and the Postmodern Abyss", *Journal of Planning Education and Research* 10(3): 189–94.

Benn, S.I. and Peters, R.S. (1959) *Social Principles and the Democratic State*. London: Allen and Unwin.

Benton, T. (1993) *Natural Relations: Ecology, Animal Rights and Social Justice*. London: Verso.

Bobbio, N. (2000) *In Praise of Meekness: Essays on Ethics and Politics*. Cambridge: Polity Press.

Braybrooke, D. and Lindblom, C.E. (1963) *A Strategy of Decision: Policy Evaluation as a Social Process*. New York: The Free Press.

Burke, E. (1774) "Speech to the Electors of Bristol", in B.W. Hill (1975) *Edmund Burke: On Government, Politics and Society*. Hassocks: Harvester Press.

Campbell, H. and Marshall, R. (1998) "Acting on Principle: Dilemmas in Planning Practice", *Planning Practice and Research* 13(2): 117–28.

Campbell, H. and Marshall, R. (1999) "Ethical Frameworks and Planning Theory", *International Journal of Urban and Regional Research* 23(3): 464–78.

Campbell, H. and Marshall, R. (2000a) "Moral Obligations, Planning and the Public Interest: A Commentary on Current British Practice", *Environment and Planning B* 27: 297–312.

Campbell, H. and Marshall, R. (2000b) "Public Involvement in Planning: Looking Beyond the One to the Many", *International Planning Studies* 5(3): 321–44.

Campbell, H. and Marshall, R. (2002) "Instrumental Rationality, Intelligent Action and Planning: American Pragmatism Revisited", in Y. Rydin and A. Thornley (eds) *Planning in the UK: Agendas for the New Millennium*, pp. 11–31. Aldershot: Ashgate.

Chambers, S. (1996) *Reasonable Democracy: Jurgen Habermas and the Politics of Discourse*. Ithaca, NY and London: Cornell University Press.

Cochran, C.E. (1974) "Political Science and the 'Public Interest'", *The Journal of Politics* 36(2): 327–55.

Davidoff, P. (1965) "Advocacy and Pluralism in Planning", *Journal of the American Institute of Planners* 31(4): 331–8.

Dewey, J. (1927) "The Public and its Problems", in J. Dewey (1984) *The Later Works, Volume 2: 1925–1927*, edited by J.A. Boydson, pp. 235–372. Carbondale and Edwardsville: Southern Illinois University Press.

Douglas, M. (1992) *Risk and Blame: Essays in Cultural Theory*. London: Routledge.

Downs, A. (1962) "The Public Interest: Its Meaning in a Democracy", *Social Research* 29.

Dryzek, J.S. (1990) *Discursive Democracy*. Cambridge: Cambridge University Press.

Dworkin, R. (1978) *Taking Rights Seriously*. London: Duckworth.

Expert Committee on Compensation and Betterment (1942) *Final Report*. London: HMSO.

Fainstein, S. (2000) "New Directions in Planning Theory", *Urban Affairs Review* 35(4): 451–78.

Flathman, R.E. (1966) *The Public Interest: An Essay Concerning the Normative Discourse of Politics*. New York: Wiley.

Foley, D. (1960) "British Town Planning: One Ideology or Three?", *British Journal of Sociology* 11: 211–31.

Forester, J. (1989) *Planning in the Face of Power*. Berkeley: University of California Press.

Forester, J. (1993) *Critical Theory, Public Policy and Planning Practice: Toward a Critical Pragmatism*. Albany: New York Press.

Forester, J. (1999a) "Reflections on the Future Understanding of Planning", *International Planning Studies* 4(2): 75–193.

Forester, J. (1999b) *The Deliberative Practitioner: Encouraging Participatory Planning Processes*. Cambridge, MA: MIT Press.

Glass, R. (1959) "The Evaluation of Planning: Some Sociological Considerations", *International Social Science Journal* XI(3): 393–409.

Gutmann, A. and Thompson, D. (1996) *Democracy and Disagreement*. Cambridge, MA: Harvard University Press.

Haar, C. (1961) *Land Planning Law in a Free Society*. Harvard, MA: Harvard University Press.

Habermas, J. (1990) *Moral Consciousness and Communicative Action*. Cambridge: Polity Press.

Hampshire, S. (1978) "Morality and Pessimism", in S. Hampshire (ed.) *Public and Private Morality*. Cambridge: Cambridge University Press.

Hampshire, S. (1983) *Morality and Conflict*. Oxford: Basil Blackwell.

Harper, T.L. and Stein, S.M. (1995) "Out of the Postmodern Abyss: Preserving the Rationale for Liberal Planning", *Journal of Planning Education and Research* 14: 233–44.

Harvey, D. (1996) *Justice, Nature and the Geography of Difference*. Oxford: Blackwell.

Harvey, D. (2000) *Spaces of Hope*. Edinburgh: Edinburgh University Press.

Healey, P. (1992) "Planning through Debate: The Communicative Turn in Planning Theory", *Town Planning Review* 63(2): 143–62.

Healey, P. (1997) *Collaborative Planning: Shaping Places in Fragmented Societies*. Basingstoke: Macmillan.

Held, V. (1970) *The Public Interest and Individual Interests*. New York/London: Basic Books.

Howe, E. (1992) "Professional Roles and the Public Interest in Planning", *Journal of Planning Literature* 6(3): 230–48.

Howe, E. (1994) *Acting on Ethics in City Planning*. New Brunswick: Rutgers, State University of New Jersey.

Innes, J.E. and Booher, D.E. (1999) "Consensus Building as Role Playing and Bricolage: Toward a Theory of Collaborative Planning", *Journal of the American Planning Association* 65(1): 9–26.

Klosterman, R. (1980) "A Public Interest Criterion", *Journal of the American Institute of Planners* 43(3): 323–33.

Lichfield, N. (1992) "From Planning Obligations to Community Impact Assessment", *Journal of Planning and Environmental Law* 1103–18.

Lichfield, N., Kettle, P. and Whitbread, M. (1975) *Evaluation in the Planning Process*. Oxford: Pergamon Press.

Lindblom, C.E. (1959) "The Science of 'Muddling Through'", *Public Administration Review* 19: 79–99.

Low, N. (1991) *Planning, Politics and the State: Political Foundations of Planning Thought*. London: Unwin Hyman.

MacIntyre, A. (1985) *After Virtue: A Study in Moral Theory*. London: Duckworth.

MacIntyre, A. (1998) *A Short History of Ethics: A History of Moral Philosophy from the Homeric Age to the Twentieth Century*. London: Routledge.

Mandelker, D.R. (1962) *Green Belts and Urban Growth: English Town and Country Planning in Action*. Madison: University of Wisconsin Press.

Meyerson, M. and Banfield, E.G. (1955) *Politics, Planning and the Public Interest: The Case of Public Housing in Chicago*. New York: Free Press.

Mill, J.S. (1861) "Utilitarianism", in M. Warnock (ed.) (1962) *Utilitarianism*, pp. 251–95. London: Collins.

Milroy, B.M. (1989) "Constructing and Deconstructing Plausibility", *Environment and Planning D* 7(3): 313–26.

Milroy, B.M. (1991) "Into Postmodern Weightlessness", *Journal of Planning Education and Research* 10(3): 181–7.

Moon, D. (1995) "Practical Discourse and Communicative Ethics", in S.K. White (ed.) *The Cambridge Companion to Habermas*, pp. 143–64. Cambridge: Cambridge University Press.

Pennock, J.R. (1962) "The One and the Many: A Note on the Concept", in C. Friedrich (ed.) *The Public Interest*. New York: Atherton Press.

Pitkin, H.F. (1967) *The Concept of Representation*. Berkeley and Los Angeles: University of California Press.

Pitkin, H.F. (1981) "Justice: On Relating Private and Public", *Political Theory* 9(3): 327–52.

Rawls, J. (1971) *A Theory of Justice*. Cambridge, MA: Harvard University Press.

Rawls, J. (1982) "Social Unity and Primary Goods", in A. Sen and B. Williams (eds.) *Utilitarianism and Beyond*, pp. 159–85. Cambridge: Cambridge University Press.

Rawls, J. (1993) *Political Liberalism*. New York: Columbia University Press.

Reade, E. (1987) *British Town and Country Planning*. Milton Keynes: Open University Press.

Reade, E. (1997) "Planning *in* the Future or Planning *of* the Future", in A. Blowers and B. Evans (eds.) *Town Planning into the 21st Century*, pp. 71–103. London: Routledge.

Rosen, F. (1983) *Jeremy Bentham and Representative Government*. Oxford: Clarendon Press.

Sandercock, L. (1998) *Towards Cosmopolis*. Chichester: Wiley.

Sandercock, L. (2000) "When Strangers become Neighbours: Navigating Cities of Difference", *Planning Theory and Practice* 1(1): 13–30.

Schön, D. (1983) *The Reflective Practitioner. How Professionals Think in Action*. Aldershot: Ashgate.

Schubert, G. (1957) "The Public Interest in Administrative Decision-Making", *American Political Science Review* 51: 346–68.

Schubert, G. (1960) *The Public Interest: A Critique of the Theory of a Political Concept*. Glencoe, IL: Free Press.

Schubert, G. (1967) "Is There a Public Interest Theory?", in C. Friedrich (ed.) *The Public Interest*. New York: Atherton Press.

Sen, A. (1979) "Personal Utilities and Public Judgements: Or What's Wrong with Welfare Economics", *The Economic Journal* 89: 537–58.

Sen, A. and Williams, B. (1982) "Introduction: Utilitarianism and Beyond", in A. Sen and B. Williams (eds.) *Utilitarianism and Beyond*. Cambridge: Cambridge University Press.

Singer, P. (1993) *Practical Ethics*. Cambridge: Cambridge University Press.

Smith, B.H. (1988) *Contingencies of Value: Alternative Perspectives for Critical Theory*. Cambridge, MA: Harvard University Press.

Sorauf, F. (1957) "The Public Interest Reconsidered", *Journal of Politics* 19(4): 616–39.

Sorauf, F. (1967) "The Conceptual Muddle", in C. Friedrich (ed.) *The Public Interest*. New York: Atherton Press.

Sugden, R. (1989) "Maximising Social Welfare: Is it the Government's Business?", in A. Hamlin and P. Pettit (eds.) *The Good Polity: Normative Analysis of the State*. Oxford: Blackwell.

Thompson, E.P. (1978) *The Poverty of Theory and Other Essays*. London: Merlin Press.

Thornley, A. (1993) *Urban Planning under Thatcherism: The Challenge of the Market*. London: Routledge.

Warnock, M. (1962) "Introduction to J.S. Mill, *Utilitarianism*", Fontana Library Edition. London: Collins.

Warren, M.E. (1995) "The Self in Discursive Democracy", in S.K. White (ed.) *The Cambridge Companion to Habermas*, pp. 167–200. Cambridge: Cambridge University Press.

Heather Campbell and Robert Marshall, "Utilitarianism's Bad Breath? A Re-evaluation of the Public Interest Justification for Planning," *Planning Theory*, 1 (2) (2002), pp. 164–86. Copyright © 2002 by Sage Publications. Reprinted by permission of Sage.

6

Planning the Capitalist City

Richard E. Foglesong

Capitalism and Urban Planning

David Harvey, a Marxist social geographer, has conceptualized urban conflict as a conflict over the "production, management and use of the urban built environment."[1] Harvey uses the term "built environment" to refer to physical entities such as roads, sewerage networks, parks, railroads, and even private housing – facilities that are collectively owned and consumed or, as in the case of private housing, whose character and location the state somehow regulates. These facilities have become politicized because of conflict arising out of their being collectively owned and controlled, or because of the "externality effects" of private decisions concerning their use. At issue is how these facilities should be produced – whether by the market or by the state, how they should be managed and by whom; and how they should be used – for what purposes and by what groups, races, classes, and neighborhoods. Following Harvey, the development of American urban planning is seen as the result of conflict over the production, management, and use of the urban built environment.

The development of this analysis depends on the recognition that capitalism both engenders and constrains demands for state intervention in the sphere of the built environment. First, let us consider some of the theories about how capitalism engenders demands for state intervention.

Sources of urban planning

Within the developing Marxist urban literature, there have been a variety of attempts to link urban conflict and demands for state intervention to the reproduction processes of capitalist society. Manuel Castells, one of the leading contributors to

Readings in Planning Theory, Third Edition. Edited by Susan S. Fainstein and Scott Campbell.
Editorial material and organization © 2012 Blackwell Publishing Ltd.
Published 2012 by Blackwell Publishing Ltd.

this literature, emphasizes the connection between state intervention in the urban development process and the reproduction of labor power.[2]

The Problem of Planning

The market system cannot meet the consumption needs of the working class in a manner capable of maintaining capitalism; this, according to Castells, is the reason for the growth of urban planning and state intervention. To the extent that the state picks up the slack and assumes this responsibility, there occurs a transformation of the process of consumption, from individualized consumption through the market to collective consumption organized through the state. This transformation entails not only an expansion of the role of the state, which is seen in the growth of urban planning, but also a politicization of the process of consumption, which Castells sees as the underlying dynamic of urban political conflict.

By contrast, David Harvey and Edmond Preteceille, writing separately, have related state intervention in the urban development process to the inability of the market system to provide for the maintenance and reproduction of the immobilized fixed capital investments (for example, bridges, streets, sewerage networks) used by capital as *means of production*.[3] The task of the state is not only to maintain this system of what Preteceille calls "urban use values" but also to provide for the coordination of these use values in space (for example, the coordination of streets and sewer lines), creating what he terms "new, complex use values."[4] François Lamarche, on the other hand, relates the whole question of urban planning and state intervention to the *sphere of circulation* and the need to produce a "spatial organization which facilitates the circulation of capital, commodities, information, etc."[5] In his view capitalism has spawned a particular fraction of capital, termed "property capital," which is responsible for organizing the system of land use and transportation; and urban planning is a complement and extension of the aims and activities of this group. In addition, and somewhat distinct from these attempts to relate urban planning to the reproduction processes of capitalist society, David Harvey has linked urban planning to the problems arising from the *uniqueness of land as a commodity*, namely the fact that land is not transportable, which makes it inherently subject to externality effects.[6]

The theories discussed above demonstrate that there are a variety of problems arising from relying upon the market system to guide urban development. At various times, urban planning in the United States has been a response to each of these problems. Yet these problems have different histories. They have not had equal importance throughout the development of planning. Moreover, not one of these problems is sufficient in itself to explain the logic of development of planning.

Constraints on urban planning

If the problems noted above arise from the workings of the market system, so that capitalism can be said to engender demands for state intervention in response to these problems, the capitalist system also constrains the realization of these demands. The operative constraint in this connection is the institution of private property. It is here that we confront what might be termed the central contradiction of capitalist urbanization: the contradiction between the social character of land and its private ownership and control. Government intervention in the ordering of the urban built environment – that is, urban planning – can be seen as a response to the social character of land, to the fact that land is not only a commodity but also a collective good, a social resource as well as a private right. Indeed, as the Marxist urban literature has sought to demonstrate, the treatment of land as a commodity fails to satisfy the social needs of either capital or labor. Capital has an objective interest in socializing the control of land in order to (1) cope with the externality problems that arise from treating land as a commodity; (2) create the housing and other environmental amenities needed for the reproduction of labor power; (3) provide for the building and maintenance of the bridges, harbors, streets, and transit systems used by capital as means of production; and (4) ensure the spatial coordination of these infrastructural facilities for purposes of efficient circulation. Yet the institution of private property stands as an impediment to attempts to socialize the control of land in order to meet these collective needs. Thus, if urban planning is necessary for the reproduction of the capitalist system on the one hand, it threatens and is restrained by the capitalist system on the other; and it is in terms of this Janus-faced reality that the development of urban planning is to be understood. Moreover, this contradiction is intrinsic to capitalist urbanization, for the impulse to socialize the control of urban space is as much a part of capitalism as is the institution of private property. Each serves to limit the extension of the other; thus, they are in "contradiction."[7] This contradiction, which will be termed the "property contradiction," is one of two that have structured the development of planning.[8]

The "property contradiction"   To state that capitalist urbanization has an inherent contradiction is *not* to predict the inevitable downfall of capitalism (although it does indicate a weakness in the capitalist structure of society that oppositional forces could conceivably exploit). Rather, it is assumed that capitalism is capable of coping with this contradiction, within limits, but that it is a continuing source of tension and a breeding ground of political conflict. Thus, our analytical interest is in the institutional means that have been devised to keep this contradiction from exploding into a system-threatening crisis. In recognizing this contradiction, we therefore gain a better appreciation of the importance, both politically and theoretically, of the institutional forms that urban planning has adopted over the course of its development, and of how (and how well) those institutional forms have responded to the contradiction between the social character of land and its private ownership and control.

In addition, recognizing this contradiction helps us to understand the patterns of alliance formation around planning issues, as well as the role of planners in mediating between different groups and group interests. For if the effort to socialize the control of urban land is potentially a threat to the whole concept of property rights, it is directly and immediately a threat to only one particular group of capitalists, those whom Lamarche terms "property capital." Included are persons who, in his words, "plan and equip space" – real estate developers, construction contractors, and directors of mortgage lending institutions.[9] It is this fraction of capital, in particular, that can be expected to oppose efforts to displace or diminish private control of urban development. Other capitalists, in contrast, may seek an expanded government role in the planning and equipping of space. For example, manufacturing capital may want government to provide worker housing and to coordinate the development of public and private infrastructure (such as utilities and railroads), and commercial capitalists may desire government restrictions on the location of manufacturing establishments. Likewise, nonowner groups have an interest in state intervention that will provide for or regulate the quality of worker housing, build parks, and improve worker transportation, for example. It is possible, therefore, for certain fractions of capital to align with nonowner groups in support of planning interventions that restrict the "rights" of urban landholders. The property contradiction thus manifests itself in the pattern of alliances around planning issues by creating, in intracapitalist class conflict, the possibility of alliances between property-owning and nonproperty-owning groups and allowing planners to function as mediators in organizing these compromises. Inasmuch as the property contradiction is inherent in the capitalist structure of society, existing independent of consciousness and will, recognition of this contradiction enables us to link the politics of planning to the structural ordering of capitalist society.

The "capitalist–democracy contradiction" The other contradiction affecting the development of urban planning is the "capitalist–democracy contradiction." If the property contradiction is internal to capitalism in that it arises out of the logic of capitalist development, the capitalist–democracy contradiction is an external one, originating between the political and economic structures of a democratic–capitalist society. More specifically, it is a contradiction between the need to socialize the control of urban space to create the conditions for the maintenance of capitalism on the one hand and the danger to capital of truly socializing, that is, democratizing, the control of urban land on the other. For if the market system cannot produce a built environment that is capable of maintaining capitalism, reliance on the institutions of the state, especially a formally democratic state, creates a whole new set of problems, not the least of which is that the more populous body of nonowners will gain too much control over landed property. This latter contradiction is conditioned on the existence of the property contradiction, in that it arises from efforts to use government action to balance or hold in check the property contradiction. Once government intervention is accepted, questions about how to organize that intervention arise: What goals should be pursued? How should they be formulated and by whom? This pattern of the capitalist–democracy contradiction following on the heels of the property contradiction is apparent in the actual history of planning, for while both contradictions have been in evidence throughout the history of planning in America, the property contradiction was a more salient generator of conflict in the earlier, pre-1940 period. The capitalist–democracy contradiction – manifested in the controversy over how to organize the planning process – has been a more potent source of conflict in the history of planning after World War II. It should also be emphasized that the capitalist–democracy contradiction is conditioned on the formally democratic character of the state, out of which the danger of government control of urban development arises. Were it not for the majority-rule criterion and formal equality promised by the state, turning to government to control urban development would not pose such a problem for capital.

Consideration of the capitalist–democracy contradiction leads us back to Offe's analysis of the internal structure of the state. Following Offe's analysis, it can be postulated that capitalism is caught in a search for a decision process, a method of policy making that can produce decisions corresponding with capital's political and economic interests. Politically, this decision process must be capable of insulating state decision making from the claims and considerations of the numerically larger class of noncapitalists, a task made difficult by the formally democratic character of the state. Economically, this decision process must be capable of producing decisions that facilitate the accumulation and circulation of capital (for example, promoting the reproduction of labor power and coordinating the building up of local infrastructure), a function that the market fails to perform and that capitalists do not (necessarily) know how to perform. Both of these problems are captured in the concept of the capitalist–democracy contradiction. The question we are led to ask, then, is, In what ways has the development of urban planning – viewed here as a method of policy formulation – served to suppress or hold in balance the capitalist–democracy contradiction in a manner conducive to the reproduction of capitalism?

Notes

1 "Labor, Capital, and Class Struggle around the Built Environment in Advanced Capitalist Societies," p. 265.
2 *Urban Question*, pp. 460–1. Castells modifies his view in his recent book, *The City and the Grass Roots*, which appeared after the manuscript of *Planning the Capitalist City* was essentially written. In this new book, Castells seeks to avoid the "excesses of theoretical formalism" that marked some of his earlier work (p. xvii). He also asserts that "although class relationships and class struggle are fundamental in understanding the process of urban conflict, they are by no means the only or even the primary source of urban social change" (p. xviii). My critical evaluation of Castells's earlier work is still valid and useful, however, since it lends emphasis and historical reference to some of Castells's own criticisms. Furthermore, my criticisms apply to a literature and a theoretical orientation that encompasses, as I point out, more than Castells's work.
3 Harvey, "The Political Economy of Urbanization in Advanced Capitalist Societies: The Case of the United States," p. 120; Preteceille, "Urban Planning: The Contradictions of

Capitalist Urbanization," pp. 69–76. For Harvey, the need for a built environment usable as a collective means of production is only one of the connections between urban planning and capitalist development; he also recognizes the need for facilities for collective consumption to aid in reproducing labor power. See, e.g., his "Labor, Capital, and Class Struggle around the Built Environment."

4 Preteceille, "Urban Planning," p. 70.

5 "Property Development and the Economic Foundations of the Urban Question," p. 86.

6 *Social Justice*, chapter 5.

7 For a discussion of this use of *contradiction*, see Godelier, "Structure and Contradiction in *Capital*," pp. 334–68.

8 Cf. Michael Dear and Allen Scott's assertion that the "urban question" (a reference to the work of Castells) is "structured around the particular and indissoluble geographical and land-contingent phenomena that come into existence as capitalist social and property relations are mediated through the dimension of urban space." They also write that planning is "a historically-specific and socially-necessary response to the self-disorganizing tendencies of *privatized* capitalist social and property relations as these appear in urban space" ("Towards a Framework for Analysis," pp. 6, 13). Cf. also, in the same volume, Shoukry Roweis's statement that "[u]rban planning in capitalism, both in theory and in practice, and whether intentionally or unknowingly, attempts to grapple with a basic question: how can *collective action* (pertinent to decisions concerning the social utilization of urban land) be made possible under capitalism?" ("Urban Planning in Early and Late Capitalist Societies," p. 170). These two theoretical analyses relate urban planning under capitalism to the problem of "collective control" – how to organize socially necessary forms of collective consumption and control in a society based upon private ownership – but they do not take note of the contradiction between capital's need for collective control in its own interest and the limits imposed by the internal structure of the *state*. This is the issue raised by Offe and which I capture in my concept of the "capitalist–democracy contradiction".

9 "Property Development," pp. 90–3.

Further Reading

Castells, Manuel. *The Urban Question*. Cambridge: MIT Press, 1977.

Dear, Michael, and Scott, Allen J., "Towards a Framework for Analysis." In *Urbanization and Urban Planning in Capitalist Society*, edited by Michael Dear and Allen J. Scott, pp. 3–18. London: Methuen, 1981.

Godelier, Maurice. "Structure and Contradiction in *Capital*." In *Ideology and Social Science*, edited by Robin Blackburn, pp. 334–68. New York: Vintage Books, 1973.

Harvey, David. "Labor, Capital, and Class Struggle around the Built Environment in Advanced Capitalist Societies," *Politics & Society* 6 (1976): 265–95.

Harvey, David. "The Political Economy of Urbanization in Advanced Capitalist Societies: The Case of the United States." In *The Social Economy of Cities*, Urban Affairs Annual, edited by Gary Grappert and Harold M. Rose, no. 9, pp. 119–63. Beverly Hills: Russell Sage, 1975.

Harvey, David. *Social Justice and the City*. Baltimore: Johns Hopkins University Press, 1973.

Lamarche, François. "Property Development and the Economic Foundations of the Urban Question." In *Urban Sociology: Critical Essays*, edited by Chris Pickvance, pp. 85–118. London: Tavistock Press, 1976.

Offe, Claus. "The Abolition of Market Control and the Problem of Legitimacy (I)." *Kapitalistate*, no. 1 (1973): 109–16.

Preteceille, Edmond. "Urban Planning: The Contradictions of Capitalist Urbanization." *Antipode* 8 (March 1976): 69–76.

Roweis, Shoukry. "Urban Planning in Early and Late Capitalist Societies." In *Urbanization and Urban Planning in Capitalist Society*, edited by Michael Dear and Allen J. Scott, pp. 159–78. London: Methuen, 1981.

7

Urban Design after *Battery Park City*
Opportunities for Variety and Vitality in Large-Scale Urban Real Estate Development

Tim Love

Somewhere between the suburban anti-sprawl agenda of the New Urbanism and the recent media focus on large-scale architecture projects such as Frank Gehry's proposal for *Atlantic Yards*, mainstream American urban design practice hums along, seemingly accepted by the media, public officials, and the academy as an appropriate, if staid, paradigm for organizing large-scale development in urban areas. When the environments that result from these plans are criticized, the culprit is thought (as it was with *Battery Park City* and *Canary Wharf*) to be the quality of the architecture and not the urban design framework. Perhaps standard urban plans are beyond reproach and have not been a focus of serious intellectual inquiry because there is a general acceptance that the traditional concept of streets and blocks should serve as the conceptual core of any city-building effort.

But what this lack of critical focus and commentary means is that the specific dimension, pattern, and logic of these streets and blocks are not questioned. Ironically, the New Urbanism, in its focus on suburban and small-town development, has a much more advanced and self-critical agenda[1] (although New Urbanism's practice models and paradigms are ill-equipped for large-scale urban development). More significantly, in the disciplinary and conceptual division between urban design's focus on "the public realm" and an architect's focus on the microprogramming of buildings, opportunities are lost for a more fine-grained planning at the ground plane.

Rather than grudging acceptance of the status quo, perhaps better designed urban frameworks provide a way both to create a more vital and diverse urbanism and to incite more innovative architectural production across a broader spectrum of American design culture. For this to occur, urban designers and architects are going

Readings in Planning Theory, Third Edition. Edited by Susan S. Fainstein and Scott Campbell.
Editorial material and organization © 2012 Blackwell Publishing Ltd.
Published 2012 by Blackwell Publishing Ltd.

to need to conspire with enlightened real-estate developers and public-policy experts to find opportunities for new planning and building paradigms at the intersection of real-estate finance logic and the regulatory context. For example, creative negotiation will be necessary to call into question the conventions of office floor-plate dimensions and urban zoning frameworks. Many urban design and architecture conventions are the result of ingrained assumptions of large American firms, habits compelled by the expediency of early phase project planning. But a new paradigm for urban design can arise with a creative coordination between building types, parcel configurations, and larger urban design frameworks.

Adopted in 1979, the *Battery Park City* master plan by Alexander Cooper and Stanton Eckstut established a durable paradigm for large-scale urban real-estate development in North America. This approach, still the primary model of urban design practice in the US for blue chip firms like SOM, Cooper Robertson & Partners, and Sasaki Associates, is a distant echo of the reengagement of the city by American architecture theorists in the late 1970s and early 1980s. This trajectory begins with Aldo Rossi's *Architecture of the City* (translated into English in 1978), Colin Rowe and Fred Koetter's *Collage City* (1978), and the brief influence of the brothers Krier (Robert and Leon) in East Coast architecture schools in the early 1980s. Instigators in this realignment included the Cornell University Department of Architecture, specifically the urban design studios run by Rowe, and the publications and programs of the Institute of Architecture and Urbanism in New York. Before this almost instantaneous embrace of both "contextualism" in architecture and the practice of "urban design" by architects, both progressive architects/theorists (e.g., Michael Graves, Peter Eisenman) and the architects favored by high cultural patrons (e.g., I.M. Pei) were primarily focused on the architectural project as an autonomous sculptural artifact. And while this is a schematic overview of a much more complex shift in the preoccupations of architects, it is important to outline because of what it now means for urban design and architecture.

The renewed focus on the city in the late 1970s and early 1980s was predicated on the spatial and morphological virtues of the traditional city. This was conditioned as much by the legibility of certain urban morphologies and patterns in the traditional city as by the Nolli map/figure-ground obsessions of Rowe and his followers. In fact, the birth of contemporary urban design as a professional discipline might be pinpointed to the mid-1980s when architects like Jaquelin Robertson and Alex Cooper practiced urban design using the figure-ground and urban poche techniques of Rowe and the Kriers. Within this conception of urbanism and urban design, the open spaces of the city, including streets, squares, and parks, are conceptualized as spatial figures "carved" out of the poche of building mass. This framework thus tends to favor shapely spatial figures such as Bath, England-like circles and crescents. The École des Beaux Arts technique of giving the poche of the plan a pink tint was adopted by urban designers who made the buildings in their urban plans a uniform pink in contrast to the lush, green, and shapely public spaces that were to constitute the "urban realm." Projects as recent as Cooper Robertson's draft master plan for Harvard's Allston campus still deploy this conceptual framework and representational technique – buildings-as-poche, figurative urban spaces, and all.

Soon after these approaches became mainstream in the mid-1980s, these tenets were quickly adopted in the North-east by both planners and architects embedded in municipal governments. Commonly held assumptions included the notion that the primary goal of city design was to create an "active urban realm" achieved by maximizing "active ground floor uses" along the edges of streets and open spaces that in turn were conceived as outdoor rooms carved from the fabric of the city. In fact, the virtues of this conception of urbanism persist to this day as the physical antidote to both postwar Modernism and suburban sprawl – its figure-ground and ideological opposites.

In addition to the unquestioned appropriateness of the urban design principles, another reason the *Battery Park City* method has endured in almost all urban plans of comparable scale is its real-estate development logic. The breaking up of large development parcels into independent "blocks," each earmarked for a single building project, achieves two objectives: The overall development can be divided into flexible phases that can easily adapt to the changing real-estate market, and by dimensioning blocks to correspond to the optimum parcel size for a typical residential or commercial development project, the resulting building is guaranteed open exposures and free access on all sides, thus promoting its value on the market. The parceled, multiphased development has the ability to attract capital on an ongoing basis. Interestingly, the flexible phasing logic of a long range commercial master plan – "In this cycle, it will need to be commercial, but in the next residential" – all but codifies a block size that persists from plan to plan. This ideal block type is typically configured for nearly square large floor-plate office buildings. The double-loaded corridor building, the multifamily building type preferred by developers, can also be efficiently accommodated within the parcel configuration by wrapping and bending the plan around the outside edges of the parcel.

The aesthetic monotony of *Battery Park City* and other similar almost finished examples, including *University Park* in Cambridge, Massachusetts, and *MetroTech* in Brooklyn, can be attributed partly to the haste of implementation of the original template. Master plans filled in relatively quickly, like the southern end of *Battery Park City*, may suffer from the look-alike architecture syndrome of a particular taste phase. Interestingly, *Canary Wharf* has had a more protracted and gradual implementation, and thus has a lively mix of Postmodern and Neo-Modern architecture, offering a pattern book of recent trends in commercial design.

Most have blamed the quality of the architecture rather than the quality of the urban design framework for the monotony of the result. At a recent waterfront conference at Yale, Dean Robert A.M. Stern followed this trend, faulting the sameness of the new slender Neo-Modernist residential towers proliferating on the Toronto waterfront, rather than the urban design of the new districts. Stern recommended a more robust decorative strategy, citing the differentiation in facade expression in the otherwise consistent prewar apartment building type that lines upper Park Avenue in New York.[2] Implicit in Stern's critique and remedy is the assumption that the logic and basic form of developer building types, the very DNA of any master plan, are a fait accompli. Worse than complicity with the forces of the real-estate market, this position suggests a strategic disengagement of architecture from the preoccupations of developers and zoning code lawyers, the professionals that in most cities are primarily responsible for shaping the massing and circulation logic of buildings.

But more than the style of the architecture, it is the monopoly of a single scale of building that is the problem. Perhaps it is now safe to say that the serial repetition of a single building type – successful in Boston's Back Bay or in Bath, England – does not work for buildings with 35,000-square-foot floor-plates. The only exception to such a rule may be Central Park West in Manhattan – the double-tower skyline looks great from *Central Park*. But insistent repetition of a single building type does not make for a socially rich street life.

A cultural and social critique of the neighborhoods that result from the *Battery Park City* method is much more complex, having to do with the monoculture meant to fill out such districts. Suffice it to say that the master developer's ability to maximize value at every stage of the phased development implementation (in office space leases, revenue from condominium sales, etc.) is predicated on the establishment and then reaffirmation of a "Class A" district. Recent public policies, such as "inclusionary zoning," which requires a certain percentage of affordable housing as part of any large development project, have helped ameliorate the situation. Similar policies needed to be adopted for retail to provide space for small-scale entrepreneurial retail, businesses often run by immigrants. Regulations that require a certain percentage of micro-retail could balance the natural tendency for large chains in large developments. The building foot-print dimensions are again much of the problem, yielding an ungainly depth for uses along active street fronts. Only the urban versions of America's big-box retailers can fill the big leasable voids, achieve the lease rates projected in the pro forma, and meet the Class A expectations of the developers.

So how do four recent and ongoing master planning efforts of a similar scope and scale offer specific opportunities for alternative design approaches that may redress some of the aesthetic and social shortcomings for prevalent urban design strategy?

Queens West and the Olympic Village, New York City: Big Architecture Is Not the Answer

An offspring of *Battery Park City* in business and political structure and design, if not in successful implementation, is the 1993 plan for *Queens West* in Long Island City. Its master plan, by Beyer Blinder Belle with Gruzen Samton, is almost identical in size, design guidelines, scope, and plan language to those for *Battery Park City*. To date, several development projects have been constructed or are in the planning stages, but given the relatively remote location of *Queens West*, the completed projects are inward-looking residential enclaves. In anticipation of the selection process for the 2012 Olympics, a competition was organized for an *Olympic Village* in the southern and undeveloped sector of the master plan. Thom Mayne emerged as winner, after which he developed the proposal in more detail. To many, including Alexander Garvin (former Managing Director of Planning for the NYC 2012 Olympic bid, and former Vice President for Planning, Design, and Development at the Lower Manhattan Development Corporation), Mayne's proposal serves as a potential counterexample and antidote to the by-now staid design of the original *Queens West* projects.[3] Interestingly, uninspiring architecture (and not the design of the framework plan) was seen as the problem with *Queens West* and aggressive architecture as the solution. Another recent example of a single-author architectural proposal for large-scale urban design is Peter Eisenman's much-lauded scheme for the air-rights over the Penn Station yards.

But both the Eisenman and the Mayne proposals are not urban design but rather very large-scale architectural works – requiring implementation by their initial authors to achieve the desired *Gesamtkunstwerk*. And in fact, there is a tipping point between the moment at which the scale of architecture can negotiate between built form and the spaces between, and both Eisenman's West Side and Mayne's *Olympic Village* proposals far exceed it. Mayne's *Diamond Ranch High School*, Louis Kahn's *Salk Institute*, Michelangelo's *Campidoglio*, and the *United Nations Building* are all examples of successful single-author chunks of coordinated urbanism. Once control by a single author exceeds this scale – in my view, Richard Meier's *Getty Center* crossed the line – it borders on the megalomaniacal, and form becomes the stand-in for the requisite variety.

I am interested rather in the realm of urban design meant to be filled in by others both because the scale exceeds the architectural but still requires physical design (not "planning"), and because it claims precisely the pragmatic territory of the *Battery Park City* method in the dynamics of the real-estate market. This complicity with market is not just an issue of efficacy but also of aesthetics – a phased project designed by many hands will result in true variety and not the artificially induced variety conjured by compositional effort. More broadly, it is valid to distinguish between these two kinds of urbanisms, given the real problems confronted by the contemporary city. Perhaps the architecture-centric schemes by Eisenman and Mayne are meant to supply the "flash value" of media-oriented architectural production, just at a much larger scale. Certainly Daniel Libeskind's galvanizing role at Ground Zero, whatever one may think of the actual proposal, proves the marketing value of this approach. But the second model for urban design, a model that distinguishes the role of urban design from that of architecture, may be the real territory for innovation.

Northpoint, Cambridge, Massachusetts: An Unbalanced Focus on Open Space Creates Polarized Urban Frameworks

Northpoint, a forty-eight-acre former train yard on the border of Cambridge, Boston, and Somerville consisting of twenty irregular small city blocks, is structured around an open-space network that integrates the Minute Man Bicycle Trail leading to the Charles River and a series of "green fingers" that penetrate the blocks. The redevelopment of this site illustrates several emerging issues that have informed more recent large-scale development. The most salient are technical and political ones provoked by the environmental remediation of brownfield sites to make them both legal and palatable for real estate development. Landscape architects have taken the conceptual lead, partly given technical issues that include grading, hydrology, and the succession of natural environments over long periods. Innovators in this area include James Corner of Field Operations and the University of Pennsylvania, which has planned the conversion of *Fresh Kills* landfill on Staten Island into an enormous regional park. Chris Reed, founder of StoSS and an instructor at the GSD, has also recently won a series of design competitions that include phased ecological processes as instigators of both the aesthetic and the underlying pragmatic argument of the design proposals.

As part of the *Northpoint* master plan, completed in 2002, Michael Van Valkenburgh and Ken Greenberg proposed a 5.5-acre "central park" as the heart of the larger green spine that both gives value to development parcels that face it and functions as conceptual centerpiece of a broader sustainable design concept.[4] Van Valkenburgh's design arguments for the park focus on its environmental and social virtues, although the published renderings of the project mostly highlight the role of the open space as a visual amenity for contiguous buildings. Certainly, a large park is an important amenity, given that three sides of the emerging neighborhood are surrounded by an elevated transportation infrastructure. (The park is being completed in phase one, along with the initial development blocks.) The sustainable design agenda became the primary marketing narrative to sell the project during the regulatory approvals process and to offer a lifestyle choice for condominium buyers.

The hurdles for regulatory approvals, already difficult given the number of jurisdictions overseeing the project, were even higher because the development entity, a joint venture between Guilford Transportation Industries of Portsmouth, New Hampshire, and Boston real-estate firm Spaulding & Slye Colliers International, was private and not under the control of a quasi-public authority like the master developers of *Battery Park City* and *Queens West*. Without "public interest" represented within the development team, community groups and single-issue advocates had additional leverage to require development-subsidized "public benefits" in exchange for development approval. *Atlantic Yards* in Brooklyn, developed by Forest City, is another example of a large-scale project initiated by a private developer rather than a public-private partnership. Forest City had to partner with several non-profit organizations and include a higher-than-typical percentage of affordable residential units to redress the perceived unbalance between the private and public benefits that would result from implementation.

More generally, the ratio between private real-estate value and public benefits has become the central negotiating point between developers and single-interest advocates/activists. Each side provides it best-case narratives, with elected officials and the affected residential communities the prime constituency for swaying the decisions of the regulators. This fundamentally political and economic negotiation has prioritized new public parks subsidized by the development financing in recent urban design plans. In fact, the politics inherent in a "parks are good – development is bad" process means that a "pro open-space" landscape architect is much more effective than a "pro buildings" architect as an advocate for urban design proposals. This is perhaps one reason that Michael Van Valkenburgh has recently found himself as the chief advocate of so many large-scale urban design projects.

The balance between parks and development can be heavily skewed one way or another depending on whether the developer is a private or public-private entity, the organizational strength of the affected community, and the original impetus for the project. It is certainly easier to add a park and reduce development rather than the other way around. The parcels reclaimed as a result of the suppression of the elevated highway that snaked through downtown Boston, for example, were finally designated in a simple 75% *open space*/25% *building parcel* ratio, despite several years of sophisticated urban planning initiatives. Michael Van Valkenburgh Associates' *Brooklyn Bridge Park* project was stalled when a decision was made in early 2006 to carve several condominium development parcels out of the project to make it "financially self-sustaining." Two arguments were offered: Revenue from the condominiums was needed to pay for park maintenance, and a residential constituency would be created for the park at Atlantic Avenue, planned as one of the major park entrances.

Unfortunately, what has resulted from these kinds of negotiations is a polarization of those who promote privatized development and those who promote unencumbered public space. The political polarization jibes almost perfectly with the one-fat-building-for-each-development-block favored by the *Battery Park* method, since in the minds of the public-space advocates, nothing within the development poche is of any public value. Yet, the best models of urbanism grow from the messy overlap of private interests and public space, as Jane Jacobs and countless other social theorists have pointed out. What is being advocated is not the fully privatized "public" spaces of Boston's *Quincy Market* or New York's *South Street Seaport*, but rather a finer-grained exchange between commerce and public space. The Italian café, the North African souk, and the Asian food market are specific examples of cultural/spatial patterns that are predicated on this condition. What is needed are urban design approaches that focus precisely on this condition of exchange rather than consider this a boundary between very different interests. This is a job for both designers and community-minded advocates. Fred Kent's *Project for Public Spaces* is one of the few groups that examine this grain of urban design; every city needs its own version.

East Bayfront, Toronto: Design the Street and Open Space Network to Instigate Creative Friction with Estate Development and Corporate Architectural Practice

The *East Bayfront Precinct Plan*, completed by Koetter Kim & Associates in November 2005, confronts several of the issues already raised, such as the open-space/development parcel balance. The project narrative is organized around the by-now requisite sustainable design theme. What is notable about this proposal is the balance it achieves between the generic *Battery Park City* master planning language of other similar proposals (including the *West Dons Precinct Plan* by Urban Design Associates, located on a large parcel adjacent to the *East Bayfront Precinct Plan*) and the overtly architectural proposals of Thom Mayne and Peter Eisenman. Koetter Kim's interest in looking more seriously at the architectural implications of urban design decisions is partly the result of pedigree. Fred Koetter was originally in Colin Rowe's orbit at Cornell and cowrote *Collage City*. In the late 1970s and early 1980s, Koetter, Susie Kim, and their team produced several urban design proposals for central Boston that owed their architectural specificity to the contemporaneous urban proposals of Leon Krien.[5] Importantly, Koetter and Kim's proposals were as much a mandate for typological innovation to solve specific urban problems as an ideological position about style.[6] (Koetter and Kim's Boston proposals predate and perhaps influenced Andrés Duany's first formulations of the New Urbanism.)

The architectural language depicted in the *East Bayfront Plan* is generically contemporary, the kind of soft Neo-Modernism prevalent in large corporate work. Bits of green fuzz are visible on roofs and setbacks in the renderings to signify an affordable green agenda. The overlap between architecture and urban design is best represented by the prescription for a south-facing arcade system that can be converted to enclosed pedestrian walkways during cold weather – an excellent example of the role of urban design as a discipline distinct from generic planning and the one-off specificity of architecture. The message here is that it is the strength of the urban framework rather than the quality of the architecture that matters.

The *East Bayfront Plan* tackles the interrelationship between block size and building typology specifically rather than generically. The plan includes a taxonomy of residential and commercial building types and how they might be accommodated within a block plan with more dimensional and proportional variety than most. In fact, the concept of using block configuration as a way to inhibit complete market flexibility, while tentative in this plan, is an important area of research for urban design. But this variety must be tested at a microeconomic level. Is each of the specific building types economically robust enough to be feasible in a market economy? Are there enough fat and flexible parcels in the overall plan to spur first-phase development, thus adding value and reducing risk for the less flexible parcels later in the development?

Consistent with the compositional language of the *Battery Park City* method, the *East Bayfront Plan* introduces inflections and exceptions into an otherwise smooth and vaguely axial grid. These exceptions are justified by existing site conditions, including the geometry of "gateway" streets (that connect the district to the city under the Gardiner Expressway) and the alignment of the expressway itself. In this case, as in many examples, the nervous ticks that provoke compositional variety do not threaten the insistent grid of the overall district. As a result, all the architecture can do is politely lay there, awaiting instructions for architectural variety from "Design Guidelines" – the typical adjunct to a master plan that qualifies cornice heights, special features at corners, and the location of building entrances, service bays, and so on.

Ken Greenberg's[7] master plan for Kendall Square in Cambridge, a precursor to his plan for *Northpoint*, pushes the irregularity of the street and parcel plan to a point that an overall grid is no longer legible – a solution originally shaped by the site's environmental problems. The streets avoid areas of major contamination to delay the costs of remediation to the individual development projects. This knowingly ad hoc strategy has benefits beyond visual variety, including its overt pragmatism (heroic and costly efforts are not required to create a resolved plan). More importantly, the idiosyncrasies of the master plan may provoke more interesting architectural responses.[8] For example, a street that dead-ends on a real-estate parcel may invite a unique programmatic response or architectural elaboration. This approach suggests a more general principle. The more specifically idiosyncratic (and pragmatic) the master plan, the less important are prescriptive design guidelines. In fact, a highly permissive, guideline-free master plan may create precisely the variety hoped for in city-building.

Rather than rely on design guidelines to frame (and some architects would say restrict or limit) the architectural options for a project built within a master plan, a master plan framework could be conceived that hardwires all the planning intentions within the infrastructure plan itself and then allows free rein for each individual development/design team. The hope is that by eliminating the possibility of design guidelines as a safety net, the infrastructure plan will need to work harder to generate a successful urban realm and will yield a higher degree of variety than the typical master plan/design guidelines framework.[9] This results partly from the additional responsibility of the master planner to design an infrastructure plan that is preloaded with juicy architectural opportunities rather than a plan that in its even-handed "correctness" can only produce monotony. In other words, one goal of the urban designer could be to set up a provocative and compelling game board for the participation of architects during the multiphased implementation of large-scale development.

Berkeley Investments' *Fort Point Portfolio*, Boston: Gentrification as a Model for Fine-Grained Ground-Level Planning

Berkeley Investments, a Boston-based real-estate development company, bought thirteen buildings, two parking garages, and several vacant parcels in the Fort Point District, a dense neighborhood of turn-of-the-century brick loft buildings immediately adjacent to downtown Boston. My firm, Utile, Inc., was hired by the developer[10] to do a comprehensive master plan that would look at reuse options for the existing building and development opportunities for the development parcels. Utile established a methodology that linked urban design to phased retail lease marketing as a way to create a neighborhood with a supportive and character-defining retail mix. The details of the plan hinged on the concept that cultural and economic reciprocities between retail at the street level and the addition of housing above would be set in motion by the establishment of the first retail.

Although there is a small residential population, the existing neighborhood is dominated by office uses; as a result, the streets are mostly deserted at night. Utile proposed new restaurants and cafés, lured to the neighborhood by below-market rents and the quality of the existing loft architecture, as a way to generate activity in the evening and create a market for condominium conversions. The plan suggested that Berkeley Investments would introduce neighborhood service retail such as a grocery store, dry cleaners, and pharmacy after developing a critical mass of residential units in existing loft buildings. Berkeley Investments would then develop residential, hotel, and office projects on infill sites in subsequent phases as real-estate values increased in the neighborhood. In this case, urban design includes the specific social engineering of the neighborhood through the careful scripting of the ground floor uses and the mix of residential and commercial uses above.

Rather than preexisting urban design paradigms, the methodology for the Fort Point plan was informed by an analysis of the initial impetus for and subsequent manifestations of gentrification in New York neighborhoods, specifically Smith Street and Williamsburg in Brooklyn, the Lower East Side, and, most recently, Bushwick in Brooklyn.[11] The question is whether naturally occurring neighborhood change, albeit shaped by real-estate speculators, can be translated to a planned process under the control of a single master developer such as Berkeley Investments.

The development of B3 (the blocks below Broad Street) in Philadelphia followed a similar strategy. Goldman Properties, led by Tony Goldman, a pioneer developer of SoHo, had acquired several contiguous parcels and prewar office buildings in the late 1990s with the idea of creating a mixed-use urban neighborhood. Rather than architects, the Goldman team[12] hired 160over90, a Philadelphia-based branding firm, to help create the blueprint for a carefully phased development of the neighborhood. In this case, a marketing and programming strategy, rather than physical design, served as the template for change. Central to the strategy was providing space "at cost" for the kinds of restaurants, galleries, and shops that would appeal to the target demographic for similar urban neighborhoods. By carefully selecting pioneer tenants, the Goldman team was functioning more like a casting director than a physical planner. To attract these tenants, 160over90's Creative Director, Darryl Cilli, chose to veer from the traditional real-estate brochure. Realizing Goldman Properties was not simply selling space but an emergent neighborhood, 160over90 created a culture magazine that could be used during the sales process. Tied to this publication was a public relations campaign that placed stories about the district in national magazines and newspapers. Subsequently, Goldman Properties has made careful and incremental additions to the neighborhood – three boutiques here, an ad agency there – while not displacing the preexisting retail that helped give the neighborhood "character" in the first place. The examples of Fort Point and B3 are rare but significant, since they suggest that the microprogramming of both ground floor uses and the occupants of the buildings above can result in a planned community with the cultural and social vitality of traditional neighbor-hoods that have arisen naturally over a longer period.

More generally, the examples of the Fort Point and the B3 plans suggest that large-scale development is occurring in existing urban neighborhoods as well as on brownfield sites, partly because of the lack of available large-scale development parcels. Unlike tabula rasa brownfield sites, these plans include both existing buildings and open parcels, and thus generate a range of building scales. This is turn may encourage a more diverse population of residents and businesses, and a more diverse group of development partners, encouraging implementation over a shorter time. The implied financing logic is that the reduction in returns caused by the smaller size of some projects within the broader mix may be offset by more aggressive absorption rates.

Ken Greenberg will be testing these financial assumptions with a new kind of parcel guideline for a development project in San Juan. In the spirit of a guided ad-hoc approach, larger blocks will require further subdivision to be determined by program and need at the time of development. The innovation is that the ultimate parcel sizes can be varied – dictated by a logic of specificity as long as the larger blocks remain permeable. This would allow and indeed encourage an overall devel-oper to acquire the larger block but would leave smaller parcels for additional phases and presumably smaller development entities. These multiple scales of development opportunities encourage several scales of economies to participate – converting one of Jane Jacobs's principles for a socially healthy neighborhood into a proactive planning strategy.

Despite the persistence of the *Battery Park City* method, several emerging trends point to new opportunities for urban design. These opportunities stem from the nature of the sites now available and attractive for large-scale real-estate development. Postindustrial sites requiring ecologically-minded remediation and districts in existing cities, usually with a critical mass of historical buildings that give character to the reengineered neighborhood, are typical. In both kinds, broader social and environmental concerns often color public perception. Creating a large public park is one of several strategies that have been deployed to find an equitable public benefit in exchange for the right to build large-scale projects. Landscape architects have taken the lead with this agenda, since they have effectively developed a narrative for park designs that combines the traditional social virtues of a public park with its new role as a healer of polluted landscapes. A drawn-out development process and the need for large developers to attract capital and tenants to projects in advance of construction necessitate robust arguments for project design decisions. This is one territory where urban designers and architects, rather than marketing consultants, can more proactively add value for developers and seize opportunities for innovative design.

At the same time, the acquisition and development of projects within existing urban districts provokes a more nuanced understanding of development and urban design by large-scale developers and the urban designers and architects who work with them. This understanding is prompted partly by the range of building sizes and types that must be accommodated in such a plan, and this diversity may also lead to a more nuanced and rich practice of urban design on tabula rasa sites. Urban infill development sites also require a more nuanced phasing strategy, since existing tenants and residents need to be considered and accommodated while larger planning moves are contemplated. The beneficial result of this approach is that the planning of specific ground floor uses and the larger public-space network that is typically the focus of urban design occur simultaneously. The ability to micro-engineer the mix of ground floor uses over a longer time may encourage a finer grain of urban design that begins with the charged boundary between buildings and street rather than the clear separation of building-as-poche and "urban realm" that was the conceptual underpinning of the *Battery Park City* method.

The inherent negative social effects of gentrification, potentially provoked when a single entity quietly buys the real estate in an urban area (whether Harvard University in Boston or Goldman Properties in Philadelphia) has to be mitigated not only with sensitive planning, but also with public policy through mechanisms such as inclusionary zoning, which fixes the percentage of affordable housing. A more balanced discourse about gentrification needs to emerge, one that avoids the polarized positions of affordable housing activists on the one hand and the champions of sanitizing versions of economic development on the other. More research needs to be done to determine other market-sensitive policies to encourage economic diversity for other use-types such as retail and office space.

More generally, there is still a place for urban design as a discipline distinct from architecture and as a vehicle for designing large city districts. Urban design conceived as single-author architectural propositions are too monolithic In contrast, I and others are supporting a method of urban design that benefits from the ad hoc compositions that naturally arise from the pragmatic planning of street networks and development parcels on complex urban sites. Our hope is that urban framework plans that aim to produce a rich enough "context" will spawn subsequent development projects that avoid architectural and social monotony. The aim is not to apply design guidelines to resolve differences but rather to put the responsibility back on the quality of the plan and thus eliminate the need for guidelines altogether. This will encourage a flowering of programmatic and aesthetic variety, and it implies that, from an urban designer's perspective, architects need to be trusted more than Andrés Duany would recommend, but not to the degree that a single architect should design an entire city district.

This reformed planning methodology needs to be organized around a sophisticated understanding of the real-estate market and justified by financial models that favor a variety of parcel sizes over a monotony of buildings and uses. A new paradigm for urban design can arise only with a careful coordination between building types, parcel configurations, and a larger urban design framework, and it requires a collaboration between architects and real-estate finance analysts who are not satisfied with the status quo. Architects, after at least fifteen years of neglecting urban design, need to follow the lead of landscape architects and reengage it as a territory for creative practice.

Notes

1 An impressive level of discussion about best-practices urban design approaches was in evidence at the most recent Congress for the New Urbanism held in Providence, Rhode Island, June 1–4, 2006.

2 Stern's comments were made during a question-and-answer period at "On the Waterfront," a conference on large-scale waterfront development, held at the Yale School of Architecture on March 31 and April 1, 2006.

3 Alexander Garvin was the organizer of the Yale School of Architecture "On the Waterfront" conference and introduced both the general session on Queens West development and Thom Mayne, one of the speakers.

4 The *Northpoint* master plan team was led by Ken Greenberg and included CBT Architects of Boston and Michael Van Valkenburgh Associates, Landscape Architects, of New York and Cambridge.

5 See "The Boston Plan: Fred Koetter and Susie Kim" in *Modulus 16, the University of Virginia Architecture Review*, 1983, 98–109 The journal serves as an excellent snapshot of the intellectual climate of the time since it contains Leon Krier's detailed reconstruction of Pliny's *Villa* and Kurt Forster's important essay on Schinkel's approach to urban design in central Berlin.

6 T. Kelly Wilson, Adjunct Associate Professor in the Department of Architecture at the Harvard Graduate School of Design, drew several of the highly detailed Boston Plan perspectives.

7 The initial Kendall Square plan was designed by Ken Greenberg with Urban Strategies, Inc. Greenberg worked on the later stages of the planning as a principal of Greenberg Consultants, Inc.

8 The *Kendall Square Plan*, approved in 1999, has now been partially filled in by buildings and landscapes by Stephen Erlich and Anschen and Allen of Los Angeles, Michael Van Valkenburgh Associates of Cambridge and New York, and most notably, the *Genzyme Headquarters* by Behnisch and Behnisch of Stuttgart.

9 For this to be a tenable framework for urban design, the infrastructure plan will need to be more specific at the ground plane while allowing for a flexibility of possible uses on the levels above. By prescribing the precise location of curb cuts for loading and parking access, for example, a street network would be generated that would be more variegated than the typical development master plan. Ideally, the full streetscape design would be finished in detail before any individual projects were initiated. As a result, a strong urban realm could act as an influential "context" in lieu of other potential form generators on tabula rasa sites.

10 The lead clients from Berkeley Investments for "The Berkeley Fort Point Portfolio: A Vision" were Young Park, President, and Rick Griffin, Executive Vice President. The plan was completed in 2005.

11 See, for example, "Psst … Have You Heard about Bushwick? How an Undesirable Neighborhood Becomes the Next Hotspot" by Robert Sullivan, *New York Times Magazine*, March 5, 2006, 108–13.

12 Craig Grossman, Director of Operations for Goldman Properties in Philadelphia, was also a key member of the development team.

Tim Love, "Urban Design after *Battery Park City*: Opportunities for Variety and Vitality in Large-Scale Urban Real Estate Developments" *Harvard Design Magazine*, 25, (Fall 2006/Winter 2007), pp. 60–9. Reproduced by permission of Tim Love.

III
Planning Types/Normative Frameworks

Introduction

What is planning theory without the city? For Susan Fainstein, it represents the arbitrary isolation of outcome and process and an inopportune detour from the intellectual history of the best urban planning thought. A purely procedural planning theory is insufficiently animated to motivate social movements towards a better city. This forced division is often codified in planning curricula: an urban theory/history course and a separate planning theory (planning-as-decision-making) course, with planning students often uninterested in the latter.

In this part's first reading, Fainstein provides a reflective historical narrative to retrace the evolution of this divide. The neglect of the urban context once burdened mid-century modernist planning theory and its rational model. Today's focus on communicative planning has come a long way from the rational planning model, yet this planning-as-discourse model is also preoccupied with the procedural role of planners. Perhaps discouraged by the challenges of reforming urban society and its larger political economy, planners instead turned their attentions to improving the democratic narratives of governance, to "speak truth to power." If you cannot directly transform the urban economic structure, you can at least transform communication. However, Fainstein notes how these inclusionary planning processes are often insufficient to achieve substantive progress in the city, and how, paradoxically, many of the notable social reforms in the city happened not through participatory grass-roots processes but rather through autocratic impositions from above. Fainstein calls for a return to a planning theory that both internally reflects on the role of planners and externally re-engages the good city as its goal. In particular, she calls for planning theory to orient around "the just city as the appropriate object of planning."

The next two essays represent foundational arguments in the intellectual history of planning theory. Each author directly attacks what was widely seen, in the early

Readings in Planning Theory, Third Edition. Edited by Susan S. Fainstein and Scott Campbell.
Editorial material and organization © 2012 Blackwell Publishing Ltd.
Published 2012 by Blackwell Publishing Ltd.

days of planning theory in the mid-twentieth century, as the dominant paradigm: comprehensive planning. This model emphasized a rational, synoptic approach, based on setting far-reaching goals and objectives. Through these two essays, their authors' names would invariably be associated with two enduring alternatives to the comprehensive model: the conservative model of incrementalism (Lindblom), and the radical-progressive model of advocacy planning (Davidoff).[1]

Charles Lindblom's 1959 article, "The Science of 'Muddling Through,'" mounted an early and highly influential attack on the foundations of comprehensive planning. If comprehensive planning was to be the unifying paradigm for the emerging postwar field of planning, this consensus did not last long. Lindblom argues that the comprehensive model required a level of data and analytical complexity that was simply beyond the grasp and ability of planners. In fact, the actual practice of planners is rarely comprehensive; by default, planners fall back on a more modest, incremental approach. Lindblom argues that planners should abandon the comprehensive model and explicitly define their efforts as incrementalism, relying on "successive limited comparisons" to achieve realistic, short-term goals. In fact, he argues paradoxically, incrementalism comprises the more scientific approach.

Incremental planning, however, has been criticized for being too timid and conservative, both reinforcing the status quo and thereby neglecting the need for transformative social change. It also shares the shortcoming of inductive thinking by assuming that short-term stimulus and response can replace the need for vision and theory. Nevertheless, the incrementalist stance has been a powerful and enduring counter-argument to traditional master planning, and its ascendance reflects a fundamental transformation in planning thought. Where once planning was grounded in a comprehensive vision of urban design and general forecasting models, it is increasingly oriented to pragmatic politics and marginal analyses of policy impacts.

If incremental planning challenged comprehensive planning's reliance on massive information and complex analysis to serve the public interest, advocacy planning attacked the fundamental notion of a single, common "public interest." Paul Davidoff, in his classic and still definitive 1965 article, "Advocacy and Pluralism in Planning," argues that unitary planning perpetuates a monopoly over planning power and discourages participation. If planning is to be inclusive, planners must advocate for the interests of the disenfranchised, since it is their interests that are overlooked under normal circumstances. Traditional planning creates at least two barriers to effective pluralism. First, planning commissions in the United States and bureaucratic planning agencies elsewhere are undemocratic and poorly suited to represent the competing interests of a pluralist society. Second, traditional city planning too narrowly addresses issues of physical planning, separating the physical from the social and thereby neglecting social conflict and inequality in the city. In this light, Davidoff's call for a move from land use to social-economic planning reflects a more general effort to shift the identity of the planner from the objective technocrat of the conservative 1950s to the engaged, social advocate of the contentious 1960s. (Paradoxically, although teachers of planning theory lament that few actually practice Davidoff's ideas, his article remains one of the most frequently read essays in all of planning.)

If earlier planning theory debates emphasized the comprehensive–incremental–advocacy divide, a focus of contemporary planning theory is on communication, dialogue and the dynamics of community input. In "Challenges of Deliberation and Participation," John Forester employs the example of planning for sustainability to argue for a better, more nuanced understanding of the related but not identical planning activities of deliberation and participation. Traditional scientific and technical approaches to sustainability are not enough, especially if disconnected from theories of governance. The sustainability challenge is thus a political as well as a technological undertaking, reconciling multiple audiences, interests, and generations.

Forester reminds us that planning is not just about finding meaning and articulating arguments, but also about taking action. Focusing on inclusive participation is not enough (even if it leads to a shared understanding) unless it also leads to effective negotiations with substantive outcomes. Too often planners conflate the two, and do not differentiate between dialogue and negotiation. He develops a practical 2 × 2 matrix (participation × deliberation) that planners can use to decode and differentiate between planning scenarios. In the end, Forester calls for planning theory not to consist of a "simplistic pronouncements of ideals" but instead to engage the challenges of practice: to help planning *do* the right thing, not just know the right thing.

We conclude this part with an excerpt from Patsy Healey's ambitious book, *Collaborative Planning: Shaping Places in Fragmented Societies*. Collaborative planning emphasizes how people construct planning problems and priorities through discussion, debate, and what Healey calls "inclusionary argumentation." Healey narrates a concise intellectual history of three planning traditions: economic, physical development, and policy analysis. These three strands, with quite separate priorities and theoretical methods, form the amalgamation that is contemporary planning thought. Importantly, successful planning requires both an institutionalist approach to understand urban and regional change and a communicative approach to foster effective practices of governance. Akin to Fainstein's argument (Chapter 8), Healey calls for bringing back these two often-divorced impulses: substantive urban theory and procedural planning theory (and in particular, collaborative planning practice). As her larger book title suggests, Healey seeks a social process that enables a fragmented, diverse and often unequal society to collectively construct a shared vision for urban life.

Note

1   Several other alternatives to the comprehensive model would later emerge: Strategic planning rejected trying to serve overly broad, vague social goals, and instead proposed a targeted form of planning that takes constraints into account. Equity planning challenged the ability of traditional planning to get at the roots of poverty and inequality

and made redistribution its principal goal. Both incremental and strategic planning share a frustration with the unwieldiness and inefficiency of comprehensive planning, while both advocacy and equity planning presume that comprehensive planning does not go far enough to deal with the unfairness of cities. More recently, communicative action challenged comprehensive planning's preoccupation with the plan as expert document and instead viewed planning as facilitating a public dialogue to define community issues and priorities.

8

Planning Theory and the City

Susan S. Fainstein

Programs in city and regional planning typically have one set of courses devoted to the process of planning (planning theory, planning methods), while another group treats the context (structure of cities and regions, urban history) and the object of planning (e.g., redevelopment policy, environmental policy) with little reference to theories of the planning process. In turn, this division of labor within the curriculum has led to a similar divide within scholarship. Consequently, much of planning theory discusses what planners do with little reference either to the sociospatial constraints under which they do it or the object that they seek to affect.

I argue in this article that such a narrow definition of planning theory results in theoretical weakness arising from the isolation of process from context and outcome. I further contend that the object of planning theory should be to formulate answers to the following questions: (1) Under what conditions can conscious human activity produce a better city for all citizens? (2) How do we explain and evaluate the typical outcomes of planning as it has existed so far? Although addressing these questions does require examination of the planner's role and strategies, it also demands exploration of the field of forces in which planners function and a formulation of what a better city might be.

Before I proceed further, three caveats are in order. First, my characterization of planning theory's insulation is a generalization that does not apply to all courses in theory or to all planning theorists.[1] I base it on the question that organized a widely attended roundtable at the 2002 meeting of the Association of Collegiate Schools of Planning (ACSP): Should planning theory and theorizing about the city be separated.[2] The roundtable started from the premise, which appeared undisputed by either the speakers or the audience, that planning theory has increasingly excluded the object of planning from its consideration. It echoed an earlier diagnosis of the problem that Robert Beauregard stated in 1990: "[Planning] theorists delved more and more into an abstract process isolated from social conditions and planning practice. ... Few planning theorists concern themselves with the physical city" (p. 211). Second, my listing of the two questions that should govern theory building in planning reflects my value orientation – that the purpose of planning is to create the just city. Although later in this article I attempt a justification of this outlook, fundamentally it arises out of a commitment that is not necessarily shared by all and to which others may not be persuaded. Third, when I use the term "the city," I do so out of convenience,[3] and by it I mean regions as well – that is, any spatially defined unit that constitutes the object of planning.

The characterization of planning theorists as disregarding the city applies most strongly to those who presently focus on prescribing normative criteria for planning practice, as well as their predecessors who sought to delineate a technical strategy for planners in the rational model, in operations research, or in various concepts of bounded rationality. The focus of the contemporary group is on communication and the roles of planners; the theorists of rationality primarily concern themselves with methodology and its limitations. At the same time, however, there has been a developing body of empirically based planning theory that does look simultaneously at planners and their spatial objects. Beginning, to name a few, with Meyerson and Banfield's book *Politics, Planning, and the Public Interest* (1955), continuing through Alan Altshuler's *The City Planning Process* (1965), Francine Rabinovitz's *City Politics and Planning* (1969), Peter Hall's *Great Planning Disasters* (1980), James Scott's *Seeing Like a State* (1998), my own book *The City Builders* (2001), and most recently Bent Flyvbjerg's *Rationality and Power* (1998), we have seen a steady stream of works that raised questions of how planners shaped urban form, the political and economic forces constraining planning, and the distributional effects of planning decisions. That these (with perhaps the exception of *Rationality and Power*) have usually not been labeled books in planning theory and assigned in planning theory courses seems largely a consequence of convenience and of the self-conscious labeling of their output as planning theory by one group of scholars in the field who concentrate on the role of the planner as mediator.[4]

The distinction between urban theory and planning theory, however, is not intellectually viable for a number of reasons, which I will elaborate in this article. They include (1) the historical roots and justification for planning, (2) the dependence of effective planning on its context, and (3) the objective of planning as conscious creation of a just city.

Historical Roots and Justification for Planning

If one examines the historical roots of planning, the question one would more likely ask is not, "Should planning theory be urban?" but rather, "Why has planning theory ceased to be urban?" The impetus for the development of planning lay in a critique of the industrial city and a desire to re-create cities according to enlightened design principles.

Whether the focus was on greenfield sites, as in Ebenezer Howard's garden city model, or on redeveloping the existing city, as in Haussmann's Paris and Burnham's City Beautiful, planning devoted itself to producing the desired object. It did so, however, without reflection on the process by which the ideal city was formulated. Its implicit theoretical arguments were about the nature of the good city rather than how one derived that concept. It was taken for granted that the function of planning was to impose a consciously chosen pattern of development upon the urban terrain; the method of making the necessary choices was not problematized. Rather, good planning was assumed to be simultaneously in the general interest and guided by experts.

To be sure, there was, during the first part of the twentieth century, some attention to process, as American progressive reformers, in their effort to rid government of bias and corruption, successfully pressed for independent planning commissions. This move, a part of a general impetus to divorce public policy determination from politics, rested on a view that a sharp line separated politics from administration and a belief that experts could develop policies in isolation from selfish interests. It incorporated the thesis, later made explicit in planning's rational model, that general goals could be stipulated in advance within a democratic political process; then, the formulation of the means to reach those goals and the process of implementing those means could be conducted impartially by disinterested appointed officials (Dror 1968; Faludi 1973). In part, it was this assumption that precipitated the recent turn in planning theory to communication, a theme to which I will return later in this article.

The development of an explicit theory directed at prescribing the planner's modus operandi began with the publication of Karl Mannheim's *Man and Society in an Age of Reconstruction* in 1935.[5] It laid the philosophical foundations for later theorizing by describing a democratic planning process that would enable experts to plan under the guidance of the public through their elected representatives. Mannheim's ambition exceeded that of *city* planning – inspired by the ideals of reform liberalism, he envisioned the national state's participation in economic and social planning. He argued that if the planning bureaucracy was subject to parliamentary control, it could apply its technical expertise to the solution of social problems without impinging on freedom:

> The new bureaucracy brought with it a new objectivity in human affairs. There is something about bureaucratic procedure which helps to neutralize the original leanings towards patronage, nepotism, and personal domination. This tendency towards objectivity may, in favourable cases, become so strong that the element of class consciousness, still present in a bureaucracy which is chosen mainly from the ranks of the ruling classes, can be almost completely superseded by the desire for justice and impartiality. (Mannheim 1935/1940, 323)

In his acceptance of the role of impartial expertise and of legislative control of planning goals, Mannheim (1935/1940) laid the foundation for the direction taken by academic planners during the postwar period:

> The subject [of physical planning] changed from a kind of craft ... into an apparently scientific activity in which vast amounts of precise information were garnered and

processed in such a way that the planner could devise very sensitive systems of guidance and control. ... Instead of the old master-plan or blueprint approach, which assumed that the objectives were fixed from the start, the new concept was of planning as a *process*. ... And this planning process was independent of the thing that was planned. (Hall 1996, 327, 329)

Famous for transforming city planning from a primarily design profession to a social science, theorists at the Universities of Chicago and Pennsylvania and their followers laid out the rational model and methods for testing policy alternatives (Sarbib 1983). They relegated public input to the goal-setting process, after which experts would reach a decision using the tools of modern statistical and economic analysis. Ironically, however, the vision of planning expertise incorporated in the rational model wholly ignored the devastating attack on positivism mounted by Mannheim himself in his essay on the sociology of knowledge. Here, in a striking foreshadowing of postmodernist/poststructuralist critique, he stated,

> For each of the participants [in a discussion] the "object" [of discourse] has a more or less different meaning because it grows out of the whole of their respective frames of reference, as a result of which the meaning of the object in the perspective of the other person remains, at least in part, obscure. ... [This approach] does not signify that there are no criteria of rightness and wrongness in a discussion. It does insist, however, that it lies in the nature of certain assertions that they cannot be formulated absolutely, but only in terms of the perspective of a given situation. ... Interests and the powers of perception of the different perspectives are conditioned by the social situations in which they arose and to which they are relevant. (Mannheim 1936, 281, 283, 284).

As applied to urban planning, Mannheim's (1936) assault on universalism denies that forecasters can assume that past experience will simply repeat itself in a new historical context and jettisons the notion of a value-free methodology. Thus, the assumptions underlying applying quantitative cost-benefit analysis to weigh alternatives within the rational model are undermined, and the use of reason and comparative analysis rather than a formally rational methodology is proposed. Mannheim is a clear precursor of Habermas in respect to this view of rationality; he differs, however, from contemporary communicative theorists in that he expects an educated elite, working within his flexible definition of reasoned reflection, to plan on behalf of society at large. His views perhaps find their most recent echo in the work of Giddens (1990). In both his explanation of people's willingness to trust expertise and in his description of reflexivity, by which knowledge circles in and out of society, Giddens presents an approach to knowledge that is neither relativist nor positivist but, as he puts it, "relationist" (or, one might say, dialectical).

If not in practice, at least within theoretical expositions of planning and in legitimations of its practice, the rational model's assumption of expertise divorced from its social base lived on, leading to the critiques of planning that developed within the social movements of the 1960s and 1970s (Fainstein and Fainstein 1974; Castells 1977, 1983; Davidoff 1965/2003).[6] These critiques were directed at both process and outcome. Even though planners were accountable to elected officials, albeit indirectly, critics accused them of being undemocratic by not consulting the people most directly affected by planning initiatives.[7]

In the areas of highways, housing development, and urban renewal, opposition was not to general goals of urban and transportation improvement. Rather, it was to the particular impacts of public programs on affected communities; these communities needed to be involved in the specifics of planning if they were to exercise any real control. The theoretical model of democracy, by which the public made its wishes known through electing representatives and then withdrew from deliberations, crumbled in the face of the actual operation of planning bureaucracies (Fainstein and Fainstein 1982). But while some of the objection was to the procedures governments used at the time, the principal concern of those resisting planning programs was with the consequences of those programs for the city. Thus, Jane Jacobs (1961) referred to the sacking of cities, and Herbert Gans (1968) analyzed the impacts of urban renewal on the displaced.

Influenced by the move toward critical theory occurring in all the social sciences at that time, the first major conference devoted explicitly to planning theory examined planning's impacts, connecting causes within the political economy with planning projects, and urban transformations.[8] Although there was a tendency in these papers to blame planners as the people most directly responsible for policies resulting in neighborhood destruction, planners were not the principal wielders of power in framing urban renewal and highway programs. Viewing planners in isolation from the political forces impinging on them unduly magnified their importance and resulted in a distorted understanding of the causes of community displacement. Perhaps, however, it was inevitable that a conference dedicated to planning theory would have such a singular focus.

Among scholars who examined planning from the vantage point of other disciplines, the approaches used by planners were regarded simply as mediating factors. Thus, the broader political economy literature examined planning within the framework of general forces and constraints. In the United States, discussions of urban redevelopment programs placed primary emphasis on what came to be labeled the urban regime (Fainstein and Fainstein 1986; Stone 1976, 1989). In Western Europe, officials of the national state allied with important economic interests were identified as the force behind large public programs for physical change (Harloe 1977; Pickvance 1976; Castells 1977).

Those writings that went beyond critique to propose new strategies for planning were tied to visions of a transformed city. The lasting influence of Jane Jacob's *Death and Life of Great American Cities* (1961) did not come from the chapters suggesting a novel form of metropolitan governance but rather derived from her suggestions concerning what makes cities work for their inhabitants. She argued that planners should examine the experience of successful cities elsewhere; she did not suggest that they simply inquire of local residents what they thought they wanted – in part because they lacked models of other approaches to urbanism. Likewise, Paul Davidoff's (1965/2003) famous argument for advocacy planning and Norman

Krumholz's (1982) defense of equity planning, while focusing on the role planners should play, tied that role to particular outcomes and relied on planning expertise as the path for reaching them. Davidoff himself led a movement for opening up the suburbs to minorities that was based on a specific view of the desirable metropolis. Krumholz (1999/2003, 228) pressed for unpopular policies like limiting public investment in downtown because of his conception of just distribution: "Equity requires that locally responsible government institutions give priority attention to the goal of promoting a wider range of choices for those Cleveland residents who have few, if any, choices."[9] For neither Davidoff nor Krumholz was participatory or deliberative democracy the principal goal, but social inclusion was – inclusion not necessarily in the discussion of what to do but inclusion in having access to the benefits of the city.

Even though the political process underlying urban renewal and highway programs was causal in creating inequitable outcomes, changing the process was not the sole goal of the critics in the streets. Rather, they desired a different model of the end result of urban programs. The demands of the urban protest movements of the period were for community control *but also* for equitable distribution of benefits, the end of displacement, and a more humane urban design than was embodied in the megaprojects then popular (Altshuler and Luberoff 2003). Greater citizen input could be instrumental in affecting urban development, but shifts away from high-rise housing projects for the poor, equally banal though more luxurious developments for the rich, and quasi-suburban downtown malls required a different vision of the city. It would be one that facilitated interaction between different groups, provided low-income people with improved housing and access to jobs and amenities, and did not privilege investment to benefit downtown business interests over neighborhood improvement.

Thus, just as in the nineteenth century, when revulsion against the squalor of the manufacturing city stimulated the modern planning movement, distaste for the form the city had taken and an idealized image of a desirable future city spurred efforts at reform. The reform movement was attacking the prevailing rational or quasi-rational model on two grounds: first, it was a misguided process; and second, it produced a city that no one wanted. The demands of reformers on the ground expressed themselves within planning theory through political economic analysis of the roots of urban inequality and through calls for democratic participation in planning.

The Context of Planning

During the 1970s, neo-Marxists emphasized the structural underpinnings that limited the potential of planning to achieve change that did not primarily support the owners of capital (Castells 1977; Harvey 1978; Fainstein and Fainstein 1979). Needless to say, this conclusion proved very discouraging to progressive planners who by then were also working for community-based organizations rather than only for city governments and developers. One response to this seeming impasse was to chart courses whereby planning could, in fact, achieve redistributional outcomes (Mier 1993; Clavel 1986; Hartman 2002). The problem, from the perspective of planning theory, was that although these efforts were rooted in an underlying normative position, their theoretical premises were rarely made explicit. In other words, exemplary remedies were presented but without describing and justifying their value premises and without a deep probing of the underlying strategies and conditions that could produce their desired results (Fainstein 1999; Sayer and Storper 1997).

The later, more theoretical response was to identify in democratic forms a way to counter structural power (Throgmorton and Eckstein 2003). This response combined with moves in other disciplines – especially philosophy and cultural studies – to scrutinize communication. Analysis of discourse dwelled on rhetorical content (deconstruction), "ways of knowing," storytelling, and the openness of the listener to the speaker. The logic was that people went along with courses of action contrary to their own best interest because of the distorting effect of communication; therefore, by speaking truth to power, employing multiple forms of discourse, and engaging all stakeholders in the communicative process, it would be possible to attain a more just outcome (Forester 1989). Where for Marx a just outcome could only occur when the economic structure was transformed, for the communicative theorists it was the product of transforming communication. But they never explained how communication could be transformed within a context of power except presumably through the power of truth telling. Yet if the powerful lose their advantages as a consequence of open communication, they are likely to either suppress unpleasant truths or to marginalize the tellers of them. Social power includes the capacity to control and channel communication and is extremely difficult to counter simply through voice.

Communicative planning theorists share with progressive political economists a skepticism concerning the usefulness of models of rationality and their associated privileging of efficiency. In many respects, the content of their critique harkens back to Mannheim's (1935/1940) assault on positivism. These theorists argue that means and ends are mutually constitutive and thus cannot be rigidly separated as they were in the rational model (Healey 1993, 1997). But, somewhat oddly given their acceptance of this proposition, they back away from a concern with ends and aim their spotlight virtually entirely on the planner's mediating role rather than on what should be done or on the context in which planning operates. Thus, for example, Judith Innes's (1996) reference to the New Jersey State Plan as resulting from a consensus-building process does not go on to evaluate the actual operation of that plan, the quality of its prescriptions, or the reasons why it has failed to achieve its objectives. In contrast, Bent Flyvbjerg (1998, 7) "caution[s] against an idealism that ignores conflict and power." In his case study of the plan for Aalborg, he focuses on how a plan that developed out of consultation and aimed at sustainability failed in its goals. He looks both at the forces that shaped the projects instituted under the plan and also at what the plan actually did rather than its rhetoric.[10]

The issue of power cannot be simply dismissed as hackneyed, as Forester (2000) does when discussing Flyvbjerg's (1998) book.[11] Rather, as Chantal Mouffe (1999, 752) argues,

> What is really at stake in the critique of "deliberative democracy" that I am proposing here is the need to acknowledge the dimension of power and antagonism *and their ineradicable character* [italics added]. By postulating the availability of [a] public sphere where power and antagonism have been eliminated and where a rational consensus would have been realized, this model of democratic politics denies the central role in politics of the conflictual dimension and its crucial role in the formation of collective identities.

There is a naïveté in the communicative approach, in its avoidance of the underlying causes of systematic distortion and its faith that reason will prevail (Neuman 2000). As Flyvbjerg (1998) points out much that is accepted as reason is simply rationalization promulgated and repeated by the powerful. Communicative theorists, to the extent that they concern themselves with how to overcome structural impediments to democratic processes, promote the establishment of institutions that are conducive to open interchange. (In this respect they resemble Mannheim [1935/1940], whose argument for an impartial bureaucracy also relied on an institutional analysis.) But without offering some kind of substantive outcome that will transpire as a consequence of institutional transformation, they are unlikely to evoke much enthusiasm for their prescription.

The ideal that everyone's opinion should be respectfully heard and that no particular group should be privileged in an interchange is an important normative argument. But it is not a sufficient one, and it does not deal adequately with the classic conundrums of democracy. These include the problems of insuring adequate representation of all interests in a large, socially divided group; of protecting against demagoguery; of achieving more than token public participation; of preventing economically or institutionally powerful interests from defining the agenda; and of maintaining minority rights. Within political theory, endless dispute has revolved around these issues, and they have by no means been resolved. Communicative planning theory typically tends to pass over them in its reliance on goodwill and to dismiss the view that the character of the obstacles to consensus building based on tolerance derive from a social context that must be analyzed:[12]

> The connection of planning to spatial policies of the state is what gives the practice of planning its specificity, whether we talk about governance, governmentality, or insurgent planning. The practices of urban/spatial/environmental/community planning are connected in diverse and changing ways to the state, its powers and resources deployed in projects of spatial management. Theories ignoring this context risk losing their explanatory potential for prescriptive futility. (Huxley and Yiftachel 2000, 339)

In the case of urban planning, that context is the field of power in which the city lies. And one path toward understanding that context is an examination of planning's outcomes and a comparison of those outcomes to a view of the just city.

In a recent reformulation of her ideas concerning collaborative planning, Healey (2003, 110) counters my argument that planners should evaluate planning practices according to normative concepts of the just city. She contends that

> concepts of the "good" and the "just" were themselves constructed through relations of knowledge and power. ... [But] the processes of articulating values and the manner in which these might become embedded in established discourses and practices were important. In other words, substance and process are co-constituted, not separate spheres. In addition, process should not be understood merely as a means to a substantive end. Processes have process outcomes. Engagement in governance processes shapes participants' sense of themselves.

I agree with her, so the question really becomes one of emphasis. The frequently made criticism of participatory planning exercises that they deteriorate into mere "talking shops" appears to me a consequence of an overemphasis on process. And while Healey (2003) correctly asserts that the concept of the just city is a social construction and develops out of discourse, it is developed at a different level of analysis from the consideration of whether a particular policy promotes justice (see Fischer 1980, 2003). Goals are not simply there to be "discovered" in the form of preferences, but neither are they redeveloped ad hoc in each interchange (Lindblom 1990; Giddens 1990). While the particular meaning of justice or fairness may assume a different form depending on situation, the ideal of justice or fairness transcends particularity (Nussbaum 2000).

Within political science there has always been a split between those who define politics as a process and those who see it in terms of who gets what, when, and how (Lasswell 1936). The "how" in the latter formulation refers to process, but the "what," which alludes to the distribution of whatever is valued, is equally important. If, as Healey (2003) says, substance and process are coconstituted, then one should not be divorced from the other, and the focus of planning theory needs to be both. The "what" for urban planners is the "right to the city" described by Henri Lefebvre (1991; see Purcell 2003). It raises questions of who owns the city, not in the sense of direct individual control of an asset but in the collective sense of each group's ability to access employment and culture, to live in a decent home and suitable living environment, to obtain a satisfying education, to maintain personal security, and to participate in urban governance. How these aims are achieved raises questions of appropriate strategies in specific circumstances, but defining the "what" is not nearly so problematic as Healey implies. Indeed, when she asserts that "an inclusionary collaborative process does not necessarily guarantee the justice of either process or material outcomes" (p. 115), she is indicating that she knows the meaning of justice independent of a specific situation.

In "Politics as a Vocation," Max Weber (1919/1958) distinguishes between an ethic of absolute means and an ethic of absolute ends. The ethic of absolute means is liberal pluralism, with its stress on tolerance and peaceful resolution of conflicts through negotiation. The ethic of absolute ends requires commitment to an overarching vision, even if adhering to it requires transgression of procedural norms. Weber contends that such a course should be rare but that it is at times necessary. Within urban planning, commitment to the just city may at times require stratagems that circumvent inclusionary processes. Many of the great advances toward the welfare state, including the origins of the German social security system and the British national health service, resulted from autocratic or bureaucratic decision making, although within a broad context of popular pressure for a more egalitarian society (Flora and Heidenheimer 1981). In arenas more closely tied to urban planning, the development of affordable housing, the placing of community-based facilities for disadvantaged populations, and the protection of the environment from toxic wastes are as likely to derive from court decisions as from deliberative democracy.

Beauregard (2003, 73) asserts that to realize a sustainable city, defined as one where environmental quality, economic growth, and social justice coexist, "the city must be governed in a way that is attentive to the shared concerns of its people." In this formulation, governance is a means to an end – sustainability – rather than simply an end in itself. Once a goal like sustainability or social justice is posited, then it becomes necessary to theorize about this goal as well as about the strategy for reaching it. Scott Campbell's (2003) article that wrestles with the trade-offs between environment, growth, and social justice, then seeks to outline solutions that encompass all three, is an example of such theorizing.

In this and other works, I have posited the just city as the appropriate object of planning (Fainstein 1997, 1999, 2000). My reasoning falls within the Rawlsian tradition, wherein social justice becomes that value that everyone would choose if one did not know where one was going to end up in the social hierarchy ("the veil of ignorance") (Rawls 1971). Harvey (1992) has argued that social justice is a widely held value that could serve to mobilize a mass movement, and a volume of essays commemorating the publication of his path-breaking work, *Social Justice and the City*, begins by asserting that "the ideal of social justice is the bedrock of any democratic society within which citizens can actively participate in a free, tolerant and inclusive political community" (Merrifield and Swyngedouw 1997, 1). The aim of that volume was to place the concept of social justice within the context of contemporary cities. The assumption, differing from Rawls's universalistic model, was that the concept of justice was situated and that theorizing about the just city actually meant theorizing about justice within particular urban milieux.

Why this kind of discussion is not the norm for planning theory rather than an obsession with the role of the planner is something of a mystery. After all, political theory examines the outcomes of governance, not just the activities of politicians; legal theory focuses on the law, not lawyers; economic theory focuses on the economy, not economists.

Perhaps this is just a question of semantics. No planning theorist would deny the importance of theorizing about urban development, and many of them, when wearing other hats, do so. But the exclusion of urban theory from planning theory courses and from books on planning theory leads toward a compartmentalization of concerns, resulting in a failure to understand the relationship between planning and the field in which it operates.

What Kinds of Theory Are Needed?

As indicated at the beginning of this article, planning theory needs to consider under what conditions conscious human activity can produce a better city (region/nation/ world) for all its citizens. Addressing such a question requires a constant concern with the interaction between planning procedures and outcomes. It also requires investigating the nature of this better city, relative to its particular history, stage of development, and context; the strategies by which it can be achieved; and the obstacles to reaching it. These inquiries in turn force an examination of how cities have developed in the past; the relationship between economic base, social structure (class, gender, and ethnicity), ideas, and governance; what role conscious policy played in producing urban form and social structure; how the system of power relations shaped policy; and the ways in which structures of power are malleable. A realistic acceptance of the power of structures does not imply a blindness to the ways in which structuration occurs (Giddens 1984; Healey 2003) or assume that structures cannot be changed. But it also accepts that they are not changed easily and that the mobilization of bias (Schattschneider 1960) is a constant of collective activity.

Even as simply a strategy, a focus on the character of the desired city and a critique of what has come before is more likely to mobilize democratic participation and popular pressure than a program extolling a particular planning process. Action depends on entrepreneurial activity; thus the new urbanists have evoked widespread interest in planning because they have something to sell – a particular vision of the good community and how to get it. On one hand, in their actual procedures when planning new communities, they tend to exclude popular participation in every- thing but decisions on décor; on the other, they have inspired supporters to press for "smart growth" and, in the venues of local planning boards, to participate enthusiastically in a process to which they were formerly indifferent.

If the just city becomes the object of planning theory, how then should we approach theory development? Leonie Sandercock presents one strategy in her book *Towards Cosmopolis* (1997). Her definition of the just city is one that is socially inclusive, where difference is not merely tolerated but treated with recognition and respect. She thus asserts that she wishes to connect "planning theory with other theoretical discourses – specifically debates around marginality, identity and difference, and social justice in the city – because these are debates which empower groups whose voices are not often heard by planners" (p. 110). John Friedmann in *The Prospect of Cities* (2002, 104) asserts the need for a utopian vision and relates it to critique:

> Utopian thinking has two moments that are inextricably joined: critique and constructive vision. The critique is of certain aspects of our present condition: injustice, oppression,

ecological devastation to name just a few. … Moral outrage over an injustice suggests that we have a sense of justice, inarticulate though it may be. … If injustice is to be corrected … we will need the concrete imagery of utopian thinking to propose steps that would bring us a little closer to a more just world.

Maarten Hajer (1995), in a book that examines how the goal of environmental sustainability has gradually penetrated society, delineates the interweaving of coalition politics, discourse, and concern with outcomes. Hajer's emphasis is on discourse but within the framework of "alternative scenarios of development" (p. 280).

In a paper called "Can We Make the Cities We Want?" I refer to Amsterdam as providing a grounded utopia – an actual city that, while not, of course, really utopia – offers a picture of possibility, at least in relation to the Anglo-American city (Fainstein 1999).[13] Martha Nussbaum (2000), in her listing of "capabilities," offers a set of general goals that can be translated into specifics depending on context. They allow the establishment of criteria by which existing places can be evaluated without demanding that all places reach these goals in the same way. Once such an evaluation is accomplished, deviation from these norms must be explained – another task for theory and one allowing multiple types of theorizing ranging from public choice (which focuses on conflicts between individual and collective rationality) to historical inquiry. Discourse unquestionably forms part of the explanation, but an understanding of the structures of power that shape discourse is a further step.

The task then for planning theory is both normative and explanatory. Here I would like to relate a personal story – thereby accepting to some degree the epistemological approach of communicative planning theory that emphasizes storytelling. When I was taking my PhD oral exam in political science at MIT, my examiner in American politics asked me what was important about the 1968 (Humphrey vs. Nixon) election. I replied that the rise of a mobilized radical right wing (embodied at that time in the candidacy of George Wallace) marked a significant change that would shape future events in a country where, until then, elections were contested at the center. My examiner informed me that I had supplied an incorrect answer. The "right" response was split-ticket voting.

To me that incident (one never forgets these kinds of offenses to one's amour propre) summarized all that was wrong with mainstream political science – its obsession with the mechanics of governance, especially voting, rather than a concern with its outcomes and the deep causes of those outcomes.[14] Finding a job in a planning department provided me with a haven where I could concern myself with what I regarded as important – the way in which public policy could benefit people who needed the mediation of government to attain a decent quality of life. Such a quest belies accusations of structural determinism. Nevertheless, policy makers are not free to act without cognizance of structural forces, even as those forces undergo long-term mutations and are susceptible to political mobilization. Thus, we come full circle – political mobilization requires a goal to mobilize about. Planning theory ought to describe that goal, along with the means of attaining it and the context in which it rests. To me, that goal is the just city, working toward it requires, as Friedmann (2000) asserts, both critique and vision. It calls for sensitivity toward process and discourse as well, but never divorced from recognition of the political-economic structure and spatial form in which we find ourselves and those to which we wish to move.

Notes

1 Robert Beauregard, John Friedmann, and Leonie Sandercock, inter alia, are notable exceptions.

2 The roundtable, in which I participated and from which this article is derived, was organized by Michael Neuman and was titled, "Is Planning Theory Urban?"

3 For the same reason we name departments "urban planning," and give degrees called "master of science in urban planning," even though such departments typically offer courses in regional planning and differentiate among types of cities.

4 The authors most often generally identified with communicative planning theory, and self-identified as planning theorists, include, inter alia, John Forester, Judith Innes, Patsy Healey, James Throgmorton, and Jean Hillier. See especially Mandelbaum, Mazza, and Burchell (1996). Andreas Faludi's early work fell into the technical rationality stream, but his more recent discussions of planning doctrine attach planning to its spatial object. I confess that in my own two theory anthologies, *Readings in Planning Theory* (Campbell and Fainstein 2003) and *Readings in Urban Theory* (Fainstein and Campbell 2002), I have preserved the distinction between planning theory and theories about the city, although the *Planning Theory* reader does include some material that considers the object of planning as well as the planning process. In my planning theory course, I use both books.

5 This book was written in German and published in Holland. The English-language edition appeared in 1940 and was substantially revised and enlarged by the author.

6 It is questionable whether planners actually followed the steps of the rational model. Rather, it acted as a "reconstructed logic" (Kaplan 1964) by which decision makers legitimated their policies. Nevertheless, it provided the justification for the highway and urban renewal programs of the time.

7 For excellent overviews of theoretical developments in this period and later, see Teitz (1996) and Hall (1996).

8 This conference took place at Virginia Polytechnic Institute and State University, Blacksburg, Virginia, May 4–5, 1978. (Papers drawn from this conference appear in Paris [1982]). A subsequent conference in April 1979 at Cornell University (see Clavel, Forester, and Goldsmith [1980] for a number of papers presented at this conference) also chiefly focused on the urban consequences of planning.

9 Krumholz is quoting from the 1975 report of the Cleveland City Planning Commission that he headed.

10 Robert Beauregard (2004) engages in a similar endeavor when examining planning for downtown Manhattan after September 11, 2001.

11 Forester's view seems to be "been there, done that." He notes that when it is shown that planning often serves the powerful "who is surprised?" (Forester 2000, 915). He wants to get past issues of structural power so as to be able to press for a more constructive strategy. He does not, however, give any convincing explanation as to how they can be ignored.

12 Healey (2003, 114) admits that while the effects of consensus-building processes may be liberating and creative, they may also be oppressive.

13 Recent events in Amsterdam, including the assassination of Theo Van Gogh, evidently over his outspoken antagonism to Muslim immigrants and angry responses to it, indicate that the social consensus on which Amsterdam's tradition of tolerance developed appears to be breaking down. The argument in my paper that relative economic equality permitted such consensus to develop did not anticipate that ethnic differences would so strongly assert themselves.

14 To be sure, many political scientists, especially including those cited at the beginning of this article who wrote about planning, do concern themselves with outcomes. And also, split-ticket voting did become more significant at that time.

References

Altshuler, Alan A. 1965. *The city planning process.* Ithaca, NY: Cornell University Press.

Altshuler, Alan A., and David Luberoff. 2003. *Mega-projects: The changing politics of urban public investment.* Washington, DC: Brookings Institution.

Beauregard, Robert A. 1990. Bringing the city back in. *Journal of the American Planning Association* 56 (2): 210–15.

Beauregard, Robert A. 2003. Democracy, storytelling, and the sustainable city. In *Story and sustainability*, ed. Barbara Eckstein and James A. Thogmorton, 65–77. Cambridge, MA: MIT Press.

Beauregard, Robert A. 2004. Mistakes were made. Rebuilding the World Trade Center, phase 1. *International Planning Studies* 9 (2–3): 139–53.

Campbell, Scott. 1983. *The city and the grassroots.* Berkeley: University of California Press.

Campbell, Scott. 2003. Green cities, growing cities, just cities? Urban planning and the contradictions of sustainable development. In *Readings in planning theory*, rev. ed., ed. Scott Campbell and Susan S. Fainstein, 435–58. Oxford, UK: Blackwell.

Campbell, Scott, and Susan S. Fainstein. 2003. *Readings in planning theory.* Rev. ed. Oxford, UK: Blackwell.

Castells, Manuel. 1977. *The urban question.* Cambridge, MA: MIT Press.

Clavel, Pierre. 1986. *The progressive city.* New Brunswick, NJ: Rutgers University Press.

Clavel, Pierre, John Forester, and William W. Goldsmith, eds. 1980. *Urban and regional planning in an age of austerity.* New York: Pergamon.

Davidoff, Paul. 1965/2003. Advocacy and pluralism in planning. In *Readings in planning theory*, rev. ed., ed. Scott Campbell and Susan S. Fainstein, 210–23. Oxford, UK: Blackwell.

Dror, Yehezkel. 1968. *Public policymaking reexamined.* San Francisco: Chandler.

Fainstein, Susan S. 1997. Justice, politics, and the creation of urban space. In *The urbanization of injustice*, ed. Andy Merrifield and Erik Swyngedouw, 18–44. New York: New York University Press.

Fainstein, Susan S. 1999. Can we make the cities we want? In *The urban moment*, ed. Sophie Body-Gendrot and Robert Beauregard, 249–72. Thousand Oaks, CA: Sage.

Fainstein, Susan S. 2000. New directions in planning theory. *Urban Affairs Review* 35 (4): 451–78.

Fainstein, Susan S. 2001. *The city builders.* Rev. ed. Lawrence: University Press of Kansas.

Fainstein, Susan S., and Scott Campbell. 2002. *Readings in urban theory.* Oxford, UK: Blackwell.

Fainstein, Susan S., and Norman I. Fainstein. 1974. *Urban political movements.* Englewood Cliffs, NJ: Prentice Hall.

Fainstein, Susan S., and Norman I. Fainstein. 1979. New debates in urban planning: The impact of Marxist theory within the United States. *International Journal of Urban and Regional Research* 3 (3): 381–403.

Fainstein, Susan S., and Norman I. Fainstein. 1982. Neighborhood enfranchisement and urban redevelopment. *Journal of Planning Education and Research* 2 (1): 11–19.

Fainstein, Susan S., and Norman I. Fainstein. 1986. Regime strategies, communal resistance, and economic forces. In *Restructuring the city*, rev. ed., ed. Susan S. Fainstein, Norman I. Fainstein, Richard Child Hill, Dennis Judd, and Michael Peter Smith, 245–82. New York: Longman.

Faludi, Andreas. 1973. *A reader in planning theory.* Oxford, UK: Pergamon.

Fischer, Frank. 1980. *Politics, values, and public policy.* Boulder, CO: Westview.

Fischer, Frank. 2003. *Reframing public policy.* Oxford: Oxford University Press.

Flora, Peter, and Arnold Heidenheimer, eds. 1981. *The development of welfare states in Europe and America.* New Brunswick, NJ: Transaction

Flyvbjerg, Bent. 1998. *Rationality and power: Democracy in practice.* Chicago: University of Chicago Press.

Forester, John. 1989. *Planning in the face of power.* Berkeley: University of California Press.

Forester, John. 2000. Conservative epistemology, reductive ethics, far too narrow politics: Some clarifications in response to Yiftachel and Huxley *International Journal of Urban and Regional Research* 24 (4): 914–16.

Friedmann, John. 2000. The good city: In defense of utopian thinking. *International Journal of Urban and regional Research* 24 (2). 459–72.

Friedmann, John. 2002. *The prospect of cities.* Minneapolis: University of Minnesota Press.

Gans, Herbert J. 1968. *People and plans.* New York: Basic Books.

Giddens, Anthony. 1984. *The constitution of society: Outline of the theory of structuration.* Cambridge, UK: Polity.

Giddens, Anthony. 1990. *The consequences of modernity.* Stanford, CA: Stanford University Press.

Hajer, Maarten A. 1995. *The politics of environmental discourse.* Oxford: Oxford University Press.

Hall, Peter Geoffrey. 1980. *Great planning disasters.* Berkeley: University of California Press.

Hall, Peter Geoffrey. 1996. *Cities of tomorrow.* Rev. ed. Oxford, UK: Blackwell.

Harloe, Michael, ed. 1977. *Captive cities.* London: Wiley.

Hartman, Chester W. 2002. *Between eminence and notoriety: Four decades of radical urban planning.* New Brunswick, NJ: Rutgers University Center for Urban Policy Research.

Harvey, David. 1978. On planning the ideology of planning. In *Planning theory in the 1980s*, ed. Robert W. Burchell and George Sternlieb, 213–34. New Brunswick, NJ: Rutgers University Center for Urban Policy Research.

Harvey, David. 1992. Social justice, postmodernism and the city. *International Journal of Urban and Regional Research* 16 (4): 588–601.

Healey, Patsy. 1993. Planning through debate: The communicative turn in planning theory. In *The argumentative turn in policy analysis and planning*, ed. Frank Fischer and John Forester, 233–53. Durham, NC: Duke University Press.

Healey, Patsy. 1997. *Collaborative planning.* London: Macmillan.

Healey, Patsy. 2003. Collaborative planning in perspective. *Planning Theory* 2 (2): 101–24.

Huxley, Margo, and Oren Yiftachel. 2000. New paradigm or old myopia? Unsettling the communicative turn in planning theory. *Journal of Planning Education and Research* 19 (4): 333–42.

Innes, Judith, 1996. Group processes and the social construction of growth management: Florida. Vermont, and New Jersey. In *Explorations in planning theory*, ed. Seymour J. Mandelbaum, Luigi Mazza, and Robert W. Burchell, 164–87. New Brunswick, NJ: Rutgers University Center for Urban Policy Research.

Jacobs, Jane. 1961. *The death and life of great American cities*. New York: Vintage.

Kaplan, Abraham. 1964. *The conduct of inquiry*. San Francisco: Chandler.

Krumholz, Norman. 1982. A retrospective view of equity planning: Cleveland, 1969–1979. *Journal of the American Planning Association* 48 (Spring): 163–74.

Krumholz, Norman. 1999/2003. Equitable approaches to local economic development. In *Readings in planning theory*, ed. Scott Campbell and Susan S. Fainstein, 224–36. Oxford, UK: Blackwell.

Lasswell, Harold D. 1936. *Politics: Who gets what, when, how*. New York: McGraw-Hill.

Lefebvre, Henri. 1991. *The production of space*. Oxford, UK: Blackwell.

Lindblom, Charles E. 1990. *Inquiry and change*. New Haven, CT: Yale University Press.

Mandelbaum, Seymour J., Luigi Mazza, and Robert W. Burchell, eds. 1996. *Explorations in planning theory*. New Brunswick, NJ: Center for Urban Policy Research.

Mannheim, Karl. 1935/1940. *Man and society in an age of reconstruction*. New York: Harcourt, Brace & World.

Mannheim, Karl. 1936. The sociology of knowledge. In *Ideology and utopia*, 264–311. New York: Harcourt, Brace & World.

Merrifield, Andy, and Erik Swyngedouw. 1997. Social justice and the urban experience: an introduction. In *The Urbanization of injustice*, ed. Andy Merrifield and Erik Swyngedouw, 1–17. New York: New York University Press.

Meyerson, Martin, and Edward C. Banfield. 1955. *Politics, planning, and the public interest; the case of public housing in Chicago*. Glencoe, IL: Free Press.

Mier, Robert. 1993. *Social justice and local development policy*. Newbury Park, CA: Sage.

Mouffe, Chantal. 1999. Deliberative democracy or agonistic pluralism? *Social Research* 66 (3): 745–58.

Neuman, Michael. 2000. Communicate this! Does consensus lead to advocacy and pluralism? *Journal of Planning Education and Research* 19 (4): 343–50.

Nussbaum, Martha. 2000. *Women and human development*. Cambridge: Cambridge University Press.

Paris, Chris, ed. 1982. *Critical readings in planning theory*. Oxford, UK: Pergamon.

Pickvance, Chris, ed. 1976. *Urban sociology*. New York: St Martin's.

Purcell, Mark. 2003. Citizenship and the right to the global city: Reimagining the capitalist world order. *International Journal of Urban and Regional Research* 27 (3): 564–90.

Rabinovitz, Francine F. 1969. *City politics and planning*. New York: Atherton.

Rawls, John. 1971. *A theory of justice*. Cambridge, MA: Harvard University Press.

Sandercock, Leonie. 1997. *Towards cosmopolis*. New York: John Wiley.

Sarbib, Jean Louis. 1983. The University of Chicago Program in Planning. *Journal of Planning Education and Research* 2 (2): 77–81.

Sayer, Andrew, and Michael Storper. 1997. Ethics unbound: For a normative turn in social theory. *Environment and Planning D: Society and Space* 15 (1): 1–18.

Schattschneider, Elmer E. 1960. *The semi-sovereign people.* New York: Holt, Rinehart & Winston.

Scott, James C. 1998. *Seeing like a state.* New Haven, CT: Yale University Press.

Stone, Clarence N. 1976. *Economic growth and neighborhood discontent.* Chapel Hill: University of North Carolina Press.

Stone, Clarence N. 1989. *Regime politics: Governing Atlanta, 1946–1988.* Lawrence: University Press of Kansas.

Teitz, Michael. 1996. American planning in the 1990s: Evolution, debate and challenge. *Urban Studies* 33 (4–5): 649–72.

Throgmorton, James A., and Barbara Eckstein, eds. 2003. *Story and sustainability: Planning, practice, and possibility for American cities.* Cambridge, MA: MIT Press.

Weber, Max. 1919/1958. Politics as a vocation. In *From Max Weber*, ed. H. H. Gerth and C. Wright Mills, 77–128. New York: Oxford University Press.

9

The Science of "Muddling Through"

Charles E. Lindblom

Suppose an administrator is given responsibility for formulating policy with respect to inflation. He might start by trying to list all related values in order of importance, for example, full employment, reasonable business profit, protection of small savings, prevention of a stock market crash. Then all possible policy outcomes could be rated as more or less efficient in attaining a maximum of these values. This would of course require a prodigious inquiry into values held by members of society and an equally prodigious set of calculations on how much of each value is equal to how much of each other value. He could then proceed to outline all possible policy alternatives. In a third step he would undertake systematic comparison of his multitude of alternatives to determine which attains the greatest amount of values.

In comparing policies he would take advantage of any theory available that generalized about classes of policies. In considering inflation, for example, he would compare all policies in the light of the theory of prices. Since no alternatives are beyond his investigation, he would consider strict central control and the abolition of all prices and markets on the one hand and elimination of all public controls with reliance completely on the free market on the other, both in the light of whatever theoretical generalizations he could find on such hypothetical economies.

Finally, he would try to make the choice that would in fact maximize his values.

An alternative line of attack would be to set as his principal objective, either explicitly or without conscious thought, the relatively simple goal of keeping prices level. This objective might be compromised or complicated by only a few other goals such as full employment. He would in fact disregard most other social values as beyond his present interest and he would for the moment not even attempt to rank the few values that he regarded as immediately relevant. Were he pressed he

Readings in Planning Theory, Third Edition. Edited by Susan S. Fainstein and Scott Campbell.
Editorial material and organization © 2012 Blackwell Publishing Ltd.
Published 2012 by Blackwell Publishing Ltd.

would quickly admit that he was ignoring many related values and many possible important consequences of his policies.

As a second step, he would outline those relatively few policy alternatives that occurred to him. He would then compare them. In comparing his limited number of alternatives, most of them familiar from past controversies, he would not ordinarily find a body of theory precise enough to carry him through a comparison of their respective consequences. Instead he would rely heavily on the record of past experience with small policy steps to predict the consequences of similar steps extended into the future.

Moreover, he would find that the policy alternatives combined objectives or values in different ways. For example, one policy might offer price level stability at the cost of some risk of unemployment; another might offer less price stability but also less risk of unemployment. Hence, the next step in his approach – the final selection – would combine into one the choice among values and the choice among instruments for reaching values. It would not, as in the first method of policy making, approximate a more mechanical process of choosing the means that best satisfied goals that were previously clarified and ranked. Because practitioners of the second approach expect to achieve their goals only partially, they would expect to repeat endlessly the sequence just described as conditions and aspirations changed and as accuracy of prediction improved.

By Root or by Branch

For complex problems the first of these two approaches is of course impossible. Although such an approach can be described, it cannot be practiced except for relatively simple problems and even then only in a somewhat modified form. It assumes intellectual capacities and sources of information that people simply do not possess, and it is even more absurd as an approach to policy when the time and money that can be allocated to a policy problem is limited, as is always the case. Of particular importance to public administration is the fact that public agencies are in effect usually instructed not to practice the first method. That is to say, their prescribed functions and constraints – the politically or legally possible – restrict their attention to relatively few values and relatively few alternative policies among the countless alternatives that might be imagined. It is the second method that is practiced.

Curiously, however, the literatures of decision making, policy formulation, planning and public administration formalize the first approach rather than the second, leaving public administrators who handle complex decisions in the position of practicing what few preach. For emphasis I run some risk of overstatement. True enough the literature is well aware of limits on human capacities and of the inevitability that policies will be approached in some such style as the second. But attempts to formalize rational policy formulation – to lay out explicitly the necessary steps in the process – usually describe the first approach and not the second.[1]

The common tendency to describe policy formulation even for complex problems as though it followed the first approach has been strengthened by the attention given to, and successes enjoyed by, operations research, statistical decision theory, and systems analysis. The hallmarks of these procedures, typical of the first approach, are clarity of objective, explicitness of evaluation, a high degree of comprehensiveness of overview, and – wherever possible – quantification of values for mathematical analysis. But these advanced procedures remain largely the appropriate techniques of relatively small-scale problem solving, where the total number of variable to be considered is small and value problems restricted. Charles Hitch, head of the Economics Division of RAND Corporation, one of the leading centers for application of these techniques, has written:

> I would make the empirical generalization from my experience at RAND and elsewhere that operations research is the art of sub-optimizing, i.e., of solving some lower-level problems, and that difficulties increase and our special competence diminishes by an order of magnitude with every level of decision making we attempt to ascend. The sort of simple explicit model which operations researchers are so proficient in using can certainly reflect most of the significant factors influencing traffic control on the George Washington Bridge, but the proportion of the relevant reality which we can represent by any such model or models in studying, say, a major foreign-policy decision, appears to be almost trivial.[2]

Accordingly I propose in this chapter to clarify and formalize the second method, much neglected in the literature. This might be described as the method of *successive limited comparisons*, I will contrast it with the first approach which might be called the rational-comprehensive method.[3] More impressionistically and briefly – and therefore generally used in this chapter – they could be characterized as the branch method and root method, the former continually building out from the current situation step by step and by small degrees; the later starting from fundamentals anew each time, building on the past only as experience is embodied in a theory, and always prepared to start completely from the ground up.

Let us put the characteristics of the two methods side by side in simplest terms (Table 9.1).

Assuming that the root method is familiar and understandable, we proceed directly to clarification of its alternative by contrast. In explaining the second we shall be describing how most administrators do in fact approach complex questions, for the root method, the "best" way as a blueprint or model, is in fact not workable for complex policy questions, and administrators are forced to use the method of successive limited comparisons.

Intertwining Evaluation and Empirical Analysis (1b)

The quickest way to understand how values are handled in the method of successive limited comparisons is to see how the root method often breaks down in *its* handling of values or objectives. The idea that values should be clarified, and in advance of the examination of alternative policies, is appealing. But what happens when we attempt

Table 9.1   Comparison of comprehensive versus incremental approaches

Rational-comprehensive (root)	Successive limited comparisons (branch)
1a Clarification of values or objectives distinct from and usually prerequisite to empirical analysis of alternative policies.	1b Selection of value goals and empirical analysis of the needed action are not distinct from one another but are closely intertwined.
2a Policy formulation is therefore approached through means-end analysis: First the ends are isolated, then the means to achieve them are sought.	2b Since means and ends are not distinct, means-end analysis is often inappropriate or limited.
3a The test of a "good" policy is that it can be shown to be the most appropriate means to desired ends.	3b The test of a "good" policy is typically that various analysis find themselves directly agreeing on a policy (without their agreeing that it is the most appropriate means to an agreed objective).

4a Analysis is comprehensive: every important relevant factor is taken into account.	4b Analysis is drastically limited:
	   i) Important possible outcomes are neglected.
	   ii) Important alternative potential policies are neglected.
	   iii) Important affected values are neglected.

5a Theory is often heavily relied upon.	5b A succession of comparisons greatly reduces or eliminates reliance on theory.

it for complex social problems? The first difficulty is that on many critical values or objectives, citizens disagree, congressmen disagree, and public administrators disagree. Even where a fairly specific objective is prescribed for the administrator there remains considerable room for disagreement on subobjectives.

Consider, for example, the conflict with respect to locating public housing, described in Meyerson and Banfield's study of the Chicago Housing Authority[4] – disagreement that occurred despite the clear objective of providing a certain number of public housing units in the city. Similarly conflicting are objectives in highway location, traffic control, minimum wage administration, development of tourist facilities in national parks, or insect control.

Administrators cannot escape these conflicts by ascertaining the majority's preference, for preferences have not been registered on most issues; indeed, there often *are* no preferences in the absence of public discussion sufficient to bring an issue to the attention of the electorate. Furthermore, there is a question of whether intensity of feeling should be considered as well as the number of persons preferring each alternative. By the impossibility of doing otherwise administrators often are reduced to deciding policy without clarifying objectives first.

Even when an administrator resolves to follow his own values as a criterion for decisions he often will not know how to rank them when they conflict with one another, as they usually do. Suppose, for example, that an administrator must relocate tenants living in tenements scheduled for destruction. One objective is to empty the buildings fairly promptly, another is to find suitable accommodation for persons displaced, another is to avoid friction with residents in other areas in which a large influx would be unwelcome, another is to deal with all concerned through persuasion if possible and so on.

How does one state even to himself the relative importance of these partially conflicting values? A simple ranking of them is not enough; one needs ideally to know how much of one value is worth sacrificing for some of another value. The answer is that typically the administrator chooses – and must choose – directly among policies in which these values are combined in different ways. He cannot first clarify his values and then choose among policies.

A more subtle third point underlies both the first two. Social objectives do not always have the same relative values. One objective may be highly prized in one circumstance, another in another circumstance. If, for example, an administrator values highly both the dispatch with which his agency can carry through its projects *and* good public relations, it matters little which of the two possibly conflicting values he favors in some abstract or general sense. Policy questions arise in forms that put to administrators such a question as: given the degree to which we are or are not already achieving the values of dispatch and the values of good public relations, is it worth sacrificing a little speed for a happier clientele, or is it better to risk offending the clientele so that we can get on with our work? The answer to such a question varies with circumstances.

The value problem is as the example shows always a problem of adjustments at a margin. But there is no practicable way to state marginal objectives or values except in terms of particular policies. That one value is preferred to another in one decision situation does not mean that it will be preferred in another decision situation in which it can be had only at great sacrifice of another value. Attempts to rank or order values in general and abstract terms so that they do not shift from decision to decision end up by ignoring the relevant marginal preferences. The significance of this third point thus goes very far. Even if all administrators had at hand an agreed set of values, objectives, and constraints, and an agreed ranking of these values, objectives, and constraints, their marginal values in actual choice situations would be impossible to formulate.

Unable consequently to formulate the relevant values first and then choose among policies to achieve them, administrators must choose directly among alternative policies that offer different marginal combinations of values. Somewhat paradoxically the only practicable way to disclose one's relevant marginal values even to oneself is to describe the policy one chooses to achieve them. Except roughly and vaguely, I know of no way to describe – or even to understand – what my relative evaluations are for, say, freedom and security, speed and accuracy in governmental decisions, or low taxes and better schools than to describe my preferences among specific policy choices that might be made between the alternatives in each of the pairs.

In summary two aspects of the process by which values are actually handled can be distinguished. The first is clear: evaluation and empirical analysis are intertwined; that is, one chooses among values and among policies at one and the same time. Put a little more elaborately one simultaneously chooses a policy to attain certain objectives and chooses the objectives themselves. The second aspect is related but distinct: the administrator focuses his attention on marginal or incremental values. Whether he is aware of it or not he does not find general formulations of objectives very helpful and in fact makes specific marginal or incremental comparisons. Two policies X and Y confront him. Both promise the same degree of attainment of objectives *a, b, c, d,* and *e.* But X promises him somewhat more of *f* than does Y, while Y promises him somewhat more of *g* than does X. In choosing between them, he is in fact offered the alternative of a marginal or incremental amount of *f* at the expense of a marginal or incremental amount of *g.* The only values that are relevant to his choice are these increments by which the two policies differ; and when he finally chooses between the two marginal values he does so by making a choice between policies.[5]

As to whether the attempt to clarify objectives in advance of policy selection is more or less rational than the close intertwining of marginal evaluation and empirical analysis, the principal difference established is that for complex problems the first is impossible and irrelevant, and the second is both possible and relevant. The second is possible because the administrator need not try to analyze any values except the values by which alternative policies differ and need not be concerned with them except as they differ marginally. His need for information on values or objectives is drastically reduced as compared with the root method; and his capacity for grasping, comprehending, and relating values to one another is not strained beyond the breaking point.

Relations Between Means and Ends (2b)

Decision making is ordinarily formalized as a means–ends relationship: Means are conceived to be evaluated and chosen in the light of ends finally selected independently of and prior to the choice of means. This is the means–ends relationship of the root method. But it follows from all that has just been said that such a means–ends relationship is possible only to the extent that values are agreed upon, are reconcilable, and are stable at the margin. Typically, therefore, such a means–ends relationship is absent from the branch method, where means and ends are simultaneously chosen.

Yet any departure from the means–ends relationship of the root method will strike some readers as inconceivable. For it will appear to them that only in such a relationship is it possible to determine whether one policy choice is better or worse than another. How can an administrator know whether he has made a wise or foolish decision if he is without prior values or objectives by which to judge his decisions? The answer to this question calls up the third distinctive difference between root and branch methods: how to decide the best policy.

The Test of "Good" Policy (3b)

In the root method a decision is "correct," "good," or "rational" if it can be shown to attain some specified objective, where the objective can be specified without simply describing the decision itself. Where objectives are defined only through the marginal or incremental approach to values described above, it is still sometimes possible to test whether a policy does in fact attain the desired objectives; but a precise statement of the objectives takes the form of a description of the policy chosen or some alternative to it. To show that a policy is mistaken one cannot offer an abstract argument that important objectives are not achieved; one must instead argue that another policy is to be preferred.

So far the departure from customary ways of looking at problem solving is not troublesome for many administrators will be quick to agree that the most effective discussion of the correctness of policy does take the form of comparison with other policies that might have been chosen. But what of the situation in which administrators cannot agree on values or objectives, either abstractly or in marginal terms? What then is the test of "good" policy? For the root method, there is no test. Agreement on objectives failing, there is no standard of "correctness." For the method of successive limited comparisons, the test is agreement on policy itself, which remains possible even when agreement on values is not.

It has been suggested that continuing agreement in Congress on the desirability of extending old age insurance stems from liberal desires to strengthen the welfare programs of the federal government and from conservative desires to reduce union demands for private pension plans. If so, this is an excellent demonstration of the ease with which individuals of different ideologies often can agree on concrete policy. Labor mediators report a similar phenomenon: the contestants cannot agree on criteria for settling their disputes but can agree on specific proposals. Similarly, when one administrator's objective turns out to be another's means, they often can agree on policy.

Agreement on policy thus becomes the only practicable test of the policy's correctness. And for one administrator to seek to win the other over to agreement on ends as well would accomplish nothing and create quite unnecessary controversy.

If agreement directly on policy as a test for "best" policy seems a poor substitute for testing the policy against its objectives, it ought to be remembered that objectives themselves have no ultimate validity other than they are agreed upon. Hence agreement is the test of "best" policy in both methods. But where the root method requires agreement on what elements in the decision constitute objectives and on which of these objectives should be sought, the branch method falls back on agreement wherever it can be found.

In an important sense, therefore, it is not irrational for an administrator to defend a policy as good without being able to specify what it is good for.

Noncomprehensive Analysis (4b)

Ideally, rational-comprehensive analysis leaves out nothing important. But it is impossible to take everything important into consideration unless "important" is so narrowly defined that analysis is in fact quite limited. Limits on human intellectual capacities and on available information set definite limits to man's capacity to be comprehensive. In actual fact, therefore, no one can practice the rational-comprehensive method for really complex problems, and every administrator faced with a sufficiently complex problem must find ways drastically to simplify. An administrator assisting in the formulation of agricultural economic policy cannot in the first place be competent on all possible policies. He cannot even comprehend one policy entirely. In planning a soil bank program, he cannot successfully anticipate the impact of higher or lower farm income on, say, urbanization – the possible consequent loosening of family ties, possible consequent eventual need for revisions in social security and further implications for tax problems arising out of new federal responsibilities for social security and municipal responsibilities for urban services. Nor, to follow another line of repercussions, can he work through the soil bank program's effects on prices for agricultural products in foreign markets and consequent implications for foreign relations, including those arising out of economic rivalry between the United States and the USSR.

In the method of successive limited comparisons, simplification is systematically achieved in two principal ways. First, it is achieved through limitation of policy comparisons to those policies that differ in relatively small degree from policies presently in effect. Such a limitation immediately reduces the number of alternatives to be investigated and also drastically simplifies the character of the investigation of each. For it is not necessary to undertake fundamental inquiry into an alternative and its consequences; it is necessary only to study those respects in which the proposed alternative and its consequences differ from the status quo. The empirical comparison of marginal differences among alternative policies that differ only marginally is, of course, a counterpart to the incremental or marginal comparison of values discussed above.[6]

Relevance as well as realism

It is a matter of common observation that in Western democracies public administrators and policy analysts in general do largely limit their analyses to incremental or marginal differences in policies that are chosen to differ only incrementally. They do not do so, however, solely because they desperately need some way to simplify their problems; they also do so in order to be relevant. Democracies change their policies almost entirely through incremental adjustments. Policy does not move in leaps and bounds.

The incremental character of political change in the United States has often been remarked. The two major political parties agree on fundamentals; they offer alternative policies to the voters only on relatively small points of difference. Both parties favor full employment but they define it somewhat differently; both favor the development of water power resources but in slightly different ways; and both favor unemployment compensation but not the same level of benefits. Similarly, shifts of policy within a party take place largely through a series of relatively small changes, as can be seen in their only gradual acceptance of the idea of governmental responsibility for support of the unemployed, a change in party positions beginning in the early 1930s and culminating in a sense in the Employment Act of 1946.

Party behavior is in turn rooted in public attitudes and political theorists cannot conceive of democracy's surviving in the United States in the absence of fundamental agreement on potentially disruptive issues, with consequent limitation of policy debates to relatively small differences in policy.

Since the policies ignored by the administrator are politically impossible and so irrelevant, the simplification of analysis achieved by concentrating on policies that differ only incrementally, is not a capricious kind of simplification. In addition, it can be argued that given the limits on knowledge within which policy makers are confined, simplifying by limiting the focus to small variations from present policy makes the most of available knowledge. Because policies being considered are like present and past policies, the administrator can obtain information and claim some insight. Nonincremental policy proposals are therefore typically not only politically irrelevant but also unpredictable in their consequences.

The second method of simplification of analysis is the practice of ignoring important possible consequences of possible policies, as well as the values attached to the neglected consequences. If this appears to disclose a shocking shortcoming of successive limited comparisons, it can be replied that, even if the exclusions are random, policies may nevertheless be more intelligently formulated than through futile attempts to achieve a comprehensiveness beyond human capacity. Actually, however, the exclusions, seeming arbitrary or random from one point of view, need be neither.

Achieving a degree of comprehensiveness

Suppose that each value neglected by one policy-making agency were a major concern of at least one other agency. In that case, a helpful division of labor would be achieved and no agency need find its task beyond its capacities. The shortcomings of such a system would be that one agency might destroy a value either before another agency could be activated to safeguard it or in spite of another agency's efforts. But the possibility that important values may be lost is present in any form of organization, even where agencies attempt to comprehend in planning more than is humanly possible.

The virtue of such a hypothetical division of labor is that every important interest or value has its watchdog. And these watchdogs can protect the interests in their jurisdiction in two quite different ways: first by redressing damages done by other agencies; and second, by anticipating and heading off injury before it occurs.

In a society like that of the United States in which individuals are free to combine to pursue almost any possible common interest they might have and in which government agencies are sensitive to the pressures of these groups, the system described is approximated. Almost every interest has its watchdog. Without claiming that every interest has a sufficiently powerful watchdog, it can be argued that our system often can assure a more comprehensive regard for the values of the whole society than any attempt at intellectual comprehensiveness.

In the United States, for example, no part of government attempts a comprehensive overview of policy on income distribution. A policy nevertheless evolves and one responding to a wide variety of interests. A process of mutual adjustment among farm groups, labor unions, municipalities and school boards, tax authorities, and government agencies with responsibilities in the fields of housing, health, highways, national parks, fire and police accomplishes a distribution of income in which particular income problems neglected at one point in the decision processes become central at another point.

Mutual adjustment is more pervasive than the explicit forms it takes in negotiation between groups; it persists through the mutual impacts of groups upon each other even where they are not in communication. For all the imperfections and latent dangers in this ubiquitous process of mutual adjustment it will often accomplish an adaptation of policies to a wider range of interests than could be done by one group centrally.

Note, too, how the incremental pattern of policy making fits with the multiple pressure pattern. For when decisions are only incremental – closely related to known policies, it is easier for one group to anticipate the kind of moves another might make and easier too for it to make correction for injury already accomplished.[7]

Even partisanship and narrowness, to use pejorative terms, will sometimes be assets to rational decision making for they can doubly ensure that what one agency neglects, another will not; they specialize personnel to distinct points of view. The claim is valid that effective rational coordination of the federal administration, if possible to achieve at all, would require an agreed set of values[8] – if "rational" is defined as the practice of the root method of decision making. But a high degree of administrative coordination occurs as each agency adjusts its policies to the concerns of the other agencies in the process of fragmented decision making I have just described.

For all the apparent shortcomings of the incremental approach to policy alternatives, with its arbitrary exclusion coupled with fragmentation when compared to the root method, the branch method often looks far superior. In the root method, the inevitable exclusion of factors is accidental, unsystematic, and not defensible by any argument so far developed, while in the branch method the exclusions are deliberate, systematic, and defensible. Ideally, of course, the root method does not exclude; in practice it must.

Nor does the branch method necessarily neglect long-run considerations and objectives. It is clear that important values must be omitted in considering policy, and sometimes the only way long-run objectives can be given adequate attention is through the neglect of short-run considerations. But the values omitted can be either long-run or short-run.

Succession of Comparisons (5b)

The final distinctive element in the branch method is that the comparisons, together with the policy choice, proceed in a chronological series. Policy is not made once and for all; it is made and remade endlessly. Policy making is a process of successive approximation to some desired objectives in which what is desired itself continues to change under reconsideration.

Making policy is at best a very rough process. Neither social scientists nor politicians nor public administrators yet know enough about the social world to avoid repeated error in predicting the consequences of policy moves. Wise policy makers consequently expect that their policies will achieve only part of what they hope and at the same time will produce unanticipated consequences they would have preferred to avoid. If they proceed through a *succession* of incremental changes, they avoid serious lasting mistakes in several ways.

In the first place past sequences of policy steps have given them knowledge about the probable consequences of further similar steps. Second, they need not attempt big jumps toward their goals that would require predictions beyond their or anyone else's knowledge, because they never expect their policy to be a final resolution of a problem. Their decision is only one step, one that if successful can quickly be followed by another. Third, they are in effect able to test their previous predictions as they move on to each further step. Lastly they can often remedy a past error fairly quickly – more quickly than if policy proceeded through more distinct steps widely spaced in time.

Compare this comparative analysis of incremental changes with the aspiration to employ theory in the root method. People cannot think without classifying, without subsuming one experience under a more general category of experiences. The attempt to push categorization as far as possible and to find general propositions that can be applied to specific situations is what I refer to with the word "theory." Where root analysis often leans heavily on theory in this sense, the branch method does not. The assumption of root analysts is that theory is the most systematic and economical way to bring relevant knowledge to bear on a specific problem. Granting the assumption, an unhappy fact is that we do not have adequate theory to apply to problems in any policy area, although theory is more adequate in some areas – monetary policy, for example – than in others. Comparative analysis as in the branch method, is sometimes a systematic alternative to theory.

Suppose an administrator must choose among a small group of policies that differ only incrementally from each other and from present policy. He or she might aspire to "understand" each of the alternatives – for example, to know all the consequences of each aspect of each policy. If so the administrator would indeed require theory. In fact, however, he or she would usually decide that *for policy-making purposes*, it was essential to know, as explained above, only the consequences of each of those aspects of the policies in which they differed from one another. For this much more modest aspiration, the administrator requires no theory (although it might be helpful, if available), for the individual can proceed to isolate probable differences by examining the differences in consequences associated with past differences in policies, a feasible program because he or she can draw on observations from a long sequences of incremental changes.

For example, without a more comprehensive social theory about juvenile delinquency than scholars have yet produced, one cannot possibly understand the ways in which a variety of public policies – say on education, housing, recreation, employment, race relations, and policing – might encourage or discourage delinquency. And one needs such an understanding to undertake the comprehensive overview of the problem prescribed in the models of the root method. If, however, one merely wants to mobilize knowledge sufficient to assist in a choice among a small group of similar policies – alternative policies on juvenile court procedures, for example – one can do so by comparative analysis of the results of similar past policy moves.

Theorists and Practitioners

This difference explains – in some cases at least – why administrators often feel that outside experts or academic problem solvers are sometimes not helpful and in turn often urge more theory on them. And it explains why administrators often feel more confident when "flying by the seat of their pants" than when following the advice of theorists. Theorists often ask administrators to go the long way round to the solution of their problems, in effect ask them to follow the best canons of the scientific method when the administrators know that the best available theory will work less well than more modest incremental comparisons. Theorists do not realize that administrators are often in fact practicing a systematic method. It would be foolish to push this explanation too far, for sometimes practical decision makers are pursuing neither a theoretical approach nor successive comparisons, nor any other systematic method.

It may be worth emphasizing that theory is sometimes of extremely limited helpfulness in policy making for at least two rather different reasons. It is greedy for facts; it can be constructed only through a great collection of observations. And it is typically insufficiently precise for application to a policy process that moves through small changes. In contrast, the comparative method both economizes on the need for facts and directs the analyst's attention to just those facts that are relevant to the fine choices faced by the decision maker.

With respect to precision of theory, economic theory serves as an example. It predicts that an economy without money or prices would in certain specified ways misallocate resources, but this finding pertains to an alternative far removed from the kind of policies on which administrators need help. On the other hand, it is not precise enough to predict the consequences of policies restricting business mergers and this is the kind of issue on which the administrators need help. Only in relatively restricted areas does economic theory achieve sufficient precision to go far in resolving policy questions; its helpfulness in policy making is always so limited that it requires supplementation through comparative analysis.

Successive Comparison as a System

Successive limited comparison is, then, indeed a method or system; it is not a failure of method for which administrators ought to apologize. Nonetheless, its imperfections, which have not been explored in this chapter, are many. For example, the method is without a built-in safeguard for all relevant values and it also may lead the decision maker to overlook excellent policies for no other reason than that they are not suggested by the chain of successive policy steps leading up to the present. Hence it ought to be said that under this method, as well as under some of the most sophisticated variants of the root method – operations research for example – policies will continue to be as foolish as they are wise.

Why then bother to describe the method in all the above detail? Because it is in fact a common method of policy formulation and is, for complex problems, the principal reliance of administrators as well as of other policy analysts.[9] And because it will be superior to any other decision-making method available for complex problems in many circumstances, certainly superior to a futile attempt at superhuman comprehensiveness. The reaction of the public administrator to the exposition of method doubtless will be less a discovery of a new method than a better acquaintance with an old. But by becoming more conscious of their practice of this method, administrators might practice it with more skill and know when to extend or constrict its use. (That they sometimes practice it effectively and sometimes not may explain the extremes of opinion on "muddling through," which is both praised as a highly sophisticated form of problem solving and denounced as no method at all. For I suspect that insofar as there is a system in what is known as "muddling through," this method is it.)

One of the noteworthy incidental consequences of clarification of the method is the light it throws on the suspicion an administrator sometimes entertains that a consultant or adviser is not speaking relevantly and responsibly when in fact by all ordinary objective evidence the person is. The trouble lies in the fact that most of us approach policy problems within a framework given by our view of a chain of successive policy choices made up to the present. One's thinking about appropriate policies with respect, say, to urban traffic control is greatly influenced by one's knowledge of the incremental steps taken up to the present. An administrator enjoys an intimate knowledge of his past sequences that "outsiders" do not share, and his thinking and that of the outsider will consequently be different in ways that may puzzle both. Both may appear to be talking intelligently, yet each may find the other unsatisfactory. The relevance of the policy chain of succession is even more clear when an American tries to discuss, say, antitrust policy with a Swiss, for the chains of policy in the two countries are strikingly different, and the two individuals consequently have organized their knowledge in quite different ways.

If this phenomenon is a barrier to communication, an understanding of it promises an enrichment of intellectual interaction in policy formulation. Once the source of difference is understood, it will sometimes be stimulating for an administrator to seek out a policy analyst whose recent experience is with a policy chain different from his own.

This raises again a question only briefly discussed above on the merits of like-mindedness among government administrators. While much of organization theory argues the virtues of common values and agreed organizational objectives, for complex problems in which the root method is inapplicable, agencies will want among their own personnel two types of diversification: administrators whose thinking is organized by reference to policy chains other than those familiar to most members of the organization and, even more commonly, administrators whose professional or personal values or interests create diversity of view (perhaps coming from different specialties, social classes, geographical areas) so that even within a single agency, decision making can be fragmented and parts of the agency can serve as watchdogs for other parts.

Notes

1 James G. March and Herbert A. Simon similarly characterize the literature. They also take some important steps, as have Simon's recent articles, to describe a less heroic model of policy making. See *Organizations* (John Wiley and Sons, 1958), p. 137.

2 "Operations Research and National Planning – A Dissent," 5 *Operations Research* 718 (October 1957). Hitch's dissent is from particular points made in the article to which his paper is a reply; his claim that operations research is for low-level problems is widely accepted.

   For examples of the kind of problems to which operations research is applied see C. W. Churchman, R. L. Ackoff and E. L. Arnoff, *Introduction to Operations Research* (John Wiley and Sons, 1957); and J. F. McCloskey and J. M. Coppinger (eds.), *Operations Research for Management*, vol. II (The Johns Hopkins Press, 1956).

3 I am assuming that administrators often make policy and advise in the making of policy and am treating decision making and policy making as synonymous for purposes of this chapter.

4 Martin Meyerson and Edward C. Banfield, *Politics, Planning and the Public Interest* (The Free Press, 1955).

5 The line of argument is, of course, an extension of the theory of market choice, especially the theory of consumer choice, to public policy choices.

6 A more precise definition of incremental policies and a discussion of whether a change that appears "small" to one observer might be seen differently by another is to be found in my "Policy Analysis," 48 *American Economic Review* 298 (June, 1958).

7 The link between the practice of the method of successive limited comparisons and mutual adjustment of interests in a highly fragmented decision-making process adds a new facet to pluralist theories of government and administration.

8   Herbert Simon, Donald W. Smithburg, and Victor A. Thompson, *Public Administration* (Alfred A. Knopf, 1950), p. 434.
9   Elsewhere I have explored this same method of policy formulation as practiced by academic analysts of policy ("Policy Analysis," 48 *American Economic Review* 298 (June, 1958)). Although it has been here presented as a method for public administrators, it is no less necessary to analysts more removed from immediate policy questions, despite their tendencies to describe their own analytical efforts as though they were the rational-comprehensive method with an especially heavy use of theory. Similarly, this same method is inevitably resorted to in personal problem solving, where means and ends are sometimes impossible to separate, where aspirations or objectives undergo constant development, and where drastic simplification of the complexity of the real world is urgent if problems are to be solved in the time that can be given to them. To an economist accustomed to dealing with the marginal or incremental concept in market processes, the central idea in the method is that both evaluation and empirical analysis are incremental.

Charles E. Lindblom, "The Science of 'Muddling Through,'" *Public Administration Review*, 19, (1959), pp. 79–88. By permission of John Wiley and Sons, Inc.

10

Advocacy and Pluralism in Planning

Paul Davidoff

The present can become an epoch in which the dreams of the past for an enlightened and just democracy are turned into a reality. The massing of voices protesting racial discrimination have roused this nation to the need to rectify racial and other social injustices. The adoption by Congress of a host of welfare measures and the Supreme Court's specification of the meaning of equal protection by law both reveal the response to protest and open the way for the vast changes still required.

The just demand for political and social equality on the part of the African-American and the impoverished requires the public to establish the bases for a society affording equal opportunity to all citizens. The compelling need for intelligent planning, for specification of new social goals and the means for achieving them, is manifest. The society of the future will be an urban one, and city planners will help to give it shape and content.

The prospect for future planning is that of a practice openly inviting political and social values to be examined and debated. Acceptance of this position means rejection of prescriptions for planning that would have the planner act solely as a technician. It has been argued that technical studies to enlarge the information available to decision makers must take precedence over statements of goals and ideals:

> We have suggested that, at least in part, the city planner is better advised to start from research into the functional aspects of cities than from his own estimation of the values which he is attempting to maximize. This suggestion springs from a conviction that at this juncture the implications of many planning decisions are poorly understood, and that no certain means are at hand by which values can be measured, ranked, and translated into the design of a metropolitan system.[1]

Readings in Planning Theory, Third Edition. Edited by Susan S. Fainstein and Scott Campbell.
Editorial material and organization © 2012 Blackwell Publishing Ltd.
Published 2012 by Blackwell Publishing Ltd.

While acknowledging the need for humility and openness in the adoption of social goals, this statement amounts to an attempt to eliminate, or sharply reduce, the unique contribution planning can make: understanding the functional aspects of the city and recommending appropriate future action to improve the urban condition.

Another argument that attempts to reduce the importance of attitudes and values in planning and other policy sciences is that the major public questions are themselves matters of choice between technical methods of solution. Dahl and Lindblom put forth this position at the beginning of their important textbook, *Politics, Economics, and Welfare.*[2]

> In economic organization and reform, the "great issues" are no longer the great issues, if they ever were. It has become increasingly difficult for thoughtful men to find meaningful alternatives posed in the traditional choices between socialism and capitalism, planning and the free market, regulation and laissez-faire, for they find their actual choices neither so simple nor so grand. Not so simple, because economic organization poses knotty problems that can only be solved by painstaking attention to technical details – how else, for example, can inflation be controlled? Nor so grand, because, at least in the Western world, most people neither can nor wish to experiment with the whole pattern of socio-economic organization to attain goals more easily won. If for example, taxation will serve the purpose, why "abolish the wages system" to ameliorate income inequality?

These words were written in the early 1950s and express the spirit of that decade more than that of the 1960s. They suggest that the major battles have been fought. But the "great issues" in economic organization, those revolving around the central issue of the nature of distributive justice, have yet to be settled. The world is still in turmoil over the way in which the resources of nations are to be distributed. The justice of the present social allocation of wealth, knowledge, skill, and other social goods is clearly in debate. Solutions to questions about the share of wealth and other social commodities that should go to different classes cannot be technically derived; they must arise from social attitudes.

Appropriate planning action cannot be prescribed from a position of value neutrality, for prescriptions are based on desired objectives. One conclusion drawn from this assertion is that "values are inescapable elements of any rational decision-making process"[3] and that values held by the planner should be made clear. The implications of that conclusion for planning have been described elsewhere and will not be considered in this chapter.[4] Here I will say that the planner should do more than explicate the values underlying his prescriptions for courses of action; he should affirm them; he should be an advocate for what he deems proper.

Determinations of what serves the public interest, in a society containing many diverse interest groups, are almost always of a highly contentious nature. In performing its role of prescribing courses of action leading to future desired states, the planning profession must engage itself thoroughly and openly in the contention surrounding political determination. Moreover, planners should be able to engage in the political process as advocates of the interests both of government and of such other groups, organizations, or individuals who are concerned with proposing policies for the future development of the community.

The recommendation that city planners represent and plead the plans of many interest groups is founded upon the need to establish an effective urban democracy, one in which citizens may be able to play an active role in the process of deciding public policy. Appropriate policy in a democracy is determined through a process of political debate. The right course of action is always a matter of choice, never of fact. In a bureaucratic age great care must be taken that choices remain in the area of public view and participation.

Urban politics, in an era of increasing government activity in planning and welfare, must balance the demands for ever-increasing central bureaucratic control against the demands for increased concern for the unique requirements of local, specialized interests. The welfare of all and the welfare of minorities are both deserving of support: Planning must be so structured and so practiced as to account for this unavoidable bifurcation of the public interest.

The idealized political process in a democracy serves the search for truth in much the same manner as due process in law. Fair notice and hearings, production of supporting evidence, cross-examination, reasoned decision are all means employed to arrive at relative truth: a just decision. Due process and two (or more) party political contention both rely heavily upon strong advocacy by a professional. The advocate represents an individual, group, or organization. He affirms their position in language understandable to his client and to the decision makers he seeks to convince.

If the planning process is to encourage democratic urban government, then it must operate so as to include rather than exclude citizens from participating in the process. "Inclusion" means not only permitting citizens to be heard. It also means allowing them to become well informed about the underlying reasons for planning proposals, and to respond to these in the technical language of professional planners.

A practice that has discouraged full participation by citizens in plan making in the past has been based on what might be called the "unitary plan." This is the idea that only one agency in a community should prepare a comprehensive plan; that agency is the city planning commission or department. Why is it that no other organization within a community prepares a plan? Why is only one agency concerned with establishing both general and specific goals for community development, and with proposing the strategies and costs required to effect the goals? Why are there not plural plans?

If the social, economic, and political ramifications of a plan are politically contentious, then why is it that those in opposition to the agency plan do not prepare one of their own? It is interesting to observe that "rational" theories of planning have called for consideration of alternative courses of action by planning agencies. As a matter of rationality, it has been argued that all of the alternative choices open as means to the ends ought be examined.[5] But those, including myself, who have recommended agency consideration of alternatives have placed upon the agency planner the burden of inventing "a few representative alternatives."[6] The agency planner has been given the duty of constructing a model of the political spectrum and charged with sorting out what he conceives to be worthy alternatives. This duty has placed too great a burden on the agency planner and has failed to provide for the formulation of alternatives by the interest groups who will eventually be affected by the completed plans.

Whereas in a large part of our national and local political practice contention is viewed as healthy, in city planning, where a large proportion of the professionals are public employees, contentious criticism has not always been viewed as legitimate. Further, where only government prepares plans and no minority plans are developed, pressure is often applied to bring all professionals to work for the ends espoused by a public agency. For example, last year a federal official complained to a meeting of planning professors that the academic planners were not giving enough support to federal programs. He assumed that every planner should be on the side of the federal renewal program. Of course government administrators will seek to gain the support of professionals outside government, but such support should not be expected as a matter of loyalty. In a democratic system opposition to a public agency should be just as normal and appropriate as support. The agency, despite the fact that it is concerned with planning, may be serving undesired ends.

In presenting a plea for plural planning I do not mean to minimize the importance of the obligation of the public planning agency. It must decide upon appropriate future courses of action for the community. But being isolated as the only plan maker in the community, public agencies as well as the public itself may have suffered from incomplete and shallow analysis of potential directions. Lively political dispute aided by plural plans could do much to improve the level of rationality in the process of preparing the public plan.

The advocacy of alternative plans by interest groups outside government would stimulate city planning in a number of ways. First, it would serve as a means of better informing the public of the alternative choices open, *alternatives strongly supported by their proponents*. In current practice those few agencies that have portrayed alternatives have not been equally enthusiastic about each.[7] A standard reaction to rationalists' prescription for consideration of alternative courses of action has been, "It can't be done; how can you expect planners to present alternatives of which they don't approve?" The appropriate answer to that question has been that planners, like lawyers, may have a professional obligation to defend positions they oppose. However, in a system of plural planning, the public agency would be relieved of at least some of the burden of presenting alternatives. In plural planning the alternatives would be presented by interest groups differing with the public agency's plan. Such alternatives would represent the deep-seated convictions of their proponents and not just the mental exercises of rational planners seeking to portray the range of choice.

A second way in which advocacy and plural planning would improve planning practice would be in forcing the public agency to compete with other planning groups to win political support. In the absence of opposition or alternative plans presented by interest groups, the public agencies have had little incentive to improve the quality of their work or the rate of production of plans. The political consumer has been offered a yes/no ballot in regard to the comprehensive plan; either the public agency's plan was to be adopted, or no plan would be adopted.

A third improvement in planning practice that might follow from plural planning would be to force those who have been critical of "establishment" plans to produce superior plans, rather than only to carry out the very essential obligation of criticizing plans deemed improper.

The Planner as Advocate

Where plural planning is practiced, advocacy becomes the means of professional support for competing claims about how the community should develop. Pluralism in support of political contention describes the process; advocacy describes the role performed by the professional in the process. Where unitary planning prevails, advocacy is not of paramount importance, for there is little or no competition for the plan prepared by the public agency. The concept of advocacy as taken from legal practice implies the opposition of at least two contending viewpoints in an adversary proceeding.

The legal advocate must plead for his own and his client's sense of legal propriety or justice. The planner as advocate would plead for his own and his client's view of the good society. The advocate planner would be more than a provider of information, an analyst of current trends, a simulator of future conditions, and a detailer of means. In addition to carrying out these necessary parts of planning, he would be a *proponent* of specific substantive solutions.

The advocate planner would be responsible to his client and would seek to express his client's views. This does not mean that the planner could not seek to persuade his client. In some situations persuasion might not be necessary, for the planner would have sought out an employer with whom he shared common views about desired social conditions and the means toward them. In fact one of the benefits of advocate planning is the possibility it creates for a planner to find employment with agencies holding values close to his own. Today the agency planner may be dismayed by the positions affirmed by his agency, but there may be no alternative employer.

The advocate planner would be above all a planner, responsible to his or her client for preparing plans and for all of the other elements comprising the planning process. Whether working for the public agency or for some private organization, the planner would have to prepare plans that take account of the arguments made in other plans. Thus, the advocate's plan might have some of the characteristics of a legal brief. It would be a document presenting the facts and reasons for supporting one set of proposals, and facts and reasons indicating the inferiority of counter proposals. The adversary nature of plural planning might, then, have the beneficial effect of upsetting the tradition of writing plan proposals in terminology that makes them appear self-evident.

A troublesome issue in contemporary planning is that of finding techniques for evaluating alternative plans. Technical devices such as cost–benefit analyses by themselves are of little assistance without the use of means for appraising the values underlying plans. Advocate planning, by making the values underlying plans more apparent, and definitions of social costs and benefits more explicit, should greatly assist the process of plan evaluation. Further, it would become clear (as it is not at present) that there are no neutral grounds for evaluating a plan; there are as many evaluative systems as there are value systems.

The adversary nature of plural planning might also have a good effect on the uses of information and research in planning. One of the tasks of the advocate planner in discussing the plans prepared in opposition would be to point out the nature of the bias underlying information presented in other plans. In this way, as critic of opposition plans, the planner would be performing a task similar to the legal technique of cross-examination. While painful to the planner whose bias is exposed (and no planner can be entirely free of bias) the net effect of confrontation between advocates of alternative plans would be more careful and precise research.

Not all the work of an advocate planner would be of an adversary nature. Much of it would be educational. The advocate would have the job of informing other groups, including public agencies, of the conditions, problems, and outlook of the group he or she represented. Another major educational job would be that of informing clients of their rights under planning and renewal laws, about the general operations of city government, and of particular programs likely to affect them.

The advocate planner would devote much attention to helping the client organization to clarify its ideas and to give expression to them. In order to make clients more powerful politically the advocate might also become engaged in expanding the size and scope of his or her client organization. But the advocate's most important function would be to carry out the planning process for the organization and to argue persuasively in favor of its planning proposals.

Advocacy in planning has already begun to emerge as planning and renewal affect the lives of more and more people. The critics of urban renewal[8] have forced response from the renewal agencies, and the ongoing debate[9] has stimulated needed self-evaluation by public agencies. Much work along the lines of advocate planning has already taken place, but little of it by professional planners. More often the work has been conducted by trained community organizers or by student groups. In at least one instance, however, a planner's professional aid led to the development of an alternative renewal approach, one that will result in the dislocation of far fewer families than originally contemplated.[10]

Pluralism and advocacy are means for stimulating consideration of future conditions by all groups in society. But there is one social group that at present is particularly in need of the assistance of planners. This group includes organizations representing low-income families. At a time when concern for the condition of the poor finds institutionalization in community action programs it would be appropriate for planners concerned with such groups to find means to plan with them. The plans prepared for these groups would seek to combat poverty and would propose programs affording new and better opportunities to the members of the organization and to families similarly situated.[11]

The difficulty in providing adequate planning assistance to organizations representing low-income families may in part be overcome by funds allocated to local antipoverty councils. But these councils are not the only representatives of the poor; other organizations exist and seek help. How can this type of assistance be financed? This question will be examined below, when attention is turned to the means for institutionalizing plural planning.

The Structure of Planning

Planning by special interest groups

The local planning process typically includes one or more "citizens" organizations concerned with the nature of planning in the community. The Workable Program requirement for "citizen participation"[12] has enforced this tradition and brought it to most large communities. The difficulty with current citizen participation programs is that citizens are more often *reacting* to agency programs than *proposing* their concepts of appropriate goals and future action.

The fact that citizens' organizations have not played a positive role in formulating plans is to some extent a result of both the enlarged role in society played by government bureaucracies and the historic weakness of municipal party politics. There is something very shameful to our society in the necessity to have organized "citizen participation." Such participation should be the norm in an enlightened democracy. The formalization of citizen participation as a required practice in localities is similar in many respects to totalitarian shows of loyalty to the state by citizen parades.

Will a private group interested in preparing a recommendation for community development be required to carry out its own survey and analysis of the community? The answer would depend upon the quality of the work prepared by the public agency, work that should be public information. In some instances the public agency may not have surveyed or analyzed aspects the private group thinks important; or the public agency's work may reveal strong biases unacceptable to the private group. In any event, the production of a useful plan proposal will require much information concerning the present and predicted conditions in the community. There will be some costs associated with gathering that information, even if it is taken from the public agency. The major cost involved in the preparation of a plan by a private agency would probably be the employment of one or more professional planners.

What organizations might be expected to engage in the plural planning process? The first type that comes to mind are the political parties; but this is clearly an aspirational thought. There is very little evidence that local political organizations have the interest, ability, or concern to establish well-developed programs for their communities. Not all the fault, though, should be placed upon the professional politicians, for the registered members of political parties have not demanded very much, if anything, from them as agents.

Despite the unreality of the wish, the desirability for active participation in the process of planning by the political parties is strong. In an ideal situation local parties would establish political platforms, which would contain master plans for community growth, and both the majority and minority parties in the legislative branch of government would use such plans as one basis for appraising individual legislative proposals. Further, the local administration would use its planning agency to carry out the plans it proposed to the electorate. This dream will not turn to reality for a long time. In the interim other interest groups must be sought to fill the gap caused by the present inability of political organizations.

The second set of organizations that might be interested in preparing plans for community development are those that represent special interest groups having established views in regard to proper public policy. Such organizations as chambers of commerce, real estate boards, labor organizations, pro- and anti-civil rights groups, and anti-poverty councils come to mind. Groups of this nature have often played parts in the development of community plans, but only in a very few instances have they proposed their own plans.

It must be recognized that there is strong reason operating against commitment to a plan by these organizations. In fact it is the same reason that in part limits both the interests of politicians and the potential for planning in our society. The expressed commitment to a particular plan may make it difficult for groups to find means for accommodating their various interests. In other terms, it may be simpler for professionals, politicians, or lobbyists to make deals if they have not laid their cards on the table.

There is a third set of organizations that might be looked to as proponents of plans and to whom the foregoing comments might not apply. These are the ad hoc protest associations that may form in opposition to some proposed policy. An example of such a group is a neighborhood association formed to combat a renewal plan, a zoning change, or the proposed location of a public facility. Such organizations may seek to develop alternative plans, plans that would, if effected, better serve their interests.

From the point of view of effective and rational planning, it might be desirable to commence plural planning at the level of citywide organizations, but a more realistic view is that it will start at the neighborhood level. Certain advantages of this outcome should be noted. Mention was made earlier of tension in government between centralizing and decentralizing forces. The contention aroused by conflict between the central planning agency and the neighborhood organization may indeed be healthy, leading to clearer definition of welfare policies and their relation to the rights of individuals or minority groups.

Who will pay for plural planning? Some organizations have the resources to sponsor the development of a plan. Many groups lack the means. The plight of the relatively indigent association seeking to propose a plan might be analogous to that of the indigent client in search of legal aid. If the idea of plural planning makes sense, then support may be found from foundations or from government. In the beginning it is more likely that some foundation might be willing to experiment with plural planning as a means of making city planning more effective and more democratic. Or the federal government might see plural planning, if carried out by local anti-poverty councils, as a strong means of generating local interest in community affairs.

Federal sponsorship of plural planning might be seen as a more effective tool for stimulating involvement of citizens in the future of their community than are the present types of citizen participation programs. Federal support could be expected only if plural planning were seen not as a means of combating renewal plans but as an incentive to local renewal agencies to prepare better plans.

The public planning agency

A major drawback to effective democratic planning practice is the continuation of that nonresponsible vestigial institution, the planning commission. If it is agreed that the establishment of both general policies and implementation policies are questions affecting the public interest and that public interest questions should be decided in accord with established democratic practices for decision making, then it is indeed difficult to find convincing reasons for continuing to permit independent commissions to make planning decisions. At an earlier stage in planning, the strong arguments of John T. Howard[13] and others in support of commissions may have been persuasive. But it is now more than a decade since Howard made his defense against Robert Walker's position favoring planning as a staff function under the mayor. With the increasing effect planning decisions have upon the lives of citizens, the Walker proposal assumes great urgency.[14]

Aside from important questions regarding the propriety of allowing independent agencies far removed from public control to determine public policy, the failure to place planning decision choices in the hands of elected officials has weakened the ability of professional planners to have their proposals effected. Separating planning from local politics has made it difficult for independent commissions to garner influential political support. The commissions are not responsible directly to the electorate, and the electorate in turn is at best often indifferent to the planning commission.

During the last decade, in many cities power to alter community development has slipped out of the hands of city planning commissions, assuming they ever held it, and has been transferred to development coordinators. This has weakened the professional planner. Perhaps planners unknowingly contributed to this by their refusal to take concerted action in opposition to the perpetuation of commissions.

Planning commissions are products of the conservative reform movement of the early part of this century. The movement was essentially anti-populist and pro-aristocracy. Politics was viewed as dirty business. The commissions are relics of a not-too-distant past when it was believed that if men of goodwill discussed a problem thoroughly, certainly the right solution would be forthcoming. We know today, and perhaps it was always known, that there are no right solutions. Proper policy is that which the decision-making unit declares to be proper.

Planning commissions are responsible to no constituency. The members of the commissions, except for their chairperson, are seldom known to the public. In general the individual members fail to expose their personal views about policy and prefer to immerse them in group decision. If the members wrote concurring and dissenting opinions, then at least the commissions might stimulate thought about planning issues. It is difficult to comprehend why this aristocratic and undemocratic form of decision making should be continued. The public planning function should be carried out in the executive or legislative office and perhaps in both. There has been some question about which of these branches of government would provide the best home, but there is much reason to believe that both branches would be made more cognizant of planning issues if they were each informed by their own planning staffs. To carry this division further, it would probably be advisable to establish minority and majority planning staffs in the legislative branch.

At the root of my last suggestion is the belief that there is or should be a Republican and Democratic way of viewing city development; that there should be conservative and liberal plans, plans to support the private market and plans to support greater government control. There are many possible roads for a community to travel, and many plans should show them. Explication is required of many alternative futures presented by those sympathetic to the construction of each such future. As indicated earlier, such alternatives are not presented to the public now. Those few reports that do include alternative futures do not speak in terms of interest to the average citizen. They are filled with professional jargon and present sham alternatives. These plans have expressed technical land-use alternatives rather than social, economic, or political value alternatives. Both the traditional unitary plans and the new ones that present technical alternatives have limited the public's exposure to the future states that might be achieved. Instead of arousing healthy political contention as diverse comprehensive plans might, these plans have deflated interest.

The independent planning commission and unitary plan practice certainly should not coexist. Separately, they dull the possibility for enlightened political debate; in combination they have made it yet more difficult. But when still another hoary concept of city planning is added to them, such debate becomes practically impossible. This third of a trinity of worn-out notions is that city planning should focus only upon the physical aspects of city development.

An Inclusive Definition of the Scope of Planning

The view that equates physical planning with city planning is myopic. It may have had some historical justification, but it is clearly out of place at a time when it is necessary to integrate knowledge and techniques in order to wrestle effectively with the myriad of problems afflicting urban populations.

The city planning profession's historical concern with the physical environment has warped its ability to see physical structures and land as servants to those who use them.[15] Physical relations and conditions have no meaning or quality apart from the way they serve their users. But this is forgotten every time a physical condition is described as good or bad without relation to a specified group of users. High density, low density, green belts, mixed uses, cluster developments, centralized or decentralized business centers are per se neither good nor bad. They describe physical relations or conditions but take on value only when seen in terms of their social, economic, psychological, physiological, or aesthetic effects upon different users.

The profession's experience with renewal over the past decade has shown the high costs of exclusive concern with physical conditions. It has been found that the allocation of funds for removal of physical blight may not necessarily improve the overall physical condition of a community and may engender such harsh social repercussions as to severely damage both social and economic institutions. Another example of the deficiencies of the physical bias is the assumption of city planners that they could deal with the capital budget as if the physical attributes of a facility could be understood apart from the philosophy and practice of the service conducted within the physical structure. This assumption is open to question. The size, shape, and location of a facility greatly interact with the purpose of the activity the facility houses. Clear examples of this can be seen in public education and in the provision of low-cost housing. The racial and other socioeconomic consequences of "physical decisions" such as location of schools and housing projects have been immense, but city planners, while acknowledging the existence of such consequences, have not sought or trained themselves to understand socioeconomic problems, their causes or solutions.

The city planning profession's limited scope has tended to bias strongly many of its recommendations toward perpetuation of existing social and economic practices. Here I am not opposing the outcomes, but the way in which they are developed. Relative ignorance of social and economic methods of analysis have caused planners to propose solutions in the absence of sufficient knowledge of the costs and benefits of proposals upon different sections of the population.

Large expenditures have been made on planning studies of regional transportation needs, for example, but these studies have been conducted in a manner suggesting that different social and economic classes of the population did not have different needs and different abilities to meet them. In the field of housing, to take another example, planners have been hesitant to question the consequences of locating public housing in slum areas. In the field of industrial development, planners have seldom examined the types of jobs the community needed; it has been assumed that one job was about as useful as another. But this may not be the case when a significant sector of the population finds it difficult to get employment.

"Who gets what, when, where, why, and how" are the basic political questions that need to be raised about every allocation of public resources. The questions cannot be answered adequately if land-use criteria are the sole or major standards for judgment.

The need to see an element of city development, land use, in broad perspective applies equally well to every other element, such as health, welfare, and recreation. The governing of a city requires an adequate plan for its future. Such a plan loses guiding force and rational basis to the degree that it deals with less than the whole that is of concern to the public.

The implications of the foregoing comments for the practice of city planning are these. First, state planning enabling legislation should be amended to permit planning departments to study and to prepare plans related to any area of public concern. Second, planning education must be redirected so as to provide channels of specialization in different parts of public planning and a core focused upon the planning process. Third, the professional planning association should enlarge its scope so as not to exclude city planners not specializing in physical planning.

A year ago at the American Institute of Planners (AIP) convention it was suggested that the AIP constitution be amended to permit city planning to enlarge its scope to all matters of public concern.[16] Members of the Institute in agreement with this proposal should seek to develop support for it at both the chapter and national level. The constitution at present states that the institute's "particular sphere of activity shall be the planning of the unified development of urban communities and their environs and of states, regions and the nation *as expressed through determination of the comprehensive arrangement of land and land occupancy and regulation thereof*."[17]

It is time that the AIP delete the words in my italics from its constitution. The planner limited to such concerns is not a city planner, but a land planner or a physical planner. A city is its people; their practices; and their political, social, cultural, and economic institutions as well as other things. The city planner must comprehend and deal with all these factors.

The new city planners will be concerned with physical planning, economic planning, and social planning. The scope of their work will be no wider than that presently demanded of a mayor or a city council member. Thus, we cannot argue against an enlarged planning function on the grounds that it is too large to handle. The mayor needs assistance, in particular the assistance of a planner, trained to examine needs and aspirations in terms of both short- and long-term perspectives. In observing the early stages of development of Community Action Programs, it is apparent that our cities are in desperate need of the type of assistance trained planners could offer. Our cities require for their social and economic programs the type of long-range thought and information that have been brought forward in the realm of physical planning. Potential resources must be examined and priorities set.

What I have just proposed does not imply the termination of physical planning, but it does mean that physical planning be seen as part of city planning. Uninhibited by limitations on their work, city planners will be able to add their expertise to the task of coordinating the operating and capital budgets and to the job of relating effects of each city program upon the others and upon the social, political, and economic resources of the community.

An expanded scope reaching all matters of public concern will not only make planning a more effective administrative tool of local government, it will also bring planning practice closer to the issues of real concern to the citizens. A system of plural city planning probably has a much greater chance of operational success where the focus is on live social and economic questions instead of rather esoteric issues relating to physical norms.

The Education of Planners

Widening the scope of planning to include all areas of concern to government would suggest that city planners must possess a broader knowledge of the structure and forces affecting urban development. In general this would be true. But at present many city planners are specialists in only one or more of the functions of city government. Broadening the scope of planning would require some additional planners who specialize in one or more of the services entailed by the new focus.

A prime purpose of city planning is the coordination of many separate functions. This coordination calls for planners with general knowledge of the many elements comprising the urban community. Educating a planner to perform the coordinator's role is a difficult job, one not well satisfied by the present tradition of two years of graduate study. Training urban planners with the skills called for in this article may require both longer graduate study and development of a liberal arts undergraduate program affording an opportunity for holistic understanding of both urban conditions and techniques for analyzing and solving urban problems.

The practice of plural planning requires educating planners who would be able to engage as professional advocates in the contentious work of forming social policy. The person able to do this would be one deeply committed both to the process of planning and to particular substantive ideas. Recognizing that ideological commitments will separate planners, there is tremendous need to train professionals who are competent to express their social objectives.

The great advances in analytic skills, for example in techniques of simulating urban growth processes, portend a time when planners and the public will be better able to predict the consequences of proposed courses of action. But these advances will be of little social advantage if the proposals themselves do not have substance. The contemporary thoughts of planners about the nature of individuals in society are often mundane, unexciting, or gimmicky. When asked to point out to students the planners who have a developed sense of history and philosophy concerning the place of individuals in the urban world, one is hard put to come up with a name. Sometimes Goodman or Mumford might be mentioned. But planners seldom go deeper than acknowledging the goodness of green space and the soundness of proximity of linked activities. We cope with the problems of the alienated citizen with a recommendation for reducing the time of the journey to work.

Conclusion

The urban community is a system composed of interrelated elements, but little is known about how the elements do, will, or should interrelate. The type of knowledge required by the new comprehensive city planner demands that the planning profession comprise groups of people well versed in contemporary philosophy, social work, law, the social sciences, and civic design. Not every planner must be knowledgeable in all these areas, but each planner must have a deep understanding of one or more of these areas and must be able to give persuasive expression to this understanding.

As members of a profession charged with making urban life more beautiful, exciting, creative, and just, we have had little to say. Our task is to train a future generation of planners to go well beyond us in its ability to prescribe the future urban life.

Notes

1 Britton Harris, "Plan or Projection," *Journal of the American Institute of Planners*, 26 (November 1960) 265–72.
2 Robert Dahl and Charles Lindblom, *Politics, Economics, and Welfare* (New York: Harper and Brothers, 1953) p. 3.
3 Paul Davidoff and Thomas Reiner, "A Choice Theory of Planning," *Journal of the American Institute of Planners*, 28 (May 1962) 103–15.
4 Ibid.
5 See, for example, Martin Meyerson and Edward Banfield, *Politics, Planning and the Public Interest* (Glencoe: The Free Press 1955) pp. 314 ff. The authors state: "By a *rational* decision, we mean one made in the following manner: 1. the decision-maker considers all of the alternatives (courses of action) open to him; ... 2. he identifies and evaluates all of the consequences which would follow from the adoption of each alternative; ... 3. he selects that alternative the probable consequences of which would be preferable in terms of his most valued ends."
6 Davidoff and Reiner, op. cit.
7 National Capital Planning Commission. *The Nation's Capital: a Policies Plan for the Year 2000* (Washington DC: The Commission, 1961).
8 The most important critical studies are Jane Jacobs, *The Life and Death of Great American Cities* (New York: Random House, 1961); Martin Anderson, *The Federal Bulldozer* (Cambridge: MIT Press, 1964); Herbert J. Gans, "The Human Implications of Current Redevelopment and Relocation Planning," *Journal of the American Institute of Planners*, 25 (February 1959) 15–26.
9 A recent example of heated debate appears in the following set of articles: Herbert J. Gans, "The Failure of Urban Renewal," *Commentary* 39 (April 1965) p. 29; George Raymond, "Controversy," *Commentary* 40 (July 1965) p. 72; and Herbert J. Gans, "Controversy," *Commentary* 40 (July 1965) p. 77.
10 Walter Thabit, *An Alternate Plan for Cooper Square* (New York: Walter Thabit, July 1961).
11 The first conscious effort to employ the advocacy method was carried out by a graduate student of city planning as an independent research project. The author acted as both a participant and an observer of a local housing organization. See Linda Davidoff, "The Bluffs: Advocate Planning," *Comment*, Dept. of City Planning, University of Pennsylvania (Spring 1965) p. 59.
12 See Section 101(c) of the United States Housing Act of 1949, as amended.
13 John T. Howard, "In Defense of Planning Commissions," *Journal of the American Institute of Planners*, 17(2) (Spring 1951) 89–95.
14 Robert Walker, *The Planning Function in Urban Government*, second edition (Chicago: University of Chicago Press, 1950). Walker drew the following conclusions from his

examination of planning and planning commissions. "Another conclusion to be drawn from the existing composition of city planning boards is that they are not representative of the population as a whole" (p. 153). "In summary the writer is of the opinion that the claim that planning commissions are more objective than elected officials must be rejected" (p. 155). "From his observations the writer feels justified in saying that very seldom does a majority of any commission have any well-rounded understanding of the purposes and ramifications of planning" (p. 157). "In summary, then, it was found that the average commission member does not comprehend planning nor is he particularly interested even in the range of customary physical planning" (p. 158). "Looking at the planning commission at the present time, however, one is forced to conclude that despite some examples of successful operations, the unpaid board is not proving satisfactory as a planning agency" (p. 165). " ... (it) is believed that the most fruitful line of development for the future would be replacement of these commissions by a department or bureau attached to the office of mayor or city manager. This department might be headed by a board or by a single director, but the members or the director would in any case hold office at the pleasure of the executive on the same basis as other department heads" (p. 177).

15 An excellent and complete study of the bias resulting from reliance upon physical or land-use criteria appears in David Farbman, "A Description, Analysis and Critique of the Master Plan," an unpublished mimeographed study prepared for the Univ. of Pennsylvania's Institute for Urban Studies, 1959–1960. After studying more than one hundred master plans Farbman wrote:

As a result of the predominantly physical orientation of the planning profession many planners have fallen victims to a malaise which I suggest calling the "Physical Bias." This bias is not the physical orientation of the planner itself but is the result of it...

The physical bias is an attitude on the part of the planner which leads him to conceive of the principles and techniques of *his profession* as the key factors in determining the particular recommendations to be embodied in his plans...

The physically biased planner plans on the assumption (conviction) that the physical problems of a city can be solved within the framework of physical desiderata: in other words, that physical problems can be adequately stated, solved and remedied according to physical criteria and expertise. The physical bias produces both an inability and an unwillingness on the part of the planner to "get behind" the physical recommendations of the plan, to isolate, examine or to discuss more basic criteria...

...There is room, then, in plan thinking for physical principles, i.e., theories of structural inter-relationships of the physical city; but this is only part of the story, for the structural impacts of the plan are only a part of the total impact. This total impact must be conceived as a web of physical, economic and social causes and effects. (pp. 22–6)

16 Paul Davidoff, "The Role of the City Planner in Social Planning," *Proceedings of the 1964 Annual Conference*, American Institute of Planners (Washington DC: The Institute, 1964) 125–31.

17 Constitution of AIP, Article II "Purposes," in *AIP Handbook & Roster – 1965*, p. 8.

Paul Davidoff, "Advocacy and Pluralism in Planning," *Journal of the American Institute of Planners*, 31 (4) (1965), pp. 544–55. Reprinted by permission of Taylor & Francis Informa UK Ltd.

11

Challenges of Deliberation and Participation

John Forester

1

The future of sustainability is tied to the future of our ability to manage interconnectedness and interdependence, and thus to our abilities to engage in cooperative, value-creating public deliberations and negotiations, essentially consensus-building in the face of deep differences of interests and values. To understand these issues, we need a better understanding of the micro-politics of planning and public participation, the relationships between our received theories and our practices, and in particular, the work of public dispute resolution and its implications for democratic deliberation and governance: in particular, we need better to understand the differences between dialogue, debate, and negotiation – and the corresponding work of facilitating a dialogue, moderating a debate, and mediating an actual negotiation (Forester 1999, 2006c).

Concerned with environmental sustainability, we must be aware not just of the power – but of the limits – of traditional scientific approaches to thinking about environmental problems – the first such limit being, perhaps, relegating serious, systematic thought about ethics and normative questions to another field altogether.

We need to worry about a second limit, too, of technical work divorced from theories of governance and deliberation. This limit is reflected in the saying that refers ironically to medical expertise: "The operation was a success, but the patient died."

So if we care about environmental quality and sustainability, we need not only technical success, but we must also be able to reconcile the perspectives, prospects, and health of not one but many patients, including ways to honor those who've come before, to respect those alive today, and to protect the life chances of those yet to come.

Readings in Planning Theory, Third Edition. Edited by Susan S. Fainstein and Scott Campbell.
Editorial material and organization © 2012 Blackwell Publishing Ltd.
Published 2012 by Blackwell Publishing Ltd.

But the history of the applied disciplines has not been kind to us. The training of doctoral students seems often narrowly archaic – as if our most promising new researchers are being trained only to talk to a few other specialists. The social sciences seem more taken with "physics envy" than with any growing respect for applied work – much less with carefully and self-critically normative work. Our professional schools remain riddled with anti-intellectualism, with theoretical fads disconnected from the entanglements and challenges of practice, and with conceptions of ethics that reduce normative thinking to simplistic pronouncements of ideals.

But by looking at the practical challenges of governance and environmental policy-making, we might learn not only theoretically but practically. We might see how our received traditions of inquiry can both help us and yet lead us astray too. We might come to see new analytic problems – and we might learn practically also about better and worse ways of handling challenges of deliberation and planning.

In what follows, we consider three central points: First, we need to integrate public participation with innovative and effective negotiation – to learn about skillfully mediated public agreements; Second, public participation, though, raises systematic, pragmatic, even seductive ambiguities that our epistemological traditions predispose us to treat as matters of meaning and argument, but not action; and third, we have a great deal to learn, accordingly, from the practice of public dispute mediators who can help us to understand democratic participation and public deliberation as processes of critically pragmatic action rather than more reductively as processes of argument and argumentation.

2

Take, first, then, the problem of integrating notions of *public participation* with *practical negotiations* in processes of environmental (or broader) governance. To pose this problem, consider a very simple but instructive two by two table that maps four possibilities that we can explore.

On the left hand side of Table 11.1 accordingly, we have below "weak or ineffective negotiation" and above we have "effective negotiations" (by "negotiation," for now, we can imagine at least attempts to avoid jointly damaging "lose-lose" outcomes and to open up possibilities of cooperative, mutual gain agreements). On the top of the table we have at the right, "minimal voice" and at the left "substantial voice." So this gives us four quite interesting possibilities.

As a first possibility, in the lower left quadrant, we have little negotiation but substantial voice, and here, we might think of public hearings: lots of people present, lots of views, if little time, lots of noise and contention, nothing being negotiated. These are public processes from hell, reflecting the meeting or institutional design from hell: there's no better way to raise and smash hopes, fuel anger and distrust, create public resentment at being shepherded through 3 minutes at a time with the de facto incentive to decide-announce-defend: in the absence of a real

Table 11.1 Integrating participation with negotiation

	High voice/participation	Low voice/participation
Effective negotiations	Mediated negotiations	Deal-making
Weak negotiations	Public hearings	Bureaucratic procedure

forum in which to discuss issues, you can only here decide what you wish to say before you've heard anyone else, you can announce it, and then you can defend it against general attacks.

As a second possibility, in the lower right quadrant, we have little negotiation and little participation, perhaps "standard bureaucratic operating procedures." Given stable problems and stable environments with well-defined expertise available, such procedures might work, but given complex and ambiguous problems, these processes benefit neither from the plurality of participation nor from the creativity of astute negotiations.

As a third possibility, in our upper right quadrant, we have effective negotiations but minimal participation. In many political contexts, this might be back room deal-making: decision-making by elites or the "old boys," deals being cut effectively for some, with many downstream left out.

This leaves us one very interesting possibility, and so we come to the upper left quadrant and the question, how to marry substantial participation, perhaps representing generations yet to come and non-human well-being of course too, with effective negotiations that create value and do not squander it, value here including concerns with justice no less than those with health and environmental quality. We should explore this quadrant in particular because we have years of recent work now that teaches us about meeting these challenges via collaborative problem solving, multi-stakeholder negotiations, and consensus-building in complex public policy settings – work from which we (desperately) need to learn, work that does indeed integrate inclusive participation with value-creating negotiations (Susskind 1994).

To learn here, we have to pay attention not simply to interdependence that forces forms of participation, not simply to plurality that forces forms of negotiation, but also to the traps of bungling participation and negotiations as we make a mess of the challenges they confront us with.

3

Now consider some of the ordinary difficulties, even ambiguities, of trying to promote such inclusion and participation and trying to get something effective and value creating done too. Here we find both practical and theoretical questions of democratic deliberation and what we can call "mediated dispute resolution" as well – but both "deliberation" and "mediation" are deeply ambiguous notions.

Suppose, then, that you are in a public meeting and the issues at hand involve any of a range of environmental or economic policy issues, for example, let us say, a meeting devoted to issues of growth and sprawl and economic incentives and global warming and energy conservation and what the city council (or national government) can do. So you hear an impassioned and thoughtful if not altogether convincing plea from Sarah Smith for tax incentives for in-fill downtown, urban development to mitigate sprawl.

Now you might have at least three quite interesting but quite ordinary questions as you listen to Sarah and wonder what to make of what she's claimed:

1. You might simply ask, "*What* is she suggesting?": Does the evidence support her? Are her claims true? How could we know? Here we have questions of the facts of the matter in the argument at hand.
2. Or you might just as reasonably ask, even if her facts are right, how do her suggestions fit with – or challenge – the institutional context at hand, "What's she (really) *suggesting*? Does the government have the authority to do what she's suggesting? Does the political support exist to mandate the policy options she's discussing? Are her recommendations justified?
3. Or you might also wonder about "What is *she* suggesting?" – in effect, "Who in the world is Sarah Smith to argue this? Is she just trying to get business for her shop downtown at the expense of housing on the Northside? Is she going to flip-flop on this suggestion as rumor has it she did before? Here we have a question less of argument and more of identity and reputation, and perhaps gendered politics as well.

Now these might be all quite reasonable questions, but they are questions that lead us in seriously different directions, and not simply by accident, because we've been trained to ask them. One raises questions of truth and refutation; the second raises questions of authority and justification; the third raises questions of self, motive and even identity.

These questions are not only deeply tied to the character of language-use and public speech itself, but to the epistemological and discursive infrastructures of our universities and their dominant philosophical traditions: first, we make claims of reference – and organize attention to "the facts" all the time; second, we can hardly speak or act at all without invoking norms selectively, as we say, "in context" – in the context, that is, of social and political institutions whose norms and conventions we enact well or poorly; and third, we embody and instantiate reputations, selves and identities, and we do all this in an "iffy" way, contingently, fluidly, but very practically, almost every time we speak or even act recognizably with one another at all.

These apparently innocuous questions are not only systematically present, but they present provinces of systematic, expectable pragmatic ambiguities, in governance conversations, in deliberative or participatory conversations, and we will return to the *absorbing pull* of this systematic ambiguity below.

But as suggested above, we have long-standing philosophical and intellectual traditions, historically, that prepare us to ask these questions and that even train us to privilege these questions:

1. For the first, we have the critical rationalist tradition and philosophies of science and practices of experimentation that refine it;
2. For the second, we have traditions of political philosophy and ethical discourse, often radically detached from critical rationalism, yet alive and well behind legal discourses and theories of justification; and
3. For the third, we have traditions of phenomenology and the human sciences that animate ethnographic and humanistic studies, the interpretive and herme- neutic disciplines that probe problems of meaning and significance, culture, identity and tradition.

4

Now, in deliberative and participatory settings, as we witness and hear rival and competing claims, invocations of interests and values – to develop, to protect, to tax, to abate taxes, and so on – we surely feel drawn to use each of these traditions of inquiry. In policy controversies we can certainly expect both passion, exaggeration and posturing, strong claims pressed as some sense opportunity but others fear and distrust those in power, as some sense money to be made and others sense environ- mental quality to be lost, perhaps forever. Faced with these passionate claims, we feel drawn to respond to them.

But even as we bring to bear these powerful and long-standing epistemological traditions, we're missing something terribly important in contexts of civic contro- versy and potential civic discovery: the critical assessment of what we can do together, how we might build a consensus to act together. We can be right, but we can fail to act well – the operation can be a success, but the patient may die. So we are missing here not only an intellectual tradition of critical pragmatism and praxis together, but we are missing the practical judgment and wisdom that mediators bring to complex public disputes.

So consider a few of the lessons that skilled mediators might teach us. Faced with these institutionally primed questions of facticity and truth, justification and legiti- macy, meaning and identity, mediators show us that we're likely to confuse three distinct discursive processes that all arise in contentious deliberative settings, and these are the processes of dialogue, debate, and cooperation (or negotiation).

In contentious situations, when we might well expect posturing and passion, it's easy to see that we might take rival claims as matters of conflicting arguments in *debate*, as we wonder who has the evidence to support their claims, or who has the more justifiable position. Or we might ask prior questions about meaning, intention, and significance: just who is this and what do they mean, where are they "coming from"?

In *dialogue*, however, we seek understanding and knowledge of the other. In *debate*, whether about "the facts" or justification, we do something else again: we're seeking to establish or refute an argument. In *negotiation* or cooperation, however, we're doing something yet different again: we're seeking an agreement upon a course of action (when no established Authority can simply impose an outcome!).

Notice that you need to act quite differently to promote each of these distinct processes: the intervener's or third party's or leader's or manager's role differs substantially here: We *facilitate* a dialogue to promote understanding. We *moderate* a debate to assess the stronger argument. But we *mediate* a negotiation to avoid lose-lose, tragedy of the commons-like traps and to agree upon action together.

So consider, finally, some of the differences between these last two practices, moderating a debate of arguments and mediating a negotiation over joint action:

Moderators take one party's blaming another as an occasion for the other to refute the claim; mediators move parties' from reciprocal blaming and defensiveness to the generation of concrete proposals responding to one another's concerns.

Moderators take appeals to deep values as positions to be defended and criticized; mediators know that parties who differ radically in their Biblical interpretations can agree practically on where the stop signs should go.

Moderators take the parties' passions to threaten rational debate; mediators take the parties passions as energy to fuel not personal attack but collaborative change.

Moderators may search for "common ground," perhaps to narrow differences; but mediators try to find and identify differences in priorities and interests that enable stakeholders to help each other – to realize not difference-splitting poor compromises but mutual gains made possible not despite but precisely *because* the parties have differing priorities.

Moderators may expect debating parties to dig in; mediators expect disputing parties to learn, to identify new interests and stakes, to invent new options in response to one another's proposals and offers.

Moderators seek the "better argument," but mediators seek to manage interdependence, to build relationships, to craft agreements on action to change the world.

So if we reduce mediating negotiations to moderating debates, we let epistemology trump ethics. We let analytic argumentation displace invention, proposal-generation, and consensus-building, the generation of practical agreement. We deconstruct rather than reconstruct. We sharpen our critical swords and substitute concern to show we are right for finding ways together to do right. We become complicit in assuming that scientific understanding or explanation alone will suffice to motivate public or collective action to bridge disputes over what should be done, and to overcome inaction in the face of such understandings, to produce commitments from relevant decision-makers actually to act. If we confuse mediation with dialogue or reduce mediation to dialogue, we risk substituting the quest for understanding for the quest for the actual implementation of the pragmatic steps to do what decision-makers and stakeholders may now believe should be done.

Achieving a common sense of issues, then, does not yet produce action together. So along with understanding, along with testing of hypotheses and knowing that the bridge will stand, that the water meets safety thresholds so we might drink it, along with knowing that our scientific bases for acting are sound, we need mechanisms to develop joint action, commitment, steps toward and through implementation, not just "talk," not just "planning," not even just "promising."

Consider, finally, Sarah Smith once more, now as a participant in a dialogue, debate, or negotiation over a given contentious issue of environmental policy or sustainability. Should Sarah engage in debate alone, she may risk a new scholasticism; in dialogue alone, she may still divorce mutual recognition from collaboratively beginning to act together, producing and implementing agreements to continue further action together. In either case she can *know* the better or desirable thing to do and yet not *do* it, either because she does not "know how" to do it or because her and others' political or moral will is too weak. As a party to a mediated agreement, in contrast, Sarah brings understanding and reason to bear in making publicly accountable commitments to act with others, beginning a flow of action with those others, especially against the backdrop of prior stalemate, impasse, or lack of coordinated environmental policy action.

Contrasting processes and practical attitudes of dialogue, debate, and negotiation can teach us, in the context of creating a sustainable future, that we must devise discursive and conversational political processes and institutions that explore possible commitments so that we not only know the right things to do but actually bring ourselves and one another *to do* those right things.

If we wish to achieve sustainability and a great deal more, we have much to learn from skilled mediators doing the challenging work of integrating diversely passionate voices with cooperative action, all without sacrificing intellectually or scientifically – integrating, then, into our governance and deliberative processes, inclusive public participation with inventive, value creating public negotiations (Forester 1999, 2006c).

Bibliography

Forester, John. 1989. *Planning in the Face of Power*. Berkeley: University of California Press.

Forester, John. 1999. *The Deliberative Practitioner*. Cambridge: MIT Press.

Forester, John. 2006a. "Policy Analysis as Critical Listening," in Robert Goodin, Michael Moran, and Martin Rein, eds. *Oxford Handbook of Public Policy*, Oxford: Oxford University Press.

Forester, John. 2006b. "Rationality and Surprise: The Drama of Mediation in Rebuilding Civil Society." in Penny Gurstein and Nora Angeles, eds. *Engaging Civil Societies in Democratic Planning and Governance*, Toronto: University of Toronto Press.

Forester, John. 2006c. "Making Participation Work When Interests Conflict: From Fostering Dialogue and Moderating Debate To Mediating Disputes." *Journal of the American Planning Association*. Fall. 72: 4, 247–56.

Forester, John. 2009. *Dealing with Differences: Dramas of Mediating Participatory Processes.* Oxford: Oxford University Press.

Forester, John. Scott Peters, and Margo Hittleman. 2005. (Practice Stories web site: http://instruct1.cit.cornell.edu/courses/practicestories).

Susskind, Lawrence. 1994. "Activist Mediation and Public Disputes." John Forester, ed. in Deborah M. Kolb and Associates. *When Talk Works: Profiles of Mediators.* San Francisco: Jossey Bass.

Susskind, Lawrence and J. Cruikshank. 1987. *Breaking the Impasse.* New York: Basic Books.

Susskind, Lawrence and J. Cruikshank. 2006. *Breaking Roberts Rules.* New York: Oxford University Press.

Susskind, Lawrence and P. Field. 1996. *Dealing With An Angry Public.* New York: Free Press.

Susskind, Lawrence, S. McKearnan and J. Thomas Larmer. eds. 1999. *The Consensus Building Handbook: A Comprehensive Guide to Reaching Agreement.* Thousand Oaks CA: Sage Publications.

John Forester, "Challenges of Deliberation and Participation," *Les Ateliers de l'Ethique* (Montreal), 1 (2) (Fall) (2008), pp. 20–5.

12

Traditions of Planning Thought

Patsy Healey

The Origins of Planning

Every field of endeavour has its history of ideas and practices and its traditions of debate. These act as a store of experience, of myths, metaphors and arguments, which those within the field can draw upon in developing their own contributions, either through what they do, or through reflecting on the field. This "store" provides advice, proverbs, recipes and techniques for understanding and acting, and inspiration – ideas to play with and develop. It may also act as a foil, against which critiques are developed and new ways of thinking brought forward. Thus, such a store provides intellectual resources. But it may also act as a constraint on intellectual innovation, by locking perceptions and understandings into particular moulds which are difficult to discard. The planning tradition itself has generally been "trapped" inside a modernist instrumental rationalism for many years, and is only now beginning to escape.

This chapter reviews the traditions of planning thought, focusing on their development in a European and American context. The objective is firstly, to identify those elements of the tradition which provide resources upon which a transformation of planning thought can build; secondly, to introduce the new communicative planning theory as a foundation for a form of collaborative planning; and thirdly, to emphasise what needs to be discarded if the transformation is to be effective.

The planning tradition is a curious one, built up through a mixture of evangelism, formal institutional practice, scientific knowledge and, increasingly, academic development. It represents a continual effort to interrelate conceptions of the qualities and social dynamics of places with notions of the social processes of "shaping places"

Readings in Planning Theory, Third Edition. Edited by Susan S. Fainstein and Scott Campbell.
Editorial material and organization © 2012 Blackwell Publishing Ltd.
Published 2012 by Blackwell Publishing Ltd.

through the articulation and implementation of policies. As John Friedmann has repeatedly pointed out, it oscillates in its emphases between a radical, transformative intention, and a role in maintaining the way cities function and governance works (Friedmann, 1973, 1987). This leads to an ambiguous relation to the social context of planning work. Planners in Europe in the 1940s and 1950s saw themselves as being at the forefront of a transforming effort, building the welfare states which would deliver a reasonable quality of life to the majority of citizens, after the horrendous experiences of war and of the economic depression before it. They were at the vanguard of a trans-forming effort (Boyer, 1983; Davies, 1972; Ravetz, 1980). Their successors, in contrast, often feel themselves operating within a complex and often uncomfortable, political and economic context, within which room for transformative manoeuvre seems slight.

Cities have been planned in one way or another, in the broadest sense of the management of organisation of space, of land and property rights and the provision of urban services, for as long as they have existed. Students of planning are still some-times taught a history of urban form, from the Greeks and Romans, through European city-states, to the present industrial and post-industrial metropolis (Mumford, 1961). This emphasises planning as the management of a product, the physical shape and form, the morphology and spatial organisation of the urban region.

However, the culture of planning as it has evolved in the past century is rooted in a much broader philosophical and social transformation, the intellectual sea change which we now label in the history of Western thought as the "Enlightenment" (Hall and Gieben, 1992). Towards the end of the eighteenth century, a whole body of ideas seemed to develop together, in science, philosophy and economics. This body of thought emphasised the value of scientific knowledge, empirical inquiry and acting in the world to improve it, a deliberate opposition to religious dogma and monarchial attitudes, upheld by a religious preoccupation with the inner life (Sennet, 1991). Enlightenment thinkers argued for the importance of individuals, as knowing subjects with rights and responsibilities, as against power through the "divine right" of kings and barons. They stressed the value of an open environment for business and commerce, as opposed to the political management of the empires and city-states of Europe at the time Contemporary western conceptions of democ-racy, based on the individual franchise, the rights of individuals to pursue their lives and livelihoods, and the primacy of profit-seeking, self-interested economic organisation were significantly shaped in this period (Hall and Gieben, 1992). Out of this climate of thought, and the marriage of science and individual freedom to industry and commerce, came the great surge of invention and expansion known as the Industrial Revolution. It also witnessed the rise of democratic states, displacing autocratic states across western societies, though there were intermittent periods of totalitarian regimes. It is this intellectual movement which these days we refer to as the project of *modernity*.

The complexity of the political and economic processes which resulted, with their mixture of positive advances in terms of wealth generation and the spread of benefits combined with gross social inequalities, systematic exclusions (of class, gender, ethnicity and race), environmental pollution and periodic collapse in market processes, led to a growing interest in the *management* of the social-spatial relations unfolding within states and cities. Faced by these dynamic and contradictory forces, arguments began to build up in favour of *planning* the trajectory of the future, rather than being perpetually vulnerable to the volatility of markets, or to the power of the big capitalist companies. The key resource for this project of planning was seen as scientific knowledge and instrumental rationality. Scientific knowledge could provide an objective basis for identifying present problems and predicting future possibilities. Instrumental rationality focused on relating *means* (how to do things) to *ends* (what could be achieved), in logical and systematic ways. Impartial reason could be used as the measure of just actions (Young, 1990). In this way, the irrationalities of market processes and of political dictatorships could be replaced with a new rationality, planning as the "rational mastery of the irrational", as Karl Mannheim put it (Mannheim, 1940).

The systematic planning of economies, of cities and of neighbourhoods thus became a growing preoccupation of national and local governments faced with the burgeoning problems generated by dynamic and often volatile economic and political conditions. It offered a "transformative mechanism" with which to change and maintain a new, more efficient and effective order to the management of urban regions and to economic management generally.

Three Planning Traditions

The culture of spatial planning as it has arrived in our times has been woven together out of three strands of thought which have grown up in the context of this inheritance. The first is that of *economic planning*, which aims to manage the productive forces of nations and regions. It is this form of planning which Mannheim had primarily in mind, linked to social policies which together would form the framework of a "welfare state". The second strand is that of the management of the *physical development* of towns which promotes health, economy, convenience and beauty in urban settings (Abercrombie, 1944; Keeble, 1952; Adams, 1994). The third is the management of *public administration* and *policy analysis*, which aims to achieve both effectiveness and efficiency in meeting explicit goals set for public agencies.

Economic planning

The tradition of economic planning is a vivid expression of the materialist and rationalist conception of a planned social order. The processes of production and distribution had to be planned to ensure efficient production and continuing growth, and, for some protagonists of economic planning, a fair distribution of the benefits of growth. It was preoccupied with both the economic failures of capitalistic market processes and their social costs.

The interest in *economic planning* arose in part from a general critique of the processes of industrial capitalism. Karl Marx mounted a devastating attack on the social costs of industrial development driven by the striving of capitalist entrepreneurs to maximise profits in competitive markets by exploiting people's labour and destroying resources (Giddens, 1987; Kitching, 1988). His analysis of capitalist processes of production, distribution and exchange was immensely powerful because it combined empirical perception with intellectual coherence, and was informed by a deeply humanitarian concern with the recovery of human dignity, which he saw attacked and degraded by the production processes he observed in nineteenth-century England (Kitching, 1988). His answer, articulated as a political programme in the *Communist Manifesto*, was to replace the market-place and the processes of production driven by capitalistic competition with a governance system which was run by the people. Initially, and in order to break the power of capitalists on governance, Marx argued that the forces representing labour should engage in "class struggle" with the objective of taking control of the state. Ultimately, the state too should wither away, leaving economic activity and governance to be managed by local communities.

Marx's political strategy underpinned the communist political movement, which gained enormous leverage in the early part of the twentieth century as labour movements across the world struggled to improve working conditions. But where communist regimes or socialist regimes, inspired by similar ideas of class struggle, came to power, they tended to reinforce the state, and the original Marxist idea of withering away was forgotten. In the economic arena, capitalist production processes were replaced with centralised planning and programming by the state, with individual enterprises driven by centrally-established production targets rather than the drive for profitability. Economic activity was typically seen to consist of a number of production sectors, usually based on a conventional division between primary, secondary and tertiary, or service industries. Co-ordination in space was subordinated to relatively independent development programmes of the different national ministries, representing economic *sectors*. In theory, production targets were to be informed by scientific research and technical understanding. In practice, building up an adequate knowledge base at the centre proved enduringly difficult and the logic of effective and efficient production quickly got replaced by a "politics of meeting targets". Further, such a concentration of economic and polit-ical power at the apex of a national system not only encouraged forms of govern-ance unresponsive to people's needs. It also provided many opportunities for corrupt practice (Bicanic, 1967). As a result, centralised "command and control" planning was increasingly discredited, from the point of view of economic effi-ciency, democratic practice and social welfare. Those who criticise planning still often have this model of planning in mind.

The communist model was not the only one which proposed replacing capital-istic economic organisation. Many writers who saw problems in large scale organisation outlined proposals for "alternative" lifestyles, characterised by forms of self-governance. These have at various times been taken up by those working within the town planning tradition (Hall, 1988). For instance, Ebenezer Howard, famous for his development of the idea of the *Garden City*, was strongly influenced by such ideas (Beevers, 1988). These ideas challenged the notion of state management and bureaucratic organisation as likely to compromise the freedom of individuals and communities to determine the conditions of their own existence. What they were searching for were ways of interacting among small groups with respect to those matters in which individuals had shared concerns. The influential planning theorist, John Friedmann (1973), describes his own intellectual odyssey from a view of planning as improving public management using the techniques of instrumental rationality, to an emphasis on collective management through interaction among small scale communities, mixing urban and rural economic and social life, a strategy of *agripolitan development*. This kind of "bottom up" economic planning represented a challenge both to capitalist societies and communist ones, and remains an important strand of thought in planning today. It has many links to the "new" radical environmental movements which are searching for different and more environmentally sustainable ways of organising economic life (Beatley, 1994; Goodin, 1992).

Meanwhile, the problems of economic organisation also came to pre-occupy the advocates of capitalist production processes and market societies. The problems here arose from the repeated experience of periodic *market failures*. The ideal of the marketplace is that it provides a mechanism for the continual readjustment of production in relation to consumers' preferences and ability to pay. It is efficient in that it encourages innovative production methods, to reduce costs and introduce new and better products, and it in theory maximises welfare, being driven by consumer demand. And all this happens without the need for complex bureaucracy and the politics which go with state management. However, this marketplace balancing act can get upset for all sorts of reasons (Harrison, 1977; Harvey, 1987). Sometimes markets can be dominated by the producers, in a situation of monopoly or oligopoly. Or there may be too few transactions and too little knowledge available about them. People may come to the marketplace with very different capacities to pay. Market processes will tend to exacerbate these inequalities. Consumers may decide not to purchase and producers not to invest in new equipment or expand production because there is too much uncertainty to predict future expenditure patterns. Or there may be problems in the supply and maintenance of goods and services that everyone benefits from but which are very costly for any one person to supply. Some of these problems are short term, and are "cleared" over time. But others are more deep-seated and can lead to a general slump in economic activity, By the middle of the twentieth century, there had been several such "depressions". The experience of these fostered ideas which suggested that economies could be "managed" to avoid market failure.

The most influential ideas at this time were those of John Maynard Keynes, who argued that economies slumped because of a crisis in consumer demand. If people did not have the resources to buy goods, and/or they did not have the confidence in their longer-term future to be prepared to invest in purchases, then production would sag. His solution, widely adopted in western economic management in the 1950s and 1960s, was to stimulate demand (Gamble, 1988; Thornley, 1991). A key element in his solution was the maintenance of "full employment", a term meaning unemployment levels of 2 to 4%, regarded by economists as representing necessary labor turnover, flexibility and availability. Such policies were buttressed by social welfare policies to assist people to acquire education, to maintain health, and to get housing. The welfare states established in the post-Second World War period in many European countries served to keep the costs of labour low for companies, while enabling reasonable wages. (They also provided benefits to workers, and could be viewed as a strategy to fend off the more radical demands which some workers' groups were advocating at the time.) These wages could then be ploughed back into the marketplace to stimulate production of consumer goods, and hence economic activity generally. In many countries, and notably Britain, the US and Australia, subsidies were provided to encourage people to purchase housing, generating the expansion of a residential development industry (see Ball, 1983).

Although rarely called planning, these demand promotion strategies created what came to be known as a "mixed economy", with economic policy – planning by another name – being driven by a mixture of economic analysis of market conditions and political sensitivity to electoral consequences. As with the centrally planned economies, the "economy" was conceptualised in terms of sectors of production. This approach provided a governance regime which seemed to have advantages for the kinds of companies and capital accumulation strategies which operated on "Fordist" production lines (Harvey, 1989; Boyer, 1991, Amin (ed.), 1994).

However, by the 1970s, these demand-stimulation strategies seemed to have run out of steam. An increasingly interrelated global economy enabled those countries with cheaper labour costs to undercut the high wage economies. Consumer demand, and its accompanying demand for state spending, was growing energetically, creating conditions of rising inflation. At the same time, new technology was reducing the demand for, and therefore the power of, labour. Meanwhile, as companies sought to cut costs to be more competitive, questions were raised about the scale of tax demands needed to support the various demand-stimulation strategies, and about the various regulations on working conditions which had built up over the years to protect labour. The Keynesian strategy seemed to have ground to a halt in "stagflation" – a situation of economic slow-down combined with rising inflation. This reaction provided fertile ground for the reappearance of liberal ideas about economic organisation. By this time, state intervention itself was seen as the problem Articulated by the neo-liberal political movements, especially in the US and Britain, new economic strategies focused on the supply side of the economy, and the reduction of constraints on adaptation and innovation (Gamble, 1988). A major objective was to reduce the role of bureaucracy and politics in the management of the economy, and to "unfetter" business from the burdens imposed upon it by the regulatory environment built up through the welfare state. Economic planning, and spatial and environmental planning, were considered one such burden, and a particular target during the period of the neo-liberal Thatcher administration in Britain in the 1980s.

Britain under the Conservative Prime Minister, Margaret Thatcher, became the arena for the wholesale introduction of these ideas. Through strategies of privatisation and deregulation, companies and market processes generally were to be freed up, to cut costs and to innovate in the globalising marketplace (Gamble, 1988; Thornley, 1991). The role of government was restricted to the management of the money supply to squeeze inflation out of national economies and to hold exchange rates at competitive positions in the international market place. Any government programmes which created "blockages" to supply-side activity were to be reduced or removed. This included "bureaucratic" regulations, such as land use controls, and the concentration of the ownership of development land in public hands in cities. The adverse social and environmental consequences of such a strategy were presented as necessary costs of transition to a more soundly-based economy, which would generate the wealth to put them right in due course. Planning, or co-ordinated economic management of the economy, in this context, was seen not just as unnecessary, but as counterproductive to the project of the recovery of a growth dynamic through market processes.

This neo-liberal strategy has had enormous influence across the world at the end of this century. It offers a way to transform governance to make it more relevant to the dynamics of contemporary economies. Its pro-active elements promote entrepreneurial rather than regulatory styles in governance (Harvey, 1989; Healey *et al.*, 1997). It suggested an end of planning, and the return of the market as the key organising principle of economic life. Yet this strategy is also running into problems. Flexible labour markets create impoverished and insecure workers, unable or afraid to spend on consumption. Individualistic competitive firm behaviour undermines the delicate relations between firms which encourage knowledge flow and creative innovation. Attention is now turning to the institutional preconditions for economic growth. The deregulation impetus itself has changed into a project of regulatory reform, changing the target and process of regulation (Vickers, 1991, Thompson *et al.*, 1991). This rediscovery of the institutional preconditions for market "health" and "vitality" has awakened interest once again in strategies which might foster economic *development*. Further, the increasing concern with environmental quality has created a climate within which there is more rather than less demand for the regulation of economic activity. So planning and the strategic management of urban region change are once again being discussed with regard to the management of economies. The causes and forms of this are discussed in more detail in Chapter 5 [original text].

Underpinning the approaches are different social theories – of class struggle for the Marxists; of communitarian self-management for the anarchists; and of individualism for the Keynesians and neo-liberals. Despite their different emphases, however, the debates and practices of economic management have shared some common characteristics. Their focus has been on the material well-being of consumers and the generation of profits for producers. Their practices have drawn on the vocabulary of neo-classical economics, even in Eastern European economies, with its metaphors of utility-maximising, rational individuals making trade-offs between their preferences. Through the science of economics, policy programmes can be developed objectively, without the need to test ideas out with the different interested parties. Governance becomes a technocratic exercise in economic management. All these assumptions are challenged by contemporary institutionalist analysis and the communicative approach now emerging in planning theory.

The debates on economic management provide a context for the discussion of the physical development of towns and cities, and the management of spatial change in urban regions, and hence for any exercise in spatial and environmental planning. But the connection between these two arenas has been persistently neglected. Economic analysis has focused on economic sectors, and has tended to neglect how economic activities occur in space and time. As a result, it has paid little attention to the co-existence of different economic activities in shared space, except at the level of the micro-analysis of labour market dynamics, or the agglomeration economies and diseconomies of particular clusters of economic activities. It was left to the field of regional economic analysis and regional location geography to articulate these connections through the elaboration of location models for urban regions. Drawing on principles developed by Von Thunen and Isard, urban region spatial organisation came to be understood as being generated by the regional economic base. This in turn created a service economy and distributed activities across space through trade-offs between transport costs and land and property values (Evans, 1985). These ideas were developed in the spatial planning field conceptually by Chadwick (1971) and McLoughlin (1969) in Britain, and more practically by Chapin (1965) in the US. They focused on the analysis and modelling of urban systems. It is the assumptions and findings of these models which have been comprehensively challenged in the fields of regional economic analysis and regional geography in recent years, contributing to the reintroduction of space, place and the institutional capacity of localities into both micro and macro economic analysis (Massey and Meegan, 1982; Harvey, 1982; Scott and Roweis, 1977). A critical contemporary challenge is to link these new understandings of the spatiality of economic process to the principles and practices of physical development planning.

Physical development planning

Whereas the economic planning tradition has been dominated by economists and political philosophers, the arena of physical development planning was shaped for many years by engineers and architects, and by utopian images of what cities could be like. Utopian dreams of urban form, and architects to build them, have been around since long before the Enlightenment. What modernity and industrial urbanisation brought with them was a more material and functional concern with the qualities of city development. These influences led to practical interest in building regulation and in the strategic regulation of the location of development. Land use zoning was introduced, aimed to prevent the pollution of residential neighbourhoods by dirty industry, and to limit development location to enable adequate services to be provided. Ways of providing infrastructure and measures for land assembly, to allow land pooling among owners, or the purchase by the state of sites needed for public projects, were also introduced in early planning systems. Urban master plans, layout plans for "greenfield" subdivision and projects for the reorganisation of the urban fabric became part of the management of the physical development process in many places from the late nineteenth century (Ward, 1994; Sutcliffe, 1981).

This of course implied affecting the structure of land and property rights and the interests of land and property owners. However, until the 1970s, and even later, there was little discussion of the nature of the development process and land and property markets in debates on physical development planning (see Healey and Barrett, 1985; Adams, 1994). These were relegated to an arena of "planning practice", concerned primarily with tools (Lichfield and Darin-Drabkin, 1980). The tools available were usually presented by the physical development planners as inadequate for the task in hand. The tradition of physical development planning instead tended to focus on broad policy objectives, and on the "ideal city" In their Utopian dreams, the most influential thinkers in the tradition harked back to the pre-Enlightenment days. They were largely disinterested in an analysis of the *processes* of physical development unfolding before them (see Hall, 1995 on Abercrombie). Instead, the idea of modernity entered into their discourse through ways of thinking about the shape and form of cities and the qualities of neighbourhood organisation. Cities were seen as an amalgam of economic, cultural and household activities. The challenge was to find a way of organising activities which was functionally efficient, convenient to all those involved, and aesthetically pleasing as well. The objective was to promote and accommodate modern life, as both a project in economic progress and an opportunity to provide good living conditions for urban populations (Healey and Shaw, 1994). The aim was to build a functionally rational city for economic and social life (Boyer, 1983). There were vigorous debates on how this could be done, which reflected different attitudes to the nature of urbanity, the proper relation between people and nature, and how far to welcome new building technologies and motorised transport. In these debates, the "British" tradition was often contrasted with the continental, the former celebrating a nostalgia for an urban form in a rural setting, and a life in balance with the natural order, as expressed in Howard's ideas for a social garden city; the latter emphasising the tradition of high density apartment life, as encapsulated in Le Corbusier's Ville Radieuse (Hall, 1988; Ward, 1994).

As a result of these influences, planning theory became in the mid-twentieth century a discussion about urban form. This generated some of the most powerful urban spatial organising ideas of the century (Keeble, 1952; Hall, 1988). The dominant idea in the British tradition has been the conception of the urban region as centripetal, focused on a city core, with a hierarchy of district and subcentres developed in an urban form which spreads out with radial routes, interlinked by concentric ringroads, and contained by a green belt to give a clearly defined urban edge. This image is particularly associated with the work of the great English planner of the first part of the twentieth century, Patrick Abercrombie (see Figure 12.1). These spatial

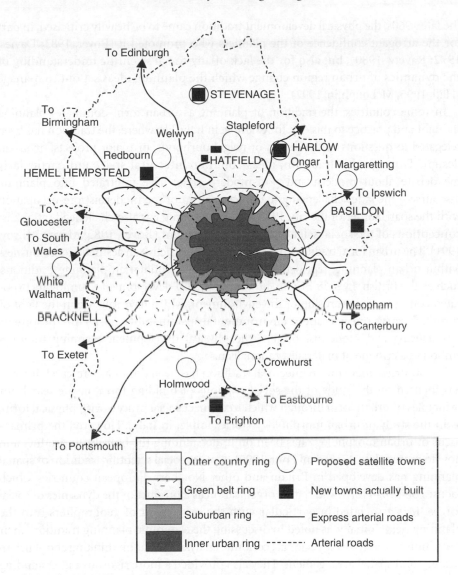

To Edinburgh

STEVENAGE

To
Birmingham

Welwyn

Stapleford

Redbourn

HARLOW

HEMEL HEMPSTEAD

HATFIELD

Ongar

Margaretting

To Ipswich

To
Gloucester

BASILDON

To South
Wales

White
Waltham

BRACKNELL

Meopham

To Canterbury

To Exeter

Crowhurst

Holmwood

To Eastbourne

To Brighton

To Portsmouth

□ Outer country ring	○ Proposed satellite towns
▨ Green belt ring	■ New towns actually built
▨ Suburban ring	—— Express arterial roads
▨ Inner urban ring	- - - - Arterial roads

Figure 12.1 Patrick Abercrombie's plan for Greater London.
Source: Wannop, 1995.

organising ideas not only provided a vocabulary of urban spatial forms. The spatial plans for particular cities have in many instances provided enduring and popular principles in local debates on the development of particular cities, for example Burnham's plan for Chicago, Abercrombie's for London and Stephenson's for Perth. Such plans have had effects by *framing* how key players in urban regions have thought about place and location (Rein and Schon, 1993; Faludi, 1996; Healey *et al.*, 1997). This is currently recognised by politicans and planners in many places in Europe, in efforts to recast spatial planning policies and practices [...]. But by the late 1960s, the physical development tradition came to be heavily criticised, in part for the arrogant confidence of the planners who promoted it (Boyer, 1983; Davies, 1972; Ravetz, 1980), but also for the lack of any social scientific understanding of the dynamics of urban region change which the planning ideas set out to manage (Hall, 1995, McLoughlin, 1992).

In some countries, the tradition of planning as urban form dominates planning thought and practice to this day, for example in Italy. Elsewhere, the tradition has been relegated to questions of the design of neighbourhoods, or major projects, or urban design. Through this tradition, ideas about architectural style, and particularly the debate about modern and post-modern style, have infiltrated into planning discourse – the latter challenging the functionalism of the modernist pre-occupation with the spatial order of the city. Post-modern thinking has also challenged rationalist conceptions of the social science of city management (Boyer, 1983; Moore Milroy, 1991). The urban form tradition has nevertheless kept active an aesthetic consciousness within urban planning, repeatedly sidelined in more utilitarian planning traditions, such as the British. Even in Britain, however, physical development planning incorporated concepts of stewardship of the environment, which have salience in the light of contemporary concerns about environmental sustainability [...] Thus, despite its rationalising and modernist origins, the physical development planning tradition embodies a critique of materialist rationalism.

In countries where the architectural tradition has been dominant, research interest has focused on the study of the social relations of building form, in the search for principles of urban form through which to connect social process with physical form, as in the study of urban morphology (for example, in Italy). However, the primary focus of urban morphology has been on understanding the built form product and how to manipulate it (Madani Pour, 1990). A more social scientific tradition of spatial planning has developed in Britain and other Northern European countries which focuses on urban form and spatial organisation as a product of the dynamics of social forces. It is associated in particular with the movement of geographers into the planning field. Initially, as noted in discussing the economic planning tradition, their contribution was to bring regional economic analysis to bear on thinking about urban strategy and spatial arrangement. They also provided a more rigorous understanding of the relationship between objectives of economic growth and quality of life, and how to manage the social processes though which these could be achieved. Such analysis had the effect of replacing discussions on idealised city form with an analysis of conditions and a prediction of *trends* which had to be accommodated, particularly in relation to accommodating the demands for better housing and for mass car ownership and use. Yet geographical analyses of the 1960s and 1970s neglected the dynamics of land and property development processes, nor was it common to recognise trends as expressions of "market processes". In more sophisticated analyses, the different dimensions of urban regions were integrated through the use of the urban systems models mentioned earlier, drawing on neo-classical forms of regional economic analysis and location theory. These were driven by the search for equilibrium relationships in urban region dynamics (Lee, 1973; Cowling and Steeley, 1973).

Such *trend planning* provided implicit support to the Keynesian demand management strategies being pursued at the level of the national economy. However, it became clear, as the stagnation of the 1970s set in, that trends could easily change. Many urban regions found their local economies undermined by the company restructuring occurring in the face of international competition (Massey and Meegan, 1982). This led to more interest being taken in how to create the conditions within which local economies could flourish rather than decline.

The increasing instability of many local economies also created problems for the process of land and property development, particularly where increasing reliance was put on private initiative, as governments began to cut back public expenditure programmes in response to their macroeconomic difficulties. This encouraged more attention to the mechanics of the property development process. Meanwhile, planners had been responding to both the increasing popular concern over environmental quality and the protection of nature, and to the realisation that welfare state policies had not eradicated poverty in the city, nor were they sensitive to the increasingly evident social diversity of urban life. By the 1980s, therefore, the physical development planning tradition was moving away from its utopian and aesthetic roots towards a form of policy analysis focused on the practical management of the dynamics of social, economic and environmental change in urban regions. [...] What makes this tradition more than just a social science of urban region change is its integration with the tradition of policy analysis.

Policy analysis and planning

The science of policy analysis is of American origin, and grew out of a search for ways of making public administration more efficient and effective. In Britain, central and increasingly local government were transformed from the late nineteenth century by the development of an administrative class at national level, with substantial capability, good pay and a commitment to a service ethic. Local government was increasingly professionalised, challenging local politics with formalised expertise (Laffin, 1986; Rhodes, 1988). On the European continent, administration was formally governed by legal rules, developed from the Napoleonic code, which gave authority to administrative action. Both systems helped to constrain the play of political power games and to limit the subversion of administrative systems to private and political party objectives, except in places such as Southern Italy, where the administrative rules were typically bypassed or surrounded with powerful alternative practices.

In the US, however, local administrations were much more open to the whims of local politics. Many US studies of local politics describe alliances within which local politicians collude with local development interests to promote speculative land profits. Logan and Molotch (1987) argued that US local governance was dominated by property development and investment interest – a *rentier* politics. Stone (1989) develops the analysis of such alliances further to examine more enduring relations between local government and business. In their discussion of local politics, Lauria and Whelan (1995) refer to such alliances as *urban regimes*. Or local government could be driven by simple political objectives of maximising electoral advantage. This was described in a famous case study of Chicago, where decisions on the location of low cost housing were made entirely with electoral advantage in mind (Meyerson and Banfield, 1955). This led to pressure to make public administration more efficient and less corrupt (Friedmann 1973). The ideal local government balanced the demands of a pluralistic polity through technical analysis and management. Policy analysis offered rational techniques for this purpose. The core of the approach developed in the 1960s focused on identifying objectives, and developing and implementing appropriate means to achieve them. Its principles drew on Herbert Simon's ideas of management by objectives, rather than by setting legal rules for administrators to follow. This approach offered flexibility to address the particularity of decision circumstances while constraining corruption by clear accountability of actions to policy criteria. The decision model was the foundation for what became known as the *rational planning process*.

The resultant debates on planning as a policy process have been enormously influential, structuring the American planning tradition, and providing a point of reference for any planning culture open to American influence. They built on the pioneering experience in regional economic development of the Tennessee Valley Authority in the 1930s, and drew on ideas about efficient business management. Models for public planning and management were developed, based on the rational relation of means to ends (Friedmann, 1973, 1987). By "rational" in this context was meant both a form of deductive logic, and the use of instrumental reason as a form of argument, drawing upon scientific analysis. As Davidoff and Reiner (1962) stress in their articulation of the approach as a "choice theory of planning", a strict separation of fact from value was to be maintained. Values were seen as originating within the political process, and were provided by the "clients" of the technicians of the policy process. Policy analysis work was seen to take place in a defined "action space", cut out from the political and institutional context in which goals were articulated (Faludi, 1973). The planner as policy analyst was a specialist in helping clients articulate their goals, and translating these into alternative strategies to maximise, or at least "satisfice", the achievement of these goals, through careful analysis and systematic evaluation.

This approach is discussed in more detail in Chapter 8 [original text]. In the US in particular, it stimulated an explosion of work on the "science" of decision-making, with much discussion on the forms the rational planning process could take and on the kinds of urban systems models which were needed to underpin analyses of the consequences of alternative actions. The model itself was challenged by those who argued that it was idealistic, with unrealistic expectations of the political willingness to stick to rational planning processes, and of the conceptual and empirical knowledge capacity to understand situations sufficiently to be able to identify and evaluate all possible alternatives. The most famous challenge was that by Charles Lindblom, who argued for an alternative approach of "disjointed incrementalism" – approaching problems in small steps rather than big steps towards grand goals (Braybrook and Lindblom, 1963). Later he argued for a more negotiative approach, a form of "partisan mutual adjustment" (Lindblom, 1965). Lindblom's ideas in this respect are an innovative precursor of the current discussion of interactive approaches to developing planning strategies.

Lindblom's arguments still propose a planning process dominated by the techniques of instrumental rationality (Sager, 1994). His approach looked rather like a sort of "market adjustment" within the public sector, produced by a form of technical analysis which drew on microeconomics rather than management theory. Other American contributions to the debate on policy processes in the later 1960s raised more fundamental questions. These focused on questions of value. In the early post-war period, there was a powerful "mood" in political debate that issues of value were no longer controversial. The West had chosen the capitalist path to peace and prosperity. Citizens were assumed to share broadly common interests, while arguing over the details of pluralistic interest conflicts. The planner or policy analyst was thus merely a technician of means committed to the values of scientifically-based and rationally-deduced policy choices, but neutral as regards ends. Davidoff and Reiner, writing in 1962, implied that this was indeed the case. But by the end of the 1960s, and linked to the rediscovery of poverty in American cities at this time, Paul Davidoff himself had come to a different view. In a famous paper, "Advocacy and pluralism in planning" (Davidoff, 1965), he argued that it was impossible for the planner to be entirely value-free as regards ends, since planners as people had values. Implicitly, he acknowledged that these values divided people. In particular, the interests of poorer people in inner-city neighbourhoods were not the same as those of local business interests. He sought a way of planning which opened up the value diversity among the plurality of interests within a political community. In this context, he argued that planners should not stay value-neutral, given that they too had sub-stantive values, values about ends. They should instead become value-conscious, declare their values and make themselves available to clients who wished to pursue such values. This approach had a powerful influence on American planning practice and thought in the early 1970s. The example from Boston quoted in Chapter 2 [original text] is taken from an example of advocacy planning inspired by Paul Davidoff.

Around the same time, the sociologist-planner Herbert Gans was arguing that planners had a moral responsibility to argue in favour of improving conditions for the disadvantaged. He argued, as Davidoff and Reiner had done, that planners needed to be aware of a double client, an employer, or "customer" for the planner's services, and, more broadly, the citizens affected by the "direct" client's proposals (Gans, 1969). Both Gans and Davidoff and Reiner were responding to the increasing political and popular interest in local environmental questions, and to the resultant pressure for more active citizen involvement in planning strategies and their implementation. In both the US and Britain, this led to ideas about the procedures for citizen partici-pation in the planning process. This in turn generated critiques which challenged the pluralistic conception of local politics, presenting it instead as a power game, in which elites held on to power which citizens struggled to gain access to. This is

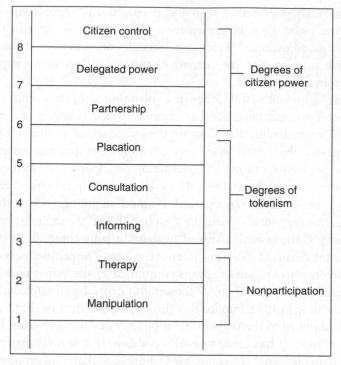

Figure 12.2 Arnstein's ladder of citizen participation.
Source: Arnstein, 1969, p. 216.

encapsulated in Sherry Arnstein's *Ladder of Citizen Participation* (1969), with its metaphoric reference to the 1968 student protests in France [Figure 12.2].

Both Davidoff and Gans assumed a pluralistic polity as idealised in dominant US political thinking at the time. They also continued to advocate the techniques of rational scientific analysis. Their objective was to shift the approach to fit the pluralistic context better. In seeking to fit the planning model to the "action space" of the institutional context, they thus shifted away from earlier conceptions of the transformative power of planning. For the urban designer planners, and for the early advocates of the rational planning process, planning approaches were in the vanguard of the transformation of cities, and the transformation of the management of local governance. Davidoff and Gans, in contrast, saw planning as a tool which citizens could use in extracting a more democratic pluralist polity from the clutches of dominant elites.

During the 1970s in the US and in Western Europe, the discussion of appropriate planning process models moved on from this position to question both the model of a pluralistic polity itself and the value of techniques based on scientific knowledge and means-oriented or "instrumental" rationality. The first was most strongly developed in Europe, and drew on Marxist-inspired theories to analyse the structural bases for the unequal distribution of power (Castells, 1977). The second challenge reached planning from several directions and reflected a much broader questioning of the role of science and instrumental reason in Western thought generally. An early paper by Rittel and Webber (1973) argued for a more interactive and enabling approach to planning since facts and values were intertwined in people's consciousness. Others, interested in how policies influenced subsequent events, in how they were "implemented", showed that policies were continually being reinterpreted by those involved in carrying them forward (Pressman and Wildavsky, 1984). British analysis argued that this negotiation and interpretation was an inherent dimension of policy work as practised. As a result, policies – that is goals, values and direction – were as likely to be articulated through the ongoing flow of events, decision and actions, as in formal exercises in policy-making (Barrett and Fudge, 1981). The former were described as a "bottom-up" view of how policies were made, to be contrasted with "top-down" formal exercises. This work explicitly emphasised the interactive nature of "doing planning work", and looked towards social exchange theory for inspiration. [...]

The Interpretive, Communicative Turn in Planning Theory

All these traditions, as they have evolved, provide pointers to the development of institutionalist analysis and communicative approaches. The economic planning tradition, as it has evolved in both national economic management and local economic development, incorporates an increasing appreciation of the institutional preconditions for economic health. The physical development planning tradition has moved both to recognise the social processes underpinning spatial organisation and urban form, and the range and complexity of the demands for local environmental management generated by interconnecting social, economic and biospheric processes. The policy analysis tradition is seeking both to escape from its predominant emphasis on instrumental reason and scientific knowledge and to incorporate greater understanding of how people come to have the ways of thinking and ways of valuing that they do, and how policy development and policy implementation processes can be made more interactive. But these directions were not unchallenged. A new reassertion of market liberal notions of governance was also emerging in parallel with these. The current period is above all one of tension between these two rapidly developing approaches in public policy.

Neo-liberal theorisation involves a reassertion of instrumental rationality, but in a narrow form grounded in microeconomics. The neo-liberal turn in public policy in Britain was promoted by the growing influence of economists in the public policy arena. This in effect abandoned the idea of policy formulation as a technical task, and concentrated instead on policy evaluation, both before policies were put into place, and in assessing their performance over time. This has generated a body of technique and evaluation criteria now used extensively by government agencies, particularly where neo-liberal policy interests predominate. It deliberately eschews a co-ordinative role with respect to public policy, leaving any necessary co-ordination to voluntaristic action, through the dynamics of market processes and community self-help. These ideas provide a foil against which the communicative approach developed in this book [the original book] is developed.

The second direction shifts the conceptual ground firmly into a phenomenological interpretation of the relationship of knowledge to action. It builds on the realisation that knowledge and value do not merely have objective existence in the external world, to be "discovered" by scientific inquiry. They are, rather, actively constituted through social, interactive processes (Berger and Luckman, 1967; Latour, 1987; Shotter, 1993). Public policy, and hence planning, are thus social processes through which ways of thinking, ways of valuing and ways of acting are actively constructed by participants.

This recognition is part of a broad wave of reflection on identity (ways of being – ontology) and the bases of knowledge (ways of knowing – epistemology) which is influencing western thought in general these days. This intellectual wave has been building up in the planning theory field since the 1970s. It is now labelled argumentative, communicative or interpretive planning theory. It has many different strands, but the key emphases are as follows:

- a recognition that all forms of knowledge are socially constructed; and that the knowledge of science and the techniques of experts are not as different from "practical reasoning" as the instrumental rationalists had claimed;
- a recognition that the development and communication of knowledge and reasoning take many forms, from rational systematic analysis, to storytelling, and expressive statements, in words, pictures or sound;
- a recognition, as a result, of the social context within which individuals form interests; individuals thus do not arrive at their "preferences" independently, but learn about their views in social contexts and through interaction;
- a recognition that, in contemporary life, people have diverse interests and expectations, and that relations of power have the potential to oppress and dominate not merely through the distribution of material resources, but through the finegrain of taken-for-granted assumptions and practices;
- a realisation that public policies which are concerned with managing co-existence in shared spaces which seek to be efficient, effective and accountable to all those with a "stake" in a place need to draw upon, and spread ownership of, the above range of knowledge and reasoning;
- a realisation that this leads away from competitive interest bargaining towards collaborative consensus-building and that, through such consensus-building practices, organising ideas can be developed and shared which have the capacity to endure, to co-ordinate actions by different agents, and to transform ways of organising and ways of knowing in significant ways, in other words, to build cultures;
- a realisation that, in this way, planning work is both embedded in its context of social relations through its day to day practices, and has a capacity to challenge and change these relations through the approach to these practices; context and practice are not therefore separated but socially constituted together.

This summary draws upon ideas developed by a number of contemporary planning theorists, notably Bengt Flyvberg, John Forester, John Friedmann, Charlie Hoch, Judy Innes, and Tore Sager. However, the planning theorists developing a communicative approach have given little attention in their work to the changing understanding of urban region dynamics evolving in regional economic analysis, urban geography and urban sociology (Lauria and Whelan, 1995). This too emphasises the active social processes through which everyday life and economic activity are accomplished. Intellectually, there are close links between the two emerging bodies of thought, grounded in the recognition of the social construction of meaning and the social embeddedness of ways of thinking and acting. A major objective of this book is to bring these two strands together and thus overcome the persistent tendency in planning thought and practice to separate the understanding of urban and regional change from the processes of governance through which political communities can collectively address their common dilemmas about what is happening to their neighbourhoods. [...]

References

Abercrombie, P. (1944) *Town and Country Planning* (Oxford: Oxford University Press (orig. publ. 1933)).

Adams, D. (1994) *Urban Planning and the Development Process* (London: UCL Press).

Amin, A. (1994) "Post Fordism: models, fantasies and phantoms of transition" in idem, *Post-Fordism: A Reader* (Oxford: Blackwell), pp. 1–40.

Arnstein, S. (1969) "The ladder of citizen participation", *Journal of the Institute of American Planners*, Vol. 35(4), pp. 216–24.

Ball, M. (1983) *Housing Policy and Economic Power* (London: Methuen).

Barrett, S. and Fudge, C. (1981) "Examining the policy–action relationship" in idem. *Policy and Action* (London: Methuen) pp. 3–32.

Beatley, T. (1994) *Ethical Land Use* (Baltimore: Johns Hopkins University Press).

Beevers, R. (1988). *The Garden City Utopia A Critical Biography of Ebenezer Howard* (London: Macmillan).

Berger, P. and Luckman, T. (1967) *The Social Construction of Reality* (Harmondsworth: Penguin).

Bicanic, R. (1967) *Problems of Planning: East and West* (The Hague: Mouton Press).

Boyer, G. (1983) *Dreaming the Rational City* (Boston, MA: MIT Press).

Boyer, R. (1991) "The eighties: the search for alternatives to Fordism", in B. Jessop, H. Kastendiek, K. Nielsen and I.K. Petersen (eds.), *The Politics of Flexibility* (Aldershot, Hants: Edward Elgar).

Braybrooke, D. and Lindblom, C.E. (1963) *A Strategy for Decision* (New York: Free Press).

Castells, M. (1977) *The Urban Question* (London: Edward Arnold).

Chadwick, G. (1971) *A Systems View of Planning* (Oxford: Pergamon).

Chapin, F.S. (1965) *Urban Land Use Planning* (Urbana: University of Illinois Press).

Cowling, T. and Steeley, G. (1973) *Sub-Regional Planning Studies: An Evaluation* (Oxford: Pergamon).

Davidoff, P. (1965) "Advocacy and pluralism in planning", *Journal of the American Institute of Planning*, Vol. 31 (Nov), pp. 331–8.

Davidoff, P. and Reiner, T. (1962) "A choice theory of planning", *Journal of the American Institute of Planners*, Vol. 28 (May), pp. 103–15.

Davies, J.G. (1972) *The Evangelistic Bureaucral* (London: Tavistock Press).

Evans, A. (1985) *Urban Economics: An Introduction* (Oxford: Blackwell).

Faludi, A. (1973) *Planning Theory* (Oxford: Pergamon).

Faludi, A. (1996) "Framing with images", *Environment and Planning B: Planning and Design*. Vol. 23, pp. 93–108.

Friedmann, J. (1973) *Retracking America* (New York: Anchor Press).

Friedmann, J. (1987) *Planning in the Public Domain* (New Jersey: Princeton University Press).

Gamble, A. (1988) *The Free Economy and the Strong State* (London: Macmillan).

Gans, H. (1969) "Planning for people, not buildings", *Environment and Planning A*, Vol. 1, pp. 33–46.

Giddens, A. (1987) *Social Theory and Modern Sociology* (Cambridge: Polity Press).

Goodin, R. (1992) *Green Political Theory* (Cambridge: Polity Press).

Hall, P. (1988) *Cities of Tomorrow* (Oxford: Blackwell).

Hall, P. (1995) "Bringing Abercrombic back from the shades", *Town Planning Review*, Vol. 66(3), pp. 227–42.

Hall, S. and Gieben, B. (1992) *Formations of Modernity* (Milton Keynes: Open University Press).

Harrison, A. (1977) *The Economics of Land Use Planning* (London: Croom Helm).

Harvey, J. (1987) *Urban Land Economics* (London: Macmillan).

Harvey, D. (1982) *The Limits of Capital* (Oxford: Blackwell).

Harvey, D. (1989) "From managerialism to entrepreneurialism: the formation of urban governance in late capitalism", *Geografisker Annaler*, Vol. 71B, pp. 3–17.

Healey, P. and Barrett, S. (eds) (1985) *Land Policy: Problems and Alternatives* (Aldershot, Hants: Gower).

Healey, P., Khakee, A., Motte, A. and Needham, B. (1997) *Making Strategic Spatial Plans: Innovation in Europe* (London: UCL Press).

Healey, P. and Shaw, T. (1994) "Changing meanings of 'environment' in the British planning system". *Transactions of the Institute of British Geographers*. Vol. 19(4), pp. 425–38.

Keeble, L. (1952) *Principles and Practice of Town and Country Planning* (London: Estates Gazette).

Kitching G. (1988) *Karl Marx and the Philosophy of Praxis* (London: Routledge).

Laffin, M. (1986) *Professionalization and Policy: The Role of the Professions in Central-Local Relationships* (Aldershot, Hants: Gower).

Latour, B. (1987) *Science in Action* (Cambridge, MA: Harvard University Press).

Lauria, M. and Whelan, R. (1995) "Planning theory and political economy: the need for reintegration", *Planning Theory*, Vol. 14, pp. 8–33.

Lee, D. (1973) "Requiem for large-scale models", *Journal of the American Planning Association*, Vol. 39, pp. 153–79.

Lichfield, N. and Darin-Drabkin, H. (1980) *Land Policy and Urban Growth* (London: George Allen & Unwin).

Lindblom, C.E. (1965) *The Intelligence of Democracy* (New York: Free Press).

Logan, J.R. and Molotch, H. (1987) *Urban Fortunes: The Political Economy of Place* (Berkeley, CA: University of California Press).

Madani Pour, A. (1990) "A study of urban form", unpublished PhD thesis. University of Newcastle.

Mannheim, K. (1940) *Man and Society in an Age of Reason: Studies in Modern Social Structure* (London: K. Paul. Trench, Trubner).

Massey, D. and Meegan, R. (1982) *The Anatomy of Job Loss* (London: Methuen).

McLoughlin, B. (1969) *Urban and Regional Planning: A Systems Approach* (London: Faber).

McLoughlin, B. (1992) *Shaping Melbourne's Future? Town Planning, the State and Civic Society* (Cambridge: Cambridge University Press).

Meyerson, M. and Banfield, E. (1955) *Politics, Planning and the Public Interest* (New York: Free Press).

Moore Milroy, B. (1991) "Into postmodern weightlessness", *Journal of Planning Education and Research*, Vol. 10(3), pp. 181–7.

Mumford, L. (1961) *The City in History* (Harmondsworth: Penguin).

Pressman, J. and Wildavsky, A. (1984) *Implementation*, 3rd edn. (Berkeley, California: University of California Press).

Ravetz, A. (1980) *Remaking Cities* (London: Croom Helm).

Rein, M. and Schon, D. (1993) "Reframing policy discourse", in F. Fischer and J. Forester (eds). *The Argumentative Turn in Policy Analysis and Planning* (London: UCL Press).

Rhodes, R. (1988) *Beyond Westminster and Whitehall: The Sub-central Governments of Britain* (London: Unwin Hyman).

Rittel, H. and Webber, M. (1973) "Dilemmas in a general theory of planning", *Policy Sciences*. Vol. 4, pp. 155–69.

Sager, T. (1994) *Communicative Planning Theory* (Aldershot, Hants: Avebury).

Scott, A.J. and Roweis, S.T. (1977) "Urban planning in theory and practice", *Environment and Planning A*, Vol. 9, pp. 1097–119.

Sennet, R. (1991) *The Conscience of the Eye: The Design and Social Life of Cities* (London: Faber).

Shotter, J. (1993) *Conversational Realities: Constructing Life through Language* (London: Sage).

Stone, C. (1989) *Regime Politics: Governing Atlanta 1946–1988* (Kansas: University of Kansas Press).

Sutcliffe, A. (1981) *Towards the Planned City* (Oxford: Blackwell).

Thompson, G., Frances, J., Levacic, R. and Mitchell, J. (1991) *Markets, Hierarchies and Networks* (Milton Keynes: Open University Press).

Thornley, A. (1991) *Urban Planning under Thatcherism* (London: Routledge).

Vickers, J. (1991) "New directions for industrial policy in the area of regulatory reform", in G. Thompson, J. Francis, R. Levacic and J. Mitchell (eds). *Markets, Hierarchies and Networks* (London: Sage) pp. 163–70.

Wannop, U. (1995) *The Regional Imperative* (Cambridge: Cambridge University Press).

Ward, S. (1994) *Planning and Urban Change* (London: Paul Chapman).

Young, I.M. (1990) *Justice and the Politics of Difference* (Princeton: Princeton University Press).

Patsy Healey, "Traditions of Planning Thought," *Collaborative Planning: Shaping Places in Fragmented Societies*. 2nd edition, 2006, chapter 1, pp. 7–30, Palgrave Macmillan.

IV

Planning in Action

Successes, Failures, and Strategies

Introduction

The three essays presented in this Part illustrate the opportunities and constraints to planners in the field, drawing upon cases in the United States, Canada, the United Kingdom, and continental Europe. The three cases develop a more nuanced and varied picture of planning outcomes. A common theme is the frequent deviation of planning practice from the logic of prevailing models, such as the "rational planning model" or the "public–private partnership." These cases remind us that planning dynamics are embedded in local contexts, that institutional arrangements and interests are complex and fluid, and that the deeper truths lie in the hard-fought details of rigorous case studies (a point Bent Flyvbjerg reiterates in this Part). As Oscar Wilde observed, "The truth is rarely pure and never simple."

The first case concerns a megaproject – part of a class of large-scale developments that promise transformative, critical mass benefits but also carry daunting costs and side effects. The argument for public–private partnerships in large-scale urban development is appealing: the public sector brings government authority, transparency and accountability to the voters, while the private sector brings entrepreneurship, innovation, and competitive cost savings. Whether such a partnership actually engenders a win-win outcome cannot be answered a priori based on ideological logic. Instead, a rigorously detailed case study investigation is required. In "Implications of Private-Public Partnerships on the Development of Urban Public Transit Infrastructure," Matti Siemiatycki examines such a partnership to build a rapid-rail project in Vancouver, British Colombia. The outcome falls far short of the ideal: the promised cost reductions due to private market pressures did not materialize, while the public sector still ended up with much of the financial risk and burden. The design was not necessarily more innovative because it was privately

Readings in Planning Theory, Third Edition. Edited by Susan S. Fainstein and Scott Campbell.
Editorial material and organization © 2012 Blackwell Publishing Ltd.
Published 2012 by Blackwell Publishing Ltd.

led. Finally, pressures to maintain confidentiality undermined the expectations for public transparency and accountability.

Siemiatycki demonstrates the power of an in-depth case study to get at the rich and complex institutional details of public–private partnerships and to show why the process fell short of expectations. By parsing and subdividing the case into fine-grained components of project costs, stakeholder interests, risk, priorities and funding streams, Siemiatycki is able to offer a rigorously differentiated evaluation of the outcomes. In the end we are left with a conundrum: how to retain public accountability and citizen deliberation in situations where confidentiality is mandated by private sector involvement in a competitive market process? The stakes are especially high with the contemporary (re)emergence of the infrastructural megaproject involving intricate contracting relationships. Such projects are redrawing the boundaries between public and private sectors, and more specifically, shifting the standard comparative advantages of the public vs. private actors. Planners should no longer assume – if they ever did – that public–private collaborations on major projects are inherently better for the public interest.

If the first case examined the efforts to privatize once-public development, the next case looks at the reverse: efforts to bring economic and place-making activity under community control. There is a long and uneven American tradition of establishing alternative community structures. James DeFilippis, in "Collective Ownership and Community Control and Development: The Long View," examines various efforts at local autonomy from the nineteenth century through the 1960s and beyond. His coverage is wide-ranging, from antebellum black communes and Robert Owen-inspired utopian socialist communities to 1960s Model Cities and Black Power efforts. His article provides both a useful history of these efforts and a series of distinctions leading to a typology of these movements (e.g., secular vs. religious; engaging or bypassing the market economy; etc.). DeFilippis also provides a cautionary tale for aspiring communitarians of today: to blithely create a structure of local/collective control without knowing the shortcomings of past efforts is both naïve and risks failure.

He concludes with a reflection on the contemporary efforts since the 1960s, including the rise of the community development corporation (CDC). DeFilippis is troubled by the tilt towards market-oriented, non-confrontational approaches that ignore the problem of entrenched power relations in communities – a trend he labels "neoliberal communitarianism." This recent evolution of the field may have arisen as a savvy, entrepreneurial adaptation in an era where "cooperation not confrontation" is the strategic maxim. For DeFilippis, this depoliticization of community development is insufficient to either achieve greater equity or to give low-income people adequate control over their lives.

We conclude this part with an essay on the practice of case study planning research itself. Bent Flyvbjerg, in "Bringing Power to Planning Research: One Researcher's Praxis Story," recounts his scholarly investigations to make two interrelated arguments on what and how planners should research. Flyvbjerg laments that planning scholars spend too much time normatively speculating about ideal cities and community participatory processes, and too little time talking about what actually happens in city planning and politics. In particular, planners too often step awkwardly around the issue of power. Emblematic of this predisposition is planning theory's frequent reading of Habermas (and his ideal speech situation) and the neglect of Nietzsche, Machiavelli and especially Foucault (and his graphic historical studies of human suffering, injustice and institutionalized cruelty). Flyvbjerg builds his argument upon his past research on planning's collision with political power – an asymmetrical encounter in which power usually trumps rationality (as in his book *Rationality and Power*, a case study of a transportation planning controversy in Aalborg, Denmark). Too often planning theorists embrace the idea of rational order and inclusive public participation to neutralize (or bypass) the messy political stuff, writing for an audience of civil servants rather than political operators. As a result, "implementation" has been frustrating (and puzzling) for so many planning theorists, since turning rationality into action requires political power. Technical information rarely carries its own, intrinsic weight in the planning process; instead, political interests manipulate, spin, suppress or elevate aspects of information for their own purposes.

Planners should therefore study what is actually happening in cities, an approach he terms "phronetic planning research." Borrowing a concept from Aristotle, Flyvbjerg views phronesis as not merely scientific knowledge, but instead practical knowledge linked to political judgment, decision-making, and action. The challenge for planners is to analyze the relationship between rationality and power in the context of real democracies. The deeper truth lies in the concrete details of specific case studies, rather than in abstract summaries. Flyvbjerg concludes with specific recommendations to make planning research more strategically relevant to both directly face these power relationships and avoid wasteful, undemocratic planning.

13

Implications of Private–Public Partnerships on the Development of Urban Public Transit Infrastructure
The Case of Vancouver, Canada

Matti Siemiatycki

Across Canada and around the world, planning processes promoting competition and free-market accountability have become increasingly popular in the delivery of public infrastructure. Most recently, the design-build-finance-operate (DBFO) style of private–public partnership has become the delivery mechanism of choice for inserting competition and free-market accountability into project planning, gaining popularity with both the right and the left of center governments and international development agencies such as the World Bank and the United Nations.

In theory, the DBFO model of private–public partnership seeks to balance the advantage of government control of the strategic allocation of scarce resources in the protection of the broad public interest, with the benefit of infusing competitive forces into the delivery of public service to increase efficiency. Proponents contend that a collaborative approach to project planning, which encourages cooperation between different levels of government and the private sector, can create win-win situations that marry community mobilization and local economic development (Miraftab 2004). In the field of urban transportation, the increasing prevalence of private–public partnerships can be seen in large part as an attempt to redress issues of political interference, weak procedural accountability, escalating construction costs, and performance shortfalls that became typical during the extended period that projects were designed, financed, and operated predominantly by the public sector (Pickrell 1992; Flyvbjerg, Bruzelius, and Rothengatter 2003). At the same time, such an approach also can be seen as an attempt by cash-strapped governments to take advantage of private-sector access to capital to finance projects, deliver innovation, and manage risk without the public sector's relinquishing control of strategic objectives as occurred under outright privatization and deregulation.

Readings in Planning Theory, Third Edition. Edited by Susan S. Fainstein and Scott Campbell.
Editorial material and organization © 2012 Blackwell Publishing Ltd.
Published 2012 by Blackwell Publishing Ltd.

And yet, to date, little academic research has been conducted in Canada to assess the implications of undertaking transportation-infrastructure delivery using a collaborative DBFO partnership approach. This is partly because DBFO private–public partnerships are a relatively new phenomenon in the Canadian transportation-planning landscape. It is also because, as Miraftab (2004) suggests, studies of private–public partnerships generally have focused on typological and logistical issues such as contract design and risk transfer while minimizing dynamics of power relations and distributional implications.

As such, despite the favorable claims of private–public-partnership supporters and the theoretical benefits proposed by prominent academics, it remains an open question whether the DBFO type of private–public partnership provides an effective tool for governments to raise necessary capital and deliver large infrastructure projects. Moreover, in practice, does the DBFO private–public-partnership approach to project delivery actually contribute to redressing issues of political influence, interest-group lobbying, poor transparency, and organizational memory that were identified by Flyvbjerg (2003), Wachs (1988), and Altshuler and Luberoff (2003) as embedded features of earlier transportation-megaproject planning processes?

To be clear, when situated within the evolving history of transportation infrastructure-delivery models, the DBFO style of private–public partnership may reveal procedural short-comings that are similar to those observed when projects are delivered using other approaches. This can lead to questions about whether the observed challenges pervade the type of model used to procure a project and are, in fact, more deeply rooted in the political, financial, governance, symbolic, and power relations that drive planning decisions. These are certainly valid concerns, and researchers for more than two decades have explored the diverse forces that support the decision to invest in a specific infrastructure project at a specific moment of strategic choice (Hall 1982; Mackett and Edwards 1998; Altshuler and Luberoff 2003; Olds 2001; Richmond 2005; Siemiatycki 2005b). However, precisely because the DBFO style of private–public partnership is the contemporary international state-of-the-art for planning and delivering transportation-infrastructure megaprojects, it seems relevant to examine this method of project delivery in isolation and explore whether the theoretical benefits are matched by the practical experience.

In exploring the questions raised about the DBFO model of project delivery, this article will proceed in two parts. The first section will review the historical evolution in public-project financing, describe the characteristics of a DBFO private–public partnership, and then identify the strengths and weaknesses of this particular project-delivery method.

The second section presents the case of the Richmond-Airport-Vancouver (RAV) urban rail project in Vancouver, British Columbia, the largest DBFO private–public partnership for an urban public-transit project ever implemented in Canada and the first of many that are currently on the drawing board (Campbell 2004). An examination of the RAV project-planning process through in-depth interviews with key participants, observations of public meetings, analysis of planning documents, and a review of media coverage of the project provides an opportunity to explore one example of the mechanistic and equity issues that underpin the application of private–public partnerships in the transit sector.

For the purpose of brevity, I will not present the case study in all its detail but instead will highlight some of the wider implications of planning through a private–public-partnership approach. Specifically, I will show that the planning of the RAV line through a DBFO private–public partnership largely has failed to achieve the desired benefits of eliminating cost escalations during the planning process, delivering greater technological innovation, or improving procedural accountability. While the results of the Vancouver experience are not statistically significant or universally generalizable to other contexts or other types of private–public partnerships, they may prove valuable in raising questions that should be asked of other projects being delivered through the DBFO private–public-partnership method.

Theory of the DBFO Private–Public Partnership

According to the United States Department of Transportation (2005), there are a variety of ways that the private and public sectors can partner to deliver infrastructure projects, which can be classified on a continuum ranging from greater public responsibility to greater private responsibility (Figure 13.1).

Traditionally, in developed countries, public-sector infrastructure projects have been delivered through a variant of the design-bid-build approach, in which the responsible public agency designed a scheme to address an identified problem, then undertook a bidding process for a private-sector concessionaire to build the system using the technology as specified by the public-sector designers, and finally, operated the system using public-sector employees once the project was constructed. Under this model of project delivery, government raised the finances to pay for the investment through debt or bond issues and repaid the capital project costs through user fees and tax revenue.

In the 1980s and early 1990s, with a mandate to cut publicsector expenditures and harness the innovative capacity of individuals working under competitive conditions, governments across the developed world encouraged the private sector to take a larger role in the financing and delivery of public-sector infrastructure. Private-sector entrepreneurs were charged with selecting the types of projects that would meet the

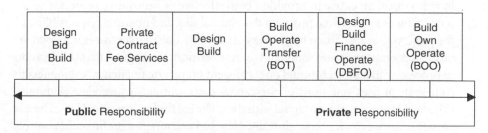

Figure 13.1 Typology of private–public partnerships.
Source: United States Department of Transportation 2005.

public interest best based on the potential to generate profits, and then they designed, financed, owned, and operated the new infrastructure. Revenue was raised through the charging of user fees, and public subsidies sometimes were offered for services such as public transit that were rarely profitable on their own.

Beginning in the early 1990s, led by initiatives in Britain, the DBFO style of private–public partnership has risen to prominence as the contemporary state-of-the-art mechanism for delivering large public-sector infrastructure projects. It has been used in transportation projects in many countries, including the United States, Australia, Canada, Britain, Ireland, Holland, and Denmark.

The DBFO private–public partnership is intended to blend the innovative capacity of private enterprises working in competitive environments with the role of government in setting specifications and supervising to ensure that performance standards are met. In the DBFO model of project delivery, the responsible public-sector agency designs a set of benefits that a project should deliver to meet a defined objective and then invites private-sector concessionaires to design a technological solution that best meets the criteria at the lowest cost. The private-sector concessionaire also is invited to finance the capital costs of the project partially or entirely, an expenditure that is repaid along with a profit by the government through user fees and subsidies where necessary durivng the course of an operating period that usually ranges from thirty to fifty years. Once the contractual period of operation is completed, the public-sector agency then either can retender or operate the system using public-sector employees (Debande 2002).

According to Flyvbjerg, Bruzelius, and Rothengatter (2003), the DBFO style of private–public partnership is seen to provide benefits in three main ways:

1. It increases the rationality of the projects that are selected for development, particularly with respect to technical specifications. This can be achieved through the use of performance specifications, whereby the government planning organization establishes a set of policy objectives to meet the public interest and then designs a tendering process so that private firms can compete to provide the best technical alternative to achieve the objectives at the lowest cost. Technological innovation is expected to arise out of the competition between different firms to best achieve the performance specifications. This is in contrast to the public-sector planner, who may have expertise in only one technology and also may have no direct incentive to provide a cost-effective or innovative project.
2. It contributes to improved procedural accountability and financial responsibility of the projects that are chosen for delivery. Again, infusing market forces into a previously noncompetitive environment is seen as critical. It is argued that the decision to proceed with a project should be contingent on private financiers' willingness to contribute at least one-third of the capital costs without a sovereign guarantee. Private contributors of risk capital with the potential for large personal losses have a greater incentive to vet proposals realistically and encourage tight financial controls during the project-development and operation phases, which could lead to more accurate appraisals and realistic decisions about whether to proceed with a given project. It also is suggested that greater private involvement could be complementary to

increased transparency and legitimate public participation, which are seen to be a central test of accountability in public-sector investments.

3. It transfers risk to the partner best able to manage it. Because of the considerable cost overruns and use variability that have characterized transportation-infrastructure megaprojects, the transfer of risk drives the DBFO private–public-partnership process. By significantly involving the private sector in the planning, financing, and operation of an infrastructure project, there is the potential to distribute different types of project risk such as construction-cost overruns and delays, interest-rate fluctuations, system performance, and patronage risk to the party that has the greatest ability and incentive to manage them. For transit projects, risk generally is divided between those related to the supply of the infrastructure and those related to demand. Transferring risk between the public and private sector is accompanied by a cost premium. This process of transferring risk in a DBFO private–public partnership differs from the more conventional public-sector project-delivery model, in which the responsible government agency and taxpayers are responsible for effectively all different types of risk.[1]

Moving from theory to practice, Table 13.1 presents a summary of the broader literature on the implications of private–public partnerships, revealing a wide

Table 13.1 Potential benefits and costs of transportation-infrastructure delivery through design-build-finance-operate (DBFO) private–public partnerships

Assertion	Source
Benefits of Private–Public Partnerships	
Evidence from Britain has shown that projects delivered using private–public partnerships have reduced development cost overruns and improved the punctuality of project completion.	HM Treasury (2003)
Financing infrastructure through private-sector capital lowers the financial burden and potential risk on the general taxpayer.	Savas (2000)
Strict contracting with the private sector to plan and develop a project can help control the urge of government officials to add expensive scope changes during the development phase that contribute to project-cost escalations following the final cost agreements.	Walker and Smith (1995); Debande (2002)
Costs of Private–Public Partnerships	
Divergent goals, methods, and objectives of different stakeholders involved in collaborative planning processes potentially can undermine the potential for participants to proceed beyond narrow self-interest.	Blumenberg (2002)
Private–public partnerships can increase the cost, complexity, and time of planning an infrastructure megaproject.	Walker and Smith (1995)
Evidence from an accounting study of 21 transportation projects delivered through private–public partnerships in the United Kingdom found serious breaches of accountability, particularly the ability of current accounting methods to provide adequate transparency of public-resource allocation.	Edwards et al. (2004)

range of potential benefits and costs to delivering infrastructure megaprojects using such an approach.

Guided by promoters in the public and private sectors as well as the academy, the narrative of collaboration is now so pervasive that private–public partnerships have become institutionalized as the project-delivery mechanism of choice within the political structures of many countries, which has been reinforced by the formation of government bureaus specifically charged with promoting and structuring partnership deals. In Canada, where both the federal and the provincial governments have formed special-purpose private–public-partnership offices, there is now considerable inertia to proceed with new infrastructure projects using the partnership approach (Siemiatycki 2005a). Examining how effective the DBFO type of private–public partnership is at delivering on the theoretical benefits will be the topic of the following section.

The DBFO Private–Public Partnership in Practice: The Case of the Richmond-Airport-Vancouver Line

This section presents the case of a DBFO style of private–public partnership used to develop a new urban rail line in Vancouver, a city region of some 2.3 million people on the west coast of Canada. The case study will begin by examining how the specifications of the RAV project were shaped and then proceed to explore the processes through which the project was approved.

Defining the project specifications: partnerships and priority setting

After years of underinvestment in urban transit infrastructure that has left a need for an estimated $7.4 billion in project spending nationally between 2004 and 2008, Canadian cities have begun to undertake a renewed period of public-transit development (Canadian Urban Transit Association 2003). And yet, as the scale and cost of transit-infrastructure projects has escalated (Flyvbjerg, Bruzelius, and Rothengatter 2003), it has become increasingly difficult for any single level of government or private-sector entity in Canada to proceed with a transportation project on its own. This situation is exacerbated in Canada, where Perl (1993) has found that administrative and fiscal responsibility for urban transportation is even more divided between the federal, provincial, and local levels of government than in other countries such as the United States and France. As such, financial and regulatory partnerships have become central to the realization of major transportation projects (McQuaid 2000). Within this context, amid the cacophony of voices calling for increased spending on specific transportation initiatives, the prioritization of the RAV project over other alternatives was rooted in its appeal to the interests of a broad range of potential funding partners.

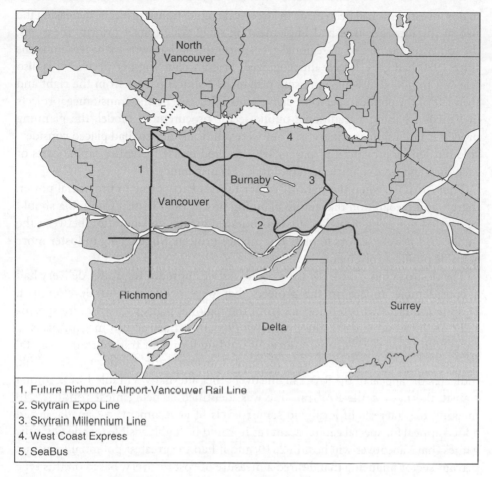

1. Future Richmond-Airport-Vancouver Rail Line
2. Skytrain Expo Line
3. Skytrain Millennium Line
4. West Coast Express
5. SeaBus

Figure 13.2   Current and future rapid-transit network in Vancouver, Canada.

For more than thirty years, planners and decision makers in greater Vancouver have been engaged in an ongoing process to establish priorities and deliver projects as part of a program to produce a modern mass-rapid-transit system in greater Vancouver. Dating back to 1975, all major strategic transportation plans in greater Vancouver have included proposals for a north-south rapid-transit connection between the growing municipality of Richmond and central Vancouver (Ladner 2004; Figure 13.2). And local transportation plans in Richmond and Vancouver called for a north-south rapid-transit alignment connecting their municipalities, although there was never agreement on an ideal route or technology.

Yet, in consecutive analyses and at repeated moments of investment, rapid transit between Richmond and Vancouver was passed over in favor of other alternatives – first for the Expo Skytrain line (a type of automated light rail) that ran east from Vancouver to Burnaby and New Westminster, and later, for the Millennium Skytrain line that ran east from Broadway along the Lougheed corridor. Perhaps more significantly, while major investments had been made in large-scale rapid-transit projects, increasing the size of the local bus fleet and implementing small-scale transit priority measures, the top two priorities of all regional-transportation and growth-management plans since 1980 had gone largely unrecognized. From a planning perspective, it is also relevant to note that while opposing provincial political parties from the right and then left of the political spectrum delivered the first two public-transit megaprojects in Vancouver using a traditional public-sector procurement model, the planning processes faced similar criticisms: They were politically driven; had placed considerable burden on provincial taxpayers, who covered nearly the entire capital costs of each line; and were characterized by a lack of transparency.

Thus, in 2001, when the right-of-center Liberal Party came to provincial power, there was a recognition that future planning processes in British Columbia should be carried out using a method that encouraged greater collaboration between the public and private sectors to plan and finance projects while trying to foster more genuine public involvement.

The desire to more centrally use a collaborative approach to project delivery had a considerable impact on the projects that were prioritized for development. Despite the fact that top priorities from the regional plans focused more specifically on improvements to the bus network than infrastructure megaprojects, a chart comparing the potential sources of funding for major transportation capital projects devised by Vancouver's regional transportation authority, Translink, indicates the appeal of the RAV rail line over other alternatives (Table 13.2). Among transit alternatives, the RAV rail line was identified as being most conducive to meeting the interests of local and senior levels of government in Canada, it had added appeal for special capital grants as it would be highly visible for the Olympic games that Vancouver will host in 2010, and it had the greatest potential to attract private-sector financing that desired a measure of cost recovery. Based on this type of analysis about potential funding sources, in 2001, the RAV line usurped other, more highly ranked local initiatives as the top regional public-transit investment priority.

While research from other jurisdictions has confirmed that the availability of financing for transportation infrastructure plays a large role in determining which projects are prioritized, it is significant that in this case, priority setting was based not only on the interests of the different levels of government but also on designing a project that would appeal to a private-sector investor (Taylor 2000; Li and Wachs 2004). The significance of the potential to attract private-sector investment in shaping project choices is revealed in the comments of Allan Davidson, regional manager, Planning and Partnerships of the British Columbia Ministry of Transportation:

> The funding [for transportation projects] comes from the Province and various other partnerships. If there are other funding partners than the province for a project, this tends to get them up on the list, because the province looks at it as we are getting a new facility at reduced cost. (Hilferink 2004, 116)

As I will illustrate in the following section, the need to design a system that would appeal to the private-sector interest for cost recovery as well as the need to attract other sources of funding resulted in a project that may not necessarily deliver the largest public benefit.

Shaping the project specifications

With the interest of multiple levels of government aligned to prioritize the development of the RAV line, attention turned to designing a process to shape the technical specifications of the project, based on the various objectives of the contributing shareholders. In 2000, the four public shareholders that agreed in principal to fund the RAV project – Translink (as the representative of the regional government), the provincial government, the federal government, and the Vancouver International Airport Authority – formed a special-project office known as RAVCO as a subsidiary of Translink to coordinate the procurement, design, financing, and implementation of the RAV project. The city of Vancouver, the city of Richmond, the greater Vancouver regional district, and the port authority were given stakeholder privileges in RAVCO since they would be affected directly by any investment decision but were not financial contributors.

Early in the planning process, RAVCO hired project-finance specialist and broker Macquarie Group, one of the global leaders in the promotion and delivery of private infrastructure provision, to examine the viability of delivering the RAV line as a private–public partnership. Macquarie's research showed that a rail rapid-transit line would be attractive to private investors as part of a DBFO private–public partnership and that the public could expect to transfer construction, maintenance, operation, and financial risk significantly to the private sector (Macquarie Group 2001).

Based on the findings of Macquarie Group's RAV study, RAVCO proceeded to design its planning and procurement strategy to accommodate the project being delivered as a private–public partnership. Specifically, RAVCO established a competitive procurement process to select the specifications of the RAV project that combined public- and private-sector collaboration (Figure 13.3).

As advocated by academics such as Flyvbjerg and his colleagues (2003) as well as many planning agencies and professional bodies (United States Department of Transportation 2004; Knight et al. 2003), the first phase of the procurement model established by RAVCO was to define a set of performance specifications for the project that were based on the policy directions and individual interests of the involved public agencies as well as consultations with the general public. This approach to project delivery was intended to provide room for private-sector innovation to deliver the most effective system technology at the lowest cost while maintaining government control to establish the direction of the project in the public interest. The use of performance specifications also may be seen as an attempt to alleviate the high incidence of political interference that shaped the route and technology selection on Vancouver's previous rapid-transit projects (Siemiatycki 2005a). As stated in RAVCO's

Table 13.2 Translink comparison of major capital projects based on suitability and potential financing sources

Project	Road			Transit			
	Fraser River Crossing/South Fraser Perimeter Road	North Fraser Perimeter Road	Major Road Network Capital Projects	Broadway West Rapid Transit Expansion	Port Moody/Coquitlam Rapid Transit Extension	Richmond/Airport Vancouver Rapid Transit Line	Trolley Bus Replacement
Issues Addressed							
Goods movement	■	■	■				
International mobility	■	?	?				
Green house gas/environment	?						■
Olympics						■	?
Livable region strategy	■	■	■	■	■	■	■
Stakeholder Interest							
Federal government	■	■	■	?	?	■	?
Provincial government	■	■	■	■	■	■	?
Translink/Greater Vancouver Regional District	■	■	■	■	■	■	■

Municipalities	Pitt Mead., M. Ridge, Surrey, Langleys, Delta	Coquitlam, New Westminster	Various Municipalities	Vancouver	Burnaby, Port Moody, Coquitlam	Richmond, Vancouver	Vancouver, Burnaby
Potential Funding Sources							
Federal — Infrastructure funds	■	■	■	■	■	■	■
Federal — Olympics							
Provincial — Partnership	■	■		■	■	■	
Provincial — Olympics						■	
Translink budget		■	■			■	■
Other (e.g., municipal)	Pitt Mead., M. Ridge, Surrey, Langleys, Delta	Coquitlam, New Westminster	Various Municipalities	Vancouver	Burnaby, Port Moody, Coquitlam	Richmond, Vancouver	Vancouver, Burnaby
Cost recovery (users)	■	?	?	■	■	■	■
P3 potential	■	?	?	?	?	■	?

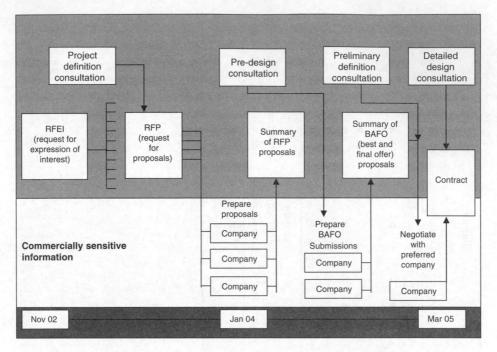

Figure 13.3 Competition and selection procurement model for the RAV line.
Source: Adapted from RAVCO (2003b).

(2003a, 26) documentation describing the procurement process, "no technology choice" was made, "leaving the opportunity for a supplier to propose a system that meets the Performance Standards and is financially feasible."

In practice, however, the collaborative approach to defining the performance specifications for the RAV line was dominated by a desire to establish the criteria so that the ultimate project selected would meet the interests of each of the participating agencies. Key areas of interest for the involved parties included the route alignment, the amount and type of grade separation from traffic, the technology, and the project-financing mechanism.

Of particular attention was the explicit inclusion of private-sector interests in directing the consideration of the project specifications and public policy. In their early discussions, the regional transportation planning authority (Translink), the provincial government, and the airport authority agreed that private-sector financing would be critical to the realization of the project. In private communications between high-ranking bureaucrats, the provincial government went as far as to make its financial contribution contingent on the project's delivery as a private–public partnership (Doyle 2002). This became official government policy and had a reflexive impact on public-policy decisions and the overall technical specifications of the RAV line (Canada Line Rapid Transit Inc. 2006).

Most notably, in 2001, based on the preliminary findings of the business-advisory consultant, Macquarie Group, RAVCO CEO Jane Bird and Translink CEO Ken Dobell (in his final days before taking up his new job in the premier's office) brought a recommendation to the Translink board that at-grade options for the RAV line be excluded from any further analysis. Among other issues, they argued that at-grade options failed to meet the requirements for private-sector involvement in a DBFO style private–public partnership. The recommendation was approved by the board. This shows that while not directly involved in the definition phase of the RAV project planning, the attractiveness of the project to a private-sector concessionaire was considered explicitly in establishing the performance criteria that would shape future design and considerably influenced the direction of public policy.

Overall, through the collaborative approach to project delivery, each partner was able to provide its own criteria on which its financial contribution and jurisdictional approval was contingent. However, not all of the partners had equal influence over the final performance specifications. In particular, a paramount concern was designing a project that met the criteria for funding from sources outside the financially constrained regional level of government, which included senior levels of government, the airport authority, and the private sector (RAVCO 2003a). For these participating organizations, the paramount concerns were building a transit system that would be a positive legacy of the Olympic Games, be unobtrusive to the surrounding community, and be conducive to attracting financing and involvement from the private sector.

To meet the interests of the key contributing agencies, when the performance specifications were released to the public in the winter of 2003, some commentators noted that they were so specifically designed based on a quick travel time, reliability requirements, a routing along Cambie Street, explicit favor for rail technology, and the need to have numerous underground segments that they left little room for innovation (Boddy 2003). As John Mills, director of Transport Canada's Pacific region policy-coordination branch, who had been involved from an early stage with RAVCO's planning of the RAV line as a representative for the federal government, noted in an interview with Dutch master's student Shanna Hilferink:

> [T]he RAV project is a case of one where there was no alternative analysis done … before a very high-level analysis was done decisions were made that discounted the Arbutus corridor and focused primarily on the Cambie corridor. So you then are stuck trying to do a multiple account evaluation basically on one corridor, that has been ordained that it must be a subway, so right off the back you are constrained in your analysis as to options. (Hilferink 2004, 145)

Thus, while RAVCO had a mandate to use performance specifications to leverage the innovative capacity of the private sector as favored by some academics and planning agencies, in practice, it appeared that the ingrained interests of the organizations involved in the project planning would limit this potential. Using rail technology along a Cambie Street route had been studied in the regional plans for more than a decade, and automated technology already was used on Vancouver's two operating rapid-transit lines, and thus, could not be seen as an innovative solution. Moreover, it appears that the adherence to a planning model that used performance specifications did not alleviate issues of political interference that had been prevalent in earlier project planning in Vancouver; instead, it simply shifted the period of political interference upstream from the design-and-procurement phase to the project-visioning phase. As I will show in the following sections, the partnership approach to transportation planning had a large impact on the potential transparency and accountability of the planning process and led to a project design that may not achieve the desired benefits for the transit system.

Delivering the RAV project using a DBFO private–public partnership

Given the institutionalization of a partnership approach to planning, it is pertinent to ask how this structure affected the habits, norms, routines, established practices, and rules that pattern behavior within the RAV project-planning process. In this section, I will turn my attention to the political process of gaining approval for the RAV line by picking up the narrative in the spring of 2003 following the completion of the project-definition report that contained the performance specifications.

Intense political and interest-group contestation always has characterized the planning of large infrastructure projects in greater Vancouver, as in other cities around the world (Altshuler and Luberoff 2003). Despite being planned through a collaborative private–public partnership approach that was meant to minimize open confrontations between the participating shareholders, the process of gaining approval for the RAV project was no exception to this trend. The case of the RAV project is an opportunity to explore one case of how the adherence to a DBFO private–public-partnership approach to transportation planning affects the potential to achieve the tenets of an accountable planning process as defined by Flyvbjerg and his colleagues (2003), which include procedural transparency, legitimate public involvement, risk transfer through private-sector financing, and a clear specification of the regulatory regime.

A defining source of conflict in the RAV planning process was embedded directly in the private–public-partnership approach to delivering the project. To maintain the integrity of the competitive tendering process to select the winning private-sector concessionaire, a planning model was established in which two parallel processes were taking place simultaneously with only limited interaction between them. These included the competition to select the winning private-sector concessionaire and the public process of gaining political approval and financial support from multiple levels of government (see Figure 13.3).

RAVCO officials acknowledged an explicit tension in undertaking the competitive procurement process as designed: "The challenge for RAVCO is balancing the public interest in disclosure and the public interest in a vibrant competitive process to procure the RAV line," a process that necessitated a considerable degree of confidentiality to maintain the integrity of the bidding (RAVCO 2004a, 7). The need for confidentiality in the DBFO private–public-partnership approach to infrastructure planning has been observed in other jurisdictions around the world (Davis 2005; Demirag, Dubnick, and Khadaroo 2004). In Ireland, for instance, where more than fifty projects have been delivered using the private–public-partnership approach, the central Private–Public Partnership Unit within the Department of Finance reported that confidentiality in DBFO projects is specifically necessary to provide the private sector with incentives to deliver innovative technologies, limit costs, protect commercially sensitive information, and encourage flexibility to re-engineer business processes (Private–Public Partnership Unit 2003).

The same arguments were put forward in the case of the RAV line in Vancouver, in which confidentiality was related particularly to the commercial sensitivity of the technologies proposed in the proponent bids and the potential for the premature release of financial information to distort the competitive tendering process, limit innovation, or weaken the public-sector position in ongoing negotiations with the private proponent. RAVCO intended to overcome the need for secrecy embedded in the DBFO private–public-partnership model by using international best practices of public disclosure, accountability, and governance, such as enhanced online posting of technical and meeting minutes, ongoing citizen engagement, and public access to internal documents under the Freedom of Information and Privacy Act (RAVCO 2004a).

Nevertheless, as will be illustrated, the explicit need for secrecy and the prevalence of commercially confidential information associated with the competitive tendering process appears to be incongruent with the need for openness and transparency associated with an accountable planning process.

The competitive selection of a private sector concessionaire   Based on the collaborative procurement model designed for the delivery of the RAV project, the design phase of the project was being guided by a competitive process to select a private-sector concessionaire that would offer the best system-design and financing package. Between the summer of 2003 and the spring of 2004, RAVCO whittled down potential proponents from a field of ten consortia led by some of the largest rail developers in the world to a short-list of two final bidders: SNC Lavalin/Serco and RAVxpress that was led by Bombardier. Both consortia proposed developing lines that were fully underground in the city of Vancouver and elevated in Richmond and on the airport lands and that used automated rail technology. SNC Lavalin/Serco also proposed a system that would operate at grade in Richmond, as desired by the local council, and that would combine manual and automated rail technology (RAVCO 2005).

While RAVCO went to some lengths to release information about the two final bids and it was reported widely that the expected capital cost of the project would be between $1.5 billion and $1.7 billion, the selection process required a high degree of secrecy about the specifications of the various proposals to limit access to commercially sensitive information, maintain the integrity of the competition between the bidders, and uphold the position of RAVCO in ongoing negotiations on specific contractual terms. This meant that during the planning process, no information was

Table 13.3 Political donations by Richmond-Airport-Vancouver (RAV) proponents

Company Name	RAV Project Involvement	Existing Interest in Private–Public Partnerships	Provincial Contribution 2001	Federal Contribution 2003
Bombardier Inc.	RAVxpress final proponent team member	Advising federal government to expand PPP model and involved in proposed PPP airport rail project in Toronto	$5,000	$139,795.22
AMEC Inc.	RAVxpress final proponent team member	Sponsor member of the Canadian Council for PPP	$12,500	$9,491
SNC-Lavalin	SNC-Lavalin/Serco final proponent team member	Involved in other private–public-partnership projects in Canada	$10,000	$91,465
KPMG Consultants	Conducted independent review of public-sector comparator	Member of the Canadian Council for PPP	$5,000	$18,926
Price Waterhouse Coopers Consultants	Conducted financial review validating PPP delivery and worked with RAVCO officials to author public-sector comparator	Sponsor member of the Canadian Council for PPP	$1,500	$15,784
Canwest Global Communications	Owner of Vancouver's two daily newspapers	Not applicable	$35,000	$3,500

Source: Elections BC (2004); Elections Canada (2004).
Note: PPP = private–public partnership.

released to the public about the exact terms of the two proposals, including the technical and design specifications of the line, the total cost of the line, the terms of the financing package, or the construction methods that would be used to build the line.

Some information also was withheld from politicians who sat on the board of the regional government and had to approve financing for the RAV project. Instead, RAVCO released a series of reports, written by consultants constrained by confidentiality clauses, that confirmed the integrity of the bid process and ensured that both of the final proposals met the standard of "value for money" as demanded by the public sector. As is typical in other jurisdictions such as Ireland and Australia, critical reports that were withheld from the public included the public-sector comparator and the value-for-money report. Together, these reports measure whether the degree of risk being transferred to the private sector as well as any innovations brought to the project outweigh the added cost of higher private-sector borrowing rates and a profit margin (Irish Department of Finance 2003; Malone 2005).

Many of the firms that conducted the critical reports were explicit supporters of private–public partnerships, some had a large stake in the proliferation of a planning model that encouraged project development through private–public partnerships, and some had donated large amounts of money to the parties in power at the provincial and federal levels of government, which, at the very least, challenged their impartiality (Table 13.3). Moreover, a number of the firms had interests in existing or future private–public-partnership projects in Canada, while others were well positioned to advise both the public sector on privatization efforts and the private sector on how to benefit from such measures.

Despite the potential for there to be the appearance of corporate conflicts of interest, requests to have the entire process reviewed during the planning stages by the auditor general of British Columbia – the agency charged with protecting the public interest with respect to government spending – were denied repeatedly. Instead, while fairness auditor Ted Hughes certified the integrity of the competitive selection process, the lack of transparency about the contents of critical technical reports had the potential to challenge public confidence in the legitimacy of the RAV planning process. As Richmond city councilor Bill McNulty commented in an interview with the *Richmond Review*, "I have some grave concerns about the consultative process. It seems the stewards of the city are being pushed aside" (van den Hemel 2004).

The public-approval process   The need for secrecy in the private bidding process had a considerable impact on the other process that was occurring simultaneously, which was the political process of arranging capital funding and jurisdictional approval from the multiple public-sector shareholders. Unlike the process of selecting the winning private proponent, which largely proceeded behind closed doors, the political-approval process was playing out in the public arena and required a high level of access to information and public consultation to enable accountable decision making. Raising the stakes, the entire political-approval process was accelerated as the race was on to have the RAV line approved so it could be built in time for the Olympic Games, a central criterion on which funding from senior levels of government was contingent.

Within the context of a collaborative approach to project delivery, there was immense pressure on each level of government to provide approvals that furthered the RAV development plan, since any level of government that refused funding would be seen as the one that scuttled a popular and necessary infrastructure project. As well, the desire to have the private-sector concessionaire partially finance the infrastructure created a sense of urgency for the public sector to solidify its financing agreements since this would influence the assessed risk of the project to private lenders, which in turn affected the interest rates that lenders would offer to the concessionaires, and ultimately, the final price of the concessionaires' bids (Bula 2004).

As the RAV project moved through the approval process, each level of government seemingly agonized about the decision of whether or not to approve the project. In a confidential report leaked to the local media, federal government officials questioned the level of risk that was being transferred to the private sector through the DBFO private–public partnership and the congestion relief and environmental benefits that would be provided by the system, yet the politicians approved it for funding (Palmer 2003). At the regional council, the project was approved by a single vote after one of the longest meetings in the organization's history, which was interrupted by an in camera session to discuss confidential information that had not been disclosed previously to the councilors. Finally, in a two-month period, the board of the regional transit authority twice rejected the project before a third vote was called hastily at which the project was approved at a total cost of $1.559 billion, of which a maximum of $1.35 billion would be from the public sector.

Six months following the approval to proceed to the final bidding stage, the low bid from the two final proponent teams came from SNC Lavalin for an underground, automated rail system at $1.899 billion, or $340 million above the total funding envelope. It also was determined that while the majority of construction risk would best be borne by the private-sector concessionaire, the public-sector agencies would be most able to manage almost all (90 percent) of the risk associated with patronage. According to Bowman (2002), this division of risk is increasingly typical in public-transit projects delivered through private–public partnerships, in which investors have come to perceive patronage as particularly unpredictable. However, by assigning the vast majority of the ridership risk to the public sector, private financiers have little incentive to assess the merits of the demand for the project since there are only minimal consequences for a wrong decision. This is significant as demand is a central component in determining the viability of a transit project yet is a component that some authors contend has been consistently overestimated intentionally to get projects started (Wachs 1986; Richmond 2005).

With considerable scope changes to remove stations and public-amenity features such as walkways from the design (which could reduce demand) as well as more money added by the public and private sectors, the line proposed by SNC Lavalin was given final approval for development in December 2004 at a total cost of $1.72 billion. Throughout the public-approval process, political incentive to continue proceeding with a complex and controversial project was generated through ongoing community consultation and public-opinion polling by RAVCO that repeatedly found a high level of support for the RAV line. However, while it appears that these measures accurately gauged public support for the RAV line, alternate polls conducted by opposing labor unions noted that there remained a general lack of understanding about the financial costs of the project or the potential risks associated with delivery as a private–public partnership (Canadian Union of Public Employees 2004).

As such, there appears to be a tension embedded in the planning of the RAV line that can be attributed at least partially to the delivery of the project as a DBFO public-private partnership. While there was a concerted effort to undertake public consultation for the RAV line during the planning process, the need for secrecy to maintain the integrity of the procurement competition as in other jurisdictions and expedience to meet the deadline of the Olympics lessened the potential for transparency, a central feature of Flyvbjerg and his colleagues' (2003) definition of accountable decision making. Moreover, as Throgmorton (1991) has observed in the planning of public-investment projects, opinion-survey research, models, and forecasts served as important rhetorical devices used by planners and project proponents to form the persuasive narratives that shaped political and public opinion.

The intersection of public and private cost creep and scope changes   Approval of the RAV line by the Translink board should have concluded the project-planning processes. But it did not. In mid-December 2004, RAVCO posted on its Web site the details of documents that would be contained in its environmental-assessment submission. While the documents were largely technical, one point stood out: 75 percent of the underground portion of the line – including in both down-town Vancouver and through a business district in South Vancouver – were going to be constructed using a cut-and-cover construction method (RAVCO 2005). Cut-and-cover construction was proposed to have numerous advantages over alternative deep-bore tunneling methods, including being less expensive, being associated with less risk of delay, and making it possible to build the stations closer to the surface, which would make access easier for system users.

However, when news of the degree to which the line was going to be built using cut-and-cover tunneling was reported in the media, it raised public alarm. Many in the community were shocked at the news, feeling that the earlier information released by RAVCO suggested that the line would be built using a less invasive deep-bore tunneling method. After exhausting the potential for a negotiated settlement with RAVCO, one business coalition legally challenged the legitimacy of the decision to build the RAV line using a cut-and-cover method on the grounds that the public had not been informed properly of this alternative during the consultation process (Greenwood 2005). The legal action was unsuccessful.

Nevertheless, according to one Translink director, David Cadman, even the board members responsible for making the final decision on the $1.72 billion transit line were unaware of exactly how much would be constructed using the cut-and-cover method, since this was considered proprietary to the SNC Lavalin bid (Smith 2005). One City of Vancouver staff member who may have had access to details of how much of the RAV line the SNC Lavalin consortium intended to construct using cut and cover was City Manager Judy Rogers, who represented Vancouver as a nonvoting member of the RAVCO board of directors. However, RAVCO board members were bound by strict confidentiality codes restricting the sharing of proprietary technical, business, financial, or legal information during the planning process. This confidentiality screen may have constrained Rogers from sharing any proprietary information about construction methods with the Vancouver city council, even if there were parts of the plan that could be to the detriment of constituents.

The level of secrecy required to maintain the integrity of the private–public-partnership delivery model calls into question whether the RAV-project governance structure threatened the fiduciary responsibility of the civil service or provided the necessary accountability to the elected officials who were responsible for deciding whether to approve the project.

The issue of the construction method was not the end of the surprises for the RAV project. Despite the use of a less expensive cut-and-cover construction method and the reduced scope of the project (the latter of which would reduce the public benefit of the project), there was another change in July 2005 when details of the final contract between RAVCO and the private consortium were announced. Instead of the $1.72 billion capital cost that had been expected when the project was approved by the Translink board in December 2004, the final price-fixed cost of the project came in at $1.9 billion, an escalation of some $180 million, or 10 percent, from when the Translink board approved the project in December 2004 and a 22 percent increase over the early cost estimates that had been used until 2003 (Boei 2005).

When details of the financial arrangement were released to the public, it appeared that the total public-sector contribution had escalated to $1.474 billion or 9 percent above Translink's approved limit. The private sector now was set to contribute about $650 million, which would be repaid over the life of the operating contract. Details of the operating contract were not released to the public. Part of the public-sector escalation was as a result of a last-minute decision to add a station to the line that previously had been eliminated to cut costs, and the public also assumed the cost of other components of the project, such as security and trolley-wire replacement, that previously had been allocated to the private concessionaire. While there are many reasons why costs escalate on large projects and while construction costs in Vancouver have risen dramatically since the 2010 Olympic Games were awarded to the city in 2003, the cost escalations experienced by the RAV project should not have been entirely unforeseeable by RAVCO planners. A confidential internal document from RAVCO's bid-evaluation committee, dated March 15, 2004, flagged the proponent that ultimately won the concession as using "very aggressive pricing" (RAVCO 2004b, 29).

Without full financial details available, it remains difficult for members of the public to assess the rate of return being paid to the private concessionaire or the actual amount and cost of transferring risk between the public- and private-sector partners. With respect to risk, however, a final surprise arose in August 2005 when it was reported that the SNC Lavalin/Serco consortium had taken on a number of new financial partners, which included the managers of the public-sector pension funds from the provinces of British Columbia and Quebec, to spread around its risk during construction. This means that the risks transferred to the private sector (a key motivation for undertaking a DBFO private–public partnership) are not entirely private as the cost of any overruns during construction would be borne partially by the public-sector employees of British Columbia and Quebec (Palmer 2005).

Conclusion

In this article, I have sought to examine the contemporary application of DBFO public-private partnerships in the provision of public services in Canada by following the narrative of one such project from its inception to the conclusion of its planning process. In piecing together the complex and detailed planning process the RAV line in greater Vancouver followed. I have highlighted the need for questions to be raised about the merits of this alternate financing and procurement model.

Specifically, this article has shown that despite the attempt by governments in British Columbia to use the DBFO private–public partnership as a mechanism to alleviate problems that had plagued earlier transit-megaproject planning in Vancouver, such as political interference, a lack of procedural transparency, and escalating costs, the outcomes in practice have not met expectations (Table 13.4). In fact, the planning of the RAV line had more similarities than differences from earlier Skytrain planning processes in greater Vancouver that were undertaken using the conventional public-sector procurement model. In this case, the theoretical benefits of a more competitive procurement process were undermined by ingrained power relations between the various parties, which ensured that while the end product was designed so that it would meet the criteria of the most financially endowed collaborators, it would not necessarily provide the greatest public benefit.

Furthermore, the case of the RAV project generally does not sustain the theoretical arguments forwarded by academics such as Flyvbjerg, Bruzelius, and Rothengatter (2003), Walker and Smith (1995), and Savas (2000) supporting DBFO private–public partnerships. The requisite level of secrecy embedded in this particular design of a competitive planning process was not compatible with the need for public transparency and accountability, and the RAV project met very few of the criteria for a meaningfully consultative process (Innes and Booher 2004). To date, the designers of the RAV procurement model in Vancouver as well as promoters of private–public partnerships in other countries such as Ireland explicitly have linked confidentiality during the planning process to improved outcomes of DBFO

Table 13.4 The theory and practice of design-build-finance-operate (DBFO) for the Richmond-Airport-Vancouver (RAV) project

Problem Observed in the Delivery of Previous Megaprojects	Proposed Solution as Part of DBFO Delivery Mechanism	Actual Outcome in the Case of the RAV Project in Vancouver
System specifications selected by public-sector bureaucrats not necessarily the most efficient over the full project life cycle; political interference in the selection of route and technology	Design a set of performance specifications and then establish a competitive process that invites private corporations to design a system that meets the standards most efficiently and cost effectively	The performance specifications were designed to meet the diverse interests of each funding partner and left little room for private-sector innovation. The route and technology selected for the RAV line had been proposed and studied for more than a decade.
	Involve a single concessionaire with both construction and project operation for a fixed period of time	
Majority of risks – including construction, performance, and ridership – were allocated to the public sector	Transfer risk from the public to the private sector through private investment of risk capital and performance payments during the operation phase of the project	The public sector assumed the majority of ridership risk. Some of the private-sector risk for construction was transferred back to segments of the public sector by partnering with public-sector pension funds.
Cost escalations during the project-construction phase, which often are exacerbated by politically motivated project-scope changes	Strict contracting with the private sector, making it more difficult to propose scope changes once project development is underway	Despite strict contracting, the final price of the RAV line escalated 22 percent during the planning process. Part of the rise in price was because of late-scope changes including the addition of a new station and a bicycle path.

| Weak transparency and accountability during the project-planning process | Make project-planning documents extensively available to politicians and the public and create different forums to foster public input and political debate about the relative merits of the project | RAV planners released more technical data than for past Skytrain projects. However, the need for confidentiality to maintain the integrity of the bidding process meant that key financial information was not released to the public (and some politicians) during the planning process. This limited the degree to which an informed discussion about the project merits could be engaged. |
| Challenge raising capital from cash-strapped governments to finance large infrastructure projects while simultaneously presenting balanced budgets | Invite the private sector to finance infrastructure investments partially or entirely, with costs recouped over the life of an operating contract | Development of the RAV line still cost some $1.25 billion in public-sector finances. Private-sector borrowing rate may be more expensive than public-sector access to capital. |

procurements such as greater innovation and lower development costs. Given these claims that are shaping the existing practice, future research is necessary to understand more thoroughly why confidentiality is seen as central to certain parts of the DBFO procurement model and whether mechanisms can be developed so that important financial and design information can be released more readily to the public during the planning process.

Additionally, the involvement of private-sector financing has not minimized development-cost escalations and scope changes, nor has it significantly lessened the burden on government balance sheets, since the public sector is still responsible for financing more than a billion dollars in initial capital costs. The subscription to a competitive delivery process using performance standards did not result in a considerably more innovative system design, as the line selected for development by SNC Lavalin will use technology and a route that have been proposed for more than a decade. And while evidence from the construction and operation phases of the project will tell how effectively risk was transferred between the public and private sectors, in the short term, it has been observed that the private sector has taken steps to disperse a portion of its risk back onto certain segments of the public.

As a single example, the findings of the RAV case study cannot be generalized to different types of planning partnerships or projects in other contexts delivered through the DBFO style of private–public partnership. Nevertheless, the experience of the RAV line raises a range of questions that should be asked as planners increasingly turn to more institutionally collaborative approaches to infrastructure megaproject delivery.

Note

1   From an economic perspective, private–public partnerships are underpinned by a value-for-money equation. On one side of the equation are the typically higher cost of a private corporation's borrowing money when compared to the lower cost for governments with a good credit rating; higher project-planning and tendering costs; and the need to pay corporate profits during both the construction and the operation phases of the project (by contrast, if a transportation system is operated by the public sector, a profit margin is not paid during this phase of the project). On the other side of the equation, the added costs of delivering the project using greater private-sector involvement are balanced against the potential benefit of a more innovative project design that delivers financial savings and added utility, the lesser burden on government to borrow money directly, and the transferring of defined risks from the public to the private sector. Given the historical experience of persistent cost overruns and demand variability that have characterized the development of transportation megaprojects, the transference of risk is a central feature guiding the private–public partnership. As with purchasing an insurance policy, the transferring of risks such as construction-cost overruns and ridership shortfalls from the public to the private sector is associated with a defined cost based on the likelihood and potential of these risks to be mitigated, and these costs are recouped from the public sector through higher bidding prices. To this end, it is proposed that when risk transfer is

considered, a project can deliver value for money even if the forecasted costs of developing the project as a private–public partnership are higher than if the project was delivered through a more conventional design-build approach.

References

Altshuler, A., and D. Luberoff. 2003. *Mega-projects: The changing politics of urban public investments*. Washington, DC: Brookings Institution.

Blumenberg, E. 2002. Planning for the transportation needs of welfare participants: Institutional challenges to collaborative planning. *Planning Education and Research* 22 (2): 152–63.

Boddy, T. 2003. Politicos see a RAV line paved with votes. *The Vancouver Sun*, August 9, F14.

Boei, W. 2005. Final RAV deal up by $180 million: Winning bidder, two new partners will cover the increase. *The Vancouver Sun*, August 3, B1.

Bowman, L. 2002. Outside the farebox. *Project Finance* 231: 42–5.

Bula, F. 2004. Secret plan to explain federal RAV funds. *The Vancouver Sun*, October 4, A1.

Campbell, G. 2004. *Speech to the B.C. Road Builders and Heavy Construction Association*. December 2, Vancouver. Retrieved from http://www.bcliberals.com/premier's_speeches/b.c._road_builders_and_heavy_construction_association/.

Canada Line Rapid Transit Inc. 2006. Canada line final project report: Competitive selection phase. Retrieved from http://www.canadaline.ca/files/uploads/docs/doc495.pdf.

Canadian Union of Public Employees. 2004. *New poll shows 74% back alternative to RAV*. Retrieved from http://www.cupe.ca/www/media/10046.

Canadian Urban Transit Association. 2003. *Report on a survey of transit infrastructure needs for the period 2004–2008*. Ottawa: Canadian Urban Transit Authority.

Davis, K. 2005. Policy forum: Financing public infrastructure PPPs and infrastructure investment. *The Australian Economic Review* 38 (4): 439–44.

Debande, O. 2002. Private financing of transport infrastructure: An assessment of the UK experience. *Journal of Transport Economics and Policy* 36 (3): 355–87.

Demirag, I., M. Dubnick, and M. I. Khadaroo. 2004. A framework for examining accountability and value for money in the UK's private finance initiative. *The Journal of Corporate Citizenship* 15: 63–76.

Dobell, K., and J. Bird. 2001. Report to board of directors: RAV project. Burnaby: Translink.

Doyle, D. 2002. *Letter to Pat Jacobsen*. June 19. Freedom of Information Request.

Edwards, P., J. Shaoul, A. Stafford, and L. Arblaster. 2004. *Evaluating the operation of PFI in roads and hospitals*. Association of Certified Chartered Accountants—research report no. 84. Retrieved from http://www.accaglobal.com/research/summaries/2270443.

Elections BC, 2004. http://www.elections.bc.ca/

Elections Canada. 2004. http://www.elections.ca/

Flyvbjerg, B. 2003. The lying game. *Eurobusiness* (June): 60–2.

Flyvbjerg, B., N. Bruzelius, and W. Rothengatter. 2003. *Megaprojects and risk: An anatomy of ambition*. New York: Cambridge University Press.

Greenwood, J. 2005. Court to decide if RAV is being done right: B.C.'s $1.7B rapid transit plan faces legal challenge. *National Post*, June 18, FP7.

Hall, P. 1982. *Great planning disasters*. Berkeley: University of California Press.

Hilferink, S. 2004. *Societal cost benefit analysis: A bridge to more efficient infrastructure decision-making?* Master's thesis, Utrecht University.

HM Treasury. 2003. PFI: Meeting the investment challenge. Retrieved from http://www. hm-treasury.gov.uk/media/648B2/PFI_604.pdf.

Innes, J. E., and D. E. Booher. 2004. Reframing public participation strategies for the 21st century. *Planning Theory and Practice* 5 (4): 419–36.

Irish Department of Finance. 2003. Assessment, approval, public sector benchmark and procurement of PPP. Presentation to the Joint Oireachtas Committee on Transportation, September 23. Retrieved from http://www.ppp.gov.ie/.

Knight, M., M. Rich, R. Green, S. Giles, and C. Amyot. 2003. Civil infrastructure systems: Technology road map. Canadian Council of Professional Engineers. Retrieved from http://www.ccpe.ca/e/files/TRMReporteng.pdf.

Ladner, P. 2004. *Numbers tell the tale in RAV line controversy: An article by NPA Councillor Peter Ladner*. Retrieved from http://www.npavancouver.ca/20040713-numbers-tell-the-tale-in-rav-l/.

Li, J., and M. Wachs. 2004. The effects of federal transit subsidy policy on investment decisions: The case of San Francisco's Geary Corridor. *Transportation* 31 (1): 43–67.

Mackett, R. L., and M. Edwards. 1998. The impact of new urban public transport systems: Will the expectations be met? *Transportation Research-A* 32: 231–45.

Macquarie Group. 2001. *PPP review of RAV rapid transit project*. Vancouver: Macquarie Group.

Malone, N. 2005. The evolution of private financing of government infrastructure in Australia—2005 and beyond. *The Australian Economic Review* 38 (4): 420–30.

McQuaid, R.W. 2000. The theory of partnership: Why have partnerships? In *Public-private partnerships: Theory and practice in international perspective*, edited by S. P. Osborne, 9–36. New York: Routledge.

Miraftab, F. 2004. Private–public partnerships: The Trojan horse of neoliberal development. *Journal of Planning Education and Research* 24 (1): 89–101.

Olds, K. 2001. *Globalization and urban change*. New York: Oxford University Press.

Palmer, V. 2003. Feds blow whistle on the RAV line. *The Vancouver Sun*, June 19, A3.

Palmer, V. 2005. Private-sector portion of RAV risk isn't so private, after all. *The Vancouver Sun*, August 10, A3.

Perl, A. D. 1993. Comparative transport finance: The institutional logic of infrastructure development in Canada, France, and the United States. Doctoral thesis, University of Toronto.

Pickrell, D. 1992. A desire named streetcar: Fantasy and fact in rail transit planning. *Journal of the American Planning Association* 58 (2): 158–76.

Private–Public Partnership Unit 2003. Presentation to the Joint Oireachtas Committee on Transport, September 23. Ireland Department of Finance. Retrieved from http://www. ppp.gov.ie/keydocs/pressreleases/.

RAVCO. 2003a. *Project definition report*. Vancouver: RAVCO.

RAVCO. 2003b. *Project delivery model*. Retrieved from http://www.ravprapidtransit.com.

RAVCO. 2004a. Minutes of a meeting of the board of directors of RAV Project Management Ltd. (RAVCO), held February 6, 2004. Retrieved December 18, 2005, from http://www. ravprapidtransit.com/files/uploads/docs/doc210.pdf.

RAVCO. 2004b. *Report of the evaluation committee*. Vancouver: RAVCO.

RAVCO. 2005. Frequently asked questions. Retrieved from http://www.ravprapidtransit. com/en/faq.php.

Richmond, J. 2005. *Transport of delight*. Akron: University of Akron Press.

Rock, C., and S. Plewes. 2002. Major capital projects: Candidates for federal funding. February 12 report to the board of directors. Retrieved from http://www.translink.bc.ca/files/board_files/meet_agenda_min/2002/02_21_02/0202021_3.2_Major_capital_report.pdf.

Savas, S. 2000. *Privatization and public-private partnerships*. New York: Seven Bridges.

Siemiatycki, M. 2005a. The making of a mega project in the neoliberal city: The case of mass rapid transit in Vancouver Canada. *City* 9 (1): 67–83.

Siemiatycki, M. 2005b. Beyond moving people: Excavating the motivations for investing in urban public transit infrastructure in Bilbao Spain. *European Planning Studies* 13 (1): 45–64.

Smith, C. 2005. RAVCO digs downtown. *The Georgia Straight*, February 3–10, p. 11.

Taylor, B. D. 2000. When finance leads planning: Urban planning, highway planning, and metropolitan freeways in California. *Journal of Planning Education and Research* 20 (2): 196–214.

Throgmorton, J. 1991. Planning as a rhetorical activity. *Journal of the American Planning Association* 59 (3): 334–46.

United States Department of Transportation. 2004. Performance specifications strategic roadmap: A vision for the future. Retrieved from http://www.fhwa.dot.gov/construction/pssr0403.htm.

United States Department of Transportation. 2005. PPP options. Retrieved from http://www.fhwa.dot.gov/ppp/options.htm.

van den Hemel, M. 2004. The bids are in. *Richmond Review*. January 29. Retrieved from http://www.yourlibrary.ca/community/RichmondReview/Archive/RR20040129/more-news.html.

Wachs, M. 1986. Techniques vs. advocacy in rapid rail transit: A study of rapid rail transit. *Urban Resources* 4 (1): 23–30.

Wachs, M. 1988. *When planners lie with numbers: An exploration of data, analysis and planning ethics*. Los Angeles: University of California.

Walker, C., and A. J. Smith. 1995. *Privatized infrastructure*. London: Thomas Telford.

14

Collective Ownership and Community Control and Development

The Long View

James deFilippis

The left in the United States suffers from a peculiar historical amnesia. Few free-school founders or food co-op enthusiasts in the sixties learned anything from their predecessors in previous decades, because they had never heard of them. The lessons of the recent past are just as obscure to the scattered activists of the present. New arrangements for living and working persist, but often in a vacuum

John Case and Rosemary Taylor, 1979

There is very little new about the solutions proposed in chapter 1 [original text] except the context in which they emerged. People in the United States have been creating forms of collective ownership and working toward the goal of local or community control for a long time. In order not to lose sight of the lessons of these histories, we need to explore them here. The histories of collective ownership, community development, and local/community control are varied and disparate, and it is the rather ambitious goal of this chapter to bring these histories together. For while these organizations, and, at times, movements, emerged at different times and in different places for different reasons, there are substantial relationships among them. Equally important, however, are the disjunctures that have existed, and which continue to exist. Beginning with the nineteenth-century American roots of collective ownership and community control, the chapter then shifts to the 1960s and discusses the emergence of the current community-development movement. It then presents the trajectory of this movement away from its organizing roots and toward greater degrees of institutionalization and professionalization. This professionalization has seen the goal of community control, and the radical politics

Readings in Planning Theory, Third Edition. Edited by Susan S. Fainstein and Scott Campbell.
Editorial material and organization © 2012 Blackwell Publishing Ltd.
Published 2012 by Blackwell Publishing Ltd.

that sometimes informed that goal, get lost in the process. The chapter concludes by discussing the implications of this history.

Co-ops, Communes, Collectives, and Community Control in American History

Nineteenth-century black communes

The history of community control in the United States has several different components, but in terms of providing the roots for the emergence of community ownership, the most important of these is the history of black "organized communities" of the nineteenth century. These communities were created primarily in the Northwest of the United States (Michigan, Indiana, Ohio, and Wisconsin) and in Southern Ontario in Canada (Pease and Pease, 1963). The goals of these organizations were to provide sites of isolation and independence from the racism of white North America, and to create a context in which individual blacks could prosper and learn to live freely. In short, "they saw in a community organization the possibility of presenting a common front to a hostile environment, and in common effort they recognized the virtue of mutual aid and assistance and the pooling of resources until such a time as the individual Negro settler could manage on his own" (Pease and Pease, 1963, pp. 16–17). As the above quote suggests, the goal of these communes, unlike their nonblack contemporaries, was not to construct forms of local socialism or communism but instead was unapologetically capitalist and individualist in purposes and organizing principles. They believed in the dominant Victorian ideals of self-help and individualism, and the goals of these communes were to train blacks to fit into what they perceived as the emergent American middle class. At the same time, the American ideal was also still enmeshed in Jefferson's vision of an agrarian populace and in a skepticism of the still barely emerging urban industrial class. So the goals of these communes were to turn freed slaves into Gentleman Farmers, and priority was given to working the soil as a means for improving the character of the individual freed slaves (although it is not clear why this would improve the character of those involved since they had come from situations where, as slaves, very often all they did was work the soil!). Started in the 1830s, these communes disappeared shortly after the end of the Civil War (with the passage of the Thirteenth Amendment to the Constitution), and their impacts on American society were largely negligible. In their assessment, Pease and Pease conclude, "what is most impressive of all about this adventure in humane salvation and massive uplift is the fact that the results were, on the whole, so tragically inconsequential" (Pease and Pease, 1963, p. 160).

These communes essentially prefigured the beliefs that Booker T. Washington disseminated during the Reconstruction Era about blacks needing to succeed in business in order to interact with whites on an equal footing. Washington continued the arguments of the communes by arguing that this equality could be realized by blacks only if they isolated themselves in order for blacks to enter into positions of authority, and then, from those segregated positions of authority, blacks could engage with whites in comparable positions (Washington, 1971). Washington, accordingly, was not an integrationist and he argued: "Let us in the future spend less time talking about the part of the city that we cannot live in, and more time making the part of the city that we live in beautiful and attractive" (quoted in Philpot, 1978, p. 209). Washington was also an unmitigated believer in the potential of capitalism to allow blacks to realize class mobility (although his capitalism was shaped by the industrial world that had developed in the time between the 1830s and his post-Civil War writing), and so he ceaselessly advocated that blacks develop industrial trade schools and become tradesmen. He stated:

> More and more thoughtful students of the race problem are beginning to see that business and industry constitute what we may call the strategic point in its solution. These fundamental professions we are able to occupy not only without resistance but even with encouragement, and from them we shall gradually advance to all the rights and privileges which any class of citizens enjoy (Washington, 1971, p. 19).

The invisibility of class structure and class conflict in his analysis is nothing short of astonishing. As we will see, Washington's arguments, in turn, provided much of the foundation for the emergence of the black capitalism and community economic-development movement of the 1960s (Halpern, 1995; Hampden-Turner, 1975; Perry, 1972).

Co-ops, communes, and utopian socialists

While the black communes emerged in the 1830s and were explicitly geared toward reproducing agrarian and mercantile capitalism in black communities, there was a parallel and yet completely different history of nineteenth-century communes and collectives that were oriented toward exactly the opposite goal – creating places outside the constraints and structures of the emergent industrial capitalist world of wage slavery and employment-based production. These "utopian" communities were attempts at local-scale communism, and they were largely divided between secular and religious communes, although there was a good deal of overlap (Nordhoff, 1993).

While the religious communes were larger in number than the secular ones, the secular communes, based on the goals of creating localized socialist communes, are the more relevant to us here. These nineteenth-century experiments with communism were ideologically a combination of Jeffersonian agrarian democracy (and his acceptance of Locke's labor theory of property) and British socialism. The work of the British socialist Robert Owen was particularly important to the creation of these communes, and he moved to the United States in 1825 to implement his ideas (Curl, 1980). Various forms of these communes grew in rural areas until shortly before the Civil War, and it has been argued that these communist experiments had a substantial impact on the young Frederich Engels in the mid 1840s (see Feuer, 1966). But they foundered in the 1850s, as greater numbers of Americans became workers in the emerging industrial economy, and the communes were unable to reach them (Curl, 1980). Efforts were made to renew this form of localized, independent communism in the 1880s and 1890s, but by then the model had been disparaged by Marx and Engels as not only unable to transform society, but also reactionary (in the sense of backward-looking). The political energy needed to resurrect it therefore proved too much to muster. In the end, these isolated, localized communes had little impact on the burgeoning industrial capitalist country of the nineteenth-century. As Oved (1988, pp. 14–15) argues, "The commune never became an integral part of the forces that formed the nation. Even when they flourished, the commune and its revolutionary lifestyle never endangered the trend of American society. Communes remained a marginal factor, and this is perhaps the reason why there was no attempt to undermine or uproot them." Thus the nineteenth-century communes – black or white, religious or secular – had little impact on the larger world around them mostly due to their goal of opting out, although the reasons differed. This lesson should have been learned by those who created the 1960s incarnations of the commune, were it not for the amnesia cited at the beginning of this chapter.

Things Come Together, Things Fall Apart: The Experience of the 1960s

These two traditions of very different kinds of communes and co-ops converged for a brief period in the mid- to late 1960s, but the convergence was short-lived, constituted by and constitutive of several other social movements. Community (or neighborhood) control reemerged as a broad set of movements in this period, but their strands remained distinct – in their goals, ideological justifications, and institutional forms. Broadly speaking, there were three different strands to this movement – the black power movement, the direct democracy movement, and the cooperative living movement – but they often overlapped, and each strand was itself not unitary but consisted of multiple components. This convergence yielded many institutional and structural innovations and changes (some shortlived, others much more durable) but for the purposes of this project, the most important institution to emerge was the "community development corporation" (CDC), which was, and is, the principle institutional vehicle for community development in the United States. But before we discuss the emergent social-movement from which sprang community development, as a programmatic idea, and the CDC, its vehicle, we need to discuss the context of American politics that both fostered these movements and severely undercut their ability to effect systematic change.

From CAAs to model cities and beyond

The federal government enacted the Economic Opportunity Act in 1964 and with it, began the well-known period of the "War on Poverty." While this war on poverty contained a diverse set of institutions, for the purposes of this discussion, the most important components of this legislation were its creation of the Office of Economic Opportunity (OEO), and a new vehicle for community-based organizing, planning, and activism, the "community action agency" (CAA). The heart of the CAA initiative was community empowerment and activism, and the underlying philosophy of the Community Action Program (CAP, which was responsible for overseeing the CAAs) was the "maximum feasible participation" of community members – particularly low-income blacks. This drive in federal policy was a complete change from its earlier practice of ignoring local communities during the early Urban Renewal programs of the 1950s. It probably, however, reflected the needs of the Democratic party to generate black involvement in formal politics as much as it was a response to the increasing demands for power by the civil-rights movement which had moved north during the late 1950s and early 1960s (Fisher, 1994).

It is unclear, at best, if within three years the CAAs were able to generate substantial community-level mobilization efforts – and this varied from city to city. In many cities, they simply became service delivery "watchdogs" whose radical potential was rather limited, while in many of the more organized and mobilized cities, the conflictual nature of the CAAs meant that it was "all conflict, all the time." And by 1967, "they were sufficiently threatening or persuasive to precipitate a change in national urban policy" (Fainstein, 1987, p. 328). This shift in policy had two particular components. First, the CAAs were to be reoriented toward economic development activities, and away from the much more broadly understood political organizing goals of their initial inception. The legislative form this shift in priorities took was that of the passage of the Special Impact Program (SIP) amendment to the OEO, which was written by Senator Robert Kennedy after his famous visit to Bedford-Stuyvesant, Brooklyn, in 1966 (Peirce and Steinbach, 1987). The SIP legislation targeted local groups for specifically economic development projects, and this program was supplemented by the Federal Community Self-Determination Act in 1969, which drove the creation of many Community Development Corporations. Although the first CDCs had actually been created somewhat earlier in 1967, and in several different cities, it was after SIP and the 1969 Self-Determination Act that they really started to grow. And this growth was accomplished because of substantial amounts of federal support (Perry, 1971).

The second component of the shift in federal policies was the enactment of the Model Cities Program, designed to place the control over antipoverty/neighborhood development policies back into the hands of city governments – and explicitly away from the hands of communities. As Halpern puts it: "Model Cities was to be community development decoupled from community action, or more specifically from community action's presumed tendency to engender conflict and disaffection"

(Halpern, 1995, p. 118). This shift indicated how threatened many city governments were by the CAP. By funding CAAs directly, the OEO and CAP were enabling community organizations to bypass city governments and connect directly to national politics and priorities. Community groups had therefore been able to jump scales, while city governments were unable to do so.

These shifts in federal policies had profound implications for the practice of community organizing at the time. Groups had to choose between becoming more professionalized development organizations or maintain their political identity. But maintaining their political identity would mean the loss of the federal and, after the Model Cities Program, local funding they had come to rely on. Either way, the potential and capacity for radical community organizing and social change was significantly undercut. As Kotler observed shortly thereafter, "The government wanted enterprise rather than political action in the neighborhood; it would move the people out of the meeting hall and put them behind cash registers" (Kotler, 1971, p. 7).

To some extent, therefore, 1960s federal neighborhood policy represented a very narrow window through which connections between community-level political organizing and community-based economic development and social service provision could be merged. But that window closed rather quickly and, in doing so, helped to solidify the divisions between organizing and development, which have come to be a dominant feature in urban politics in the last quarter century.

Black power and black capitalism

While the federal government was both supporting and limiting the opportunities for community empowerment in the 1960s, one of the most powerful forces in driving issues of community control was the emergent "black power" movement, a product of the civil-rights movement, which had been mobilizing since at least the early 1950s. A significant strand of the black-power movement was the drive for "community control" (Altshuler, 1970; Carmichael and Hamilton, 1967). The movement for "community control," which was race-based, had two distinct components. First it dealt specifically with issues of government decentralization and black participation and control. This was particularly true for issues of education and policing. Second, it addressed the control over economic relations between blacks and whites. While the former segment represented a substantial set of issues and conflicts in American cities (see Fainstein and Fainstein, 1976, for a discussion of these), the latter of these two helped drive the creation of the CDC and also foreshadowed the central issue of this project: Can people acting in their communities control the economic relationships that connect them to the rest of the world?

There was not a clear, unifying underlying rationale of the economic component of the community control movement, and instead there was a variety of programs, goals, and ideals. This, of course, echoed the long-standing debates by black leaders about how to structure, organize, and promote black economic development. The 1960s version of this argument was made from a variety of different positions, ranging from direct community ownership by CDCs in black neighborhoods, to co-operative ownership by blacks, to individually owned forms of capital accumulation by blacks. Despite the debates about what form black ownership should take, some of its most visible proponents were decidedly ambivalent about it. Roy Innis, the director of the Congress of Racial Equality (CORE), was one of the principal proponents of black ownership, and his arguments, which exemplify the incoherence of this ambivalence, deserve to be quoted at length here. He stated:

> In the new focus on economic control, there has been much talk about something called 'black capitalism' ... There is no such animal. Capitalism, like socialism, is an economic and political philosophy that describes the experience of Europeans and their descendants – Americans. Blacks must innovate, must create a new ideology. It may include elements of capitalism, elements of socialism, or elements of neither: *That is immaterial.* What matters is that it will be created to fit our needs. (Innis, 1969, pp. 52–3, emphasis added)

This ambivalence led, fairly quickly, to a reassertion of Booker T. Washington's Reconstruction Era arguments about the central role of black entrepreneurialism and capitalism in the realization of power within the black community. So despite powerful criticisms of black capitalism (see Boggs, 1970; Kain and Persky, 1971, Sturdivant, 1969) it became, through its promotion by OEO policies, the Nixon administration, and the lack of clarity about issues of ownership by leaders in black communities, the dominant form of black economic "community" control by the end of the 1960s. It should also be noted that the Community Self-Determination Act was co-authored by CORE and the Nixon presidential campaign, and the politics surrounding its passage were a peculiar combination of black power advocates and Rockefeller Republicans (see McClaughry, 1969). As Harold Cruse perceptively noted at the time, this segment of the black power movement, "is *nothing but the economic and political philosophy of Booker T. Washington given a 1960s militant shot in the arm and brought up to date*" (Cruse, 1969, p. 114, emphasis in original). Community control, in its economic guise, remarkably quickly became an argument in support of black capitalism, and advocates for both consciously and unconsciously conflated these two goals (Allen, 1969; Faux, 1971; Green and Faux, 1969; McKersie, 1968; Perry, 1972). The radical potential of demands for black economic power thus became co-opted and transformed into simply a debate about how best to reproduce capitalist practices in black urban neighborhoods. The road of collective *community* control and empowerment was not taken (Shipp, 1996). A substantial political opportunity was lost.

Direct democracy and neighborhood government

While the community control argument was being presented by black-power activists and theorists, a nominally comparable but substantively different argument was being presented by those advocating neighborhood control and neighborhood government. These activists and writers were advocating govern-ment decentralization as a means to politically empower the citizens of urban areas. In short, this movement represented another incarnation of the Jeffersonian liberal traditional of populism and small-scale participatory government. As Wilson put it, "It is primarily at the neighborhood level that meaningful [i.e., potentially reward-ing] opportunities for the exercise of urban citizenship exist" (Wilson, 1968, p. 28). Jane Jacobs similarly wrote from Toronto, "The governments of large modern cities are not only incomprehensibly complex today, but also their direct effects on citi-zen's lives are now so ubiquitous that they cannot help but fail when their functions are centrally organized. Many functions must be decentralized and brought under direct, continuing control of local communities" (quoted in Repo, 1977, p. 48).

But perhaps the strongest supporter of the neighborhood democracy movement was Milton Kotler, who would eventually become the executive director of the National Association of Neighborhoods. He was clear about what he saw as, "the radical politics of local control" (Kotler, 1969), as a rejection of both the centralized welfare policies of the New Deal/Great Society variety, and the central role of class in leftist politics. Both of these should be replaced, he argued, by an embrace of the Ancient Greek view of humans as almost inherently political beings mixed with a twentieth-century perspective on the declining ability of humans to act as such (see Arendt, 1958). He argued that "True radicalism issues from a practical view of man's political nature, rather than a theoretical view of the state. Its object is to shape the state to fit the present purpose of popular struggle – local rule – not to reshape man to fit a theoretical state. For the left to engage in a politics of liberty requires that it free itself of the modern heritage of revolution and address the principles of local control" (Kotler, 1969, p. 96). Thus, like the black community control movement, when push came to shove, not only did the neighborhood government movement fail to address issues of capital and class relations, it actually embraced the capitalist political economy, albeit with a rejection of its bureaucratized and centralized Keynesian form.

This was, in short, a movement for localized democracy as an end in itself, not a movement to use the framework of local democracy for changes in larger-scale, *or even local*, economic structures and relations. The movement for neighborhood control was not without its political victories and, together with the state-centered wing of the black community control movement, it did affect some institutional changes, most notably in the creation of Boston's "Little City Halls," and New York City's (now defunct) school districts and Community Boards (Fainstein and Fainstein, 1976). But even these institutional victories did not mark a substantial wresting of control from municipal governments by neighborhoods (Marcuse, 1987).

Co-ops, communes, and collectives

At the same time that the efforts for black power and direct democracy were being undertaken, the history of communal and collective ownership entered a new phase. During the 1960s, various forms of collective ownership were being created. These efforts tended to be small in scale and very localized in their goals and orientations. Also, the collectives tended to be centered around the institutions of social-service provision and social reproduction: Free schools, communal housing and, consumer co-operatives were the primary forms of this re-emergence. The goals of these forms of collectives ranged from the fairly apolitical cooperatives (see Dodge, 1964) to "counterinstitutions" of the New Left. Adherents of the latter wanted to construct a new society, and took seriously Mao's story of the old man who shocked his neighbors by moving a mountain one stone at a time as a parable of how small changes can have a cumulative impact on society. They wanted, in short, to "live the revolution" (Moberg, 1979).

At the same time, this was largely a movement of disaffected middle-class white Americans, and was not predicated on a complex analysis of class or race structures. The co-ops', and communes', small size (often no bigger than a communal house in a city) belied their criticisms of the larger society and their conscious goal of using the new institutions as a model to transform that society. Alternative (i.e., collectively owned and controlled) institutions were created throughout the country, but despite their political content, these counterinstitutions were only loosely connected to the larger political movements of the time. This was partly a function of their limited size but also a result of how they constructed themselves in the form of communes. Communes tend to be separatist and closed, which does not easily translate into connected components of a larger movement. In her analysis of American communes, Cavan (1976) found these two attributes (along with the voluntary involvement of their members) to be what characterize communes in the first place, and what distinguishes them from other small-scale social networks and subsocieties. All of this resulted in the demise of most of the communes in the 1970s, and many of the education and social-service reforms initiated became parts of the larger bureaucratic structures that these groups emerged as an "alternative" to in the first place. The echoes of the nineteenth-century communes' experiences were striking. Both were unable to substantially transform society because change cannot be affected by simply "opting out," but instead requires direct confrontations with the structures that govern the political economy. This is an issue that we will return to later in this project.

Opportunities lost

The possibilities of connecting these three separate movements, all struggling for local control, albeit in somewhat different forms, were always fairly slim. And in many basic ways, they were fighting for different goals and had very different constituencies. But, at the same time, they were conscious political efforts to create institutions in which local-scale actors had greater control over their lives. They also shared a rhetorical belief in "community" participation and control. Participatory democracy was, stated or unstated, a central goal of these groups, and it was this goal that brought these activists together, on paper at least in the form of books written at the time (see, in particular, Benello and Roussopoulos, 1971).

At the same time, their understandings of capital and class were extremely limited and none of these forms of local control directly confronted capital or even adequately theorized capitalism. In this way, the movements failed to appreciate the inherent importance of capital and class relations in structuring the American political economy. As Ira Katnelson (1981) argues in his exceptional book, this failure to understand class leads to movements sliding into the prefigured "trenches" of American urban politics in which *class* is dealt with at work, and *community* is dealt with at home – and both are dealt with inadequately. And in sliding into those trenches, the invisibility of class in American public life is reproduced. This set the community and neighborhood control efforts up to either disappear or become institutionally co-opted. And this is largely what happened in the 1970s and 1980s.

From Community Control to Community-Based Development: 1970 to the Present

The period that stretches from the early 1970s to the present has often been described as one in which there is a general decline in the levels of local-scale political organizing, or the "death of urban politics" referred to in chapter 1 [original text]. While there is certainly a degree of truth to this statement, it is also an oversimplification of local and community politics. Instead, this period can better be described as one in which there has been an increasing disassociation of explicitly political community organizing from community development. Both continue, but they are too often conflated, with the latter being assumed to stand for the former. As such, CDCs are no longer seen as vehicles for community control but instead are characterized as sources for "community-based" activities like housing or "development." This divide, which began in the 1960s with the changing funding priorities of the OEO splitting CDCs from CAAs, is reproduced and strengthened with each generation of community development and organizing groups. But I am getting ahead of myself, and I must first discuss the trends in community or, more appropriate to the time, neighborhood organizing in the 1970s.

Neo-Alinskyism and the neighborhood movements of the 1970s

Often described as distinct from what had come in the preceding decade, local politics in the 1970s is better understood as having evolved from the earlier period, particularly from the direct democracy strand of organizing. Local politics were dominated in this decade by what has been called "the neighborhood movement" (*Social Policy*, 1979). In truth, this was less a movement than a diverse set of localized responses to particular issues that largely stemmed from people's attempts to protect their neighborhoods from threats and encroachments from without. Accordingly, the politics of the organizations in this "movement" varied tremendously, largely in relation to the character of the threat from without and the perceived sources of that threat.

As this "Backyard Revolution" (Boyte, 1980) was taking place, a set of populist organizations emerged that were large in scale (often state- or nation-wide) and relatively unencumbered by an ideologically defined set of goals. The principal intellectual figure in this movement was Saul Alinsky who, although he had been organizing in Chicago since before World War II, had emerged nationally as a prominent critic of the explicitly socialist and race-based organizing efforts of the 1960s. Instead, he and his organization, the Industrial Areas Foundation (IAF), argued for a brand of organizing that assumed that the only long-term goal should be the mobilization of people to take power for themselves. After working for the Congress of Industrial Organizations (CIO) in the late 1930s, he argued that working-class political organizing needed to be free of the ideological framework of class, and that:

> It is not just trying to deal with the factory manager, but with every element and aspect, whether it be political, economical or social that makes up the life of the worker so that instead of viewing itself as a separate section of the American people engaged in a separate craft in a particular industry, it will think of itself as an organization of *American citizens* (Alinsky, 1969, p. 36, emphasis in original).

With his prominence in the late 1960s and 1970s (and for excellent discussions of the goals and importance of Alinsky-style organizing, see Fisher, 1994, pp. 138–55; and Stein, 1986), the work of Alinsky and the IAF played a central role in the emergence of national groups such as the Association of Community Organizations for Reform Now (ACORN) and statewide groups such as Massachusetts Fair Share (Delgado, 1986; Perlman, 1979).

These groups were run by largely white, primarily middle-class staffs and organizers, and the organizers often had little experience with politics and conflict, except what they learned in their training by these groups. The model of organizing was basically the same in every locality: local people would meet with organizers from the national organization to discuss their concerns and then work to mobilize larger numbers of people in those localities to address these problems. The national organizer, therefore, brings no agenda to the locality but instead allows the issues, and the solutions, to be defined by those within the locality. The recipe, therefore, was for a situation in which the IAF was working nationally to mobilize people, but its local-scale organizations, lacking any coherent ideological framework, became about neigh-borhoods "getting what they could." This, however, left them poorly positioned to deal with larger social forces, processes, and changes. In this model, the goals of community control and community empowerment remained, but rather than being seen as means to an end, they became ends in and of themselves. And in this way, it theoretically and practically overlapped with the neighborhood control movement of the late 1960s.

This left neighborhood organizations in the position of being particularly vulnerable to co-optation. This is essentially what happened as the 1980s emerged, and these groups evolved from confrontational organizations to developers. This evolution, which will be discussed shortly, was actually prefigured by the transformation of one of Alinsky's own groups in Chicago, The Woodlawn Organization (TWO). This organization, founded in 1961, was rather militant and held rent strikes and mobilized protests and picket lines, but by the early 1970s the organization had already been transformed into functionally acting as a CDC (Fish, 1973; Fisher, 1994; Jones, 1979). While the group realized early successes, it lacked enough vision to build on those successes when the area continued to decline and suffer from disinvestment and arson. Fish (1973) argued that the group's survival was an important achievement, but it is not clear how its survival affected any significant changes or even necessarily benefited the Woodlawn area.

To say, however, that politically progressive organizing did not occur in the 1970s would be both unfair and an oversimplification of local politics at the time. First, while the neo-Alinsky style organizers were self-avowedly "nonideological" in perspective, their goals of increased participation in, and the democratization of, urban politics were certainly laudable. They were also explicitly confrontational. They recognized that there are inherent conflicts in society, and understood that power is only appropriated through struggle. Second, there were powerful, community based efforts to prevent the displacement of low-income residents by the continued construction of roads through inner-city neighborhoods, and by the last remnants of the Urban Renewal program's demolition (which formally ended in 1973 but, given the lag time associated with government construction projects, dragged on through to the late 1970s). Third, substantial political and legal victories were realized by those who struggled against the practice of financial institution redlining, and the efforts of these organizers yielded the 1975 passage of the Federal Home Mortgage Loan Disclosure Act and the 1977 Community Reinvestment Act (Squires, 1992).

CDCs: professionalization and a new generation

While the neighborhood movement was emerging in the 1970s, the older CDCs were themselves undergoing significant changes, with a new set of "2nd generation" (Peirce and Steinbach, 1987; Zdenek, 1987) CDCs growing from the roots of the antiredlining and urban renewal fights that had taken place. The older CDCs were facing uneven outcomes, as some grew while others failed. They shared a common experience, however, in which the sense of community control of enterprise continued to decline in importance as profit-making increasingly became the dominant goal. This was partly driven by the difficult realities of the markets these groups were operating within. This problem surfaced almost immediately (see Sturdivant, 1971), and continues today, but was also a function of the changing priorities of the OEO which, despite being on its last political legs, was still the dominant source of financial support for these "1st generation" CDCs. In one of the last policy statements from the OEO about the SIP program, issued in 1974, the agency stated, "All things being equal, ventures with a greater employment potential should be given higher priority than those with smaller employment potential, but in the short term job creation should not be pursued as an objective at the sacrifice of venture profits" and "In order to produce benefits for low-income impact area residents, however, the institution-building and venture development efforts of the CDC require the participation of the non-poor in managerial and leadership roles" (quoted in Berndt, 1977, p. 137). The OEO, however, was not long for this world, and the Nixon administration terminated the agency and the CDC program was shifted to the newly created Community Services Administration. The first-generation CDCs were therefore left to deal with this loss of funding and, in accordance with the ideologies of black capitalism and the priorities that had been established by the OEO and President Nixon, they did so by becoming increasingly individualist and entrepreneurial in their orientation and goals.

Evaluations written during the 1970s, which for all intents and purposes were the first real evaluations of the CDCs created in the late 1960s, indicate the extent to which community control had become less important relative to the goal of economic development. Kelly (1977) conducted a survey of the members of the boards of directors of the CDCs created by OEO funding, and found that only 35 percent of the board members considered, "Providing opportunities for community-controlled ownership of businesses and property" one of their three highest priorities (Kelly, 1977, p. 25). In fact, in her analysis of community economic development, she plainly stated: "the community economic development movement in no way opposes or contradicts the American tradition of individual entrepreneurship" (Kelly, 1977, p. 21). A similar observation was made by Berndt (1977) who described the Bedford-Stuyvesant Restoration Corporation (the CDC that emerged from Robert Kennedy's tour through the neighborhood) as being run like General Motors. This should not have been surprising, because the people running it were the chair of Mobil Oil and the president of Citibank (Stoecker, 1997).

The second generation CDCs created in the late 1970s and the early 1980s came out of a different tradition from that of the first generation. Whereas the first generation was founded largely through government sponsorship, this second generation emerged out of protest movements that became organizations (see Piven and Cloward, 1977, for a useful framework for understanding the distinctions between movements and organizations). In becoming CDCs, they transformed themselves from being confrontational in their dealings with city governments, schools, banks and other local expressions of power, to cooperative in those relationships as they became more immersed in the structures against which they were originally protesting (Fulton, 1987; Gittell, 1980; Lenz, 1988).

Shelterforce magazine, one of the primary forums for discussion of CDCs and community organizing efforts, observed that there tended to be a three-step process to the transformation of oppositional community organizations to CDCs in the late 1970s and early 1980s. First, the groups emerge out of opposition to something (redlining, displacement, etc.). Second, the groups become somewhat more proactive, and begin direct political lobbying of city halls to enact their agendas. Third, the groups realize the limits of public money, and begin working to fulfill their agenda themselves (Fulton, 1987). While this description is a rather crude one, it nonetheless fairly accurately describes a process which was not actually one of political co-optation, but instead one of professionalization. These groups were not created to fundamentally transform the structures that govern the urbanization process. They emerged out of localized problems and conflicts, and it was not ideologically inconsistent to deal with local-scale problems as a developer rather than an adversarial activist. These transformations were not, therefore, normative. Instead they were merely programmatic.

Nonprofits for hire: the 1980s and 1990s[1]

The 1980s and 1990s marked the coming of age for community development, as the number of CDCs grew rapidly, along with a heightened public awareness of their existence and activities and an increased set of burdens and expectations placed upon them. This growth of activity has been evident both in the number of CDCs and in their average size. While only about 150 first-generation CDCs were created in the late 1960s and early 1970s (and many failed within a few years), by the early 1980s another 500 to 750 second-generation CDCs had been created (Zdenek, 1987). The number of CDCs exploded in the 1980s, and an additional 1,000 CDCs were created between 1981 and 1987 (Peirce and Steinbach, 1987). The number of CDCs nationwide, therefore, essentially grew at modest, but significant, rate through the end of the 1960s and the 1970s, and beginning in the late 1970s and early 1980s began to grow much more rapidly. This growth continued through the decade, and by the early 1990s more than 2,000 were operating nationwide (de Souza Briggs, Mueller, and Sullivan, 1997). This rapid growth has since continued, and there are currently roughly 3,600 CDCs (National Congress for Community Economic Development, 2002).

The growth of CDCs has been accompanied by significant changes in their structures, goals, and relationships with the public and private for-profit sectors. First, CDCs grew in the 1980s in spite of, and partially in reaction to, the shrinking desire of the public sector to provide goods of collective consumption – particularly affordable housing. The disappearance of Urban Development Action Grants (UDAGs) and project-based Section 8 funding are two of the most notable and visible examples of this decline in federal support for inner-city areas. Shrinking public resources left CDCs directly facing the impacts of these cutbacks, and thus helped create many more CDCs out of community-based political organizations. Local governments, [...], exacerbated this loss of federal money by increasingly withdrawing from the provision of social services and housing in the 1980s. CDCs thus filled the vacuum left by the state – both at the local and federal levels. And while CDCs are rightfully best known for producing housing, their role is, and was, not limited to just affordable housing, as CDCs branched out into the areas of social-service provision, education, and health and child care (Vidal, 1996).

The second transformation emerges from the first. Because of the decline in public-sector support, funding for CDCs and CDC activities went from a "one-stop shopping" toward more "creative" forms of financing, often referred to as "patchwork" financing (Vidal, 1997). CDCs increasingly found themselves in the 1980s and 1990s putting together the funding for projects from a variety of sources, such as private investments made to receive a Low-Income Housing Tax Credit (after 1986), financial institution loans made to satisfy CRA requirements, grants from foundations, etc. This patchwork financing has furthered the process of professionalization in community development, because the financial-management capacities it requires greatly exceed those of the prior, single-source financing.

Such expertise has often come from the national intermediaries that were constructed in the late 1970s and early 1980s. In the space of four years, 1978–1981, the four most important intermediaries/foundations in community development were created. These are: the Neighborhood Reinvestment Corporation (NRC), formed by the federal government; the Local Initiatives Support Corporation (LISC), started by the Ford Foundation; the Fannie Mae Foundation, created by Fannie Mae; and the Enterprise Foundation, the product of real-estate magnate, and sometime urban utopian, Jim Rouse. Together they finance, provide technical assistance for, and generally shape the structure of the community-development industry. They are key institutions in both the growth of CDCs and in their increasing professionalization.

Together, this growing network of localized CDCs, their larger-scale foundation support, and other not-for-profit voluntary associations, have created a situation in which CDCs in many poor neighborhoods and localities have functionally become "the Shadow State" (Wolch, 1990). They provide the goods of collective consumption that formerly virtually defined municipal government functions. This role has been embraced not only by CDCs themselves, but by the state, as it willingly walks away from the provision of these services, and looks to the community-based sector to fill in the holes it has left behind (DeFilippis, 1997). It is also important to note that this public sector retreat, and the growth of the not-for-profit sector in public life, has been actively promoted by both the Democratic and Republican parties. And in 1996, while Newt Gingrich was wondering aloud about the movie *Boys Town* and the use of not-for-profit orphanages as a solution to the "problems" of children of welfare parents, president Clinton was leading a weekend-long celebration of "volunteerism" in Philadelphia. These events are merely emblematic, and represent the broad (if often only rhetorical) support for not-for-profits by both parties.

At the same time, most of whatever remained of the radical politics that were part of the context from which CDCs emerged in the 1960s, was lost, as they became increasingly part of the urban political machinery and political organizing receded further from their goals and mission. The Ford Foundation's definitive guide to community development in the 1980s put it – without any sense of apology: "with rare exceptions, the 1960s are now as much history for them (CDCs) as for the rest of American society. One can't very well hurl his body into the path of an oncoming bulldozer when he (or she) is the developer" (Peirce and Steinbach, 1987, p 8). That guide was tellingly called *Corrective Capitalism*.

Community development today

As has already been suggested, the community-development industry in the 1990s and 2000s has progressed along much the same lines that had been established in the earlier periods. In the last decade, the field has been dominated by various programmatic initiatives or trends focused on how to best go about "doing" community development. This has included discussions of "community-based assets," "capacity-building," "consensus organizing" and "social capital construction," among others. Rather than discuss these initiatives individually, it is perhaps more useful to explain the perspectives, aims, and objectives that they all share.

First, these initiatives are unambiguously market-based in their larger goals and programmatic details. This perspective has probably been made most explicit by Michael Porter through his Initiative for a Competitive Inner City and in a set of articles (Porter, 1995, 1997) which argued that, "a sustainable economic base can be created in inner cities only as it has been elsewhere. through private, for-profit initiatives, and investments based on economic self-interest and genuine competitive advantage" (Porter, 1997, p. 12). But Porter is far from alone in making these arguments, and the dominant argument at this point is that for CDCs to be successful, not only must they adopt an explicitly entrepreneurial set of goals and practices, but they must also work with the corporate sector (Bendick and Egan, 1991; Berger and Steinbach, 1992; Carr, 1999; Grogan and Proscio, 2000; Peirce and Steinbach, 1987; Taub, 1990; Tholin, 1994; Vidal, 1992, 1996). This point is highlighted by the trajectory of Paul Grogan, who was the president of LISC for over a decade and then founded CEOs for Cities (Herbert, 2001).

The second shared attribute of community development theory and practice in the last decade is a promotion of nonconfrontational forms of engagement and organizing. Community development is now a collaborative process, and the older, more conflictual ideals of black power, and neo-Alinsky-style organizing have been rejected (Epstein, 1996). Michael Eichler, the president of the Consensus Organizing Institute, which has received a great deal of attention in the field (see Gittell and Vidal, 1998), described a project that the Institute had worked on as having, "demonstrated the essential attribute of consensus organizing: instead of taking power from those who have it, consensus organizers build relationships in which power is shared for mutual benefit Cooperation, rather than confrontation became the modus operandi for solving a neighborhood problem" (Eichler, 1998). Within the current understanding of cooperation, there is almost contempt for past organizing efforts, and Grogan and Proscio state, "The community organizing and planning of that period (the 1960s) was soon squandered on divisive or extremist political tactics, including the in-your-face style of protest that Tom Wolfe famously dubbed, 'mau-mauing'" (Grogan and Proscio, 2000, p. 66). The dominant understanding is thus that low-income inner-city residents have a shared set of interests with the larger society they exist within, and organizing and development should be structured accordingly. Power relations are therefore downplayed or completely ignored in this framework.

While it might seem a bit paradoxical, given the neo-liberal market orientation described above, the current period in community development is also characterized by a powerful reassertion of the idea of *community*, and a particular version of *communitarianism* (see Sites, 1998). This communitarian framework is one which posits a belief that there are shared interests among individuals in a community, and thus community development should be about creating the social relationships that allow those mutual goals to be realized. This form of communitarianism thus mirrors consensus-based organizing, in that the assumption is of shared interests; the difference is one assumes it for relations between people in the community and the rest of the world, and the other for relations between people within a community. There are two principal figures in this understanding of community. The first is John McKnight, who has argued for a framework of community development centered around "community-based assets" (Kretzmann and McKnight, 1993; McKnight, 1995; see also Shragge and Fisher, 2001). The second is Robert Putnam, whose work on social capital (Putnam, 1995, 1996, 2000) has become almost axiomatic in community-development theory and practice (see DeFilippis, 2001). Not only do both of them argue that relations within communities tend to be largely "win-win" relations, but both take that framework one step farther to assume that *individual* gains and interests in the community are synonymous with *collective*, or community, gains and interests. Both also largely assume that communities are functions of, and defined by, the attributes and relationships of people within them. Thus not only does this particular form of communitarianism fit with consensus or nonconfrontational organizing, but it also fits with the neoliberal, market-based perspectives and policies that govern community development activity.

Together these three perspectives, which dominate the theory and practice of community development, can best be described as a form of *neoliberal communitarianism*. This neoliberal communitarianism has, at its core, a belief that society is conflict-free, and it gets this from both halves of its theoretical framework. It also represents the fruition of the depoliticization of community development that came with its split from community organizing in the late 1960s. This depoliticization also needs to be understood as both a product, and producer, of their support from the public sector. The political logic of CDCs in American politics has therefore come full circle. The federal government, which initiated the movement for community development by sponsoring often radical political organizations working toward community control and empowerment, now supports CDCs exactly because they are no longer connected to any radical political movement. And the goals of CDCs have also come full circle. Initially conceived as vehicles that would use the market as a means to the end of community empowerment and control, they have now become vehicles for the market, in which the goal of community control is not even an issue.

Problems in Neoliberal Communitarian Community Development Theory and Practice

All of this would be fine, and not warrant any objection here, if this understanding of community development had demonstrated itself capable of accomplishing the two goals of this project: to allow low-income people to have more control over their economic lives, and to do so in ways which equitably improve the lives of people in low-income communities. Unfortunately, it has failed in achieving, or moving toward, both of these goals. Admittedly, community development has produced a substantial volume of adequate affordable housing for low-income people over the last thirty years. And certainly the lives of thousands of low-income people have benefited significantly because of this. But all too often, the reality has been that community-development efforts have failed to visibly or measurably improve the larger communities in which they are located. Instead, we are faced, as Lenz put it, with "the terrible paradox of thriving organizations and dying communities," or, more morbidly, "the operation was successful, but the patient died" (Lenz, 1988, p. 25). The persistence of these problems led Stoecker to observe that "the continuing critiques of CDCs across three decades suggest that more is at issue than imperfect practice" (Stoecker, 1997, p. 4). He is certainly right. The problems are much more fundamental and require a complete rethinking of community development. Community development needs to reconnect with its goals of community control, but it must do in a way that understands capital, capitalism, and class in American society.

The theoretical problems relate to both halves of the neoliberal communitarian framework, and they will be addressed in turn. First, the interests of capital should not be assumed to be synonymous with the interests of communities. I do not subscribe to the view that capital and community *necessarily* have the diametrically opposing interests of exchange value and use value (respectively), and some forms of capital are very much *within* communities. But given the lack of capital owned and controlled by low-income people, however, the use value vs. exchange value is usually the case. Capital is interested in the extraction of profit, which is needed to reproduce itself and to generate wealth for the *individuals* who own it. This is inherently true in capitalism. We should no more assume the shared interests of black inner-city business owners and their workers than we would the shared interests of Nike and its sweatshop workers in Indonesia. And while both the local business owners and their workers might share an interest in a community (because of their local dependence on it), that in no way eliminates their inherent respective class interests.

Second, capitalism is about competition – both between and within classes. And while capitalist economies are not zero-sum games, they still, like all forms of competition, unquestionably produce winners and losers. Given this reality, it is exceedingly unlikely that low-income people in inner-city areas would be able to succeed in many competitions with their wealthier, better-educated, and more politically powerful, suburban (or urban gentrifier) counterparts. This is especially true if the playing field for the competition is the free market, which has already produced such uneven results. Uneven development is an inherent component of capitalism, and one of the primary geographic manifestations of its competitive structure. Only by ignoring this geographical and historical truism can we assume that underdeveloped places and spaces can be developed by the free market for the gains of people within them.

Third, given the histories of capital disinvestment and decline in most inner-city neighborhoods, more often than not, any investment capital in them will need to come from the outside. The potential for inner-city residents to control their own economic lives therefore immediately gets undercut by a framework that relies on free-market investments into the inner-city. Embracing the market leaves control over capital and economic development firmly and squarely beyond the reach of people in the inner-city.

The communitarian half of the framework is comparably fundamentally flawed, and in similar ways. First, the individual is *not* the same as the group. We cannot assume that individual gains and interests are the same as those of the larger community. This point is especially valid in low-income urban neighborhoods. As Blakely and Small astutely observe in their critique of Porter, "there is little connection between [individual] work and better outcomes for ghetto dwellers or for their communities. The signals are very clear. To move up economically requires moving out. As a result, the link between job and social betterment is lost collectively as achievers move out of the ghetto" (Blakely and Small, 1996, p. 166).

Second, the communitarian perspective assumes that people in a community share common interests simply by virtue of living in the same area. But clearly communities are diverse, conflict-laden, and contested places and spaces. For interests to be shared requires the construction of shared interests – not the a priori assumption of their existence. Landlords and renters, business owners and workers, and service providers and recipients are all fairly obvious examples of how interests are not shared by people in a community. They demonstrate that individuals' self-interest cannot be "added up" to yield a community's interests. Not only does this assumption of shared or mutual interests deny the various forms of exploitation and conflict that occur between people in a community, it also ignores how oppressive communities can be to people who are in some way defined as "different" (see Young, 1990, for a thorough discussion of these issues).

Third, communities are not simply the products of the attributes of the people within them. Instead, [...], for localities, communities are the products of a complex set of much larger-scale social relationships. Citibank (for instance) and its lending practices, state governments and their education financing policies, communities with soon-to-be emigrants in other countries, are all very real examples of how America's urban communities are products of a whole host of relations that extend geographically well beyond the place of the community. These relations are often contentious (school funding issues being a classic example), and are always imbued with issues of power. Only by ignoring these vitally important, power-laden connections can we assume that communities are the products of the attributes of the individuals that live and work within them.

Along with concerns over the processes of globalization and capital mobility, it was in reaction to this fundamentally flawed framework for community development that this current project emerged. But this is also why the failures of the 1960s community control efforts warranted such attention here. At the substantial risk of telescoping history, the current problems of CDCs stem from the flaws of the framework that inspired their formation. The contemporary forms of community development only represent a deepening of those problems – not their creation.

Concluding Comments

I want to end this chapter by discussing three moments from 1999, which highlight the contemporary political state of community development. The first is an extended memo in the *Neighborworks Journal*, which is the journal of the NRC, by James Carr, senior vice-president of the Fannie Mae Foundation. In it he issued a call for "A New Paradigm for Community Reinvestment." The new paradigm called for greater collaboration between community developers and outside investors and businesses. It included a promotion of the idea of place-marketing in which community development projects could take on names such "The Woodlands," "Celebration" and "Redwood Shores." He even stated, "some of these places could be treated as urban blank slates, where the development takes on an image the investors choose" (Carr, 1999, p. 21). In this new paradigm, the first role for government is to, "assist private firms to extract value from community assets" (Carr, 1999, p. 22) – which is a far cry from government supporting community control or equitable development.

The second "moment" comes from the substantial gutting of the Community Reinvestment Act, which occurred in the fall of 1999. The CRA was a product of long-standing community organizing efforts in the 1970s, and its enactment as a national regulatory policy in 1977 needs to be understood as a major victory for organizers at the time. After years of political pressure from banks to eliminate it, or substantially mitigate its regulatory powers, the fight came to a head in 1999. The problem was that by 1999 the community organizations that had worked so hard to see it enacted had long since become CDCs. As such, they were unable or unwilling to mobilize much constituency to save it. To be fair, ACORN did have some demonstrations and protests, but the political battle was largely waged as one of "our lobbyists" vs. "their lobbyists." The outcome, therefore, was never seriously in doubt.

Finally, that summer I was at a meeting at the Urban Justice Center in New York planning a march from Washington, DC, to New York City as part of the now-international Economic Human Rights Campaign. In the course of the discussion, one of the issues that arose was contacting other community organizations who might be sympathetic to the march in order to solicit their support. One of the people in the room (John Krinsky, who had researched Mutual Housing Associations and Community Land Trusts, while at the Community Service Society [...]) suggested that one of the groups we should contact about this march was the Association of Neighborhood and Housing Development (ANHD). ANHD is the principal trade association for CDCs in New York City. The response from the roomful of thirty local community and political organizers to the mention of its name was a unanimous, "Who?"

Note

1   The title of this section subheading is taken from the title of smith and Lipsky's 1993 book.

References

Alinsky, S. 1969 (1946). *Reveille for Radicals*. New York: Random House.
Allen, L. 1969. Making capitalism work in the ghettos. *Harvard Business Review*, May–June: 83–92.
Altshuler, A. 1970. *Community Control*. New York: Pegasus.
Arendt, H. 1958. *The Human Condition*. Chicago: University of Chicago Press.
Bendick, M. and M. L. Egan. 1991. *Business Development in the Inner-City. Enterprise with Community Links*. New York: Community Development Research Center/New School for Social Research.
Benello, C. G. and D. Roussopoulos (eds.), 1971. *The Case For Participatory Democracy: Some Prospects for a Radical Society*. New York: Grossman Publishers.
Berger, R. and C. Steinbach. 1992. *A Place in the Marketplace: Making Capitalism Work in Poor Communities*. Washington, DC: National Congress for Community Economic Development.
Berndt, H. L. 1977. *New Rulers in the Ghetto: The Community Development Corporation and Urban Poverty*. Westport, CT: Greenwood Press.
Blakely, E. J. and L. Small. 1996. Michael Porter: New Gilder of Ghettos. *Review of Black Political Economy*. Fall/Winter, 161–83.
Boggs, J. 1970. *Racism and the Class Struggle*. New York: Monthly Review Press.
Boyte, H. 1980. *The Backyard Revolution. Understanding the New Citizen Movement*. Philadelphia: Temple University Press.
Carmichael, S. and C. V. Hamilton. 1967. *Black Power*. New York: Vintage.
Carr, J. 1999. Community, Capital and Markets: A New Paradigm for Community Reinvestment. *The Neighborworks Journal*, summer: 20–3.
Case, J. and R. C. R. Taylor. 1979. *Co-ops, Communes & Collectives: Experiments in Social Change in the 1960s and 1970s*. New York: Pantheon Books.
Cavan, R. S. 1976 *Communes, Historical and Contemporary*. New Delhi: Vikas.
Cruse, H. 1969. *Rebellion or Revolution*. New York: Apollo Books.
Curl, J. 1980. *History of Work Cooperation in America: Cooperatives, Cooperative Movements, Collectivity, and Communalism from Early America to the Present*. Berkeley, CA: Homeward Press.
de Souza Briggs, X., E. Mueller, and M. Sullivan. 1997. *From Neighborhoods to Communities: The Social Impacts of Community Development Corporations*. New York: Community Development Research Center New School for Social Research.
DeFilippis, J. 1997. Community, locality, and the transformation of inter-scale relations in the American political economy. Paper presented at the Annual Meeting of the Political Geography Specialty Group of the Association of American Geographers. San Marcos, TX. April.
DeFilippis, J. 2001. The myth of social capital in community development. *Housing Policy Debate*. 12(4): 781–806.
Delgado, G. 1986. *Organizing the Movement: The Roots and Growth of ACORN* Philadelphia: Temple University Press.
Dodge, P. J. 1964. *People Help Themselves through Cooperatives*. New York: Public Affairs Committee.
Eichler, M. 1998. Look to the future, learn from the past. *Shelterforce Online*. September/October. http://www.nhi.org/online/issues/101/eichler.html
Epstein, R. 1996. The de-activist. *City Limits*. October: 18–23.

Fainstein, N. and S. Fainstein. 1976. The future of community control. *The American Political Science Review* 70: 905–23.

Fainstein, S. 1987. Local mobilization and economic discontent. In M. P. Smith and J. Feagin (eds.). *The Capitalist City*. Cambridge, MA: Blackwell.

Faux, G. 1971. *CDCs: New Hope for the Inner City*. New York: Twentieth Century Fund.

Feuer, L. S. 1966. The influence of the American Communist colonies on Engels and Marx. *The Western Political Quarterly*, September, 19(3): 456–74.

Fish, J. H. 1973. *Black Power, White Control: The Struggle of the Woodlawn Organization in Chicago* Princeton, NJ: Princeton University Press.

Fisher, R. 1994. *Let The People Decide: Neighborhood Organizing in America. Updated Edition.* New York: Twayne Publishers.

Fulton, W. 1987. Off the barricades, into the boardrooms. *Planning*, August: 11–15.

Gittell, M. 1980. *The Limits to Citizen Participation: The Decline of Community Organizations.* Beverly Hills, CA: Sage.

Gittell, R. and A. Vidal. 1998. *Community Organizing: Building Social as a Development Strategy*. Thousand Oaks, CA: Sage.

Green, G. and G. Faux. 1969. The social utility of black nterprise. In W. Haddad and D. Pugh (eds.). *Black Economic Development*. Englewood Cliffs, NJ: Prentice Hall.

Grogan, P. and T. Proscio. 2000. *Comeback Cities*. New York: Westview Press.

Halpern, R. 1995. *Rebuilding the Inner City: A History of Neighborhood Initiatives to Address Poverty in the United States*. New York: Columbia University Press.

Hampden-Turner, C. 1975. *From Poverty to Dignity*. Garden City, NY: Anchor Press.

Herbert, B. 2001. Championing cities. *New York Times*, April 26.

Innis, R. 1969. Separatist Economics: A New Social Contract. In W. F. Haddad and G. D. Pugh (eds.). *Black Economic Development*. Englewood Cliffs, NJ: Prentice Hall.

Jones, D. J. 1979. Not in my community: The neighborhood movement and institutionalized racism. *Social Policy* 10(2): 44–7.

Kain, J. F. and J. J. Persky. 1971. Alternatives to the gilded ghetto. In R. W. Bailey (ed.). *Black Business Enterprise: Historical and Contemporary Perspectives*. New York: Basic Books.

Katznelson, I. 1981. *City Trenches: Urban Politics and the Patterning of Class in the United States*. Chicago: University of Chicago Press.

Kelly, R. M. 1977. *Community Control of Economic Development*. New York: Praeger.

Kotler, M. 1969. *Neighborhood Government: The Local Foundations of Political Life.* Indianapolis. IN: Bobbs-Merrill Company.

Kotler, M. 1971. The Politics of Community Economic Development. *Law and Contemporary Problems* 36: 3–12.

Kretzmann, J. and J. McKnight. 1993. *Building Communities from the Inside Out: A Path Toward Finding and Mobilizing a Community's Assets*. Chicago: ACTA Publications.

Lenz, T. 1988. Neighborhood development: Issues and models. *Social Policy*, spring: 24–30.

Marcuse, P. 1987. Neighborhood Policy and the Distribution of Power: New York City's Community Boards. *Policy Studies Journal*, 16(2): 277–89.

McClaughry, J. 1969. Black Ownership and National Politics. In W. F. Haddad and G. D. Pugh (eds.). *Black Economic Development*. Englewood Cliffs. NJ: Prentice Hall.

McKersie, R. B. 1968. Vitalize black enterprise. *Harvard Business Review*, September–October: 88–99.

McKnight, J. 1995. *The Careless Society: Community and Its Counterfeits*. New York: Basic Books.

Moberg, D. 1979. Experimenting with the Future: Alternative Institutions and American Socialism. In J. Case and R. Taylor (eds.). *Co-ops, Communes and Collectives: Experiments in Social Change in the 1960s and 1970s*. New York: Pantheon Books.

National Congress for Community Economic Development. 2002. *Member Information*. Washington, DC: published by author.

Nordhoff, C. 1993. *American Utopias*. Stockbridge, MA: Berkshire House, cop.

Oved, I. 1988. *Two Hundred Years of American Communes*. New Brunswick, NJ: Transaction Books.

Pease, W. H. and J. H. Pease. 1963. Black *Utopia; Negro Communal Experiments in America*. Madison: State Historical Society of Wisconsin.

Peirce, N. and C. Steinbach. 1987. *Corrective Capitalism: The Rise of America's Community Development Corporations*. New York: Ford Foundation.

Perlman, S. 1979. *A Theory of the Labor Movement*. Philadelphia: Porcupine Press.

Perry, S. 1971. A note on the genesis of the Community Development Corporation. In C. G. Benello and D. Roussopoulos (eds.). *The Case For Participatory Democracy: Some Prospects for a Radical Society*. New York: Grossman Publishers.

Perry, S. 1972. Black institutions, Black separatism, and ghetto economic development. *Human Organization* 31(3): 271–9.

Philpott, T. 1978. *The Slum and the Ghetto: Neighborhood Deterioration and Middle Class Reform, Chicago, 1880–1930*. New York: Oxford University Press.

Piven, F. P. and R. Cloward. 1977. *Poor People's Movements: Why They Succeed, How They Fail*. New York: Pantheon Books.

Porter, M. 1995. The competitive advantage of the inner city. *Harvard Business Review* 73 (May/June): 55–71.

Porter, M. 1997. New Strategies for Inner-City Economic Development. *Economic Development Quarterly* 11(1): 11–27.

Putnam, R. 1995. Bowling alone: America's declining social capital. *Journal of Democracy* 6: 65–78.

Putnam, R. 1996. The strange disappearance of civic America. *The American Prospect*, winter: 34–48.

Putnam, R. 2000. *Bowling Alone*. New York: Simon and Schuster.

Repo, M. 1977. The fallacy of community control. In J. Cowley, A. Kaye, M. Mayo, and M. Thompson (eds.) *Community or Class Struggle?* London: Stage 1.

Shipp, S. 1996. The road not taken: Alternative strategies for Black economic development in the United States. *Journal of Economic Issues* 30(1): 79–95.

Shragge, E. and R. Fisher, 2001. Community development practices: New forms of regulation and/or potential for social change. Paper presented of the annual meeting of the Urban Affairs Association. Detroit, April.

Sites, W. 1998. Communitarian theory and community development in the United States. *Community Development Journal* 33(1): 57–65.

Social Policy. 1979. *Organizing Neighborhoods*: Special Issue. September/October.

Squires, G. (ed.), 1992. *From Redlining to Reinvestment: Community Responses to Urban Disinvestment*. Philadelphia: Temple University Press.

Stein, A. 1986. Between Organization and Movement: ACORN and the Alinsky Model of Community Organizing. *Berkeley Journal of Sociology* 31: 93–115.

Stoecker, R. 1997. The CDC Model of Urban Redevelopment. *Journal of Urban Affairs* 19(1): 1–22.

Sturdivant, F. D. 1969. The Limits of Black Capitalism. *Harvard Business Review*. January–February: 122–8.

Sturdivant, F. D. 1971. Community Development Corporations: The Problem of Mixed Objectives. *Law and Contemporary Problems* 36: 35–50.

Taub, R. 1990. *Nuance and meaning in community development. Finding community and development*. New York: Community Development Research Center/New School for Social Research.

Tholin, K. 1994. *Community Development Financial Institutions: Investing in People and Communities*. Chicago: Woodstock Institute.

Vidal, A. 1992. *Rebuilding communities. A National Study of Urban Community Development Corporations*. New York: Community Development Research Center/New School for Social Research.

Vidal, A. 1996. CDCs as Agents of Neighborhood Change. The State of the Art. In D. Keating, et al. (eds.). *Revitalizing Urban Neighborhoods*. Lawrence: University of Kansas Press.

Vidal, A. 1997. Can Community Development Re-Invent Itself: *Journal of the American Planning Association,* autumn: 429–38.

Washington, B. T. 1971 (1907). *The Negro in Business*. New York: AMS Press.

Wilson, J. Q. 1968. The urban unease: community vs. city. *The Public Interest* 12 (summer): 25–40.

Wolch, J. 1990. *The Shadow State: Government and Voluntary Sector in Transition*. New York: The Foundation Center.

Young, I. M. 1990. *Justice, and the Politics of Difference*. Princeton: Princeton University Press.

Zdenek, R. 1987. Community Development Corporations. In S. Bruyn and J. Mechan (eds.). *Beyond the Market and the State: New Directions in Community Development*. Philadelphia: Temple University Press.

James deFilippis, "Collective Ownership and Community Control and Development: The Long View," from *Unmaking Goliath,* 2004, chapter 2, pp. 37–59, 163, Routledge.

15

Bringing Power to Planning Research

One Researcher's Praxis Story

Bent Flyvbjerg

The Inevitable Question of Power

Friedmann (1998), in a recent stocktaking article on planning research, identifies what he calls "perhaps the biggest problem" in theorizing and understanding planning (p. 249). This problem, according to Friedmann, is "our ambivalence about power." He rightly argues that this ambivalence exists in all major schools of planning thought from the rational planning paradigm to the knowledge/action theory of planning to the communicative paradigm. Furthermore, Friedmann says, one "of the things I would do differently today" in thinking about planning is introducing "the incvitable question of power" (p. 250). Friedmann closes his article by encouraging planning researchers to ponder the question of power with a point of departure in what is *actually* happening in city politics and planning, as opposed to what we *normatively* would like to see happen, the latter being the classic and problematic approach of planning research:

> I would like to urge those of us who are committed to the further development of planning theory to build relations of power – and especially enabling power – into our conceptual framework. This will be done more readily once we ground our theorizing in the actual politics of city-building. (pp. 252–3)

Unlike political science and sociology, the field of planning research still lacks a regular body of central monographs and articles that place power relations at their core. Valuable contributions are emerging, however, from scholars like Crush (1994), Fischler (1998), Hajer (1995), Richardson and Jensen (2000), and Yiftachel and

Readings in Planning Theory, Third Edition. Edited by Susan S. Fainstein and Scott Campbell.
Editorial material and organization © 2012 Blackwell Publishing Ltd.
Published 2012 by Blackwell Publishing Ltd.

Huxley (2000). The works of Forester (1989, 1999), Healey (1997), and other communicative theorists also talk about power. But because of their focus on Habermasian communicative rationality, they tend to remain strongly normative and procedural without the substantive understanding of *Realpolitik* and real rationality that characterizes studies of power (Flyvbjerg 1998a). My own work is an attempt at contributing to the kind of development Friedmann now encourages by introducing to planning research an intellectual tradition that is particularly strong on issues of power. This tradition runs from Aristotle to Machiavelli to Nietzsche to Foucault (Flyvbjerg 1992, 1996, 1998b, 2001; Flyvbjerg and Richardson 1998). In what follows, I will explain how I came to work with issues of power, and I will give an illustration of how the praxis-oriented methodology I have developed to study power in planning may be employed in practice. I call this methodology "phronetic planning research" after the Aristotelian concept *phronesis*.

Something Happened

One summer, something happened that would prove consequential to my professional trajectory in life. I was employed as a student intern with the newly established Regional Planning Authority with Ribe County Council in Denmark. Parliament had just passed the first law on nationwide regional planning, and the counties were in the process of preparing the first generation of regional plans. The atmosphere was one of novelty and aspiration. As a planner-to-be, I felt I was in the right place at the right time.

The central question of the regional planning exercise was the classic one of whether future development should be encouraged chiefly in the main urban centers or whether development should be decentralized and take place in smaller towns. My job was to carry out a survey of social, educational, and health services with the purpose of finding arguments for and against centralization and decentralization in these three sectors. One of the arguments I found was in a British study showing how young children's performance in school decreases with increasing distance between home and school. The study was presented in a well-known textbook with an instructive figure documenting the negative correlation between distance and learning (Abler, Adams, and Gould 1971). "Thus it would appear," the authors concluded, "that there are good psychological as well as economic reasons for minimizing the school journeys of young children" (Abler, Adams, and Gould 1971, 478). This might be seen as an argument for decentralized schools, that is, many schools close to where the children live, as opposed to fewer schools with longer distances to travel between home and school. I included this information and the figure in my draft report together with many other results that might count as pros and cons in the County Council's decision regarding whether to centralize or decentralize urban development.

After approval from my boss, my report was sent for comment to the administrative heads of the county's social, educational, and health services, respectively. When they returned the report, there was plenty of red ink on its pages. The text and figure about young children's performance in school was crossed out, among other things. A note in the margin, in finickly handwriting, read, "Cancel, may not apply in Denmark," followed by the initials of the county director of schools. The director may well have been right about this, of course, but going through his corrections, it became clear they had a peculiar pattern: knowledge that could be taken as arguments for a geographically decentralized school structure had to go, while knowledge that supported a decision to centralize the schools could stay in the report. The school administration had already unofficially decided on centralization, and the Regional Planning Authority was not allowed to interfere with knowledge that might question the wisdom of the decision. Our report had to show that centralization was desirable.

From the way the matter was handled – with a certain tension in the air; things that could not be said had to be done – it was clear to me that something important was going on. Later, I experienced a similar episode as an intern with the Ministry of Environment in Copenhagen. We had not learned about this in planning school. Our education was based on the Baconian dictum that "knowledge is power," knowledge is important. The university itself was built on that assumption. As students, we were not exposed to knowledge that addressed the question of whether it is true that knowledge is always important or what decides whether knowledge gets to count as knowledge or not. Such questions were not asked.

Today, we would say that our education lacked reflexivity on this point. However, in my practical work I had seen, on one hand, that knowledge can be so important that people in powerful positions find it worth their while to repress it. On the other hand, I had also seen examples of knowledge being so weak that this repression actually succeeded. I had seen knowledge being marginalized by power and power producing the knowledge that served its purposes best. I concluded that knowledge about the phenomena that decide whether economic, social, geographic, or other knowledge gets to count as important is at least as important as that knowledge itself. If you are not knowledgeable about the former, you cannot be effective with the latter. Even if it would take me more than a decade before I could express my experiences in scholarly formulas, I had, in fact, already found my professional interest in planning: the relationship between rationality and power, truth and politics.

Later, as a university lecturer, I found that planning, democracy, and modernity have a "blind spot" in their reflexivity regarding the relationship between rationality and power. Ideals seem to block the view to reality. Modern democratic constitutions typically prescribe a separation of rationality and power, much like the untenable separation of fact and value in conventional social and political thinking. The ideal, which often remains unrealized, prescribes that first we must know about a problem, then we can decide about it. For example, first the planners investigate a policy problem, then they inform the city council, who decides on the problem. Power is brought to bear on the problem only after we have made ourselves knowledgeable about it. In reality, however, power often ignores or designs knowledge at its convenience. A consequence of the blind spot is that the relationship between rationality and power gets little attention in the research literature. There is a large gray area between rationality and power, which is underinvestigated. This is the area where the sort of thing takes place that happened with the schools in Ribe County. The literature contains many studies of rationality and some of power, but much fewer of the relationship between the two.

I decided that as a scholar, I would study this gray area. Accepting the ideal that planning and democratic decisions should be rational and informed – an ideal to which I subscribe – should clearly not keep us from trying to understand how rationality and power relate in real planning in real democracies. First, I wanted to study the phenomenon that modern ideals of how rationality and power ought to relate – and such ideals are centrally placed in planning in any democracy – are often a far cry from the realities of how rationality and power actually relate, with only weak guiding power and impact from ideals to reality. Second, I wanted to focus on what can be done about this problem. I decided to study these issues not only in theory but also in practice. I figured that a focus on concrete cases in particular contexts would help to better understand planning practice. And I reckoned that such an understanding is necessary for changing planning practice in a direction that would leave less scope for the kind of undemocratic power-knowledge relations I had witnessed in Ribe and elsewhere. Eventually, I decided to study how rationality and power shape planning in the town where I live and work, Aalborg, Denmark.

Aalborg and Florence

Aalborg is the main urban commercial, administrative, and cultural center for northern Jutland, a region of a half-million people, idyllically adjoined by the North Sea to the west and the Baltic Sea to the east. A typical medium-sized European city. Aalborg has a high-density historical center that is several centuries old. When I moved to Aalborg to start teaching in the university there, a major urban preservation project was being implemented in the city center. Aalborg, like many other European cities, was overrun by cars, and the city government had decided to do something about it. The project they were implementing was aimed at preserving the character of the historical downtown area; radically improving public transportation; enhancing environmental protection; developing an integrated network of bike paths, pedestrian malls, and green spaces; and developing housing stock. Specifically, automobile traffic was to be reduced by one-third in the downtown area. With these measures, city government was a good decade ahead of its time in trying to cut a path to what would later be known as "sustainable development." The planning exercise they had just started would become known as the award-winning Aalborg Project; it would become one of the town's most sensitive and enduring political and planning issues for a decade and a half, and it would be recommended by the Organization for Economic Cooperation and Development (OECD) as a model for international adoption on how to integrate environmental and social concerns into city politics and planning, including how to deal with the car in the city.

I had heard about the plans for the Aalborg Project previously, but I only began to consider the project as a potential candidate for my own research when, as a newcomer, I mused about the many changes happening to the urban landscape. Some of these were hard to explain rationally; for instance, how certain regulations aimed at reducing car traffic were repeatedly being reorganized. If there was logic to the reorganizations, it escaped me, and I got curious. I did a pilot study of the Aalborg Project and then an actual study, covering almost fifteen years in the life of the project. The results of the research are described in Flyvbjerg (1998b). In what follows, I will focus not on the results of the study as such. Instead, I will illustrate the method I employed, which, after Aristotle's concept *phronesis*, I call phronetic planning research. *Phronesis* goes beyond both analytic, scientific knowledge (*episteme*) and technical knowledge or know-how (*techne*) and involves judgments and decisions made in the manner of a virtuoso social and political actor. The method is more fully described, with theoretical argument, in Flyvbjerg (2001). The examples that follow are necessarily brief and selective. For a deeper understanding. I refer the reader to the two books.

I wanted Aalborg to be to my study what Florence was to Machiavelli's – no other comparison intended. I wanted to write what Machiavelli calls the *verita effelluale*, effective truth, of planning and democracy in Aalborg, that is, a truth that holds the potential to affect the reality it uncovers. In so doing, I hoped to contribute to the discussion of planning and democracy, in Aalborg and elsewhere. Aalborg would be a laboratory for understanding the real workings of power and what they mean for our more general concerns of social and political organization. In carrying out the study, I employed what Peattie (2001) calls "dense data case studies." The case story, accordingly, can neither be briefly recounted nor summarized in a few main results. The story is itself the result. It is a "virtual reality," so to speak, of planning at work. Not the only reality, to be sure, and a reality to be interpreted differently by different readers. But for the reader willing to enter this reality and explore the life and death of the Aalborg Project from beginning to end, the payback is meant to be a sensitivity to issues of planning, democracy, rationality, and power that cannot be obtained from theory. Students can safely be let loose in this kind of reality, which provides a useful training ground with insights into practice that academic teaching often does not provide.

Where Are We Going?

In studying Aalborg, I took my point of departure in four value-rational questions that stand at the core of phronetic planning research:

1. Where are we going with planning and democracy in Aalborg?
2. Who gains and who loses, by which mechanisms of power?

3. Is this development desirable?
4. What should be done?

The questions are asked and answered by planning researchers on the basis of their attitude to what they study. This attitude is not based on idiosyncratic moral or personal preferences but on a context-dependent common worldview and interests among a reference group, well aware that different groups typically have different worldviews and interests and that there exists no general principle by which all differences can be resolved.

In the Aalborg study, the main sources for answering the questions were archival data, interviews, participant observation, and informants. For a while, I had my own desk and coffee mug with the city department for planning and environment, just as I was a frequent visitor with the other actors in the Aalborg Project. Empirically, I wanted the study to be particularly deep and detailed because I wanted to test the thesis that the most interesting phenomena, and those of most general import, would be found in the most minute and most concrete of details. Or to put the matter differently, I wanted to see whether the dualisms general/ specific and abstract/concrete would vanish if I went into sufficiently deep detail. Nietzsche (1968a), who with Machiavelli is one of the pioneers in the study of power, advocates "patience and seriousness in the smallest things" (p. 182, sec. 59) and stresses the importance of detail when he says that "all the problems of politics, of social organization, and of education have been falsified through and through ... because one learned to despise 'little' things, which means the basic concerns of life itself" (Nietzsche 1969, 256, sec. 10). Rorty (1985) is similarly emphatic that "the way to re-enchant the world ... is to stick to the concrete" (p. 173). Both Nietzsche and Rorty seem right to me. And, for reasons I will touch upon below, I definitely wanted to reenchant my work. I saw the Aalborg case as being made up of the type of little things that Nietzsche talks about. Indeed, I saw the case itself as such a thing, as what Nietzsche calls a "discreet and apparently insignificant truth," which, when closely examined, would reveal itself to be pregnant with paradigms, metaphors, and general significance, what Nietzsche calls "cyclopean monuments" (Foucault 1984, 77). Let us now see what these terms might mean in practical planning research.

One day in the city archives, I was searching for material on the genealogy of the Aalborg Project. I was "meticulously and patiently" poring over some of the tens of thousands of pages of "entangled and confused" documents, which made up the archival side of the case and which often were "scratched over and recopied many times," as Nietzsche (1969) and Foucault (1984, 76–7) said I should be doing when doing genealogy. At one point, a particular document attracted my attention. It was the minutes from a meeting about the planning of a major new thoroughfare in Aalborg's city center. I was trying to understand the context of the Aalborg Project and was studying urban policy and planning in Aalborg in the years immediately prior to the launching of the project. At first, I did not know exactly why this particular set of minutes drew my attention more than the many other pages I was perusing that day in the archives. In particular, five lines of text, buried within the minutes under the fifth of six items on the meeting agenda, kept alerting me. Here is how the five lines read in full:

> Before November 13, the City Center Group must organize a meeting plan for orientation of the following groups:
>
> a. The [City Council] Technical Committee.
> b. The Chamber of Industry and Commerce.
> c. The Police. (Technical Department City Center Group 1974, 2)

The City Center Group is a group of officials responsible for planning and policy in downtown Aalborg, and the three groups listed for orientation – no more and no less – are the external parties that the City Center Group decides to inform about what the group has in mind for the new thoroughfare in the center. I could not come to grips with what it was about this text that kept exciting my attention, and I moved on to other documents. Later in the day, I returned to the five lines and asked myself, "a, b, and c, yes, but the ABC of what?" I did not get any further, however. This went on for several days. I kept returning to the text, but to no avail. I felt like you sometimes do when you look at a certain gestalt-type figure with a hidden image. You know the image is there, but you cannot see it; it will not become a gestalt. And the harder you try, the more difficult the task seems to be.

Then one day, when I returned to the document one more time, in a flash, I finally saw the image: here is a private interest group, the Chamber of Industry and Commerce, sandwiched between two constitutionally determined powers. On one side, there is the *political power* of the democratically elected City Council Technical Committee, representing the political parties of the council in matters of planning and environment. On the otherside, there is the *executive power* of the police. What is a private interest group doing in the middle of such company? Does its inclusion here not constitute a deeply problematic deviation from democratic standards? And, finally, the question with monumental potential of Nietzsche's "cyclopean" kind; could the abc-list be indicative of the ABC of power in Aalborg? Did I have here, in fact, an image of the tripartition and separation of powers à la Aalborg?

The minutiae of the five lines of text and the questions they sparked would prove invaluable for understanding the Aalborg Project and for answering the four basic value-rational questions above. Following this approach, and documenting case after case of special treatment of the Chamber of Industry and Commerce by elected and administrative city officials, I eventually established that only by factoring in the hidden power relations between the chamber and the city government could I begin to understand the curious changes to the urban landscape that had first made me interested in the Aalborg Project. In relation to the central traffic and environment component of the project, the rationality of the chamber could be summarized in the following three propositions: (1) What is good for business is good for Aalborg;

(2) people driving automobiles are good for business, ergo; (3) what is good for people driving automobiles is good for Aalborg, whereas, conversely, what is bad for auto drivers is bad for Aalborg. In short, "the car is king" was the rationality of the chamber.

In contrast, the rationality of the Aalborg Project – or, to be more precise still, the rationality of its planners – was built on the basic premise that the viability of downtown Aalborg as the historic, commercial, and cultural center of the city and of northern Denmark could be secured if, and only if, automobile traffic was significantly reduced in the city center. The fate of the Aalborg Project would be decided by these two rationalities fighting it out, and the group who could place the most power behind their interpretation of what was rational and what was not would win. Below we will see how. Here, I will note only that in this fight over rationality and power, the Chamber of Industry and Commerce – through century-old and well-maintained relations of power – was able to position itself as a clandestine advisory board to top officials in the municipal administration. "You know, we had the possibility to change the proposals [the planners] came up with," a former chairperson of the chamber explained to me in a startlingly frank interview (unless otherwise stated, all interviews were carried out by me). The chamber secretly reviewed and negotiated changes to the Aalborg Project before proposals for the project were presented to the politicians on the City Council Technical Committee and to the council itself. This happened despite the fact that by law and constitution it was the politicians who were supposed to make the decisions that the chamber was now making with administrative officials. The chamber preferred things this way, needless to say, "for it has turned out that if [the proposals] first reach the Technical Committee, and are presented there and are to be discussed in the City Council, then it is almost impossible to get them changed," as the chamber ex-chairperson clarified for me.

The power relations I uncovered through interviews, in the archives, and with the help of my informants are too complex to be accounted for here. Enough is to say that they were of a premodern kind that could not be defended publicly vis-à-vis standards of modern democracy, similar to what Putnam (1993) found for planning in Italy in regions with weak civic traditions. In a sense, there was both too much and too little democracy in Aalborg. When I evaluated the city government against conventional standards of representative democracy, I found there was too much democracy, because the Chamber of Industry and Commerce was participating where it should not be in the role of what it itself was eager to stress was not a "supreme city council," which is exactly what it was. Its participation was distorting the outcomes of representative democracy and transforming the rationality of the Aalborg Project. When, on the other hand, I evaluated the city government against more recent ideas of stakeholder and citizen participation approaches to democracy, I found too little democracy, because involving only one stakeholder is clearly not enough when others are affected and wish to be involved.

For these and for other reasons given in *Rationality and Power* (Flyvbjerg 1998b), my answer to the first of the four value-rational questions ("Where are we going with planning and democracy in Aalborg?") was a clear, "Astray."

Who Gains and Who Loses, by Which Mechanisms of Power?

In answering the second question, "Who gains and who loses, by which mechanisms of power?" I was particularly interested in the interplay between rationality and power in defining winners and losers. Let me give just one example, though at some length, of how I addressed this question.

Above, I mentioned the "car is king" rationality of the Chamber of Industry and Commerce. The city planners were aware of the barriers this rationality might create for the Aalborg Project. Therefore, at one stage in the project, they decided to try and shoot down the chamber's rationality by agreeing to do a shopping survey of where customers in downtown Aalborg came from and which means of transportation they used. The Chamber of Industry and Commerce had been claiming over and over, like a mantra, that 50 to 60 percent of gross revenues, if not more, in the city center's shops came from customers driving cars and that policies and plans that were hostile to drivers would thereby lead to a reduction in retail earnings. When the survey was done, it showed, in stark contrast to the chamber's claim, that each of the three groups – (1) motorists; (2) pedestrians, bicyclists, and moped drivers; and (3) users of public transportation – accounts for equal shares of gross revenues.

Aalborg Stiftstidende, the local newspaper interviewing the chairperson of the Chamber's City Center Committee, tells its readers that the chairperson "acknowledges being astonished as to how many customers use public transportation." At the same time, however, the chairperson points out that one should not look at total gross revenues alone but should examine the share of specialty goods as compared with the share of sales of staples and so on. According to the chairman, who owns a specialty shop himself, this is because (1) it is the specialty shops that distinguish a center more than the sales of groceries, and (2) specialty goods generate the largest share of earnings. Specialty goods are thus more important for the retailers and for the downtown economy than are other types of goods.

The chairperson also cites these factors in an interview I did with him, in which he comments on my interpretation of the survey results as rendered above:

> CHAIRPERSON: Well, it shows that you, too, have not understood [the results of the survey]. Because what counts for the city's retailers is not the giant sales which lie in the supermarkets' food sections. If you subtract them, you will obtain other percentages. And the purchases made by those driving their cars have a *much, much* higher average. It is the specialty goods which create the gross earnings, the profits. It is the specialty goods which create a center at all. If the specialty goods are not found in a center, then you get an American-style situation. Slums. Food products make up a very large part of sales. Try and subtract them and then analyze where the earnings come from.
>
> INTERVIEWER: Has the chamber tried to do that?
>
> CHAIRPERSON: Oh yes, yes. We also presented it to the municipality. I think that we reach a figure where those driving cars make up far more than

50 percent of the specialty goods trade. Now specialty goods also include clothes, and so on. It is hardly so marked for clothes. But as soon as you go over to genuine specialty goods [i.e., excluding clothes and other textiles], then the proportion of drivers gets very, very large.

INTERVIEWER: Are everyday goods not so important for a center?

CHAIRPERSON: No, because it is only a question of supplying the local residents, right? It certainly has nothing to do with creating an atmosphere in a town. This is not what makes a town fun and nice to be in and interesting to walk around in. (Flyvbjerg 1998b, 110–11)

But even if we allow for the revamped categories, which the chairperson of the Chamber's City Center Committee proposes, he still overestimates the significance of automobile drivers. Their share of purchases in downtown Aalborg is not "much, much higher" or "far more than 50 percent." Subtracting both conventional goods and clothes and textiles from gross revenues and then examining the remaining sector of pure specialty goods, as the chairperson proposes, it appears that motorists account for 45 percent of the revenues in this group of goods. Since pure specialty goods constitute 33 percent of total earnings, the share of specialty goods purchased by drivers thus comprises but 15 percent of gross revenues (i.e., 45 percent of 33 percent). Were we to accept the chairperson's argument, it would mean that city policy makers ought to accord highest priority to the specific activities (specialty shopping) of a specific customer group (drivers) who contribute only 15 percent of the total sales in downtown Aalborg. Even when seen from a narrow sales point of view, such a policy would seem problematic. However, through a complicated web of influences and rationalizations that cannot be accounted for here, this is precisely what the actual policy becomes in Aalborg (Flyvbjerg 1998b, 109–12).

In contrast to the Chamber of Industry and Commerce, the city planners view the results of the shoppers' survey as hard evidence against the chamber's views and in favor of their own strategy: the bicyclists, those on mopeds, pedestrians, and those using public transportation must be accorded higher priorities in downtown Aalborg, say the planners; the interests of those driving private cars must be downgraded. It therefore seems strongly misleading and unusually provocative to the planners when the *Aalborg Stiftstidende* chooses to report on the shopping survey with the following four-column headline: "Aalborg's Best Customers Come Driving in Cars." The headline is misleading, inasmuch as drivers are shown much less significant as a customer group than originally thought. After all, the text of the article makes clear that two-thirds of total sales are made to people who do *not* come to the shops by car. Headline and text thus convey two opposing messages, as if two different people wrote them – which is probably the case, the text by a reporter and the headline by an editor.

For the planners, this misleading headline is the straw that breaks the camel's back. It is captions like these, together with a number of very critical editorials about the Aalborg Project, that force the head of the Aalborg Project, a conservative alderman who heads the city's administration for planning and environment, to uncharacteristically complain about lack of fairness in the paper's coverage of the project.[1] The alderman explains in an interview:

> I think that I, not I but everyone here in the house [the city's headquarters for planning and environment], hardly received a totally fair treatment [in the press]. I think that a line was already in place, coming from *Aalborg Stiftslidende* among others, that this [project] was garbage. (Flyvbjerg 1998b, 114)

The chief of city planning now wants to strike back at both the *Aalborg Stiftslidende* and the Chamber of Industry and Commerce. He is fed up with both of them. Normally, it is the official policy of the city not to reply to press criticism unless asked. But the planning chief asks permission from the alderman to submit a long comment to the paper. He has, in fact, written it. First, the alderman says no, according to an in-house source. Then the chief tries again, and the alderman gives in. He now says that if the chief absolutely wants to, he can submit the comment, as long as it is as his personal opinion. Here is an excerpt from the proposed commentary by the chief of city planning written for the *Aalborg Sliftslidende*.

> One cannot ... talk about, for example, the purchases of drivers being dominant in relation to those of other road users, bus passengers, or pedestrians. ... It is just as important to plan for bus passengers, bicyclists, and pedestrians, who taken together make up 65% of the purchases. Parenthetically, it can be mentioned that [the chamber] has stated to the *Stiftslidende* that public transportation is more important than what the Chamber of Industry and Commerce had expected, (which must logically imply that they have overestimated the importance of one or more of the other traffic forms (perhaps the driving of private cars)) [parentheses in original].... The City Council has resolved that major new roads and extensions of existing roads in the dense part of the city must be avoided, which accords well with many other tendencies in society, including the interest in maintaining the urban environment, improving traffic safety, and converting from private to public transportation.
>
>   The instruments of planning, as previously mentioned, therefore consist of regulating traffic within the possibilities accorded by the existing street area; that is, removing the unwanted through-traffic and other measures which can lead extraneous vehicles out to the main traffic arteries as directly as possible.
>
>   When the Chamber of Industry and Commerce, in its alternative to the city center project, calls attention to the fact that private cars should be able to drive unhindered through the downtown area, that parking conditions be improved, that public transportation be expanded, that bicycles and motorbikes have unhindered access everywhere (outside the pedestrian streets), that the conditions for "non-vehicular" road users be improved, that retail deliveries can operate without problems, that better conditions be created for pedestrians – all this together with the establishment of more green areas, expansion of housing, maintenance of downtown functions, more jobs, and better public services, then it is a list of wishes which everyone could put their name to. The problem lies in fulfilling, within the existing framework, the often contradictory goals. Priorities must be set, and it must be accepted that it will entail restrictions on freedom within one domain to achieve important advantages in

others…. In my opinion, the report on shopping in the city center does not produce any need to propose changes in the planning objectives. On the contrary. I think that [these objectives] have been confirmed on many points. (Flyvbjerg 1998b, 114–15)

The chief of city planning never publishes his article, however. He explains why:

CHIEF OF CITY PLANNING: It was a kind of self-criticism, you know. It didn't promote the case, and now we had just received a certain amount of goodwill from the Chamber of Industry and Commerce. So there was no reason to dig [trenches].

INTERVIEWER: But was it you yourself who decided that the article would not appear?

CHIEF OF CITY PLANNING: Yes! (Flyvbjerg 1998b, 115)

The goodwill of the Chamber of Industry and Commerce that the chief talks about is explained by the fact that the shopping survey has opened the chamber's eyes to the fact that there are other groups of customers than those driving private cars. And these other groups put significant amounts of cash into the shopkeepers' cash registers. However, the chief of city planning and his staff are mistaken in their evaluation of the chamber's goodwill. In fact, the chamber draws a fundamentally different conclusion from the shoppers' survey than the planners, a conclusion that they do not understand until it is too late. The chamber's leadership realizes that there are indeed other important customers than those who drive cars. And this causes the chamber to reduce or withdraw its previous criticism of those subprojects aimed at improving conditions for pedestrians, bicyclists, public transportation, and so on, such as pedestrians malls, a network of bicycle paths, and a large bus terminal. After the publication of the shopping survey, the previous harsh criticism of these subprojects simply ceases.

Nevertheless, the chamber's view of reality is not structured by the same analytic rationality as that of the chief of city planning and his staff. The chamber therefore does not draw the same conclusions about trade-offs and priorities as the planning chief. The chamber wants "to have their cake and eat it too," as the alderman for planning and environment would later put it.

In other words, there exists a single survey and two interpretations. The planners interpret the survey as solid, analytic documentation for the Aalborg Project's downgrading of automobile traffic and its upgrading of public transportation and nonautomotive forms of transport to achieve environmental improvements and improved traffic safety. For the chamber, however, the survey documents the possibility to increase earnings for the city's shops by improving conditions for nonautomotive and public transportation *without* reducing car access. It is a classically clear example of an evaluation that is dependent on the eyes of the beholder.

Empirically speaking, the survey results are not interesting in themselves. They may or may not reveal a single reality, but that is not important. Rather, the interpretations of the survey results are important. And the decisive aspect in relation to the fate of the Aalborg Project is not whether the one or the other interpretation is correct, rational, or true but which party can put the greatest power behind its interpretation. The interpretation, which has the stronger power base, becomes Aalborg's truth, understood as the actually realized physical, economic, ecological, and social reality.

The stronger power base turns out to be that of the chamber, which, by means of a multiplicity of clever strategies and tactics, successfully blocks most of the city's measures for reducing auto traffic while, as said, allowing measures that facilitate walking, biking, and the use of public transportation. The chamber thus confirms a basic Nietzschean insight regarding power and interpretation, namely, that interpretation is not only commentary, "Interpretation is itself a means of becoming master of something" and "all subduing and becoming master involves a fresh interpretation" (Nietzsche 1968b, 342, sec. 643; 1969, 77, sec. 2.12). With the help of the very survey that the planners carried out to disprove the Chamber of Industry and Commerce, the chamber came up with a fresh interpretation of the Aalborg Project – and became master of the project.

In this manner, power defined a reality in which the winner was the business community in downtown Aalborg, who, via their strategy of opposing measures to restrict cars combined with acceptance of improvements for public transportation, pedestrians, and bicyclists, have seen an increase in retail sales in downtown Aalborg following the implementation of the Aalborg Project, while sales figures declined at the national level during the same period.

With roughly a 50 percent increase in bicycle and public transportation in downtown Aalborg during the first decade of the project, and without a projected 35 percent decline in automobile traffic, but an increase instead, the actual situation stood in sharp contrast to what was envisioned. Without the downgrading of automobiles, the pressure on downtown road space has produced harmful effects on environment, traffic safety, and traffic flow. It was this very situation that the Aalborg Project was supposed to prevent but that it has instead exacerbated. Thus, the losers in the struggle over the Aalborg Project were those citizens who live, work, walk, ride their bikes, drive their cars, and use public transportation in downtown Aalborg, that is, virtually all of the city's and the region's half-million inhabitants plus many visitors. Every single day, residents, commuters, and visitors in downtown Aalborg were exposed to increased risks of traffic accidents substantially higher than the national average and the planners' projections. They were also exposed to higher levels of noise and air pollution, and a deteriorating physical and social environment. The taxpayers were also losers, because the considerable funds and human resources used in the Aalborg Project have largely been wasted.

The rationality and interests of one group, the Chamber of Industry and Commerce, was allowed to penetrate and transform the project. The main viewpoints of the chamber have overlapped with the views of the Aalborg Police Department and the *Aalborg Stiftslidende*. As the *Stiftslidende* has a near monopoly on the printed press in Aalborg, and as the police hold a powerful position in questions of traffic policy, this threefold overlapping of interests has endowed the chamber's viewpoints with a special impact.

The *Realpolitik* for the Aalborg Project was shaped by these interests in classic Machiavellian style, while the *formal* politics in democratically elected bodies like the City Council have had only minor impact on the project. Rational, deliberative democracy gave way to premodern, tribalistic rule by the strongest. Distorted relations of power produced a distorted project. Power thus defined a reality in which the *real* Aalborg Project, that which has become reality, deviates from, and on principal objectives directly counteracts, the *formal* Aalborg Project, which was ratified by the City Council with a 25–1 vote, but which exists only on paper.

Briefly summarized, my untangling of the web of rationality-power relations in the Aalborg Project showed that while power produces rationality and rationality produces power, their relationship is asymmetrical. Power has a clear tendency to dominate rationality in the dynamic and overlapping relationship between the two. Paraphrasing Pascal, one could say that power has a rationality that rationality does not know. Rationality, on the other hand, does not have a power that power does not know. The result is an unequal relationship between the two. Illegitimate rationalization and not rationality came to dominate the fate of the Aalborg Project (Flyvbjerg 1998b, 225–36).

Is It Desirable?

The third value-rational question is whether the situation depicted in answering the first two questions is desirable. My answer to this was, No.

I did not need ideals of strong democracy or strong ecology to support this conclusion. Most, if not all, informed persons who subscribe to the ground rules of democracy and who agree with the 25–1 majority on the City Council, which ratified the environmental objectives of the Aalborg Project, would also have to agree with my analysis that the development that I had uncovered was neither desirable nor justifiable. Thus, my analysis could not be easily rejected on grounds of being idiosyncratic. This was deliberate and strategically important, because as I moved on to answering the fourth question – What should be done? – I wanted as broad popular support as possible for my conclusions and suggestions for action.

I already mentioned above Francis Bacon's dictum that knowledge is power. This dictum expresses the essence of Enlightenment thinking. "Enlightenment is power," and the more enlightenment – the more rationality – the better. The Aalborg study shows that Bacon is right; knowledge is power. But the study also shows that the inverse relation between power and knowledge holds and that empirically, as opposed to normatively, it is more important: "Power is knowledge." In this sense, the study stands Bacon on his head. It shows how power defines what gets to count as knowledge. It shows, furthermore, how power defines not only a certain conception of reality. It is not just the social construction of rationality that is at issue here; it is also the fact that power defines physical, economic, social, and environmental reality itself.

Modernity relies on rationality as the main means for making democracy and planning work. But if the interrelations between rationality and power are even remotely close to the asymmetrical relationship depicted in the Aalborg case – which the tradition from Thucydides, Machiavelli, and Nietzsche tells us they are – then rationality is such a weak form of power that democracy and planning built on rationality will be weak, too. The asymmetry between rationality and power makes for a fundamental weakness of modernity and of modern democracy and planning. The normative emphasis on rationality leaves the modern project as ignorant of how power works as the guardians of the Aalborg Project and therefore as open to being dominated by power. Relying solely on rationality therefore risks exacerbating the very problems modernity attempts to solve.

This weakness of modernity and of democracy and planning needs to be reassessed in light of the context-dependent nature of rationality, taking a point of departure in thinkers like Machiavelli, Nietzsche, and Foucault. The Aalborg study shows constitution writing and institutional reform based on communicative rationality à la Jürgen Habermas to be inadequate. To enable democratic thinking and the public sphere to make a real contribution to democratic planning and action, we have to tie them back to what they cannot accept in much of communicative planning theory: power, conflict, and partisanship. This, then, was the next step in my work with the Aalborg Project: to become a partisan, to face conflict, and to exercise power.

What Should Be Done?

In deciding on my praxis in relation to the Aalborg Project. I reasoned that if the arrangements and outcomes of city politics and planning in Aalborg were not publicly justifiable, as my studies showed they were not, then, perhaps, I could help change things for the better, if only modestly, by calling public attention to my results. *Better* is defined here simply as being more democratic and more effective in fulfilling the objectives of the Aalborg Project as ratified by the City Council. In this way, my studies would become part of the power relations they had uncovered.

I already mentioned that I chose to study the relationship between rationality and power because this particular area of research was relatively unexplored and because I hoped to help improve the reflexivity of planning on this point. By the time I began the Aalborg study, however, another, more personal, motive had come along. Campbell (1986, 128–9), Lindblom (1990), Lindblom and Cohen (1979, 84), and others have noted that the development of social research is inhibited by the fact that researchers tend to work with problems in which the answer to the question, "If you are wrong about this, who will notice?" is "Nobody." Bailey (1992) calls the outcome of this type of research "'so what' results" (p. 50). I had now been a planning researcher long enough to be only too familiar with the problem of "so what results." At one point, I considered leaving the university altogether because of this problem. Planning research, like other social science, does not have natural science's link to technological development and has only sporadic political relevance or support. Planning research, therefore, seemed to me too isolated from what is important in life to be worth the effort of a lifetime's work. Nonetheless, I chose to stay and tried to solve my problem, in part by gradually developing and practicing the methodology described in Flyvbjerg (2001). Phronetic planning research would be my antidote to the "so what" problem.

Instead of natural science's relevance to technological development, I would conduct phronetic research in ways that would make it relevant to practical politics, planning, and administration. I tried to secure such relevance by adopting two basic criteria. First, I would choose to work with problems that are considered problems not only in the academy but also in the rest of society. Second, I would deliberately and actively feed the results of my research back into the political, administrative, and social processes that I studied. For reasons I will return to below, at one stage I called this way of working "research on the body."

Employing this approach in the Aalborg study has been a challenge and has worked much better than I had reason to expect when I first began to develop it. One day, for example, I found myself in a studio of the Danish Radio (DR), participating in a direct, national broadcast about preliminary results from my study. To get my feet wet and to gain step-by-step experience with the phronetic methodology, I had published partial results of my research as I went along. "Trial balloons," I called them. This was the second time I sent up a balloon, and one of the results that drew public attention, locally and nationally, was the fact that whereas the Aalborg City Council had decided with the Aalborg Project that higher-than-average traffic accidents for the many bicyclists in the city center were cause for special concern and must be reduced by 30 to 40 percent, now – several years into the implementation of the project – I documented that instead of the planned reduction, there was a steep increase in accidents. Moreover, the increase had happened without politicians and planners noticing. They, quite simply, were not monitoring the project on which they had spent millions for planning and implementation. I also showed how the increase in accidents was caused by city officials allowing the rationality of the Chamber of Industry and Commerce to slowly, surely, and one-sidedly influence and undermine the rationality of the Aalborg Project as explained above. Participating in the radio broadcast were also the alderman for planning and environment, the chairman for the local chapter of the Danish Cyclist's Federation – a force to be reckoned with in a bicycle nation like Denmark – and two interviewing journalists. When the journalists asked the alderman what he thought about the results of my study, he pulled from his briefcase a sheet of statistics, waved it, and said to the nation that here he held proof that my data were wrong.

This, of course, is as bad as it gets for a scholar. We are paid to be that group in society that is best equipped to produce data, knowledge, and interpretations of the highest validity and reliability. This is a main basis of our credibility and existence. Consequently, if someone questions that credibility, our existence is at issue.

The journalists immediately turned to me and asked for my reaction to the alderman's attack. The green light on my microphone went on, I crossed my fingers for luck under the table and answered that if there were any errors in my numbers, they must originate with the police, who does the registration of traffic accidents on location, or with the Danish Highway Administration, who maintains the national database for traffic accidents. When the broadcast was over, I went to my office and prepared a large package for the alderman containing the raw computer printouts of my data and other details of my analyses plus a cover letter asking the alderman to please identify the errors he said I had made. Three weeks later, the material was returned to me with a message stating that the alderman's staff had been able to identify no errors. The same day, I wrote a short press release stating the facts of the matter to clear myself of the accusations of poor scholarship. That evening on television, I watched the alderman retract his accusations. The next day, the printed media carried the story, and I was in the clear again.

There were other incidents like this, and I mention them here to emphasize four things. First, and most important, this way of working helps effectively to begin the dialogue with groups outside of academia, which is at the heart of phronetic research. Some groups and individuals, like the alderman above, may not be interested in beginning a dialogue; they would rather do without the extra attention, transparency, and accountability it entails. In the Aalborg case, they would have preferred to turn a blind eye on the traffic accidents and environmental problems; in other cases, the issues will be something else. But the very raison d'étre of phronetic research is to help society see and reflect, and transparency and accountability are key prerequisites for this and for democracy. Where there is resistance to seeing and hearing, the dialogue may need to be jump-started, as was the case in Aalborg. Nevertheless, after some initial difficulties, a real dialogue was established that went on for several years and covered many aspects of planning, politics, and administration in Aalborg.

Second, the dialogic approach to research is also effective in ensuring that research results reach the relevant target groups. This is a question of effective communication. The highly specialized media of scholarly journals and monographs are well suited for reaching academic audiences. But they are lacking when it comes to the target groups that are relevant in the practical world of planning, politics, and administration. Here public dialogue, including communication via everyday media, is necessary.

Third, the dialogic approach generates the type of outside stakeholders in the research that we need to get beyond the stigma of "so what results." I here understand a stakeholder to be an organization, a group, or a person with an interest in the outcomes of the research. The stakeholders care about the research, for good and for bad, some as supporters and some as antagonists.

Fourth and finally, your senses are definitely sharpened when you carry out your research with the knowledge that upon publication, people with an interest in the results might do what they can to find errors in your work, like the alderman and his staff did with my analyses of the Aalborg Project. For me, the consequence is a state of heightened awareness in data collection and processing that helps take the drudgery and dullness out of these activities. External scrutiny is also an excellent motivation for achieving the highest levels of validity and reliability: facts and data have to be handled with excruciating accuracy, and interpretations have to be clear and balanced. Otherwise, the work will be self-defeating and not allowed to count as a voice in the phronetic dialogue that it is aimed at.

Because of the stakes involved and because of the engagement with other actors, you experience an almost bodily responsibility for, and involvement in, the research. This engagement seems to me to enhance the learning process, which is in the best of the traditions of experiential learning and very different from didactics and theory. Learning becomes embodied. I understand from colleagues in the field of education that recent research corroborates the experience that human learning is generally more effective with this type of engagement and with an excited sensory system; that learning is more effective when the proprioceptors are firing, so to speak. This is why, as said, I called my methodology "research on the body," here understood not as research with the body as an object of study but as research that is embodied and where researchers experience, on their own bodies, society's reactions to their research.

As a consequence of my trial balloons and the debates they generated, when later I published the Aalborg study in earnest – in the two-volume, 640-page Danish edition of *Rationalitet og Magt* – the alderman and other actors with stakes in the Aalborg Project knew that they would not get away with postulating another reality for my research than what could be documented. That type of tactics may work in politics, but it rarely does in research. Therefore, the debate about the Aalborg Project, although still spirited, now became much less polemical and more dialogic. For instance, the alderman and I would give back-to-back talks about the project, each presenting our views, followed by discussion, in and out of Aalborg. Our "road show," we would eventually call it. The alderman and his staff began to listen to the research instead of fighting it; they realized the research was influencing public opinion about their work, and soon they were ready to make changes in the Aalborg Project.

Reaching the dialogic mode of communication is crucial for practicing phronetic research in a democratic society. Polemics typically does not facilitate democracy but is more closely related to the tactics of rhetoric and antagonistic power play. Dialogue, on the other hand – not necessarily detached and without combat, but with respect for other parties and a willingness to listen – is a prerequisite for informed democratic decision making. And dialogue is the vehicle by means of which research can best hope to inform the democratic process, whereas polemics has only limited use for research in achieving its goals. Thus, to be effective, phronetic researchers avoid polemics and look for dialogue. They also look for how they themselves may contribute to establishing the conditions for dialogue where such conditions are not already present.

The debate about the Aalborg Project, which again was both local and national and this time also spilled over into Sweden and Norway, now placed so much attention on the Aalborg Project that it became hard for the city government to continue to defend the project and refuse to be held accountable for what was going wrong with it. At the practical level, this was the situation I had hoped to bring about by publishing the Aalborg study. The aim of exposing dubious social and political practices through phronetic research is, in Foucault's (1981) words, as quoted in Miller (1993), precisely to bring it about that practitioners no longer know what to do "so that the acts, gestures, discourses that up until then had seemed to go without saying become problematic, difficult, dangerous" (p. 235). For the Aalborg Project, my study led to transparency, transparency led to public attention, and public attention led to accountability. And after accountability, no more Aalborg Project. Or, to put it more accurately, after accountability, another Aalborg Project, since the problems in downtown Aalborg had not disappeared by any means. Quite the opposite; they had been exacerbated and needed to be taken care of more than ever.

The alderman put it like this in an interview:

> I simply took the consequence of Flyvbjerg's study, and I could see that the process we had been through [with the Aalborg Project] could in any case not be allowed to happen again. I let myself be much inspired by [the idea that] now we must have a broad popular element [in city planning] so that it did not proceed on those power positions [which had dominated the Aalborg Project]. (Petersen 1993, 44)

Foucault said about his work that practitioners are not likely to find constructive advice or instructions in it; they would find only the kind of problematizations mentioned above. Such problematizations are useful and may lead to action and change in themselves. But unlike Foucault, based on my problematizations of the Aalborg Project, I reconstructed a set of planning and policy measures for how city governments may significantly reduce their risk of ending up with the type of counterproductive, wasteful, and undemocratic plans and policies seen in Aalborg (Flyvbjerg 1991, 1993).

One of seven key measures I proposed was the use of planning councils in the decision-making process, not as detached Habermasian or Cartesian fora devoid of power but as devices that acknowledge and account for the working of power and for the passionate engagement of stakeholders who care deeply about the issues at hand (for the other six measures, see Flyvbjerg 1993, 194–7). I developed the idea from a set of semi-institutionalized, semisecret, and often intense meetings that were already being held on a regular basis between city officials and the Aalborg Chamber of Industry and Commerce. The problem with these meetings was that only a single stakeholder was invited to participate; this was one reason why decisions became unbalanced. But from the meeting minutes and from my interviews with participants, I could see that such meetings were not necessarily a bad idea in themselves. The interactions they involved resulted in additional information and in ideas that proved useful in the decision-making process. And the collaboration between project owner and stakeholder led to external support for aspects of the project that might not have gained support without stakeholder participation. Finally, real negotiations and real decisions with real commitments took place in the meetings.

In my version of a planning council, however, it would be open to not only one stakeholder but to all stakeholders in addition to all other interested and affected parties. Moreover, as the composition of such councils and decisions about who should count as stakeholders are clearly political acts, I suggested that city government take an active role in identifying participants and in facilitating their involvement with councils with the purpose of ensuring that discussions and decisions would be as democratic and have as wide support as possible. I suggested that planning councils should be active in the decision-making process from beginning to end, from policy idea to design of plans, to political ratification, to practical implementation.

When the alderman and his staff decided to end the Aalborg Project and to build something new on its ruins, they looked to the measures I had proposed. Eventually, they launched a new round of planning under the name "Aalborg Better Town" (*Aalborg Bedre By*), including the use of planning councils, now called "planning panels." City officials took an active part in identifying external parties to participate on the panels instead of staying locked with the ideas and initiatives of the Chamber of Industry and Commerce.

In the process of starting up the panels, officials also contacted me and encouraged me to become a panel member. In this way, I would be able to use my knowledge about Aalborg to improve the new planning. I was tempted but felt I had to choose between roles. Also, at this time, I was moving into another area of research, namely, that of megaproject planning and decision making. I was keen to see what the phronetic research methodology honed on the Aalborg Project might do in this field. Instead of becoming an expert on Aalborg and local planning, I wanted to get back on the steep part of the learning curve, as when I began the Aalborg study, and I deliberately chose megaproject planning as a contrast to Aalborg: I wanted to move from local issues to national and international ones, and from small projects to very big and very expensive ones (Skamris and Flyvbjerg 1997; Bruzelius, Flyvbjerg, and Rothengatter 1998; Flyvbjerg, Bruzelius, and Rothengatter 2003). Right or wrong, I decided not to participate in the planning panels. Nevertheless, when a few years later, the European Union in Brussels awarded Aalborg its European Planning Prize for the new planning, I could not help but feel – however impudent this might seem to others and to myself – that in a small way, perhaps I had a share in what had transpired. Triumphing over 300 nominees from all over the European Union, Aalborg received the prize for having developed what the jury viewed as an innovative and democratic urban policy and planning with particular emphasis on the involvement of citizens and interest groups.

Conclusion

What typifies a work in phronetic planning research is that for a particular area of concern, it focuses analysis on praxis in answering the four value-rational questions that have given structure to this article: (1) Where are we going? (2) Who gains and who loses, by which mechanisms of power? (3) Is this development desirable? (4) What should be done? The questions can be answered in different ways for a given area of interest, depending on perspective. And since there is always an urban politics in a democracy, the praxis that works in one situation does not necessarily work in another. Thus, there exists neither one fixed methodology for doing phronetic planning research nor only one typical example of such work, nor one kind of praxis related to it. To the extent that the example given in this article may be an example to follow, this would be mainly as regards the questions asked, with their focus on power, values, and praxis. It would not necessarily be for the answers given, because such answers will vary from context to context. The article is, as the title says, only one researcher's story. It is hoped that other researchers will develope other narratives. We need them as points of reference for praxis in planning research. The aim is not to tell planners in the usual manner how we think *they* can make a difference but to understand how *we* ourselves may make a difference with the work we do.

Note

1 The City Council has thirty-one members, among whom four alderman/-women plus one mayor are elected, each holding a powerful position with responsibility for a large budget and a large staff in each of five municipal main areas of policy and administration.

References

Abler, Ronald, John Adams, and Peter Gould. 1971. *Spatial organization: The geographer's view of the world*. Englewood Cliffs, NJ: Prentice Hall.

Bailey, Mary Timney. 1992. Do physicists use case studies? Thoughts on public administration research. *Public Administration Review* 52 (1): 47–54.

Bruzelius, Nils, Bent Flyvbjerg, and Werner Rothengatter. 1998. Big decisions, Big risks: Improving accountability in mega projects. *International Review of Administrative Sciences* 64 (3): 423–40.

Campbell, Donald T. 1986. Science's social system of validity-enhancing collective belief change and the problems of the social sciences. In *Metatheory in social science: Pluralisms and subjectivities*, edited by Donald W. Fiske and Richard A. Shweder, 108–35. Chicago: University of Chicago Press.

Crush, Jonathan. 1994. Scripting the compound: Power and space in the South African mining industry. *Environment and Planning D: Society and Space* 12 (3): 301–24.

Fischler, Raphael. 1998. Toward a genealogy of planning: Zoning and the welfare state. *Planning Perspectives* 13 (4): 389–410.

Flyvbjerg, Bent. 1991. 90'ernes trafikplanlægning for miljø, sundhed og bæredygtighed (Traffic planning in the 90s for environment, health, and sustainability). *Miljø og Tehnologi: Nordisk Tidsskrift for Miljøteknik, -forvaltning og -politik* 6 (1): 28–32.

Flyvbjerg, Bent. 1992. Aristotle, Foucault and progressive *phronesis*: Outline of an applied ethics for sustainable development. *Planning Theory* 7–8: 65–83.

Flyvbjerg, Bent. 1993. Når demokratiet svigter rammes miljøet (When democracy fails, the environment is hurt). In *Plauera für en bärkraftig urveckling: 21 nordiska forshare ger sin syn*, edited by Benny Kullinger and Ulla-Briu Strömberg, 187–97. Stockholm: Byggforskningsrådet.

Flyvbjerg, Bent. 1996. The dark side of planning: Rationality and *Realrationalität*. In *Explorations in planning theory*, edited by Seymour J. Mandelbaum, Luigi Mazza, and

Robert W. Burchell, 383–94. New Brunswick, NJ: Center for Urban Policy Research Press.

Flyvbjerg, Bent. 1998a. Empowering civil society: Habermas, Foucault, and the question of conflict. In *Cities for citizens: Planning and the rise of civil society in a global age*, edited by Mike Douglass and John Friedmann, 185–211. New York: John Wiley.

Flyvbjerg, Bent. 1998b. *Rationality and power: Democracy in practice*. Chicago: University of Chicago Press.

Flyvbjerg, Bent. 2001. *Making social science matter: Why social inquiry fails and how it can succeed again*. Cambridge, UK: Cambridge University Press.

Flyvbjerg, Bent, Nils Bruzelius, and Werner Rothengatter. 2003. *Megaprojects and risk: An anatomy of ambition*. Cambridge, UK: Cambridge University Press.

Flyvbjerg, Bent, and Tim Richardson. 1998. In search of the dark side of planning theory, Paper presented at the Third Oxford Conference on Planning Theory, 2–4 April 1998, Oxford Brookes University, Oxford, UK.

Forester, John. 1989. *Planning in the face of power*. Berkeley: University of California Press.

Forester, John. 1999. *The deliberative practitioner: Encouraging participatory planning processes*. Cambridge, MA: MIT Press.

Foucault, Michel. 1981. *Colloqui con Foucault*. Salerno, Italy: 10/17 Cooperative Editrice.

Foucault, Michel. 1984. Nietzsche, genealogy, history. In *The Foucault reader*, edited by Paul Rabinow, 76–100. New York: Pantheon.

Friedmann, John. 1998. Planning theory revisited. *European Planning Studies* 6 (3): 245–53.

Hajer, Maarten A. 1995. *The politics of environmental discourse: Ecological modernization and the policy process*. Oxford, UK: Clarendon.

Healey, Patsy. 1997. *Collaborative planning: Shaping places in fragmented societies*. London: Macmillan.

Lindblom, Charles. 1990. *Inquiry and change: The troubled attempt to understand and shape society*. New Haven, CT: Yale University Press.

Lindblom, Charles, and David K. Cohen, 1979. *Usable knowledge: Social science and social problem solving*. New Haven, CT: Yale University Press.

Miller, James. 1993. *The passion of Michel Foucault*. New York: Simon & Schuster.

Nietzsche, Friedrich. 1968a. *The anti-Christ*. Harmondsworth, UK: Penguin.

Nietzsche, Friedrich. 1968b. *The will to power*. New York: Vintage.

Nietzsche, Friedrich. 1969. *On the genealogy of morals*. New York: Vintage.

Peattie, Lisa. 2001. Theorizing planning: Some comments on Bent Flyvbjerg's *Rationality and Power*. *International Planning Studies* 6 (3): 257–63.

Petersen, Morten Rugtved. 1993. Bfornyelse: Bypolitik og beslutninger. Master's thesis, Department of Development and Planning, Aalborg University, Aalborg, Denmark.

Putnam, Robert D., with Robert Leonardi and Raffaella Y. Nanetti. 1993. *Making democracy work: Civic traditions in modern Italy*. Princeton, NJ: Princeton University Press.

Richardson, Tim, and Ole B. Jensen. 2000. Discourses of mobility and polycentric development: A contested view of European spatial planning. *European Planning Studies* 8 (4): 503–20.

Rorty, Richard, 1985. Habermas and Lyotard on postmodernity. In *Habermas and modernity*, edited by Richard J. Bernstein, 161–75. Cambridge, MA: MIT Press.

Skamris, Mette K., and Bent Flyvbjerg. 1997. Inaccuracy of traffic forecasts and cost estimates on large transport projects. *Transport Policy* 4 (3): 141–6.

Technical Department City Center Group, Aalborg Municipality. 1974. Minutes of meeting. 1 November, Aalborg, Denmark.

Yiftachel, Oren, and Margo Huxley. 2000. Debating dominance and relevance: Notes on the "communicative turn" in planning theory. *International Journal of Urban and Regional Research* 24 (3): 907–13.

V
Social Justice
Race, Gender, Class

Introduction

This group of readings examines the challenges of planning in an era of diversity, multiculturalism, and identity politics. Focusing on race, class, gender, and sexuality, the authors each provide a distinctive analysis of unequal access, marginalization, and paths towards social justice.

We begin with a chapter excerpted from Iris Marion Young's 2000 book *Inclusion and Democracy*. This book builds upon her seminal 1990 book, *Justice and the Politics of Difference,* in which she rejected communitarianism as enforced homogeneity with xenophobic, anti-urban tendencies. Her vision of urban life was one in which social relations affirm group differences, rather than fusing into a single identity. City life became "the being together of strangers," and supported "unassimilated otherness" (echoing the Jane Jacobs ideal of city streets and their ability to handle strangers).

In the text reproduced here, Young extends the idea of "the politics of difference" and outlines an effective set of conceptual distinctions regarding structural vs. cultural group differences. She argues that critics have wrongly reduced the politics of difference to "identity politics" (i.e., the expression of cultural meaning). Although she recognizes that identity politics (in which marginalized groups assert alternative, positive group images) can have a positive function, she also contends that it has the potential to be counterproductive. She does not, however, regard cultural conflict as the defining issue of group relations. Rather, her primary focus is on the structural foundations of the politics of difference. The assertion of group identity is not usually a stand-alone cultural goal, but instead is usually linked to group demands for substantive, structural outcomes: access to better education, housing, work opportunities, social services, and so forth. Finally, Young challenges the common perception that society has only two choices in the face of social differences: either devolution to a competition among private interests or the complete sublimation of difference in the name of social cohesion. This is, for Young, a false dichotomy. The expression of group identity need not invariably cause social fragmentation and a loss of the collective public good. She instead argues for a third path, where civility does not require the suppression of difference, and where a shared public space can be shaped beyond parochial interests. Young argues against a forced consensus of political debate and provides an alternative perspective to envision civic spaces that foster diversity and difference while facilitating a shared civic political culture. (One sees here a contemporary variation of Paul Davidoff's influential 1960s criticism of a false unitary "public interest"; see his "Advocacy and Pluralism in Planning," Chapter 10.)

In "The Minority-Race Planner in the Quest for a Just City," June Manning Thomas examines the promises and shortcomings of recruiting more underrepresented minorities to the ranks of planners in the larger pursuit of social justice. Through her interviews with minority planners, Thomas explores the complex roles and conflicted challenges faced by these professionals. Their voices add a rich detail and nuance to her analysis. Thomas concludes that increasing minority participation in the profession is not a guarantee of greater urban equality: the evidence that the composition of planning staffs makes a substantive difference is often inconclusive, particularly so with influencing outcomes. That said, Thomas finds evidence that minority-race planners do make a difference with process. These planners often play a bridge role between city government and the minority community, increasing lines of communication and advocating for marginalized communities. However, this exceptional role has a potentially debilitating downside: the bridge position can place the minority planner in an awkward, difficult role, overworked and marginalized by (often white) co-workers. Stronger minority presence on planning staffs alone may not be sufficient to overcome the entrenched, institutionalized inequality in many communities. In these situations, the culture of "deep differences" also requires more structural, systemic reforms to achieve the just city.

Gender politics has emerged as a powerful and transformative theme in urban planning. The historical forces behind an emerging feminist planning theory are numerous, including the larger feminist movement, women re-entering the labor force in large numbers, more women planners and professors, parallels between the civil rights movement and the feminist movement, and links with intellectual movements such as postmodernism, multiculturalism and post-structuralism. Planning's communicative action critique of the singular expert voice resonates with the feminist challenge to the male-voice-as-universal default. The feminist perspective intersects with numerous issues in urbanism: the differing uses of urban space by men and women; threats to personal safety of women in cities; structural discrimination against women in economic development; the transportation needs of women beyond the traditional "journey to work"; more fluid boundaries between the personal and the political (e.g., between home and wage work); the connections between the experience of gender differences, racial differences, and the cultural politics of diversity.

Dolores Hayden, in "Nurturing: Home, Mom, and Apple Pie," (excerpted from her book *Redesigning the American Dream*), traces the connections between gender roles, family life, and the structure of American neighborhoods. Specifically, she argues that the traditional suburban model built for a nineteenth-century nuclear family structure is not appropriate to contemporary society. The perpetuation of this housing pattern undermines progress for women and nontraditional households. To trace the suburban model historically, Hayden articulates three prototypes of organizing household work: home as haven, the industrial strategy, and the neighborhood strategy. The haven approach is to increase the efficiency of household work, glorify woman's traditional sphere of work in the home, and isolate a woman (housewife) in a suburban cottage in a garden, far from the toils of the city and its wage economy. At the other end of the scale is the industrial strategy, which views housework as a vestige of the pre-industrial craft production era, requiring modernization through mass production, standardization, and separation of home and work. That is, it shifts traditional housework (cooking, laundry, education, and childcare) into a factory setting.

Hayden takes the middle path between these two extremes. She advocates the neighborhood strategy, with producer cooperatives, shared childcare, and other household work activity done at the neighborhood scale. This third path seeks to empower women while retaining local initiative and to balance scale economies (of the industrial strategy) with the benefits of personalized nurturing and child rearing (of the home as haven strategy). The challenge for planners and architects is to design communities – and to retrofit existing suburbs – to encourage cooperation and collaboration at this decentralized scale. (Interestingly, in her combined social, environmental, and design critique of suburbia, and in her choice of the neighborhood scale, Hayden's writings anticipate many of the New Urbanist ideals.)

In "Planning as a Heterosexist Project," Michael Frisch shifts the focus from gender to sexual preference – a theme that most planning texts have awkwardly avoided. Frisch challenges two prevailing assumptions about planning: that the field is neutral about sexuality; or that sexuality is not relevant to planning (i.e., planning does not intrude into private spaces and private affairs, and since sex is private, it is not in the domain of planning.) Frisch sees, in planning's historical origins, a Victorian impulse to turn chaos into order. Planning, in its search for order, reinforces standards about normal behavior, and excludes marginal behavior and activities in cities. Thus, homosexuality is equated with disorder in the city. These sexual preference biases are incorporated into zoning, housing rights, and norms and expectations about the public realm, civic spaces and the right to privacy. Frisch attacks the construction of heterosexuality (as pleasure, as procreation, as based in natural sex differences) as a totalizing concept that sets the default and excludes all alternatives. This article serves as an object lesson for planners working in diverse communities: the professional stance of looking away from marginalized urban groups is not a neutral, non-discriminatory stance; instead, it reinforces the majority group (and all its practices and traditions) as the status quo and delegitimizes all other behavior.

16

Inclusion and Democracy

Iris Marion Young

[…]

2.   Social Difference Is Not Identity

Those who reduce group difference to identity implicitly use a logic of substance to conceptualize groups. Under this logic a group is defined by a set of essential attributes that constitute its identity as a group. Individuals are said to belong to the group in so far as they have the requisite attributes. On this sort of account, the project of organizing in relation to group-based affiliation and experience requires identifying one or more personal or social attributes which make the group what it is, shared by members of the group, and which clearly exclude others. Identifying the group of Latinos, for example, means finding the essential attributes of being Latino, such as biological connection, language, national origin, or celebration of specific holidays. Saying that gay people are a group, to take another example, means identifying the essential attributes that members of the group share that make the group a group. In their efforts to discover the specificities of their group-based social positions and forge relations of solidarity among those similarly located, group-based social movements themselves have sometimes exhibited these essentializing tendencies. We did not need to wait for neo-republican or socialist critics of "identity politics" to point out the problems with such identity claims. Group-differentiated political movements themselves, along with their theoreticians, have developed sophisticated critiques of such tendencies.[1]

Readings in Planning Theory, Third Edition. Edited by Susan S. Fainstein and Scott Campbell.
Editorial material and organization © 2012 Blackwell Publishing Ltd.
Published 2012 by Blackwell Publishing Ltd.

Whether imposed by outsiders or constructed by insiders to the group, attempts to define the essential attributes of persons belonging to social groups fall prey to the problem that there always seem to be persons without the required attributes whom experience tends to include in the group or who identify with the group. The essentialist approach to defining social groups freezes the experienced fluidity of social relations by setting up rigid inside-outside distinctions among groups. If a politics of difference requires such internal unity coupled with clear borders to the social group, then its critics are right to claim that such politics divides and fragments people, encouraging conflict and parochialism.

A politics that seeks to organize people on the basis of a group identity all members share, moreover, must confront the fact that many people deny that group positioning is significant for their identity. Some women, for example, deny reflective awareness of womanly identity as constitutive of their identity, and they deny any particular identification with other women. Many French people deny the existence of a French identity and claim that being French is nothing particularly important to their personal identities; indeed, many of these would be likely to say that the search for French identity that constitutes the personal identities of individual French men and women is a dangerous form of nationalism. Even when people affirm group affinity as important to their identities, they often chafe at the tendency to enforce norms of behaviour or identity that essentialist definitions of the groups entail.

Thirdly, the tendency to conceive group difference as the basis of a common identity which can assert itself in politics implies for many that group members all have the same interests and agree on the values, strategies, and policies that will promote those interests. In fact, however, there is usually wide disagreement among people in a given social group on political ideology. Though members of a group oppressed by gender or racial stereotypes may share interests in the elimination of discrimination and dehumanizing imagery, such a concern is too abstract to constitute a strategic goal. At a more concrete level members of such groups usually express divergent and even contradictory interests.[2]

The most important criticism of the idea of an essential group identity that members share, however, concerns its apparent denial of differentiation within and across groups. Everyone relates to a plurality of social groups; every social group has other social groups cutting across it. The group "men" is differentiated by class, race, religion, age, and so on; the group "Muslim" differentiated by gender, nationality, and so on. If group identity constitutes individual identity and if individuals can identify with one another by means of group identity, then how do we deal theoretically and practically with the fact of multiple group positioning? Is my individual identity somehow an aggregate of my gender identity, race identity, class identity, like a string of beads, to use Elizabeth Spelman's metaphor. In addition, this ontological problem has a political dimension: as Spelman, Lugones, and others argue, the attempt to define a common group identity tends to normalize the experience and perspective of some of the group members while marginalizing or silencing that of others.[3]

Those who reduce a politics of difference to "identity politics", and then criticize that politics, implicitly use a logic of substance, or a logic of identity, to conceptualize groups. In this logic an entity is what it is by virtue of the attributes that inhere in it, some of which are essential attributes. We saw above that attempts to conceptualize any social group – whether a cultural group like Jews, or structural groups like workers or women – become confused when they treat groups as substantially distinct entities whose members all share some specific attributes or interests that do not overlap with any outsiders. Such a rigid conceptualization of group differentiation both denies the similarities that many group members have with those not considered in the group, and denies the many shadings and differentiations within the group.

By conceiving social group differentiation in relational rather than substantial terms, we can retain a description of social group differentiation, but without fixing or reifying groups. Any group consists in a collective of individuals who stand in determinate relations with one another because of the actions and interactions of both those associated with the group and those outside or at the margins of the group.[4] There is no collective entity, the group, apart from the individuals who compose it. A group is much more than an aggregate, however. An aggregate is a more or less arbitrary collection of individuals according to one or more attributes; aggregation, when it occurs, is from the point of view of outsiders, and does not express a subjective social experience. Insurance companies may aggregate smokers for the purposes of actuarial tables, and the Cancer Society may aggregate persons known to have contributed to health insurance advocacy groups. When constituted as aggregates, individuals stand in no determinate relations to one another. The members of groups, however, stand in determinate relations both to one another and to non-members. The group, therefore, consists in both the individuals and their relationships.

Associations are one kind of group. An association is a group that individuals purposefully constitute to accomplish specific objectives. These may be as minor and transient as forming a neighbourhood welcoming committee or as grand and long-lasting as a constitutional state. Certainly associations are constituted relationally. Their members or affiliates stand in certain relations with one another around particular objectives, and those relations are often defined by explicit rules and roles, although many of the relationships in associations will also be informal and tacit. The argument of this chapter requires conceptualizing *social* groups, however, as distinct from associations.[5]

Considered relationally, a social group is a collective of persons differentiated from others by cultural forms, practices, special needs or capacities, structures of power or privilege. Unlike associations, social groups are not explicitly constituted. They emerge from the way people interact. The attributes by which some individuals are classed together in the "same" group appear as similar enough to do so only by the emergent comparison with others who appear more different in that respect. Relational encounter produces perception of both similarity and difference. Before the British began to conquer the islands now called New Zealand, for example, there was no group anyone thought of as Maori. The people who lived on those islands saw themselves as belonging to dozens or hundreds of groups with different lineage and relation to natural resources. Encounter with the English, however, gradually changed their perceptions of their differences; the English saw them as similar to each other in comparison to the English, and they found the English more different from them than they felt from one another.

In a relational conceptualization, what makes a group a group is less some set of attributes its members share than the relations in which they stand to others. On this view, social difference may be stronger or weaker, it may be more or less salient, depending on the point of view of comparison. A relational conception of group difference does not need to force all persons associated with the group under the same attributes. Group members may differ in many ways, including how strongly they bear affinity with others of the group. A relational approach, moreover, does not designate clear conceptual and practical borders that distinguish all members of one group decisively from members of others. Conceiving group differentiation as a function of relation, comparison, and interaction, then, allows for overlap, interspersal, and interdependence among groups and their members.[6]

Groups differentiated by historic connection to territories and by culture have received the most attention both in recent political theory and practical politics, for example in nationalist politics, on the one hand, and in efforts to institute multicultural policies, on the other. Cultural groups are differentiated by perceived similarity and dissimilarity in language, everyday practices, conventions of spirituality, sociability, production, and the aesthetics and objects associated with food, music, buildings, the organization of residential and public space, visual images, and so on. For those within it or who practice it, culture is an environment and means of expression and communication largely unnoticed in itself. As such, culture provides people with important background for their personal expression and contexts for their actions and options. Culture enables interaction and communication among those who share it. For those unfamiliar with its meanings and practices, culture is strange and opaque. Cultural difference emerges from internal and external relations. People discover themselves with cultural affinities that solidify them into groups by virtue of their encounter with those who are culturally different in some or many respects. In discovering themselves as distinct, cultural groups usually solidify a mutual affinity and self-consciousness of themselves as groups.

Political conflict between cultural groups is common, of course. Outsiders condemn or denigrate a group's practices or meanings, and/or assert the superiority of their own, sometimes attempting to suppress the denigrated group's practices and meanings, and impose its own on them. It is important to remember, however, that much of the ground for conflict between culturally differentiated groups is not cultural, but a competition over territory, resources, or jobs. The last chapter of this book [original text] focuses on some issues of cultural difference by examining contemporary arguments about liberal nationalism and self-determination. Later in this chapter I will discuss the politics of multiculturalism as a kind of "identity politics".

More important for the central argument of this chapter, however, is the concept of *structural*, as distinct from cultural, group. While they are often built upon and intersect with cultural differences, the social relations constituting gender, race, class, sexuality, and ability are best understood as structural.[7] The social movements motivated by such group-based experiences are largely attempts to politicize and protest structural inequalities that they perceive unfairly privilege some social segments and oppress others. Analysing structural difference and structural inequality, then, helps to show why these movements are not properly interpreted as "identity politics" I turn, then, to an account of structural differentiation.

3. Structural Difference and Inequality

Appeal to a structural level of social life, as distinct from a level of individual experience and action, is common among social critics.[8] Appeal to structure invokes the institutionalized background which conditions much individual action and expression, but over which individuals by themselves have little control. Yet the concept of structure is notoriously difficult to pin down. I will define social structure, and more specifically structural inequality, by rebuilding elements from different accounts.

Marilyn Frye likens oppression to a birdcage. The cage makes the bird entirely unfree to fly. If one studies the causes of this imprisonment by looking at one wire at a time, however, it appears puzzling. How does a wire only a couple of centimetres wide prevent a bird's flight? One wire at a time, we can neither describe nor explain the inhibition of the bird's flight. Only a large number of wires arranged in a specific way and connected to one another to enclose the bird and reinforce one another's rigidity can explain why the bird is unable to fly freely.[9]

At a first level of intuition, this is what I mean by social structures that inhibit the capacities of some people. An account of someone's life circumstances contains many strands of difficulty or difference from others that, taken one by one, can appear to be the result of decision, preferences, or accidents. When considered together, however, and when compared with the life story of others, they reveal a net of restricting and reinforcing relationships. Let me illustrate.

Susan Okin gives an account of women's oppression as grounded in a gender division of labour in the family. She argues that gender roles and expectations structure men's and women's lives in thoroughgoing ways that result in disadvantage and vulnerability for many women and their children. Institutionally, the entire society continues to be organized around the expectation that children and other dependent people ought to be cared for primarily by family members without formal compensation. Good jobs, on the other hand, assume that workers are available at least forty hours per week year round. Women are usually the primary caretakers of children and other dependent persons, due to a combination of factors: their socialization disposes them to choose to do it, and/or their job options pay worse than those available to their male partners, or her male partner's work allows him little time for care work. As a consequence the attachment of many women to the world of employment outside the home is more episodic, less prestigious, and less well paid than men's. This fact in turn often makes women dependent on male earnings for primary support of themselves and their children. Women's economic dependence gives many men unequal power in the family. If the couple separates, moreover, prior dependence on male earnings coupled with the assumptions of the judicial system makes women and their children vulnerable to poverty. Schools', media, and employers' assumptions all mirror the expectation that domestic work is done primarily by women, which assumptions in turn help reproduce those unequal structures.[10]

This is an account of gender difference as structural difference. The account shows gender difference as structured by a set of relationships and interactions that act together to produce specific possibilities and preclude others, and which operate in a reinforcing circle. One can quarrel with the content or completeness of the account. To it I would add, for example, the structures that organize the social dominance of norms of heterosexual desire, and the consequences of this heterosexual matrix for people of both sexes and multiple desires. The example can show at an intuitive level the meaning of structural social group difference. Social groups defined by race or class are also positioned in structures; shortly I will elaborate these examples. Now I will systematize the notion of structure by building up definitions from several social theorists.

Peter Blau offers the following definition. "A social structure can be defined as a multidimensional space of differentiated social positions among which a population is distributed. The social associations of people provide both the criterion for distinguishing social positions and the connections among them that make them elements of a single social structure."[11] Blau exploits the spatial metaphor implied by the concept of structure. Individual people occupy varying *positions* in the social space, and their positions stand in determinate relation to other positions. The structure consists in the connections among the positions and their relationships, and the way the attributes of positions internally constitute one another through those relationships.

Basic social structures consist in determinate social positions that people occupy which condition their opportunities and life chances. These life chances are constituted by the ways the positions are related to one another to create systematic constraints or opportunities that reinforce one another, like wires in a cage. Structural social groups are constituted through the social organization of labour and production, the organization of desire and sexuality, the institutionalized rules of authority and subordination, and the constitution of prestige. Structural social groups are relationally constituted in the sense that one position in structural relations does not exist apart from a differentiated relation to other positions. Priests, for example, have a particular social function and status in a particular society by virtue of their structured and interdependent relations with others who believe they need specialists in spiritual service and are willing to support that specialization materially. The prestige associated with a caste, to take another example, is bought only through reproduced relations of denigration with lower castes. The castes exist by virtue of their interactive relations with one another, enacted and re-enacted through rituals of deference and superiority enforced through distributions, material dependencies, and threats of force.

More generally, a person's social location in structures differentiated by class, gender, age, ability, race, or caste often implies predictable status in law, educational possibility, occupation, access to resources, political power, and prestige. Not only do each of these factors enable or constrain self-determination and self-development, they also tend to reinforce the others. One reason to call these structural is that they are relatively permanent. Though the specific content and detail of the positions and relationships are frequently reinterpreted, evolving, and even contested, the basic social locations and their relations to one another tend to be reproduced.

It is certainly misleading, however, to reify the metaphor of structure, that is, to think of social structures as entities independent of social actors, lying passively around them, easing or inhibiting their movement. On the contrary, social structures exist only in the action and interaction of persons; they exist not as states, but as processes. Thus Anthony Giddens defines social structures in terms of "rules and resources, recursively implicated in the reproduction of social systems".[12] In the idea of the duality of structure, Giddens theorizes how people act on the basis of their knowledge of pre-existing structures and in so acting reproduce those structures. We do so because we act according to rules and expectations and because our relationally constituted positions make or do not make certain resources available to us.

Economic class is the paradigm of structural relations in this sense. Understood as a form of structural differentiation, class analysis begins with an account of positions in the functioning of systems of ownership, finance, investment, production, and service provision. Even when they have shares of stock or participate in pension funds, those who are not in a position to live independently and control the movement of capital must depend on employment by others in order to gain a livelihood. These positions of capitalist and worker are themselves highly differentiated by income and occupation, but their basic structural relation is an interdependency; most people depend on employment by private enterprises for their livelihoods, and the owners and managers depend on the competence and co-operation of their employees for revenues. Important recent scholarship has argued that a bipolar understanding of economic class in contemporary societies is too simple, and we must also analysis the structural differences of professional and non-professional employees, as well as self-employed, and those more or less permanently excluded from employment.[13]

People are born into a particular class position, and this accident of birth has enormous consequences for the opportunities and privileges they have for the rest of their lives. Without a doubt, some born to wealth-owner families die paupers, and others born poor die rich. Nevertheless, a massive empirical literature shows that the most consistent predictor of adult income level, educational attainment, occupation, and ownership of assets is the class situation of one's parents. While class position is defined first in terms of relations of production, class privilege also produces and is supported by an array of assets such as residence, social networks, access to high-quality education and cultural supplements, and so on. All of these operate to reinforce the structural differentiations of class.

Defining structures in terms of the rules and resources brought to actions and interactions, however, makes the reproduction of structures sound too much like the product of individual and intentional action. The concept of social structure must also include conditions under which actors act, which are often a *collective* outcome of action impressed onto the physical environment. Jean-Paul Sartre calls this aspect of social structural the *practico-inert*.[14] Most of the conditions under which people act are socio-historical: they are the products of previous actions, usually products of many co-ordinated and unco-ordinated but mutually influenced actions over them. Those collective actions have produced determinate effects on the physical and cultural environment which condition future action in specific ways. As I understand the term, social structures include this practico-inert physical organization of buildings, but also modes of transport and communication, trees, rivers, and rocks, and their relation to human action.

Processes that produce and reproduce residential racial segregation illustrate how structural relations become inscribed in the physicality of the environment, often without anyone intending this outcome, thereby conditioning future action and interaction. A plurality of expectations and actions and their effects operate to limit the options of many inner-city dwellers in the United States. Racially discriminatory behaviour and policies limit the housing options of people of colour, confining many of them to neighbourhoods from which many of those whites who are able to leave do. Property-owners fail to keep up their buildings, and new investment is hard to attract because the value of property appears to decline. Because of more concentrated poverty and lay-off policies that disadvantage Blacks or Latinos, the effects of an economic downturn in minority neighbourhoods are often felt more severely, and more businesses fail or leave. Politicians often are more responsive to the neighbourhoods where more affluent and white people live; thus schools, fire protection, policing, snow removal, garbage pick-up, are poor in the ghetto neighbourhoods. The spatial concentration of poorly maintained buildings and infrastructure that results reinforces the isolation and disadvantage of those there because people are reluctant to invest in them. Economic restructuring independent of these racialized processes contributes to the closing of major employers near the segregated neighbourhoods and the opening of employers in faraway suburbs. As a result of the confluence of all these actions and processes, many Black and Latino children are poorly educated, live around a higher concentration of demoralized people in dilapidated and dangerous circumstances, and have few prospects for employment.[15]

Reference to the physical aspects of social structures helps to lead us to a final aspect of the concept. The actions and interactions which take place among persons differently situated in social structures using rules and resources do not only take place on the basis of past actions whose collective effects mark the physical conditions of action. They also often have future effects beyond the immediate purposes and intentions of the actors. Structured social action and interaction often have collective results that no one intends, and which may even be counter to the best intentions of the actors.[16] Even though no one intends them, they become given circumstances that help structure future actions. Presumably no one intends the vulnerability of many children to poverty that Okin argues the normal gender division of labour produces.

In summary, a structural social group is a collection of persons who are similarly positioned in interactive and institutional relations that condition their opportunities and life prospects. This conditioning occurs because of the way that actions and interactions conditioning that position in one situation reinforce the rules and resources available for other actions and interactions involving people in the structural positions. The unintended consequences of the confluence of many actions often produce and reinforce such opportunities and constraints, and these often make their mark on the physical conditions of future actions, as well as on the habits and expectations of actors. This mutually reinforcing process means that the positional relations and the way they condition individual lives are difficult to change.

Structural groups sometimes build on or overlap with cultural groups, as in most structures of racialized differentiation or ethnic-based privilege. Thus cultural groups and structural groups cannot be considered mutually exclusive or opposing concepts. Later I will elaborate on the interaction of cultural groups with structures, in the context of evaluating what should and should not be called identity politics. Not all ethnic or cultural group difference, however, generates structural group difference. Some structural difference, moreover, is built not on differences of cultural practice and perception, but instead on bodily differences like sex or physical ability. Some structures position bodies with particular attributes in relations that have consequences for how people are treated, the assumptions made about them, and their opportunities to realize their plans. In so far as it makes sense to say that people with disabilities are a social group, for example, despite their vast bodily differences, this is in virtue of social structures that normalize certain functions in the tools, built environment, and expectations of many people.[17]

People differently positioned in social structures have differing experiences and understandings of social relationships and the operations of the society because of their structural situation. Often such differences derive from the structural inequalities that privilege some people in certain respects and relatively disadvantage others. Structural *inequality* consists in the relative constraints some people encounter in their freedom and material well being as the cumulative effect of the possibilities of their social positions, as compared with others who in their social positions have more options or easier access to benefits. These constraints or possibilities by no means determine outcomes for individuals in their ability to enact their plans or gain access to benefits. Some of those in more constrained situations are particularly lucky or unusually hard-working and clever, while some of those with an open road have bad luck or squander their opportunities by being lazy or stupid. Those who successfully overcome obstacles, however, cannot be judged as equal to those who have faced fewer structural obstacles, even if at a given time they have roughly equivalent incomes, authority, or prestige.

[...]

5. What Is and Is Not Identity Politics

Some critics of a politics of difference wrongly reduce them to "identity politics". They reduce political movements that arise from specificities of social group difference to assertions of group identity or mere self-regarding interest. Often group-conscious social movements claim that social difference should be taken into account rather than bracketed as a condition of political inclusion for furthering social justice. Yet the label "identity politics" is not entirely misplaced as a characterization of some claims and self-conceptions of these movements. Now I want to sort out those concerns and public activities plausibly called identity politics from those that are not.

Historically excluded or dominated groups all have organized discourses and cultural expressions aimed at reversing the stereotypes and deprecations with which they claim dominant society has described them. Politically conscious social movements of indigenous people, for example, promote a positive understanding of indigenous governance forms, technology, and art, as a response to colonialist definitions of "civilized" institutions and practices. Many African Americans in the United States historically and today cultivate pride in the ingenuity of African American resistance institutions and cultural expression as a response to the invisibility and distortion of their lives and experience they have seen in dominant discourses. Where dominant understandings of femininity equate it with relative weakness and selfless nurturing, some feminists have reinterpreted typically womanly activities and relationships as expressions of intelligence and strength. Interpretations and reinterpretations of typical experiences and activities of group members in response to deprecating stereotypes can rightly be called "identity politics". They are often expressed in cultural products such as novels, songs, plays, or paintings. Often they are explicit projects that individual persons take up as an affirmation of their own personal identities in relation to group meaning and affinity with others identified with the group. Their function is partly to encourage solidarity among those with a group affinity, and a sense of political agency in making justice claims to the wider society.

Any movements or organizations mobilizing politically in response to deprecating judgements, marginalization, or inequality in the wider society, I suggest, need to engage in "identity politics" in this sense. Working-class and poor people's movements have asserted positive group definition in this sense as much as gender, racialized, or colonized groups. Such solidarity-producing cultural politics does consist in the assertion of specificity and difference towards a wider public, from whom the movement expects respect and recognition of its agency and virtues. The public political claims of such groups, however, rarely consist simply in the assertion of one identity as against others, or a simple claim that a group be recognized in its distinctiveness. Instead, claims for recognition usually function as part of or means to claims against discrimination, unequal opportunity, political marginalization, or unfair burdens.

Another kind of movement activity often brought under the label "identity politics", however, I find more ambiguous. The project of revaluation and reclaiming identity often involves individual and collective exploration of the meaning of a cultural group's histories, practices, and meanings. Many people devote significant energy to documenting these meanings and adding to their creative expression in music, visual images, and written and visual narratives. The exploration of positioned experience and cultural meaning is an important source of the self for most people. For this reason exploring the expressive and documentary possibilities especially of

cultural meaning is an intrinsically valuable human enterprise, and one that contributes to the reproduction of social groups. In themselves and apart from conflict
and problems of political and economic privilege or civil freedom, however, these
are not *political* enterprises. To the extent that social movements have mistaken these
activities for politics, or to the extent that they have displaced political struggles in
relation to structural inequalities, critics of identity politics may have some grounds
for their complaints.

Projects of the exploration of cultural meaning easily become political, however,
under at least the following circumstances. (1) Sometimes people find their liberty
to engage in specific cultural practices curtailed, or they face impediments in forming associations to express and preserve their cultural identity. (2) Even where there
is social and cultural tolerance, sometimes political conflict erupts over educational
practices and curricular context because different groups believe they are entitled
to have their children learn their cultural practices and meanings in public schools.
(3) Even when they have a formal liberty to explore their affinity group meanings,
engage in minority practices, and form associations, sometimes groups find that
they cannot get access to media, institutions, and resources they need to further
their projects of exploring and creating cultural meaning. These are all familiar and
much discussed conflicts often brought under the rubric of "multicultural" politics.
I do not wish to minimize the difficulty and importance of working through such
issues. The point here is that most group-based political claims cannot be reduced
to such conflicts concerning the expression and preservation of cultural meaning.

Charles Taylor's theory of the politics of recognition is a very influential interpretation of a politics of difference. Taylor argues that cultural group affinity, as well as
respect for and preservation of their culture, is deeply important to many people
because they provide sources of their selves. A person lacks equal dignity if a group
with which he or she is associated does not receive public recognition as having
equal status with others. Some political movements thus seek recognition in that
sense, as a claim of justice.[18] While I agree that claims for recognition and respect for
cultural groups judged different are often made and are claims of justice, I disagree
with Taylor and those who have taken up his account that misrecognition is usually
a political problem independent of other forms of inequality or oppression. On his
account, groups seek recognition for its own sake, to have a sense of pride in their
cultural group and preserve its meanings, and not for the sake of or in the process of
seeking other goods. But I do not believe this describes most situations in which
groups demand recognition. Where there are problems of lack of recognition of
national, cultural, religious, or linguistic groups, these are usually tied to questions
of control over resources, exclusion from benefits of political influence or economic
participation, strategic power, or segregation from opportunities. A politics of
recognition, that is, usually is part of or a means to claims for political and social
inclusion or an end to structural inequalities that disadvantage them.

Political movements of African Americans today have been interpreted by many
as "identity politics". An examination of some of the central claims made by African
American activists, however, puts such a label into question. Many African Americans

call for stronger measures to prevent race-motivated hate crimes and to pursue and punish those who commit them. Agitation continues in many cities to make police more accountable to citizens, in an effort to prevent and punish abuse and arbitrary treatment which African Americans experience more than others. African American politicians and activists continue to argue that institutional racism persists in the American educational, labour market, and housing allocation system, and that more active measures should be taken to enforce anti-discrimination and redistribute resources and positions for the sake of the development of disadvantaged African American individuals and neighbourhoods. Making many of these claims involves asserting that African Americans as a group are positioned differently from other people in American society, and sometimes activists also assert a pride in African American cultural forms and solidarity. The primary claims of justice, however, refer to experiences of structural inequality more than cultural difference.

What of movements of indigenous people? Indigenous politics certainly does entail a claim to recognition of the cultural distinctness of these groups. Indigenous peoples everywhere have suffered colonialist attempts to wipe out their distinct identities as peoples. They have been removed, dispersed, killed, their languages, religious practices, and artistic expression suppressed. They demand of the societies that continue to dominate them recognition and support for their distinct cultures and the freedom to express and rejuvenate those cultures. Colonialist oppression of indigenous people has involved not only cultural imperialism, however, but at the same time and often in the same actions deprivation of the land and resources from which they derived a living, and suppression of their governing institutions. As a result of conquest and subsequent domination and economic marginalization, indigenous people today are often the poorest people in the societies to which they are connected. Primary indigenous demands everywhere, then, are for self-determination over governance institutions and administration of services, and restoration of control over land and resources for the sake of the economic development of the people. Self-determination also involves cultural autonomy.

The "identity" assertions of cultural groups, I suggest, usually appear in the context of structural relations of privilege and disadvantage. Many Muslims in Europe or North America, for example, assert their right to wear traditional dress in public places, and make claims of religious freedom.[19] Many Middle Eastern, North African, and South Asian migrants claim that Germany, the Netherlands, or France ought to accept them with their difference as full members of the society in which they have lived for decades, where their children were born and now live marginal youthful lives. Many of them experience housing, education, and employment discrimination, are targets of xenophobic acts of violence or harassment, and are excluded from or marginalized in political participation. In this sort of context claims for cultural recognition are rarely asserted for their own sake. They are part of demands for political inclusion and equal economic opportunity, where the claimants deny that such equality should entail shedding or privatizing their cultural difference.

Let me review one final example of political claims of justice critics often deride as divisive identity politics: political claims of gay men and lesbians. Especially after internal movement criticisms of efforts to "identify" what it means to "be" gay, more people whose desires and actions transgress heterosexual norms, and who find affinities with gay and lesbian institutions, would deny that they have or express a "gay identity" they share with others. They do claim that they ought to be free to express their desires and to cultivate institutions without hiding, and without fear of harassment, violence, loss of employment, or housing. Many claim, further, that same-sex partners should have access to the same material benefits in tax law, property relations, and access to partner's employment benefits as heterosexual couples can have through marriage. For the most part, these claims of justice are not "identity" claims. Nor are they simple claims to "recognition". They are claims that they should be free to be openly different from the majority without suffering social and economic disadvantage on account of that difference.

To summarize, I have argued in this section that some group-based political discourses and demands can properly be labelled "identity politics". Sometimes groups seek to cultivate mutual identification among those similarly situated, and in doing so they may indeed express conflict and confrontation with others who are differently situated, against whom they make claims that they wrongfully suffer domination or oppression. Such solidarity-forming "identity politics" is as typical of obviously structurally differentiated groups such as economic classes, however, as of marginalized cultural groups. Multicultural politics concerning freedom of expression, the content of curricula, official languages, access to media, and the like, moreover, can properly be called "identity politics". Most group-conscious political claims, however, are not claims to the recognition of identity as such, but rather claims for fairness, equal opportunity, and political inclusion.

Critics of the politics of difference worry about the divisiveness of such claims. There is no question that such claims often provoke disagreement and conflict. When diverse groups makes claims of justice, however, we cannot reject them simply on the grounds that others' disagreement with or hostility to them produces conflict. Norms of inclusive communicative democracy require that claims directed at a public with the aim of persuading members of that public that injustices occur must be given a hearing, and require criticism of those who refuse to listen. Appeals to a common good that exhort people to put aside their experienced differences will not promote justice when structural inequality or deep disagreement exist. I shall now argue that such group-based conflict or disagreement is more likely to be avoided or overcome when a public includes differently situated voices that speak across their difference and are accountable to one another.

6. Communication across Difference in Public Judgement

We can now return to arguments such as Elshtain's that a politics of difference endangers democracy because it encourages self-regarding parochialism and destroys a genuine public life. Elshtain conceptualizes genuine democratic process as one in which participants assume a public mantle of citizenship which cloaks the private and partial and differentiated, on the one hand, and enters an impartial and unitary realm, on the other. Either politics is nothing but competition among private interests, in which case there is no public spirit; or politics is a commitment to equal respect for other citizens in a civil public discussion that puts aside private affiliation and interest to seek a common good. I believe that this is a false dichotomy.

Difference, civility, and political co-operation

When confronted so starkly with an opposition between difference and civility, most must opt for civility. But a conception of deliberative politics which insists on putting aside or transcending partial and particularist differences forgets or denies the lesson that the politics of difference claims to teach. If group-based positional differences give to some people greater power, material and cultural resources, and authoritative voice, then social norms and discourses which appear impartial are often biased. Under circumstances of structural social and economic inequality, the relative power of some groups often allows them to dominate the definition of the common good in ways compatible with their experience, perspective, and priorities. A common consequence of social privilege is the ability of a group to convert its perspective on some issues into authoritative knowledge without being challenged by those who have reason to see things differently. Such a dynamic is a major way that political inequality helps reproduce social and economic inequality even in formally democratic processes.

It is especially ironic that some critics on the left, such as Gitlin and Harvey, reject a politics of difference, and argue that class offers a vision of commonality as opposed to the partiality of gender or race. For those aiming to speak from the perspective of the working class have long argued that the economic and social power of the capitalist class allows that class perspective to dominate political and cultural institutions as well, and to pass for a universal perspective. The capitalist class is able to control deliberative modes and policy decisions for the sake of its interests and at the same time to represent those interests as common or universal interests. On this account, the only way to expose that such claims to the common good serve certain particular interests or reflect the experience and perspective of particular social segments primarily is publicly to assert the interests not served by the allegedly common policies, and publicly to articulate the specificity of the experiences and perspectives they exclude. Claims by feminists that the formulation and priorities of issues often assume masculine experience as normative, or by racialized or ethnic minorities that the political agenda presumes the privilege and experience of majorities, are extensions of this sort of analysis. To the degree that a society is in fact differentiated by structural relations of privilege and disadvantage, claims that everyone in the society has some common interests or a common good must be subject to deep scrutiny, and can only be validated by critical discussion that specifically attends to the differentiated social positions.

At least while circumstances of structural privilege and disadvantage persist, a politics that aims to promote justice through public discussion and decision-making must theorize and aim to practise a third way, alternative to either private interest competition or difference-bracketing public discussion of the common good. This third way consists in a process of public discussion and decision-making which includes and affirms the particular social group positions relevant to issues. It does so in order to draw on the situated knowledge of the people located in different group positions as resources for enlarging the understanding of everyone and moving them beyond their own parochial interests.[20]

It is simply not true that, when political actors articulate particularist interests and experiences and claim that public policy ought to attend to social difference, they are necessarily asserting self-regarding interests against those of others. Undoubtedly groups sometimes merely assert their own interests or preferences, but sometimes they make claims of injustice and justice. Sometimes those speaking to a wider public on behalf of labour, or women, or Muslims, or indigenous peoples make critical and normative appeals, and they are prepared to justify their criticisms and demands. When they make such appeals with such an attitude, they are not behaving in a separatist and inward-looking way, even though their focus is on their own particular situation. By criticizing the existing institutions and policies, or criticizing other groups' claims and proposals, they appeal to a wider public for inclusion, recognition, and equity. Such public expression implies that they acknowledge and affirm a political engagement with those they criticize, with whom they struggle.

Critics who emphasize appeals to a common good are surely right to claim that workable democratic politics requires of citizens some sense of being together with one another in order to sustain the commitment that seeking solutions to conflict under circumstances of difference and inequality requires. It is far too strong, however, to claim that this sense of being together requires mutual identification. Nor should such togetherness be conceived as a search for shared interests or common good beyond the goal of solving conflicts and problems in democratically acceptable ways. Trying to solve problems justly may sometimes mean that some people's perceived interests are not served, especially when issues involve structural relations of privilege. Even when the most just solutions to political problems do not entail promoting some interests more than others, fairness usually involves co-ordinating diverse goods and interests rather than achieving a common good.

Political co-operation requires a less substantial unity than shared understandings or a common good, [...]. It requires first that people whose lives and actions affect one another in a web of institutions, interactions, and unintended consequences acknowledge that they are together in such space of mutual effect. Their conflicts and problems are produced by such togetherness. The unity required by political co-operation also entails that the people who are together in this way are committed to trying to work out their conflicts and to solve the problems generated by their collective action through means of peaceful and rule-bound decision-making. Political co-operation requires, finally, that those who are together in this way understand themselves as members of a single polity. That means only that they conduct their problem-solving discussions and decision-making under agreed-upon and publicly acknowledged procedures.

These unity conditions for democratic decision-making are certainly rare enough in the world, difficult both to produce and maintain. Common good theorists no doubt fear that attending to group differences in public discussion endangers commitment to co-operative decision-making. Perhaps sometimes it does. More often, however, I suggest, groups or factions refuse co-operation because, at least from their point of view, their experience, needs, and interests have been excluded or marginalized from the political agenda, or are suppressed in discussions and decision-making. Only explicit and differentiated forms of inclusion can diminish the occurrence of such refusals, especially when members of some groups are more privileged in some or many respects.

Notes

1   For some examples of critiques of essentialism and a politics of identity from within theories and movements that support a politics of difference, see Elizabeth V Spelman, *Inessential Woman* (Boston: Beacon Press, 1988); Anna Yeatman, "Minorities and the Politics of Difference", in *Postmodern Revisions of the Political* (New York: Routledge, 1994); Michael Dyson, "Essentialism and the Complexities of Racial Identity", in David Theo Goldberg (ed), *Multiculturalism* (Cambridge, Mass. Blackwell, 1994); Steven Seidman, "Identity and Politics in a 'Postmodern' Gay Culture", in *Difference Troubles; Queering Social Theory and Sexual Politics* (Cambridge: Cambridge University Press, 1997).

2   Compare Anne Phillips, *The Politics of Presence* (Oxford: Oxford University Press, 1995), ch. 6.

3   Spelman, *Inessential Woman*; Maria Lugones, "Purity, Impurity and Separation", *Signs. A Journal of Women in Cultural and Society*, 19/2 (Winter 1994), 458–79.

4   For an account of groups as constituted relations, see Larry May, *The Morality of Groups* (Chicago: University of Chicago Press, 1988); and *Sharing Responsibility* (Chicago: University of Chicago Press, 1993).

5   In earlier work I have distinguished these three terms, aggregates, associations, and social groups, and I rely on these conceptualizations here. See *Justice and the Politics of Difference* (Princeton: Princeton University Press, 1990), ch. 2.

6   Martha Minow proposes a relational understanding of group difference; see *Making All the Difference* (Ithaca, NY: Cornell University Press, 1990), pt. II. I have referred to a relational analysis of group difference in *Justice and the Politics of Difference*, ch. 2; in that earlier formulation, however, I have not distinguished group affiliation from personal identity as strongly as I will later in this chapter. For relational understandings of group difference, see also William Connolly, *Identity/Difference* (Ithaca, NY: Cornell University Press, 1993), and Chantal Mouffe, "Democracy, Power and the 'Political'", in Seyla Benhabib (ed.), *Democracy and Difference* (Princeton: Princeton University Press, 1996).

7   The following effort to articulate the naming of structural social groups and use that concept to argue against an "identity politics" interpretation of the claims of difference-based social movements is partly motivated by a desire to think through further some of the issues raised in an exchange I have had with Nancy Fraser See Fraser, "From Redistribution to Recognition? Dilemmas of Justice in a 'Post-Socialist' Age", *New Left Review*, 212 (July–Aug, 1995), 68–99; and Iris Marion Young, "Unruly Categories: A Critique of Nancy Fraser"s Dual Systems Theory', *New Left Review*, 222 (Mar–Apr, 1997), 147–60. Fraser's

initial paper importantly reminded theorists of justice and multi-culturalism of issues of structural oppression and possible transformation. Fraser herself oversimplifies the meaning of a politics of difference as identity politics, however, and I believe inappropriately dichotomizes issues of culture and structure.

8   See e.g., William Julius Wilson, *When Work Disappears* (New York: Knopf, 1997); see also Jean Hampton, *Political Philosophy* (Boulder, Colo.: Westview Press, 1997), 189–90.

9   Marilyn Frye, 'Oppression', in *The Politics of Reality* (Trumansburg, NY: Crossing Press, 1983).

10   Susan Okin, *Justice, Gender and the Family* (New York: Basic Books, 1989).

11   Peter Blau, *Inequality and Heterogeneity* (New York: Free Press, 1977), 4.

12   Anthony Giddens, *The Constitution of Society* (Berkeley University of California Press, 1984).

13   For a clear and thorough account of class in a contemporary Marxist mode, see Eric Olin Wright, *Class Counts* (Cambridge: Cambridge University Press, 1997).

14   Jean-Paul Sartre, *Critique of Dialectical Reason*, trans. Alan Sheridan-Smith (London: New Left Books, 1976), bk. 1, ch. 3.

15   See Douglas Massey and Nancy Denton, *American Apartheid* (Cambridge, Mass: Harvard University Press, 1993).

16   Sartre calls such effects counter-finalities; see *Critique of Dialectical Reason*, 277–92.

17   Anita Silvers develops a thorough and persuasive account of why issues of justice regarding people with disabilities should focus on the relation of bodies to physical and social environments, rather than on the needs and capacities of individuals called disabled. See Silvers, 'Formal Justice', in Anita Silvers, David Wasserman, and Mary B. Mahowald (eds.), *Disability, Difference, Discrimination Perspectives on Justice in Bioethics and Public Policy* (Lanham, Md.: Rowman & Littlefield, 1998).

18   Taylor, 'Multiculturalism and the Politics of Recognition'.

19   See Joseph Carens and Melissa Williams, 'Muslim Minorities in Liberal Democracies: Justice and the Limits of Toleration', in Carens (ed), *Culture, Citizenship, and Community: A Contextual Exploration of Justice as Evenhandedness* (Oxford: Oxford University Press, 2000).

20   I find the conception of deliberative democracy elaborated by James Bohman a version of this third way Bohman criticizes communitarian or neo-republican interpretations of publicity and deliberation as requiring too much consensus. He constructs a weaker version of publicity and legitimacy that are explicitly open to social difference and inequality which recognizes that ideals of impartiality and common good are problematic in complex democracies with cultural differences and structural inequalities. See *Public Deliberation* (Cambridge, Mass.: MIT Press, 1996). In some of his most recent work Jürgen Habermas has shifted from a more unifying view to one which emphasizes more the need to attend to social differences. See 'Does Europe Need a Constitution? Reponse to Dieter Grimm', and 'Struggles for Recognition in the Democratic Constitutional State', both in *The Inclusion of the Other. Studies in Political Theory* (Cambridge, Mass.: MIT Press, 1998).

Iris Marion Young, "Inclusion and Democracy," *Inclusion and Democracy*, 2000, pp. 87–99, 102–11, Oxford University Press.

17

The Minority-Race Planner in the Quest for a Just City

June Manning Thomas

Ann Markusen once suggested that the urban planning profession is losing the battle with economics for the shaping of urban space in part because planners value equity as a normative criterion, whereas economics values market efficiency. Efficiency has won out in whatever war of values might have taken place (Markusen, 2000). While it may be true that planners value equity, any such commitment may run counter to political and social conditions. Furthermore, either widely accepted tools are not available to create such equity, or political conditions in fact support inequitable, purposeful oppression. These situations have emerged in several very different contexts around the world (Bollens, 1999, 2004; Fainstein, 2005; Flyvbjerg, 2002; Forester, 2000; Yiftachel, 2006; Yiftachel and Ghanem, 2004).

One modest but tangible way to help bring about equity in the urban context may be to ensure that the ranks of professional planners include diversity in race and ethnicity, particularly in urban societies where severe inequities by race and ethnicity exist. Diversity in the urban planning profession and the connection between diversity and the "just city" are not topics that have recently received a great deal of attention in the scholarly planning literature, but professional diversity would seem to be one visible, tangible, and basic measure of the profession's commitment to social equity. If the urban planning profession cannot itself reflect commitment to social equity in the form of its own demographics, it could seem contradictory for professional planners to argue for social equity in society at large.

This article will explore possible reasons for focusing on the diversity – in this article, we will largely address racial diversity, particularly in the United States – of the profession as we continue to dialogue about the just city, and we will discuss some of the subtleties of circumstance that may make the diversity of the profession difficult to

Readings in Planning Theory, Third Edition. Edited by Susan S. Fainstein and Scott Campbell.
Editorial material and organization © 2012 Blackwell Publishing Ltd.
Published 2012 by Blackwell Publishing Ltd.

maintain. Racial diversity could conceivably bring tangible benefits to the workplace and to the community, especially in those social contexts characterized by racial conflict or segregation. If this potential contribution is to unfold, however, we will need to come to terms with the difficult work contexts which may face minority-race planners, and with the possible need to address dysfunction within these contexts before attempting to address dysfunction within the world at large. After offering a few definitions related to race, we will explore these issues by considering the theoretical background of the "just city", as well as initial thoughts concerning the means for reaching such a city. We will reference as well the results of interviews with a few African American US planners, to gain some sense of the challenges that may face minority-race planners in their work environments in at least one country, the US.

Minority-Race People

In this discussion, we reference "minority-race", "race", and "ethnicity" because of a lack of better language. We continue to use these terms only because they have social meaning to many people today, but their scientific meaning is vague, and meaning varies by nation or continent. "Race" is a social construct with little biological justification. Its modern usage arose only a few hundred years ago in order to justify the economic oppression of darker-skinned people under conditions of slavery, colonialism, and industrialization, and it serves particularly poorly as a concept in societies characterized by populations of diverse origins which have intermarried.[1] In the US, the context for much of the discussion of this article, definitions are sometimes fluid but race remains a powerful concept because of a cultural reality: people continue to treat others differently because of perceived race, with particularly strong distinctions between "black" or African American and "white" or Caucasian, even though both of these categories include extensive mixture and variation (Farley et al., 2000; Hirschman, 2004; Moses, 2004). Furthermore, centuries of different treatment, by individuals and by institutions, have left a lasting mark on the urban landscape, with far different circumstances for people perceived to be of minority race or ethnicity in terms of living conditions, residential patterns, and social and economic opportunities, particularly for those of low income (Wilson, 2003).

While in some national contexts "ethnicity" is a good substitute for "race", this is not necessarily true in the US. "Ethnicity" often refers to tribal, national, regional, language grouping or other variations which may be less physically obvious than the popular conception of race (Hirschman, 2004). Yiftachel (2006) has argued that ethnic divisions, more so than racial divisions, are particularly difficult in the Southern and Eastern parts of the world. He suggests that the North and West – meaning North America and Western Europe – benefit from a number of basic liberties and social welfare provisions that make life even for their disadvantaged racial minorities relatively more stable than life for many oppressed ethnic groups in Southern and Eastern places such as Israel, apartheid South Africa, Eastern Europe, and many other countries.

While this is undoubtedly true, the economic, social, and spatial divisions by race and ethnicity in his designated North and West – particularly in US cities – pose continuing, ongoing dilemmas that have yet to be resolved and may not be resolved in the foreseeable future. Planners will probably have much less credibility and efficacy in helping to bring about social equity in situations of racial or ethnic division or conflict if their membership is composed largely of the dominant race or ethnicity, or if their planning work environments do not support the effective functioning of members of minority races or ethnic groups as planning professionals. These are two variants of the phenomenon wherein planners in conflict-laden societies have found it necessary to negotiate difficult shoals of allegiance and reform, or in fact have become tools of the state used to create and legitimize situations of spatial control of oppressed racial, ethnic, or religious groups (Bollens, 1999, 2000; Yiftachel, 2000).

The postmodern era celebrates non-exclusion, and so it is unfortunate that it is necessary to raise yet again this topic of racial diversity in the profession. The main reason is not to hold on to modernist or structuralist notions of binary reality that Soja (1997) referred to as outmoded – that is, to view everything in exclusionary terms of black or white, worker or capitalist, immigrant or native, male or female – but rather to ground dialogue in the reality of the fragmented metropolis and to understand that the "politics of difference" (Merrifield, 1997) is a messy affair, requiring focused attention and effort. In the US, it is not surprising that professional organizations such as the American Planning Association (APA) (2005a, 2005b, 2006a, 2006b) and the American Institute of Certified Planners (AICP) (2005b) have witnessed or participated in continued dialogue about racial diversity in the profession.

The Ends

In this discussion of the just city, it is important to consider both means and ends. By ends we refer to the goal that planners are trying to achieve in today's cities and urban regions, and means refers to the process by which this goal is attained. Ends and means may be interrelated, contingent upon one another and dynamic according to situation (Healey, 2003).

Concerning the goal of a just city, first we must note that values such as equity or justice may not be so much universal as individualized, necessitating that we take great care in analyzing the context under consideration (Watson, 2006). Furthermore, definitions are not simple matters. The definition of justice, for example, varies according to conditions of knowledge and power, or context (Healey, 2003; Young, 1990), with not a little confusion caused by successively varying historical understandings of the meaning of the concept of justice, dating from Aristotle to Marx to Rawls and beyond (Fleischacker, 2004; Merrifield and Swyngedouw, 1997; Stein and Harper, 2005). Some Marxists or political economists may eschew "justice" as a vague moralism, while some liberal scholars may champion the concept but strip their discussion of urban context or means of implementation (Katznelson, 1997).

Nevertheless, it is still possible to argue that planners should strive for the "just city" as a main end or goal of planning action (Fainstein, 2000, 2005; Krumholz and Forester, 1990; Harvey, 2003; Krumholz and Clavel, 1994). Fainstein argues that planning theory should take "an explicitly normative position concerning the distribution of social benefits" (Fainstein, 2000: 467). She presents a definition of the "just city" that is twofold, looking at both process and product: "A theory of the just city values participation in decision making by relatively powerless groups and equity of outcomes" (Fainstein, 2000: 468).[2] It is this dualistic definition that we use in this article.

Focusing on results or "equity of outcomes" – as opposed to process – is an important component of this definition, even though the power of planning to shape outcomes is and always has been limited (Fainstein, 2005). Outcomes often stem from processes during which powerful economic interests dominate decision-making, a fact which has taught us to beware of actions touted as being in the "public interest" which nevertheless have led to grossly inequitable results for vulnerable populations. Scholars such as Paul Davidoff and Norman Krumholz have called for advocacy and equity planning, approaches which focus on process but also on equity of results in the field, particularly for the disadvantaged (Davidoff, 1965; Krumholz and Forester, 1990). Their work helps keep us on track, although it is important to note that they have not focused on the social structures that underlie uneven distribution, a situation described by Fainstein in her criticism of "post-structural"[3] thinkers, who have "identified the way in which space embodies power without necessarily locating its source in particular groups of people" (Fainstein, 1997: 26). It is one thing to identify with the disadvantaged, as did Davidoff, but it is another to recognize and analyze which people and organizations are in power, creating the situation that leads to others' disadvantage. The work of political economists such as Harvey remind us that economic considerations, particularly structural manifestations of economic power, influence the outcomes we see in cities (Harvey, 1973, 1992; Watson, 2006).

Watson has explicitly examined the usefulness of normative theories such as the just city for oppressed residents of urban South Africa, warning that solutions supposedly designed for social justice (such as the destruction of substandard housing) may indeed work to the detriment of people seeking autonomy (as in intentional informal settlements; Watson, 2002). She has also argued that current forms of justice as defined and promoted by authors such as Rawls and Habermas assume conditions of liberalism and universality which do not fit non-Western contexts, particularly situations characterized by "deep differences" (Watson, 2006). Building on Bollens's work concerning fractured urban societies (Bollens, 2004), she has seen the situation of "deep difference" – which appears to be growing in part because of the uneven development that accompanies globalization, leading to enhanced fragmentation by race, income, class, and other categories – as particularly problematic because of vastly different value systems that accompany growing social disjuncture around the world. Although she argues that no universal definition of justice exists, she too urges planners to undertake efforts that create just outcomes, and she references several of Harvey's suggestions, such as creation of social organizations and economic systems that minimize the exploitation of labor, and action that recognizes the ecological impact of social projects (Watson, 2006).

Leonie Sandercock has suggested that diversity is part of the goal in urban contexts (Sandercock, 2003). She defines a just city as one in which everyone is treated with respect, no matter their race, ethnicity, nationality, gender, class, or sexual orientation. During some such discussions of diversity, however, race may be submerged under the larger umbrella of multiculturalism.[4] This in itself is a problem because some dilemmas (ethnic oppression in some parts of the world, racial oppression in North America, poverty) are much more deeply ingrained within key social and economic institutions than other forms of inequity (Catlin, 1993; Thomas and Darnton, 2006; Thomas and Ritzdorf, 1997; Yiftachel, 2006). Therefore, a simple call for respect for all kinds of difference may not be enough to address the concerns of those suffering the longest and deepest inequities. This situation, too, reminds us of Fainstein's warning that post-structuralist thought, although rightly concerned about social injustice, may place too much emphasis on diversity as opposed to political action and economic equality (Fainstein, 1997).

The goal of the "just city" appears to be important even if a commonly accepted definition of what this means may not exist. Even without transparency of definition, at least one professional organization in what Yiftachel calls the North-West, the AICP in the US, has adopted a Code of Ethics (2005a) which refers to "social justice" as a legitimate goal for planners. One of several main principles of that code states: "We shall seek social justice by working to expand choice and opportunity for all persons, recognizing a special responsibility to plan for the needs of the disadvantaged and to promote racial and economic integration." If we assume that the just city, characterized by some form of "equity" of outcomes, is indeed an important goal or "end" for urban planning, how are we to reach it?

The Means

The above discussion suggests that the definition of means to reach the "just city" will vary by national or regional (continental or sub-continental) context. For the US, the AICP Code assumes that the means is clear: planners must simply plan for the disadvantaged and promote integration, as well as "urge the alteration of policies, institutions, and decisions that oppose such needs" (AICP, 2005a). This is essentially the approach of "equity planning", as well (Krumholz and Forester, 1990), with an important difference in assumptions. The US professional code does not mention political context, has conceptual roots in the faith in expertise characteristic of the rational process, and implies that the practice of planning can help lead to "social justice" if this is so mandated by the professional organization. The code gives no guidance about what to do when principles of loyalty (to employers and other powers-that-be) and social reform (for the disadvantaged) *compete*, a not-uncommon situation for planners. This code also does not address the simple question of how to insure that a planner has the motivation or ability to pursue social justice when local contexts argue against this. Krumholz (and his co-authors) clearly knew that the political context was complicated, and these writings attempted to educate planners about the essential nature of social justice and its promotion, but again the issue of motivation was barely addressed (Krumholz and Clavel, 1994; Krumholz and Forester, 1990).

Davidoff's conception of advocacy planning suggested that planners recognize the presence of multiple publics, and provide professional services for disadvantaged populations, but these concepts of advocacy (Davidoff, 1965) arose at a time in the US history when federal programs such as Model Cities provided disadvantaged central-city residents with the resources and autonomy necessary to hire planning services, a situation that seldom exists in modern times (save for developmentally advanced organizations such as certain community development corporations). Theorists of neither equity planning nor advocacy planning addressed the possible danger of planners focusing on social equity as philanthropic act rather than collaborative endeavor among equals.

Communicative (Innes, 1995, 1996) and collaborative (Healey, 2003) planning have emerged as popular vehicles for addressing the concerns of multiple parties in situations characterized by competing values and interests. These paradigms clearly have drawbacks in situations of uneven power, however, a situation that has been explored in the planning theory literature (Flyvbjerg, 2002; Watson, 2002; Yiftachel, 2006). To put the commentary simply, some people are more powerful than others, and the less powerful are usually disadvantaged in any dialogue or collaboration that might take place. Although these authors rely upon a Foucaultian framework and so they surely understand that power is always manifest (Gutting, 2005), the question is whether the innately uneven distribution of power can be suspended at least while deliberations are under way.

Flyvbjerg (2002) has offered possible strategies for overcoming such manifestations of power, such as exploring the abuse of power, and then publicizing and moving to counteract injustice, an approach which he has modeled in Denmark concerning transportation plans for the central business district of the city of Aalborg. Denmark, however, is more homogeneous than several other countries in the North and West, and exhibits relatively few internal differences of the kind Watson describes as "deep differences". Flyvbjerg's ability to publicize his research in the local Danish media, revealing the negative effects of an established pattern of power, in effect illustrates Watson's point that not all contexts offer equivalent opportunities for reform.

For societies characterized by long-standing inequities, reflected in an urban landscape fractured by major differences in social and economic opportunity, with patterns of racial or other segregation that affect all aspects of daily life, the following questions are very important: what might motivate a planner to seek to work for the goal of the just city? How can we find or train planners willing to overcome the strictures of bureaucratic complacency and seek to work at least in part to enhance either the outcome or process of the just city? For it does little good to promote the goal of social justice if means for insuring or encouraging practice which leads to social justice are not at hand.

Here is where, among a collection of strategies, we might place recruitment and retention of members of the minority-race population into the ranks of the planning profession. The desired behavior – which for the sake of shorthand discussion we might term *advocacy*, by which we mean the promotion of the just city as defined by Fainstein in citations above – can be exhibited by any one, of any race, gender, ethnicity, nationality, or any other criterion, and we should expect support for principles of social justice from all planners of good conscience. Inevitably, however, some will be more motivated in this direction than others.

Hypothetically, we might expect that a profession which contained representatives of populations disadvantaged *for that societal context* might very well find its responsiveness towards social justice *in that society* to be enhanced. In modern South Africa, for example, it would seem to be very difficult for the urban planning profession to attend to the needs of social justice in the spatial reorganization of urban society if the former ethnic and racial victims of apartheid did not also become lead politicians or members of the planning profession, or at least become involved in the planning process, and develop the knowledge, will, and motivation needed to help steer decision-making toward the goal of social justice. This is not to suggest that professional inclusion is a sufficient condition – in modern South Africa, for example, economic conditions of inequality and underdevelopment are so entrenched that largely black governmental leadership and increasingly inclusionary planning have generated progress but have not yet been able to bring about equitable cities (Lund and Skinner, 2004; Ozler, 2007; Parnell, 2004) – but rather that it is a necessary one. In apartheid South Africa and in Israel, and in other places characterized by "deep difference" backed by rule of law (Yiftachel and Ghanem, 2004), it is not clear that the racial and ethnic characteristics of planners would matter at all.

In at least the North American context, however, particularly in metropolitan areas severely fractured by race and poverty lines or their intersections – as is the case in US metropolitan areas, which have many such intersections (Wilson, 2003) – it would seem to make sense to recruit to the profession members of the society's most marginalized racial minorities. Many large metropolitan areas still reflect high levels of racial segregation, with central cities typically containing much larger percentages of minority races than surrounding suburbs, and the level of racial segregation is particularly high in Midwestern and Northeastern metropolitan areas such as Detroit, Chicago, and New York City (Farley et al., 2000). Although subtle barriers such as municipal fragmentation and socio-economic stratification supported by tools such as zoning and inadequate public transportation often reinforce informal barriers, particularly for the poor, gains in civil rights legislation and popular perception have loosened racial constraints supported by law, and blatant racial discrimination in such matters as formal access to housing is not legally defensible. Differences are deep, therefore, but not so deep or so entrenched legally as to be insurmountable.

The Minority-Race Planner

It is of course not so much the race or ethnicity of planners as their orientation and skill sets that are important. Forester (2000) has noted that planners will increasingly need to work with social inequalities, and they will need to be aware of the role of race, gender, and ethnicity. He suggests that planning does not need complacent bureaucrats, but rather people who "speak articulately to the realities of poverty and suffering, deal with race, displacement, and histories of underserved communities in ways that do not leave people's pain at the door" (Forester, 2000: 259). Given this situation, planners of many different racial or ethnic backgrounds could meet these criteria concerning the ability to "deal with race" and to address problems of poverty, displacement, and insufficient service without leaving "people's pain at the door" – a possible reference to advocacy – and all minority-race planners would not necessarily have the ability to do so. However, it would seem conceptually reasonable to assume that some minority-race planners could prove to have particularly useful skills related to these specific tasks, perhaps because of bonds of culture, history, community, or sentiment. If so, agency effectiveness could be diminished if racial minorities were severely underrepresented in the planning profession.

In a remarkable book chapter on urbanization and injustice, Marshall Berman (1997) once wrote about the political value of African American rap, an art form that was perhaps purest in its earliest state, before violent tendencies took over certain "gangsta rap" practitioners. As he described the early characteristics of this phenomenon, rap was once a way for disenfranchised, disadvantaged ghetto youth to address the circumstances of their confinement in ways eloquent and focused. He noted that the humble but sophisticated lyrics written by the first wave of rappers said a lot of what we need to know about power and protest in the contemporary US, and this form soon became popular for a wide range of people around the world who wanted to speak from the street. If black youth raised in the ghetto have special skills or insights which enable them to represent the truth of disadvantage in creative ways, might not planners living as racial minorities in a severely fragmented metropolis have comparable effects in the milieu of urban planning and decision-making?

And yet underrepresentation by both race and gender has been a problem in the past. In Canada and the US, diversity by gender has grown over the last few years, although not as rapidly as might be expected given the increasing presence of women in planning student populations (Rahder and Altilia, 2004). The presence of racial minorities, however, is low relative to total population figures. In the US, the body of professional planners, APA, probably includes fewer than 10 percent racial minorities, compared with over 30 percent of the general population. In 2004, APA estimated that 2.7 percent of its members were black or African American, 2.9 percent Asian, and 2.2 percent Hispanic (APA, 2005a). This situation has led the professional planning organization in the US to initiate a series of strategies designed to increase recruitment and retention of racial minorities in the planning profession (APA, 2005a).

Does the presence of racial minorities in the urban planning profession better lead to the "end" of the just city? To this simple question it would be hard to reply "yes". The conceptual difficulties of claiming this would be several, but the main problem is the required indication that planners who are racial minorities somehow help produce better outcomes leading to a just city than planners who are not. Berman (1997), Merrifield (1997) and Soja (1997) among others have warned against the tendency to claim exclusion of reform sensibility or binary thinking characteristic of modernism, that is to claim that "just us" (of a certain race or of certain disadvantages) can bring about positive social change, a position which can cause serious problems of isolation and exclusion. To be sure, a few planning narratives have suggested that the race of the planner can have a positive effect on planning results. Two primary US examples are Catlin (1993), who argued that his African American heritage was of decided advantage in the quest for just solutions to the planning problems of Gary, Indiana, and Thomas (1997), who offered narrative accounts of black planners who saw themselves as the best representatives of the black community during the battles in Detroit over urban renewal during the 1950s and 1960s, and who logged limited successes in changing the outcomes of specific urban renewal projects to the benefit of predominantly African American communities. Other supportive commentary for such a concept is difficult to find, however.

Another problem with answering such a question in the affirmative is that it implies that a planner's efforts can change conditions of injustice in the urban context, *and* that the race or ethnicity of the planner affects this effort. Although efforts to correct injustice do exist, some would argue that the political economy is in effect rigged to subvert true reform, and some evidence supports this claim (Fainstein, 1997; Logan and Molotch, 2007; Soja, 1997).[5] This would logically be true regardless of the genetic background of the planner, and indeed one might argue that planners who are racial minorities in situations of uneven opportunity may have much less personal power to move the system than planners who are not.

While much of the above commentary concerning the just city and minority-race planners stems from conceptualization, it is possible to envision empirical research designed to explore these thoughts. In some allied disciplines, researchers have found that the race of the professional does appear to lead to more just outcomes for minority-race communities; this is not exactly the same as a just city, but it comes closer than several alternatives. The most prominent of such examples of research would be in public administration. In one branch of public administration scholars have pursued a concept known as "representative bureaucracy", referring to the relative presence of various classes, educational levels, etc. in government service (Brudney et al., 2000; Lim, 2006; Meier, 1975; Murray et al., 1994; Sowa and Selden, 2003). One subset of research studies looks at racial diversity within government as being of particular benefit for racial-minority communities, for several tangible reasons. Often based on a number of large-scale survey questionnaires, this research suggests that minority communities may gain greater access and better service results when served by a public sector which includes representatives of their racial group (Brudney et al., 2000; Sowa and Selden, 2003).

One potential step between conceptualization and extensive empirical work comparable to that in public administration would be to carry out qualitative research designed to explore the processes at work from the perspective of a few individuals belonging to some subset, such as, here, minority-race planners. Creswell (1994) describes this approach particularly well. As he noted, such a qualitative approach could start with theory – as, in this case, the possibility that minority-race planners make unique contributions but face unique challenges – but not *test* the theory so much as explore possibilities for further inquiry. The examples he cites often reflect interviews with or intense study of a very few individuals or cases (Creswell, 1994). In such studies, the aim is not to generalize to any population or to proclaim "findings" but rather to further clarify the issues at play (beyond, in this case, the author's own thoughts).

The author identified a few African American planners to interview in the fall of 2006, based on questions informed by the representative bureaucracy literature and the need to explore this concept of the "just city". The attempt was not to represent all black American planners, but rather to anchor theory in reality by seeing how a few such planners reacted to in-depth questions concerning the interconnections of race and the planning profession, an area not well explored, and to identify issues needing further research (APA, 2005a; Hoch, 1994). These six were "representative" of only their subset: graduates from one urban planning program in Michigan, representing perhaps a fourth of the group who had graduated from that program between 1990 and 2001 and who could be traced, and about one-half of this university's black graduates in that cohort who were working for in-state public agencies.[6] We chose these planners not because of any outstanding professional accomplishments or expressions of content or discontent, but rather because of their accessibility to the author, their work experience in a US state where at least moderate if not "deep" difference – racial segregation and greatly unequal life circumstances – are known to exist (Darden et al., 2007; Farley et al., 2000; Orfield and Luce, 2003), their employment by public sector agencies, and the fact that they had been in the field (since at least 2001) long enough to be at least tentatively "established". The six were located throughout the state, but all had at least some experience working as a planner in metropolitan Detroit, an area characterized by extensive historical and contemporary racial segregation, inequality, and antagonism (Farley et al., 2000; Sugrue, 1996; Thomas, 1997).

When asked directly if their work benefited the needs of African American or other minority communities, these Michigan planners were able to offer very few specific examples of such benefit. One transportation planner mentioned his ability to facilitate a project involving an Indian tribe more quickly than had been the case before, and he directly credited this to his personal experience with disadvantage as a minority, but his explanation focused more on process than on product. "Being black in this country, you are able to understand how to sympathize with people when they are put out. When they are being worked against for the wrong reasons ... I could be seen as more sensitive to their needs." Another planner referred to her work with HOPE VI, again citing her ability to advocate for the needs of the local residents and help complete the project. Such examples, however, do sound more process-oriented than product-oriented, since they apparently focus on communication and access rather than on altered results.

For the second category of concern, process or means, we have suggested that the presence of minority-race urban planners may offer distinct advantages for certain kinds of work. The workplace diversity literature notes tangible benefits of a diverse work staff for the internal workings of organizations and for their work in society at large. Although much is yet to be learned and documented about this process, specific benefits internal to the workplace seem to include improvement in functionality and creativity. For example, the presence of a diverse workforce may bring ideas and strategies to the organization that would not otherwise be present. Wise and Tschirhart (2000) review this burgeoning "diversity in the workplace" literature and summarize these arguments. Other, related sources suggest that diverse workers create more effectiveness in the field for some professions. Social work scholars have explicitly determined that effective practitioners need to understand oppression and value diversity, in part by developing "cultural competency", and they have developed models of classroom training which help future practitioners develop necessary skills and sensibilities (Marsh, 2004; Min, 2005; Schmitz et al., 2001). Such efforts could conceivably benefit from the presence in social work of professionals who already have, because of their personal background, facility with the culture experiencing oppression.

When we asked these black Michigan planners how their work benefited minority communities, their process-oriented answers suggested that they saw themselves as playing an important role in improving processes. These planners became extremely animated and detailed when describing their contributions to the process of inclusion for minority-race or low-income communities. One of the questions that seemed to elicit the most response was: "What are the particular advantages or disadvantages associated with being a black planner in your workplace, or in the areas you serve?"

The commentary that erupted is too detailed to explain fully here, but two main categories of response related to these planners' ability: 1) to defend the interests of the minority or disadvantaged community within the agency, and 2) to serve as a bridge, that is to link communication between urban communities and planning agencies. Concerning the defense of community function, several of these planners were very assertive in their stated belief that they were able "watch out for" the interests of low-income minority communities. A typical account would relate to a specific project, such as a transportation project involving a community with a high proportion of minorities, where the planner found himself or herself explaining to his or her colleagues that public meetings would have to be held at times convenient to the working-class residents, and the planner attributed this greater sensitivity to the planner's minority race. One planning agency staffer discussed the reactions of her majority-race colleagues to the presence of representatives of the minority-race central city on a multi-jurisdictional board, and suggested that the central-city residents were treated by majority-race planners as "retards, but they are city officials, experts, planners, engineers and they have a background in doing quality work for decades now". This planner claimed that without her presence this casual dismissal of the minority-race representatives' opinion would go unchallenged.

Concerning the "bridge" function, the second major category, several of these planners indicated that they communicated with underrepresented populations better than their colleagues. One said "you figure that you can work better with your kind". Another noted: "I feel like when I do go to Detroit or smaller communities that feel like they don't have a voice, it is easier for me to build a relationship with those communities. And it doesn't necessarily have to be a black community, it could be the Latino community, it could be a poorer community." She felt that her "sincerity" was stronger than that of most planners. "I can't say it is for all blacks in the planning profession, 'cause there might be some sincere other folks as well." Speaking of her colleagues in one former job, located in a predominantly black city, and apparently linking race and motivation, she commented: "they were all black planners and [therefore] they all felt compelled to really do something for the greater good."

One noted that his white colleagues saw him as a bridge:

> In the field, sometimes as an African American you are always expected to be able to deal with urban environment issues and you are kind of a guide. You may get tagged to do certain things because some of your white counterparts might not feel comfortable working in these areas.

This planner saw a distinct disadvantage to being one of a few blacks in the workplace; colleagues relied upon him to serve as a bridge, oblivious to his other work commitments. Other black planners offered specific examples of community residents, rather than themselves or their colleagues, offering the opinion that black planners served as a bridge. One planner noted that, when her white colleagues went to a particular public meeting with a large number of low-income racial minorities, the planners came back to the office and reported that no one seemed to have anything to say about the issue the planners were trying to discuss. When the black planner went to meet with the same population, however, she heard a flood of opinions, which apparently had been saved until she – perceived either as a part of the community or as a more sensitive ear – arrived.

These few accounts suggest that it is important to explore whether indeed a special role exists for minority-race planners to assist with the process of inclusion, by facilitating enhanced participation by disadvantaged minorities, helping to fulfill one half of Fainstein's definition of what a theory of a just city "values" (2000: 468). But the interviewed planners, and the literature, suggest that a steep price may be paid for these apparent benefits.

Researchers in other professional fields have noted the possible problems. In the medical field, a recently published study of African American internal medicine physicians in six states outlined the substantial experience of race-related challenges for interviewed physicians. Among the implications of race was the emergence of what the researchers called "racial fatigue", born of persistent experiences of racial discrimination and distrust, and leading to several negative consequences for their personal and professional lives (Nunez-Smith et al., 2007).

Public administration researchers have found that those racial minorities working in the public sector (and offering better service to racial minority communities) may pay a price. One of the first public administration scholars to describe that price was Adam Herbert (1974), whose work laid the groundwork for more recent research (Murray et al., 1994). According to what is known as the "Herbert thesis", minority public administrators can find themselves facing at least six key dilemmas. The first 1) is that their workplace may expect them to comply with official policies, but those policies could be in conflict with the goals of the minority community. Two other concerns were: 2) they are likely to be assigned to marginal job categories which deal with minority issues but true resolution of those issues could be very difficult to achieve; and 3) they may experience pressure from their colleagues to support the organization and its goals rather than to support the minority community's interests. Finally, three other concerns were: 4) the minority community expects them to be accountable to that community, in spite of their work situation demanding accountability to the organization; 5) they may indeed feel a strong personal commitment to carry out policies that promote the interests of that community; but 6) they may also feel pressure to ignore the interests of the community in order to advance in their personal careers (Murray et al., 1994). Such professionals must decide how to respond when competing goals confront them in their work, and their work may indeed suffer because of the effort involved.

In terms of the Herbert thesis, our interview questions asked about only three dimensions of the six listed above – concerning system demands (the first problem listed above), community accountability (the fourth listed), and personal commitment (the fifth) – but respondents offered comments, on their own, about other dimensions as well, particularly concerning colleague pressure.

It appeared that the pressures described by the Herbert thesis did apply to these black planners in Michigan. To a series of questions about system demands, accountability, and personal commitment, several respondents noted that they were indeed feeling pressure and conflicting demands at their work-places, serious enough to cause at least two of the six to consider leaving the field.

System demands largely related to the expectation that the planner conform to the policies of the agency, even if he or she perceived those policies to be harmful, or not helpful, to the black community. For example, one planner noted that his organization was supposed to look at impacts on the community of its actions, and that it gave lip service to this goal, but that the agency appeared to have a blind side when it came to certain decisions related to a project that could pose great difficulties for a nearby minority or low-income community. Another planner recalled the reaction when she specifically asked to study an issue that related to the health of a project's nearby low-income community, populated in large part by Hispanics; she was told that such concerns were "a lot of crap". Asked to rate their organizations' "dedication to seeking minority community input and participation", on a 10-point scale, the six gave responses ranging from 1 to 10, with an average of 5.5. Efforts to change the culture of the organizations seemed futile, however: one person noted, "it's difficult to move an organization of this size".

Concerning community accountability, these planners saw themselves as accountable to the "minority community", which in the case of one respondent actually made up the majority of her community or area of jurisdiction. They rated their role as "actively advocating on behalf of and providing leadership to increase minority or disadvantaged community participation and input" from 8 to 10, with an average for the six of 9.1. However their perception was that either they had to persuade their majority-race colleagues and supervisors to include the minority community in meaningful ways, or the reaction of their fellow planners blocked their efforts to engage, or at least respect, representatives of that community who attempted to participate in decision-making. One example is the previously referenced situation of a planner's constant need to remind his colleagues that daytime "participation" meetings were of no use to working-class people.

As far as "personal commitment" was concerned, these planners saw themselves as highly motivated and committed to advocating within their agency for the needs of minority or economically disadvantaged groups, and several gave personal accounts of such commitments. When asked whether they would suggest the profession as an option for students choosing a career, these planners' responses indicated a high level of personal commitment and dedication to their profession, at least before they encountered such difficulties. Concerning recruitment, five of the six indicated that they would recommend planning as a career for young students, and the sixth said he would not but only because "there are better ways to effect change". One made comments arguing for representatives of several races and age groups, such as: "We need more color represented and I would say that for every race … and we have a poor planning system because it is underrepresented by the population that we have." He went on to argue: "You need a champion for you to say, I'm a black person, I understand your problems and that goes a long way …". Another commented that:

> I think having blacks in planning that are committed to civic pride and service and who can really stand firm whatever their belief would definitely help the future of communities … it's really important to keep that diversity in there because you're not dealing with monotone populations, you know. You're dealing with diverse populations these days.

In addition to such accounts, several respondents offered personal stories of their attraction to the profession speaking to the issue of motivation: they indicated that they entered planning because they were responding directly to the conditions of poverty and disinvestment which affected their own minority-race neighborhoods.

Yet these respondents felt insecure in their efforts. One interviewee mentioned, several times in his interview, the danger of being "pigeon-holed" if he pressed too hard on behalf of minority or disadvantaged communities. Another interviewee frankly felt harassed because of his efforts to support low-income disadvantaged minority populations, and at least one of his colleagues – also interviewed for this study – agreed that she perceived the colleague as being regularly harassed because he was an outspoken black male. Several told stories of what they perceived as flagrant mistreatment by their colleagues or supervisors, such as the planner who commented that:

> there are a lot of white men in planning and they really don't trust or feel that blacks are capable of making higher-level decisions that most planners have to. I think that sometimes black planners are very honest in their assessment of what's really going on and people don't like that.

Some interviewees questioned how long they would be able to work at their agency under these conditions.

Diversifying the Profession

These planners indeed found the workplace itself challenging, and felt that system demands and other pressures unique to minority-race planners stymied their efforts to promote the cause of social justice. The theme that emerged most often was that they felt that they offered a unique perspective concerning the special needs of minority communities, as well as low-income communities of any race. They saw themselves as serving the agency in special ways, and serving particularly minority communities in special ways. They claimed that they were highly motivated to enter the profession because of the perception of severe inequalities in their own communities. But they did not feel supported, by the planning agency or by their colleagues, in their work for social equity.

At least in Michigan, and by implication perhaps in the US, and possibly beyond, the planning profession may need minority-race (or minority-ethnic, etc.) planners in order to help create local conditions of access in those processes necessary for a just city. Yet the effective presence of such racial minorities in the profession may face major barriers, not a few of which exist on the job. Little justification exists for any claim that only minority-race planners can bring about just results, the "ends" we discussed earlier. Neither can it be argued that only minority-race planners can work in minority-race contexts or create better access for minority-race communities; the necessity of fighting for social justice should rest with all planners. As a practical matter, however, in deeply conflicted contexts, communities disadvantaged in some way may very well look at the diversity of local urban planners as a symbol of access or "means" toward the goal of social justice. Minority-race planners may see themselves as having a special role to play in the process of local decision-making, and it is entirely conceivable that the perceptions of local minority-race communities may reinforce that tendency. But if minority-race planners cannot survive in the profession, their potential to assist with the process of social change is stillborn.

As we have noted, these thoughts need further exploration and research. Yet if our conceptualization of the issues is correct, one theory to be tested is that minority-race planners in fragmented metropolitan areas can help improve the planning process for minority-race people in matters such as access and connection. If this is indeed true, then at least one appropriate course of action would appear to be fairly obvious. This would be to enhance efforts in minority-race recruitment, in educational programs as well as professional settings, in the reasonable hope that such acts will give greater voice to those who have little. Another theory to be tested is that such minority-race planners face major institutional barriers to their success and effectiveness comparable to those identified by researchers in other professions (Murray et al., 1994; Nunez-Smith et al., 2007). If this is indeed true, much wider institutional and bureaucratic reform would be necessary, far beyond simply recruiting racial minorities to the profession. Corrective action would necessitate examining the social and institutional contexts of planning organizations, in order to discern and correct those barriers which minority-race planners face and which threaten retention, recruitment, and job effectiveness.

Notes

1 "Minority" as a sole descriptor, without linkage to race as in "minority-race", is problematic; it collapses together a number of categories of social groups which may have little in common with each other. Some have therefore called for social scientists to abolish use of the term (Wilkinson and Butler, 2002). In the context of the US, the focus of much of this article, minority-race people may be considered to be those of African American, American Indian, Asian, and other specific racial backgrounds as defined by the US Census Bureau (2008). "Race" (or racial background) is also a problematic concept, however. Former thinking that humanity is composed of separate and fairly exclusionary racial categories such as "black", "white", "Asian", etc. has begun to yield to scientific evidence that humanity forms a continuum not easily classified, and to the social reality that many people have ancestral backgrounds from several different "races" (Hirschman, 2004). Hirschman recommends replacing the concept of "race" with "ethnicity", but he recognizes the complexities of this suggestion, particularly for purposes such as national censuses.

2 Although we could further explore the term "equitable", we may for this article infer the concept of "fair" and clarify that this does not mean absolute equality in services or outcomes, which is not possible in a democratic society, and quite possibly not in any society.

3 Fainstein (1997) uses post-structuralism as a term inclusive of several theoretical approaches which tend to focus on cultural criticism rather than a strong political-economy analysis.

4 As is gender; see Rahder and Altilia (2004).

5 Some evidence suggests the contrary, arguing that planners can bring about positive change; see in particular, Krumholz and Clavel (1994).

6 Michigan does not have a large number of minority-race planners, with minority-race attendance at statewide planning conferences notably lacking, and the state professional

planning chapter does not have a major initiative to enhance racial diversity in planning, as does California (Dinwiddie-Moore, 2006). The six people interviewed were in positions of reasonable responsibility (none were in entry-level jobs, and two headed small planning divisions), and were known to work in locations of potential interest: state, regional, or local agencies with mixed-race staff, covering jurisdictions with at least some racial mixture. Three were women, and all graduated from the accredited planning program referenced. Four had an undergraduate degree in urban planning, and the other two had higher degrees in planning. All 60- to 90-minute interviews were taped, transcribed, and analyzed through formation of categories of responses suggesting certain patterns, as described in Creswell (1994). The author has maintained communication with the three women over some period of years, allowing for a more in-depth knowledge of their careers.

References

American Institute of Certified Planners (AICP) (2005a) Code of Ethics. Adopted 19 March 2005, available online at: [http://www.planning.org/ethics/conduct.html], accessed 2007.

American Institute of Certified Planners (AICP) (2005b) 'Introduction' to Educational Testing Service, 'The Technical Report for the Minority Pass Rate Project', March, available online as part of document at: [www.planning.org/certification/pdf/minorityreport.pdf.], accessed 2006.

American Planning Association (2005a) 'APA Diversity Task Force Report', M. Silver and R. Barber, co-chairs, American Planning Association, available online at: [http://www.planning.org/diversity/index/htm], accessed 2006.

American Planning Association (2005b) 'Diversity Summit, APA National Conference PowerPoint', available online at: [http://www.planning.org/diversity/index/htm], accessed 2006.

American Planning Association (2006a) available online at: [http://www.planning.org/diversity/index.htm], accessed 2006.

American Planning Association (2006b) 'Diversity Subcommittee Status Report', 23 April, available online at: [http://www.planning.org/diversity/index/htm], accessed 2006.

Berman, M. (1997) 'Justice/Just Us: Rap and Social Justice in America', in A. Merrifield and E. Swyngedouw (eds) *The Urbanization of Injustice*, pp. 161–79. New York: New York University Press.

Bollens, S. (1999) *Urban Peace-building in Divided Societies: Belfast and Johannesburg.* Boulder, CO: Westview Press.

Bollens, S. (2000) *On Narrow Ground: Urban Policy and Ethnic Conflict in Jerusalem and Belfast.* Albany: State University of New York Press.

Bollens, S. (2004) 'Urban Planning and Intergroup Conflict: Confronting a Fractured Public Interest', in B. Stiftel and V. Watson (eds) *Dialogues in Urban and Regional Planning*, pp. 209–46. London and New York: Routledge.

Brudney, J.L., Hebert, F. and Wright, D. (2000) 'From Organizational Values to Organizational Roles: Examining Representative Bureaucracy in State Administration', *Journal of Public Administration Research and Theory* 10(3): 491–512.

Catlin, R. (1993) *Racial Politics and Urban Planning: Gary Indiana 1980–1989.* Lexington: University Press of Kentucky.

Creswell, J. (1994) *Research Design: Qualitative & Quantitative Approaches*. Thousand Oaks, CA: SAGE.

Darden, J., Thomas, R. and Stokes, C. (eds) (2007) *The State of Black Michigan*. East Lansing: Michigan State University Press.

Davidoff, P. (1965) 'Advocacy and Pluralism in Planning', *Journal of the American Institute of Planners* 31: 331–7.

Dinwiddie-Moore, J. (2006) 'California's Efforts to Encourage Diversity', PowerPoint available online at: [www.planning.org/diversity/resources.htm], accessed 2007.

Fainstein, S. (1997) 'Justice, Politics and the Creation of Urban Space', in A. Merrifield and E. Swynegedouw (eds) *The Urbanization of Injustice*, pp. 18–44. New York: New York University Press.

Fainstein, S. (2000) 'New Directions in Planning Theory', *Urban Affairs Review* 35(4): 451–78.

Fainstein, S. (2005) 'Planning Theory and the City', *Journal of Planning Education and Research* 25(2): 121–30.

Farley, R., Danziger, S. and Holzer, H. (2000) *Detroit Divided*. New York: Russell Sage Foundation.

Fleischacker, S. (2004) *A Short History of Distributive Justice*. Cambridge, MA: Harvard University Press.

Flyvbjerg, B. (2002) 'Bringing Power to Planning Research: One Researcher's Praxis Story', *Journal of Planning Education and Research* 21 (4): 353–66.

Forester, J. (2000) 'Why Planning Theory? Educating Citizens, Recognizing Differences, Mediating Deliberations', in L. Rodwin and B. Sanyal (eds) *The Profession of City Planning: Changes, Images and Challenges: 1950–2000*, pp. 253–60. Rutgers, NJ: Center for Urban Policy Research.

Gutting, G. (2005) *Foucault: A Very Short Introduction*. Oxford: Oxford University Press.

Harvey, D. (1973) *Social Justice and the City*. London: Edward Arnold.

Harvey, D. (1992) 'Social Justice, Postmodernism and the City', *International Journal of Urban and Regional Research* 16(4): 588–601.

Harvey, D. (2003) 'The Right to the City', *International Journal of Urban and Regional Research* 27(4): 939–41.

Healey, P. (2003) 'Collaborative Planning in Perspective', *Planning Theory* 2(2): 101–23.

Herbert, A.W. (1974) 'The Minority Administrator: Problems, Prospects, and Challenges', *Public Administration Review* 34(6): 556–63.

Hirschman, C. (2004) 'The Origins and Demise of the Concept of Race', *Population and Development Review* 30(3): 385–415.

Hoch, C. (1994) *What Planners Do: Power, Politics and Persuasion*. Chicago, IL: Planner's Press.

Innes, J. (1995) 'Planning Theory's Emerging Paradigm: Communicative Action and Interactive Practice', *Journal of Planning Education and Research* 14(4): 183–9.

Innes, J. (1996) 'Planning through Consensus Building: A New View of the Comprehensive Planning Ideal', *Journal of the American Planning Association* 62(4): 460–72.

Katznelson, J. (1997) 'Social Justice, Liberalism, and the City: Considerations on David Harvey, John Rawls, Karl Polanyi', in A. Merrifield and E. Swyngedouw (eds) *The Urbanization of Injustice*, pp. 45–64. New York: New York University Press.

Krumholz, N. and Clavel, P. (1994) *Reinventing Cities: Equity Planners Tell Their Stories*. Philadelphia, PA: Temple University Press.

Krumholz, N. and Forester, J. (1990) *Making Equity Planning Work: Leadership in the Public Sector*. Philadelphia, PA: Temple University Press.

Lim, H. (2006) 'Representative Bureaucracy: Rethinking Substantive Effects and Active Representation', *Public Administration Review* 66(2): 193–204.

Logan, J. and Molotch, H. (2007) *Urban Fortunes: The Political Economy of Place*, 20th anniversary edn. Berkeley: University of California Press.

Lund, F. and Skinner, C. (2004) 'Integrating the Informal Economy in Urban Planning and Governance: A Case Study of the Process of Policy Development in Durban, South Africa', *International Development Planning Review* 26(4): 431–56.

Markusen, A. (2000) 'Planning as Craft and as Philosophy', in L. Rodwin and B. Sanyal (eds) *The Profession of City Planning*, pp. 261–74. Rutgers, NJ: Center for Urban Policy Research.

Marsh, J. (2004) 'Social Work in a Multicultural Society', *Social Work* 49(1): 5–6.

Meier, K. (1975) 'Representative Bureaucracy: An Empirical Analysis', *American Political Science Review* 69(2): 526–42.

Merrifield, A. (1997) 'Social Justice and Communities of Difference: A Snapshot from Liverpool', in A. Merrifield and E. Swyngedouw (eds) *The Urbanization of Injustice*, pp. 200–22. New York: New York University Press.

Merrifield, A. and Swyngedouw, E. (1997) 'Social Justice and the Urban Experience: An Introduction', in A. Merrifield and E. Swyngedouw (eds) *The Urbanization of Injustice*, pp. 1–15. New York: New York University Press.

Min, J. (2005) 'Cultural Competency: A Key to Effective Future Social Work with Racially and Ethnically Diverse Elders', *Families in Society* 86(3): 347–58.

Moses, Y. (2004) 'The Continuing Power of the Concept of "Race"', *Anthropology & Education Quarterly* 35(1): 146–8.

Murray, S., Terry, L., Washington, C. and Keller, L. (1994) 'The Role Demands and Dilemmas of Minority Public Administrators: The Herbert Thesis Revisited', *Public Administration Review* 54(5): 409–17.

Nunez-Smith, M., Curry, C., Bigby, B., Berg, D., Krumholz, H. and Bradley, E. (2007) 'Impact of Race on the Professional Lives of Physicians of African Descent', *Annals of Internal Medicine* 146(1): 45–52.

Orfield, M. and Luce, T. (2003) 'Michigan Metropatterns: A Regional Agenda for Community and Prosperity in Michigan', Michigan Area Research Corporation report, available online at: [http://www.metroresearch.org/maps/region_maps/michigan_1c.pdf], accessed 2007.

Ozler, B. (2007) 'Not Separate, Not Equal: Poverty and Inequality in Post-Apartheid South Africa', *Economic Development and Cultural Change* 55(3): 487–529.

Parnell, S. (2004) 'Building Developmental Local Government to Fight Poverty: Institutional Change in the City of Johannesburg', *International Development Planning Review* 26(4): 377–99.

Rahder, B. and Altilia, C. (2004) 'Where Is Feminism and Planning Going? Appropriation or Transformation?', *Planning Theory* 3(2): 106–16.

Sandercock, L. (2003) *Cosmopolis II: Mongrel Cities*. London: Continuum.

Schmitz, C., Stakeman, C. and Sisneros, J. (2001) 'Educating Professionals for Practice in a Multicultural Society: Understanding Oppression and Valuing Diversity', *Families in Society* 82(6): 612–22.

Soja, E. (1997) 'Margin/alia: Social Justice and the New Cultural Politics', in A. Merrifield and E. Swyngedouw (eds) *The Urbanization of Injustice*, pp. 180–99. New York: New York University Press.

Sowa, J. and Selden, S. (2003) 'Administrative Discretion and Active Representation: An Expansion of the Theory of Representative Bureaucracy', *Public Administration Review* 63(6): 700–10.

Stein, S. and Harper, T. (2005) 'Rawls's "Justice as Fairness": A Moral Basis for Contemporary Planning Theory', *Planning Theory* 4(2): 147–72.

Sugrue, T. (1996) *The Origins of the Urban Crisis: Race and Inequality in Postwar Detroit.* Princeton, NJ: Princeton University Press.

Thomas, J. (1997) *Redevelopment and Race: Planning a Finer City in Postwar Detroit.* Baltimore, MD: Johns Hopkins University Press.

Thomas, J. and Darnton, J. (2006) 'Social Diversity and Economic Development in the Metropolis', *Journal of Planning Literature* 21(2): 1–16.

Thomas, J. and Ritzdorf, M. (eds) (1997) *Urban Planning and the African American Community: In the Shadows.* Thousand Oaks, CA: SAGE.

United States Census Bureau (2008) Definitions of race in glossary online at: [http://factfinder.census.gov/home/en/epss/glossary_r.html], accessed 2008.

Watson, V. (2002) 'The Usefulness of Normative Planning Theories in the Context of Sub-Saharan Africa', *Planning Theory* 1(1): 27–52.

Watson, V. (2006) 'Deep Difference: Diversity, Planning and Ethics', *Planning Theory* 5(1): 31–50.

Wilkinson, D. and Butler, J. (2002) 'The Clinical Irrelevance and Scientific Invalidity of the "Minority" Notion: Deleting It from the Social Science Vocabulary', *Journal of Sociology and Social Welfare* 29(2): 21–34.

Wilson, W.J. (2003) 'Race, Class and Urban Poverty: A Rejoinder', *Ethnic and Racial Studies* 26(6): 1096–114.

Wise, L.R. and Tschirhart, M. (2000) 'Examining Empirical Evidence on Diversity Effects: How Useful Is Diversity Research for Public-sector Managers?', *Public Administration Review* 60(5): 386–94.

Yiftachel, O. (2000) 'Social Control, Urban Planning and Ethno-class Relations: Mizrahi Jews in Israel's "Development Towns"', *International Journal of Urban and Regional Research* 24(2): 418–38.

Yiftachel, O. (2006) 'Re-engaging Planning Theory? Towards "South-Eastern" Perspectives', *Planning Theory* 5(3): 211–22.

Yiftachel, O. and Ghanem, A. (2004) 'Understanding "Ethnocratic" Regimes: The Politics of Seizing Contested Territories', *Political Geography* 23: 647–76.

Young, I. (1990) *Justice and the Politics of Difference.* Princeton, NJ: Princeton University Press.

18

Nurturing
Home, Mom, and Apple Pie

Dolores Hayden

Home fires are brightest,
Home ties are strongest,
Home lives are happiest,
Home loves are dearest.

American sampler

M is for the many things she gave us,
O is because she's the only one…

Alberta Hunter

Home is where the heart is. Home, sweet home. Whoever speaks of housing must also speak of home. The word embraces both physical space and the nurturing that takes place within it. Few of us can separate the ideal of home from thoughts of mom and apple pie, mother love and home cooking. Rethinking home life involves rethinking the spatial, technological, cultural, social, and economic dimensions of sheltering, nurturing, and feeding people. These activities, often discussed by men as if they had existed unchanged from the beginning of time, unsmirched by capitalist development, technological manipulation, or social pressures, require expert analysis. Sociologist Arlie Hochschild's *The Second Shift* and economist Nancy Folbre's *The Invisible Heart* break new ground in analyzing the complexities of domestic work.[1] Yet among feminist activists, mother love and home cooking have long been celebrated targets. It is understood that "Home, sweet home has never meant housework, sweet housework," as Charlotte Perkins Gilman put it in the 1890s. It has also been clear that mothering is political. Lily Braun, the German socialist feminist, wrote: "After the birth of my son, the problems of women's liberation were no longer mere theories. They cut into my own flesh."[2] That was 1901. The United States has

Readings in Planning Theory, Third Edition. Edited by Susan S. Fainstein and Scott Campbell.
Editorial material and organization © 2012 Blackwell Publishing Ltd.
Published 2012 by Blackwell Publishing Ltd.

been slower than the rest of the world to reach a more egalitarian political position on domestic life. Most industrialized nations have developed complex legislation to support women workers with paid maternity leave and quality child care. The U.S. has not.

Nurturing men and children has traditionally been women's work. A brief accounting reveals the many separate tasks involved. Home cooking requires meals prepared to suit the personal likes and dislikes of family members. It is also one of the most satisfying and creative aesthetic activities for many women and men. Housecleaning requires sweeping, vacuuming, washing, polishing, and tidying the living space. Laundry requires sorting, washing, drying, folding or ironing, and putting away clean clothes and linens. Health care begins at home, where home remedies and prescribed medicines are distributed. Mental health also begins at home, when homemakers provide emotional support so that all family members make successful connections and adjustments to the larger society. This is crucial not only for the education of [the] young, but also for adults, who must sustain the pressures of earning a living, and for the elderly, who need emotional support in their frail years.

Equally important are those ties to kin and community that maintain the social status and ethnic identity of the household. Maintenance of these ties often includes cultural rituals – the preparation of Thanksgiving dinners, Seders, Cinco de Mayo celebrations – with all the food, clothing, and special objects associated with each event. Recreation is another home task: arranging for children's play, team sports, birthday parties, and family vacations. In urban societies, recreation also means arranging family experiences of nature, such as visits to parks or camping trips.

Economist Heidi Hartmann has estimated that a good home life for a family of four requires about sixty hours of nurturing work per week.[3] That work may have been more physically arduous in the past, but never more complex. Beyond the house and the immediate neighborhood, home life includes the management of extensive relationships with stores, banks, and other commercial service facilities, and with public institutions such as schools, hospitals, clinics, and government offices. Part of homemaking involves seeing that each family member's myriad personal needs are fully met. The new dress must be the right size. The new fourth grade teacher must understand a child's history of learning difficulties. Sometimes relationships with stores or institutions turn into adversarial ones. If the new car is a lemon, if the grade school isn't teaching reading fast enough, if the hospital offers an incorrect diagnosis, if the social security benefit check is late, then the stressful nature of the homemaker's brokering work between home, market, and state is exacerbated.

Italian social theorist Laura Balbo has written brilliantly about the key roles women play in sustaining these three sectors of modern society. Not only do homemakers make the bridge between commercial services, government bureaucracies, and the family, they are also low-paid providers of service performing heroic feats of overtime in the commercial or state sectors.[4] Much women's nurturing work requires a high level of skill, understanding, judgment, and patience. Yet when this work is conducted in the private home, women's time and skills often go unrecognized.

Traditionally, marriage has been a homemaker's labor agreement – and a rather vague one at that – to provide personal service and nurturing to a man and children in exchange for financial support. Homemakers, as the one group of workers for whom no legal limits on hours, pension benefits, health insurance, or paid vacations have ever applied, have often found that the only time their work of cooking, cleaning, and nurturing compelled attention was when it was *not* done.

While "man's home is his castle," a woman often lacks any private space in her home. Society defines the ideal home as a warm, supportive place for men and children, but for homemakers it has always been a workplace, where a "woman's work is never done." While women may have gourmet kitchens, sewing rooms, and so-called master bedrooms to inhabit, even in these spaces the homemaker's role is to service, not to claim autonomy and privacy. There has been little nurturing for homemakers themselves unless they break down. In crises, women have looked to other women for emotional support. This may be the informal help acknowledged by homemaker and author Erma Bombeck, who dedicated one of her books to the other homemakers in her car pool: the women who, "when I was drowning in a car pool threw me a line … always a funny one."[5] Women's support may also come from mothers, sisters, female friends, and female kin, who traditionally rally in crises. It may come from the range of services provided by the feminist movement, such as discussion groups, crisis centers, health centers, and hostels. Or it may come from husbands and children who finally notice when their wives and mothers break down.

American urban design, social policy planning, and housing design have seldom taken the complexity of homemaking into account. To rethink private life, it is essential to be explicit about the range of needs that homes and homemakers fulfill. Home life is the source of great cultural richness and diversity in an immigrant nation. Home life is also the key to social services – education, health, mental health. And home life is the key to successful urban design, in the patterning of residential space, commercial space, and institutional space, so that the linkages between home, market, and state can be sustained without undue hardship.

Yet in the last half-century, the cultural strength of home has been debated. The success of the family in providing socialization for children has been challenged. The failure of many residential neighborhoods has been noted.[6] A conservative movement for "family values" has been mounted, without much interest in defining this term. In light of the extensive literature on such topics as divorce and family violence, it is surprising to see how few alternative models of home life are discussed in a serious, sustained way. Many critics fail to distinguish between the traditional male-headed family and other models of family life. Others welcome new models but fail to record the struggles to transform the male-headed family that feminists have waged for at least two hundred years.[7] Innovative, egalitarian housing strategies that lead to new forms of housing cannot be developed without a reformulation of the traditional family and its gender division of work. Americans interested in debating these issues can consider the history of three alternative models of home.

Three Models of Home

In the years between 1870 and 1930, home life provoked a phenomenal amount of political debate. Because this topic linked the Woman Question to the Labor Question, it attracted the attention of housewives, feminist activists, domestic serv-ants, inventors, economists, architects, urban planners, utopian novelists, visionar-ies, and efficiency experts. Housework, factory work, and home were all susceptible to restructuring in the industrial city. Women and men of all political persuasions generally agreed that burdensome household work, as it had been carried out in the pre-industrial houses of the first half of the nineteenth century, left most women little time to be good wives and mothers. Industrial development was transforming all other work and workplaces, and it was expected that domestic work and residen-tial environments would be transformed as well. Activists raised fundamental ques-tions about the relationships between women and men, households and servants. They explored the economic and social definitions of "woman's work." They also raised basic questions about household space, public space, and the relationship between economic policies and family life concretized in domestic architecture and residential neighborhoods.

Many proposed solutions drew, in one way or another, on the possibilities suggested by new aspects of urban and industrial life: new forms of specialization and division of labor, new technologies, new concentrations of dwelling units in urban apartment houses or suburban neighborhoods. But domestic theorists also had to deal with a number of unwelcome consequences of these new developments: hierarchy in the workplace, replacement of handcraft skills by mechanization, erosion of privacy in crowded urban dwellings, and development of conspicuous domestic consumption in bourgeois neighborhoods. Although life in the isolated household was burdensome, inefficient, and stifling, many reformers feared that the socialization of domestic work would deprive industrial society of its last vestige of uncapitalized, uncompetitive, skilled work. That is, they worried about mother love and home cooking.

For the most part, the major domestic strategies of the time have been ignored or misunderstood by both historians and political theorists. William O'Neill, in his popular book *Everyone Was Brave*, scathingly condemned the leaders of the American nineteenth-century woman's movement as "weak and evasive" activists, completely unable to tackle the difficult ideological problem of the family. He called them frustrated women who never understood that a revolution in domestic life was needed to achieve feminist aims.[8] Betty Friedan, in her 1981 book *The Second Stage*, reiterated O'Neill's views approvingly, as support for her mistaken belief that twentieth-century feminists were the first to introduce serious concern for domestic life into political organizing.[9] Some contemporary writers still dismiss any serious theoretical concern with housework as a waste of time; they look to wage work to liberate women, much as Bebel did in 1883 and Lenin in 1919.[10]

Almost all American women involved in politics between 1870 and 1930 saw domestic work and family life as important theoretical and practical issues. The material feminists argued that no adequate theory of political economy could develop without full consideration of domestic work.[11] They debated both businessmen and Marxists with an eloquence that has rarely been equaled. The years between 1870 and 1930 produced three major strategies for domestic reform: Catharine Beecher's capitalist haven strategy, a Marxist industrial strategy, and the material feminists' neighborhood strategy. Finding a new approach requires that all of these strategies, and the experiences of trying to implement them, are clearly understood.

The haven strategy

The leading exponent of the home as haven, Catharine Beecher, explained the technological and architectural basis of a refined suburban home beginning in the 1840s ... she proposed to increase the effectiveness of the isolated housewife and to glorify woman's traditional sphere of work. Beecher devoted her energy to better design. The housewife would be equipped with an efficient kitchen, adequate running water, and effective home heating and ventilation. She would have a better stove. In *The American Woman's Home*, Beecher suggested that the housewife devote more of her labor to becoming an emotional support for her husband and an inspiring mother for her children. Self-sacrifice would be her leading virtue. The home, a spiritual and physical shelter from the competition and exploitation of industrial capitalist society, and a training ground for the young, would become a haven in a heartless world. Beecher believed this division of labor between men and women would blunt the negative effects of industrial society on male workers. She argued that both rich and poor women, removed from competition with men in paid work, would find gender a more engrossing identification than class.

For Beecher, it was extremely important that the housewife do nurturing work with her own two hands. As she performed many different tasks each day, she was to be a sacred figure, above and beyond the cash nexus. Her personal services as wife and mother were beyond price. The biological mother was presented as the only focus for her children's needs. The virtuous wife was presented as the only one who could meet her husband's needs as well. The spatial envelope for all of this exclusive nurturing was a little cottage in a garden. Nature surrounding the home reinforced belief in a woman's natural, biologically determined role within it. Beecher also showed how domesticity could be adapted to a tenement apartment or a single teacher's residence.

The industrial strategy

The German Marxist, August Bebel, in his classic book *Women Under Socialism* (1883), wanted to move most traditional household work into the factory, abolishing women's domestic sphere entirely. Bebel argued: "The small private kitchen is, just like the workshop of the small master mechanic, a transition stage, an arrangement by which time, power and material are senselessly squandered and wasted ... in the future the domestic kitchen is rendered wholly superfluous by all the central institutions for the preparation of food."[12] He also predicted that just as factory kitchens would prepare dinners, and large state bakeries would bake pies, so mechanical laundries would wash clothes and cities would provide central heating. Children would be trained in public institutions from their earliest years. Women would take up industrial employment outside the household, and the household would lose control of many private activities. The effects of industrialization would be general, and women would share in the gains and losses with men, although their new factory work would probably be occupationally segregated labor in the laundry or the pie factory. A life of dedication to greater industrial production and the socialist state would reward personal sacrifice in the Marxist version of the industrial strategy.

In Bebel's version of home life, both nature and biology disappear in favor of industrial efficiency. Bebel believed that nurturing work should be done by women, but he tended to see women as interchangeable service workers. The demand that women nurture with a personal touch, so central to Beecher, was replaced by a sense that any day-care worker could offer a substitute for mother love and any canteen worker could serve up a substitute for home cooking. The spatial container for this interchangeable, industrial nurturing was to be the apartment house composed of industrial components and equipped with large mess halls, recreation clubs, child-care centers, and kitchenless apartments. Of course, service workers would need to be constantly on duty to keep these residential complexes running, but Bebel did not consider this service as labor of any particular value or skill. He underestimated the importance of the socialized home as workplace, even as he recognized the private home as workshop.

The neighborhood strategy

Midway between the haven strategy and the industrial strategy, there was a third strategy. The material feminists led by Melusina Fay Peirce wanted to socialize housework under women's control through neighborhood networks. In contrast to the advocates of the haven approach, who praised woman's traditional skills but denied women money, or the advocates of the industrial approach, who denied women's traditional skills but gave women wages, the material feminists argued that women should be paid for what they were already doing. As Jane Cunningham Croly put it in Stanton and Anthony's newspaper, *The Revolution*: "I demand for the wife who acts as cook, as nursery-maid, or seamstress, or all three, fair wages, or her rightful share in the net income. I demand that the bearing and rearing of children, the most exacting of employments, shall be the best paid work in the world."[13]

Material feminists agreed that women were already doing half the necessary labor in industrial society and should receive half the wages. They believed that women would have to reorganize their labor to gain these demands. The first reason for organizing was to present a united front; the second was to utilize the possibility of new technologies and the specialization and division of labor, in order to perfect their skills and to shorten their hours. Peirce argued that "it is just as necessary, and just as honorable for a wife to earn money as it is for her husband," but she criticized the traditional arrangement of domestic work as forcing the housewife to become a "jack-of-all-trades."[14]

Peirce's proposed alternative was the producers' cooperative. She envisioned former housewives and former servants doing cooking, baking, laundry, and sewing in one well-equipped neighborhood workplace. Women would send the freshly baked pies, the clean laundry, and the mended garments back to their own husbands (or their former male employers) for cash on delivery. Peirce planned to overcome the isolation and economic dependency inherent in the haven approach, and the alienation inherent in the industrial approach. While revering woman's traditional nurturing skills and neighborhood networks as the material basis of women's sphere, Peirce proposed to transform these skills and networks into a new kind of economic power for women by elevating nurturing to the scale of several dozen united households.

Peirce also overcame another great flaw in the haven approach. In the early 1870s, there were very few appliances, aside from Beecher's own inventions and architectural refinements, to help the housewife who worked alone. Almost all of the major advances, such as clothes-washing machines, dishwashers, refrigerators, and new kinds of stoves, were being developed for commercial laundries, breweries, hotels, hospitals, and apartment houses. They were designed to serve fifty to five hundred people, not one family. Peirce proposed, like Bebel, to use this technology, but to use it at the neighborhood scale, in a community workplace.

Peirce understood economic activity as both industrial production and human reproduction. She argued that her cooperative housekeeping strategies would lead to complete economic equality for women, because men could sustain farming and manufacturing while women ran the new, expanding areas of retail activity and service industries, in addition to their old standby, household production.[15] Thus she retained a gender division of labor but planned to revise national measures of productive economic activity. In this part of her analysis, Peirce anticipated Richard Ely, Helen Campbell, and Ellen Swallow Richards, who attempted, beginning in the 1880s and 1890s, to introduce home economics (or domestic economy) into academic debates and public policy as the "economics of consumption" on an equal plane with the economics of production.[16] All of the material feminists knew what many later Marxist and neoclassical economists alike have tended to forget: it is not the wage that defines work, it is the labor.

When Catharine Beecher, August Bebel, and Melusina Peirce framed their views of what the industrial revolution should mean to domestic life, they set up models of women's work and family life marked by all the hopes and fears of the mid-nineteenth century. They accepted gender stereotypes so strong that not one of these three models incorporated any substantial male responsibility for housework and child care. Yet Beecher's and Bebel's models of home continued to shape home life and public policy for over a century. The haven strategy and the industrial strategy became the ruling paradigms for domestic life in capitalist and in state socialist societies where the paid employment of women was a fact, not a hope or a fear.[17] Neither model of home life incorporated any substantial critique of male exclusion from the domestic scene. Both models disconnected household space from other parts of the industrial city and its economy. Attempts to repair their conceptual difficulties accelerated in the years after World War I, but neither model has undergone the total revision that would enable planners of housing, jobs, and services to create the spatial settings for modern societies where the paid employment of women is essential.

As a result, women have become disadvantaged workers in both capitalist and state socialist societies. If we look at the evolution of these two models, we see that there have been many ingenious modifications and ideological surprises as capitalists attempted to industrialize the haven strategy or state socialists attempted to domesticate the industrial strategy. The neighborhood strategy of Peirce met a rather different fate. Its adherents advanced their cause effectively in the United States and Europe, creating many interesting small experiments. As a result, they extended their argument for justice and women's liberation, but never had to provide a framework for government policy.

The evolution of all three models of home in different societies during the twentieth century reveals a great deal about capitalism and the role of the state in advanced capitalist societies, socialism and the role of the state in state socialist societies, and feminism and the persistence of male economic control of female labor. It is a story far too complex to be told in full here, yet a brief review may provoke readers of many different political persuasions. While the story does not deal at all with the fate of home life in economically developing nations, it may be read as a cautionary tale for any nation just beginning to make policies about housing and the employment of women. In the American context, the history of the three models of home may suggest ways to salvage the housing stock we now have while leaving the Victorian conventions of gender behind.

Modifying Beecher's Haven Strategy

Miniaturized technology and household engineering

The first to modify the house as haven were manufacturers who introduced industrially produced appliances and products into the home. These were profitable extensions of the market economy, presented as aids to the hardworking homemaker. What is astonishing is that these inventions eroded the autonomy of women at least as much as they contributed to saving women's labor. Eventually the haven strategy produced not a skilled housewife happy at home, supported by her husband's "family" wage, but a harried woman constantly struggling to keep up standards.

The years since 1900 have seen the production of privately owned clothes washers, clothes dryers, refrigerators, gas and electric stoves, freezers, dishwashers, toasters, blenders, electric ovens, food processors, vacuum cleaners, and electric brooms.[18] Many of these appliances were the result of an extended campaign to miniaturize earlier hotel technology in the post-World War I era, and their potential for lightening household labor was tremendous. Unfortunately manufacturers began their sales of all such appliances and home improvements by advertising in women's magazines with themes of fear and guilt.[19] "For the health of your family ... keep your foods sweet and pure, free from odors, impurities, and contamination," read the copy for McCray Sanitary Refrigerators. "Don't apologize for your toilet! Modernize it," said Pfau Manufacturing Company. Women were also told that liberation could be bought: "Electricity has brought to women a new freedom [represented by the figure of Liberty, wearing a crown and classical drapery] ... the easy scientific method of cleaning with the Western Electric Vacuum cleaner."[20] The "laboratory-clean home" was what the housewife had to achieve.

In the first three decades of the twentieth century, industrial engineers and home economists joined forces to show housewives how to apply Frederick Taylor's factory-oriented, time-and-motion studies to their tasks at home. Since there had been no division and specialization of labor in the home, the industrial paraphernalia of task analysis with stopwatches made housewives into split personalities. They were the "managers" supervising their own speedup. As Christine Frederick put it, "Today, the woman in the home is called upon to be an executive as well as a manual laborer."[21] Or as one woman complained, "The role of the housewife is, therefore, analogous to that of the president of a corporation who would not only determine policies and make overall plans but also spend the major part of his time and energy in such activities as sweeping the plant and oiling the machines."[22]

Household engineers made women feel guilty for not doing tasks fast enough. Advertisers made both men and women feel guilty through emotional blackmail. Men were told that if they loved their wives, they owed it to them to buy particular appliances. Women were told that if they bought certain items, men would love them more. "Man seeks no club, when the home has a Hub," wrote one stove manufacturer. The American response to such ad campaigns was extensive purchasing, but researchers who have studied time budgets find that conflicts within the home continued and the work of the "haven" housewives was still "never done." Jo Ann Vanek reported in her 1974 survey in *Scientific American* that household standards had risen but women's time had not been saved.[23] To take just one example, Vanek showed that the full-time urban or rural housewife spent more hours doing laundry in the 1970s than in the 1920s, despite all the new washing machines, dryers, bleaches, and detergents. Why? Her family had more clothes and wanted them cleaner. The classic "ring around the collar" commercials of the 1960s dramatized the issue. A husband and his five-year-old son jeered at a woman for using a detergent that could not remove the stains on their shirt collars. Her response – to buy a new product – exemplified the ways that conflict within a family was exploited. Manufacturers often present ownership of multiple appliances as an integral part of a rising standard of living. This is misleading: many appliances require more labor than they save.

The popularity of gourmet cooking, the expansion of houses, and the increasing complexity of home furnishings have also contributed to an increasing demand for female labor hours in the home. Another development launched in the 1920s, which continued into the twenty-first century, was the creation of a culture of mothering that demanded intense attention to children at every stage of their development. Although the numbers of children were shrinking, mothers were expected to spend more time with each one. When American manufacturers introduced television, many households used it as a baby-sitting machine. However, television created as many problems as it solved, since children listened to endless commercials for candy and toys. Some inventions are better eliminated from home life.

Commercial services

When increasing numbers of American housewives and mothers entered the paid labor force in the 1960s and 1970s, and commercial services became a fast-growing sector of the economy, there was a second major modification of the haven strategy. In 1978, it was estimated that Americans spent a third of their food budgets in restaurants and fast-food establishments. From 1970, when Americans spent $6 billion on fast food, until 2000, when they spent over $110 billion (an almost twenty-fold increase), fast-food logo buildings have lined the highways.[24] The proportion of restaurant food eaten by two-earner couples was, as might be expected, higher than for one-earner couples with a full-time housewife. A McDonald's slogan, "A Mom making time," captured the mood of some customers. "It's nice to feel so good about a meal," sang Colonel Sanders' chorus. "We're cooking dinner in your neighborhood," ran the folksy copy line for a California chain of fast-food restaurants. Happy family life and the consumption of industrially produced meals have collided, just as political liberation for women and the purchase of electrical appliances meshed as themes in the 1920s.

Harland Sanders, the goateed Kentucky colonel dressed in a white suit with a black string tie, smiles at motorists from the street corners and roadsides of America. A man who started his career in 1929, running a small cafe behind a gas station in Corbin, Kentucky, he became the king of the take-out chicken business in the late 1950s. By 2000, Colonel Sanders' Kentucky Fried Chicken franchised 10,800 businesses doing $8.9 billion worth of fast food annually, worldwide.[25] When fast food came of age as one of many commercial services supported by working women and their families, Sanders became a hero as an entrepreneur. When Sanders died in 1980, his body lay in the rotunda of the state capitol in Frankfort. In Louisville, his hometown, the flags on city buildings were flown at half-staff. But was Sanders a hero to women? His franchises employed thousands of non-union women at low wages to prepare and serve his industrial food products. These commercial services and products filled in for home cooking, but they drained a woman's salary. One woman's precarious haven was sustained by the products of another woman's small wages in this fast-growing sector of the market economy. Those theorists who argued that such commercial services "liberated" women considered only the consumer and not the producer. Of course, the quality and price of commercial fast food varies greatly, as do the costs and conditions of production. In 2000, upscale businesses run by professional cooks, with catchy names like "A Moveable Feast" and "Perfect Parties," offer a range of carefully prepared soups, main courses, and desserts to affluent households whose members have no time to create elegant dinners.

Almost as common as the fast-food place on the corner is the commercial child-care facility. Profit-making child care is also big business. Most are independent operations run by licensed day-care providers. The fastest growing group are more carefully calculated to run as franchises, such as the Kinder Care chain, with 1,240 centers in thirty-nine states and the United Kingdom. Their education director in 1980 was an ex–Air Force colonel who designed a program for children in the chain's standardized plastic schoolhouses.[26] At the high end, expensive day-care services may provide development child care for the children of affluent families. At the low end, many in-home, "family" day-care centers exist.

Other types of profitable, personalized commercial services now offered to the home-as-haven include private cooks, nurses, maids, baby-sitters (long employed by the affluent), and Internet grocery-shopping services. One, called nyerrands.com, advertised in 2001, "Give us your to do list." Their fees are $30 per hour for waiting around for home deliveries, 20 percent of the bill for drugstore or grocery errands, and 25 percent of the bill for category-killer discount stores like Costco. Should you require "life management" assistance such as cleaning your closets or organizing your refrigerator, services in most big cities will provide a price quote on demand. The bargain end of the spectrum on personal service is the maid franchise operation. Such services pay workers extremely low wages. When author Barbara Ehrenreich went on assignment as a maid, she received $6.65 an hour, while customers were charged $25 an hour.[27]

Employer benefits and state services

American employers may provide services to workers who are mothers when there are bonanza profits to be made; the state intervenes to provide services to employed women when there are wartime labor shortages. These crisis times reveal just how much can be gained by supporting women's economic activities … Kaiser Shipyards in Vanport City, Oregon, was an impressive demonstration of how employers could make a difference for women. In less than one year, Kaiser management created a dazzling array of inducements for mothers with children to take on jobs as welders, riveters, and heavy construction workers. Almost sixty years later, American women workers still lack national legislation requiring that all employers treat women as valued workers and offer similar programs.

In 1993, the United States enacted the Family and Medical Leave Act. It requires employers with over fifty workers to provide up to twelve weeks of unpaid leave for "certain family and medical reasons," including childbirth, adoption, and the need to care for a spouse, child, or parent who is seriously ill, as well as a serious health condition of the worker. An international study of 152 countries in 1998 showed that 80 percent offered *paid* maternity leave. A European official commented sadly on the U.S., "it's a do-it-yourself maternity plan."[28] Since employers provide no pay, only affluent workers would be able to take time off. Mother and fathers who want a year off to bond with a new baby and create a secure attachment are out of luck.

The child-care situation is no better. A national day-care bill was passed by both houses of Congress in 1971, only to be vetoed by Richard Nixon, who argued that he was defending the American family. The need for developmental child care has been fought by conservatives, who fail to appreciate that while 65 percent of the mothers of children under six are in the paid labor force, only a small percent of the children of employed mothers enjoy quality child care.[29] Most parents have to struggle to find anything. Latch-key children are on the rise. When the topic turns to welfare mothers, the lack of day care becomes a clear example of inept policy. Welfare reformers in the Clinton era told women they must get off welfare and find paid employment. Often there was no public day care and no adequate provision for commercial child-care expenses, which might take a third or half of a woman's pay.

Experiments in flex-time, or flexible work schedules, have been heavily publicized as employers' initiatives to help employed parents at little cost to themselves. So have experiments in telecommuting, or work at home on the Internet. Such arrangements do not eliminate the double day, they merely make it less logistically stressful. Flexible work schedules are worth campaigning for, but trade unions and women's groups recognize they are only a small part of a broader solution to women's double workload.

Swedish parent insurance

It is instructive to mention Swedish benefits, which guarantee women and men workers more rights to economic support for parenting. Gender equality was not the only motivation for their legislation. Politicians agreed that more Swedish women in the paid labor force were preferable to large numbers of guest workers (migrant laborers) for political reasons. So, during the 1960s and 1970s, elaborate maternity insurance, child-care provisions, and incentives to employers evolved in order to avoid bringing guest workers from Southern Europe into the country in large numbers. Eventually, by 1999, 70 percent of Swedish women had joined the paid labor force; Swedish Parent Insurance was a monument to their economic importance to the nation, and to their role as mothers.

Swedish Parent Insurance, established in 1974, provides for economic benefits and leaves from paid work for either new mothers or new fathers. As Sheila Kamerman, a specialist in the comparative analysis of social welfare programs, has described it, "this is a universal, fully paid, wage-related, taxable cash benefit." It now covers the year after childbirth. Either parent can remain home to care for the infant. Kamerman explains how it might work: "A woman might use the benefit to cover four months of full time leave and stay home. Then each might, in turn, work two months at half time, followed by two months at three-quarter time (a six-hour day). Employers are required to accept part-time employment as part of this benefit, for childcare purposes." When only 10 percent of the eligible men used this benefit in 1976, the Swedish government appointed a Father's Commission to recommend changes. New legislation added thirty days of leave for fathers only. Men had to use it during the child's first year, or lose it. Men also got an additional benefit which provided ten days leave at the time of birth, and eighteen days of paid leave per child for either parent to care for sick children at home. In some parts of Sweden, Kamerman notes that workers will also come to the house to care for a sick child so that both parents may go to work, and another Swedish program has offered state subsidies for employers who hire women in fields dominated by men, or hire men in fields dominated by women. Sweden has recognized that there may be economic disruption caused by giving equal work to women and men, where jobs previously were segregated. This legislation makes it possible for employers to recoup some of the cost of this social change.[30] This is the kind of economic equity that can improve the lives of both women and men.

Male participation

One last attempt to modify the round of tasks for the housewife in the U.S. has been the call for male participation. Training boys for housework and child care, and insisting that adult men take part, educates them and improves their skills. Imaginative projects along these lines include grade-school courses for boys on how to take care of babies and YWHA play groups for fathers and children.[31] Both traditional consciousness-raising and these new courses reveal to men and boys the skills needed for nurturing, the time involved, and the role that space plays in isolating the nurturer. They find that kitchens are often designed for one worker, not two; that supermarkets are designed for the longest possible trip, not the shortest; and that men's rooms, like women's rooms, need a safe place where a diaper can be changed. Men who do housework and parenting then begin to see the patterns of private and public life in the divided American city.

  In the United States, we have had active struggle for male participation in housework since the 1970s. Yet sociological studies suggest that American men do only 10 percent to 15 percent of household work (a smaller percentage than children contribute) and women still bear the brunt of 70 percent, even when both members of a couple are in the paid labor force. Sociologist Arlie Hochschild reported in *The Second Shift* that employed women averaged 15 hours more of housework and child care per week than men, a finding consistent from the 1980s through the 1990s. Indeed, economist Heidi Hartmann suggests that men actually demand eight hours more service per week than they contribute.[32] Other studies have found that the work week of American and Canadian women is 21 hours longer than that of men.[33]

A closer look at male behavior in different classes reveals common gender stereotypes underlying the struggle over housework within the family. Men pretend to be incompetent or they call the jobs trivial.[34] They may also have very heavy overtime (whether at executive or blue-collar jobs) and argue that their time is always worth more than a woman's time. Men may also find that even if they do participate, a couple with young children still can't manage alone if both partners are employed full-time. An even more insurmountable problem to male participation is the absence of men in many households.[35] Men's reluctance to take part in nurturing the next generation is only part of the problem. In many cases the ideal of male involvement has blinded many angry women to the severe logistical problems presented by the house itself. Women's hope for male cooperation, some time in the distant future, obscures the need for sweeping spatial and economic reforms.

Modifying Bebel's Industrial Strategy

In the same way that Beecher's haven strategy of keeping domestic work out of the market economy was slowly eroded, so Bebel's ideal strategy for the state socialist world has also been betrayed by the retention of a second shift of private life and home cooking. Bebel argued that only a comprehensive program of industrial development for all women, including the design of new services and new housing forms, could improve women's position.[36] This has never been realized. Domestic drudgery accompanied industrial work for women; it did not wither away under the "dictatorship of the proletariat," just as the state did not.

Between the 1950s and the 1990s, one might have expected more comprehensive planning of services in state socialist countries such as Cuba, China, and the former Soviet Union, where the state owned the factories, ran the shops, ran the day care, ran the transit, and owned the housing. At the state's discretion, day care and other services could be located in the factory or in the residential neighborhood. Indeed, day care, other social services, and even the factory itself could be placed in the residential neighborhood. Despite this potential ability to meet employed women's needs, such decisions were not usually made in ways that increased women's autonomy.

The house for the new way of life

The first opportunity for fulfilling Bebel's ideal occurred in the Soviet Union, after the October Revolution of 1917. Lenin and Alexandra Kollontai led Bolshevik support for housing and services for employed women. They argued for the transformation of the home by the state and experimented with these ideas as the basis for national housing policy. Lenin, in *The Great Initiative*, wrote about the need for housing with collective services in order to involve women in industrial production: "Are we devoting enough attention to the germs of communism that already exist in this area [of the liberation of women]? No and again no. Public dining halls, creches, kindergartens – these are exemplary instances of these germs, these are those simple, everyday means, free of all bombast, grandiloquence and pompous solemnity, which, however, are *truly* such that they can *liberate women*, truly such that they can decrease and do away with her inequality vis-a-vis man in regard to her role in social production and public life." Lenin conceded that, "these means are not new, they have (like all the material prerequisites of socialism) been created by large-scale capitalism, but under capitalism they have firstly remained a rarity, secondly – and particularly important – they were either hucksterish enterprises, with all the bad sides of speculation, of profit-making, of deception, of falsification or else they were a 'trapeze act' of bourgeois charity, rightly hated and disclaimed by the best workers."[37] Following Lenin's encouragement, the new regime developed a program of building multifamily housing with collective services, beginning with competitions by architects to generate new designs for the "House for the New Way of Life."

While the competition had a strong intellectual impact on designers of mass housing all over the world, ultimately, few of the projects were built as intended. The USSR lacked the technology and the funds to follow through on its commitment to urban housing under Lenin. Under Stalin, the commitment itself dissolved. Stalin's ascendancy in the 1930s ended the official policy of women's liberation. Divorce and abortion were made difficult; "Soviet motherhood" was exalted, and experiments in collective living and new kinds of housing ended. Only the most minimal support for women's paid labor-force participation was provided: day care in large, bureaucratic centers stressing obedience, discipline, and propaganda.

Soviet motherhood

As a result, women in the USSR were encouraged to join the paid labor force without recognition of their first job in the home. In 1980, Anatole Kopp, a specialist in Soviet housing, concluded that "Soviet society today has but little connection with the fraternal, egalitarian, and self-managing society dreamed of by a few during the short period of cultural explosion which followed the Revolution." Workers lived in small private apartments in dreary, mass housing projects, where miles and miles of identical buildings had been constructed with industrialized building systems. Individual units were cramped and inconvenient. Appliances were minimal. Laundry was done in the sink; cooking on a two-burner countertop unit without oven. Refrigerators were rare status symbols for the favored elite. "Soviet architecture today well reflects daily life in the USSR ... It reflects the real condition of women in the Soviet Union – a far cry from the idyllic pictures once painted by Alexandra Kollontai."[38]

Research on the time budgets of women and men in the former Soviet Union showed the extent of inequality: 90 percent of all Soviet women between the ages of twenty and forty-nine were in the paid labor force. While women's housework time decreased somewhat between 1923 and 1966, men's time spent in housework did not increase. As a result, women's total work week was still seventeen hours longer than men's.[39] Moscow was one of the few cities in the world to provide enough day care for the children of all employed mothers, but while this allowed women to function as full-time paid workers (51 percent of the Soviet Union's labor force), their housing was not designed to include either Bebel's industrialized housekeeping services or American kitchen appliances.[40] So, one could compare women's work in the United States and the former Soviet Union. The USSR emphasized state subsidized day care and women's involvement in industrial production. The U.S. emphasized commercial day care and women's consumption of appliances and commercial services. In both cultures, the majority of married women had two jobs, worked 17–21 hours per week more than men, and earned about 60 to 75 percent of what men earned. The "new way of life" in the USSR was as elusive as the "new woman" in the U.S.

Housewives' factories in Cuba and China

The situation for employed women has been quite similar in other state socialist countries whose economic development was influenced by the Soviet Union. Given that standing in long lines to purchase scarce food supplies and consumer goods has long been a problem for housewives in state socialist societies, Cuba developed the Plan Jaba or Shopping Bag Plan in the early 1970s to permit employed women to go to the head of lines in crowded stores. However pragmatic the Plan Jaba was, as a solution to the woman's double day as paid worker and mother, and as a solution to the hours of queuing, one could hardly call it a major theoretical innovation. The publicity given to it as a fine example of socialist liberation for women was over-done. In much the same vein, Cuba also offered employed women special access to rationed goods and factory laundry services.[41] Such services cannot correct more basic problems. The location of factories in neighborhoods was not a service to women but a disservice when the well-located factories offered only low-paid work for women. In Cuba, a textile factory staffed primarily by low-paid women was located in the Alamar housing project outside Havana; a shoe factory staffed by low-paid women was placed in the José Martí neighborhood in Santiago. In addition, the large and well-designed day-care centers in housing projects employed only women as day-care workers, at low salaries, because child care was considered a woman's job.

Chinese examples of residential quarter planning for employed women are similar. During the Great Leap Forward, so-called housewives' factories were located in residential neighborhoods. The female workers received low wages and worked in relatively primitive industrial conditions. All this was justified for some time as a transitional stage of national economic development. However, in 1980, the Chinese planned an entire new town, which included new housewives' factories, to accompany a large new steel plant for male workers who would earn much higher wages.[42] Chinese residential neighborhoods, like the Cuban ones, have also employed women as day-care workers and community-health workers at very low wages. So, while the socialization of traditional women's work proceeded at a rapid rate to support women's involvement in industrial production, both the industrial workers and the service workers remained in female ghettos, and female responsibility for nurturing work remained the norm.

During the last three decades, women in state socialist countries have raised the issue of male participation, as have their counterparts in the United States. Cuban women developed a strong critique of what they call the "second shift," or their responsibility for housework once the paid shift is over. A cartoon shows an agricultural worker with a mound of sugar cane she has just cut, saying "Finished! Now to cook, wash, and iron!" As a result of such campaigns, the Cuban Family Code of 1974 was written. In principle, it aimed at having men share what was formerly "women's work." In practice, the law depended upon private struggle between husband and wife for day-to-day enforcement. Men feigned incompetence, especially in the areas of cooking and cleaning. The gender stereotyping of low-paid jobs for women outside the home, in day-care centers for example, only reinforced the problem at home. Some Cuban men made an effort, but many argued that domestic sharing could wait for the next generation. While Communist Party policy urged male cadres to assume half the domestic chores, Heidi Steffens, a writer for *Cuba Review*, recounted a popular mid-1970s anecdote. A well-known member of the Central Committee of the party took over the job of doing the daily laundry, but he insisted that his wife hang it out and bring it in from the line, since he didn't want the neighbors to see his loss of *machismo*.[43] The power of *machismo* was also evident when men cited pressure to do "women's" work as one of their reasons for emigration.[44]

In China, where there have also been general political policies that housework should be shared, the ambience is even less supportive. Sometimes the elderly – more often a grandmother than a grandfather – will fill in. The history of party pronouncements on housework can be correlated with the need to move women into or out of the paid labor force. When a party directive instructed male members not to let themselves be henpecked into too much domestic activity at the expense of their very important political work, it was clear that full male participation in housework was a distant goal rather than a reality.[45] In state socialist countries, as in capitalist ones, the hope of male participation hides the inadequacy of the basic model concerning work and home. It encourages both women and men to think that the next generation might negotiate a better solution, rather than to consider the overall inadequacies of spatial and economic planning.

Modifying Peirce's Neighborhood Strategy

While the haven strategy and the industrial strategy suffered slow disintegration into the double day, Melusina Peirce's neighborhood strategy of material feminism never became mainstream. Like Bebel and Beecher, she failed to incorporate male participation in housework and child care, but at least she had a strong economic reason for the exclusion. Peirce wanted to overcome the isolation of housewives, the lack of specialization of tasks, the lack of labor-saving technology, and the lack of financial security for any woman who had spent a lifetime in domestic labor. She saw men as a threat to women's traditional economic activities and wanted women to defend and expand their household activities on their own terms, rather than have them taken over by men's commercial enterprises.

In 1868, Peirce herself organized a bakery, laundry, grocery, and sewing service in Cambridge, Massachusetts.[46] In the next half-century, dozens of other experiments were conducted, including a family dining club in Warren, Ohio, from 1903 to 1923, and a Cleaning Club in Northbrook, Illinois, in the late 1940s. In Massachusetts, between 1926 and 1931, Ethel Puffer Howes made an even more ambitious experiment, providing models of community-run services: a cooperative dinner kitchen for the home delivery of hot food, a cooperative nursery school, a home helpers' bureau, and a job placement advisory service for Smith graduates. As the head of the Institute for the Coordination of Women's Interests at Smith College, Howes believed that her model institutions could be recreated throughout the nation by housewives who also wished to enter paid employment. Unfortunately, during the Depression, prejudice against women's employment, combined with the Smith College faculty's suspicions that Howes' ideas were unacademic, ended this project after five years of successful operation.

Recruiting adequate capital to initiate change was a consistent problem for all of these neighborhood experiments. Some housewives' experiments failed because husbands found their wives demands for pay too expensive – they believed that marriage was a labor contract, making housewives' labor free. Other experiments – including some that lasted the longest – relied on ties between neighbors and kin but involved little money changing hands. This tradition of housewives' neighborly sharing of tasks moved too slowly for many nineteenth-century feminists who attempted to push the neighborhood strategy in the direction of more businesslike enterprises run by professional women. They believed that the increasing employment of women outside the home could provide the paid jobs and paying customers necessary to transform traditional domesticity. Yet while more cash was a resource, the neighborhood organization of women suffered as a result.

In the 1890s the idea of neighborhood domestic reform as "good business" became quite popular when the American feminist Charlotte Perkins Gilman proposed the construction of special apartment houses for employed women and their families. In *Women and Economics*, she noted that employed women required day care and cooked-food service to enjoy home life after a day of paid work, and argued that if any astute business woman were to construct an apartment hotel with these facilities for professional women and their families, it would be filled at once. She believed that female entrepreneurs would find this "one of the biggest businesses on earth."[47]

Service houses, collective houses, and cooperative quadrangles

Gilman's work was translated into several European languages, and her argument was taken up by many European women and men looking for a better approach to housing. The builder Otto Fick constructed the first "service house" in Copenhagen in

1903, a small apartment house occupied by tenants who enjoyed food service, cleaning, and laundry service. The building was explicitly designed for married women in the paid labor force, but Fick thought career and motherhood incompatible and prohibited children.[48] A second fault can be seen in Fick's claim that he was the "inventor of a new mode of living which simultaneously has all the features of a profitable business venture."[49] His claim depended upon residents paying the service personnel low wages and making a profit on the market price of shares in the residents' association when they sold out. Nevertheless, Fick achieved a level of social and technological innovation that Gilman had only proposed, and his project operated until 1942.[50]

Another successful design for live/work housing was developed in Sweden in the 1930s. In 1935, feminist Alva Myrdal (later awarded the Nobel Prize for her work on world peace) collaborated with architect Sven Markelius to create housing with work space, food service, and child care. Their project in the center of Stockholm included fifty-seven small apartments of very elegant design. Some of them could also be used as offices or studios. Not only did Markelius design these, he moved into the building himself and served as an unofficial handyman for thirty years, in order to make sure everything about the building worked, and to demonstrate his commitment to social housing.[51]

In 1945, *Life* magazine praised this project as a model for post–World War II reorganization of American housing: the reporter suggested that Americans should copy its design for women in the wartime labor force who wished to continue their careers.[52] The only disadvantage was that most residents did not wish to leave after their children were grown, and new parents could not find space in the building. The day-care center ultimately had to take in neighborhood children as well as residents' children to stay in business. The restaurant food became less economically competitive when cheap eating places appeared in large numbers in the city.

Olle Enkvist, a Stockholm contractor who became involved with the combination of housing and services, built the collective houses Marieberg (1944), Nockebyhove (1951), Blackeberg (1952), and Hasselby (1955–56). All had restaurants and full child care. Unlike Fick, who believed in joint stock ownership by a residents' association, Enkvist owned these buildings as benign landlord. His success was measured in long waiting lists of prospective tenants. After his death there were numerous tenant confrontations with the new management, especially when, in the 1970s, the new management wished to close the collective dining rooms because they didn't generate as much profit as the rental apartments. This probably would have seemed most ironic to Enkvist, who decided against delivery systems for cooked food (such as the elevators Fick had used for food) on the grounds that a large dining room with private family tables was more conducive to social contacts. Hasselby tenants did prove they could cater for themselves without losing money (serving about one hundred people daily for three years), but management found this level of participation cumbersome and decided to eject the tenants. The turmoil of decollectivization then led to the impression that these projects were social or financial failures, although many functioned smoothly for thirty years. Their main failure was that the landlord did not turn a high profit.[53]

In England, Gilman's arguments were taken up by Ebenezer Howard, founder of the Garden Cities movement, who proposed the "cooperative quadrangle" as the basis of new town planning in 1898.[54] Howard's cooperative quadrangles were to be composed of garden apartments served by a collective kitchen, dining room, and open space. They were designed to release women from household drudgery in the private home, and between 1911 and 1930 several of these projects were built for various constituencies, including single female professionals and the elderly, as well as two-earner couples. Howard himself lived in Homesgarth, a cooperative triangle at Letchworth. The quadrangles never became the standard housing available in the Garden Cities, but they did provide some very successful alternative projects within these new towns. In time, their dining rooms also seemed expensive compared to local restaurants. After World War I, Clementina Black of London argued for the postwar adoption of "Domestic Federations" similar to Howard's designs.[55] After World War II, Sir Charles Reilly, Member of Parliament and head of the School of Architecture at Liverpool University, also proposed a plan for reconstruction that incorporated many of the features of Howard's cooperative quadrangles.[56] He organized neighborhoods of duplex houses around nurseries, community kitchens, and open spaces.

Apartment hotels

In the United States, Gilman's ideas were reflected in the apartment hotels built between 1898 and 1930 in major cities. Mary Beard, the well-known historian, lived in one such apartment hotel with her husband and children; they were located on the bus line to the New York Public Library. Knowing that three meals a day would be served to her family, she was able to hop on the bus and tend to her research. Georgia O'Keefe lived in a similar hotel with good light for painting. For less affluent women, Finnish and Jewish workers' housing cooperatives provided child care, bed-sitting rooms for the elderly, and tea rooms adjacent to family apartments.[57] The Workers Cooperative Colony in the Bronx, organized and owned by workers in the needle trades, was an early example of this kind of project in the mid-1920s. Again, the cost of providing services with well-paid unionized service workers made competition with commercial groceries, restaurants, and laundries difficult.

Cash or community?

All these attempts to define supportive residential communities for employed women and their families ran into two related economic difficulties. First, the economic value of housework was never adequately understood. Second, the economic value of the new services was unclear, in relation both to the old-fashioned system of hiring personal servants and the new commercial services and industrial products developed for haven housewives. Such services, when produced by low-paid female workers, were cheaper, if less intimate and desirable, than community-generated alternatives.

Economies of scale worked in favor of the nationally distributed products and services, even if they were impersonal. Once the substitution of cash for personal participation by residents had been arranged, the difference between industrial and neighborhood services might be difficult to discern. So professional women, if they attempted to buy services, had to be very careful to treat the women service workers well. Otherwise, they wound up closer to Colonel Sanders, year by year.

Family allowances and wages for housework   In much the same way, housewives struggling for economic independence through the neighborhood strategy found themselves closer to the haven strategy if they focused on wages and omitted the ideal of reshaping household work in community form. Eleanor Rathbone, an economist, feminist, and Member of Parliament in England, formed a club to lobby for wages for wives as early as 1918.[58] Some Americans also supported this cause in the 1940s.[59] Rathbone started by seeking a decent wage for housework; in the late 1940s, she won for mothers the Family Allowance: a small subsidy for a second child and any additional ones. Inspired by the concept of Family Allowances, and the potential of organizing to increase them, some British feminists revived the idea of larger payments for housework in the early 1970s. Led by Selma James, a group called Wages for Housework demanded that the state pay wages to all women for their housework. To attract supporters, the organizers ran skits about women's work in urban neighborhoods on market days. They passed out free potholders with their slogan to remind women of the campaign for wages every time they picked up a hot pot. They used union techniques of insisting on wages, wages, wages. "Just give us the money. All we want is the money," James incanted at one meeting.

Wages for Housework organized effectively among welfare recipients and single-parent mothers. They created special suborganizations: Lesbians for Wages for Housework, and Black Women for Wages for Housework. The campaign developed successful recruiting tactics, but there was no mass movement. Organizers demonstrated the value of a housewife's day but their emphasis was on cash. Their campaigns had some of the weaknesses of American welfare-rights organizing of the 1960s. Wages for Housework did not confront the isolated home as haven, the setting for housework. They accepted females as domestic workers and identified the welfare state (rather than employers or husbands) as the primary target of their activities. Furthermore, they included sexual services as "all in a day's work" for the housewife. This made it easy to organize angry women who felt sexually exploited, but the model of wife as paid maid and prostitute made it difficult to articulate a more sophisticated position on male-female relationships.

Wages for Housework never lacked vitality, even if it lacked subtlety. A china bank in the shape of a rolling pin, made in the 1940s, carried the message of the earlier British feminists, "If women were paid for all they do, there'd be a lot of wages due."[60] But just as Rathbone had found a wage for haven housewives politically impossible in the 1940s, so it was in the 1970s. Even if they had won, financial recognition from the state for the work of homemaking would not have been enough to transform the haven housewife's situation.

Trade-A-Maid   Gary Trudeau's *Doonesbury* cartoon on "Trade-A-Maid" schemes, in which American haven housewives swap chores, points out this problem as well. As Nichole, the "Alternate Life Stylist," explains it, "Housewife A and her best friend, Housewife B, spend weekdays cleaning each other's home. Their respective husbands pay for their services, just as they would for those of a first-class maid."[61] The employed wives then become eligible for Social Security and for tax deductions on cleaning equipment. They receive cash but neither husband suffers loss of family income since the swap means both wives are paid equally. However, they still work in isolation, since receiving a wage for housework (whether paid by individual husbands or by the state) does not transform the home as haven, nor does it utilize the full range of technologies available in twentieth-century society. "It's illegal, though, right?" worries the interviewer. "Not yet," says Nichole.

NICHE   Another American proposal captures the essence of the neighborhood strategy and avoids the question of industrial technologies by stressing the value of women offering social services to each other in the neighborhood. In 1977, Nona Glazer, Lindka Mjaka, Joan Acker, and Christine Bose suggested institutionalizing housewives' cooperative services by establishing government funding for Neighbors in Community Helping Environments (NICHE).[62] In *Women in a Full Employment Economy*, they explained how to start Neighborhood Service Houses, where women would supervise children's play, care for sick children, facilitate repair service to homes, encourage bartering, distribute hot meals, and work with battered women, abused children, and rape victims. In return for providing these family and community services, women would receive at least a minimum wage. This proposal recognized that women's cooperation to socialize homemaking tasks could transform women's experience. NICHE also saw economic recognition of domestic labor as essential, but it did not involve proposals for male participation. Since NICHE was relying on the state to provide the wages, they had selected almost as difficult a program as the Wages for Housework campaigns. In a Democratic administration concerned about full employment the proposal looked possible; when Republicans took office and slashed social services, the proposal looked even more relevant, but funding appeared impossible.

Complexity

All of these campaigns to transform models of home life underscore the need for complex social, economic, and environmental innovations. Successful solutions would reward housework and parenting as essential to society, incorporate male responsibility for nurturing, build on existing networks of neighbors, kin, and friends, and incorporate new technologies, in order to promote equality for women within a more caring society. Yet before any specific policy changes can be proposed, it is essential to recognize the consistent economic and spatial failures that marred previous attempts. Beecher's and Bebel's models were too simplistic. If Beecher's glorification of the homemaker attempted to recover a pre-industrial past, Bebel's rejection of the homemaker embraced the fantasy of a totally industrial future. As public policy, these strategies led to ironies compounded upon ironies; after a century, women had gotten the worst of both worlds, having been economically disadvantaged by the double day and spatially manipulated by the refusal of designers and planners to treat the home as a workplace.

Yet the most humiliating aspect of women's experience as nurturers was not their economic or spatial frustration, but the suppression of the neighborhood approach to home life, in order that the haven and industrial strategies could be presented as modern. The advocates of neighborhood networks were attacked as socialist sympathizers in the United States in the 1920s, and as bourgeois deviationists who should be expelled from the Communist Party in Germany and the USSR. Women have had warmed-over Beecher presented to them as women's liberation through Western Electric vacuum cleaners and Colonel Sanders; warmed-over Bebel presented as women's liberation through the Plan Jaba and the housewives' factories. Full recognition of what women actually contribute to society in the current century is essential to recover nurturing from the domain of corporate or bureaucratic planning. No one has put the problem of nurturing more succinctly than Melusina Peirce: "Two things women must do somehow, as the conditions not only of the future happiness, progress, and elevation of their sex, but of its bare respectability and morality. 1st. They *must* earn their own living. 2nd. They *must* be organized among themselves."[63] If this is still the best advice to women about how to deal with their traditional work, two huge areas of concern remain, architecture and economics. The three models of home life that have characterized nurturing have also had strong implications for housing design and for economic productivity, as house forms and systems of national accounting have reflected underlying ideas about the nature of home.

Notes

1   Ellen Malos, ed., *The Politics of Housework* (London: Virago Press, 1980); Nancy Folbre, *The Invisible Heart: Economics and Family Values* (New York: The New Press, 2001); Arlie Russell Hochschild, *The Second Shift* (1989; New York: Avon Books, 1997), includes a bibliography of recent scholarship.

2   Lily Braun, *Frauenarbeit und Hauswirtschaft* (Berlin, 1901); Dolores Hayden, *The Grand Domestic Revolution: A History of Feminist Designs for American Homes, Neighborhoods, and Cities* (Cambridge, Mass.: MIT Press, 1981), 291–305.

3   Hartmann has pioneered the analysis of women's labor time in the home, as the basis for her analysis of the family as a site of class and gender conflict usually ignored by liberal theorists. Heidi I. Hartmann, "The Family as the Locus of Gender, Class, and Political Struggle: The Example of Housework," *Signs: Journal of Women in Culture and Society* 6 (Spring, 1981), 366–94.

4   Laura Balbo, "The Servicing Work of Women and the Capitalist State," in *Political Power and Social Theory* (New York: Basic Books, 1981); Laura Balbo, "Crazy Quilts: Rethinking the Welfare State Debate from a Woman's Perspective," mimeographed, GRIFF, Milan, Italy, 1981; Laura Balbo and Renate Siebert Zahar, *Interferenze* (Milan: Feltrinelli, 1979).

5   Erma Bombeck, *The Grass is Always Greener Over the Septic Tank* (New York: Fawcett, 1977), 5. Billed as "the exposé to end all exposés – the truth about the suburbs," this book can be read as a bunch of little jokes, or as an unconscious but revealing indictment of numerous planning and design failures, and housewives' struggles to overcome them. A more serious attack is John Keats, *The Crack in the Picture Window* (Boston: Houghton Mifflin, 1957).

6   Literature on the family is reviewed in Hartmann, "The Family as the Locus of Gender, Class, and Political Struggle," 365–8.

7   Among the traditional family's defenders is Christopher Lasch, *Haven in a Heartless World: The Family Besieged* (New York: Basic Books, 1976).

8   William O'Neill, *Everyone Was Brave: A History of Feminism in America* (1969; New York: Quadrangle, 1971), 358.

9   Betty Friedan, *The Second Stage* (New York: Summit, 1981), 43, 83.

10 August Bebel, *Women under Socialism*, tr. Daniel De Leon (1883; New York: Schocken, 1971), 338–9; V. I. Lenin, *The Emancipation of Women* (New York: Progress Publishers, 1975), 69.

11 Hayden, *Grand Domestic Revolution*, 3–5.

12 Bebel, *Women Under Socialism*, 338–9.

13 Jane Cunningham Croly, letter to Elizabeth Cady Stanton, printed in *The Revolution* 3 (May 27, 1869), 324.

14 Melusina Fay Peirce, "Cooperative Housekeeping II" (second of five articles), *Atlantic Monthly* 22 (Dec. 1868), 684.

15 Melusina Fay Peirce, "Cooperative Housekeeping III," *Atlantic Monthly* 23 (Jan. 1869), 29–30.

16 Mari Jo Buhle, "A Republic of Women: Feminist Theory in the Gilded Age," paper read at the 1981 meeting of the American Historical Association, 4–7; also *Lake Placid Conference on Home Economics, Proceedings* (Lake Placid, N.Y., 1903, 1907).

17 Thomas Kuhn, *The Structure of Scientific Revolutions* (1962; Chicago: University of Chicago Press, 1973); "Second Thoughts on Paradigms," in *The Essential Tension: Selected Studies in Scientific Tradition and Change* (Chicago: University of Chicago Press, 1977), 293–319.

18 Susan Strasser, *Never Done: A History of American Housework* (New York: Pantheon Books, 1982), is an excellent work.

19 Ruth Schwartz Cowan, "The 'Industrial' Revolution in the Home: Household Technology and Social Change in the 20th Century," *Technology and Culture* 17 (Jan. 1976), 1–23.

20 Carol Miles, "The Craftsman Ideal of Home Life," unpublished paper, 1981.

21 Christine Frederick, *Household Engineering: Scientific Management in the Home* (Chicago: American School of Home Economics, 1920), 92.

22 Edith Mendel Stern, "Women Are Household Slaves," *American Mercury* (Jan. 1949), 71.

23 Jo Anne Vanek, "Time Spent in Housework," *Scientific American* (Nov. 1974), 116–20.

24 "U.S. Dines Out Despite Prices," *Boston Globe* (Oct. 25, 1978), 75; Eric Schlosser, *Fast Food Nation: The Dark Side of the All-American Meal* (Boston: Houghton Mifflin, 2001), 3.

25 Kentucky Fried Chicken Website, http://www.kfc.com/about/kfcfacts.htm (June 2001); Edith Evans Asbury, "Col. Harland Sanders, Founder of Kentucky Fried Chicken Dies," *New York Times* (Dec. 17, 1980), 29.

26 Kinder Care Web site, http://www.kindercare.com (June 2001); "A Big, Big Business," *Southern Exposure* 8 (Fall 1980), 36–40; Joseph Lelyveld, "Drive-in Day Care," *New York Times Magazine* (June 5, 1977), 110.

27   Barbara Ehrenreich, *Nickel and Dimed: On [Not] Getting By in America* (New York: Metropolitan Books, 2001), 72.

28   U.S. Department of Labor, "FMLA Compliance Guide," http://www.dol.gov/esa/public/regs/compliance/whd/1421.htm (July 2001); "U.S. Maternity Plans Pale in Comparison to Other Nations," *Washington Post* (Feb. 15, 1998), http://www.chron.com/content/chronicle/nation/98/02/16/ maternityleave.2-0.html (July 2001).

29   Kristin Moore and Sandra Hofferth, "Women and Their Children," in R. Smith, ed., *The Subtle Revolution: Women at Work* (Washington, D.C.: Urban Land Institute, 1979), 125–58; U.S. Department of Labor, Bureau of Labor Statistics, "Employment Characteristics of Families in 2000," April 2001, ftp://ftp.bls.gov/pub/news.release/famee.txt (June 2001); Nancy S. Barrett, "Women in the Job Market: Unemployment and Work Schedules," in Smith, ed., *The Subtle Revolution*, 88–90.

30   Sheila B. Kamerman, "Work and Family in Industrialized Societies," *Signs* 4 (Summer 1979), 644–5; Statistics Sweden, "Employment Rates for EU Member States, 1999," March 2001, http://www.scb.se/eng/omscb/eu/syssel sattning.asp (June 2001); Ann Crittenden, *The Price of Motherhood* (New York: Metropolitan Books, 2001), 244–6.

31   Ari Korpivaara, "Play Groups for Dads," and Alison Herzig and Jane Mali, "Oh, Boy! Babies!" in *Ms.* 10 (Feb. 1982), 52–8.

32   Sarah Fenstermaker Berk, "The Household as Workplace," in G. Wekerle, ed., *New Space for Women* (Boulder, Colo.: Westview, 1980), 70; Nona Glazer-Malbin, "Review Essay: Housework," *Signs* 1 (Summer 1976), 905–22; Nadine Brozan, "Men and Housework: Do They or Don't They?," *New York Times* (Nov. 1, 1980), 52; Clair Vickery, "Women's Economic Contribution to the Family," in Smith, ed., *The Subtle Revolution*, 159–200; Arlie Hochschild and Anne Machung, "Afterwood" to the 1997 edition of *The Second Shift* (1989; New York: Avon, 1997), 279; Nona Glazer, *Women's Paid and Unpaid Labor: The Work Transfer in Health Care and Retailing* (Philadelphia: Temple University Press, 1993); Hartmann, "The Family as the Locus of Gender, Class, and Political Struggle," 383.

33   Hartmann, "The Family as Locus," 380; Crittenden, *The Price of Motherhood*, 22.

34   Mainardi, "The Politics of Housework," in Robin Morgan, ed., *Sisterhood Is Powerful* (New York: Vintage, 1970), 447–54.

35   The majority of American men stop paying child support within two years of a divorce settlement, according to Kathryn Kish Sklar, "Women, Work, and Children, 1600–1980," paper read at the Third Annual Conference on Planning and Women's Needs, UCLA, Urban Planning Program, Feb. 21, 1981.

36   Bebel, *Women under Socialism*, 344–9.

37   Vladmir I. Lenin, *The Great Initiative*, quoted in Vladimir Zelinski, "Architecture as a Tool of Social Transformation," *Women and Revolution* 11 (Spring 1976), 6–14.

38   Anatole Kopp, "Soviet Architecture Since the 20th Congress of the C.P.S.U.," paper delivered at the Second World Congress of Soviet and East European Studies, 1980, 12–13.

39   Michael Paul Sacks, "Unchanging Times: A Comparison of the Everyday Life of Soviet Working Men and Women between 1923 and 1966," *Journal of Marriage and the Family* 39 (Nov. 1977), 793–805.

40   Alice H. Cook, *The Working Mother: A Survey of Problems and Programs in Nine Countries*, 2nd ed. (1978; Ithaca, N.Y.: New York State School of Industrial and Labor Relations, 1975), 8.

41   Carollee Benglesdorf and Alice Hageman, "Women and Work," in "Women in Transition," special issue of *Cuba Review* 4 (Sept. 1974), 9.

42   I was shown this project by planners in April 1980 when I visited China as a guest of the Chinese Architectural Society.

43   Heidi Steffens, "A Woman's Place," *Cuba Review* 4 (Sept. 1974), 29.

44   Geoffrey E. Fox, "Honor, Shame, and Women's Liberation in Cuba: Views of Working-Class Emigré Men," in A. Pescatello, ed., *Female and Male in Latin America* (Pittsburgh: University of Pittsburgh Press, 1973). I visited Cuba in 1979 and also observed male refusal to do housework in many situations.

45   Delia Davin, *Woman-Work: Women and the Party in Revolutionary China* (Oxford, England: Clarendon Press, 1976); Elisabeth J. Croll, "Women in Rural Production and Reproduction in the Soviet Union, China, Cuba, and Tanzania: Case Studies," in *Signs*, special issue on Development and the Sexual Division of Labor, 7 (Winter 1981), 375–99.

46   Hayden, *Grand Domestic Revolution*, 66–89, 208–27, 266–77.

47   Charlotte Perkins Gilman, *Women and Economics* (Boston: Maynard and Small, 1898); Hayden, *Grand Domestic Revolution*, 182–205. An early translation of Gilman in an architectural journal is "La Maison de Demain," *La Construction Moderne* 5 (Nov. 1914), 66–8.

48   Erwin Muhlestein, "Kollektives Wohnen gestern und heute," *Architese* 14 (1975), 4–5.

49   Otto Fick, "The Apartment House Up To Date," *Architectural Record* 22 (July 1907), 68–71.

50   Dick Urban Vestbro, "Collective Housing Units in Sweden," *Current Sweden*, Svenska Institutet, Stockholm, publication no. 234 (Sept. 1976), (6), 6–7.

51   Ibid.

52   "Sweden's Model Apartments: Stockholm Building is Wonderful for Wives Who Work," *Life* 18 (Mar. 12, 1945), 112–14.

53   Muhlestein, "Kollektives," 6–8; Vestbro, "Collective Housing," 8–11.

54   Hayden, *Grand Domestic Revolution*, 230–7.

55   Clementina Black, *A New Way of Housekeeping* (London: W. Collins Sons, 1918).

56   Lawrence Wolfe, *The Reilly Plan* (London: Nicholson and Watson, 1945).

57   Hayden, *Grand Domestic Revolution*, 251–61.

58   Ann Oakley, *Woman's Work: The Housewife Past and Present* (New York: Pantheon, 1974), 227–9.

59   Kay Hanly Bretnall, "Should Housewives Be Paid a Salary?," *American Home* 37 (Feb. 1947), 15–16.

60   Wages for Housework Collective, *All Work and No Pay* (London: Falling Wall Press, 1975), 5; also see Malos, ed., *The Politics of Housework*, for a full analysis of this movement.

61   Gary B. Trudeau, *Doonesbury*, "And Now, Here's Nichole," in Ann E. Beaudry, ed., *Women in the Economy* (Washington, D.C.: Institute for Policy Studies, 1978), 61.

62   Nona Glazer, Lindka Mjaka, Joan Acker, Christine Bose, *Women in a Full Employment Economy* (1977), mimeo.

63   Melusina Fay Peirce, "Cooperative Housekeeping," *Atlantic Monthly* 23 (March 1869), 297.

19

Planning as a Heterosexist Project

Michael Frisch

Urban planning is "a conscious effort to direct social processes to attain goals" (Fainstein and Fainstein 1996, 265–66). Urban planning then is a social project. Typically, planners characterize their work as being for the public good. In their Plan of Chicago, Burnham and Bennett ([1909] 1993, 1) characterized their plan as "the means whereby the city may be made an efficient instrument for providing all its people with the best possible conditions of living." Yet, recent scholarly work shows that planning may be used in multiple ways. Flyvbjerg (1998) presents planning as rationalization produced by the exercise of power. Planning within this context becomes more reflective of existing power relations than of positive social action. Fogelsong (1986) shows how planning facilitates capital accumulation often to the detriment of working people. Yiftachel (1998) goes further along this line of reasoning. He views planning as a process of social control and argues that planning has a "dark side of oppression" applied to people along many possible divisions, including class, race, ethnicity, gender, and sexual orientation. Thomas (1994) illustrates this dynamic in terms of race in her review of postwar planning in Detroit. Feminist writers have explored this aspect of planning in terms of urban design (Hayden 1981), zoning (Ritzdorf 1986), and planning theory itself (Sandercock and Forsyth 1992). In this article, I explore how urban planning works to promote heterosexuality at the expense of lesbian and gay people.

What does urban planning have to do with sexual orientation? Often, planning academics argue that the "community's interest in morals" has not played a large role in development of zoning laws and regulations (Anderson 1968, 468). Contrary to this notion, recent work increasingly shows how planning laws were enacted to control immoral sexuality and especially women's sexuality

Readings in Planning Theory, Third Edition. Edited by Susan S. Fainstein and Scott Campbell.
Editorial material and organization © 2012 Blackwell Publishing Ltd.
Published 2012 by Blackwell Publishing Ltd.

(Wilson 1992; Hooper 1998; Wirka 1998). Planning under apartheid acted to regulate by race and sexuality (Elder 1998). I will show how planning discourse advances heterosexuality and suppresses homosexuality through notions such as order, public, family, reproduction, and nature. Based on this discourse, planning strengthens spaces, places, and institutions that exclude on the basis of perceived orientation. Urban planning is, thus, a heterosexist project. An inclusionary urban planning must address this exclusiveness. The inclusive project would create communities where lesbians, gay men, bisexuals, and transgendered people are accepted as full citizens (Richardson 1998). In such communities, "queer spaces" might be planned rather than repressed.

Both urban planning and categories of sexual orientation are products of the late nineteenth century and early twentieth century. While a form of urban planning existed before capitalist development, modern planning and capitalism are deeply intertwined (Fogelsong 1986). Parallel to and influenced by this development is the rise of categories of sexual orientation. Social scientists described homosexuals as pathological, and the category heterosexual was developed as the inverse "normal" state (D'Emilio and Freedman 1988). Today, direct connections between the development and promotion of these categories and modern planning are hard to find. Planning discourse assumes heterosexuality, thereby leaving homosexuality closeted and coded. Foucault and Sedgwick provide methodologies for dealing with this absence (Foucault 1976; Sedgwick 1990). I find the codes of sexual difference in the central dualisms assumed within the writings, laws, and regulation that constitute the discourse of planning. These planning dualisms include order/disorder, public/private, household/family, production/reproduction, and natural/artificial. By analyzing relations of sexual difference within these dualisms of planning discourse, I show that planning fundamentally promotes heterosexuality and represses homosexuality. I argue that an inclusive planning would promote (not just tolerate) multiple sexual orientations. Only the promotion of homosexuality can undo the damage done by planning over the past century (Sedgwick 1993). Aspects of this inclusive planning are found in the reconstructive nature of lesbian and gay communities.

I start by reviewing the existing literature on planning and queer communities. The few works that have addressed sexual orientation within planning have looked at case studies rather than at planning's role. I briefly discuss the rise of the categories of heterosexuality and homosexuality. I show how mechanisms of repression including homosexual panic and the closet maintain heterosexist domination. This leads to the definition of a heterosexist project. I examine the work of the heterosexist project within three dualisms: order/disorder, family/household, and public/private. First, I look at concepts of order and disorder within the work of Geddes and Mumford. In their works, I find a direct and explicit connection between urban planning and efforts to control sexuality. Then, I discuss how heterosexist notions of kinship exclude lesbians and gays within the context of housing and zoning. Lesbians and gays are households not families, and this distinction is written into land use law and promoted by the zoning system. Third, I examine the fluidity of queer space to reveal relations within the public and private dichotomy. Here, planning is shown to be repressive of these spaces. The rise of these spaces reflects resistance to the heterosexual order. Finally, I conclude by presenting very briefly some general principles of planning inclusive of sexual difference.

What Is a Heterosexist Project? Definitions and a Review of the Planning Literature

I have already used multiple definitions to describe identities of sexual orientation (Rubin, 1992). For example, I use the terms *queer* and *lesbian and gay* interchangeably throughout much of this article. Lesbians and gays redefined the word *queer* as inclusive of a spectrum of sexual orientations to avoid being forced to choose an identity (Warner 1993). In the next section, I clarify my terms and identify central concepts used throughout the rest of the article.

Definitions: Heterosexual

The term *heterosexual* commonly refers to eroticism between people of a different sex. Yet, heterosexuality contains more social meanings. Katz (1995, 13–14) identifies three basic universal assumptions about heterosexuality: the procreative necessity of it, its basis in natural sex differences, and its potential for creating pleasure. These notions about heterosexuality are assumed to have always existed. Heterosexuality is regarded as normal. With these assumptions, heterosexuality becomes a total concept, eliminating options and alternatives (Gibson-Graham 1998).

Yet, homosexuals and heterosexuals have not always existed as categories. Modern sexual identities can be traced back to nineteenth-century efforts at classifying human activity and behavior within "scientific" notions of the day (Sedgwick 1990). The word *heterosexual* did not exist before 1868 and possibly as late as 1892 (Katz 1995). Katz (1995, 34) continues that "ways of ordering the sexes, genders, and sexualitics have varied radically." While men had sex with men in the past, such activities were imbued with much different meanings than they have today. Strangely, the first use of the term *heterosexual* found by Katz was in an 1868 letter concerning sex law reform. The letter compared both heterosexuality and homosexuality to "normal sexuality," and all of these terms had different meanings then than they do today (p. 52). Similarly, as used by Kiernan in the first published reference to the word in the United States, both homosexuality and heterosexuality referred to "perversions" (pp. 19–20). Only gradually did heterosexuality lose its pejorative nature (p. 88). Through the works of Kraft-Ebbing. Freud, and Ellis, heterosexuality became the opposite of homosexuality by representing "normal" sex (Katz 1995; Weeks 1977). Thus, the modern terminology arose out of the new fields of psychology and social science.

The development of an identity requires the connection of the terms and ideas with people. D'Emilio (1993) points to capitalism as the producer of these identities. While same-sex activity occurred prior to capitalism, "there was no social space that allowed men and women to be gay" (p. 470).[1] Work occurred within the family unit. D'Emilio argues that only with the rise of wage labor was it possible for someone to establish a life as an individual (p. 470). Large industrial cities provided both the cover and the supply of similar individuals (p. 471). Finally, Foucault (1976) integrates these two streams showing the interplay between the fascination with categories of pathologies and the capitalist production of identities as commodities. Thus, modern sexual identities arose in the nineteenth century, connected to processes of capitalist urban development.

Definitions: The closet

The universal assumptions of procreative necessity, natural sex difference, and pleasure continue to define heterosexuality. For example, on 10 November 1997, the attorney general of Vermont, a liberal state, issued a long brief using the argument that the maintenance of procreation requires the denial of marriage rights to same-sex couples (Planet Out 1997). Heterosexuality is promoted everywhere, from television to churches and schools. Heterosexuality is not a choice; it is compulsory (Rich [1982] 1993). Compulsory institutions need enforcement mechanisms. The closet is one such mechanism.

What is the closet? Closetedness is "a speech act of silence" (Sedgwick 1990, 3). Rich ([1982] 1993, 238) calls the closet the "rendering invisible of the lesbian possibility." Initially, lesbians and gays construct the closet as an "information management strategy" to minimize the negative effects of the social stigma surrounding homosexuality (Escoffier 1997). Yet, control of the closet slips from the individual to institutions. The "don't ask, don't tell" policy of the armed forces institutionalizes the closet (Signorile 1991). Society enforces the closet through violence (Escoffier 1997). Gays and lesbians know this violence firsthand. Gay bashing is a common occurrence in many American cities (Berrill 1992). This violence extends to murder and, in its most gruesome form, genocide as in Nazi Germany (Plant 1986). Beyond the body, the closet extends to written accounts of homosexual existence. Adrienne Rich points out that earlier in this century, it was common to destroy records of homosexuality. In the middle of the twentieth century, a professional conference of psychologists did not even use the word *homosexuality*; instead the "H" problem was discussed (Duberman 1991). The closet silences homosexuality and subordinates it to heterosexuality.

This silence raises a procedural problem. How can I examine the interaction of planning and sexual orientation if much of the record is repressed and destroyed? Foucault (1976, 27) offers some of the procedural answers:

> Silence itself – the things one declines to say, or is forbidden to name, the discretion that is required between different speakers – is less the absolute limit of discourse, the other side from which it is separated by a strict boundary, than an element that functions alongside things said, with them and in relation to them within overall

strategies. There is no binary division to be made between what one says and what one does not say; we must try to determine the different ways of not saying such things, how those who can and those who cannot speak of them are distributed, which type of discourse is authorized, or which form of discretion is required in either case. There is not one but many silences, and they are an integral part of the strategies that underlie and permeate discourse.

When there is no record of homosexuality in a planning discourse, I look at how heterosexuality is presented and not presented. What positions are taken and avoided? The lack of direct references to sexual orientation in a discourse does not negate my argument (Sedgwick 1990). The work is in finding the indirect references and structured silences that have a heterosexist source.

Definitions: What is a heterosexist project?

Finally, what do I mean by project? Omi and Winant (1994, 56) define a project as "the work of linking structure and representation." In discussing racial formation, they define a racial project as "simultaneously an interpretation, representation, or explanation of racial dynamics, and an effort to reorganize and redistribute resources along particular racial lines" (p. 56). A racial project is racist only if "it creates or reproduces structures of domination based upon essentialist categories of race" (p. 71).[2] Adopting their model, planning is not only a sexual project. Because of the repetition of the three heterosexual assumptions within planning discourse, planning is heterosexist. Zoning, housing rights, and our sense of the public realm are built around heterosexual constructs of family, work, and community life. Planning reproduces structures of heterosexual domination.

A quick review of recent work in planning and urban studies

Serious work on lesbian and gay topics in planning and urban studies has only occurred in the past fifteen years.[3] Earlier, if the topic of homosexuality was broached, it was presented in the terms of deviance as in case studies developed in the thirties by the urban ecology school of sociology (Johnson 1997). Castells and Murphy published the first early work on the topic in 1982. Castells (1983) then used this study of the rise of the San Francisco gay male community in his book on urban grassroots movements. As the gay community develops a sense of place and culture, it creates the potential for dynamic urban transformation. However, the potential for transformation is lost when members of the gay community bargain away their power through interest group politics, acting solely in their own short-term interests rather than reaching out to other potential allies to accomplish long-term goals (pp. 169–70). Gay community politics must be viewed within the lens of the heterosexist project of planning. The extent of institutionalized repression may lead some members of the lesbian and gay community to get what they can when they can get it. Institutional change via an inclusive urban planning may be a necessary prerequisite to the creation of long-term urban transformation.

Castells's (1983) remarks about how gender differences between lesbians and gay men affect the articulation of their communities in space and place have led to many responses. Castells argued that lesbians establish social and interpersonal networks, are poorer than men, organize politically in forms less focused on existing structures, and have fewer choices of work and residence. In contrast, gay men seek to dominate space. Lesbians in his analysis become placeless, while gay political organizing becomes place dependent (p. 140). Critiques of this work have focused on the various individual components of Castells's argument. Lesbian community formation does seem to be more a social process consisting of networks of friends and colleagues rather than a physical process (Valentine 1993a, 1993b, 1995; Forsyth 1997). The lower economic status of lesbians combined with gender discrimination may limit their transactions within the urban land market and thus limit the establishment of lesbian institutions (Badgett 1995a, 1995b; Forsyth 1997). Yet, lesbian places may be identified if the analyst knows how to read the evidence (Adler and Brenner 1992, Wolfe 1992; Rothenberg 1995; Valentine 1995; Bouthillette 1997; Forsyth 1997). Heterosexist assumptions contained within planning limit lesbians' visibility (Wolfe 1992; Peake 1993). Thus, "making the invisible visible" is an important strategy of resistance (Barnett 1993; Sandercock 1998).

The role of gay men in the gentrification of San Francisco has also prompted responses to Castells's case study. Castells (1983, 158–9) identified three forces leading to urban rehabilitation: gay professionals hire renovators to do the job, gay realtors discover the gay market both in terms of labor to perform the renovation and the demand for urban renovation, and finally collectives form to do the renovation work themselves. The depth of social relations in each factor raises the possibility of urban transformation. In contrast, Knopp sees the gay role in urban transformation less positively. First, Lauria and Knopp (1985) set the terms for this work by nothing Altman's (1982) description of the spatial differential of oppression and the rise of a spatial process of homosexualization. The rise of a "gay" identity becomes a new division of consumption. In his analysis of New Orleans gentrification, Knopp (1990b) sees gays as oppressors used by capital to facilitate gentrification. Knopp (1990a) divides gays into two communities, one aligned with capital and one resistant to capital. However, Knopp's early work (1987, 1990a, 1990b, 1992) is limited by the lack of analysis of how heterosexism determines the rules of capitalist development (1995, 1998). While gay men have access to male privilege via the closet (Gluckman and Reed 1997; Jacobs 1997; Richardson 1998), they face significant income losses due to sexual orientation discrimination (Badgett 1995b). I will show how plans, laws, and regulations guiding urban development assume heterosexuality. Significant resistance to oppression is necessary even within exploitative gay gentrification processes.

Finally, in a work published in the important volume edited by Sandercock (1998) – *Making the Invisible Visible* – Moira Kenney reviews the context of gay and lesbian experience in the city. She begins to relate urban planning history to the important new findings of a whole generation of historians studying pre-Stonewall lesbian and gay communities (for example, see D'Emilio 1983; Bérubé 1990; Faderman 1991; Chauncey 1995, 1996, 1997; Beemyn 1997). These historians point out the existence of many lesbian and gay communities stratified by race and class and point to multiple strategies of resistance (DuBrow 1998). In a later part of this article, I will use material from these histories as well as from geographical and architectural work on queer space to delineate planning as an agent of repression of such space. Kenney (1998) identifies three directions for incorporating lesbian and gay experience within planning history: identification of lesbian and gay planners, a deeper analysis of discrimination fostered by planning, and strategies of resistance and appropriation. By describing how planning works as a heterosexist project, I help explain the reticence of lesbian and gay planners to come out, reveal instruments of discrimination, and begin developing components of an inclusive planning.

Planning as a Heterosexist Project

How does planning lead to heterosexist domination? First, I show an explicit link between the modern ideology of heterosexism and modern urban planning through Patrick Geddes and Lewis Mumford. Their notions of order and disorder related to both sexuality and cities. I then discuss two other dualisms within planning: household/family and public/private. Notions of heterosexual domination expressed explicitly in the Geddes-Mumford link are implied within the planning discourses around these dualisms. Planners developed land use regulations and zoning to protect families as the site of heterosexuality from people with "indulgent lifestyles" (Baar 1992). Lastly, I examine public/private through the lens of new notions of queer space. Queer space challenges the public realm by making private use of public space. Planners work to destroy these queer spaces and render them safe for heterosexuals. Through each of these cases, planning reinforces heterosexist assumptions about life.

Order/disorder

Modern city planning grew out of an impulse "to bring order out of chaos" (Burnham and Bennett [1909] 1993, 1). Chauncey (1995, 137–8), in *Gay New York*, summarizes this rise:

> In the closing decades of the nineteenth century and the opening decades of the twentieth, an extraordinary panoply of groups and individuals organized to reform the urban moral order. Although their efforts rarely focused on the merging gay world,

most of them had a significant effect on its development. Some sought to reconstruct the urban landscape itself in ways that minimize the dissipating effects of urban disorder: reforming the tenements, putting up new residential hotels in which single men and women could lead moral lives, creating parks to reintroduce an element of rural simplicity and natural order to the city, building playgrounds and organizing youth clubs to rescue young people from city streets and gangs, and constructing grand boulevards and public buildings that would inspire a new order in the city itself and command respect for an orderly society.

This movement constructed the heterosexual order of life out of the disorder of the city. This impulse is directly expressed via the writings of Patrick Geddes and Lewis Mumford. In his history of planning, Peter Hall (1988) celebrates Geddes as an early synthesizer of modern planning impulses. Geddes developed the concept of the regional survey leading to the saying "survey before plan" (p. 142). Mumford was a disciple of Geddes. In their writings, there is an explicit link between heterosexuality and planning

Patrick Geddes was more than an early planner. He was trained as a botanist and made significant contributions to biology as well as the emerging disciplines of sociology, planning, and public health. His biological work applied a form of evolutionary theory to sex and reproduction, and he contributed articles on these topics to one of the great editions of the *Encyclopedia Britannica* (Geddes 1886a, 1886b). According to Geddes, the uniting of female and male sex forces "express the highest outcome of the whole activities of the organism – the literal blossoming of the individual life" (Geddes 1886b, 724). While he did not label it, what we would call heterosexuality, Geddes describes as the pinnacle of human existence.

Geddes and his collaborator J. Arthur Thomson wrote a book further developing this evolutionary approach to sexuality and reproduction (Geddes and Thomson 1890). Based on their scientific expertise, they were asked to comment on social aspects of sex in a 1912 pamphlet (Thomson and Geddes 1912). In this work, they emphasize that humans are "social animals" (Thomson and Geddes 1912, 18). They argue that "the complexity of human social organization tends to segregate a large fraction of the population from the normal expression of sex-impulses" (Thomson and Geddes 1912, 20). Yet, we are also rational beings; we can control our environment and control sexuality creating "more normal life-opportunities for its normal members" (Thomson and Geddes 1912, 20). They continue along these lines, arguing for generosity in judgments since

many of our social conditions are dismally abnormal, and are directly provocative of abnormalities in sexual expression. In illustration, we may refer to frequent deficiency in one of the primary needs of family life – namely, room. The crowding together of inmates of both sexes and of various ages is still excessive for well-nigh half the nation, is often hideous and the impossibility of privacy creates situations which are revolting. (p. 24)

They view the rise of single, unattached adults in the city as worse than family overcrowding:

> More subtle, yet more severe and disastrous, provocatives to sexual irregularities than those of family overcrowding alone are those found in those social arrangements which leave large numbers of adults temporarily or permanently unmated. (p. 26)

Yet, their liberalism in judgment extends only to an occasional lapse in behavior. They argue that "sexually vicious habits of mind and body" are "evil and destructive" both to individuals and to society (Thomson and Geddes 1912, 29). They narrowly define "normal sex-expression" and emphasize self-control (Thomson and Geddes 1912, 43). Then, Thomson and Geddes (1912) define what is not normal:

> There are the terrible volumes of sexual pathology. There is sexual hyperaesthesia or the abnormal exaggeration of sexual excitability, an exaggeration all but universal in some measure through all our civilizations. There is auto-eroticism or masturbation, which often wrecks both body and mind; there are loathsome and sinister perversions of the attractions between the sexes and repulsive fleshly attractions between those of the same sex; there is the nemesis of uncontrolled sexuality which may make an old man a satyr or a terror to little children; and if these and other hells be escaped by the persistently uncontrolled, there is that of a mind that is preoccupied with lustful thoughts and pictures, and of an eye which betrays itself in its lecherousness. (p. 44)

They refer to masturbation and homosexuality in the same context as pedophiles and pornography. They see all of these "perversions" as abnormal and in need of individual and societal control. While not labeled as such, their view of heterosexuality expresses each of Katz's three assumptions of heterosexuality: biological difference, pleasure potential, and procreative necessity.

Thomson and Geddes (1912) promote two forms of control over sexuality. The first is self-control through marriage, morals, and rational thought (p. 45). The second mode of control is social organization through the use of planning in both its social and physical forms. They promote Jane Addams and her settlement house work as capable of producing "real and substantial uplift to the cause of youth and the bettering of cities" (p. 42). They also make explicit mentions of the potential of city planning to improve the conditions that create abnormal sexuality. They lament that the Town Planning Act recently passed by Parliament and the various garden cities schemes have done so little, when the need is so great (p. 25). Planning by providing space and emphasizing rationality creates an order that produces heterosexuality.

Lewis Mumford idolized Geddes. Through the Regional Planning Association of America, Mumford popularized the concept of regional planning along with Geddes's approach to planning (Luccarelli 1995). Mumford himself talks about how Geddes makes the connection between the (heterosexual) order of life and planning. This next passage shows the degree of Mumford's admiration:

The depletion of vitality, the arrest of growth, the domination of the living by the non-living, the persistence of fixity and habit over flexibility and purposive change – against all these forms of disintegration Geddes endlessly battled. Geddes was on the side of life, wherever it was threatened or besieged. Into the piled-up tenement districts of Edinburgh he brought gardens; into the plague ridden streets of Indian cities, he brought cleanliness; into the cram ridden school of verbalistic empaperment he brought the regional survey, which sent the student out into the city and the country-side, seeing with his own eyes the realities behind his academic abstraction; into the movement for sexual development, with which he sympathized, he brought the sense of family, the need for children, the acceptance of mature responsibilities. With the wand of life he tapped the rock and made water flow forth. (Mumford 1944, 384–5)

Like magic, Geddes brought order into cities and the family. Note how Mumford's phrase "the movement for sexual development" encapsulates the assumptions of heterosexuality. Within one sentence, Mumford has connected planning and hetero-sexuality.

When Mumford does address homosexuality, it is connected to death and disorder. In the following passage, he applies his mid-century view to homosexuality as represented in ancient Greece:

In sexual life if love were a purposeless welling forth of appetites, homosexual love might seem as reasonable as heterosexual love – and in turn heterosexual love might become as unashamingly sterile. All the irrationalities of human love, however, move eventually toward a goal more imperative than pleasure: the conception and nurture of children, the perpetuation of the race. The very mechanisms of sex are adapted to that higher reason: the mystery of life itself, seeking its own extension and perpetuation. Even when the love of a man and a woman has no direct biological issue, their passion and their deepening loyalty symbolize and anticipate that final outcome: the triumph of life. And as long as the ancient forms of fertility are not violated, the relationship may be a fruitful and life-exalting one. In Greece the practice of homosexuality and infanticide might seem to have cold reason on their side; yet they were profoundly hostile to life. (Mumford 1944, 24)

According to Mumford, heterosexuality promotes the natural order of things. Each of Katz's three universal heterosexist assumptions operates in this passage. Natural sex differences are referenced in the "adaptive mechanisms of sex." Sex would not have its meaning without its relation to procreation. Procreation as the "triumph of life" defines sex as the site of pleasure. Finally, not only are homosexual practices "purposeless" and "unashamingly sterile," Mumford goes on to put them on the same level as baby killing.

These passages raise questions about other metaphors used by Mumford. In his remarks following the horrors of World War II, the atomic bomb, and the Holocaust, Mumford (1951, 283) makes several references that, while they do not explicitly mention homosexuality and heterosexuality, place the source of the evil on the breaking of the heterosexual order:

The violence and evil of our time have been, when viewed collectively, the work of loveless men: impotent men who lust after sadistic power to conceal their failure as lovers: repressed and frustrated men, lamed by unloving parents, and seeking revenge by taking refuge in a system of thought or a mode of life into which love cannot intrude: at best people whose erotic impulses have been cut off from the normal rhythms of life, self-enclosed atoms of erotic exploit, incapable of assuming the manifold responsibilities of lovers and parents through all stages of life, unwilling to accept the breaks and abstentions of pregnancy, making sexual union itself an obstacle to the other forms of social union that flow out of family life.

This passage has an unspoken homophobic bent within the writing. The "normal rhythms of life" fits within Geddes's conception of natural sex difference and male and female function. Geddes saw homosexuality as separated from the natural functions of male and female. This separation might be described as "self-enclosed atoms of erotic exploit." Homosexuality represents sterility and these men become "impotent." Mumford seems to be implying a connection between homosexuality and the disorder created by the evil and violence of our century.

Thus, while planners did not focus on "the emerging gay world," they did focus on explicitly structuring life for heterosexuality. Two of the great historical planners, Geddes and Mumford, saw planning as a means of bringing order into life. They explicitly connected heterosexuality with this order.

Family/household

How did planners create order for heterosexuality? In this next section, I show how planners encouraged the development of land use regulation and zoning that would protect the family. Just as we have to bring order to the city, we must bring order to the family. Thus, arguments for the adoption of single-family zoning speak of protecting the family. Throughout these texts supporting zoning, writers make an unspoken assumption that through marriage, the family becomes the site of natural heterosexuality for procreation and pleasure. In contrast to the single-family home, proponents of single-family zoning see apartments as the site of immoral activity. Apartments contain households. Finally, I show that similar to the unspoken acceptance of Katz's assumptions of heterosexuality, the definition of the family remained unchallenged until the sixties.

Early court cases supporting the application of zoning in cities relied on the same reasoning used by Geddes and Mumford. However, in most of these quotations the underlying purpose of controlling sexuality remains closeted. It is up to us to decode the references. For example, Gellen (1985, 112) quotes a 1925 California Supreme Court decision, *Miller v. Board of Public Works of the City of Los Angeles*:

> ... that justification for residential zoning be nested on the protection of the civic and social value of the American home. The establishment of such districts is for the general welfare because it tends to promote and perpetuate the American home. It is

axiomatic that the welfare and indeed the very existence of a nation depends upon the character and caliber of its citizenry. The character and quality of manhood and womanhood are in large measure the result of home environment.

According to this decision, zoning is necessary to protect the "American home." The judges continue: "with [home] ownership comes stability, the welding together of family ties, and better attention to the raising of children" (p. 113). Home is the site of the family. The judges argue that the family is the source of sex-differentiated human character. These characteristics are "the foundation of good citizenship" and thus contribute to an orderly society (p. 112). With planning, we may influence child development and thereby create heterosexuals.

Planning creates order for heterosexual families. This reasoning led to the Supreme Court's *Euclid v. Ambler* decision in 1926 that institutionalized zoning in the United States. Gellen (1985, 112) notes how Bettman, in his brief submitted on the case, "underscored the deterministic relationship between environment and moral character." According to Bettman's brief,

> the essential object of promoting what might be called orderliness in the layout of cities is not the satisfaction of taste, or aesthetic desires, but rather the promotion of those beneficial effects upon health and morals which come from living in orderly and decent surroundings. ... The man who seeks to place his home for his children in an orderly neighborhood is not motivated so much by considerations of taste or beauty as by the assumption that his children are likely to grow mentally, physically, and morally more healthful in such a neighborhood than in a disorderly, noisy, slovenly, blighted and slumlike neighborhood. (Gellen 1985, 112)

The "moral health of children" in families requires zoning. Following this logic, the Supreme Court ruled in *Euclid v. Ambler* (1926) that "exclusion of buildings devoted to business, trade, etc. from residential districts bears a rational relation to the health and safety of the community." Support for this conclusion was found in the "suppression and prevention of disorder" (*Euclid v. Ambler* 1926). What remains unsaid by the Court is that disorder includes homosexuality. Yet, as I have shown previously, homosexuality was a part of the disorder of the city that planners were aiming to control. With this case, zoning then becomes a legal tool of sexual control.

The approval of zoning went beyond just the development of districts distinguished by land use. Zoning created special areas for single-family buildings. The Supreme Court explicitly targeted apartments in *Euclid v. Ambler*: "the apartment house is a mere parasite, constructed in order to take advantage of the open spaces and attractive surroundings created by the residential character of the district" (Mandelker, Cunningham, and Payne 1995, 86). Once again, there is an unspoken understanding that crowded conditions create socially abnormal development. Yet, the fear of apartments went beyond just crowded conditions but actually included direct issues of social control. Baar (1992) traces the history of this bias against apartments and shows that opposition against apartment buildings began in the 1890s. He finds that opponents of multifamily housing saw apartments as favoring people with "indulgent lifestyles" (p. 41). Objections to apartments went beyond creation of play area for children (Gellen 1985, 111). Apartment living

> encouraged a lifestyle in which women were not home-bound and in which children were exposed to single men and women of different social backgrounds and cultural values. Social workers and housing reformers alike believed that exposure to the lifestyles of the unattached had a detrimental effect on the moral development of young children, especially girls. (Gellen 1985, 111)

Following this line of reasoning, the Ohio Lower Appellate Court ruled in *Morris v. East Cleveland* in favor of single-family zoning. Part of the court's reasoning was that in apartment houses, "the number of people passing in and out render immoral practices therein more difficult of detection and suppression" (Baar 1992, 45). Not only was the single-family house the designated site of heterosexuality, planners suppressed apartments as sites of difference. Apartments housed indulgent, immoral people. Apartments prevented surveillance of residents' activities. Apartments housed households not families.

After the legal foundations of planning were established, suburbs, the site of new development, also became the sites of planning practice. Fishman (1987) argues that suburbs developed as sites of exclusion based on class. Post-World War I suburbs developed with the principles and tools of planning formed a response to the same "bourgeois anxieties" that led to late-nineteenth-century railway suburbs. Practices such as large-lot zoning and deed restrictions were used to control apartments and thus control households. Apartment houses could legally be excluded from these new communities. Apartments then were an urban phenomena while single-family homes were suburban. Thus, suburban development excludes on the basis of sexual orientation as well as class.

The legalistic family/household distinction did not arise until the 1960s (Mandelker, Cunningham, and Payne 1995). At this time, "many municipalities began to change the definition of family in their ordinances to exclude or limit the number of person unrelated by blood, marriage or adoption who might constitute a family for zoning purposes" (Mandelker, Cunningham, and Payne 1995, 260). Alternative household formations became a more public phenomena at this time, and communities responded to limit their spread into single-family districts (*Village of Belle Terre v. Borass 1974*). People with little control, those with indulgent lifestyles, still could live in apartments. By design, these apartments were separated from the real families in their single-family homes. Thus, what emerges as a "nonfamily" household in the sixties was closeted before that time. As gays and lesbians fight for family rights of custody, adoption, and marriage, the outlines of the unspoken limits of family become more defined. By raising private "family" issues publicly, lesbians and gays challenge the modern heterosexual order imposed by planning.

Public/private

In my urban design class, someone characterized planning as the study of the spaces between the buildings. While the speaker meant to illustrate the relevance of a figure ground drawing, he also meant that planning deals with mediating the space between the public, represented by the street, and the private, represented by the interior of the building. Inside the building, if it is a single-family home, lies the family – a heterosexual space protected as I have shown by land use regulations developed by planners. Outside lies the public realm. Lesbians and gay men make private use of this public space. In this next section, I examine how lesbians and gay men have used public space. Planning and public authorities respond to these uses through benign repression such as rezoning and outright closure of spaces or through stronger forms of repression including arrest and imprisonment of the offending parties. The advent of the lesbian and gay rights movement has reduced this repression. Yet, the dichotomy of private versus public still exists in the law. The semilegal status of homosexuality threatens the stability of any lesbian or gay community formed within a city.

The industrial city was characterized by crowding both in public and private. Anonymity became possible. People traveled to the cities to find work. They were functionally alienated from the institutions of land, household production, and extended family relations that marked precapitalist development (D'Emilio 1993). The city attracted large numbers of people either single or temporarily single. The new immigrant faced alienation in the workplace but also at home. Immigrants were separated from traditional culture and social norms all in an alien space. Diversions arose to entertain the masses. Mumford (1938, 267) characterized them as "the poisons of vicarious vitality." He goes on "to sum up these diversions":

> to counteract an intolerable preoccupation with arithmetical abstractions and mechanical instruments, an almost equally abstract interest in the stomach and the sexual organs, divorced from their organic relations. To counteract boredom and isolation, mass spectacles: to make up for biological inferiority, a series of collective games and exhibitions, based on withering specializations of the body. In short the metropolis is rank with forms of negative vitality. (p. 271)

Recent work by lesbian and gay historians shows the existence of gay culture at the turn of the century. In his history of gay New York, Chauncey (1995) describes a gay subculture operating out of taverns and on the streets of the city itself. He goes on to tie regulation of this culture to reform efforts inclusive of planning:

> The policing of gay culture in the early twentieth century was closely tied to the efforts of these societies to police working-class culture more generally. The societies' efforts to control the streets and tenements and to eliminate the saloon and brothel were predicated on a vision of an ideal social order centered in the family. (Chauncey 1995, 138–9)

What we now see as representative of gay culture, Mumford saw as a "form of negative vitality." Planning laws and procedures regulate streets, tenements, and building uses to limit these forms.

Why then was planning necessary to keep the heterosexual order? Gay men, and to some extent lesbians too, used public space for their own private purposes. Faderman (1991) shows how working-class women first entered saloons, thereby taking advantage of public amusements. Working-class lesbians formed the nucleus of early lesbian bar culture. Faderman shows other patterns of lesbian space within women's social networks, softball teams, same-sex colleges, bohemia, and hobo life. Gay men met each other on the street, in parks, and in public areas (Chauncey 1996). This pattern repeated itself in multiple urban areas. For example, Johnson (1997) describes the rise of "Fairytown" in Chicago. Gays adapted their strategies to the place. Within the car-oriented society of Flint, gays cruised a circuit in their cars (Retzloff 1997). In times of greater repression, such use of public space became coded:

> Given the risks involved in asserting a visible presence in the streets, most gay people chose not to challenge the conventions of heterosexual society so directly. But they resisted and undermined them nevertheless by developing tactics that allowed them to identify and communicate with one another without alerting hostile outsiders to what they were doing. … Other gay men developed codes that were intelligible only to other men familiar with the subculture. (Chauncey 1995, 187)

The use of slang or the wearing of a certain type of tic or scarf signaled "sisterhood" to other gay men. Thus, public space becomes queer space. When society increases repression, these spaces become more fluid, as gays adopt codes to define space rather than using place.

Society responded to overt expression of homosexuality through repression. There was always the threat of violence. More lawful means of repression also existed. Laws passed to control prostitution were used against gay men. Society made it illegal for gay men to cruise. New York went as far to make "degeneracy" a crime in 1923. The law defined degeneracy as "frequenting about any public place soliciting men for the purpose of committing a crime against nature or other lewdness" (Chauncey 1995, 185–6). Over the years, hundreds of men were arrested and charged with this crime.

Planning provided the means of another type of repression. In her classic, *The Death and Life of Great American Cities*, Jane Jacobs (1961) shows how planning acts to repress these public expressions of homosexuality. In her section on parks, she uses the four squares of Penn's Philadelphia to illustrate her point about how the activities at the edge of the park determined the successfulness of the park. As Jacobs points out, one of these parks was used by nonheterosexuals:

> Several decades ago, Washington Square became Philadelphia's pervert park, to the point where it was shunned by office lunchers and was an unimaginable vice and crime problem to park workers and police. In the mid-1950s it was torn up, closed for more than a year, and redesigned. In this process, its users were dispersed, which was the intent. (pp. 92–3)

The dictionary still defines *pervert* as referring to people who prefer anything other than "normal coitus" (Merriam-Webster, Inc. 1986). No doubt, in 1961. Jacobs' use of *perverts* refers to gay men. In contrast, Chauncey (1995, 180) describes in more enlightened language how gay men use parks:

> Cruising parks and streets provided many young men and newcomers to the city with a point of entry into the rest of the gay world, which was sometimes hidden from men looking for it by the same codes and subterfuges that protected it from hostile straight intrusions.

This passage further explains why the city of Philadelphia had to act in Jacobs' example. Cruisy parks provided an entrance point to the city within the closet. Through meeting other gay people, codes were taught and secrets revealed. Gays recruited in parks. This public behavior threatens the heterosexual order. As Jacobs shows, cities respond to this threat by shutting down the place.

Furthermore, the repression is not restricted to the public sphere. In many states, it is illegal to break the heterosexual order in private. Sodomy laws regulate private behavior. However, married people have a right to privacy established in a series of cases following *Griswold v. Connecticut* (Garrow 1994). Based on these precedents, laws regulating heterosexual sodomy (within marriage) have been overturned. In 1986, the Supreme Court in *Bowers v. Hardwick* reaffirmed the right to regulate private homosexual behavior. The Court ruled "that no connection between family, marriage, or procreation on the one hand and homosexual activity on the other has been demonstrated" (Garrow 1994, 663). The Court's ruling again reaffirmed the central assumptions of heterosexuality with family denoting natural sex difference, marriage revealing the allowed site of pleasure, and procreation explicitly expressed. Privacy only exists within heterosexuality.

This lack of basic privacy rights has public implications. Present repression sometimes combines land use regulations forbidding uses prohibited by law with references to constitutional sodomy laws prohibiting homosexual behavior. In places with sodomy laws, some view being openly queer as living with intent to break the law. These people have legal justification then to discriminate in the areas of accommodation, employment, housing, and land use. Without a gay rights law, such discrimination is legal (Hunter, Michaelson, and Stoddard 1992). In such places, zoning may be used to prevent lesbian and gay businesses. Thus, regulation of private behavior has public consequences within the realm of planning.

This repression has dire implications for lesbians and gay men. Before the advent of gay rights laws, "every evening spent in a gay setting, every contact with another gay man or lesbian, every sexual intimacy carried a reminder of the criminal penalties that could be exacted at any moment" (D'Emilio 1983, 49). At the height of the repression in the fifties, thousands lost their jobs and thousands were kicked out of the military (D'Emilio 1983). This repression still resonates today. Lesbians who experienced the repression of the 1950s "have little faith that the progress that has come about through the gay liberation movement is here to stay" (Faderman 1991,

157). The institution of the closet developed as a survival strategy for lesbians and gays. Fear of reprisals still keeps many lesbians and gays in the closet.

The atmosphere of repression also affected the development of lesbian and gay institutions. Lesbians and gays used public spaces on the edges of society where the mainstream would not notice. Jacobs notes this tendency in 1961:

> The perverts who completely took over Philadelphia's Washington Square for several decades were a manifestation of this city behavior in microcosm. They did not kill off a vital and appreciated park. They did not drive out respectable users. They moved into an abandoned place and entrenched themselves. As this is being written, the unwelcome users have successfully been cleared away to find other vacuums, but this act has still not supplied the park with a sufficient sequence of welcome users. (p. 98)

The development of institutions provides a fixity to otherwise fluid spaces created by just queer uses of public space. Faderman (1991, 161) describes the lesbian bar as a dark secret nighttime place usually located in dismal areas. Other locations for the lesbian and gay institutions include bohemian neighborhoods such as Greenwich Village and Harlem of the 1920s (Chauncey 1995). The seeking out of edge spaces and "border vacuums" in lesbian and gay community formation goes beyond multiplying the rent gap and gentrification. It is connected to a process of private appropriation of public space (Bell 1995; Binnie 1995). Creating fixity also requires making public what was private. Someone has to come out of the closet to develop a queer institution. Often, these institutions and businesses are treated as "adult" establishments. Planning processes with a strict separation of public and private enforce heterosexist notions of public and private.

I have shown how notions of public and private work differently depending on sexual orientation. Heterosexuals have a right to privacy. Heterosexual notions of the public realm emphasize separations of public and private. Planning acts on these notions in redevelopment projects and in developing and enforcing land use regulations. Planning empowers heterosexuality. "Where there is power, there is resistance" (Foucault 1976, 95). Creating an inclusive planning means challenging the strict separation between the two spheres. Lesbian and gays within planning live out this challenge when they "come out." Each act of coming out is a form of resistance.

Conclusion: A Queer Inclusive Planning?

Urban planning produces structures that enforce and reinforce heterosexuality. Geddes and Mumford explicitly saw planning as a means of social regulation of sexuality. The legal justification for zoning and the resultant forms of suburban development explicitly promote heterosexuality. These laws, regulations, and processes continue to operate today even in a liberal state with a gay rights law such as New Jersey. Further work needs to address the role of heterosexuality in other planning dualisms such as production/reproduction and rural/urban. Knopp (1998) has begun this project in his latest work by addressing the interplay between class and sexual orientation within cities. New work in cultural geography also expands on these ideas (Nast and Pile 1998).

The heterosexist project of planning raises implications for lesbian and gay politics. The battle for lesbian and gay rights starts with breaking the silence and coming out. Yet, coming out does not change the heterosexual structures guiding urbanization and community formation. One popular writer on gay politics, Michelangelo Signorile, treats urbanization as a force independent of sexual orientation. He emphasizes gay men's own self-oppression and extols a suburban ideal. He goes as far as to say that "it's true that most gay men in urban America are not living a life of enforced heterosexuality" (Signorile 1997, 27). This view minimizes the extent of heterosexual structuralization of place. The city organizes perceptions, regulates social relations between people, and forms the categories among which we end up divided (Grosz 1998). The places in which "out" gay men live are still structured for heterosexuals. Instead, lesbians and gays need to ask as the feminists did in the late seventies, What would the inclusive city look like (Hayden 1981)? By asking this question, we might begin to develop new structures inclusive of lesbians and gay men.

Planning as a queer inclusive project

What would queer inclusive planning look like? Richard Sennett (1970) described some of the possibilities in his book *The Uses of Disorder*. In the book, he traces the development of a myth of "communal solidarity" that is behind many modern planning measures (p. 48). Instead of building on measures that create exclusion, he wants to create urban areas with a "multiplicity of contact points" (p. 57). Only dense urban areas have the relative instability required to keep up social mixing (p. 152). Sennett wants to increase complexity and conflict in the city, whereby the only solution is common engagement and social interaction (pp. 147–8). Finally, he calls for a reduction in "family intensity" hoping to draw people into interaction outside of familial and protected surroundings (pp. 168–9). It is not enough to create spaces that are separate but equal. Rather, we must try to create spaces of interaction.

Feminist writers provide some of the detailed programs to achieve the inclusive city (Sandercock and Forsyth 1992; Ritzdorf 1993; Sandercock 1998). Ritzdorf (1986, 26) calls for changes in zoning ordinances such as the redefinition of family, the allowance of work at home, the adoption of accessory apartment ordinances, and the allowance of day care in all zones. Hayden (1984, 204) reexamines designs for congregate housing as a way to reorganize life to empower women. She also calls for dividing large single-family homes into duplexes and triplexes (Hayden 1981, 183). Finally, Stacey (1996) explicitly redefines family to include lesbians and gays. According to Stacey. "the postmodern family condition of pluralism and flexibility should represent a democratic opportunity in which individuals' shared capacities, desires and conviction could govern the character of their gender, sexual and family relationship" (p. 37). This opportunity would be partially accomplished by the extension of marriage rights to lesbians and gays (p. 107).

We must also address the myths of heterosexuality. For example, many lesbians and gay men are parents. Challenging myths requires deconstruction, though deconstruction alone is not enough. We must recognize difference and give it equal status (Fraser 1997). Recognition implies something more than tolerance (Sedgwick 1993). This recognition challenges our conceptions of the public realm. An inclusive planning would treat lesbians and gays as full citizens (Richardson 1998). Planning is a constructive activity (Fainstein and Fainstein 1996). We have the tools to begin the inclusive project.

Notes

1   Many writers have noted identities based on same-sex relationships in history and in traditional societies (Trumbach 1977; Boswell 1980; Halperin 1989). The dynamics of these identities differ from lesbian and gay identities within modern capitalist societies (D'Emilio 1993).
2   This concept of a project is similar to DeLauretis's (1987) concept of "technology," when she writes about film as a technology of gender. Planning can also be seen as a technology of sex.
3   Sociological and cultural studies slowly began appearing in the seventies (see, for example, Humphreys 1970; Harry 1974; Katz 1976; Weeks 1977; Levine 1979). Many of these studies form the basis of what became lesbian and gay studies and queer studies.

References

Adler, S., and J. Brenner. 1992. Gender and space: Lesbians and gay men in the city. *International Journal of Urban and Regional Research* 16 (1): 24–33.

Altman, D. 1982. *The homosexualization of America, the Americanization of the homosexual.* New York: St Martin's.

Anderson, R. M. 1968. *American law of zoning.* Rochester, NY: Lawyer's Cooperative Publishing.

Baar, K. 1992. The national movement to halt the spread of multifamily housing, 1890–1926. *Journal of the American Planning Association* 58 (1): 39–48.

Badgett, M. V. L. 1995a. Gender, sexuality and sexual orientation: All in the feminist family? *Feminist Economics* 1 (1): 121–39.

Badgett, M. V. L. 1995b. The wage effects of sexual orientation discrimination. *Industrial and Labour Relations Review* 48 (4): 726–35.

Barnett, B. M. 1993. Invisible southern black women leaders in the civil rights movement: The triple constraints of gender, race and class. *Gender & Society* 7 (2): 162–82.

Beemyn, B., ed. 1997. *Creating a place for ourselves.* New York: Routledge.

Bell, D. 1995. Perverse dynamics, sexual citizenship and the transformation of intimacy. In *Mapping desire,* edited by D. Bell and G. Valentine, 304–17. New York: Routledge.

Berrill, K. T. 1990. Anti-gay violence and victimization in the United States: An overview. *Journal of Interpersonal Violence* 5 (3): 274–94.

Berrill, K. T. 1992. Anti-gay violence and victimization in the United States: An overview. In *Hate crimes: Confronting violence against lesbians and gay men,* edited by G. Herek and K. Berrill. Newbury Park, CA: Sage.

Bérubé, A. 1990. *Coming out under fire: The history of gay men and women in World War Two.* New York: Free Press.

Binnie, J. 1995. Trading places. In *Mapping desire,* edited by D. Bell and G. Valentine, 182–99. New York: Routledge.

Boswell, J. 1980. *Christianity, social tolerance, and homosexuality.* Chicago: University of Chicago Press.

Bouthillette, A.-M. 1997. Queer and gendered housing. In *Queers in space,* edited by G. B. Ingram et al., 213–32. Seattle, WA: Bay Press.

Bowers v. Hardwick, 478 U.S. 186 (1986).

Buruham, D. H., and E. H. Bennett. [1909] 1993. *Plan of Chicago.* New York: Princeton Architectural Press.

Castells, M. 1983. *The city and the grassroots.* Berkeley: University of California Press.

Castells, M., and K. Murphy. 1982. Cultural identity and urban structure: The spatial organization of San Francisco's gay community. In *Urban policy under capitalism,* edited by N. Fainstein and S. Fainstein, 243–57. Beverly Hills, CA: Sage.

Chauncey, G. 1995. *Gay New York, gender, urban culture and the making of the gay male world, 1890–1940.* New York: Basic Books.

Chauncey, G. 1996. Privacy could only be had in public: Gay uses of the street. In *Stud, architectures of masculinity,* edited by J. Sanders, 224–67. New York: Princeton Architectural Press.

Chauncey, G. 1997. The policed: Gay men's strategies of everyday resistance in Times Square. In *Creating a place for ourselves,* edited by B. Beemyn, 9–25. New York: Routledge.

DeLauretis, T. 1987. The technology of gender. In *Technologies of gender. Essays on theory. Film and fiction,* edited by T. DeLauretis. Bloomington: Indiana University Press.

D'Emilio, J. 1983. *Sexual politics, sexual communities: The making of a homosexual minority in the United States.* Chicago: University of Chicago Press.

D'Emilio, J. 1993. Capitalism and gay identity. In *The lesbian and gay studies reader,* edited by H. Abelove et al., 467–76. New York: Routledge.

D'Emilio, J., and E. B. Freedman. 1988. *Intimate matters, a history of sexuality in America.* New York: Perennial Library.

Duberman, M. 1991. *About time, exploring the gay past.* Expanded and rev. ed. New York: Meridan.

DuBrow, G. L. 1998. Feminist and multicultural perspectives on historic preservation planning. In *Making the invisible visible, a multicultural planning history,* edited by L. Sandercock, 57–77. Berkeley: University of California Press.

Elder, G. S. 1998. The South African body politic: Space, race and heterosexuality. In *Places through the body,* edited by H. J. Nast and S. Pile, 153–64. New York: Routledge.

Escoffier, J. 1997. The political economy of the closet: Notes toward an economic history of gay and lesbian life before Stonewall. In *Homo economics, capitalism community and lesbian and gay life,* edited by A. Gluckman and B. Reed, 123–34. New York: Routledge.

Euclid v. Ambler, 272 U.S. 365 (1926).

Faderman, L. 1991. *Odd girls and twilight lovers.* New York: Penguin.

Fainstein, S., and N. Fainstein. 1996. City planning and political values: An updated view. In *Readings in planning theory,* edited by S. Campbell and S. Fainstein, 265–87. Malden, MA: Blackwell.

Fishman, R. 1987. *Bourgeois utopias: The rise and fall of suburbia.* New York: Basic Books.

Flyvbjerg, B. 1998. *Rationality and power: Democracy in practice.* Chicago: University of Chicago Press.

Fogelsong, R. 1986. *Planning the capitalist city.* Princeton, NJ: Princeton University Press.

Forsyth, A. 1997. Out in the valley. *International Journal of Urban and Regional Research* 21 (1): 38–61.

Foucault, M. 1976. *The history of sexuality*. Translated by Robert Hurley. 1978. New York: Vintage.

Fraser, N. 1997. Justice as parity of participation. Talk given at Rutgers University, November, New Brunswick, New Jersey.

Garrow, D. J. 1994. *Liberty and sexuality*. New York: Macmillan.

Geddes, P. 1886a. Reproduction. In *Encyclopedia Britannica*, 9th ed., vol. 20, 413–22. New York: Scribner.

Geddes, P. 1886b. Sex. In *Encyclopedia Britannica*, 9th ed., vol. 21, 720–24. New York, NY: Scribner.

Geddes, P., and J. A. Thomson. 1890. *The evolution of sex*. New York: Henry Holt.

Gellen, M. 1985. *Accessory apartments in single-family housing*. New Brunswick, NJ: Center for Urban Policy Research.

Gibson-Graham, J. K. 1998. Queer(y)ing globalization. In *Places through the body*, edited by H. J. Nast and S. Pile, 23–11. New York: Routledge.

Gluckman, A., and B. Reed, eds. 1997. *Homo economics, capitalism community and lesbian and gay life*. New York: Routledge.

Grosz, E. 1998. Bodies-cities. In *Places through the body*, edited by H. J. Nast and S. Pile, 42–51. New York: Routledge.

Hall, P. G. 1988. *Cities of tomorrow: An intellectual history of urban planning and design in the twentieth century*. Oxford, UK: Basil Blackwell.

Halperin, D. 1989. *One hundred years of homosexuality and other essays on Greek love*. New York: Routledge.

Harry, J. 1974. Urbanization and the gay life. *Journal of Sex Research* 10 (3): 238–47.

Hayden, D. 1981. What would a non-sexist city be like? In *Women and the American city*, edited by C. Stimpson. Chicago: University of Chicago Press.

Hayden, D. 1984. *Redesigning the American dream*. New York: Norton.

Hooper, B. 1998. The poem of male desire. In *Making the invisible visible, a multicultural planning history*, edited by L. Sandercock. 227–54. Berkeley: University of California Press.

Humphreys, L. 1970. *Tearoom trade: Impersonal sex in public spaces*. Chicago: Aldine.

Hunter, N. D., S. E. Michaelson, and T. B. Stoddard. 1992. *The rights of lesbians and gay men* (an ACLU handbook). 3d ed. Carbondale: Southern Illinois University Press.

Jacobs, J. 1961. *The death and life of great American cities*. New York: Random House.

Jacobs, M. P. 1997. Do gay men have a stake in male privilege? In *Homo economics, capitalism community and lesbian and gay life*, edited by A. Gluckman and B. Reed, 165–84. New York: Routledge.

Johnson, D. K. 1997. The kids of Fairytown. In *Creating a place for ourselves*, edited by B. Beemyn, 97–113. New York: Routledge.

Katz, J. N. 1976. *Gay American history*. New York: Thomas Crowell.

Katz, J. N. 1995. *The invention of heterosexuality*. New York: Plume.

Kenney, M. 1998. Remember, Stonewall was a riot: Understanding gay and lesbian experience in the city. In *Making the invisible visible, a multicultural planning history*, edited by L. Sandercock, 120–32. Berkeley: University of California Press.

Knopp, L. 1987. Social theory, social movements and public policy: Recent accomplishments of the gay and lesbian movements in Minneapolis, Minnesota. *International Journal of Urban and Regional Research* 11 (2): 243–61.

Knopp, L. 1990a. Exploiting the rent gap: The theoretical significance of using illegal appraisal schemes to encourage gentrification in New Orleans. *Urban Geography* 11 (1): 48–64.

Knopp, L. 1990b. Some theoretical implications of gay involvement in the urban land market. *Political Geography Quarterly* 9 (4): 337–58.

Knopp, L. 1992. Sexuality and the spatial dynamics of capitalism. *Environment and Planning D: Society and Space* 10: 651–69.

Knopp, L. 1995. Sexuality and urban space. In *Mapping desire*, edited by D. Bell and G. Valentine, 149–61. New York: Routledge.

Knopp, L. 1998. Sexuality and urban space, gay male identity politics in the United States, the United Kingdom and Australia. In *Cities of difference*, edited by R. Fincher and J. M. Jacobs, 149–76. New York: Guilford.

Lauria, M., and L. Knopp. 1985. Toward an analysis of the role of gay communities in the urban renaissance. *Urban Geography* 1(2): 152–69.

Levine, M. 1979. Gay ghetto. *Journal of Homosexuality* 4: 363–77.

Luccarelli, M. 1995. *Lewis Mumford and the ecological region*. New York: Guilford.

Mandelker, D. R., R. A. Cunningham, and J. M. Payne. 1995. *Planning and control of land development*, 4th ed. Charlottesville, VA: Michie Law Publishers.

Merriam-Webster, Inc. 1986. *Webster's ninth new collegiate dictionary*. Springfield, MA: Merriam-Webster, Inc.

Mumford, L. 1938. *The culture of cities*. New York: Harcourt Brace.

Mumford, L. 1944. *The condition of man*. New York: Harcourt Brace.

Mumford, L. 1951. *The conduct of life*. New York: Harcourt Brace.

Nast, H. J., and S. Pile, eds. 1998. *Places through the body*. New York: Routledge.

Omi, M., and H. Winant. 1994. *Racial formation in the United States*. New York: Routledge.

Peake, D. 1993. Race and sexuality, challenging the patriarchal structuring of urban social space. *Environment and Planning D: Society and Space* 11: 415–32.

Planet Out. 1997. E-mail news service of 11/11/97.

Plant, R. 1986. *The pink triangle: The Nazi war against homosexuals*. New York: Holt.

Retzloff, T. 1997. Cars and bars: Assembling gay men in postwar Flint Michigan. In *Creating a place for ourselves*, edited by B. Beemyn. 224–52. New York: Routledge.

Rich, A. [1982] 1993. Compulsory heterosexuality and lesbian existence. In *The lesbian and gay studies reader*, edited by H. Abelove et al., 227–54. New York: Routledge.

Richardson, D. 1998. Sexuality and citizenship. *Sociology* 32 (1): 83–100.

Ritzdorf, M. 1986. Women and the city: Land use and zoning. *Urban Resources* 3 (2): 23–27.

Ritzdorf, M. 1993. The fairy's tale, teaching planning and public policy in a different voice. *Journal of Planning Education and Research* 12 (2): 99–110.

Rubin, G. 1992. Thinking sex: Notes for a radical theory of the politics of sexuality. In *Pleasure and Danger: Exploring female sexuality*, edited by C. Vance, 267–319. New York: Routledge.

Rothenberg, T. 1995. "And she told two friends" lesbian creating urban social space. In *Mapping desire*, edited by D. Bell and G. Valentine, 165–81. New York: Routledge.

Sandercock, L., ed. 1998. *Making the invisible visible, a multicultural planning history*. Berkeley: University of California Press.

Sandercock, L., and A. Forsyth. 1992. Gender: A new agenda for planning theory. *Journal of the American Planning Association*, 58(1): 49–59.

Sedgwick, E. K. 1990. *Epistemology of the closet*. Berkeley: University of California Press.

Sedgwick, E. K. 1993. How to bring your kids up gay. In *Fear of a queer planet*, edited by M. Warner, 69–81. Minneapolis: University of Minnesota Press.

Sennett, R. 1970. *The uses of disorder: Personal identity and city life*. New York: Norton.

Signorile, M. 1991. *Queer in America*. New York: HarperCollins.

Signorile, M. 1997. *Life outside*. New York: HarperCollins.

Stacey, J. 1996. *In the name of the family*. Boston: Beacon.

Thomas, J. M. 1994. Planning history and the black urban experience: Linkage and contemporary implications. *Journal of Planning Education and Research* 14 (1): 1–14.

Thomson, J. A., and P. Geddes. 1912. *Problems of sex*. New York: Moffet Yard.

Trumbach, R. 1977. London's sodomites: Homosexual behavior and western culture in the eighteenth century. *Journal of Social History* 11: 10–34.

Valentine, G. 1993a. Desperately seeking Susan: A geography of lesbian friendships. *Area* 25 (2): 109–21.

Valentine, G. 1993b. (Hetero)sexing space: Lesbian perceptions and experiences of everyday spaces. *Environment and Planning A* 11 (4): 395–412.

Valentine, G. 1995. Out and about. Geographies of lesbian landscapes. *International Journal of Urban and Regional Research* 19 (1): 96–107.

Village of Belle Terre v. Borass, 416 U.S. 1 (1974).

Warner, M., ed. 1993. *Fear of a queer planet*. Minneapolis: University of Minnesota Press.

Weeks, J. 1977. *Coming out: Homosexual politics in Britain from the nineteenth century to the present*. New York: Quartet Books.

Wilson, E. 1992 *The sphinx in the city: Urban life, the control of disorder, and women*. Berkeley: University of California Press.

Wirka, S. M. 1998. City planning for girls: Exploring the ambiguous nature of women's planning history. In *Making the invisible visible, a multicultural planning history*, edited by L. Sandercock, 150–62. Berkeley: University of California Press.

Wolfe, M. 1992. Invisible women in invisible places: Lesbians, lesbian bars, and the social production of people/environment relationships. *Architecture and Behavior* 8 (2): 137–50.

Yiftachel, O. 1998. Planning and social control: Exploring the dark side. *Journal of Planning Literature* 12 (4): 395–420.

Michael Frisch, "Planning as a Heterosexist Project," *Journal of Planning Education and Research* 21 (3) (2001) pp. 254–66. Copyright © 2001 by Sage Publications.
Reprinted by permission of Sage Publications.

VI

Planning Goals

Justice, Conflict, and the Right to the City

Introduction

This part includes four readings on the divergent priorities of planning: sustainability, planning ethics, community participation through discursive politics, and preserving the public interest embodied in public places. The authors challenge prevailing assumptions embedded in received models of public policies, priorities, and places. Each addresses a shortcoming of the traditional, rational comprehensive model of planning, whether it is its simplistic notion of democratic public spaces, its lack of subtlety about ethical conflicts, its presumption of objective technical expert knowledge, or its shortcomings in dealing with the complex challenge of sustainable development.

We begin the part with a discussion of the growing commitment to sustainability development in planning. In "Green Cities, Growing Cities, Just Cities? Urban Planning and the Contradictions of Sustainable Development," Campbell questions whether the idea of sustainability is a useful rallying cry for the urban planning profession. Its broad promises attract a wide and hopeful following, but also undercut its strategic credibility. The remarkable consensus in favor of the idea is encouraging but also reason for skepticism, since sustainability can mean many things to many people without requiring commitment to any specific policies. The danger is that in the end, though all will endorse the principle of sustainability, few will actually practice it. The result would be simply superficial, feel-good solutions: by merely adding "sustainable" to existing planning documents (sustainable zoning, sustainable economic development, sustainable transportation planning, sustainable housing, and so on), this would create the illusion that we are actually doing sustainable planning. (This is reminiscent of the addition of the term "comprehensive" to planning 50 years ago – or "strategic" planning in the 1980s.)

Readings in Planning Theory, Third Edition. Edited by Susan S. Fainstein and Scott Campbell.
Editorial material and organization © 2012 Blackwell Publishing Ltd.
Published 2012 by Blackwell Publishing Ltd.

The author argues for a broader definition of sustainability. He develops the idea of the "planner's triangle" to distinguish the field's three fundamental goals – economic development, environmental protection, and social justice – and more importantly, to articulate the resulting conflicts over property, resources, and development. At the theoretical center of this triangle lies the sustainable city, but the path to this elusive center is neither direct nor simple; instead, as the struggle for sustainability becomes more advanced, it will also become more sharply contentious, since it will involve increasingly explicit and sobering trade-offs between interest groups in society.

The next reading is not a conventional academic essay on planning theory, but instead the official AICP "Code of Ethics and Professional Conduct." The American Institute of Certified Planners (AICP), part of the American Planning Association (APA), adopted this version of the code in 2005 and further revised it in 2009. Not all planners, or even all APA members, are subject to the code. Instead, it applies specifically to planners certified under AICP. That said, the code does put forth a concise, explicit statement to guide planners through ethical and professional dilemmas. As with the old (1992) code, this current AICP Code places the public interest as the planner's primary obligation. Students of planning theory can learn much by juxtaposing the AICP code with contemporary planning theory literature (contained in this volume and elsewhere). How well does the code engage the key principles and debates within planning theory, such as the tensions between public and private planning, social justice, sustainability, diversity, communicative action, globalization, and conflicting conceptions of the public interest, to name but a few? How does the code – in covering both broad, aspirational principles and more enforceable rules and procedures – tackle the perennial tension within planning between the short-term, administrative demands of the job and long-term, reformist visions of the good city? Such official institutional statements, rewritten and revised over time by many hands and laden with bullet points, may lack the singularly daring, lyrical, polemical voice of a solo visionary planner/intellectual. However, such codes do embody (for better or for worse) a pluralistic agreement, developed through collective compromise, of a profession that seeks to both inspire and regulate its members. Part carrot and part stick, reconciling ambitious reform with cautious professionalism, a professional code of ethics and conduct may be a more accurate measure of the current state of planning thought than any single scholarly statement.

In "Public Policy as Discursive Construct: Social Meaning and Multiple Realities," the political scientist Frank Fischer argues for an alternative approach to public policy that emphasizes the social construction of political values and priorities. Unlike the physical world, the social world is intrinsically bound to meaning, and thus the causal explanation model from the natural sciences is a poor model for the social sciences. That said, though meaning is constructed it is neither arbitrary nor any less "real." Meaning is deeply entrenched in social and political structures. Fischer embraces the term "post-empiricist," not as a rejection of empirical research per se, but instead as a rejection of the uncritical and exclusive acceptance of all empirical measures and observations as incontrovertible and fixed. Resonating with

Davidoff's critique (Chapter 10) of a singular "public interest" through forced consensus, Fischer warns against the mistaken interpretation of existing social values and meanings as universal, a stance that too often leads to the codification of dominant group values as the norm. Social meaning reinforces structures of privilege and inequality.

Fischer's theoretical approach has direct implications for political action. Citizens are not only the products of their social environment, but also potential change agents of this environment. This reflexive relationship is a two-way street of cause and effect: if ideas and norms are socially constructed, then they are not fixed but instead open to reconstruction. Since power and authority are linked to social meaning, then social change requires challenging and changing meaning. If the old progressive motto was "question authority," then the post-empiricist version might be to "question assumptions" (i.e., challenge authority by challenging social meanings). Fischer uses the example of poverty to illustrate how the path to reforming anti-poverty policies lies in changing the meaning and definition of poverty itself. Overall, the larger aspiration is deliberative democracy: providing people the time and space to collectively discuss, construct and change meaning, building upon their diverse range of experiences. This deliberative process goes beyond mere voting (which is bound by preset categories) to enable the public to shape the agendas of political debates and define their own categories.

Serving the public interest, for urban planning, translates into developing and preserving public spaces. Shifting levels of public space serve as a proxy barometer of society's changing commitment to civil society. The loss of public spaces – through privatization, securitization, or excessive regulation – symbolizes the shrinking, fragmentation and privatization of the public interest, with political consequences for civil liberties. In "The Mauling of Public Space," Margaret Kohn examines the threats to public spaces, not by authoritarian regimes, but rather through technology, suburbanization, the automobile culture, and particularly the changing landscape of retail. The title contains an obvious *double entendre*, as Kohn examines the shifting role of the American shopping mall and its displacement of public downtown streets, sidewalks, and plazas as the center of public life. Kohn retraces the shopping mall's emergence through the history of free-speech court cases and the frequent prohibition of political speech in malls. One sees in these cases the shifting lines between public and private spaces – and the tensions between the impulse to create controlled, safe private shopping environments and the public's need for open, messy spaces of access. Too often the courts base their pro-private property decisions on an antiquated understanding of the role of the mall – which originally attracted brief visits for the single purpose of shopping, but have long since been retooled to provide an omnibus shopping-dining-leisure-entertainment experience over many hours. (And with the current emergence of free standing big box retail, arranged along a pedestrian-hostile power center strip, it is even harder to superimpose here the model of the public town square; at least the Victor Gruen-style postwar shopping mall contained vestiges of the old public spaces in the form of a central courtyard and walkways.)

Kohn is troubled by the way that prevailing notions of public speech and civil discourse are not only tethered to old technologies (e.g., the daily newspaper, network television), but also to old forms of public spaces – spaces that are rarely constructed in this era of edge cities, exurban housing estates and self-contained communities. And the public has largely embraced this loss of public openness without a fuss, comfortably enjoying the mall's soothing apolitical calm. For Kohn, the abstract call for "ideal speech situations" is not enough: robust democracies require free political debate – an activity that takes place in lively public spaces. Rather than building consensus, free speech is valuable because it can disrupt the all too comfortable consensus found in these depoliticized spaces.

20

Green Cities, Growing Cities, Just Cities?

Urban Planning and the Contradictions of Sustainable Development

Scott Campbell

In the coming years planners face tough decisions about where they stand on protecting the green city, promoting the economically growing city, and advocating social justice. Conflicts among these goals are not superficial ones arising simply from personal preferences. Nor are they merely conceptual, among the abstract notions of ecological, economic, and political logic, nor a temporary problem caused by the untimely confluence of environmental awareness and economic recession. Rather, these conflicts go to the historic core of planning, and are a leitmotif in the contemporary battles in both our cities and rural areas, whether over solid waste incinerators or growth controls, the spotted owls or nuclear power. And though sustainable development aspires to offer an alluring, holistic way of evading these conflicts, they cannot be shaken off so easily.

This chapter uses a simple triangular model to understand the divergent priorities of planning. My argument is that although the differences are partly due to misunderstandings arising from the disparate languages of environmental, economic, and political thought, translating across disciplines alone is not enough to eliminate these genuine clashes of interest. The socially constructed view of nature put forward here challenges the view of these conflicts as a classic battle of "man versus nature" or its current variation, "jobs versus the environment." The triangular model is then used to question whether sustainable development, the current object of planning's fascination, is a useful model to guide planning practice. I argue that the current concept of sustainability, though a laudable holistic vision, is vulnerable to the same criticism of vague idealism made thirty years ago against comprehensive planning. In this case, the idealistic fascination often builds upon a romanticized view of pre-industrial, indigenous, sustainable cultures – inspiring visions, but also of limited

Readings in Planning Theory, Third Edition. Edited by Susan S. Fainstein and Scott Campbell.
Editorial material and organization © 2012 Blackwell Publishing Ltd.
Published 2012 by Blackwell Publishing Ltd.

modern applicability. Nevertheless, sustainability, if redefined and incorporated into a broader understanding of political conflicts in industrial society, can become a powerful and useful organizing principle for planning. In fact, the idea will be particularly effective if, instead of merely evoking a misty-eyed vision of a peaceful ecotopia, it acts as a lightning rod to focus conflicting economic, environmental, and social interests. The more it stirs up conflict and sharpens the debate, the more effective the idea of sustainability will be in the long run.

The paper concludes by considering the implications of this viewpoint for planning. The triangle shows not only the conflicts, but also the potential complementarity of interests. The former are unavoidable and require planners to act as mediators, but the latter area is where planners can be especially creative in building coalitions between once-separated interest groups, such as labor and environmentalists, or community groups and business. To this end, planners need to combine both their procedural and their substantive skills and thus become central players in the battle over growth, the environment, and social justice.

The Planner's Triangle: Three Priorities, Three Conflicts

The current environmental enthusiasm among planners and planning schools might suggest their innate predisposition to protect the natural environment. Unfortunately, the opposite is more likely to be true: our historic tendency has been to promote the development of cities at the cost of natural destruction: to build cities we have cleared forests, fouled rivers and the air, leveled mountains. That is not the complete picture, since planners also have often come to the defense of nature, through the work of conservationists, park planners, open space preservationists, the Regional Planning Association of America, greenbelt planners, and modern environmental planners. Yet along the economic–ecological spectrum, with Robert Moses and Dave Foreman (of *Earth First!*) standing at either pole, the planner has no natural home, but can slide from one end of the spectrum to the other; moreover, the midpoint has no special claims to legitimacy or fairness.

Similarly, though planners often see themselves as the defenders of the poor and of socio-economic equality, their actions over the profession's history have often belied that self-image (Harvey 1985). Planners' efforts with downtown redevelopment, freeway planning, public–private partnerships, enterprise zones, smokestack-chasing and other economic development strategies don't easily add up to equity planning. At best, the planner has taken an ambivalent stance between the goals of economic growth and economic justice.

In short, the planner must reconcile not two, but at least three conflicting interests: to "grow" the economy, distribute this growth fairly, and in the process not degrade the ecosystem. To classify contemporary battles over environmental racism, pollution-producing jobs, growth control, etc., as simply clashes between economic growth and environmental protection misses the third issue, of social justice. The "jobs versus environment" dichotomy (e.g., the spotted owl versus Pacific Northwest

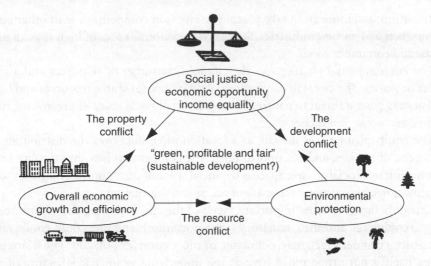

Figure 20.1 The triangle of conflicting goals for planning, and the three associated conflicts. Planners define themselves, implicitly, by where they stand on the triangle. The elusive ideal of sustainable development leads one to the center.

timber jobs) crudely collapses under the "economy" banner the often differing interests of workers, corporations, community members, and the national public. The intent of this chapter's title is to focus planning not only for "green cities and growing cities," but also for "just cities."

In an ideal world, planners would strive to achieve a balance of all three goals. In practice, however, professional and fiscal constraints drastically limit the leeway of most planners. Serving the broader public interest by holistically harmonizing growth, preservation, and equality remains the ideal; the reality of practice restricts planners to serving the narrower interests of their clients, that is, authorities and bureaucracies (Marcuse 1976), despite efforts to work outside those limitations (Hoffman 1989). In the end, planners usually represent one particular goal – planning perhaps for increased property tax revenues, or more open space preservation, or better housing for the poor – while neglecting the other two. Where each planner stands in the triangle depicted in Figure 20.1 defines such professional bias. One may see illustrated in the figure the gap between the call for integrative, sustainable development planning (the center of the triangle) and the current fragmentation of professional practice (the edges). This point is developed later.

The points (corners) of the triangle:
The economy, the environment, and equity

The three types of priorities lead to three perspectives on the city: The economic development planner sees the city as a location where production, consumption, distribution, and innovation take place. The city is in competition with other cities for markets and for new industries. Space is the economic space of highways, market areas, and commuter zones.

The environmental planner sees the city as a consumer of resources and a producer of wastes. The city is in competition with nature for scarce resources and land, and always poses a threat to nature. Space is the ecological space of greenways, river basins, and ecological niches.

The equity planner sees the city as a location of conflict over the distribution of resources, of services, and of opportunities. The competition is within the city itself, among different social groups. Space is the social space of communities, neighborhood organizations, labor unions: the space of access and segregation.

Certainly there are other important views of the city, including the architectural, the psychological, and the circulatory (transportation); and one could conceivably construct a planner's rectangle, pentagon, or more complex polygon. The triangular shape itself is not propounded here as the underlying geometric structure of the planner's world. Rather, it is useful for its conceptual simplicity. More importantly, it emphasizes the point that a one-dimensional "man versus environment" spectrum misses the social conflicts in contemporary environmental disputes, such as loggers versus the Sierra Club, farmers versus suburban developers, or fishermen versus barge operators (Reisner 1987; Jacobs 1989; McPhee 1989; Tuason 1993).[1]

Triangle axis 1: The property conflict

The three points on the triangle represent divergent interests, and therefore lead to three fundamental conflicts. The first conflict – between economic growth and equity – arises from competing claims on and uses of property, such as between management and labor, landlords and tenants, or gentrifying professionals and long-time residents. This growth–equity conflict is further complicated because each side not only resists the other, but also needs the other for its own survival. The contradictory tendency for a capitalist, democratic society to define property (such as housing or land) as a private commodity, but at the same time to rely on government intervention (e.g., zoning, or public housing for the working class) to ensure the beneficial social aspects of the same property, is what Richard Foglesong (1986) calls the "property contradiction." This tension is generated as the private sector simultaneously resists and needs social intervention, given the intrinsically contradictory nature of property. Indeed, the essence of property in our society is the tense pulling between these two forces. The conflict defines the boundary between private interest and the public good.

Triangle axis 2: The resource conflict

Just as the private sector both resists regulation of property, yet needs it to keep the economy flowing, so too is society in conflict about its priorities for natural resources. Business resists the regulation of its exploitation of nature, but at the same time needs regulation to conserve those resources for present and future demands. This can be called the "resource conflict." The conceptual essence of natural resources is therefore the tension between their economic utility in industrial society and their ecological utility in the natural environment. This conflict defines the boundary between the developed city and the undeveloped wilderness, which is symbolized by the "city limits." The boundary is not fixed; it is a dynamic and contested boundary between mutually dependent forces.

Is there a single, universal economic–ecological conflict underlying all such disputes faced by planners? I searched for this essential, Platonic notion, but the diversity of examples – water politics in California, timber versus the spotted owl in the pacific Northwest, tropical deforestation in Brazil, park planning in the Adirondacks, greenbelt planning in Britain, to name a few – suggests otherwise. Perhaps there is an *Ur-Konflikt*, rooted in the fundamental struggle between human civilization and the threatening wilderness around us, and expressed variously over the centuries. However, the decision must be left to anthropologists as to whether the essence of the spotted owl controversy can be traced back to Neolithic times. A meta-theory tying all these multifarious conflicts to an essential battle of "human versus nature" (and, once tools and weapons were developed and nature was controlled, "human versus human") – that invites skepticism. In this discussion, the triangle is used simply as a template to recognize and organize the common themes; to examine actual conflicts, individual case studies are used.[2]

The economic–ecological conflict has several instructive parallels with the growth–equity conflict. In the property conflict, industrialists must curb their profit-increasing tendency to reduce wages, in order to provide labor with enough wages to feed, house, and otherwise "reproduce" itself – that is, the subsistence wage. In the resource conflict, the industrialists must curb their profit-increasing tendency to increase timber yields, so as to ensure that enough of the forest remains to "reproduce" itself (Clawson 1975; Beltzer and Kroll 1986; Lee, Field, and Burch 1990). This practice is called "sustained yield," though timber companies and environmentalists disagree about how far the forest can be exploited and still be "sustainable." (Of course, other factors also affect wages, such as supply and demand, skill level, and discrimination, just as lumber demand, labor prices, transportation costs, tariffs, and other factors affect how much timber is harvested.) In both cases, industry must leave enough of the exploited resource, be it human labor or nature, so that the resource will continue to deliver in the future. In both cases, how much is "enough" is also contested.

Triangle axis 3: The development conflict

The third axis on the triangle is the most elusive: the "development conflict," lying between the poles of social equity and environmental preservation. If the property conflict is characterized by the economy's ambivalent interest in providing at least a subsistence existence for working people, and the resource conflict by the economy's ambivalent interest in providing sustainable conditions for the natural environment, the development conflict stems from the difficulty of doing both at once. Environment–equity disputes are coming to the fore to join the older dispute about economic growth versus equity (Paehlke 1994, pp. 349–50). This may be the most challenging conundrum of sustainable development: how to increase social equity and protect the environment simultaneously, whether in a steady-state economy (Daly 1991) or not. How could those at the bottom of society find greater economic opportunity if environmental protection mandates diminished economic growth? On a global scale, efforts to protect the environment might lead to slowed economic growth in many countries, exacerbating the inequalities between rich and poor nations. In effect, the developed nations would be asking the poorer nations to forgo rapid development to save the world from the greenhouse effect and other global emergencies.

This development conflict also happens at the local level, as in resource-dependent communities, which commonly find themselves at the bottom of the economy's hierarchy of labor. Miners, lumberjacks, and mill workers see a grim link between environmental preservation and poverty, and commonly mistrust environmentalists as elitists. Poor urban communities are often forced to make the no-win choice between economic survival and environmental quality, as when the only economic opportunities are offered by incinerators, toxic waste sites, landfills, and other noxious land uses that most neighborhoods can afford to oppose and do without (Bryant and Mohai 1992; Bullard 1990, 1993). If, as some argue, environmental protection is a luxury of the wealthy, then environmental racism lies at the heart of the development conflict. Economic segregation leads to environmental segregation: the former occurs in the transformation of natural resources into consumer products; the latter occurs as the spoils of production are returned to nature. Inequitable development takes place at all stages of the materials cycle.

Consider this conflict from the vantage of equity planning. Norman Krumholz, as the planning director in Cleveland, faced the choice of either building regional rail lines or improving local bus lines (Krumholz et al. 1982). Regional rail lines would encourage the suburban middle class to switch from cars to mass transit; better local bus service would help the inner-city poor by reducing their travel and waiting time. One implication of this choice was the tension between reducing pollution and making transportation access more equitable, an example of how bias toward social inequity may be embedded in seemingly objective transit proposals.

Implications of the Planner's Triangle Model

Conflict and complementarity in the triangle

Though I use the image of the triangle to emphasize the strong conflicts among economic growth, environmental protection, and social justice, no point can exist alone. The nature of the three axial conflicts is mutual dependence based not only on opposition, but also on collaboration.

Consider the argument that the best way to distribute wealth more fairly (i.e., to resolve the property conflict) is to increase the size of the economy, so that society will have more to redistribute. Similarly, we can argue that the best way to improve environmental quality (i.e., to resolve the resource conflict) is to expand the economy, thereby having more money with which to buy environmental protection. The former is trickle-down economics; can we call the latter "trickle-down environmentalism"? One sees this logic in the conclusion of the Brundtland Report: "If large parts of the developing world are to avert economic, social, and environmental catastrophes, it is essential that global economic growth be revitalized" (World Commission on Environment and Development 1987). However, only if such economic growth is more fairly distributed will the poor be able to restore and protect their environment, whose devastation so immediately degrades their quality of life. In other words, the development conflict can be resolved only if the property conflict is resolved as well. Therefore, the challenge for planners is to deal with the conflicts between competing interests by discovering and implementing complementary uses.

The triangle's origins in a social view of nature

One of the more fruitful aspects of recent interdisciplinary thought may be its linking the traditionally separate intellectual traditions of critical social theory and environmental science/policy (e.g., Smith 1990; Wilson 1992; Ross 1994). This is also the purpose of the triangle figure presented here: to integrate the environmentalist's and social theorist's world views. On one side, an essentialist view of environmental conflicts ("man versus nature") emphasizes the resource conflict. On another side, a historical materialist view of social conflicts (e.g., capital versus labor) emphasizes the property conflict. By simultaneously considering both perspectives, one can see more clearly the social dimension of environmental conflicts, that is, the development conflict. Such a synthesis is not easy: it requires accepting the social construction of nature but avoiding the materialistic pitfall of arrogantly denying any aspects of nature beyond the labor theory of value.

Environmental conflict should not, therefore, be seen as simply one group representing the interests of nature and another group attacking nature (though it often appears that way).[3] Who is to say that the lumberjack, who spends all his or her days among trees (and whose livelihood depends on those trees), is any less close to nature than the environmentalist taking a weekend walk through the woods? Is the lumberjack able to cut down trees only because s/he is "alienated" from the "true" spirit of nature – the spirit that the hiker enjoys? In the absence of a forest mythology, neither the tree cutter nor the tree hugger – nor the third party, the owner/lessee of the forest – can claim an innate kinship to a tree. This is not to be an apologist for clear-cutting, but rather to say that the merits of cutting versus preserving trees cannot be decided according to which persons or groups have the "truest" relationship to nature.

The crucial point is that all three groups have an interactive relationship with nature: the differences lie in their conflicting *conceptions* of nature, their conflicting *uses* of nature, and how they incorporate nature into their systems of values (be they community, economic, or spiritual values). This clash of human values reveals how much the ostensibly separate domains of community development and environmental protection overlap, and suggests that planners should do better in combining social and environmental models. One sees this clash of values in many environmental battles: between the interests of urban residents and those of subsidized irrigation farmers in California water politics; between beach homeowners and coastal managers trying to control erosion; between rich and poor neighborhoods, in the siting of incinerators; between farmers and environmentalists, in restrictions by open space zoning. Even then-President George Bush weighed into such disputes during his 1992 campaign when he commented to a group of loggers that finally people should be valued more than spotted owls (his own take on the interspecies equity issue). Inequity and the imbalance of political power are often issues at the heart of economic–environmental conflicts.

Recognition that the terrain of nature is contested need not, however, cast us adrift on a sea of socially-constructed relativism where "nature" appears as an arbitrary idea of no substance (Bird 1987; Soja 1989). Rather, we are made to rethink the idea and to see the appreciation of nature as an historically evolved sensibility. I suspect that radical environmentalists would criticize this perspective as anthropocentric environmentalism, and argue instead for an ecocentric world view that puts the Earth first (Sessions 1992; Parton 1993). It is true that an anthropocentric view, if distorted, can lead to an arrogant optimism about civilization's ability to reprogram nature through technologies ranging from huge hydroelectric and nuclear plants down to genetic engineering. A rigid belief in the anthropocentric labor theory of value, Marxist or otherwise, can produce a modern-day Narcissus as a social-constructionist who sees nature as merely reflecting the beauty of the human aesthetic and the value of human labor. In this light, a tree is devoid of value until it either becomes part of a scenic area or is transformed into lumber. On the other hand, even as radical, ecocentric environmentalists claim to see "true nature" beyond the city limits, they are blind to how their own world view and their definition of nature itself are shaped by their socialization. The choice between an anthropocentric or an ecocentric world view is a false one. We are all unavoidably anthropocentric; the question is which anthropomorphic values and priorities we will apply to the natural and the social world around us.

Sustainable Development: Reaching the Elusive Center of the Triangle

If the three corners of the triangle represent key goals in planning, and the three axes represent the three resulting conflicts, then I will define the center of the triangle as representing sustainable development: the balance of these three goals. Getting to the center, however, will not be so easy. It is one thing to locate sustainability in the abstract, but quite another to reorganize society to get there.

At first glance, the widespread advocacy of sustainable development is astonishing, given its revolutionary implications for daily life (World Commission 1987; Daly and Cobb 1989; Rees 1989; World Bank 1989; Goodland 1990; Barrett and Bohlen 1991; Korten 1991; Van der Ryn and Calthorpe 1991). It is getting hard to refrain from sustainable development; arguments against it are inevitably attached to the strawman image of a greedy, myopic industrialist. Who would now dare to speak up in opposition? Two interpretations of the bandwagon for sustainable development suggest themselves. The pessimistic thought is that sustainable development has been stripped of its transformative power and reduced to its lowest common denominator. After all, if both the World Bank and radical ecologists now believe in sustainability, the concept can have no teeth: it is so malleable as to mean many things to many people without requiring commitment to any specific policies. Actions speak louder than words, and though all endorse sustainability, few will actually practice it. Furthermore, any concept fully endorsed by all parties must surely be bypassing the heart of the conflict. Set a goal far enough into the future, and even conflicting interests will seem to converge along parallel lines. The concept certainly appears to violate Karl Popper's requirement that propositions be falsifiable, for to reject sustainability is to embrace nonsustainability – and who dares to sketch that future? (Ironically, the nonsustainable scenario is the easiest to define: merely the extrapolation of our current way of life.)

Yet there is also an optimistic interpretation of the broad embrace given sustainability: the idea has become hegemonic, an accepted meta-narrative, a given. It has shifted from being a variable to being the parameter of the debate, almost certain to be integrated into any future scenario of development. We should therefore neither be surprised that no definition has been agreed upon, nor fear that this reveals a fundamental flaw in the concept. In the battle of big public ideas, sustainability has won: the task of the coming years is simply to work out the details, and to narrow the gap between its theory and practice.

Is sustainable development a useful concept?

Some environmentalists argue that if sustainable development is necessary, it therefore must be possible. Perhaps so, but if you are stranded at the bottom of a deep well, a ladder may be impossible even though necessary. The answer espoused may be as much an ideological as a scientific choice, depending on whether one's loyalty is to Malthus or Daly. The more practical question is whether sustainability is a useful concept for planners. The answer here is mixed. The goal may be too far away and holistic to be operational: that is, it may not easily break down into concrete, short-term steps. We also might be able to *define* sustainability yet be unable ever to actually measure it or even know, one day in the future, that we had achieved it. An old eastern proverb identifies the western confusion of believing that to name something is to know it. That may be the danger in automatically embracing sustainable development: a facile confidence that by adding the term "sustainable" to all our existing planning documents and tools (sustainable zoning, sustainable economic development, sustainable transportation planning), we are *doing* sustainable planning. Conversely, one can do much beneficial environmental work without ever devoting explicit attention to the concept of sustainability.

Yet sustainability can be a helpful concept in that it posits the long-term planning goal of a social–environmental system in balance. It is a unifying concept, enormously appealing to the imagination, that brings together many different environmental concerns under one overarching value. It defines a set of social priorities and articulates how society values the economy, the environment, and equity (Paehlke 1994, p. 360). In theory, it allows us not only to calculate whether we have attained sustainability, but also to determine how far away we are. (Actual measurement, though, is another, harder task.) Clearly, it can be argued that, though initially flawed and vague, the concept can be transformed and refined to be of use to planners.

History, equity, and sustainable development

One obstacle to an accurate, working definition of sustainability may well be the historical perspective that sees the practice as pre-existing, either in our past or as a Platonic concept. I believe instead that our sustainable future does not yet exist, either in reality or even in strategy. We do not yet know what it will look like; it is being socially constructed through a sustained period of conflict negotiation and resolution. This is a process of innovation, not of discovery and converting the nonbelievers.

This point brings us to the practice of looking for sustainable development in pre-industrial and nonwestern cultures (a common though not universal practice). Searching for our future in our indigenous past is instructive at both the philosophical and the practical level (Turner 1983; Duerr 1985). Yet it is also problematical, tapping into a myth that our salvation lies in the pre-industrial sustainable culture. The international division of labor and trade, the movement of most people away from agriculture into cities, and exponential population growth lead us irrevocably down a unidirectional, not a circular path: the transformation of pre-industrial, indigenous settlements into mass urban society is irreversible. Our modern path to sustainability lies forward, not behind us.

The key difference between those indigenous, sustainable communities and ours is that they had no choice but to be sustainable. Bluntly stated, if they cut down too many trees or ruined the soil, they would die out. Modern society has the options presented by trade, long-term storage, and synthetic replacements; if we clear-cut a field, we have subsequent options that our ancestors didn't. In this situation, we must *voluntarily choose* sustainable practices, since there is no immediate survival or market imperative to do so. Although the long-term effects of a nonsustainable economy are certainly dangerous, the feedback mechanisms are too long-term to prod us in the right direction.

Why do we often romanticize the sustainable past? Some are attracted to the powerful spiritual link between humans and nature that has since been lost. Such romanticists tend, however, to overlook the more harsh and unforgiving aspects of being so dependent on the land. Two hundred years ago, Friedrich Schiller (1965, p. 28) noted the tendency of utopian thinkers to take their dream for the future and posit it as their past, thus giving it legitimacy as a cyclical return to the past.[4] This habit is not unique to ecotopians (Kumar 1991); some religious fundamentalists also justify their utopian urgency by drawing on the myth of a paradise lost. Though Marxists don't glorify the past in the same way, they, too, manage to anticipate a *static* system of balance and harmony, which nonetheless will require a cataclysmic, revolutionary social transformation to reach. All three ideologies posit some basic flaw in society – be it western materialism, original sin, or capitalism – whose identification and cure will free us from conflict. Each ideology sees a fundamental alienation as the danger to overcome: alienation from nature, from god, or from work. Each group is so critical of existing society that it would seem a wonder we have made it this far; but this persistence of human society despite the dire prognoses of utopians tells us something.

What is the fallout from such historical thinking? By neglecting the powerful momentum of modern industrial and postindustrial society, it both points us in the wrong direction and makes it easier to marginalize the proponents of sustainable development. It also carries an anti-urban sentiment that tends to neglect both the centrality and the plight of megacities. Modern humans are unique among species in their propensity to deal with nature's threats, not only through flight and burrowing and biological adaptation, nor simply through spiritual understanding, but also through massive population growth, complex social division of labor, and the fundamental, external transformation of their once-natural environment (the building of cities). Certainly the fixation on growth, industry, and competition has degraded the environment. Yet one cannot undo urban-industrial society. Rather, one must continue to innovate through to the other side of industrialization, to reach a more sustainable economy.

The cyclical historical view of some environmentalists also hinders a critical understanding of equity, since that view attributes to the environment a natural state of equality rudely upset by modern society. Yet nature is inherently neither equal nor unequal, and at times can be downright brutal. The human observer projects a sense of social equity onto nature, through a confusion, noted by Schiller, of the idealized future with myths about our natural past. To gain a sense of historical legitimacy, we project our socially constructed sense of equality onto the past, creating revisionist history in which nature is fair and compassionate. Society's path to equality is perceived not as an uncertain progress from barbarism to justice, but rather as a return to an original state of harmony as laid out in nature. In this thinking, belief in an ecological balance and a social balance, entwined in the pre-industrial world, conjures up an eco-Garden of Eden "lost" by modern society.[5]

It will be more useful to let go of this mythic belief in our involuntary diaspora from a pre-industrial, ecotopian Eden.[6] The conflation of ecological diasporas and utopias constrains our search for creative, urban solutions to social–environmental conflict. By relinquishing such mythic beliefs, we will understand that notions of equity were not lying patiently in wait in nature, to be first discovered by indigenous peoples, then lost by colonialists, and finally rediscovered by modern society in the late twentieth century. This is certainly not to say that nature can teach us nothing. The laws of nature are not the same thing, however, as natural law, nor does ecological equilibrium necessarily generate normative principles of equity. Though we turn to nature to understand the context, dynamics, and effects of the economic–environmental conflict, we must turn to social norms to decide what balance is fair and just.

How, then, do we define what is fair? I propose viewing social justice as the striving towards a more equal distribution of resources among social groups across the space of cities and of nations – a definition of "fair" distribution. It should be noted that societies view themselves as "fair" if the *procedures* of allocation treat people equally, even if the *substantive* outcome is unbalanced. (One would hope that equal treatment is but the first step towards narrowing material inequality.) The environmental movement expands the space for this "equity" in two ways: (1) intergenerationally (present versus future generations) and (2) across species (as in animal rights, deep ecology, and legal standing for trees). The two added dimensions of equity remain essentially abstractions, however, since no one from the future or from other species can speak up for their "fair share" of resources. Selfless advocates (or selfish ventriloquists) "speak for them."

This expansion of socio-spatial equity to include future generations and other species not only makes the concept more complex; it also creates the possibility for contradictions among the different calls for "fairness." Slowing worldwide industrial expansion may preserve more of the world's resources for the future (thereby increasing intergenerational equity), but it may also undermine the efforts of the underdeveloped world to approach the living standards of the west (thereby lowering international equity). Battles over Native American fishing practices, the spotted owl, and restrictive farmland preservation each thrust together several divergent notions of "fairness." It is through resolving the three sorts of conflicts on the planner's triangle that society iteratively forms its definition of what is fair.

The path towards sustainable development

There are two final aspects of the fuzzy definition of sustainability: its path and its outcome. The basic premise of sustainable development is one that, like the long-term goal of a balanced U.S. budget, is hard not to like. As with eliminating the national debt, however, two troubling questions about sustainable development remain: How are you going to get there? Once you get there, what are the negative consequences? Planners don't yet have adequate answers to these two questions; that is, as yet they have no concrete strategies to achieve sustainable development, nor do they know how to counter the political resistance to it.

On the *path* towards a sustainable future, the steps are often too vague, as with sweeping calls for a "spiritual transformation" as the prerequisite for environmental transformation. Sometimes the call for sustainable development seems to serve as a vehicle for sermonizing about the moral and spiritual corruption of the industrial world (undeniable). Who would not want to believe in a holistic blending of economic and ecological values in each of our planners, who would then go out into the world and, on each project, internally and seamlessly merge the interests of jobs and nature, as well as of social justice? That is, the call to planners would be to stand at every moment at the center of the triangle.

But this aim is too reminiscent of our naive belief during the 1950s and 1960s in comprehensive planning for a single "public interest," before the incrementalists and advocacy planners pulled the rug out from under us (Lindblom 1959; Altshuler 1965; Davidoff 1965; Fainstein and Fainstein 1971). I suspect that planners' criticisms of the sustainable development movement in the coming years will parallel the critique of comprehensive planning thirty years ago: The incrementalists will argue that one cannot achieve a sustainable society in a single grand leap, for it requires too much social and ecological information and is too risky. The advocacy planners will argue that no common social interest in sustainable development exists, and that bureaucratic planners will invariably create a sustainable development scheme that neglects the interests both of the poor and of nature. To both groups of critics, the prospect of integrating economic, environmental and equity interests will seem forced and artificial. States will require communities to prepare "Sustainable Development Master Plans," which will prove to be glib wish lists of goals and suspiciously vague implementation steps. To achieve consensus for the plan, language will be reduced to the lowest common denominator, and the pleasing plans will gather dust.

An alternative is to let holistic sustainable development be a long-range goal; it is a worthy one, for planners do need a vision of a more sustainable urban society. But during the coming years, planners will confront deep-seated conflicts among economic, social and environmental interests that cannot be wished away through admittedly appealing images of a community in harmony with nature. One is no more likely to abolish the economic–environmental conflict completely by achieving sustainable bliss than one is to eliminate completely the boundaries between the city and the wilderness, between the public and private spheres, between the haves and have-nots. Nevertheless, one can diffuse the conflict, and find ways to avert its more destructive fall-out.

My concern about the *ramifications* of a sustainable future is one that is often expressed: steady-state, no-growth economics would be likely to relegate much of the developing world – and the poor within the industrialized world – to a state of persistent poverty. The advocates of sustainable development rightly reject as flawed the premise of conventional economics that only a growth economy can achieve social redistribution. And growth economics has, indeed, also exacerbated the environment's degradation. However, it is wishful thinking to assume that a sustainable economy will automatically ensure a socially just distribution of resources.[7] The vision of no-growth (commonly thought not universally assumed to characterize sustainable development) raises powerful fears, and planners should be savvy to such fears. Otherwise, they will understand neither the potential dangers of steady-state economics nor the nature of the opposition to sustainable development.

Rethinking/redefining sustainable development

Despite the shortcomings in the current formulation of sustainable development, the concept retains integrity and enormous potential. It simply needs to be redefined and made more precise. First, one should avoid a dichotomous, black-and-white view of sustainability. We should think of American society not as a corrupt, wholly unsustainable one that has to be made pure and wholly sustainable, but rather as a hybrid of both sorts of practices. Our purpose, then, should be to move further towards sustainable practices in an evolutionary progression.

Second, we should broaden the idea of "sustainability." If "crisis" is defined as the inability of a system to reproduce itself, then sustainability is the opposite: the long-term ability of a system to reproduce. This criterion applies not only to natural ecosystems, but to economic and political systems as well. By this definition, western society already does much to sustain itself: economic policy and corporate strategies (e.g., investment, training, monetary policy) strive to reproduce the macro- and micro-economies. Similarly, governments, parties, labor unions, and other political agents strive to reproduce their institutions and interests. Society's shortcoming is that as it strives to sustain its political and economic systems, it often neglects to sustain the ecological system. The goal for planning is therefore a broader agenda: to sustain, simultaneously and in balance, these three sometimes competing, sometimes complementary systems.[8]

Third, it will be helpful to distinguish initially between two levels of sustainability: specific versus general (or local versus global). One might fairly easily imagine and achieve sustainability in a single sector and/or locality, for example, converting a Pacific Northwest community to sustained-yield timber practices. Recycling, solar power, cogeneration, and conservation can lower consumption of nonsustainable resources. To achieve complete sustainability across all sectors and/or all places, however, requires such complex restructuring and redistribution that the only feasible path to global sustainability is likely to be a long, incremental accumulation of local and industry-specific advances.

What this incremental, iterative approach means is that planners will find their vision of a sustainable city developed best at the conclusion of contested negotiations over land use, transportation, housing, and economic development policies, not as the premise for beginning the effort. To first spend years in the hermetic isolation of universities and environmental groups, perfecting the theory of sustainable development, before testing it in community development is backwards. That approach sees sustainable development as an ideal society outside the conflicts of the planner's triangle, or as the tranquil "eye of the hurricane" at the triangle's center. As with the ideal comprehensive plan, it is presumed that the objective, technocratic merits of a perfected sustainable development scheme will ensure society's acceptance. But one cannot reach the sustainable center of the planner's triangle in a single, holistic leap to a pre-ordained balance.

The Task Ahead for Planners: Seeking Sustainable Development within the Triangle of Planning Conflicts

The role of planners is therefore to engage the current challenge of sustainable development with a dual, interactive strategy: (1) to manage and resolve conflict; and (2) to promote creative technical, architectural, and institutional solutions. Planners must both negotiate the procedures of the conflict and promote a substantive vision of sustainable development.

Procedural paths to sustainable development: Conflict negotiation

In negotiation and conflict resolution (Bingham 1986; Susskind and Cruikshank 1987; Crowfoot and Wondolleck 1990), rather than pricing externalities, common ground is established at the negotiation table, where the conflicting economic, social, and environmental interests can be brought together. The potential rewards are numerous: not only an outcome that balances all parties, but avoidance of heavy legal costs and long-lasting animosity. Negotiated conflict resolution can also lead to a better understanding of one's opponent's interests and values, and even of one's own interests. The very process of lengthy negotiation can be a powerful tool to mobilize community involvement around social and environmental issues. The greatest promise, of course, is a win–win outcome: finding innovative solutions that would not have come out of traditional, adversarial confrontation. Through skillfully led, back-and-forth discussion, the parties can separate their initial, clashing substantive demands from their underlying interests, which may be more compatible. For example, environmentalists and the timber industry could solve their initial dispute over building a logging road through alternative road design and other mitigation measures (Crowfoot and Wondolleck 1990, pp. 32–52).

However, conflict resolution is no panacea. Sometimes conflicting demands express fundamental conflicts of interest. The either-or nature of the technology or ecology may preclude a win–win outcome, as in an all-or-nothing dispute over a proposed hydroelectric project (Reisner 1987) – you either build it or you don't. An overwhelming imbalance of power between the opposing groups also can thwart resolution (Crowfoot and Wondolleck 1990, p. 4). A powerful party can simply refuse to participate. It is also hard to negotiate a comprehensive resolution for a large number of parties.

Planners are likely to have the best success in using conflict resolution when there is a specific, concise dispute (rather than an amorphous ideological clash); all interested parties agree to participate (and don't bypass the process through the courts); each party feels on equal ground; there are a variety of possible compromises and innovative solutions; both parties prefer a solution to an impasse; and a skilled third-party negotiator facilitates. The best resolution strategies seem to include two areas of compromise and balance: the procedural (each party is represented and willing to compromise); and the substantive (the solution is a compromise, such as multiple land uses or a reduced development density).

Procedural paths to sustainable development: Redefining the language of the conflict

A second strategy is to bridge the chasms between the languages of economics, environmentalism, and social justice. Linguistic differences, which reflect separate value hierarchies, are a major obstacle to common solutions. All too often, the economists speak of incentives and marginal rates, the ecologists speak of carrying capacity and biodiversity, the advocate planners speak of housing rights, empowerment, and discrimination, and each side accuses the others of being "out of touch" (Campbell 1992).

The planner therefore needs to act as a translator, assisting each group to understand the priorities and reasoning of the others. Economic, ecological and social thought may at a certain level be incommensurable, yet a level may still be found where all three may be brought together. To offer an analogy, a Kenyan Gikuyu text cannot be fully converted into English without losing something in translation; a good translation, nevertheless, is the best possible way to bridge two systems of expression that will never be one, and it is preferable to incomprehension.

The danger of translation is that one language will dominate the debate and thus define the terms of the solution. It is essential to exert equal effort to translate in each direction, to prevent one linguistic culture from dominating the other (as English has done in neocolonial Africa). Another lesson from the neocolonial linguistic experience is that it is crucial for each social group to express itself in its own language before any translation. The challenge for planners is to write the best translations among the languages of the economic, the ecological, and the social views, and to avoid a quasi-colonial dominance by the economic *lingua franca*, by creating equal two-way translations.[9]

For example, planners need better tools to understand their cities and regions not just as economic systems, or static inventories of natural resources, but also as *environmental systems* that are part of regional and global networks trading goods, information, resources and pollution. At the conceptual level, translating the economic vocabulary of global cities, the spatial division of labor, regional restructuring, and technoburbs/edge cities into environmental language would be a worthy start; at the same time, of course, the vocabulary of biodiversity, landscape linkages, and carrying capacity should be translated to be understandable by economic interests.

This bilingual translation should extend to the empirical level. I envision extending the concept of the "trade balance" to include an "environmental balance," which covers not just commodities, but also natural resources and pollution. Planners should improve their data collection and integration to support the environmental trade balance. They should apply economic–ecological bilingualism not only to the content of data, but also to the spatial framework of the data, by rethinking the geographic boundaries of planning and analysis. Bioregionalists advocate having the spatial scale for planning reflect the scale of *natural* phenomena (e.g., the extent of a river basin, vegetation zones, or the dispersion range of metropolitan air pollution); economic planners call for a spatial scale to match the *social* phenomena (e.g., highway networks, municipal boundaries, labor market areas, new industrial districts). The solution is to integrate these two scales and overlay the economic and ecological geographies of planning. The current merging of environmental Raster (grid-based) and infrastructural vector-based data in Geographic Information Systems (GIS) recognizes the need for multiple layers of planning boundaries (Wiggins 1993).

Translation can thus be a powerful planner's skill, and interdisciplinary planning education already provides some multilingualism. Moreover, the idea of sustainability lends itself nicely to the meeting on common ground of competing value systems. Yet translation has its limits. Linguistic differences often represent real, intractable differences in values. An environmental dispute may arise not from a misunderstanding alone; both sides may clearly understand that their vested interests fundamentally clash, no matter how expressed. At this point, translation must give way to other strategies. The difficulties are exacerbated when one party has greater power, and so shapes the language of the debate as well as prevailing in its outcome. In short, translation, like conflict negotiation, reveals both the promises and the limitations of communication-based conflict resolution.

Other procedural paths

Two other, more traditional approaches deserve mention. One is political pluralism: let the political arena decide conflicts, either directly (e.g., a referendum on an open space bond act, or a California state proposition on nuclear power), or indirectly (e.g., elections decided on the basis of candidates' environmental records and promised legislation). The key elements here, political debate and ultimately the vote, allow much wider participation in the decision than negotiation does. However, a binary vote cannot as easily handle complex issues, address specific land-use conflicts, or develop subtle, creative solutions. Choosing the general political process as a strategy for deciding conflict also takes the process largely out of the hands of planners.

The other traditional strategy is to develop market mechanisms to link economic and environmental priorities. Prices are made the commonality that bridges the gap between the otherwise noncommensurables of trees and timber, open space and real estate. The marketplace is chosen as the arena where society balances its competing values. This economistic approach to the environment reduces pollution to what the economist Edwin Mills (1978, p. 15) called "a problem in resource allocation." This approach can decide conflicts along the economic–environmental axis (the resource conflict), but often neglects equity. However, the market does seem to be dealing better with environmental externalities than it did ten or twenty years ago. Internalizing externalities, at the least, raises the issues of social justice and equity: e.g., who will pay for cleaning up abandoned industrial sites or compensate for the loss of fishing revenues due to oil spills. The recent establishment of a pollution credit market in the South Coast Air Quality Management District, for example, is a step in the right direction – despite criticism that the pollution credits were initially given away for free (Robinson 1993).

The role of the planner in all four of these approaches is to arrange the procedures for making decisions, not to set the substance of the actual outcomes. In some cases, the overall structure for decision-making already exists (the market and the political system). In other cases, however, the planner must help shape that structure (a mediation forum; a common language), which, done successfully, gives the process credibility. The actual environmental outcomes nevertheless remain unknowable: you don't know in advance if the environment will actually be improved. For example, environmentalists and developers heralded the Coachella Valley Fringe-Toed Lizard Habitat Conservation Plan as a model process to balance the interests of development and conservation; yet the actual outcome may not adequately protect the endangered lizard (Beatley 1992, pp. 15–16). Similarly, although the New Jersey State Development Plan was praised for its innovative cross-acceptance procedure, the plan itself arguably has not altered the state's urban sprawl.

The final issue that arises is whether the planner should play the role of neutral moderator, or of advocate representing a single party; this has been a long-standing debate in the field. Each strategy has its virtues.

Substantive paths to sustainable development: Land use and design

Planners have substantive knowledge of how cities, economies, and ecologies interact, and they should put forth specific, farsighted designs that promote the sustainable city. The first area is traditional planning tools of land-use design and control. The potential for balance between economic and environmental interests exists in design itself, as in a greenbelt community (Elson 1986). Sometimes the land-use solution is simply to divide a contested parcel into two parcels: a developed and a preserved. This solution can take crude forms at times, such as the "no-net-loss" policy that endorses the dubious practice of creating wetlands. A different example, Howard's turn-of-the-century Garden City (1965), can be seen as a territorially symbolic design for balance between the economy and the environment, though its explicit language was that of town–country balance. It is a design's articulated balance between the built development and the unbuilt wilderness that promises the economic–environmental balance. Designs for clustered developments, higher densities, and live-work communities move toward such a balance (Rickaby 1987; Commission of the European Communities 1990; Hudson 1991; Van der Ryn and Calthorpe 1991). Some dispute the inherent benefits of the compact city (Breheny 1992). A further complication is that not all economic–environmental conflicts have their roots in spatial or architectural problems. As a result, ostensible solutions may be merely symbols of ecological–economic balance, without actually solving the conflict.

Nevertheless, land-use planning arguably remains the most powerful tool available to planners, who should not worry too much if it does not manage all problems. The trick in resolving environmental conflicts through land-use planning is to reconcile the conflicting territorial logics of human and of natural habitats. Standard real estate development reduces open space to fragmented, static, green islands – exactly what the landscape ecologists deplore as unable to preserve biodiversity. Wildlife roam and migrate, and require large expanses of connected landscape (Hudson 1991). So both the ecological and the economic systems require the interconnectivity of a critical mass of land to be sustainable. Though we live in a three-dimensional world, land is a limited resource with essentially two dimensions (always excepting air and burrowing/mining spaces). The requirement of land's spatial interconnectivity is thus hard to achieve for both systems in one region: the continuity of one system invariably fragments continuity of the other.[10] So the guiding challenge for land-use planning is to achieve simultaneously spatial/territorial integrity for both systems. Furthermore, a sustainable development that aspires to social justice must also find ways to avoid the land-use manifestations of uneven development: housing segregation, unequal property-tax funding of public schools, jobs–housing imbalance, the spatial imbalance of economic opportunity, and unequal access to open space and recreation.

Substantive paths to sustainable development: Bioregionalism

A comprehensive vision of sustainable land use is bioregionalism, both in its 1920s articulation by the Regional Planning Association of America (Sussman 1976) and its contemporary variation (Sale 1985; Andrus et al. 1990; Campbell 1992). The movement's essential belief is that rescaling communities and the economy according to the ecological boundaries of a physical region will encourage sustainability. The regional scale presumably stimulates greater environmental awareness: it is believed that residents of small-scale, self-sufficient regions will be aware of the causes and effects of their environmental actions, thereby reducing externalities. Regions will live within their means, and bypass the environmental problems caused by international trade and exporting pollution.

The bioregional vision certainly has its shortcomings, including the same fuzzy, utopian thinking found in other writing about sustainable development. Its ecological determinism also puts too much faith in the regional "spatial fix": no geographic scale can, in itself, eliminate all conflict, for not all conflict is geographic. Finally, the call for regional self-reliance – a common feature of sustainable development concepts (Korten 1991, p. 184) – might relegate the regional economy to underdevelopment in an otherwise nationally and internationally interdependent world. Yet it can be effective to visualize sustainable regions within an interdependent world full of trade, migration, information flows and capital flows, and to know the difference between *healthy interdependence* and *parasitic dependence*, that is, a dependence on other regions' resources that is equivalent to depletion. Interdependence does not always imply an imbalance of power, nor does self-sufficiency guarantee equality. Finally, the bioregional perspective can provide a foundation for understanding conflicts among a region's interconnected economic, social and ecological networks.

Other substantive paths

One other approach is technological improvement, such as alternative fuels, conservation mechanisms, recycling, alternative materials, and new mass transit design. Stimulated by competition, regulation, or government subsidies, such advances reduce the consumption of natural resources per unit of production and thereby promise to ameliorate conflict over their competing uses, creating a win–win solution. However, this method is not guaranteed to serve those purposes, for gains in conservation are often cancelled out by rising demand for the final products. The overall increase in demand for gasoline despite improvements in automobile fuel efficiency is one example of how market forces can undermine technologically-achieved environmental improvements. Nor, importantly, do technological improvements guarantee fairer distribution.

The role of the planner in all these substantive strategies (land use, bioregionalism, technological improvement) is to design outcomes, with less emphasis on the means of achieving them. The environmental ramifications of the solutions are known or at least estimated, but the political means to achieve legitimacy are not. There also is a trade-off between comprehensiveness (bioregions) and short-term achievability (individual technological improvements).

Merging the substantive and procedural

The individual shortcomings of the approaches described above suggest that combining them can achieve both political and substantive progress in the environmental–economic crisis. The most successful solutions seem to undertake several different resolution strategies at once. For example, negotiation among developers, city planners, and land-use preservationists can produce an innovative, clustered design for a housing development, plus a per-unit fee for preserving open space. Substantive vision combined with negotiating skills thus allows planners to create win–win solutions, rather than either negotiating in a zero-sum game or preparing inert, ecotopian plans. This approach is not a distant ideal for planners: they already have, from their education and experience, both this substantive knowledge and this political savvy.

In the end, however, the planner must also deal with conflicts where one or more parties have no interest in resolution. One nonresolution tactic is the NIMBY, Not In My Back Yard, response: a crude marriage of local initiative and the age-old externalizing of pollution. This "take it elsewhere" strategy makes no overall claim to resolve conflict, though it can be a productive form of resistance rather than just irrational parochialism (Lake 1993). Nor does eco-terrorism consider balance. Instead, it replaces the defensive stance of NIMBY with offensive, confrontational, symbolic action. Resolution is also avoided out of cavalier confidence that one's own side can manage the opposition through victory, not compromise ("My side will win, so why compromise?"). Finally, an "I don't care" stance avoids the conflict altogether. Unfortunately, this ostensible escapism often masks a more pernicious NIMBY or "my side will win" hostility, just below the surface.

Planners: Leaders or Followers in Resolving Economic–Environmental Conflicts?

I turn finally to the question of whether planners are likely to be leaders or followers in resolving economic–environmental conflicts. One would think that it would be natural for planners, being interdisciplinary and familiar with the three goals of balancing social equity, jobs, and environmental protection, to take the lead in resolving such conflicts. Of the conflict resolution scenarios mentioned above, those most open to planners' contributions involve the built environment and local resources: land use, soil conservation, design issues, recycling, solid waste, water treatment. Even solutions using the other approaches – environmental economic incentives, political compromise, and environmental technology innovations – that are normally undertaken at the state and federal levels could also involve planners if moved to the local or regional level.

But the planners' position at the forefront of change is not assured, especially if the lead is taken up by other professions or at the federal, not the local, level. The lively debate on whether gasoline consumption can best be reduced through higher-density land uses (Newman and Kenworthy 1989) or through energy taxes (Gordon and Richardson 1990) not only reflected an ideological battle over interpreting research results and the merits of planning intervention, but also demonstrated how local planning can be made either central or marginal to resolving environmental–economic conflicts. To hold a central place in the debate about sustainable development, planners must exploit those areas of conflict where they have the greatest leverage and expertise.

Certainly planners already have experience with both the dispute over economic growth versus equity and that over economic growth versus environmental protection. Yet the development conflict is where the real action for planners will be: seeking to resolve both environmental and economic equity issues at once. Here is where the profession can best make its unique contribution. An obvious start would be for community development planners and environmental planners to collaborate more (an alliance that an internal Environmental Protection Agency memo found explosive enough for the agency to consider defusing it) (Higgins 1993, 1994). One possible joint task is to expand current public–private partnership efforts to improve environmental health in the inner city. This urban-based effort would help planners bypass the danger of environmental elitism that besets many suburban, white-oriented environmental organizations.

If planners move in this direction, they will join the growing environmental justice movement, which emerged in the early 1980s and combined minority community organizing with environmental concerns (Higgins 1993, 1994). The movement tries to reduce environmental hazards that directly affect poor residents, who are the least able to fight pollution, be it the direct result of discriminatory siting decisions or the indirect result of housing and employment discrimination. The poor, being the least able to move away, are especially tied to place and therefore to the assistance or neglect of local planners. Understandably, local civil rights leaders have been preoccupied for so long with seeking economic opportunity and social justice that they have paid less attention to inequities in the local environment. The challenge for poor communities is now to expand their work on the property conflict to address the development conflict as well, that is, to challenge the false choice of jobs over the environment. An urban vision of sustainable development, infused with a belief in social and environmental justice, can guide these efforts.

Yet even with the rising acceptance of sustainable development, planners will not always be able, on their own, to represent and balance social, economic, and environmental interests simultaneously. The professional allegiances, skills, and bureaucracies of the profession are too constraining to allow that. Pretending at all times to be at the center of the planner's triangle will only make sustainability a hollow term. Instead, the trick will be for individual planners to identify their specific loyalties and roles in these conflicts accurately: that is, to orient themselves in the triangle. Planners will have to decide whether they want to remain outside the conflict and act as mediators, or jump into the fray and promote their own visions of ecological-economic development, sustainable or otherwise. Both planning behaviors are needed.

Notes

1 A curious comparison to this equity–environment–economy triangle is the view of Arne Naess (1993), the radical environmentalist who gave Deep Ecology its name in the 1970s, that the three crucial postwar political movements were the social justice, radical environmental, and peace movements, whose goals might overlap but could not be made identical.

2   Perhaps one can explain the lack of a universal conflict in the following way: if our ideas
of the economy, equity, and the environment are socially/culturally constructed, and if
cultural society is local as well as global, then our ideas are locally distinct rather than
universally uniform.

3   For planners, if one is simply "planning for place," then the dispute about suburban
housing versus wetlands does indeed reflect a conflict between an economic and an
environmental use of a specific piece of land. But if one sees this conflict in light of
"planning for people," then the decision lies between differing social groups (e.g., environmentalists, fishermen, developers) and between their competing attempts to incorporate the piece of land into their system and world view. (This classic planning
distinction between planning for people or for place begs the question: Is there a third
option, "planning for nonpeople, i.e., nature"?)

4   Schiller, using Kant's logic, recognized 200 years ago this human habit of positing the
future on the past: "He thus artificially retraces his childhood in his maturity, forms for
himself a *state of Nature* in idea, which is not indeed given him by experience but is the
necessary result of his rationality, borrows in this ideal state an ultimate aim which he
never knew in his actual state of Nature, and a choice of which he was capable, and
proceeds now exactly as though he were starting afresh. ... "

5   Some radical ecologists take this lost world a step further and see it not as a garden, but
as wilderness (e.g., Parton 1993).

6   I use the term diaspora to mean the involuntary dispersal of a people from their native
home, driven out by a greater power (Hall 1992). The curious nature of the diaspora
implied by the environmental world view is that it is ambiguously voluntary: western
positivistic thinking is the villain that we developed, but that eventually enslaved us.
Then, too, diasporas invariably combine dislocations across both time and space, but the
mythic "homeland" of this environmental diaspora is only from an historical era, but
from no specific place.

7   The reverse may also not be automatic. David Johns (1992, p. 63), in advocating a broad
interspecies equity, reminds us that not all forms of equity go hand-in-hand: "The
nature of the linkages between various forms of domination is certainly not settled, but
deep ecology may be distinct in believing that the resolution of equity issues among
humans will not automatically result in an end to human destruction of the biosphere.
One can envision a society without class distinctions, without patriarchy, and with cultural autonomy, that still attempts to manage the rest of nature in utilitarian fashion
with resulting deterioration of the biosphere.... But the end of domination in human
relations is not enough to protect the larger biotic community. Only behavior shaped by
a biocentric view can do that."

8   The ambiguity of the term sustainable development is therefore not coincidental, given
that reasonable people differ on which corner of the triangle is to be "sustained": a fixed
level of natural resources? current environmental quality? current ecosystems? a hypothetical pre-industrial environmental state? the current material standards of living?
long-term economic growth? political democracy?

9   These issues of language and translation were raised by Ngũgi wa Thiong-o and Stuart
Hall in separate distinguished lectures at the Center for the Critical Analysis of
Contemporary Cultures, Rutgers University (March 31 and April 15, 1993).

10 Conservationists have in fact installed underpasses and overpasses so that vulnerable
migrating species can get around highways.

References

Altshuler, Alan. 1965. The Goals of Comprehensive Planning. *Journal of the American Institute of Planning* 31, 3: 186–94.

Andrus, Van, et al., eds. 1990. *Home: A Bioregional Reader*. Philadelphia and Santa Cruz: New Catalyst/New Society.

Barrett, Gary W., and Patrick J. Bohlen. 1991. Landscape Ecology. In *Landscape Linkages and Biodiversity*, edited by Wendy E. Hudson. Washington, DC and Covelo, CA: Island Press.

Beatley, Timothy. 1992. Balancing Urban Development and Endangered Species: The Coachella Valley Habitat Conservation Plan. *Environmental Management* 16, 1: 7–19.

Beltzer, Dena, and Cynthia Kroll. 1986. *New Jobs for the Timber Region: Economic Diversification for Northern California*. Berkeley: Institute of Governmental Studies, University of California.

Bingham, Gail. 1986. *Resolving Environmental Disputes: A Decade of Experience*. Washington, DC: The Conservation Foundation.

Bird, Elizabeth Ann R. 1987. The Social Construction of Nature: Theoretical Approaches to the History of Environmental Problems. *Environmental Review* 11, 4: 255–64.

Breheny, M. J., ed. 1992. *Sustainable Development and Urban Form*. London: Pion.

Bryant, Bunyan, and Paul Mohai, eds. 1992. *Race and the Incidence of Environmental Hazards*. Boulder, CO: Westview Press.

Bullard, Robert D. 1990. *Dumping in Dixie: Race, Class, and Environmental Quality*. Boulder, CO: Westview Press.

Bullard, Robert D., ed. 1993. *Confronting Environmental Racism: Voices from the Grassroots*. Boston: South End Press.

Campbell, Scott. 1992. Integrating Economic and Environmental Planning: The Regional Perspective. Working Paper No. 43, Center for Urban Policy Research, Rutgers University.

Clawson, Marion. 1975. *Forests: For Whom and For What?* Washington, DC: Resources for the Future.

Commission of the European Communities. 1990. *Green Paper on the Urban Environment*. Brussels: EEC.

Crowfoot, James E., and Julia M. Wondolleck. 1990. *Environmental Disputes: Community Involvement in Conflict Resolution*. Washington, DC and Covelo, CA: Island Press.

Daly, Herman E. 1991. *Steady State Economics*. 2nd edition, with new essays. Washington, DC and Covelo, CA: Island Press.

Daly, Herman E., and John B. Cobb, Jr. 1989. *For the Common Good: Redirecting the Economy toward Community, the Environment, and a Sustainable Future*. Boston: Beacon Press.

Davidoff, Paul. 1965. Advocacy and Pluralism in Planning. *Journal of the American Institute of Planners* 31, 4: 544–55.

Duerr, Hans Peter. 1985. *Dreamtime: Concerning the Boundary between Wilderness and Civilization*. Oxford: Basil Blackwell.

Elson, Martin J. 1986. *Green Belts: Conflict Mediation in the Urban Fringe*. London: Heinemann.

Fainstein, Susan S., and Norman I. Fainstein. 1971. City Planning and Political Values. *Urban Affairs Quarterly* 6, 3: 341–62.

Foglesong, Richard E. 1986. *Planning the Capitalist City*. Princeton: Princeton University Press.

Goodland, Robert. 1990. Environmental Sustainability in Economic Development – with Emphasis on Amazonia. In *Race to Save the Tropics: Ecology and Economics for a Sustainable Future*, edited by Robert Goodland. Washington, DC and Covelo, CA: Island Press.

Gordon, Peter, and Harry Richardson. 1990. Gasoline Consumption and Cities – A Reply. *Journal of the American Planning Association*. 55, 3: 342–5.

Hall, Stuart. 1992. Cultural Identity and Diaspora. *Framework* 36.

Harvey, David. 1985. *The Urbanization of Capital*. Baltimore: Johns Hopkins University Press.

Higgins, Robert R. 1993. Race and Environmental Equity: An Overview of the Environmental Justice Issue in the Policy Process. *Polity*, 26, 2 (Winter): 281–300.

Higgins, Robert R. 1994. Race, Pollution, and the Mastery of Nature. *Environmental Ethics*, 16, 3 (Fall): 251–64.

Hoffman, Lily. 1989. *The Politics of Knowledge: Activist Movements in Medicine and Planning*. Albany: SUNY Press.

Howard, Ebenezer. 1965. *Garden Cities of To-Morrow* (first published in 1898 as *To-Morrow: A Peaceful Path to Real Reform*). Cambridge, MA: MIT Press.

Hudson, Wendy E., ed. 1991. *Landscape Linkages and Biodiversity*. Washington, DC and Covelo, CA: Island Press.

Jacobs, Harvey. 1989. Social Equity in Agricultural Land Protection. *Landscape and Urban Planning* 17, 1: 21–33.

Johns, David. 1992. The Practical Relevance of Deep Ecology. *Wild Earth* 2, 2.

Korten, David C. 1991. Sustainable Development. *World Policy Journal* 9, 1: 157–90.

Krumholz, Norman, et al. 1982. A Retrospective View of Equity Planning: Cleveland, 1969–1979, and Comments. *Journal of the American Planning Association* 48, 2: 163–83.

Kumar, Krishan. 1991. *Utopia and Anti-Utopia in Modern Times*. Oxford and Cambridge, MA: Basil Blackwell.

Lake, Robert. 1993. Rethinking NIMBY. *Journal of the American Planning Association* 59, 1: 87–93.

Lee, Robert G., Donald R. Field, and William R. Burch, Jr., eds. 1990. *Community and Forestry: Continuities in the Sociology of Natural Resources*. Boulder, CO: Westview Press.

Lindblom, C. E. 1959. The Science of Muddling Through. *Public Administration Review* 19 (Spring): 79–88.

Marcuse, Peter. 1976. Professional Ethics and Beyond: Values in Planning. *Journal of the American Institute of Planning* 42, 3: 264–74.

McPhee, John. 1989. *The Control of Nature*. New York: Farrar, Straus, Giroux.

Mills, Edwin S. 1978. *The Economics of Environmental Quality*. New York: Norton.

Naess, Arne. 1993. The Breadth and the Limits of the Deep Ecology Movement. *Wild Earth* 3, 1: 74–5.

Newman, Peter W. G., and Jeffrey R. Kenworthy. 1989. Gasoline Consumption and Cities – A Comparison of U. S. Cities with a Global Survey. *Journal of the American Planning Association* 55, 1: 24–37.

Paehlke, Robert C. 1994. Environmental Values and Public Policy. In *Environmental Policy in the 1990s*, 2nd edition, edited by Norman J. Vig and Michael E. Kraft. Washington, DC: Congressional Quarterly Press.

Parton, Glenn. 1993. Why I am a Primitivist. *Wild Earth* 3, 1: 12–14.

Rees, William. 1989. *Planning for Sustainable Development*. Vancouver, BC: UBC Centre for Human Settlements.

Reisner, Marc. 1987. *Cadillac Desert: The American West and its Disappearing Water*. New York: Penguin Books.

438 *Scott Campbell*

Rickaby, P. A. 1987. Six Settlement Patterns Compared. *Environment and Planning B: Planning and Design* 14: 193–223.

Robinson, Kelly. 1993. The Regional Economic Impacts of Marketable Permit Programs: The Case of Los Angeles. In *Cost Effective Control of Urban Smog*, Federal Reserve Bank of Chicago (November): 166–88.

Ross, Andrew. 1994. *The Chicago Gangster Theory of Life: Ecology, Culture, and Society.* London and New York: Verso.

Sale, Kirkpatrick. 1985. *Dwellers in the Land: The Bioregional Vision.* San Francisco: Sierra Club Books.

Schiller, Friedrich. 1965. *On the Aesthetic Education of Man* [translated by Reginald Snell]. Originally published in 1795 as *Über die Ästhetische Erziehung des Menschen in einer Reihe von Briefen.* New York: Friedrich Unger.

Sessions, George. 1992. Radical Environmentalism in the 90s. *Wild Earth* 2, 3: 64–7.

Smith, Neil. 1990. *Uneven Development: Nature, Capital and the Production of Space.* Oxford, UK: Blackwell.

Soja, Edward. 1989. *Postmodern Geographies: The Resurrection of Space in Critical Social Theory.* London and New York: Verso.

Susskind, Lawrence, and Jeffrey Cruikshank. 1987. Mediated Negotiation in the Public Sector: The Planner as Mediator. *Journal of Planning Education and Research* 4: 5–15.

Sussman, Carl, ed. 1976. *Planning the Fourth Migration: The Neglected Vision of the Regional Planning Association of America.* Cambridge, MA: MIT Press.

Tuason, Julie A. 1993. Economic/Environmental Conflicts in 19th-Century New York: Central Park, Adirondack State Park, and the Social Construction of Nature. Unpublished manuscript, Dept. of Geography, Rutgers University.

Turner, Frederick W. 1983. *Beyond Geography: The Western Spirit Against the Wilderness.* New Brunswick, NJ: Rutgers University Press.

Van der Ryn, Sim, and Peter Calthorpe. 1991. *Sustainable Communities: A New Design Synthesis for Cities, Suburbs and Towns.* San Francisco: Sierra Club Books.

Wiggins, Lyna. 1993. Geographic Information Systems. Lecture at the Center for Urban Policy Research, Rutgers University, April 5.

Wilson, Alexander. 1992. *The Culture of Nature: North American Landscape from Disney to the Exxon Valdez.* Cambridge, MA and Oxford, UK: Blackwell.

World Bank. 1989. *Striking a Balance: The Environmental Challenge of Development.* Washington, DC.

World Commission on Environment and Development (The Brundtland Commission). 1987. *Our Common Future.* Oxford: Oxford University Press.

Scott Campbell, "Green Cities, Growing Cities, Just Cities? Urban Planning and the Contradictions of Sustainable Development," *Journal of the American Planning Association,* 62 (3) (Summer 1996), pp. 296–312.

21

AICP Code of Ethics and Professional Conduct

American Institute of Certified Planners

Adopted March 19, 2005
Effective June 1, 2005
Revised October 3, 2009

The Executive Director of APA/AICP is the Ethics Officer as referenced in the following.

We, professional planners, who are members of the American Institute of Certified Planners, subscribe to our Institute's Code of Ethics and Professional Conduct. Our Code is divided into three sections:

Section A contains a statement of aspirational principles that constitute the ideals to which we are committed. We shall strive to act in accordance with our stated principles. However, an allegation that we failed to achieve our aspirational principles cannot be the subject of a misconduct charge or be a cause for disciplinary action.

Section B contains rules of conduct to which we are held accountable. If we violate any of these rules, we can be the object of a charge of misconduct and shall have the responsibility of responding to and cooperating with the investigation and enforcement procedures. If we are found to be blameworthy by the AICP Ethics Committee, we shall be subject to the imposition of sanctions that may include loss of our certification.

Section C contains the procedural provisions of the Code. It (1) describes the way that one may obtain either a formal or informal advisory ruling, and (2) details how a charge of misconduct can be filed, and how charges are investigated, prosecuted, and adjudicated.

Readings in Planning Theory, Third Edition. Edited by Susan S. Fainstein and Scott Campbell.
Editorial material and organization © 2012 Blackwell Publishing Ltd.
Published 2012 by Blackwell Publishing Ltd.

The principles to which we subscribe in Sections A and B of the Code derive from the special responsibility of our profession to serve the public interest with compassion for the welfare of all people and, as professionals, to our obligation to act with high integrity.

As the basic values of society can come into competition with each other, so can the aspirational principles we espouse under this Code. An ethical judgment often requires a conscientious balancing, based on the facts and context of a particular situation and on the precepts of the entire Code.

As Certified Planners, all of us are also members of the American Planning Association and share in the goal of building better, more inclusive communities. We want the public to be aware of the principles by which we practice our profession in the quest of that goal. We sincerely hope that the public will respect the commitments we make to our employers and clients, our fellow professionals, and all other persons whose interests we affect.

A: Principles to Which We Aspire

1.   Our overall responsibility to the public

Our primary obligation is to serve the public interest and we, therefore, owe our allegiance to a conscientiously attained concept of the public interest that is formulated through continuous and open debate. We shall achieve high standards of professional integrity, proficiency, and knowledge. To comply with our obligation to the public, we aspire to the following principles:

a) We shall always be conscious of the rights of others.
b) We shall have special concern for the long-range consequences of present actions.
c) We shall pay special attention to the interrelatedness of decisions.
d) We shall provide timely, adequate, clear, and accurate information on planning issues to all affected persons and to governmental decision makers.
e) We shall give people the opportunity to have a meaningful impact on the development of plans and programs that may affect them. Participation should be broad enough to include those who lack formal organization or influence.
f) We shall seek social justice by working to expand choice and opportunity for all persons, recognizing a special responsibility to plan for the needs of the disadvantaged and to promote racial and economic integration. We shall urge the alteration of policies, institutions, and decisions that oppose such needs.
g) We shall promote excellence of design and endeavor to conserve and preserve the integrity and heritage of the natural and built environment.
h) We shall deal fairly with all participants in the planning process. Those of us who are public officials or employees shall also deal evenhandedly with all planning process participants.

2. Our responsibility to our clients and employers

We owe diligent, creative, and competent performance of the work we do in pursuit of our client or employer's interest. Such performance, however, shall always be consistent with our faithful service to the public interest.

a) We shall exercise independent professional judgment on behalf of our clients and employers.
b) We shall accept the decisions of our client or employer concerning the objectives and nature of the professional services we perform unless the course of action is illegal or plainly inconsistent with our primary obligation to the public interest.
c) We shall avoid a conflict of interest or even the appearance of a conflict of interest in accepting assignments from clients or employers.

3. Our responsibility to our profession and colleagues

We shall contribute to the development of, and respect for, our profession by improving knowledge and techniques, making work relevant to solutions of community problems, and increasing public understanding of planning activities.

a) We shall protect and enhance the integrity of our profession.
b) We shall educate the public about planning issues and their relevance to our everyday lives.
c) We shall describe and comment on the work and views of other professionals in a fair and professional manner.
d) We shall share the results of experience and research that contribute to the body of planning knowledge.
e) We shall examine the applicability of planning theories, methods, research and practice and standards to the facts and analysis of each particular situation and shall not accept the applicability of a customary solution without first establishing its appropriateness to the situation.
f) We shall contribute time and resources to the professional development of students, interns, beginning professionals, and other colleagues.
g) We shall increase the opportunities for members of underrepresented groups to become professional planners and help them advance in the profession.
h) We shall continue to enhance our professional education and training.
i) We shall systematically and critically analyze ethical issues in the practice of planning.
j) We shall contribute time and effort to groups lacking in adequate planning resources and to voluntary professional activities.

B: Our Rules of Conduct

We adhere to the following Rules of Conduct, and we understand that our Institute will enforce compliance with them. If we fail to adhere to these Rules, we could receive sanctions, the ultimate being the loss of our certification:

1. We shall not deliberately or with reckless indifference fail to provide adequate, timely, clear and accurate information on planning issues.

2. We shall not accept an assignment from a client or employer when the services to be performed involve conduct that we know to be illegal or in violation of these rules.

3. We shall not accept an assignment from a client or employer to publicly advocate a position on a planning issue that is indistinguishably adverse to a position we publicly advocated for a previous client or employer within the past three years unless (1) we determine in good faith after consultation with other qualified professionals that our change of position will not cause present detriment to our previous client or employer, and (2) we make full written disclosure of the conflict to our current client or employer and receive written permission to proceed with the assignment.

4. We shall not, as salaried employees, undertake other employment in planning or a related profession, whether or not for pay, without having made full written disclosure to the employer who furnishes our salary and having received subsequent written permission to undertake additional employment, unless our employer has a written policy which expressly dispenses with a need to obtain such consent.

5. We shall not, as public officials or employees; accept from anyone other than our public employer any compensation, commission, rebate, or other advantage that may be perceived as related to our public office or employment.

6. We shall not perform work on a project for a client or employer if, in addition to the agreed upon compensation from our client or employer, there is a possibility for direct personal or financial gain to us, our family members, or persons living in our household, unless our client or employer, after full written disclosure from us, consents in writing to the arrangement.

7. We shall not use to our personal advantage, nor that of a subsequent client or employer, information gained in a professional relationship that the client or employer has requested be held inviolate or that we should recognize as confidential because its disclosure could result in embarrassment or other detriment to the client or employer. Nor shall we disclose such confidential information except when (1) required by process of law, or (2) required to prevent a clear violation of law, or (3) required to prevent a substantial injury to the public. Disclosure pursuant to (2) and (3) shall not be made until after we have verified the facts and issues involved and, when practicable, exhausted efforts to obtain reconsideration of the matter and have sought separate opinions on the issue from other qualified professionals employed by our client or employer.

8. We shall not, as public officials or employees, engage in private communications with planning process participants if the discussions relate to a matter over which we have authority to make a binding, final determination if such private communications are prohibited by law or by agency rules, procedures, or custom.

9. We shall not engage in private discussions with decision makers in the planning process in any manner prohibited by law or by agency rules, procedures, or custom.

10. We shall neither deliberately, nor with reckless indifference, misrepresent the qualifications, views and findings of other professionals.

11. We shall not solicit prospective clients or employment through use of false or misleading claims, harassment, or duress.

12. We shall not misstate our education, experience, training, or any other facts which are relevant to our professional qualifications.

13. We shall not sell, or offer to sell, services by stating or implying an ability to influence decisions by improper means.

14. We shall not use the power of any office to seek or obtain a special advantage that is not a matter of public knowledge or is not in the public interest.

15. We shall not accept work beyond our professional competence unless the client or employer understands and agrees that such work will be performed by another professional competent to perform the work and acceptable to the client or employer.

16. We shall not accept work for a fee, or pro bono, that we know cannot be performed with the promptness required by the prospective client, or that is required by the circumstances of the assignment.

17. We shall not use the product of others' efforts to seek professional recognition or acclaim intended for producers of original work.

18. We shall not direct or coerce other professionals to make analyses or reach findings not supported by available evidence.

19. We shall not fail to disclose the interests of our client or employer when participating in the planning process. Nor shall we participate in an effort to conceal the true interests of our client or employer.

20. We shall not unlawfully discriminate against another person.

21. We shall not withhold cooperation or information from the AICP Ethics Officer or the AICP Ethics Committee if a charge of ethical misconduct has been filed against us.

22. We shall not retaliate or threaten retaliation against a person who has filed a charge of ethical misconduct against us or another planner, or who is cooperating in the Ethics Officer's investigation of an ethics charge.

23. We shall not use the threat of filing an ethics charge in order to gain, or attempt to gain, an advantage in dealings with another planner.

24. We shall not file a frivolous charge of ethical misconduct against another planner.

25. We shall neither deliberately, nor with reckless indifference, commit any wrongful act, whether or not specified in the Rules of Conduct, that reflects adversely on our professional fitness.

26. We shall not fail to immediately notify the Ethics Officer by both receipted Certified and Regular First Class Mail if we are convicted of a "serious crime" as defined in Section D of the Code; nor immediately following such conviction shall we represent ourselves as Certified Planners or Members of AICP until our membership is reinstated by the AICP Ethics Committee pursuant to the procedures in Section D of the Code.

American Institute of Certified Planners, *ACIP Code of Ethics and Professional Conduct*. Adopted March 19, 2005; revised Oct. 3, 2009, Parts A and B. http://www.planning.org/ethics/ethicscode.htm

22

Public Policy as Discursive Construct
Social Meaning and Multiple Realities

Frank Fischer

The starting point for a postempiricist discursive alternative to contemporary policy inquiry begins with the recognition that the human and physical realms are inherently different. The reason has to do with social meaning. Whereas physical objects have no intrinsic meaning structures, human actors actively construct their social worlds. They do so by assigning meaning to events and actions, both physical and social. Human experience, as such, is enveloped in a non-material social, cultural, and personal realm of thought and meanings.

It is not that all people are constructing and reconstructing their worlds all of the time. On the contrary, most of the time we live in a social world into which we were born, a world of meaning generally taken for granted by the people who live in it. Given their socialization, it comes to them more or less as a given, fixed reality and they treat it as such. People realize, of course, the world was established before they arrived. The point is that many of the ideas and social understandings upon which their world was constructed are difficult to recognize or identify. They are typically buried in everyday practices and accepted as part of the nature of things. Indeed, for many, these ideas and beliefs come to give the impression of being natural, or perhaps obvious, in the language of the everyday world. Even when people do have an appreciation of these ideas and meanings, the original meanings of their forefathers are not immediately or obviously accessible to them. It may be the case that these ideas or meanings were appropriate at that time, but no longer relevant or right for a new generation and its social circumstances. For instance, it is common today in the Western world to accept that women are equal to men and should have the same rights. But, as feminists are quick to point out, numerous laws and practices still in existence have their origins in a time when women were seen as inferior.[1]

Readings in Planning Theory, Third Edition. Edited by Susan S. Fainstein and Scott Campbell.
Editorial material and organization © 2012 Blackwell Publishing Ltd.
Published 2012 by Blackwell Publishing Ltd.

One of the main features of the politics of social change – indeed often the main feature – is the calling of particular meanings into question. Movements concerned with issues such as civil rights, women's liberation, or environmental protection have organized their struggles around calling attention, to underlying social assumptions and their less obvious implications for contemporary life.[2] Thus, while most of us are first and foremost products of our social environment, we also can be agents affecting the world in which we live. Not everybody assumes the role of agent of social and political change. But the activities of those who do are among the main objects of political inquiry.

If the first principle of a phenomenological or interpretive perspective is an emphasis on meanings in the construction and understanding of social reality, the second is that social meanings are always potentially open to reconstruction and change. The social world of the individual or the collective is constantly enlarged by new experiences and thoughts; it is continuously in the process of evolving through reflection, practices, and communication with others. Changing over time through the interaction of people's cognitive schemes with their social environment, the social world is an interpretive linkage of social perceptions, recollections, and expectations, all of which are grounded in subjective experience and understanding of the social and physical realms.

This understanding of social reality has profound import for the way we approach the study of social and political inquiry. Based on social meanings – motives, intentions, goals, purposes, values, and so forth – social action is constructed through language and, as such, its analysis has more in common with history and literature than with physical science. Rather than seeking proofs through formal logic and empirical experimentation, the investigation of social action requires the use of metaphoric processes that pull together and connect different experiences based on perceived similarities. The meaning of a social experience is assessed in terms of its position in the larger patterns of which it is a part, be it a situation, a social system, or an ideology.

Because social meanings change, there can be no fixed or lasting set of meanings associated with the actors and events that constitute social and political life. To be sure, some meanings can last for generations and be approached as relatively fixed. But there are no firm social categories in which positivists can empirically anchor their methods. Even when social meanings last for longer durations, they still have to be seen as related to a particular time and place. This is to say, there can be no universal interpretations that are applicable without reference to social context.

The neglect of this basic nature of social reality by empiricist social science has had profound implications for political and policy inquiry. The failure to carefully connect or relate empirical findings to the social understandings of those under investigation is a root cause of the problem. By treating the meanings of their findings as clear or evident, empiricist social scientists assign to them in effect the social understandings of the dominant social groups. In a world of dominant and subordinate groups, this practice wittingly or unwittingly supports the conception of the socio-political world advanced by social and political elites. This failure to translate empirical findings into a set of social meanings germane to the full play of politics underlies the charge of social irrelevance that has plagued sociology, political science, and, yes, even economics. If the pretence that empirical findings speak for themselves has managed to endure in ivory tower social science, it becomes a problem rather quickly in an applied field of inquiry such as policy analysis, where the explicit goal is to facilitate real-world decision processes. These processes, as we see below, are entirely interwoven with dominant and competing systems of social meaning.

Despite the continuing dominance of empiricism in the social and policy sciences, the implications of social science's neglect of the value-laden social meanings inherent in social and political action has long been understood by the critics, in particular political philosophers and interpretive social scientists. That this polemic still has to be engaged, despite recognition of the methodological implications associated with dealing with meaningful action, is more than a little astonishing. The endurance of empiricism in the face of the success of this critique only under-scores the power of a scientific ideology.

Basic to the postempiricist critique has been an analytical differentiation between two fundamental traditions of knowing – causal explanation of the type sought by the physical sciences (concerned with establishing relations between causes and effects) and the kind of social understanding central to the social world. Because the arguments for scientific causal explanation are best known, [...], we concentrate here on the concept of social understanding.

The Phenomenology of Social Action

Whereas positivist-oriented empirical analysis aims at causal explanation and prediction of behaviour, social understanding requires a teleological explanation related to goals and purposes. In the traditions of sociology, following the great German sociologist Max Weber, such explanation is referred to as the process of *Verstehen*. *Verstehen* identifies the process of rendering facts *understandable* by interpreting their meanings in the light of relevant social goals and values.

The origins of *Verstehen* sociology can be traced to philosophers and social scientists influenced by the philosophy of phenomenology. Although the label "phenomenologist" captures a somewhat mixed group, by and large the works of Alfred Schutz (1967) and his followers, especially Berger and Luckmann (1966), have been seminal in the interpretivist debate with the positivist approach. The special value of the phenomenological movement has been its deep-seated critique of social science inquiry itself. No other theoretical orientation has devoted as much effort to the explication of the distinction between the social and physical worlds and the methodologies appropriate to each.

The crucial question of a phenomenological interpretive social science revolves around the applicability of objective, empirically oriented methods to the subjec-tively based problems of the social world. Concerned fundamentally with the role of social meaning, the interpretivist objection to the use of physical science techniques is that the physical world possess no intrinsic meaning structure. As Schutz (1962: 5) explained, it is up to the physical scientists "to determine which sector of the universe of nature which facts and which events therein, and which aspects of such facts and events are topically relevant to their specific purpose". The data and events within the observational field of the physical scientist do "not 'mean' anything to the molecules, atoms and electrons therein".

The social realm, unlike the physical realm, is inherently laden with subjective meaning. For the social inquirer, the observational field has "a particular meaning and relevance structure for the human beings living, thinking and acting therein. The human subjects have preselected and preinterpreted this world by a series of commonsense constructs which determine their behavior, define the goal of the actions [and] the means available – which help them find their bearings in their natural and socio-cultural environment and to come to grips with it" (Schutz 1962: 5–6). Thus, the social world is an organized universe of meaning experienced and interpreted by everyday social actors. Social knowledge is in significant part the product of these common-sense interpretations that, when combined with the social actors' personal experience, forms an orientation toward the everyday world that is taken for granted.

The social actor's constructs, as first-order constructs of social reality, pose a fundamental methodological implication for social scientists. Unlike physical scientists, social scientists cannot establish from the outside which events and facts are interpretationally relevant to the actor's own specific purposes. The constructs of social science must take the form of second-order constructs. The crux of the problem, as such, is how to establish and maintain a systematic relationship between social scientists' second-order explanations and the everyday first-order explanations of the social actors under investigation.

The failure of the empiricist approach is its inability to incorporate an adequate account of the social actor's subjective understanding of the situation. By focusing on the observable dimensions of a social phenomenon, empiricists observe the social world from a different angle from that of their subjects. The empiricists' models, in short, tend to be constructed around the researcher's own implicit assumptions and value judgements about reality. They thus drift away from the social context by tacitly substituting their own view of the relevant aspects of the situation for the social actors' understanding of the social realities. These tacit value assumptions are usually difficult to observe since they are buried in the foundations of the empiricists' theoretical model.

To accurately explain social phenomena, the investigator must first attempt to understand the meaning of the social phenomenon from the actor's perspective. Such an understanding is derived by interpreting the phenomenon against the social actor's own motive and values. A good example is offered by the policy analytic approach of Schuman (1982). Following the theoretical insights of Schutz, Schuman conducted a phenomenological examination of higher education policy in the United States by letting the students speak for themselves.

Schuman's goal was to reveal the everyday meanings of going to a university for both college students and those who chose not to attend. After reviewing the standard kinds of statistically-based explanations about why students are said to go to college – mainly to earn a better living – he showed through extensive interviews that such objective analysis cannot capture the much more complicated sets of reasons and motives involved in decisions to both go to and stay in college. Economics-related statistics simply missed the intricate web of reasons and motives that bear on such decisions. Letting the students speak for themselves revealed the statistics to be accurate, but not right. As Schuman (1982: 29) puts it, they are not wrong, but at the same time you can't say that they are correct. The problem with such statistical explanations, he shows, is that they deal with only a very small part of the student's reality and thus go astray because of exclusion. In short, the meaning of these statistics as they relate to the students can be understood only by examining them in terms of the configuration of factors that structure their personal social context. To know what college means to people, he argues, we must get them to reveal both their way of seeing the world and the world in which they are living.

Despite the many misunderstandings that have surrounded this process of *Verstehen*, it does not signal a return to an explanatory technique based on empathy or intuitive understanding of the motives and reasons behind observed social action (Morrow and Brown 1994). From Schutz's perspective, *Verstehen* is not an instrument of explanation but rather a process of concept formation employed in arriving at an interpretive understanding of social phenomena. The focus of the interpretive process is on the social actor's meaning rather than the intuitive or empathic mental processes of the observer. Interpretive understanding, in this respect, does not deny the need for verification, as implied by intuitive conceptions of *Verstehen*. Instead, it calls attention to the fact that any method that permits the observer to select and interpret social facts in terms of his or her own private value system can never produce a socially relevant, valid theory.

A couple of illustrations can help to clarify this point. If the empiricist social scientist wants to explain why Mr X is more actively engaged in politics than Ms Y, he or she may appeal to an empirically established causal finding in the empirical literature: men are more active politically than women. The interpretive political scientist, however, is likely to ask whether this type of causal reference really provides sufficient information to enable one to understand the situation. Most people confronted with this question would ask to be supplied with additional information. What are Mr X's reasons and motives for his political involvement? Does he seek to gain moral approbation? Is he determined to protect certain strongly held beliefs? Does he think political involvement will further his business career?

The limitation of a causal explanation is even better illustrated in historical situations. Take the case of Neville Chamberlain's action at Munich in 1938. Would it be productive to ask: what always causes a Chamberlain at a Munich in 1938 to do exactly the sort of thing the actual Chamberlain did there and then? (Dray 1957). The interpretivist's contribution here is to show that the historian works to marshal the facts and norms of the situation to illustrate that Chamberlain's actions can be explained as the logical outcome of a specific configuration of factors. The task is to demonstrate that, given certain motives and purposes, it was (or was not) logical for the man to act in a specific way in such a situation.

Inquiring into social meaning is not to be understood as an uncontrollable or indeterminable aspect of social discourse. Aimed at mutual understanding through acculturation and commonly shared social learning, social understanding can in many cases be subjected to tests of valid inference. Because of the intermingling of factual and normative elements, though, such inferential tests generally follow a different path from those rendered by empirical analysis. The nature of the process can be nicely illustrated with a courtroom analogy. In a court trial, subjective perceptions of facts and reasons are submitted to a number of inferential and documentary tests. The judge and the jury, for example, do not simply impute reasons and motives to the defendant, however plausible they may sound. Documentary evidence and testimony must be produced in support of an explanation formulated in terms of "reasons" for behaviour rather than causes in the strict sense of the term. The verdict is reached by bringing together the external evidence and the defendant's publicly stated subjective intentions. It is the task of the judge and the jury to interpret the defendant's social behaviour against a reconstruction of what they take to be the facts.

Following this line of argument, it can scarcely be said that interpretive understandings are arbitrary. Although answers are not worked out by rigid adherence to the scientific methods of demonstration and verification, interpretive understandings can be based on the giving of reasons and the assessment of arguments. In such analysis, the task is to show how certain circumstances *logically* entitle a specific opinion or way of viewing things. The relationship of the belief to a decision or action is not external and contingent (like causes) but internal and logical. Even though such argumentation is not based on certainty in the scientific sense, it is possible to have a significant degree of confidence in a well-reasoned interpretation of social action [...].

The Social Construction of Reality

Whereas phenomenology is basically a philosophical orientation that has shaped the interpretivist perspective in the social sciences, the interpretivist emphasis on multiple social realities has given rise to various theoretical lines of investigation. The contemporary variant most important to postempiricist policy analysis is social constructionism, also more simply referred to as constructionism. Social constructionism refers to the varying ways in which the social realities of the world are shaped and perceived (Gergen 1999). Although there are theoretical differences among those who call themselves social constructionists, they share a common concern for how people assign meaning to the world.

The idea of social constructionism has it origins in the sociology of knowledge (Berger and Luckmann 1966; Mannheim 1936). Most basically, it is an inquiry into the ways objects are seen through different mental structures or world views, how they are interpreted in different social circumstances and understood during different historical periods. Because social constructs are so much a part of our way of life, it is often difficult to recognize them as constructions. Their identification and explication, for this reason, relies heavily on the interpretive or hermeneutic methods of social inquiry [...].

The social constructionist approach is of particular relevance to policy analysis for two reasons. One is its major influence on the field of science and technology studies, a focus of inquiry with direct bearing on the methods and techniques of policy science (Latour and Woolgar 1979; Jasanoff 1990). Such theorists examine the ways in which scientific facts, experiences, events, and beliefs are constructed and certified to be true or valid. [...] [T]he most basic insight of such work is that the very objects of inquiry are constituted through a mix of physical objects and social interactions. Science, for this reason, is seen to be better explained as a social process with similarities to many other social processes, rather than an objective methodology removed from social and subjective concerns. For example, those things taken to be the concepts and theories of the field are the product of a social consensus process among elite members of the scientific community rather the discovery and proof of a fixed social reality per se. The facts of science are thus determined as much by the assumptions underlying them as they are by empirical observations. The point is derived from studies of the physical science, but applies even more to the social sciences.

The other relevant way in which social constructionism has played a major theoretical role is the focus on social problems in sociology, an area of study closely related to public policy (Best 1989; Gusfield 1981; 1989). In so far as public policies are designed to address social problems, it is in many ways the same topic only dressed up somewhat differently. Originally, social problem theorists assumed that the existence of social problems such as drug addiction or crime were the direct outcomes of readily identifiable, visible objective social conditions. Contemporary constructionists now see them to be the products of activities of political or social groups making claims about putative conditions to public officials and agencies, with the recognition of the grievance depending on the success of their rhetorical campaign. Whereas social scientists, in the first instance, were regarded as experts employing scientific methods to locate and analyse those moral violations and advise policy-makers on how to best cope with them, such problems in the constructivist view result from a sequence of events that develop on the basis of collective social definitions.

Best (1989), for example, points to three primary foci in the studying of the construction of social problems; the claims, the claims-makers, and the claims-making process. In the case of environmental politics, Hannigan (1995: 54–5), following Best, shows the ways the environmental problem is socially constructed as a multifaceted construction which welds together a clutch of philosophies, ideologies, scientific specialities, and policy initiatives. He argues that six factors are forged together in the construction of the environmental problem: (1) scientific authority for and validation of claims; (2) existence of a popularizer who can bridge environmentalism and science; (3) media attention in which the problem is framed as novel and important; (4) dramatization of the problem in symbolic and visual terms; (5) economic incentives for taking positive action; and (6) emergence of an institutional sponsor who can ensure both legitimacy and continuity. Put differently, even if ozone levels in the atmospherc increase, without an effective interplay of these six factors drawing public attention to it, the ozone hole will not be a worrisome topic of public concern, let alone make it onto the political agenda. That is, from a political perspective, the problem would not exist.

Such constructionist analysis of social problems closely parallels the concerns and considerations that come into play in the policy agenda-setting process generally, involving first with how an issue comes to be identified and defined and, second, how it gets on the political and governmental agendas (Cobb and Elder 1972; 1983; Clemons and MacBeth 2001: 175–233). In this sense, the constructionist perspective on social problems analyses the first step of the policy agenda-setting process, especially problem definition. A useful analytic example in the policy literature is offered by Linder (1995: 208–30), who offers a framework of categories for identifying the rhetorical and problem elements involved in the social construction of a policy problem. Examining the public controversies in the US over the health risks posed by living in proximity to the electric and magnetic fields created by power lines, he demonstrates how the rhetorical elements of problem construction can be identified in terms of four analytic categories:

- the nature of the argumentative appeals and warrants (for example, as moralist or paternalistic premises);
- how scientific claims are treated in the controversy (for example, as decisive evidence or partisan advocacy);
- the image of the public underlying the rhetoric (for example, as victims or potential issue activists); and
- the image of the electro and magnetic fields (for example, as toxin hazard or socially perceived risk).

Linder then delineates four policy-analytic elements embedded in each of the rhetorical constructions:

- the policy objective (for example, health protection or the public's right-to-know);
- the type of policy intervention (for example, regulatory control or research support);
- the policy instrument (for example, limits on exposures or a public information campaign); and
- the objectionable errors (for example, false negatives or false positives).

Politics in a World of Multiple Realities

As the foregoing discussion makes clear, politics is about social meanings. It is about politicians, interest groups, and citizens who hold multiple and changing social meanings about the political actions and events that transpire in the world in which they operate. Indeed, the creation of meaning is a crucial dimension in the political manoeuvre for advantage: the construction of beliefs about events, policies, leaders, problems, and crises that rationalize or challenge existing inequalities. Such meaning creation is basic to the mobilization of support for particular actions as well as to efforts to immobilize the political opposition. While intimidation and coercion help to counter political resistance, the most basic strategy for generating support in a democratic system is the evocation of social and political interpretations that legitimize the desired course of action. Designed either to threaten or reassure – or both, depending on the interests of competing groups – such interpretations encourage people to be actively supportive or at minimum to remain quiescent.

Despite the fact that symbols and the multiple meanings create problems for the systematic empirical study of politics and public policy, there is no escaping their central role in the world of political action. Even though politics is generally discussed and pursued in practical terms, particularly in terms of consequences, it is always at the same time about the social meanings of problems and events. As every politician, journalist, or historian knows, political controversy and strategic behaviour turns on conflicting interpretations of events and actions. Political leaders are judged to be tyrannical or benevolent, economic and social policies as exploitative or just, and so on. Although the process takes different forms, it is witnessed throughout the ages in all political cultures.

Where do these social meanings come from? This is not an easy question. One thing is clear, though: they do not spring from thin air. Social meanings are the products of interactions among social actors. People decide the meaning of statements by considering them from the perspectives of others significant to them, through either direct communicative encounters or the "inner speech" process involving imagined conversations with their intended or would-be interlocutors.

The social meaning upon which political discourses turn are mainly derived from moral or ideological positions that establish and govern competing views of the good society. Although contemporary parties and groups go to considerable effort to avoid explicit use of ideological language – more so in the United States than in Europe – the struggle over the allocation of political benefits and costs is always enveloped in the ideological contest. A political claim thus reflects and reinforces an ideology, a subject, and a reality. For example, those who accept and support the electoral outcomes of contests between the Republican and Democrat Parties in the United States wittingly or unwittingly sustain a construction of a world that generally treats the issues of class, race, gender, and inequality as secondary concerns.

Both the material and social worlds get their specific social meanings from the symbols of a world view or ideology. The language, objects, and rituals to which those in politics respond are more than abstract ideas. A symbol typically carries a range of diverse, often conflicting meanings that are an integral part of particular social or material situations. The experience of the symbols stands for the material condition and vice versa. Although the social-psychological processes through which this happens are not fully understood, the material foundations of the symbol is generally evident. Languages, objects, and actions that evoke social meanings presuppose that the evocation is a function of particular material and social conditions. Every sign, as Edelman (1988: 9) puts it, exercises its effect because of the specific content of privilege, disadvantage, frustration, aspiration, hope, and fear in which it is experienced.

Recognizing the degree to which linguistic symbols structure our understanding of politics is the first step in seeing that political language *is* in important ways political reality itself. As the medium of symbols, it is generally the language about political events, not the events themselves, that people experience. Even the political events that we personally witness take their meaning from the language that portrays them. For both participants and observers there is no other reality.[3]

Thus the potency of political language does not stem from its mere descriptions of a real world, as empiricists have maintained. Rather, it comes from its reconstruction of the world – its interpretations of past experiences, its evocation of the unobservable aspects in the present, and constructions of possibilities and expectations for the future. These features make language a powerful constitutive force within politics. And, as such, the ability to use it effectively is an essential resource in the unfolding of the political process.

By compelling us to examine the subtle connections between social meaning and language, the constructionist perspective makes us aware that the potential ambiguity of statements about social action invariably carries different meanings in different settings. For this reason, the analyst must carefully attend to the speaker's political language. As Edelman (1988: 104) explains, the use of political language is a clue to the speaker's view of reality at the time, just as an audience's interpretation of the same language is a clue to what may be a different reality for them. If there are no conflicts over meaning, the issue is not political, by definition.

This position is in no way intended to imply that all political arguments are either equally valid or entirely relative, [...]. The point is to recognize and appreciate that social situations and the discourses about them create political arguments that cannot be finally verified or falsified. Because a social problem is not a verifiable entity but a construction that furthers ideological interests, its explanation is bound to be part of the process of construction rather than a set of falsifiable propositions (Edelman 1988: 18). In short, a society of multiple realities and relative standards are all we ever achieve (Edelman 1988: 111). It is a reality that social scientists must accept and learn to deal with.

In so far as the aspects of events, leaders, and policies that most decisively affect current and future social well-being are uncertain or unknowable, the political language that depicts them is necessarily ambiguous. Even when there is consensus about an action or a statement, there will be conflicting assumptions about the causes of developments, the intentions of interest groups and public officials, and the consequences of the specific event. It is thus not just what can be observed that shapes public action and political support, but what must be assumed, supposed, or constructed. Is the president or prime minister a well-meaning leader who represents the common people's aspirations against the elitist liberals and intellectuals, or is he a front man for mean-spirited corporate executives and a menace to the poor? The answer depends on political ideology and social assumptions.

Reason and rationalizations are thus intertwined. There is no way to establish the validity of any of these positions that can necessarily satisfy those who have a material or moral reason to hold a different view. Indeed, given the intertwining of facts and interests, the hallmark of political argument is the near-impossibility of marshalling evidence that can persuade everyone. Pervasive in such argumentation are contradictions, ambiguities, and rhetorical evocations that reflect the material situations and ideological orientations of the political participants. In short, it is not reality in an observable or testable sense that shapes social consciousness and political action, but rather the ideas and beliefs that political language helps evoke about the causes of satisfactions and discontents.

To be sure, language is only one aspect of a political situation, but it is a critical one. Through language political phenomena are interpretively fitted into narrative accounts that supply them with social meanings acceptable to particular audiences and their ideologies. Although they are susceptible to political criticism, firmly held narratives manage time and again in suspending belief or critical judgement, in sustaining opposition, or marshalling political support despite events that create doubts that put them in question (Edelman 1988).

Even though there is nothing new about the role of symbols in politics, this emphasis on symbols takes on special meaning in the modern age of the mass media. As postmodernists point out, politics today has become something of a spectacle. In the study of politics we are especially indebted to Murray Edelman (1988) for this perspective, who in many ways was a postmodernist ahead of his time.

The Political Spectacle as Hyperreality

Politicians and the media, as Edelman has shown, have turned contemporary politics into a political spectacle that is experienced more like a stage drama rather than reality itself. Based on socially constructed stories designed more to capture the interest of the audience than to offer factual portrayal of events, the political spectacle is constituted by a set of political symbols and signifiers that continuously construct and reconstruct self-conceptions, the meaning of past events, expectations for the future, and the significance of prominent social groups. As an interpretation reflecting the diverse social situations of its audiences and the language and symbols to which they are exposed, the political spectacle attributes meanings to social problems, political leaders, and enemies that rationalize and perpetuate political roles, statuses, and ideologies. The spectacle of politics is a modern-day fetish, a creation in part of political actors that come to dominate the thoughts and activities of both its audience and the actors themselves.

The best-known example of the political spectacle is the American-style presidential campaign, which focuses more on the horse race than on the issues themselves. For at least a year before a presidential election the media turn the contest into a virtual soap opera that comes to fascinate a large portion of the society, despite its banality. For many observers, it has lead to the near collapse of the American political culture (Agger 1990).

Postmodern analysis identifies this spectacle as part of the hyperreality that characterizes much of contemporary American society and increasingly European youth culture as well. Hyperreality pertains to a situation in which words, symbols, and signs are increasingly divorced from direct experiences in the social world. It refers, as such, to a process in postmodern society in which "symbols can be thought of as float[ing] away ... to procreate with other symbols" (Fox 1995).

This free play of signifiers is based on the marketing and advertising practices of post-industrial society, where the design of products to which symbols have been attached become too complex for the consumer to master (Jameson 1992). As symbols lose their moorings, marketers take advantage of this and manipulate them by attaching them to other symbols. Thus, as Fox (1995) puts it, machines become sexy, cleaning fluids repair dysfunctional families, and to purchase a particular brand of coloured carbonated water is to signify membership in a generation.[4]

As signs increasingly break away from the objects or events they were designed to denote, any sort of concrete or empirical conception of reality loses its influence over them. In the process, such signs can in a certain way be understood to have a life of their own outside everyday experiential reality. Like sports celebrities and movie stars, politicians increasingly operate in this realm, especially evidenced in electoral campaigns. As public relations consultants and spin doctors manipulate the symbols of a media-driven political process, political symbols increasingly evince tenuous relations to the objects and events traditionally taken to be reality. One of the most interesting images of this state of affairs is drawn by the French philosopher Baudrillard (1989) in his book *America*. More than a little cynically, he offers a portrait of the American family travelling along the open highway in an automobile whose windows have been replaced by television screens.

Not all citizens are duped by such linguistic manipulations, but many do seem to take hyperreality to be reality itself. For those who recognize these manipulations, it has the effect of turning many of them off to politics generally. A phenomenon of considerable concern to serious observers of the political scene, its manifestations are decreasing levels of citizen participation, dwindling levels of voter turn-out, indifference to important issues, poor understanding of the issues, and low levels of civic involvement, among other things.

The Social Meanings of Public Policies

Maynard-Moody and Kelly (1993: 71) describe the policy process as a struggle over the symbols we invoke and the categories into which we place different problems and solutions, because ultimately these symbols and categories will determine the action that we take. On this view, a political community is made up of citizens who live in a web of independent associations fused together through shared symbols. In such a community, people envisage ideas about the good society and struggle for common, shared interests as well as their own personal interests (Stone 1988). Unlike contemporary policy analysis, such an interpretive policy analysis rejects the idea that individual interests are simply given. The analyst needs to account for how citizens get their images of the world in which they live, how they are socially constructed, and the ways these images shape individual interests and policy preferences.

Earlier we defined policy as a political agreement on a course of action or (inaction) designed to resolve or mitigate problems on the political agenda. This agreement, as Heclo (1972) explains, is an intellectual construct rather than a self-defining phenomenon. Discursively constructed, there can be no inherently unique decisions, institutions, or actors constituting a public policy that are only to be identified, uncovered, and explained. Public policy, as such, is an analytical category with a substantive content and cannot be simply researched; more fundamentally, it has to be interpreted. Hence, as Majone (1989: 147) adds, our understanding of a policy and its outcomes cannot be separated from the ideas, theories, and criteria by which the policy is analysed and described.

From a constructivist perspective, the basic political agreement upon which a policy rests refers to an understanding based on a set of normative and empirical beliefs. As Stone (1988) makes clear, the standard production model of policy fails to capture the nature of this understanding. The essence of policymaking, as she writes, is the struggle over ideas and their meanings. Recognizing that shared meanings motivate people to action and meld individual striving into collective action, ideas are the medium of exchange in policymaking, a mode of influence even more powerful than money, votes, or guns. As such, policymaking is a constant discursive struggle over the definitions of problems, the boundaries of categories used to describe them, the criteria for their classification and assessment, and the meanings of ideals that guide particular actions.

Each policy-related idea is an argument, or rather a set of arguments, favouring different ways of looking at the world. The task of the analyst is to examine the multiple understandings of what otherwise appears to be a single concept, in particular how these understandings are created and how they are manipulated as part of political strategy. Uncovering the hidden arguments embedded in each policy concept, Stone (2002) explains, can illuminate and even at times resolve the political conflicts that would otherwise only appear to be on the surface of the issue.

Conventionally, policy is described in instrumental terms as a strategic intervention to resolve or assist in resolving a problem. From this perspective, as we have seen, policy is analysed objectively in terms of efficiency or effectiveness. And this is not entirely wrong. But it neglects the fact that the very same policy is a symbolic entity, the meaning of which is determined by its relationship to the particular situation, social system, and ideological framework of which it is a part. As Yanow (1996) puts it, policies are neither symbolic nor substantive. They are both at once. Even purely instrumental intentions are communicated and perceived through symbolic means (Yanow 1996:12). The creation and implementation of a policy is about the creation of symbols, with programme names, organizations and rituals, with even the design and decor of buildings being part of the language. In this formulation, notions of cause and effect need not disappear, as critics of interpretive analysis often suggest, but the focus on such relationships does not take precedence over interpretive analysis.

Much of the best constructivist research has to do with determining what is considered a policy problem and what is not, or what in policy studies is usually discussed as agenda-setting. In the constructionist view, the problems which governments seek to resolve are not just considered to have an "objective" base in the economy or material structure of the society, but are also constructed in the realm of public and private discourse. They do not come into existence simply because they are there, or for their implications for well-being. As Edelman puts it (1988: 12), such problems come into discourse and therefore into existence as reinforcements of ideologies, not simply because they are there or because they are important for well-being.

The ideologies and values underlying policies are often reflected in symbols. Created through language and communicative interaction, such symbols signify the meanings of particular events and offer standards for judging what is good and bad. Edelman (1977; 1988), for example, illustrates how words such as "welfare" generate images that cause people to reject the claims of groups in need of social assistance. Because the interests of competing groups give rise to diverging meanings, as Edelman (1988: 15) puts it, national security is a different problem for each of the parties concerned with it, such as the various branches of the arms forces, the General Dynamics Corporation, that firm's workers, the Women's International Leagues for Peace and Freedom, and potential draftees. In this sense, a problem is the result of negotiations among groups with competing definitions. This can, of course, be understood as interest group politics, but it differs from the standard approach that sees each group pursuing its own interest in a particular context. Here groups have different interests, but they also define the problems and interests differently.

Given these subjective and less observable dimensions of policy, it is difficult to justify the conventional modes [of] rational analysis. On those rare occasions when social well-being is not closely linked to value differences and objectives are comparatively non-controversial, the standard technical approach to policy analysis – adjusting efficient means to political ends – can play a role. In the real world of policy politics, though, the majority of the situations involve much more than the logic of effective means to achieve social goals. Moreover, means and ends are often inherently connected in such ways that make it difficult to see which is which is, for example, the death penalty a means to a necessary end, or it is an evil end unto itself? It depends on whom you ask.

What is more, the reasons political actors generally offer for their policy objectives are rationalizations designed to persuade particular audiences. Ideological arguments, writes Edelman (1988: 115), are typically advanced through a dramaturgy of objective description, which masks the performative function of political language. In the name of such description, the acceptability of the policy argument ultimately depends on how effectively it succeeds in rationalizing the situation of its intended audience.

Although conventional policy analysis is devoted to uncovering and deciding objective facts, policy turns less on the *facts* of a controversy than on the meanings that it generates. Indeed, it is precisely that events are assigned different meanings by different groups that makes them politically controversial. Even when groups can come to an agreement on disputed facts, the question of what these facts mean to the situation is still open. A question such as whether drug addiction originates from the social inadequacies of the drug addicts themselves or is the product of particular social pathologies of life in poor neighbourhoods does not lend itself to unambiguous empirical answers.

To be sure, political news coverage and politicians' speeches about policy issues lead people to believe that policies are about factual problems and solutions. But the political construction of policy problems attaches them, both explicitly and implicitly, to normative symbols of right or wrong, good and bad. Conservatives, for example, often search for and insist on policy solutions that fit their ideological emphasis on free market-oriented solutions, regardless of the characteristics of the particular problem. Independently of its demonstrated effectiveness in dealing with a problem, a solution that emphasizes a greater role for government will be opposed as leading to the wrong kind of society. It is in this sense that a solution often goes out looking for a problem to solve.

Rather than taking the actions and assertions of politicians and policymakers as straightforward statements of intent, accounts of policy problems and issues are thus seen as devices for generating varying presuppositions about the social and political events rather than factual claims. While the concept of a fact is not rendered meaningless, policy actions have to first and foremost be seen as resting on interpretations that reflect and sustain particular beliefs and ideologies. To be sure, empirical data and information play a role in policymaking, but their meaning is determined by how they fit into the particular arguments of an ideological framework. While the policy analyst can investigate the empirical dimensions of a problem and inform the political players of their findings, these research findings cannot be confused with an explanation of policy polities. The meaning of the "facts" to the political actors is determined by political discourses and these meanings are what the political struggle is first and foremost about. The social problems that enter the policy process are thus social constructions built on an intermingling of empirical findings with social meanings and ideological orientations. To understand how a particular condition becomes constructed as a problem, the range of social constructions in the discourses and texts about it need to be explored in the situational context from which they are observed.

Furthermore, problems and the policies designed to deal with social problems are important determinants of which actors will have the authority and power to deal with the issues they raise.[5] As Baumgartner and Jones (1983) point out, when a policy is presented as dealing with a technical problem, professional experts will tend to dominate the decision process. When the political, ethical, or social dimensions are seen to be the primary characteristics, a much larger group of participants usually becomes actively involved.

Often social conditions fail to become problems because powerful political groups can strategically manoeuvre to block measures that benefit a particular group. The effective long-term strategy, however, is ideological. When the ideological premises for or against an action are embedded in the existing discourses, people will accept them as part of how the world works and not recognize them as ideological. To people who see black people as inferior, discrimination is not a problem.

Because there are generally long-standing agreements on many social practices, only a limited number of the many potential problems actually become problems. Perhaps the most powerful influence of news, discussion, and writing about policy problems is the immunity from notice and criticism they provide for serious conditions that are not on the accepted agenda for political consideration. By naming a policy one way rather than another, diverse and contradictory responses to a spectrum of political interests can be either revealed or hidden. Because an emphasis on policy inconsistencies and differences can generate unwanted political conflicts, policy names are often designed to reassure or assuage citizens and politicians. Politicians, for example, speak of peace-keepers rather than deadly missiles. In this way, policies portray accomplishments, while masking problematic actions and counter-productive strategies that offset or reverse claims of success. Similarly, Edelman (1971) has shown the ways in which political elites and opinion-makers frequently respond to social and economic problems by symbolic political actions designed to reassure the public without dealing concretely with the problems. Through the symbolic manipulation of political language, political leaders at times create public expectations that can be satisfied by symbols of political action rather than action itself.

Finally, it is important to recognize that ambiguous meanings often have important political functions. Seeking to satisfy different interest groups at the same time, government policies often comprise a sequence of ambiguous claims and actions that contain logical inconsistencies. Given the would-be irrationality of the process, policy scientists have devoted a good deal of energy to developing strategies for circumventing this inconvenient aspect of political reality. What they have generally missed, however, is the degree to which such work enables conflicting groups to find ways to live with their differences. By helping to bring together citizens with varying policy preferences, ambiguity often facilitates cooperation and compromise. Enabling politicians to blur or hide problematic implications of controversial decisions, ambiguity can assist in sidestepping barriers that otherwise block consensus-building. People who benefit from the same policy but for different reasons can more easily find ways to agree. As Cobb and Elder (1983) explain, the ambiguity of symbols provides a vehicle through which diverse motivations, expectations, and values are synchronized to make collective action possible.

Numerous studies have shown the way legislatures seek to satisfy demands to do something about problems by passing vague statutes with ambiguous meaning. Legislators can placate both sides in a conflict by rhetorically supporting one side of the issue but making the actual decision more in the favour of the other side. By helping both sides feel better off with a policy agreement, legislators can facilitate negotiation and compromise by allowing opponents on both sides of an issue to proclaim success from a single policy decision. Because ambiguity allows participants to read themselves into collective programmes and actions, individuals can reconcile their own ambivalent and inconstant attitudes. In this way, the ambiguity of symbols helps coalitions form where pure material interests would divide potential members. It can quell resistance to policies by reassuring at the same time as the actual policies divide.

[…]

Notes

1 A good example is employment practices. Why, for example, do women still get less pay than men for the same job?
2 Environmentalists, for instance, have shown that nature has been defined differently at different times by different people. Where industrialists have viewed the environment as a source of natural resources to be exploited for productive gain. American Indians and other aboriginal groups have understood the environment to be mother earth and sought to live in harmonious balance with its natural requirements.
3 To put it more concretely, although we organize disciplines around the study of political systems and political economies, nobody has ever seen one of these entities. We can only see various pieces of the whole. Our understandings of these broader systems are interpretive constructions based on these partial views.
4 Fox applies this provocative perspective to the "reinventing government" effort to reform public administration during the Clinton administration.
5 Cobb and Elder (1983) write that the question of who communicates what to whom, and how, and with what effects goes to the crux of the political process.

References

Agger, B. (1990). *The Decline of Discourse: Reading, Writing, and Resistance in Postmodern Capitalism*. New York: Falmer.

Baudrillard, J. (1989). *America*. New York: Verso Books.

Baumgartner, F. and Jones, B. (1983). *Agendas and Instability in American Politics*. Chicago: University of Chicago Press.

Berger, P. and Luckmann, T. (1966). *The Social Construction of Reality: A Sociology of Knowledge*. London: Penguin Books.

Best, J. (1989). *Images of Issues: Typifying Contemporary Social Problems*. New York: Aldine De Gruyter.

Clemons, R. S. and McBeth, M. K. (2001). *Public Policy Praxis*. Englewood Cliffs, NJ: Prentice Hall.

Cobb, R. W. and Elder, C. D. (1972). *Participation in American Politics: The Dynamics of Agenda-Building*. Boston: Allyn and Bacon.

Cobb, R. W. and Elder, C. D. (1983). *The Political Uses of Symbols*. New York: Longman.

Dray, W. (1957), *Laws and Explanation in History*. Oxford: Oxford University Press.

Edelman, M. (1971). *Politics as Symbolic Action: Mass Arousal and Quiescence*. New York: Academic Press.

Edelman, M. (1977). *Political Language: Words that Succeed and Policies That Fail*. New York. Academic Press.

Edelman, M. (1988). *Constructing the Political Spectacle*. Chicago: Chicago University Press.

Fox, C. J. (1995). "Reinventing Government as Postmodern Symbolic Politics". Paper presented at the Annual Meeting of the American Society of Public Administration, San Antonio, Texas, 22–6 July.

Gergen, K. J. (1999). *An Invitation to Social Construction*. Thousand Oaks, CA. Sage.

Gusfield, J. (1981). *The Culture of Public Problems*. Chicago: University of Chicago Press.

Gusfield, J. (1989). "Constructing the Ownership of Social Problems: Fun and Profit in the Welfare State", *Social Problems*, 36(5): 431–41.

Hannigan, J. A. (1995). *Environmental Sociology: A Social Constructivist Perspective*. London: Routledge.

Heclo, H. (1972). "Review Article: Policy Analysis". *British Journal of Political Science*, 2: 83–108.

Jameson, F. (1992). *Postmodernism. Or the Cultural Logic of Late Capitalism*. Durham, NC: Duke University Press.

Jasanoff, S. (1990). *The Fifth Branch: Science Advisors as Policymakers*. Cambridge, MA: Harvard University Press.

Latour, B. and Woolgar, S. (1979). *Laboratory Life*. Newbury Park, CA: Sage.

Linder, S. (1995). "Contending Discourses in the Electric and Magnetic Fields Controversy: The Social Construction of EMF Risk as a Public Problem". *Policy Sciences*, 28: 209–30.

Majone, G. (1989). *Evidence, Argument, and Persuasion in the Policy Process*. New Haven: Yale University Press.

Mannheim, K. (1936). *Ideology and Utopia*. New York: Harcourt, Brace and World.

Maynard-Moody, S. and Kelly, M. (1993). "Stories Public Managers Tell About Elected Officials: Making Sense of the Politics-Administration Dichotomy", in B. Bozeman (ed.), *Public Management. The State of the Art*. San Francisco: Jossey-Bass.

Morrow, R. A. and Brown, D. (1994). *Critical Theory and Methodology*. Thousand Oaks, CA: Sage.

Schuman, D. (1982). *Policy Analysis, Education, and Everyday Life*. Lexington, MA: D. C. Heath.

Schutz, A. (1962). *Collected Papers*. Vol. 1. (ed. M. Natanson). The Hague: Martinus Nijhoff.

Schutz, A. (1967). *The Phenomenology of the Social World*. Evanston, IL: Northwestern University Press.

Stone, D. A. (1988). *Policy Paradox and Political Reason*. Glenview, IL: Scott, Foresman and Company.

Stone, D. A. (2002). *Policy Paradox: The Art of Political Decision-Making* (2nd edn). New York. W. W. Norton.

Yanow, O. (1996). *How Does a Policy Mean? Interpreting Policy and Organizational Actions*. Washington, DC: Georgetown University Press.

Frank Fischer, "Public Policy as Discursive Construct: Social Meaning and Multiple Realities," from *Reframing Public Policy*, 2003, pp. 48–64, Oxford University Press.

23

The Mauling of Public Space

Margaret Kohn

In his book *Edge City*, Joel Garreau tells the story of Bridgewater Township, a community of about forty thousand people located in New Jersey. Like earlier cities that were situated at the intersection of transportation routes, it owes its location to the confluence of two superhighways, routes 287 and 78. Although Bridgewater was originally a bedroom community for professionals who worked in New York, it gradually developed its own local economy with offices, businesses, and services. What it lacked was a sense of place. Local residents dreamed of a town center, some composite of a New England village green and a Tuscan piazza, a place where old people could gossip, young people could *farsi vedere* (make oneself seen), and mothers could bring young children while getting a latté, a sandwich, or some postage stamps. After more than a decade of discussion, in 1988 they inaugurated Bridgewater Commons, a mall.

Ironically, the Bridgewater Commons Mall was not originally the initiative of commercial real estate developers. It was the compromise reached by the community agency committed to maintaining the small town's quality of life and avoiding the strip-mall aesthetic. Individual retailers could not provide the capital necessary to implement a comprehensive plan that included environmentally sensitive landscaping and rational traffic management. More important, a traditional downtown could not guarantee the most highly prized amenities: safety, cleanliness, and order.

The Bridgewater Commons and hundreds of supermalls like it have long troubled architects and critics who bemoan the homogeneity, sterility, and banality of the suburbs. Approaching the mall primarily as an aesthetic or even a sociological issue, however, overlooks the enormous political consequences of the privatization of public space. Public sidewalks and streets are practically the only remaining available

Readings in Planning Theory, Third Edition. Edited by Susan S. Fainstein and Scott Campbell.
Editorial material and organization © 2012 Blackwell Publishing Ltd.
Published 2012 by Blackwell Publishing Ltd.

sites for unscripted political activity. They are the places where insurgent political candidates gather signatures, striking workers publicize their cause, and religious groups pass out leaflets. It is true that television, newspapers, and direct mail constantly deliver a barrage of information, including political leaflets. But unlike the face-to-face politics that takes place in the public sphere, these forms of communication do not allow the citizen to talk back, to ask a question, to tell a story, to question a premise. The politics of the public sphere requires no resources – except time and perseverance. Public spaces are the last domains where the opportunity to communicate is not something bought and sold.

And they are rapidly disappearing. These places are not banned by authoritarian legislatures. Their disappearance is more benign but no less troubling. The technology of the automobile, the expansion of the federal highway system, and the growth of residential suburbs have changed the way Americans live. Today, the only place that many Americans encounter strangers is in the shopping mall. The most important public place is now private. And this is probably not an accident.

The privatization of public space poses a number of conceptual challenges for public policy makers. Is it ownership or use that determines whether a particular place is truly private? How should the right to private property be weighed against the legitimate state interest in sustaining a public sphere? Does it violate the First Amendment if a shopping mall prohibits orderly political speech?

The US Supreme Court has tried to answer these questions in a series of decisions that have determined government policy defining the public sphere. The Supreme Court's doctrine in "the shopping mall cases" reflects a growing unwillingness to engage the broader political issues emerging from rapid social change.

The Shopping Mall Cases

The Supreme Court addressed the implications of private ownership of quasi-public spaces in a series of cases decided between 1946 and 1980. The Court first considered the issue in 1946 in *Marsh v. Alabama*, which dealt with a Jehovah's Witness who was arrested for distributing religious pamphlets in the business district of a company-owned town. The majority decided that the arrest violated the freedom of the press and freedom of religion guaranteed by the First Amendment and applied to the states under the Fourteenth Amendment. The opinion, written by Justice Hugo Black, emphasized that all citizens must have the same rights, regardless of whether they live in a traditional municipality or a company-owned town. He noted that a typical community of privately owned residences would not have had the power to pass a municipal ordinance forbidding the distribution of religious literature on street corners. Why then, should a corporation be allowed to do so?

The company – Gulf Shipbuilding Corporation – based its argument on the common law and constitutional right to private property. If an individual does not have to allow Jehovah's Witnesses into her home, why should the company have to allow them on its property? The court, however, rejected this logic. It cited a long list of precedents – cases involving bridges, roads, and ferries – to establish that the right to private property is not absolute. Especially when a private company performs public functions, it opens itself up to greater government scrutiny and regulation. Given that the town was freely accessible to outsiders, it implicitly invited in the general public, thereby voluntarily incurring quasi-public obligations. The concept of "invitee" went on to play an important role in desegregation cases. According to the Court in *Marsh v. Alabama*, "The more an owner, for his advantage, opens up his property for use by the public in general, the more do his rights become circumscribed by the statutory and constitutional rights of those who use it."

The opinion concluded that property rights must be weighed against other state interests. Justice Black emphasized that a democracy had a compelling state interest in maintaining free and open channels of communication so that all of its residents could fulfill their duties as citizens: "To act as good citizens they must be informed. In order to enable them to be properly informed their information must be uncensored." A concurring opinion by Justice Felix Frankfurter stated that fundamental civil liberties guaranteed by the Constitution must have precedence over property rights.

Based on the reasoning in *Marsh v. Alabama*, it would seem that the right to free speech would apply to other private arenas that were similarly open to a broader public. In the 1972 decision *Lloyd v. Tanner*, the Court considered whether First Amendment guarantees extended to the shopping mall. This time, however, the majority upheld the mall's policy forbidding the distribution of handbills on its premises. The owners could exclude expressive conduct, even if it did not disrupt the commercial functions of the mall. Writing for the majority, Justice Lewis Powell argued that a shopping mall was not the functional equivalent of a company town because it was not a space where individuals performed multiple activities. It was simply devoted to shopping. Although it was true that the shopping mall implicitly invited the general public onto its premises, this did not transform it into a public space. According to Powell, political activists misunderstood the invitation if they turned the mall into a public forum: the invitation to the public was only to shop. Moreover, since the First Amendment only limited "state action" there was no constitutional basis to apply it to private entities.

In *Lloyd v. Tanner* the Court did not overrule *Marsh v. Alabama*; instead it emphasized how the two cases differed. The mall was no company town. Basically, the Court concluded that activists had other opportunities to engage in political activity. They could make use of the public roads and sidewalks on the perimeter of the shopping mall. The assumption was that citizens had other chances to be exposed to diverse ideas and viewpoints. Because they presumably spent, at most, part of their day at the shopping mall, they could become informed citizens elsewhere.

Although the Court tried to emphasize the differences between the two cases, it actually modified its view of the relevant doctrine. In the *Lloyd* decision, there was no idealistic discussion of the free exchange of ideas necessary to maintain an informed citizenry. Rather than considering the goal of the First Amendment – presumably to foster the free expression characteristic of a democracy – the Court focused narrowly on the supposed absence of state action. It decided that private property does not "lose its private character merely because the public is generally invited to use it for designated purposes."

It is puzzling that the justices in *Lloyd* did not really analyze the logic of *Marsh v. Alabama* on the critical issue of state action. In the company-town case, Justice Black suggested that the enforcement of state criminal trespass laws constituted state action. If the state may make no law abridging the freedom of speech, then it cannot pass a criminal-trespass statute penalizing a citizen simply for engaging in non-disruptive expression in a place where she would be legitimately allowed to enter. This same logic was used in a much more famous case, *Shelley v. Kraemer*, which was decided by the same court in 1948. In that case, the Supreme Court struck down a restrictive covenant preventing residents from selling their homes to blacks. Although the contract was undeniably private, it could not be enforced without "the active intervention of the state courts, supported by the full panoply of state power." According to this decision, private actors could not use the police and the courts to enforce practices that violate constitutional rights. In *Lloyd v. Tanner*, the Supreme Court decided to overlook these precedents, assuming a much narrower definition of what constitutes state action.

The last shopping mall case. *Pruneyard Shopping Center v. Robins* (1980), dealt with a group of high school students who attempted to gather signatures for a petition protesting a United Nations resolution condemning Zionism. The California State Supreme Court originally found in favor of the students, ruling that the state's criminal-trespass law would constitute state action for the purposes of the First Amendment protections. The shopping mall owners appealed to the US Supreme Court, claiming that their Fifth Amendment right not to be deprived of "private property, without due process of law" was violated by the California decision. They argued that the mall was no public forum. To require the mall to allow political solicitation was tantamount to "taking without just compensation." The owners also claimed that the right to exclude others is an essential component of the definition of private property.

The *Pruneyard* decision, which governs to this day, articulated a mediating position. The Supreme Court rejected the mall owners' claim to absolute dominion over their property. Again drawing upon a long history of precedents regarding public regulation of private property, the court concluded that the due process clause only required that the laws "not be unreasonable, arbitrary, or capricious and that the means selected shall have a real and substantial relation to the objective sought." The right to exclude others would only be decisive if the mall owners could prove that allowing orderly political speech would substantially decrease the economic value of their property.

The Court, however, also rejected the students' claims to protection under the free speech clause of the First Amendment. Since the facts of the case were substantially the same as those in *Lloyd v. Tanner*, the Court saw no reason to reconsider the issue. It still insisted that the mall was private and therefore outside of the reach of the Bill of Rights. But there was a second issue at stake. The students had challenged the shopping center's policy under both the US and the California State Constitutions. The language of the California free speech clause was more expansive. Article 1, section 2, of the California Constitution provides

> Every person may freely speak, write and publish his or her sentiments on all subjects, being responsible for the abuse of this right. A law may not restrain or abridge liberty of speech or press.

The US Supreme Court found that there was no reason why a state or federal statute or constitutional provision could not guarantee access to the public areas of private malls. This finding was consistent with an earlier decision, *Hudgens v. National Labor Relations Board* (1976), which held that striking workers had no First Amendment right to picket in a mall, but they could assert such a right under federal labor relations laws protecting the processes associated with collective bargaining. Since the *Pruneyard* decision, fourteen states have considered whether their own state constitutions protect expressive conduct in shopping malls. Only five – California, Oregon, New Jersey, Colorado, and Massachusetts – recognized broader protections for speech.

Privatization and Public Policy

More than twenty years have passed since the *Pruneyard* decision. Although the law has not changed in that period, society has. There is something quaint and anachronistic about reading the old shopping mall cases. They describe the world we take for granted as something new and marvelous, and they could not even imagine the world we will soon live in. Writing in 1972, Justice Powell described the Lloyd Center in Portland Oregon like this:

> The Center embodies a relatively new concept in shopping center design. The stores are all located within a single large, multi-level building complex sometimes referred to as the "Mall." Within this complex, in addition to the stores, there are parking facilities, malls, private sidewalks, stairways, escalators, gardens, an auditorium, and a skating rink. Some of the stores open directly on the outside public sidewalks, but most open on the interior privately owned malls. Some stores open on both. There are no public streets or public sidewalks within the building complex, which is enclosed and entirely covered except for the landscaped portions of some of the interior malls.

This futuristic mall had sixty shops and a thousand parking spaces. Compared to today's supermalls, Lloyd Center is a neighborhood corner store. By 1990, there were more than three hundred mega-supermalls, each with at least five department stores and three hundred shops. The West Edmonton Mall has more than 800 shops, 11 department stores, 110 restaurants, 20 movie theaters, 13 night clubs, a chapel, a large hotel, and a lake.

In 1972, the Court concluded that this new concept in shopping – "sometimes referred to as the 'Mall'" – in no way resembled a company town. It seemed obvious that a mall was simply devoted to a single activity – shopping – while a town was defined by the physical proximity of diverse spaces and activities – housing and services, leisure and work, consumption, education, and production. A mall is a place you visit; a town is a place in which you live. But this has been slowly changing. Industry watchers report that by 1999 the average mall visit lasted four hours, up from an hour two decades before.

The mall has become an entertainment mecca, a major employer, and a premier vacation destination. The Travel Industry Association of America reported that shopping is the number one vacation activity in America. The Mall of America in Bloomington, Minnesota, attracts 37.5 million visitors annually. Its hundreds of retail establishments are not the only draw – it has a wedding chapel, the nation's largest indoor amusement park, a post office, a police station, and a school.

The mall is also a workplace. The West Edmonton Mall has more than fifteen thousand employees. Although they do not manufacture automobiles or aircraft carriers, they do produce the spiral of fantasy, desire, and consumption that is now North America's number one export.

The mall is becoming not only a genuinely multi-use facility, but a completely self-contained utopia of suburban life. In the morning the doors open to waiting seniors, the famous mall-walkers who appreciate the controlled climate, cleanliness, and safety. At night, the security guards have to herd out the lingering teenagers, who are in no rush to go home to their monotonous housing developments. The mall is clearly the nodal point of social life, but is it a town?

An April 1999 survey by the journal *Shopping Center World* found that half of the 150 new projects under construction are multi-use malls. Some of these are New Urbanist inspired developments that try to mimic the appeal of old-fashioned downtown areas. They link higher density housing with office and retail space, all unified by architectural cues that evoke the turn of the century. Fifty of the new multi-use malls include office space, libraries, housing, or hotels.

One such project is in the new Towers at Zona Rosa, a shopping mall situated ten minutes from downtown Kansas City. Although the plan relies on thirty thousand square foot department stores to anchor the retail plaza, it also includes loft-style apartments situated above boutiques and cafés. Underground parking, decorative street lamps, indigenous plants, and outdoor tables are among the lifestyle-enhancing amenities. As theme parks, megamalls, and gated communities merge, nostalgic recreations of the village green replace actual public space.

Living at the mall might still seem unusual, but it is a culmination of a dynamic that has been accelerating throughout the 1990s – the emergence of what Joel Garreau has called edge cities. The growth of edge cities reflects a complete transformation of the spatial structure of postwar American life. The typical pattern of bedroom communities situated along the outskirts of urban cores is disappearing. He reports that Americans no longer sleep in the suburbs and work in the city. In dozens of cities, including Houston, Boston, Tampa, and Denver, there is more office space outside of the central business district than within it. This new office space is built in edge cities – suburbs that now incorporate millions of square feet of commercial development.

There are undoubtedly positive sides to this development. As more companies relocate to the suburbs, the average American's commute time decreases. But as workplaces become more and more decentralized, the density needed to support public transportation like commuter railroads also disappears. Although your suburban office park may be closer to your home, it is probably not served by the subway. It becomes ever more commonplace to move from home to office to shopping mall in the automobile. The edge city citizen need never traverse public space. It becomes possible to spend an entire day or lifetime without encountering street corners, bus stops, or park benches.

The new edge city geography poses a challenge to the doctrine established by the Supreme Court. If private space takes on a public character in cases like the company town when it colonizes every aspect of life, then it is time to reconsider the character of the mall. But this is unlikely to happen. As recently as 1992, the Supreme Court held that labor organizers had no right to try to contact potential members by passing out leaflets in the parking lot of a Lechmere's store – this despite the fact that the only alternative space was a forty-six-foot-wide grassy strip separating the lot from the highway. In 1999, the Minnesota State Supreme Court heard a challenge from an animal rights group that was prevented from peacefully protesting in the common area of the 4.2-million-square-foot Mall of America. The protestors argued that the mall was a public space because it had been heavily subsidized by the state, which provided $186 million in public financing. The Justices found that "neither the invitation to the public to shop and be entertained ... nor the public financing used to develop the property are state action for the purposes of free speech" under the Minnesota Constitution.

Politics and Public Space

This string of defeats is a setback for political activists and proponents of an active public life. But it could have the unintended consequence of channeling debate over privatization into the public arena and out of the closed chambers of the Court. If judicial intervention will not protect the public sphere, then political action still presents an alternative. Congress or state legislatures could pass statutes mandating that malls of a certain size must provide access to community groups. They could also establish guidelines to extend broader protections for political activity. One way to do this would be to pass legislation applying speech and petition guarantees to the functional equivalents of traditional public forums. As indicated in the *Pruneyard* decision, there is no constitutional provision that would invalidate these kinds of laws. Because labor unions are dependent on tactics like the picket line, they would be powerful proponents of such a law and useful allies for other activist groups fighting to maintain access to public space. As the Seattle-inspired euphoria wanes, the struggle for such legislation could unify labor and other social movements.

Even in areas where such tactics were unsuccessful at the state level, it would still be possible to adopt similar strategies at the local level. The obvious place to start is to support downtown business districts and other public places that still encourage diversity and invite political activity. But this individualist solution, by itself, is naïve. Collective action is also necessary. When new, large-scale mall developments are proposed, citizens have the most leverage to demand some form of continued public access. The support of local government agencies, town councils, and planning boards is crucial for a project on the scale of the modern mall. By building and upgrading roads, modifying zoning, and approving permits, localities still have bargaining power over some aspects of development. They could negotiate a policy guaranteeing free access to a community booth or public courtyard in the mall.

Why are these tactics seldom even employed, let alone successful? Although malls like the one in Bridgewater manage to preserve natural oases like "Mac's Brook," they fail to protect oases of public openness in a privatized world. This is not only the fault of greedy developers. Most people do not value the disruption and unease caused by other peoples' political speech. One of the appeals of the mall is precisely that it provides an environment carefully designed to exclude any source of discomfort. The soothing lighting, polished surfaces, pleasant temperature, and enticing displays are not the only allure; part of the fantasy involves entering a world where no homeless person, panhandler, or zealot can disturb the illusion of a harmonious world.

In the mauling of public space, democratic theorists have confronted extremely sophisticated marketing experts, and the democratic theorists have lost. The political theorists who are most concerned with democracy have failed to offer a compelling rationale to challenge the privatization of public space. By concentrating on the value of speech rather than the importance of space, they turn the public sphere into an abstraction. We need to engage in more careful reflection on the reasons why we should protect free speech and public space.

In academic circles, theorists argue that deliberation between citizens is the most promising way to reach rational political decisions. Moreover, they stress that rational, public-spirited discussions are necessary to legitimate democratic procedures and make sure that politics does not degenerate into mere struggles over power. These theories of deliberative democracy are indebted to Jürgen Habermas's influential work on the ideal speech situation: if everybody plays fair, tells the truth, speaks respectfully, and only makes claims in the name of the general good, then a rational consensus could emerge.

At first, it seems like this emphasis on "deliberative democracy" is precisely what is needed to reinvigorate our commitment to the public sphere, to street corners with soap boxes and speakers, or at least their modern equivalents. These theories offer the perfect justification of the speech clause of the First Amendment. But the concept of deliberation will not be useful if it emphasizes the rationality that emerges from the ideal speech situation. Let's face it. Nothing approaching the ideal speech situation ever happens in the mall. The ideal speech situation is basically an extremely idealized depiction of the norms of scholarly journals or conferences. We need free speech and public places not because they help us, as a society, reach a rational consensus, but because they disrupt the consensus that we have already reached too easily. While reasonable arguments often just reinforce distance, public space establishes proximity. This proximity has distinctive properties that democratic theorists often overlook. We can learn something from facing our fears that we cannot learn from debating principles. The panhandler and the homeless person do not convince us by their arguments, but their presence conveys a powerful message. They reveal the rough edges of our shiny surfaces. The union picketer and right-to-lifer confront us with meaningful and enduring conflict. Provocative speech cannot be something that happens elsewhere – in academic journals, conferences, mass mailings, and highly scripted town meetings. Sometimes it must be in your face for it to have any impact. For a robust democracy we need more than rational deliberation; we need public places that remind us that politics matter.

In New Jersey, at least, malls will be part of this public space. That is the implication of a decision reached by the New Jersey State Supreme Court on June 13, 2000. In a unanimous vote, the court held that Mill Creek, a New Jersey mall, could not restrict free speech by forbidding political groups from leafleting. Although the owners could place reasonable restrictions on expressive conduct to make sure that politics did not disrupt the commercial activities of the mall, they could not deny access to the only place left in New Jersey where there is an opportunity for face-to-face contact with large groups of people. By a circuitous route, the dream of Bridgewater will come true and the residents will get their commons.

Margaret Kohn, "The Mauling of Public Space," *Dissent*, 48, 2, (Spring, 2001), pp. 71–7.

VII
Planning in a Globalized World

Introduction

This final part turns to planning theory's evolution and adaptation in a globalizing world. The four readings examine the internationalization and exporting of planning theory (Ward), the enduring role of community-level political action in the face of globalization (Evans), the potential convergence and deviations of urbanization patterns in the US and China (Zhang and Fang), and the building of an alternative planning theory around pressing urban issues of the global "south-east" regions rather than the standard "north-west" (Yiftachel).

In "Re-examining the International Diffusion of Planning," Stephen Ward asks a basic question: how do planning ideas morph and adapt as they move across borders? Using a rich array of examples, Ward observes no single model of diffusion. Instead, he develops a useful typology of six variants, from voluntary borrowing to authoritarian imposition. Understandably, the power relationship between exporter and importer of planning concepts heavily shapes the nature of the diffusion. Planning ideas are not always imported unadulterated: they are often filtered, diluted, altered, or subverted. Diffusion frequently leads to innovation in which local ideas, institutions, and capacities are incorporated (a classic example: Howard's Garden City idea from 1898 started in England but travelled around the world and morphed along the way). In this import/export network of planning ideas, the trade patterns have shifted over time, reflecting changes in economic power, political might, and technology. Looking to the future, we can expect the shifting urban hierarchy of political and financial power around the globe to further realign the marketplace and trading routes of planning ideas. (Oren Yiftachel picks up on this theme of the realignment of planning theory's intellectual geography.)

Readings in Planning Theory, Third Edition. Edited by Susan S. Fainstein and Scott Campbell.
Editorial material and organization © 2012 Blackwell Publishing Ltd.
Published 2012 by Blackwell Publishing Ltd.

In a rapidly urbanizing world of seven billion people, constructing livable, sustainable cities with adequate housing, water, sanitation and accessibility is a daunting task. For Peter Evans, this undertaking best happens at the community level – a scale of political action that remains robust and relevant even in a global era of information and commerce. In the concluding chapter from his edited book, *Livable Cities? Urban Struggles for Livelihood and Sustainability*, Evans distills lessons from case study cities in Asia, the Americas and Europe against the theoretical backdrop of markets, human agency and political ecology. The communities with the most success in creating livable spaces do not have one single defining characteristic or institution, but rather a complex, synergistic ecology of positive capacities, including a shared history and common cultural ties. However, this ability goes beyond the standard conception of "social capital" to include a broader set of dynamics. And one often finds an interactive effect: strong communities are more able to achieve livability and this local struggle for more livable conditions itself builds community. By contrast, though non-governmental organizations (NGOs) play an important role as allies, they often follow rather than drive community development. The role of the state is decidedly mixed, both aiding and hindering reform. Poor urban communities face particular challenges: with restricted access to economic and political networks, they often suffer loss of land and other resources when middle-class residents seek to improve their own quality of life. Moreover, the poor's engagement with sustainability is more complicated and ambivalent given conflicting priorities and needs: livable spaces that integrate healthy livelihoods and sustainable material practices is, for Evans, "a key to making poor communities effective agents of livability."

Stephen Ward asked how planning ideas from one country translate into another; in the next essay Yan Zhang and Ke Fang ambitiously compare the two seemingly opposite cases of urban strategies in the United States and China. Urban renewal was a defining (and arguably destructive) tool of postwar American urban policy; are contemporary inner-city redevelopment programs in China taking the same approach? Or, as the authors ask, "Is history repeating itself?"

The short answer is not exactly. These two processes are happening in clearly divergent stages of demographic and industrial development: China is intensifying its city development at a time of rapid urbanization, industrialization, rural-urban migration and liberalization of land markets. In contrast, postwar American urban renewal came after a century of industrialization: the long-standing urban-industrial machine had slowed, decentralized to suburbs, automated, and given way to services, leaving partially abandoned central cities. In addition, the federal government took a stronger lead in American urban renewal than the current central government does in China. Finally, the standard understanding of public–private partnerships (shaped largely by redevelopment experience in the United States and Europe) has a very different connotation in China (where the public and private are tightly intertwined and boundaries are blurry).

That said, Zhang and Fang see a compelling commonality between the Chinese and US urban experiences: at the core are the shared dynamics of urban growth machines, which exploit the complementary land use and financial powers of public and private actors to catalyze large-scale urban development projects. Real estate becomes a driving force of local economic development. In both cases, growth machines also threaten to displace local communities. Zhang and Fang are particularly troubled by the shortage of pushback, community input, and transparency in the Chinese cities, which lack the "checks and balances" that eventually slowed and redirected American postwar urban renewal programs. However, growth machines are contradictory: they are self-sustaining, but they also plant the seeds of their own vulnerability. They expand through the mutually reinforcing dynamics of their various public and private elements, but they also increase social tension and opposition, foreshadowing trouble ahead for China's urban "growth machines in-the-making."

The final essay in this part continues the theme of comparative urbanization, or more precisely, the urgency to develop vital, relevant planning theories for the rapidly urbanizing "south-eastern" regions of the world. In "Re-engaging Planning Theory? Towards South-Eastern, Perspectives," Oren Yiftachel expresses frustration with the blind spots of "north western" (i.e., Anglo American) planning theory, especially its inability to adequately engage a central challenge of non-western, non-northern societies: land use disputes arising from ethnic conflict and disagreements over "homelands."

Yiftachel links his argument to a critique of communicative action planning theory, which he views as less relevant outside the developed world of the "north-west" and has distracted the planning field from more directly engaging the substantive issues in urban policies. For Yiftachel, too much planning theory is preoccupied with the limiting subfield of analyzing the thinking and communication of planning professionals. (This conclusion resonates with both the Fainstein and Forester essays in this volume.) To understand the pressing urban challenges in the south-eastern regions of the world, one needs to look far beyond the formal professional circles of urban planners and develop a more complex understanding of the urban development process and its multiple actors, of which formal planners are only a small part.

Yiftachel's essay is provocative and should launch a lively debate regarding alternative directions for planning theory and the promises and pitfalls of applying conventional planning ideas to emerging urban areas of the world. To rephrase Yiftachel's argument using the terminology of international trade, he is essentially arguing for a shift away from an export-base model of north-western planning theory and towards a model of "theory import substitution": south-eastern societies will initially generate their own planning theories, but then move also into exporting these ideas, eventually leading to a reverse flow of planning ideas back to the north-west.

24

Re-examining the International Diffusion of Planning

Steven V. Ward

An intriguing footnote in the life of Ildefons Cerdà, author of the 1859 plan for Barcelona's *Eixample* (Extension), is that Georges-Eugène Haussmann, simultaneously engaged on the remodelling of Paris, is reported to have offered to buy Cerdà's plans and studies (Estapé, 1996, p. 55). Cerdà apparently refused, saying that he had drawn them up for Catalonia. If true, and the evidence rests on family recollection rather than a documentary source, this episode suggests that there was some degree of international linkage at a very early stage in the development of modern planning. In turn, Cerdà's refusal to sell may also partially explain why his remarkable innovatory work including, in 1867, the *Teoría General de la Urbanización* (General Theory of Urbanization), effectively the first modern theoretical work on urban planning, had a negligible international impact.

Within a few decades, however, there was abundant evidence that much more effective international flows of ideas and practices were becoming well established (Albers, 1997; Collins and Collins, 1965; Sutcliffe, 1981). Many cities, in Europe and beyond, sought to replicate the great new boulevards which Haussmann had driven through the old Paris at the behest of his Emperor. The emerging practices of *Stadterweiterungen* (town extension) in Germany, associated particularly with Reinhard Baumeister and Joseph Stübben, were also beginning to attract interest in Britain and the United States. So too was the notion of a more organic approach to town design, developed by Camillo Sitte and, to a lesser extent, Charles Buls from Austria and Belgium respectively. In England, Ebenezer Howard contributed a conceptually rich vision of the garden city in 1898, soon to be given a tangible form at Letchworth. Other seminal works followed in the new century, from Eugène Hénard and Tony Garnier in France, Charles Mulford Robinson and Daniel Burnham

Readings in Planning Theory, Third Edition. Edited by Susan S. Fainstein and Scott Campbell.
Editorial material and organization © 2012 Blackwell Publishing Ltd.
Published 2012 by Blackwell Publishing Ltd.

in the United States, Raymond Unwin in England, and Patrick Geddes in Scotland. Reflecting the nationalities of the authors of most of these works, four main innovatory planning traditions – Germany (*Städtebau*), Britain (town planning), France (*urbanisme*) and the United States (city planning) – were clearly apparent by 1914.

The key point, however, is that virtually all these works and the ideas they contained were also part of an emergent international discourse of planning. Written in German, French or English, many were translated within a few years of their publication into at least one other of the three languages. Some also appeared in other languages as well. The ideas they contained were interpreted, albeit selectively, into specific national contexts by a host of intermediaries throughout the world. Individual planners began to work in other countries, taking with them their own national planning conceptions and, in some cases, receiving others.

These early years set a pattern for the twentieth century. Despite the disruptive effects of major wars, internationalism has remained a powerful theme in urban planning. The dominant centres of innovation and patterns of emulation have not remained static, however. The balance of exchange between the main innovatory nations has shifted. Everywhere the influence of American ideas and practices has strengthened, paralleling the United States' rise to world dominance (Cody, 1998). The creation of the Soviet Union in 1917 unleashed a periodically innovative planning tradition, influential to some extent in Western Europe in the 1930s and 1940s and more directly so in Eastern Europe in the third quarter of the century.

Yet planning innovation has not been the exclusive prerogative of world powers. New innovators such as the Netherlands and Scandinavia emerged, to some extent replacing Germany as its influence waned in the Nazi years and their aftermath (e.g. Hall, 1991). Moreover, the decline of formal colonialism since 1945 has been paralleled by a weakening of the direct influence of British and French planning. A neo-colonialism built around foreign aid and international institutions such as the United Nations or the World Bank has, however, perpetuated a mainly (but not entirely) one way flow of planning ideas and practices from the developed to the developing world (e.g. Armstrong, 1987; Okpala, 1990; Sanyal, 1990). The European Union has also tried to play an important role in producing convergence in the planning repertoires of its member states (Williams, 1996).

International Diffusion as a Historical Theme

Not surprisingly, the international character of the twentieth century planning movement has been a strong theme in historical writing. In particular, historians have been obliged to consider how and why planning ideas and practices came to spread between different countries. The best known works in English dealing with this theme are Anthony Sutcliffe's *Towards the Planned City* (1981) and Peter Hall's *Cities of Tomorrow* (1988, revised 1996). In fact, there is a significant volume of other work from many countries dealing to some extent with diffusion. The main concern has been to show how their principal subject, usually a particular city, country or group of countries, encountered key planning ideas or practices from elsewhere. This is apparent, for example, in Freestone (1989), Home (1997), King (1976, 1990), Smets (1977), Watanabe (1980, 1992). Wynn (1984), Yeoh (1996) and Yerolympos (1996).

Another approach to diffusion is that found in Buder (1991), Gold (1997) and Hardy (1991). These works have explored how the ideas and practices of particular planning traditions (namely the garden city and modern movements) have spread to different countries. In other cases the emphasis has been much more the exchange of planning ideas and practices, implying more complex diffusional flows between particular places. We can find this expressed in Albers (1997), Bosma and Hellinga (1997), Hall, P. (1996), Hall, T. (1997). Schubert (1997) and Sutcliffe (1981). It has also been the subject of a major international conference on planning history held in Tokyo in 1988 (TIPHC, 1988).

But, whatever the exact treatment of diffusion, we can identify three major concerns recurring throughout all these studies:

1. The mechanisms of diffusion. For example, key personalities, reformist or professional milieux, intergovernmental actions.
2. The extent to which ideas and practices are changed in their diffusion. How are they applied in specific national settings and why are differences apparent?
3. The fundamental causation of diffusion. For example, how much does it mirror the larger economic, political or cultural contexts of international relations? How far is the "text" of planning's international diffusion more autonomous or reliant on chance actions?

No universal answers to these questions have emerged from historical studies and planning historians have adopted a variety of perspectives. We can illustrate this by reference to three planning historians whose work has been particularly influential. Thus Peter Hall's narrative, though acknowledging the role of structure and context, is largely one of great men with big ideas that spread because of the potency of message and the charisma and energy of those who carried it. By contrast, Anthony King's explanation rests much more on the global hegemony of Western imperialism, exporting its conception of planning in both the colonial and post-colonial eras. Between these two, Sutcliffe's account of the emergence of urban planning in the great powers of the late nineteenth century acknowledges both the larger impersonal forces and charismatic visionaries. Yet he stresses the critical intermediary role of the reformist and expert milieux, where imported ideas were distilled into locally relevant practices.

It will be immediately clear, however, that these different perspectives are not merely products of the interpretative stances of the historians concerned. They reflect real differences in the experiences of different countries. India's encounters with external planning models, the basis of King's work, were objectively different to those of Western Europe or the United States. In contrast to the pattern of promiscuous borrowing of external models that was typical amongst the latter group, planning in imperial India was externally imposed from one source.

Significantly, when he deals with New Delhi, Nairobi or Lusaka, Hall readily acknowledges the central importance of this imperial domination. Here, at least, the ideas of the great men were triumphant because they were imposed by colonial power.

A wider review of writing about countries that were neither the major Western world powers nor their colonies increases this sense of real variety in experiences of diffusion. Thus the planning histories of southern European countries or the smaller countries of north western Europe, of Japan or the self-governing white Dominions of the British Empire typically show a high dependence on externally developed planning models. Yet such models were certainly not imposed in the classic imperial manner, without opportunity for indigenous political discretion. We can go further and note a growing awareness of the many subtleties of colonial planning, between imperial powers, between different parts of their Empires, and over time (e.g. Home, 1997; Wright, 1991). Also, it is clear that post-colonial experiences of planning imported as part of foreign aid, though replicating many features of the colonial era, have differed in some important respects.

These cases underline the general point that diffusion needs to be understood as highly variable, rather than as a single, uniform process. All the major dimensions of diffusion – the agencies and mechanisms by which it occurs, the extent to which ideas and practices are changed and, though it is more a matter of interpretation, its fundamental causation – have shown great diversity. Without denying that there will always be unique features in every episode of diffusion, it is possible (and indeed valuable) to generalize the different varieties.

A Typology of Diffusion

The remainder of the chapter elaborates on this general point, drawing widely on relevant historical writing to develop a typology for the diffusion of planning. It consists of a series of "ideal types" of episodes of diffusion, highlighting salient features and giving some examples that reflect these features. Table 24.1 summarizes the different types. They fall into two distinct groups – "borrowing" and "imposition" – each having three types. This grouping thus marks a fundamental distinction between those episodes of diffusion where the "importing" country has the greater role in shaping and controlling the diffusion process (borrowing) and those where the "exporting" country is the main determining force (imposition).

As this rather implies, the essential basis of the typology is that of context, specifically the power relationship between the countries originating and receiving planning models, is always of critical importance. By power relationship is meant simply the degree of domination, however expressed, of the one by the other. The individual types are, of course, rather generalized and certainly do not capture the subtleties of actual diffusion episodes. They merely represent the principal gradations of borrowing and imposition during the twentieth century. Thus the great Western powers, equivalents and rivals rather than deferential to each other, borrowed in creative rather than slavish fashion. Where the sense of deference was greater, then the borrowing became progressively less selective.

Table 24.1 Typology of diffusion

Type	Indigenous Role	External Role	Typical Mechanisms	Level of Diffusion	Key Actors	Potential for Distinctiveness	Characteristic Examples
Synthetic borrowing	Very high	Very low	Indigenous planning movements plus wide external contacts	Theory and practice	Indigenous	Very high	Major countries of Western Europe and USA
Selective borrowing	High	Low	External contact with innovative planning traditions	Practice and some theory	Indigenous	High	Smaller countries of Western Europe
Undiluted borrowing	Medium	Medium	Indigenous deference to innovative external planning traditions	Practice with little or no theory	External with some indigenous	Fairly Low	Dominions of British Empire, Japan, and some European examples
Negotiated imposition	Low	High	Dependence on external planning tradition(s)	Practice	External with some indigenous	Low	Aid-dependent countries (e.g. Africa)
Contested imposition	Very low	Very high	High dependence on one external planning tradition	Practice	External	Low	"Enlightened" colonial planning
Authoritarian imposition	None	Total	Total dependence on one external planning tradition	Practice	External	None	Newly subjugated territories

As deference graded into dependence, in colonial or post-colonial situations, then the power balance and the diffusional type shifted to imposition. Yet there are degrees of dependence and thus of imposition. In most cases receiving countries have been able to negotiate or contest the process of external imposition, thereby moderating its nature. However, in extreme cases, few in number in this century, dominance has been so complete as to eliminate any hint of indigenous modification. In all such situations the power balance, whether measured in governmental, economic or cultural terms, was very uneven as between the dominated colony and dominant imperial power. Among the rival great Western powers in the early twentieth century, however, the power relationship was more nearly equal.

Diffusion by Borrowing

Synthetic borrowing

Most familiar is the type of diffusion which has occurred between the main innovative planning traditions. As we have already noted of the early years, the patterns have typically been very open. Each of these innovatory countries drew on several external planning models, while the other innovators for their part borrowed back from them. To a greater extent than in other types of diffusion, the trade in ideas was closer to a state of balance. Before 1914, for example, Britain borrowed heavily from German town extension, zoning and organic approaches to urban design. In turn, the Germans (having already borrowed British public health innovations) looked admiringly on British housing design and, above all, the garden city. The United States, for its part, borrowed German zoning, the British garden city, and the French approach to grand urban design. It gave back to Europe the notion of the city-wide master plan and the grand approach to urban landscape design.

One of the key points about this form of diffusion is that the borrowed external models have typically been filtered through highly developed indigenous reformist movements and professional expertise. This filtering process has tended to deconstruct the models, breaking them down into component elements, and integrating them with planning ideas and practices that are already present. This deconstruction has occurred both consciously and unconsciously, through misunderstanding or partial understanding. In either case, though, the outcome has been that the diffused models were almost never transferred unaltered. Indigenous ideas and ideas already received from other sources were combined with newly-received models to create something distinctive and new. The overall effect was a process of synthetic innovation, with the further possibility that the resultant innovations might themselves be diffused elsewhere.

The history of the neighbourhood unit provides a classic example of how this process operated. The starting point was Britain, with Ebenezer Howard's indicative but barely elaborated concept of the 5000 population ward within his larger formulation of the garden city. It was, however, Clarence Perry in the United States who fashioned it into a workable physical model, sticking to Howard's 5000 population, in the 1920s. These ideas were further elaborated to reflect the growing importance of automobile traffic by Henry Wright and Clarence Stein. Their efforts culminated in the Radburn layout in the late 1920s.

Both ideas then spread back to Western Europe, where they were further overlain with new aspects and meanings. For the moment, Radburn principles were not applied, although there were signs of some German interest, especially in Hermann Jansen's road safety residential plans of the late 1920s (Hass-Klau, 1992). In Britain, however, planners were becoming more concerned with the neighbourhood as a device to promote social cohesion. Increasingly more ambitious objectives, involving a social class mix, were gradually added. Particularly influential was Barry Parker's plan for the Wythenshawe satellite town in Manchester, part of the garden city mainstream. Meanwhile in the Soviet Union there were some innovations that echoed Perry's ideas, though without apparent knowledge of Western developments (Tetlow, 1959). British modernists, in the shape of the MARS (Modern Architectural Research) group, began to experiment with Soviet-influenced neighbourhood ideas in the later 1930s (Gold, 1997). These two strands came together in the 1940s. Neighbourhoods, now with a notional population of up to 10,000, occupied a central place in Britain's wartime and early postwar plans, particularly in the first new towns.

American and British thinking had by then begun to influence planners in Sweden during the early 1940s. As a neutral country, Sweden suffered less wartime privation than other parts of Europe. This allowed it to assume an especially important role in the empirical elaboration of neighbourhood ideas in the immediate postwar years. Accordingly, Swedish experience became extremely important in the physical design of neighbourhoods. By 1947, variants of Radburn layouts were being planned, a few years before their first British use (Parsons, 1992). By 1950, Swedish experiences had also shown that 10,000 was far too low a population for an effective social unit in an affluent society (Sidenbladh, 1964).

Meanwhile, Dutch planners secretly replanning the devastated city of Rotterdam during the Nazi occupation had already come to similar conclusions but for quite different reasons (Lock, 1947). Aware to some extent of pre-war thinking on neighbourhood units but without knowledge of the important Anglo-American developments of the 1940s, the Rotterdam planners had already by 1945 proposed a socially mixed neighbourhood unit of 20,000. This reflected some very specific features of Dutch society, relating to the church's extensive role in social provision. Although planners from other countries, ever fascinated by Rotterdam's reconstruction, soon became aware of this variant of the neighbourhood, it did not seem as generalizable as the Swedish experience.

The most extraordinary aspect of the diffusion of the neighbourhood unit at this time involved its deployment in wartime Nazi Germany. Thus planners in Hamburg particularly made extensive use of a concept called the "local group as neighbourhood cell" (Schubert, 1995). This reflected the idiosyncrasies of Nazi ideology, yet it also leaned on the Anglo-American concept of the neighbourhood. In part, this connection reflected pre-war links. Yet there was also a keen awareness of wartime developments in London and other cities. Via neutral Stockholm, the German intelligence services had secured copies of Patrick Abercrombie's plans for London, making them available to Hamburg's chief planner. The similarities ensured that, stripped of their Nazi overtones, they could therefore be perpetuated into the postwar years.

After 1945 all versions of the idea became the subject of even more international cross-fertilization, with Radburn principles being widely adopted and adapted. However enough has been said to show how this synthetic process gave an innovative dimension to diffusion, in circumstances where planning models came into countries which already had highly developed planning traditions.

Selective borrowing

Where innovatory synthesis of imported and existing ideas and practices has been lacking, diffusion has often taken the form of a rather simpler process of borrowing. A characteristic feature of this non-innovatory borrowing has been a relatively shallow engagement within the importing country with the theoretical and conceptual bases of the borrowed model. This has limited the possibilities of deconstructing the ideas and reassembling them, with other ideas, to make something different. Instead planners in the receiving country have tended, rather atheoretically, to emulate specific aspects of external planning practice in a simple and direct manner.

This is not to say, however, that the borrowing has necessarily been slavish or uncritical. There has often been some degree of selection. Parts of the borrowed model may be discarded if they seem less appropriate. The main point, though, is that the importing country has added nothing significant to what is imported. In turn this offers little that is sufficiently distinctive for other countries to borrow. Yet countries which habitually borrow selectively may sometimes play an important intermediary role, facilitating the movement of innovations between more distinctive (and possibly competitive) planning traditions.

In fact, this type of diffusion episode can be found throughout the century in many different countries. It is, perhaps, most characteristic of the development of planning in the smaller and less powerful Western and Central European countries. These countries would have enjoyed fairly good access to more than one of the major innovative planning traditions. Typically they would also have had reformist movements pressing for planning and substantial indigenous professional expertise. Together these were capable of exercising some discretion over what was borrowed from external planning models. Yet the critical mass needed to innovate in more thoroughgoing fashion was absent.

A good example is Belgium. This small country was not entirely devoid of genuine innovation of international significance. Yet its planning tradition depended heavily on external sources of theory and practice, mainly French, German and British (Smets, 1977). Thus Parisian Haussmannism was emulated in the later nineteenth century (Hall, 1997). The early twentieth century brought growing awareness of the British garden city tradition, implemented through a combination of French-style social housing organizations and the British co-partnership model. More generally, Belgium (along with Switzerland) apparently played significant parts in moving British and German urban reformist ideas into the Francophone world (Claude, 1989). Another case is Norway, where traditional dependence on Swedish design in the early twentieth century was leavened, though not supplanted, by other influences, especially from Britain, the United States, France and the Netherlands (Lorange and Myhre, 1991). Again, however, no significant innovations arose from these borrowings.

Yet it would be incorrect to imply that selective borrowing has occurred only in smaller countries. Although there has always been a strong tendency in the major innovative planning traditions to use imported models in a more adaptive fashion, episodes of selective borrowing can be found everywhere. A recent example would be the rapid adoption throughout the developed world of the American approach to waterfront redevelopment. Pioneered in cities such as Baltimore and Boston in the 1970s, the model had by the 1990s appeared throughout Europe and beyond, with varying (but often very close) correspondence to the originals (Breen and Rigby, 1996).

Overall, however, examples of this type do not negate the main point: if synthetic innovation has been the dominant means of receiving externally generated ideas and practices, the cumulative result will be a national planning tradition that soon becomes distinct. If selective borrowing has been usual, particularly from more than one source, then differences will certainly arise, but more slowly. The cumulative result will also appear as an altogether more derivative planning tradition.

Undiluted borrowing

This derivative quality has been even more marked where external ideas and practices have been received without conscious selectivity – where the borrowing, in other words, is undiluted. In such cases, the tendency has been to receive not just individual ideas or innovations but substantial packages of planning practice. As this implies, such borrowing has been rather uncritical and frequently with only very limited awareness of the full range of alternative external planning models that are available. In turn, this reflects a rather underdeveloped indigenous planning movement and, quite often, a high reliance on foreign planners to supply leadership. There is a real difference here from previous types, where imported ideas and practices were filtered through indigenous planning movements (and in some cases, intermediate countries).

This diffusional type has been characteristic of countries which exhibit a more general deference to ideas arising in those countries from which they borrow. The relationship between the two parties is therefore markedly more uneven than in the previous two types. Yet we should not exaggerate the aspect of external dependence.

This type should be still understood, very definitely, as *borrowing*, clearly implying that the power to make decisions remains in the importing country.

The clearest examples of undiluted borrowing have undoubtedly been the white settled Dominions of the British Empire, whose early encounters with twentieth century planning came largely through the prism of British experience (Ward, 1997). These were self governing by the time modern planning thought and practice developed. Yet they had relatively small populations, underdeveloped reform movements and limited professional resources. When combined with more general ethnic and cultural affinities, these factors created a strong initial dependence on planning models from the imperial homeland. At varying rates, this was then overlain with what, initially at least, was an almost equally uncritical admiration for ideas and practices from the United States.

Canada borrowed uncritically from British planning in the first two decades of the century, to the extent of adopting planning legislation and founding a British-style professional body for planning (Simpson, 1983). Then, in the 1920s, American influences, often copied in an equally direct way, became dominant, coinciding exactly with the American replacement of Britain as the main foreign investor in Canada (Ward, 1999). After 1945, there was a resurgence of British planning (though not economic) influences. Yet external ideas were by then being received in a more critical and selective fashion. Canadian awareness of other European planning traditions, particularly the French, also increased.

There were many similarities between Canada and Australia. In the latter, however, British connections were dominant for much longer (Freestone, 1989; 1997). In part, this reflected the persistence of Australia's economic and cultural ties with Britain. Nor was the American model as conveniently located as it was for Canadian planners, who often found it easier to consult American planners than fellow Canadians. Thus the Australian planning system developed very much in the British image, with extensive British professional leadership. Although there was early awareness of American planning models (most strongly apparent in the chosen plan for the new federal capital at Canberra), it was not until the 1960s that they even began to match the extent of British influence.

Yet we should not see undiluted borrowing as a manifestation only of late imperialism. It could also arise in quite different circumstances, sometimes even in countries with relatively advanced planning traditions. Thus the replanning of the historic French city of Reims, devastated in World War One, became an exercise in scientific American city planning. United States' wartime relief had brought a leading American planner, George B. Ford, on the scene who quickly assumed technical dominance in the reconstruction debate (Bédarida, 1990; Wright, 1991). Ironically, very similar circumstances at almost exactly the same time allowed the French *urbaniste*, Ernest Hébrard, to assume an even more dominant role in the replanning of Thessaloniki in Greece, following its destruction by fire in 1917 (Yerolympos, 1996). The resultant plan was a grand exercise in French urban design. Such uncritical absorption of external models was not usual in either country, however, especially France.

An example of a more habitual uncritical borrowing that did not depend on imperial ties or emergency situations, was early twentieth century Japan. Here Western, especially German, British and American, planning practices were borrowed and applied with a surprising lack of adaptation to Japanese conditions (Hein and Ishida, 1998; Watanabe, 1988, 1992). The context was the rapid modernization of Japan from the later nineteenth century, which encouraged a fairly systematic trawling of the advanced Western countries for progressive practices which could be adopted.

What was particularly striking, however, was the rather imperfect conceptual grasp of the models that were being received. Having only a weakly developed reformist movement and professional skills in planning, the possibilities of conscious selection or synthesis were quite limited. Initially, at least, Western planning was copied quite slavishly, the only adaptations arising unconsciously from misunderstanding. In some aspects, what was borrowed was an even purer version of Western ideas than was actually adopted in the West. The land readjustment proposals incorporated in the first Japanese planning legislation of 1919, for example, were a more radical version of the widely admired German *Lex Adickes* than the German parliament had been prepared to adopt (Ishida, 1988).

Over time Japanese planning began to assume a more distinctive character, not least because Japanese planners, unlike those in Australia, had always looked to the West as a whole. Even so, as late as the 1950s, Tokyo's planners were still directly mimicking a planning model drawn directly from another country (TMG, 1994). This was the archetypal British metropolitan planning solution, with encircling green belt and planned decentralization. Ironically, the Tokyo plan was very similar to proposals for Sydney adopted a decade earlier and on the point of being substantially abandoned (Winston, 1957). The Japanese plan proved even more short-lived. In both cases the failures reveal the weakness of over reliance on imported models. They failed entirely to grasp political and growth realities that were quite different to those of British cities.

Diffusion by Imposition

The dangers of inappropriate transfers were (and are) much higher when the balance of power is such that the exporting country can exert more control than the importing country over the diffusion process. Thus, instead of authorities in the importing countries deciding themselves what they wish to borrow from foreign planning repertoires, relevant agencies in the exporting countries make the key decisions. This inherently limits the opportunities for local participation in the planning process within the countries receiving planning. Even more than in cases of undiluted borrowing, the importing countries will typically have very underdeveloped planning and reform movements. They will also be heavily, often almost totally, reliant on imported planning expertise. In most cases, of course, imposition is symptomatic of colonial or neo-colonial relationships. Beyond these underlying characteristics, there have been several distinct varieties of diffusion through imposition.

Negotiated imposition

The post-colonial period for many former colonies in some cases encouraged greater scepticism about external planning ideas. The more affluent and determined former colonies were quickly able to cross that critical divide between imposition and borrowing. In Singapore, for example, the post-independence State constructed a distinctive form of planning that borrowed freely from Western planning practice (Perry, Kong and Yeoh, 1997). The original base was British, yet ideas and practices were seemingly drawn from a variety of sources. They were applied, however, with a relentless discipline rarely matched in the West, inspired by distinctively Asian social and political ideologies.

Yet Singapore was exceptional, not least because of an extraordinary material progress that no other recent ex-colonies have matched. Many other ex-colonies in Asia and, above all, in Africa experienced a mode of diffusion that can be called negotiated imposition. It was characterized by continued dependence on external technical expertise and, often more importantly, material aid. Nominally the independent governments actually took the decisions about the acceptance of external aid and assistance. Yet such was the extent of dependence that the process went beyond borrowing. If these countries wanted the aid, the technical assistance went along with it. The offer could scarcely be refused.

It was a diffusional relationship that perpetuated some aspects of colonialism. At the outset, at least, there were slightly more options. In cases where the transition to independence had been peaceful and without active resentment, planning and aid flowed smoothly from former colonial masters. Thus from the late 1940s many British and French consultants began to find work in former colonies in this way, funded substantially by their own governments or United Nations agencies (e.g. MLCERG, 1997). Independence could also mean seeking aid and expertise from sources other than (or at least, in addition to) former colonial masters. Indonesia, for example, turned sharply away from the Netherlands for fifteen years after independence (van der Heiden, 1988). While maintaining fairly strong connections with Britain, India began to develop other linkages (Evenson, 1989). Its great size and economic and strategic potential gave it a negotiating power in external dealings that few other underdeveloped ex-colonies possessed. Yet smaller countries such as Tanzania also avoided some of the worst features of neo-colonialism by seeking aid and expertise from several countries (Armstrong, 1987).

These developments had implications for the international planning influence of Western countries which had not been formal colonial powers. Here was one of the principal ways in which the international planning influence of the United States grew (Cody, 1998). Yet less dominant affluent countries such as Canada, Australia, the Scandinavian countries and Western Germany, not lately major colonial powers, similarly exported their own conceptions of planning from the 1960s. Countries from the communist bloc sometimes used comparable methods to increase their influence in parts of Africa and Asia.

More recently there has been a growing tendency for international bodies such as the United Nations Centre for Human Settlements (Habitat) and the World Bank to play important roles (Okpala, 1990). These have purveyed generalized Western-determined planning and development solutions, premised increasingly on economic liberalization. The disappearance in the 1980s of a communist alternative and the wider effects of global economic change have strengthened this latest variant of imposition. Although at the technical level, the export of foreign planning aid is now being undertaken more sensitively than ever before, with growing emphasis on indigenous expertise, the wider sense of imposition remains very strong. The scope for negotiation, apparently so great in the bright confident morning of independence, has narrowed.

Contested imposition

Countries where planning has been externally imposed often, though not invariably, have underdeveloped civil societies. This, with the absence of both elective democratic government and indigenous reformist movements, has been a key part of the colonial experience. Yet such formidable obstacles, although they seriously weakened the possibilities of any formal negotiation of what was proposed by colonial powers, did not condemn the recipient population to absolute passivity. A more typical situation within long established colonial empires was indigenous obstruction of externally imposed planning projects. Measures that were particularly repugnant to local interests and sensitivities might well provoke rioting or other forms of protest. More typically, indigenous populations might simply abuse or superimpose their own meanings or customary uses on external planning forms.

The case of colonial Singapore, which has been meticulously documented (Yeoh, 1996), provides a particularly good example of this. A British colony, its highly urbanized character made it an early target for British sanitary and planning ideas. From 1913, when municipal elections were abolished, authority was vested in a nominated body which proved more amenable to the "progressive" principles of British-style municipal management (undertaken by British professionals). Yet this apparent authoritarianism was actually rather more subtle in operation. Nominations included a growing number of the indigenous population. This approach gave influence to those Europeanized Singaporeans who could be expected broadly to support the British town planning model. At the same time they also had to mediate between the indigenous population as a whole and colonial authority. In effect, this usually meant trying to contain opposition.

Reality, however, was more complex. Wholesale zoning powers sought for the Singapore Improvement Trust founded in 1927 were compromised by property interests of all races. However, there was strong and persistent Asian opposition by both owners and occupiers to the more modest proposals to open up what to British eyes were congested districts. Similarly attempts effectively to anglicize public space by limiting street trade proved practically impossible to enforce. Conflicts were particularly strong where planning proposals affected indigenous sacred spaces.

The pattern in French colonies, at least showpieces such as Morocco or Indo-China, was supposed to be different (Wright, 1991). By the time of World War One, the official imperial ideology had become an enlightened approach called "associationism". In planning terms, this involved modern colonial built forms, yet planned in styles that were supposed to defer to indigenous culture. Moreover they were developed as new settlements alongside indigenous traditional communities, without any direct intention to replace them. The rigid racial segregation that was typical of British imperial planning was also rejected. The intention was that the indigenous population would gradually realize the superiority of the new settlements, planned by leading French *urbanistes*, and increasingly use and occupy these spaces themselves. It promised, at least, a different social geography to that of the British colonial city, which rested on the separatist concept of the "dual mandate" (Home, 1997).

Yet the French strategy also acknowledged the potential tensions with the colonized peoples and sought to avoid them, though without actually involving indigenous viewpoints. Despite physical results that were often impressive, the overall outcomes scarcely lived up to the ideals. Invariably the financial benefits of these planned urban developments went overwhelmingly to French interests. Only small numbers of the indigenous elite were able to embrace fully the spirit of "associationism" And, though it took different forms, colonial planning was challenged, actively and passively, by the majority of indigenous people. Thus in Indo-China, enlightened *urbanisme* could not tame the rising indigenous challenge to the colonizers in major cities such as Saigon and Hanoi. Around Moroccan cities such as Casablanca, burgeoning indigenous *bidonvilles* (shack communities) were soon challenging the colonial planning process.

As the case of Indo-China shows, the contesting of externally imposed planning was an integral part of a much wider process of challenging imperial dependence. This link with struggles for national self-determination confers a wider resonance on the planning history of these countries. It contains, too, some faint glimmerings of that conscious exercise of critical selectivity that was the hallmark of diffusion in the Western heartlands of planning innovation and their immediate neighbours.

Authoritarian imposition

The most acute type of imposition has occurred in situations of extreme repression. Characteristic of this type of diffusion would be externally imposed planning proposals and methods of enforcement which grant few if any concessions to established indigenous interests. This can sometimes lead to a curious phenomenon whereby "purer" expressions of one country's planning approach may appear elsewhere, in lands appropriated as colonies. Invariably, conquering powers are far less compromised in overriding indigenous democratic or property rights than in the imperial homeland.

Perhaps the most extreme example of this phenomenon was the short-lived Nazi replanning of the provinces of Poland incorporated into the German Reich in the early 1940s (Fehl, 1992). Seeking to impose a new regional order, the planners of the SS (amongst them the geographer Walter Christaller) adopted a version of Ebenezer Howard's social city that had been entirely stripped of its original social reformist meanings. In this form it became the basis for a new Germanic ethnic template, to be implemented by seizure of indigenous property, forced depopulation, slave labour, and extermination. Jews alone suffered such wholesale dispossession within Germany proper, where most existing property rights were treated more respectfully.

Another example was the imposition of Japanese notions of planning (in effect, the rather imperfectly assimilated pastiche of Western planning ideas) on its colonies, Taiwan, Korea and Manchuria (Hein, 1998). Again, such planning efforts were frequently far more interventionist than anything undertaken in the imperial homeland. Thus Taiwan had building controls from 1895 and housing laws from 1900, well in advance of comparable developments in Japan. By the 1930s, land readjustment in the Japanese colonies was also being undertaken in a far more draconian fashion, without compensation, than would have been tolerated in Japan itself.

There were comparable episodes of planning in other colonial settings. Thus the early planning of Algeria, though skilfully undertaken by French military engineers, was a heavy handed exercise of imperial power, without concession to indigenous society or culture (Malverti and Picard, 1991). Similar charges have been laid against the British, especially in the most grandiose exercises in imperial planning such as New Delhi (Irving, 1981). Yet extreme authoritarianism, without reference to indigenous sentiments, has actually been quite rare in twentieth century colonial planning. As we have seen, indigenous populations were not usually meekly accepting of these alien forms of planning, imposed through imperial power.

Conclusions and Speculations

Amongst the impositional forms of diffusion, context – the power relationship between the "exporter" and the "importer" of planning – has clearly assumed the central role in shaping the diffusion experience. The relationship was absolute in authoritarian imposition but increasingly modified by other factors as we ascend the categories in Table 24.1. Effectively, the influence of context would tend to increase as the power relationship between the originating and receiving countries became more uneven. Where the power relationship was more even or favoured the receiving country, however, indigenous reformist milieux could be expected to play a more important and autonomous role, often adapting what was imported. Further down Table 24.1, however, the likelihood of adaptation was much lower. There was instead a stronger likelihood that purer versions of the exported model might appear than had been found in its country of origin.

The role of individuals as independent variables in the diffusion process remains less amenable to generalization, however. Key individuals could become significant if not primary determinants in all diffusion types. Clearly, though, the way they could exert influence would vary according to context. The more authoritarian nature of colonial power probably gave the individuals in whom that power was vested the greatest scope to shape outcomes. Where indigenous reformism was more established, the extent of the individual's role would depend on the persuasive appeal of his/her proposals, particularly within reformist and professional milieux.

A more human way of expressing this explanatory problem is to go back to the story in the introduction. If Cerdà *had* sold his work to Haussmann, or at least made greater efforts to promote his pioneering *Teoría* outside Spain, perhaps the course of international planning history might have been different. Barcelona might have become a mecca of late nineteenth century planning, alongside Paris, Frankfurt, Birmingham and Chicago. On the other hand, it is doubtful whether one individual can ever surmount the limits imposed by context. Spain's terminal decline as a world power in the late nineteenth century would almost certainly have prejudiced reformers in other countries against adopting any Spanish ideas, whatever their intrinsic merits. It certainly ruled out colonial demonstrations of the kind that played such a key part in the international spread of British and French planning during the twentieth century.

Today, paradoxically, Barcelona's planning and other lessons are being widely studied, borrowed and, to varying degrees, adapted in both the post-industrial and Hispanic developing worlds (Borja, 1996). The context has now shifted to remarkable global economic success, underpinned by progressive reformism and dazzling professional expertise. Cerdà's modern equivalent has been the city's charismatic and visionary recent Mayor, Pasqual Maragall. Unlike Cerdà, however, Maragall has played on the world stage, importing and adapting external planning models (for example, from Baltimore) and, even more, promoting the international spread of the Barcelona model.

Now, of course, we accept globalization as a reality of everyday life. The jet airliner, satellite telecommunications, and the internet have accelerated an internationalization of information that was originally made possible by the steamship, the railway, the mechanized printing press, the postal service, and the telegraph. Throughout the world the lessons of Barcelona (or indeed any other admired planning model) can today be examined more conveniently than ever before. Even past, unrecognized lessons can finally be diffused – Cerdà would doubtless be astonished to learn that it is now possible to buy video cassettes with commentaries in several languages, explaining his great plan for the *Eixample*.

Despite all this, the likelihood is that, in most respects, the diffusion of planning will continue as before. Modern communications certainly allow borrowing to be more rapid, more comprehensive, and less spatially bounded. Yet the process is being driven (as it always was to some extent) by economic imperatives. Throughout the world, cities are now exposed to the full rigours of global market forces. Their leaders seek planning models from successful cities everywhere in the continual battle to win or retain highly mobile international capital. In Beirut, for example, now rebuilding itself after a destructive civil war to regain its role as the Middle East's main international centre, planners have quite deliberately drawn on the widest possible range of Western planning expertise and models (Gavin and Maluf, 1996). Despite occasional echoes of French colonial links, this borrowing process is, however, largely orchestrated by Lebanese interests.

More generally, the effective ending of all but the final vestiges of formal colonialism in the last years of the century may perhaps reduce the extent of impositional diffusion. We may, at least, see a shift to more negotiative forms than have been typical for much of the twentieth century. Yet colonialism continues to cast a long shadow of dependence over the poorest parts of the world, especially in Africa. For many countries, saddled with huge external debt burdens and lacking sufficient indigenous reformist and professional resources, diffusion will necessarily continue to be an externally-determined process. Nor is it certain even that the more authoritarian forms of imposition have entirely gone. Thus the chronic instability of post-imperial or post-communist nationalism in disputed regions of the Balkans and Middle East is bringing a reordering of settlement, enforced by military power.

Yet, while such trends are regrettable, there is also an emergent type of impositional diffusion by consent that can be welcomed. The European Union is the clearest example, where powerful affluent countries have lately begun to defer (rhetorically, at least) to mutually agreed models for environmental management and planning that transcend the nation state. Such initiatives recall the spirit of internationalism that characterized many European planning movements at the beginning of the twentieth century. There are much weaker signs that the same spirit has also found global expression in the recent Earth Summits. If (and this is a very big "if") tangible achievement follows, then one of the promises of twentieth century planning may finally be fulfilled. Whether or not this occurs, however, there is much about how planning diffusion occurs that will not change. Fundamentally, it will continue to be shaped by the endlessly fascinating mix of context, reformist and professional milieux, and individual action that largely determined its course during the twentieth century.

References

Albers, G. (1997) *Zur Enwicklung der Stadtplanung in Europa: Begegnungen, Einflüsse, Verflechtungen.* Wiesbaden: Vieweg.

Armstrong, A. (1987) Tanzania's expert-led planning: An assessment *Public Administration and Development,* 7, pp. 261–71.

Barker, J.M. (ed.) (1997) *Old Institutions – New Images.* Proceedings of the International Conference, John Curtin International Institute, Perth: Curtin University.

Bédarida, M (1990) La "renaissance des cités" et la mission de Geo B. Ford, in Gaudin, J.P. (ed.) *Villes Réfléchies: Histoire et Actualité des Cultures Professionelles dans l'Urbanisme.* Dossiers des Seminaires, Techniques, Terntoires et Societes, no. 11/12, Paris: Délégation à la Recherche et à l'Innovation, Ministère de l'Equipement, du Logement, des Transports et de la Mer, pp. 33–42.

Borja, J. (ed.) (1996) *Barcelona: An Urban Transformation Model 1980–1995* Urban Management Series Volume 8. Quito: Urban Management Programme.

Bosma, K. and Hellinga, H. (eds.) (1997) *Mastering the City 1. North-European City Planning 1900–2000*. Rotterdam: NAI Publishers/EFL Publications.

Breen, A. and Rigby, D. (1996) *The New Waterfront: A Worldwide Success Story*. London: Thames and Hudson.

Buder, S. (1991) *Visionaries and Planners: The Garden City Movement and the Modern Community*. New York: Oxford University Press.

Claude, V. (1989) Sanitary engineering as a path to town planning: The singular role of the *Association générale des hygiénistes et techniciens municipaux* in France and the French-speaking countries, 1900–1920. *Planning Perspectives*, 4, pp. 153–66.

Cody, J. (1998) Private hands and public gloves: Options for globalizing US planners, 1945–1975, in Freestone (ed.), pp. 95–100.

Collins, G.R. and Collins, C.C. (1965) *Camillo Sitte and the Birth of Modern City Planning*. London: Phaidon.

Estapé, F. (1996) Ildefons Cerdà I Sunyer, in Palà, M. and Subirés, O. (eds.) *1856–1999 Contemporary Barcelona Contemporánea*. Centre de Cultura Contemporànea de Barcelona: Barcelona, pp. 53–5.

Evenson, N. (1989) *The Indian Metropolis A View Toward the West*. New Haven: Yale University Press.

Fehl, G. (1992) The Nazi Garden City, in Ward, S.V (ed.) *The Garden City: Past, Present and Future*. London. E & FN Spon, pp. 88–106.

Freestone, R. (1989) *Model Communities: The Garden City Movement in Australia*. Melbourne. Nelson.

Freestone, R. (1997) The British connection: Convergence, divergence and cultural identity in Australian urban planning history, in Barker (ed.), pp. 61–70.

Freestone, R. (ed.) (1998) *The Twentieth Century Urban Planning Experience: Proceedings of the 8th International Planning History Society Conference and 4th Australian Planning/ Urban History Conference*. Sydney: University of New South Wales.

Gavin, A. and Maluf, R (1996) *Beirut Reborn: The Restoration and Development of the Central District*. London: Academy Editions.

Gold, J.R. (1997) *The Experience of Modernism: Modern Architects and the Future City 1928–1953*. London: E & FN Spon.

Hall, P. (1996) *Cities of Tomorrow: An Intellectual History of Urban Planning and Design in the Twentieth Century*. Updated edition. Oxford: Blackwell.

Hall, T. (ed.) (1991) *Planning and Urban Growth in the Nordic Countries*. London: E & FN Spon.

Hall, T. (1997) *Planning Europe's Capital Cities Aspects of Europe's Nineteenth Century Urban Development*. London: E & FN Spon.

Hardy, D. (1991) *From Garden Cities to New Towns: Campaigning for Town and Country Planning, 1891–1946*. London: E & FN Spon.

Hass-Klau, C. (1992) *The Pedestrian and City Traffic*. London: Belhaven.

Hein, C. (1998) Japan and the transformation of planning ideas: Some examples of colonial plans, in Freestone (ed.), pp. 352–7.

Hein, C. and Ishida, Y. (1998) Japanische Stadtplanung und ihre deutsche Wurzeln. *Die Alte Stadt.* 3. pp. 189–211.

Home, R (1997) *Of Planting and Planning: The Making of British Colonial Cities.* London: E & FN Spon.

Irving, R.G. (1981) *Indian Summer: Lutyens, Baker and Imperial Delhi.* New Haven: Yale University Press.

Ishida, Y (1988) Some failures in the transference of Western planning systems to Japan, in TIPHC, pp. 543–55.

King, A.D. (1976) *Colonial Urban Development: Culture, Social Power and Environment.* London: Routledge.

King, A.D. (1990) *Urbanism, Colonialism and the World-Economy: Cultural and Spatial Foundations of the World Economic System.* London: Routledge.

Lock, M. (1947) *Reconstruction in the Netherlands: An Account of a Visit to Post-War Holland by Members of the Town Planning Institute.* London: Jason.

Lorange, E. and Myhre, E. (1991) Urban planning in Norway, in Hall, T. (ed.), pp. 116–66.

Malverti, X. and Picard, A. (1991) Algeria: Military genius and civic design. *Planning Perspectives,* 6, pp. 207–236.

MLCERG (Max Lock Centre Exhibition Research Group) (1997) *Max Lock 1909–1988: People and Planning. An Exhibition of His Life and Work.* London: University of Westminster.

Okpala, D.C.I. (1990) The roles and influences of external assistance in the planning, development and management of African human settlements systems. *Third World Planning Review,* 12, pp. 205–29.

Parsons, K.C. (1992) American influence on Stockholm's post World War II suburban expansion. *Planning History,* 14 (1), pp. 31–14.

Perry, M., Kong, L. and Yeoh, B. (1997) *Singapore: A Developmental City State.* Chichester: John Wiley.

Sanyal, B. (1990) Knowledge transfer from poor to rich cities: A new turn of events. *Cities,* 7, pp. 31–6.

Schubert, D. (1995) Origins of the neighbourhood unit idea in Great Britain and Germany. Examples from London and Hamburg. *Planning History,* 17(3), pp. 32–40.

Schubert, D. (1997) *Stadterneuerung in London und Hamburg: Eine Stadtebaugeschichte zwischen Modernisierung und Disziplinierung.* Wiesbaden: Vieweg.

Sidenbladh, G. (1964) Planning problems in Stockholm, in Planning Commission of the City of Stockholm, *Stockholm Regional and City Planning.* Stockholm: Planning Commission of the City of Stockholm, pp 55–64.

Simpson, M.A. (1983) *Thomas Adams and the Modern Planning Movement: Britain, Canada and the United States, 1920–1940.* London: Mansell.

Smets, M. (1977) *L'Avènement de la Cité Jardin en Belgique: Histoire de l'Habitat Social en Belgique de 1830 à 1930.* Bruxelles: Pierre Mardaga.

Sutcliffe, A. (1981) *Towards the Planned City: Germany, Britain, the United States and France, 1780–1914.* Oxford: Blackwell.

Tetlow, J.D. (1959) Sources of the neighbourhood idea. *Journal of the Town Planning Institute,* 45, pp. 113–15.

TIPHC (Third International Planning History Conference) (1988) *The History of International Exchange of Planning Systems.* Tokyo: City Planning Institute of Japan/ Planning History Group.

TMG (Tokyo Metropolitan Government) (1994) *A Hundred Years of Tokyo City Planning*. TMG Municipal Library no 28 Tokyo: TMG.

van der Heiden, C.N. (1988) Foreign influence on Dutch planning doctrine, in TIPHC. pp. 89–112.

Ward, S.V. (ed.) (1992) *The Garden City: Past, Present and Future*. London E. and F.N. Spon.

Ward, S.V. (1997) A paradoxical persistence? British influences on Canadian and Australian urban planning, in Barker (ed.), pp. 51–60.

Ward, S.V. (1999) The international diffusion of planning. A review and a Canadian case study. *International Planning Studies*, 4, pp. 53–77.

Watanabe, S.J. (1980) Garden City Japanese style. The case of Den-en Tosh Company Ltd 1918–1928, in Cherry, G.E. (ed.), *Shaping an Urban World*. London: Mansell, pp. 129–43.

Watanabe, S.J. (1988) Japanese vs Western urban images: Western influences on the Japanese architectural profession, 1910–1920s, in TIPHC, pp. 568–84.

Watanabe, S.J. (1992) The Japanese Garden City, in Ward (ed.), pp. 69–87.

Williams, R.H. (1996) *European Union Spatial Policy and Planning*. London: Paul Chapman.

Winston, D. (1957) *Sydney's Great Experiment*. Sydney: Angus and Robertson.

Wright, G. (1991) *The Politics of Design in French Colonial Urbanism*. Chicago: Chicago University Press.

Wynn, M. (ed.) (1984) *Planning and Urban Growth in Southern Europe*. London: Mansell.

Yeoh, B.S.A. (1996) *Contesting Space: Power Relations and the Urban Built Environment in Colonial Singapore*. Kuala Lumpur: Oxford University Press.

Yerolympos, A. (1996) *Urban Transformations in the Balkans (1820–1920): Aspects of Balkan Town Planning and the Making of Thessaloniki*. Thessaloniki: University Studio Press.

25

Political Strategies for More Livable Cities
Lessons from Six Cases of Development and Political Transition

Peter Evans

[...]

Communities

The initial intuition that communities are the place to start is thoroughly reinforced by these studies. In each one, communities come to the fore as agents of livability both in the sense of trying to secure livelihood and in the sense of defending the urban environment against degradation. Wat Chonglom takes livability into its own hands, turning its thoroughly degraded location into a livable community. Los Belvederes wrests a foundation for livelihood from a hostile state and tries (albeit unsuccessfully) to do it in a way that will not prejudice the sustainability of the larger urban region. O'Rourke [1997; O'Rourke and Brown 1999] finds that community pressure is the most important check on industrial pollution in Vietnam. In Taiwan, communities are the key political force in the fight against industrial pollution and the most important political counterweights to overdevelopment. In São Paulo, it is a local community – Eldorado – that spearheads the fight to protect the Billings reservoir from the "accumulationist" strategy of degradation promoted by the state and private industry. In Gille's case, it is the political impotence of the local communities that makes dumping toxic industrial wastes a "rational" economic strategy for the Budapest Chemical Works.

Given this fundamental role, the question of community empowerment comes immediately to the fore. What gives communities the capacity to act? What gives them the capacity to prevail in the face of what Douglass calls the "manifold, seemingly

Readings in Planning Theory, Third Edition. Edited by Susan S. Fainstein and Scott Campbell.
Editorial material and organization © 2012 Blackwell Publishing Ltd.
Published 2012 by Blackwell Publishing Ltd.

unrelenting forces [that] challenge the viability of low-income communities"? Is there evidence that communities' capacity for collective action is likely to be robust over time? Or is community action an anachronism, left over from a more place-based world, likely to wither in the face of the social dislocations and concentration of power that are the hallmark of the information age (cf. Castells 1997)?

The social and political assets of communities as revealed in these studies are consistent with a "social capital" perspective and suggest important extensions to that perspective. As would be expected, shared longevity of residence and common cultural ties are associated with the ability to act collectively. The residents of Wat Chonglom, who epitomize effective collective action, have for the most part been living together in the same slum community for a quarter of a century, share the same religion (Buddhism), and in many cases come from the same province of origin. O'Rourke's most successful community, Dona Bochang, is similar. A shared history going back almost fifty years and a shared, actively practiced, minority identity (Catholic) underlie its ability to act cohesively.

Likewise, again consistent with a social capital perspective, the existence of an associational life helps. Churches, like Dona Bochang's (or Wolgoksa-dong's), are one source of associational life, but there are others. Keck shows how Eldorado's long-established neighborhood association helped nurture and make effective a strong sense of identification with the locale. The residents of Wat Chonglom are actively involved in a multiplicity of neighborhood committees. In Hsiao and Liu's study, the membership of the Chihshan Yen community's housewives in the Homemakers' Union Environmental Protection Foundation help knit the community together.

While the long-standing social ties and associational life emphasized by a social capital perspective produce the expected positive effects, other dynamics are also at work. On the one hand, one of the communities that would seem most socially "traditional" – Gille's Garé – is also one of the most powerless (at least pre-1989). On the other hand, there are examples in which cohesion and the capacity for collective action seem to be "bootstrapped" rather than based on a long-standing endowment of social capital. In Pezzoli's analysis of Los Belvederes, community is created out of the struggle for land. To be sure, a number of community members had previous experience with organizations and collective action, but in Los Belyederes social capital is less a heritage and more a consequence of the experience (and necessity) of working together.

Even when a community has the advantage of initial endowments of social capital, the positive effects of collective action are important. In Wat Chonglom, Douglass and his collaborators emphasize, the sense of efficacy gained through the successful execution of projects was central to enhancing community cohesion and capacity for future collective action. These studies argue for a reciprocal relation between social capital and collective action. Social capital helps make collective action possible, but collective action is an important source of social capital.

These studies do not suggest that the demise of "traditional" communities will mark the end of communities as important political actors. They suggest that contemporary urban communities can construct the capacity for collective action and that the experience of engaging in struggles for livability is a good way to construct it. They also suggest that the capacity for collective action may emerge, even in unlikely communities, once the achievement of some common end seems like a feasible possibility. The transformation that Gille reports in Garé is the nicest example. Freed from repressive central political control after 1989 and stimulated by the arrival of new leadership, a community that had appeared socially and politically dead began an active pursuit of its collective interests.

Just as these studies caution us against overemphasizing the extent to which the capacity for collective action is a historical endowment, they also underline inescapable differences across communities depending on the social and the human resources that they can command. Throughout these studies, the danger of talking about "communities" without specifying their socioeconomic status is clear. Urban middle-class communities are privileged – privileged in the human resources that they can draw on internally and privileged in their linkages to elites and elite organizations. While all communities share place-based interests in preserving the city as habitat, poor communities have only a precarious claim on the right to livelihood, and this separates them from their more privileged middle-class counterparts.

The contrasting positions of poor and middle-class communities come through most clearly in Hsiao and Liu's analysis of Taipei. Here middle-class communities fight to maintain the quality of life in their neighborhoods, while the poor must struggle to maintain any foothold in the city at all. In the most vivid case – the eviction of the poor from the cemetery-slum in Kang-Le – the green space to improve quality of life comes directly out of the poor's living space. An analogous kind of conflict occurs in relation to pollution as illustrated by Gille's tale of how better-connected communities are likely to export degradation to sociopolitically isolated "wasteland" communities like Garé. Given the political advantages of more affluent, educated communities, conflicting community interests are likely to be resolved at the expense of poorer communities, exacerbating their marginalization.

Even when the interests of poor and middle-class communities are not so directly in conflict, poor communities have a harder time defending themselves against degradation. The problem is as much lack of linkages as a lack of economic resources per se. O'Rourke's contrast of the poor and slightly better-off communities affected by the pollution of the Lam Thao fertilizer plant illustrates the point nicely. The poorer, more distant community lacks the education and sophistication necessary to make its claim in a legally effective way and, more important, is bereft of effective ties to higher levels of the political apparatus.

While recognizing the magnitude of the obstacles that poor communities face in realizing their interests, it is important not to underestimate their political capacity. With little in the way of resources beyond determination and some prior organizing experience, the residents of Los Belvederes started from "homes" of rocks and cardboard, survived repeated evictions, created a community of permanent homes, and eventually secured schools, sewers, and a legally recognized right to their land. Poverty did not stop Wat Chonglom from remaking itself in a more livable vein. Even the persistently oppressed squatters of Wolgoksa-dong managed to defend themselves against eviction and force the delivery of a variety of city services.[1] Poor communities are political actors, and often very effective ones, despite the odds stacked against them.

The most complex and interesting consequences of the differences between poor and middle-class communities revolve around the relations of these communities to issues of environmental sustainability. Poor and middle-class communities both play important roles acting on behalf of sustainability, but poor communities relate to sustainability in particularly complex and ambivalent ways.

These studies provide a variety of compelling illustrations of how poverty puts poor communities on the front lines of battles for sustainability. Affluent communities don't live at the back walls of polluting factories; toxic wastes are not dumped in their backyards. Nor do affluent communities have to worry about forcing city administrations to provide them with water or to extend sewers into their neighbor-hoods. Being forced to confront degradation directly puts poor communities in the position of fighting battles that are essential to their immediate interests but simultaneously on behalf of the general interests of society in sustainability.

When the community next to Viet Tri Chemicals arrives at the factory gates to complain that the factory's effluents have killed their fish, they are protecting their immediate livelihood interests, but they are also creating pressure for the factory to reduce its emissions, and in that way they benefit the entire city and its hinterland. When the favelas of São Paulo fight to have SABESP extend water and sewer lines into their neighborhoods, they are fighting for their immediate interests, but they are also fighting to reduce the chance of cholera and other public health risks that affect the entire city. No less than rural communities defending forests and rivers, urban communities can be simultaneously self-interested political actors and agents of a universal interest in greater sustainability.

If the immediate interests of poor communities always paralleled universal interests in sustainability, the political analysis of urban livability would be more straightforward (and more optimistic). Unfortunately, the limited livelihood options available to poor communities often put them in the position of having to pursue interests that are in direct contradiction to larger interests in sustainability. Keck's story of the poor communities that have occupied the ecologically sensitive area surround São Paulo's Guarapiranga dam is a prime example. In this case, there is a clear contradiction between the only strategy left open to these communities to gain affordable housing and the ecological sustainability of the city's watershed. As members of the Paulista environmental movement put it trenchantly: "A small number of people can't be allowed to endanger the water supply of 12 million people" […]. The communities of Los Belvederes are part of a similar contradiction. As Pezzoli explains, their successful efforts to carve out possibilities for livelihood in the face of the hostile socioeconomic environment of Mexico City also make them contributors to the potentially disastrous depletion of the aquifers on which the entire city depends for its water supply.

The relation of middle-class communities to sustainability issues is different. Middle-class residents pursuing their livelihoods as individuals may have equally (or greater) negative effects on sustainability – given their greater propensity to consume energy and generate waste, especially once they become enmeshed in "car culture." Nonetheless, the collective mobilization of middle-class communities is rarely focused on anti-sustainability projects. To the contrary, when middle-class communities act collectively, it is more likely to be on the side of sustainability. As Hsiao and Liu point out, middle-class people may be attached to their cars, but they demonstrate against parking lots.

When sustainability issues do capture the attention of middle-class communities – which is generally when their accustomed "quality of life" is threatened – their privileged position gives them extra leverage. Keck's description of the role of the community of Eldorado is an archetypal example. When São Paulo's Billings reservoir began to smell, the well-to-do residents of Eldorado were in a good position to spearhead the campaign not just to clean up the reservoir but to reverse the approach to water management that sent the pollution to Billings in the first place. Their mobilization was less likely to evoke the wrath of the military regime's security apparatus than similar activities on the part of a working-class community. Eldorado could draw on sophisticated community members such as Fernando Vitor, who understood the media and the legal system and were themselves part of the local political system. It could also count on a variety of useful linkages – as, for example, with engineers who provided free technical advice [...].

An important commonality cuts across poor and middle-class communities. In both, issues related to sustainability stimulate public, collective involvement. This is true of middle-class communities from Hungary [...] to Taiwan [...]. It is also true of poor communities from Vietnam [...] to Mexico [...]. This mutually reinforcing relation between collective action and sustainability is one of the hopeful threads that runs through all six studies. Sustainability issues lend themselves to collective action, and collective organization is likely to direct community attention toward sustainability issues.

Fully realizing the potential for mobilization around issues of sustainability is a greater challenge in the case of poor communities. Their position on the front lines of struggles against degradation gives them special importance as agents of livability. At the same time, the frequency with which they are put in the position of sacrificing sustainability in order to secure livelihood undercuts this potential. Finding ways to resolve the latter contradiction is one of the principal challenges to the politics of livability. This is what makes Pezzoli's study of Los Belvederes such a fascinating case. The vision of the *colonia ecológica productiva* (CEP) opened the possibility of resolving livelihood problems without threatening the ecological resources of the Ajusco preserve. Even though implementation proved inviable in the end, it remains one of the most imaginative attempts at reorienting a quest for livelihood in an ecological direction.

The example of Los Belvederes also demonstrates how politically powerful ecological claims can be for poor communities. The idea of the CEP enabled Los Belvederes to attract extralocal allies and project its demands onto a citywide political stage. If it had not so quickly proved infeasible, the CEP might have proved an urban analogy to the idea of rural "extractive reserves," which enabled disempowered Brazilian peasants to build quite an effective set of transnational alliances with First World NGOs around the same time (see Keck 1995; Keck and Sikkink 1998). When poor communities succeed in linking livelihood struggles to the universalistic goal of ecological sustainability, the political balance shifts in their favor.

Convincing connections between livelihood struggles and sustainability goals are a key to making poor communities effective agents of livability. The challenge of making such connections also underscores the implausibility of achieving livability on the basis of community empowerment alone. Communities supply the fundamental energy for change and hold environmental strategies to the fundamental test of improved well-being at the level of day-to-day experience, but their energy and experiential grounding must be complemented by broader sets of ideas and organization.

Intermediary Organizations: NGOs and Political Parties

Many kinds of intermediaries serve to connect the struggles of individual communities with the surrounding political and social milieu in these studies: universities, churches, social movement organizations,[2] NGOs (in the strict sense of formal, translocal organizations with some professional staff and independent fund-raising capabilities), and political parties. All of them are important, but two will be the principal focus of the analysis here: NGOs and political parties.

Formally organized, translocal NGOs are not nearly as ubiquitous in these studies as one might expect from their salience in the general literature on environmental activism. In some cases, such as Vietnam, Korea, and Hungary pre-1989, the relative absence of NGOs reflects effective state efforts to restrict their activities. In other contexts, such as Bangkok and São Paulo, NGOs are widely active, but for some reason they don't emerge as central actors in our cases. When they do appear, however, they play a crucial role in magnifying the ability of communities to realize livelihood goals and, even more important, in connecting livelihood and sustainability issues.

Pezzoli's analysis of Los Belvederes again provides the most striking example. Without the local NGO, Grupo de Tecnología Alternativa (GTA), community activists in Los Belvederes would never have been able to credibly project the conceptualization of the CEP. Once formulated, the CEP idea drew Los Belvederes to the attention of Austrian environmentalists and gave the community the political clout that goes with access to the media. This combination of providing access to a broader range of ideas and supplying connections to a network of other potentially supportive organizations is the archetypal NGO contribution.

O'Rourke's Tae Kwang shoe factory provided an even more powerful "NGO effect." In this case, the community of workers was completely outmatched in its local environment by the power of the Nike subcontractor that employed them. Once their situation came to the attention of a transnational network of NGOs, one of the key sources of the local company's power – its ties to transnational capital – became an Achilles' heel. Once transnational connections were made, the core of Nike's economic power – its universally known brand name – could be leveraged against it. As in the case of Los Belvederes, NGOs were able to transform immediate local struggles over the working environment into a specific instance of universal issues, in this case human rights and social justice.

Environmental NGOs were also central to the quest for livability in Taiwan, but in this case, Hsiao and Liu's analysis reveals weaknesses as well as strengths. Unlike the NGOs involved with Los Belvederes or in the Nike case, environmental NGOs in Taiwan have, according to Hsiao and Liu, "remained silent on issues relating to the urban poor." Middle-class concerns with quality of life are extended to the countryside, but Taiwanese NGOs seem blind to the idea that livelihood and sustainability issues must be joined together in order to generate a viable politics of livability. The Taipei case implies that if overcoming the potential contradictions between livelihood struggles and sustainability issues is a central problem in making poor communities better agents of livability, then overcoming the tendency to privilege sustainability issues at the expense of questions of the livelihood and the well-being of poor communities is the central issue for environmental NGOs.

The role of political parties is both more ubiquitous and more complex than that of NGOs. These six studies contain examples of all of the negative effects on independent community mobilization traditionally attributed to political parties – co-opting community leaders, constructing "clientelistic" networks that demobilize both leaders and their constituents, dividing and distracting communities by involving them in self-interested partisan conflicts, and so on. At the same time, there are a significant number of instances in which political parties, especially opposition parties, support communities' pursuit of greater livability.

Dominant parties are more likely to be part of the problem than part of the solution. In Korea and Hungary, for example, the positive functions of dominant parties for communities in pursuit of livability are hard to find. In at least one surprising case, however, the dominant party seems to provide useful alternative ways of getting to state agencies. In O'Rourke's description, certain local organizations of the Vietnamese Communist Party deliver community grievances upward in an unexpectedly capillary fashion. Obviously, representation is combined with control, with the balance depending on particular local circumstances, but the possibility of positive linkages via even a dominant party cannot be dismissed out of hand.

One important traditional role for party politicians is to act as intermediary between communities and the state agencies that supply infrastructure and services to communities. This relationship can bring with it the divisive and demobilizing side effects (as Pezzoli argues in relation to the PRI's "Community Development Program" for Ajusco), but the negative political effects must be balanced against the positive effects of the infrastructure itself. In both the Mexico City and São Paulo cases, the extent to which even "illegal" communities were able to negotiate the provision of services from the state is impressive. Political parties played a central role in these negotiations.

Opposition parties may be less effective at providing traditional services, but they deliver more positive political side effects. When opposition parties become strong enough to win local or state-level elections, they do two important things. First, when they grow out of a base in social and community movements, opposition parties support increased participation by communities and social movement groups. Second, they challenge the exclusive emphasis on accumulation that generally characterizes the discourse of dominant parties (and the economic elites that support them). These effects can be seen both in Asia (Taiwan) and in Latin America (Mexico and Brazil).

In Taipei, the emergence of political competition and opposition parties made challenging the degrading strategies of economic accumulation politically feasible. Given the KMT's unremitting pursuit of accumulation at any cost and its tightly constructed alliances with dominant economic elites, the opposition Democratic Progressive Party (DPP) really had little choice other than to include more emphasis on livability in its definition of development. The DPP's historic ties to the environmental movement made it a natural to bring environmental politics more to the fore, giving community groups and social movements a powerful ally in their fights for parks and preservation. (Of course, as more DPP leaders got into office, their ties with the environmental movement sometimes had the negative effect of dampening the movement's enthusiasm for protesting these officials' own infringements on sustainability.)

Despite the PRI's traditional rhetorical emphasis on welfare, the PRD (Partido Revolucionario Democratico) in Mexico City found itself in a position not unlike the DPP's: the party had to find an alternative base to counter the formidable alliance of ruling party and private capital. Greater openness to unaffiliated community and social movement groups made political sense. In São Paulo, although there was no real dominant party to contend with at the end of military rule, the election of an opposition governor in 1982 had a similarly invigorating effect on the politics of livability. The new Montoro government was willing to think about new forms of watershed management. In addition, according to Keck, "environmental organizations credit Montoro with providing space in which they could organize."

This is not to say that the rise of opposition parties is inevitably linked to greater ideological emphasis on livability. Despite the high hopes surrounding the return to civilian rule in Korea in 1987, the politicians of the former opposition have proved almost as thoroughly (if less repressively) attached to the old politics of accumulation as their military predecessors were. Likewise, despite the important role played by the environmental movement in undermining the Communist Party's hegemony in Hungary, the new parties that emerged after the transition seem to have little interest in an agenda of livability. Even in the case of Taiwan's DPP, as Hsiao and Liu point out, opposition politicians have proved themselves far from immune to the lure of overdevelopment in pursuit of world city status.

Likewise, even when opposition parties are willing to raise the banner of livability, their sponsorship may be flawed by their political roots. The DPP in Taipei and the Workers' Party (Partido dos Trabalhadores, or PT) in São Paulo illustrate contrasting ways in which parties can go astray. In the case of the DPP, Hsiao and Liu make it clear that the party carries with it the flaws of the environmentalist NGOs that were its early allies. Like them, the party is strong on parks and preservation but relatively indifferent to the livelihood of poor communities. Similarly, the PT ended up mirroring the contradictions of the working-class communities that are its principal base. In theory, the PT should have been exceptionally effective in helping community groups to find strategies that would integrate livelihood struggles with sustainability issues. The PT has a much longer history of working with the poor and marginalized communities than the DPP and PRD. In addition, the PT could count a number of activists from the environmental movement among its membership. In practice, however, the PT was unable to formulate a strategy that would reconcile these two constituencies. While its environmentalist constituency was condemning the invasions of reservoir areas, its community-based militants were prominent among the leadership of the invaders [...]. Rather than the party becoming a vehicle for resolution of the contradictions between livelihood and sustainability issues, the contradictions became an organizational problem for the party itself.

If parties are not the uniformly nefarious actors that they were sometimes portrayed to be in the literature on urban community struggles, they are, even under the best of circumstances, imperfect intermediaries, certainly not solutions in themselves. Parties (particularly opposition parties) can, however, provide two kinds of support. At the macro level, they can open political space for communities and other social movement groups to participate in debates over rules and policies. They also create discursive space enabling imaginaries to extend beyond the standard monolithic emphasis on development and accumulation. At the micro level, they can provide organizational niches that give innovative community leaders extra leverage. In São Paulo, Virgílio Farias used his position in the environment department of the local PT administration to organize one of the Movimento de Defesa da Vida's important early campaigns. The PRD victory in Mexico City gave Ajusco's Hipólito Bravo López a chance to develop his leadership skills and experiment with new ways of building his community's external linkages.

Suggesting that parties are the solution to communities' needs for external linkages would be foolish. Control, clientelism and co-optation, and the quest for partisan advantage play much too large a role in the repertoires of even progressive parties. Nonetheless, it would be equally foolish for activists and community leaders to ignore the possibilities that party structures afford and the ways that oppositional parties can open up the larger political environment for new discourses and new forms of participation.

Overall, the external connections that intermediaries provide play an essential role in enabling communities to become effective agents of livability. Romantic visions in which individual communities can somehow resolve problems of livelihood and sustainability on their own are analytically misguided and a political disservice.

Douglass et al.'s (2002) analysis of the case of Wat Chonglom and its implications for other slum communities in Bangkok makes the point best. Wat Chonglom is the best example among all of the six studies of the successful self-reliant pursuit of livability. Yet Douglass and his collaborators are clear that external connections – primarily in the form of two university professors and the outside loan that they helped the community arrange – played a catalytic role in moving the community onto a trajectory of enhanced livability. Furthermore, they are equally clear that even in Bangkok, where the state encourages self-reliance, Wat Chonglom is the exception that proves the rule, and "attempts to follow the self-reliant model in other slum communities revealed the model's limitations."

Self-reliant internal organization gives poor communities the capacity to make effective use of external linkages, but intermediary organizations still have an essential role to play. They bring new ideas and strategic inputs that magnify the returns of internal efforts. They help communities find ways to reconcile their limited livelihood options with sustainability. They improve the odds in uneven conflicts between urban communities and those who see the city as a place to accumulate money and power rather than as a place to live. They are likely to be a crucial component in any assemblage of actors capable of producing greater livability.

Allies and Enemies in the State

Even in a globalized world, the predilections and capacities of states have a powerful effect on the prospects of communities looking for livability. Yet if political parties are ambiguous organizations, states are ambiguous actors in even more complicated ways. These six studies reveal states as congregations of agencies, filled with both opponents and allies of projects of livability. The internal mix of agencies varies across states and over time.

While there is much variation among these states, there is also an important commonality. The one thing that this variegated set of developing and transitional states – capitalist and state socialist, democratic and authoritarian – shares most clearly is an "accumulationist" bias. From pretransition state socialist Hungary to transitional Vietnam to developmentalist Taiwan to corporatist Mexico to "savage capitalist" Brazil, all of these states appear to be dominated by a surprisingly similar focus on the accumulation of wealth and productive capacity within their borders. The KMT happily allies with developers destroying Taipei's hillsides in hopes that new luxury housing will help turn the city into a world city. Potential damage to industrial production is the only viable "environmentalist" argument in Budapest. The core of São Paulo's water policy from the 1940s to the 1960s was trying to ensure that utility companies could generate enough power to fuel industrial growth, even if it meant pumping sewage into the city's reservoir. The domination of the state's imaginary by this "accumulationist" project makes it that much clearer why communities must be the driving forces behind livability goals.

In other dimensions, variation outweighs commonality. In Douglass's portrayal the Korean and Thai states have contrasting defects. The Korean state is oppressive to an extent that makes it next to impossible for self-initiated community-level organizations to thrive. Communities rise in self-defense – as for example under the threat of eviction – but the kind of rich associational life that would foster capacity for collective action on behalf of livability is stifled. At the same time, the Korean state is quite efficient in delivering public infrastructure and even amenities to poor communities like Wolgoksa-dong. The Thai state, while allowing local initiatives to flourish where they can (as in Wat Chonglom), is ineffectual in providing the kind of support and infrastructure that poor communities need to transform local living situations.

Gille replicates a similar contrast in her comparison of the Hungarian state during the state socialist period with the state in its post-1989 incarnation. By eliminating all possibilities for voice on the part of disadvantaged local communities in the pre-1989 period, the state paved the way for ecological disasters like the toxic waste dump in Garé. By withdrawing from active participation in livability issues in the post-1989 period, the state left these same communities without the organizational, political, and material resources that they needed to resolve their problems.

Communities can't do without states. There is no dearth of examples in these studies of how the power of the state is used to impose degradation on communities and to smother community-based projects of livability. Yet communities suffer as much from the incapacity of the state to implement its own projects of livability as they do from its excessive capacity to facilitate projects of accumulation at the expense of livelihood and sustainability.

Communities need capable public institutions desperately, but, unfortunately, they need states quite different from the ones that currently confront them. The question is how that difference might be reduced. The apparent inability of existing states to combine capacity for effective public action with openness to grassroots initiatives and responsiveness to community needs defines what is lacking in existing public institutions. Political efforts to restructure existing state apparatuses at the national level are admirable endeavors, worth pursuing but unlikely to produce the desired combination of capacity and openness in the foreseeable future. Efforts to transform city administrations are more promising, but local governments will still sit in the shadow of national rules and power. Less ambitious, but more likely to produce concrete results, are what might be called "jujitsu tactics" – efforts to leverage the conflicts and contradictions that already exist within state apparatuses to shift the balance of state action toward livability.

Jujitsu tactics are based on the premise that most public institutions are both collections of organizations, some of which actually have a vested interest in promoting livability, and aggregations of individual incumbents, some of whom are potential allies. Even state apparatuses with relatively effective forms of hierarchical coordination are fraught with conflicts among competing projects and organizations. The balance of power among these competing interests within the state depends in part on the effectiveness of their allies in society. If communities, NGOs, and other institutions can make more effective use of potential allies and find ways to strengthen the position of these allies in their conflicts within the state, prospects for livability increase substantially.

As would be expected, those parts of the state apparatus that have the most direct relations to the task of accumulation tend to be the best developed and most powerful. Those concerned with livability are weaker and less developed. O'Rourke [1997; O'Rourke and Brown 1999] characterizes Vietnam's environmental agencies as "very young and very weak," "underfunded and understaffed." He observes, not surprisingly, that "in internal government battles, environmental agencies generally lose." He illustrates the point by noting the consistent inability of the Hanoi Department of Science, Technology, and Environment (DOSTE) to make any headway against the power of the Department of Industry (DOI), having failed to shut down a single one of the DOI's two hundred factories, despite clear environmental violations (as in the case of Ba Nhat). Hsiao and Liu [1997] paint a similar picture of the Taiwanese Environmental Protection Agency's unequal battle against the accumulationist thrust of the mainstream ministries. Any effort to boost the state's contribution to livability must start by recognizing this discouraging differential.

Despite their relative weakness, allies within the state are still crucial resources for communities and other social groups working to secure livelihood and sustainability. This is especially the case when communities mobilize against powerful private interests. Their success ultimately depends on their ability to gain allies within the state. Again this is laid out most clearly in O'Rourke's cases. None of his communities can win by simply confronting the polluting firms themselves. Only when direct community pressure is combined with some kind of support from the state does victory become a possibility.

State agencies vary by level as well as by function. Confronted with an accumulationist government at the national level, communities are often able to find allies at the local level. In Taiwan, when alliance with the national KMT regime was hopeless, the municipal-level DPP government of Taipei was an ally on at least some issues. In Vietnam, communities' environmental concerns are a nuisance from the point of view of the national Ministry of Industry but a priority for local officials in Viet Tri City. The point is not that all local administrations are arrayed on the side of livability; they may well turn out to be the creatures of local contractors and developers. The point is that splits between the interests of local and central administrations are another point of potential leverage for communities.

The contribution of allies within the state apparatus may not be in terms of the direct exercise of political power. State agencies, or networks of individuals within state agencies, may, like NGOs, become sources of new ideas or imaginaries. The best example is the Solução Integrada, which plays a role in Keck's story of São Paulo's watershed almost as important as the role of the CEP in Pezzoli's account of Los Belvederes. The Solução Integrada, devised in the mid-1970s by a state technocrat who saw himself as a nationalist working in the service of society rather than as a technician, was still invoked by community activists fifteen years later as proof that the pollution of Billings reservoir was not an inevitable consequence of the city's growth.

The middle-level "whistle-blowers" in Gille's description of Hungary are a different sort of example of how individuals and networks within the state apparatus can offer intangible resources in livability struggles. Gille [1998] points out that when the Hungarian state did allow environmental considerations to deflect its accumulationist agenda, it was because middle-level technocrats with sustainability concerns managed to get the ear of officials in more powerful parts of the state apparatus. Likewise, in the rare cases when community mobilization around environmental issues emerged in pre-1989 Hungary, information from allies working within local government played a crucial role in getting things started.

Those inside the state who are trying to make cities more livable depend on the existence of mobilized communities just as much as communities and social movements depend on allies within the state. As O'Rourke points out, the ability of environmental agencies to overcome the resistance of their opponents within the state depends on the political vitality of community demands. Without active communities, agencies and individuals within the state have no political case to counter the primacy of accumulation.

Keck's [1995] analysis of the Solução Integrada is a nice illustration of how much generators of ideas within the state apparatus need mobilized communities if they hope to turn their ideas into realities. However technically compelling and compatible with the long-run general interests of the city Rodolfo Costa e Silva's plan might have been, the interests of the electrical utilities and the governor's relatives easily checkmated it in the absence of community pressure. Even during the Montoro administration in São Paulo, when, according to Keck, technocrats favorable to the Solução Integrada were hegemonic within the bureaucracy, they were unable to prevail.

The complementarity between what is possible from within the state apparatus and what can be done from outside is evident. Those working inside the state apparatus command technical expertise and the legitimacy that goes with it. They lack the political legitimacy that communities can command, as well as the determination that comes from being forced to endure the day-to-day effects of degradation.

"State-society synergy" is not just an abstract concept. It is shorthand for the myriad concrete relationships of mutual support that connect communities, NGOs, and social movements with individuals and organizations inside the state who put a priority on livelihood and sustainability. Keck's description of São Paulo's "water networks" offers a vivid picture of state-society synergy made concrete: "Activists within and outside the state have formed ties and shared ideas in community groups, environmental organizations, universities, and technical agencies, their loose linkages sustaining a vision of water policy centered on preserving the quality of the water supply and the contribution of local water sources to the metropolitan area's quality of life." [Keck 2002: 168]

State-society synergy does not, however, mean an absence of conflict between communities and state agencies. Paradoxically, conflict is likely to be first and foremost with agencies that are supposed to be part of the solutions. Communities and NGOs are more likely to find themselves attacking environmental agencies and social service organizations for "not doing their jobs" than they are to try to mobilize against the Ministry of Industry for doing its job in an effective but tunnel-vision way. This makes good political sense. Potential allies are both more vulnerable and more likely to change their ways than agencies with opposing agendas and constituencies. Dramatic and aggressive actions to force environmental or state sanitation agencies to do their job – actions such as dumping dead fish on the agencies' front steps – may not seem "synergistic" on the surface, but they are as important to the process as quieter, more obviously collaborative relations.

Unlike markets, states – even relatively undemocratic states – can be held accountable. You can fight with them. Having somewhere to direct demands, someone to hold responsible who is supposed to be able to deliver redress, is a key ingredient in making mobilization seem worthwhile. Thus, even when they play an adversarial role, states can be important catalysts to the mobilization of communities. For Vietnamese communities fighting against industrial pollution, the passage of the 1994 environmental law and the creation of state agéncies with environmental responsibilities was important, not so much because the agencies were able to enforce the regulations but because the communities now had a legitimate target at which to direct their grievances. For Garé, in would-be neoliberal Hungary, the withdrawal of the state left them with no one against whom their claims could be pressed.

Once the evolution of people's living circumstances appears to depend only on "market forces," no one is responsible and collective mobilization seems nonsensical. Los Belvederes illustrates the point. As long as the community's demands were directed primarily against the state, collective mobilization made sense. Solidarity was essential to the struggle for legalization. Mobilization also made sense as a means of securing collective goods from the state, such as the materials to build milk stores and schools. Once legalization was achieved, the residents began to relate to the housing market as individuals, and internal conflicts dissipated the social capital built up over years of collective action.

The web of relations that tie state and society together around issues of livability is intricate and convoluted. Livability depends on the extent to which communities and other groups in civil society that are trying to make cities livable can build ties with people and agencies within the state who share the same agenda. How likely this is to occur depends, in turn, on the effects of the shifting global context, more specifically on the consequences of the twin transitions to market orientation and electoral democracy.

Effects of the Twin Transitions

The introductory chapter to this volume [original text] juxtaposed two pictures of the changing global context. On the one hand, there was the triumphalist vision in which the twin transitions were in themselves the solution. On the other, there was Castells's daunting vision of the global networks that compose the "space of flows" and seem to ensure the dominance of interests inimical to livability. Both visions agreed on the increasing structural dominance of global markets. Neither left much room for agency on the part of groups fighting for urban livability. After looking at these six studies, a different picture emerges.

Nothing in these studies negates the idea that global markets are having a fundamental impact on how Third World cities work, but they hardly support that triumphalist view that markets are in themselves answers to problems of livelihood and sustainability. Certainly the two cases that witnessed the most dramatic moves in the direction of market orientation – Vietnam and Hungary – offer little in support of the triumphalists. In Hungary, where hopes were highest that market orientation would bring reductions in degradation, Gille shows that degradation was intimately connected to market-conforming economic strategies; she suggests that it was a lack of political accountability more than a lack of market orientation that led to communist degradation. Nor does O'Rourke find evidence that increased market orientation is driving "ecological modernization" in Vietnam.

None of this is to say that the contemporary mode of accumulation is qualitatively more threatening to sustainability than its predecessors were. The current quest for world-city status is no more environmentally destructive than the strategies of import-substituting industrialization that were in vogue a half century ago, or the reliance on extractive exports that dominated Third World economic strategies in the nineteenth century. If current economic expansion is more ecologically threatening than past growth, it is because populations several times as dense and cities hundreds of times larger make the achievement of ecological sustainability correspondingly more pressing, but there is no evidence in these studies that current accumulation strategies themselves are inherently more degrading.

The negative impact of the global economy in these studies is more political than it is economic. The desire to construct policies that will advantage cities in global markets leads those in power to ignore problems of livability and sustainability. This is most obvious in the case of Taiwan's desire to make Taipei a regional winner in the contest for global city status. Hungarian officials' failure to anticipate the toxic by-products of the Budapest Chemical Works' economic success represents an earlier version of the same problem. Because BCW was singularly effective (relative to other local firms) in relating to global markets, the toxic impact of its strategy was ignored.

After looking at these studies, the paramount question is not whether global markets are the solution. They are not. The question is whether the second of the twin transitions – electoral democracy – can compensate for the tendency of global markets to divert policy makers from questions of livability. The immediate answer is probably not, but the evolution of the political context does seem to be moving in a positive direction.

The institutionalization of electoral politics as the dominant mode of determining political succession has expanded the space for political mobilization at the community level in almost all of the countries examined here. Even though party competition and the leaders it produces do not usually focus on livability, they are less likely to disrupt and repress self-initiated local efforts at making cities more livable. The space for community-level mobilization created by democratization is made easier to use by other, complementary institutional changes.

Complementing new space for mobilization, there have been important additions to the state-level institutional instruments available to those interested in sustainability. We can lament the relative weakness of environmental agencies, but it is important to remember that most of these agencies didn't exist at all two or three decades ago. The same is true of laws constraining accumulation in the name of sustainability. The authors of these studies comment on the panoply of sweeping new laws that have been put in place from Brazil to Taiwan to Vietnam. If these laws were actually enforced, there would be a monumental improvement on the sustainability front. Of course, they are not, and outrage is an appropriate response. Yet, as in the case of the still ineffectual state agencies, these legal rules must be seen as potentially powerful tools, whose utilization depends on building the political foundations that will make them real.

There is also one less tangible but unquestionably positive change in the global context. The ubiquity with which environmental discourse has become part of politics, even in cities where degradation continues apace, is impressive. The political efficacy of the CEP idea in Mexico City, the popularity of the campaign to clean up the Tietê in Saˉo Paulo, and the convictions of Vietnamese peasants that they have a right to a cleaner environment all reflect a positive change in the global ideological context.

Two cautionary notes should be raised before coming to positive conclusions. First, it is important to note what might be called the "transition effect." These cases suggest an association between transitions to electoral democracy and the effervescence of environmental organizations. Authoritarian regimes under fire seemed to find environmental movements the least threatening among the possible oppositional movements and therefore allowed them to gain a vanguard position during the transition. Hungary and Taiwan are the best examples.

Hsiao and Liu underline the fact that environmental movements played an important pioneering role in providing opportunities for civic mobilization during Taiwan's transition to electoral democracy. Gille observes that in Hungary, "from about 1987 to 1990, the state showed an unprecedented openness to environmental initiatives," and because of that, more general democratic demands were expressed indirectly, through environmental protests. What is disturbing about the "transition effect," especially in the Hungarian case, is that once environmentalism "lost its potential for filling in for other political issues," activists and their technocratic allies abandoned the movement, in some cases disavowing sustainability concerns altogether.

The fact that sustainability retains its political charisma in cases where the transition to elections is well past (Brazil) and where the transitions to electoral rule is not yet in sight (Vietnam) is reassuring. Nonetheless, it is important not to confuse a temporary transition effect with a long-term, secular trend in the direction of increasing the political impact for movements focused on environmental issues.

The second cautionary note involves a problem that transcends transitional regimes and is therefore more serious. If the openness of otherwise authoritarian regimes to environmental demands is striking, middle-class indifference to social justice arguments as a basis for livelihood demands is equally so. The Taiwanese case has already been underlined as a prime example. Hsiao and Liu see middle-class movements focused on "quality of life" kinds of sustainability demands as likely to treat the livelihood demands of poorer communities with callous disregard rather than as part of a general movement for more livable cities.

If the global ideological context has become more favorable to the introduction of sustainability issues, it may well have become less permeable to the interjection of the social justice concerns that are essential to the pursuit of livability. It is hard to find evidence for a burgeoning of social movements and NGOs on the livelihood side comparable to their blossoming on the environmental side. This is a serious problem and underlines again the potential benefits of uniting immediate livelihood struggles with broader sustainability issues. Demonstrating that local fights to improve living conditions are simultaneously in service of universal sustainability goals is the best way to endow them with ideological clout.

Despite these two cautionary notes, there is no overall evidence that states are becoming more rapaciously committed to accumulation than they have been in the past, or that the political-legal matrices within which struggles over livability must be fought are less favorable today than they were a generation ago. If neither the macrolevel political-legal context nor the general thrust of economic policies has regressed, and if space for political action on behalf of livability has, if anything, expanded in recent decades, the question must be: How can this space best be exploited?

Ecologies of Actors and the Pursuit of Livability

The persistent resilience of community efforts to make their own corners of the city more livable is as impressive as the obstacles they confront. It is impossible to read the stories of Los Belvederes, Wat Chonglom, Dona Bochang, or even the thoroughly oppressed Wolgoksa-dong and the "wasteland" Garé, and conclude that the political battle for livability is over. Place-based agency turns out to be hard to kill. At the same time, it is clear from these studies that calls for community empowerment will not, in themselves, produce the kind of progress toward livability that is needed. Mobilized communities are not enough.

The concept of an "ecology of agents" that was put forward in the introductory chapter can now be given more content. Like Castells's vision of the "network society," the idea of ecologies of local political agents focuses on the power of connections rather than the capacities of individual actors. Though it does not negate the existence of Castells's space of flows, this imagery focuses on a more modest set of networks, with very different aims, rooted in the "space of places." While more modest, the constellations of actors that are the focus of these studies still have the potential to collectively effect change, if only they can figure out how to better exploit the social and ideological resources at their disposal.

Each type of actor – communities, intermediary organizations, and state agencies – has a complementary contribution to make to the fight for livability. The capacity of each depends on its internal coherence as well as the aggregated experience and ability of its individual members, but the power of each to effect change also depends fundamentally on its relations to the others. State agencies depend on political pressure from communities. NGOs without a community base lack legitimacy. Communities without external ties are politically weak and parochial. Only when this constellation of actors functions in an interconnected, complementary way does it have a chance of making cities more livable.

Interconnection can take two forms. Formal linkages and alliances officially connect groups, organizations, agencies, or other social entities. Networks of individuals operate within organizations and agencies and, more important, trespass the boundaries of groups and formal organizations and thereby make it easier to bring disparate entities together. The key is nurturing those networks and alliances that are particularly oriented toward pursuing livability.

The process of building these networks and alliances is already under way, as these six studies make clear. But too many opportunities for building ties, making connections, and exploiting potential synergies are being overlooked. They are overlooked because categorical divisions and lack of a shared cultural framework blind actors to complementary possibilities. Technocrats underestimate the extent to which they need communities; community leaders dismiss those working in the state as bureaucrats; NGOs dismiss both ordinary citizens and technocrats as pedestrian and shortsighted. Communities and NGOs are suspicious of supporting plans to increase the capacity of state agencies as long as construction firms and real estate developers appear to be the state's dominant interlocutors. Those working in state agencies are reluctant to jeopardize the privileged status of technocratic qualification by granting legitimacy to community inputs.

For cities to become more livable, groups and individuals inside and outside of the state must become more conscious of the necessity of looking for complementarities, forging alliances, and bridging differences that separate the multiple agendas that are part of livability. Bureaucrats must be open to direct democratic demands, regardless of how inconvenient and unreasonable they might be. Communities must be willing to provide political backing for increasing the capacity of state agencies, despite the risk that the capacity might be misused or captured. NGOs must use their greater political and institutional flexibility to build ties in both directions. Perhaps most important, actors both inside and outside of the state must be on the lookout for new institutional forms – such as Keck's basin committees – that hold the promise of transcending old impasses.

The vision of agency that emerges here is not revolutionary. It is built on the accretion of small changes – filling a gap in a network so that it becomes more robust; using a network to give activists a head start on a contested issue by sharing crucial information; discovering which public agency is likely to be vulnerable to pressure and taking advantage of that vulnerability; finding new ways to think about the governance of key collective goods, such as drinking water. The battles won through this kind of accretive process are important not just because of their contribution to livability but also because winning them simultaneously builds both institutional infrastructure and capacity for collective action.

Is this strategic vision of communities, organizations, and individuals, interconnected in synergistic ways, playing complementary roles that cumulate, sufficient to trump the admittedly weighty forces undermining the quest for livability? Perhaps not, but they are certainly strategies worth exploring, especially for those with a "passion for the possible."[3]

Notes

1 Conversely, it is important not to exaggerate the extent of middle-class privilege. The educated middle-class community around Ba Nhat Chemicals was less successful in securing redress than the poor agriculturalists around the Lam Thao plant (although not less successful than the agriculturalists' even poorer cousins across the river).

2 Social movement organizations (sometimes referred to as SMOs) are more local and less professionalized than NGOs. They may expand out from a base in particular communities to make connections to other communities, or they may start as issue-based groups. The Billings Defense Committee and the Movimento de Defesa da Vida [...] are good examples of social movement organizations.

3 See the discussion of Hirschman's "possibilism" at the end of chapter 1 [original text].

References

Castells, Manuel. 1997. *The Power of Identity*. Vol. 2 of *The Information Age: Economy, Society, and Culture*. Oxford: Blackwell.

Douglass, Mike, Orathal Ard-am, and Ik Ki Kim. 2002. "Urban Poverty and the Environment: Social Capital and State-Community Synergy in Seoul and Bangkok." In *Livable Cities? Urban Struggles for Livelihood and Sustainability*, Ed. P. Evans, Chapter 2. Berkeley: University of California Press.

Gille, Zsuzsa. 1998. "Conceptions of Waste and the Production of Wastelands: Hungary since 1948." In *Environmental Issues and World-System Analysis*. Ed. W. Goldfrank, D. Goodman, and A. Szasz. Westport, Conn.: Greenwood Press.

Hsiao, Hsin-Huang Michael, and Hwa-Jen Liu. 1997. "Land-Housing Problems and the Limits of the Non-Homeowners Movement in Taiwan." *Chinese Sociology and Anthropology* 29:42–65.

Keck, Margaret. 1995. "Social Equity and Environmental Politics in Brazil: Lessons from the Rubber Tappers of Acre." *Comparative Politics* 27(4): 409–24.

Keck, Margaret. 2002. "From Tribal village to Global Village: Indian Rights and International Relations in Latin America." *American Political Science Review* 96(2): 462–3.

Keck, Margaret, and Kathryn Sikkink. 1998a. *Activists beyond Borders: Advocacy Networks in International Politics*. Ithaca, N.Y.: Cornell University Press.

O'Rourke, Dara. 1997. "Smoke from a Hired Gun: A Critique of Nike's Labor and Environmental Auditing in Vietnam as Performed by Ernst and Young." Published on the Internet at www.corpwatch.org/trac/nike/ernst/

O'Rourke, Dara, and Garrett Brown. 1999. "Beginning to Just Do It: Current Workplace and Environmental Conditions at the Tae Kwang Vina Nike Shoe Factory in Vietnam." Published on the Internet at www.globalexchange.org/ economy/corporations/nike/vt.html, March 14.

Peter Evans, "Political Strategies for More Livable Cities: Lessons from Six Cases of Development and Political Transition," from *Livable Cities?: Urban Struggles for Livelihood and Sustainability*, 2001, pp. 223–46, University of California Press.

26

Is History Repeating Itself?
From Urban Renewal in the United States to Inner-City Redevelopment in China

Yan Zhang and Ke Fang

Introduction: Why Compare Apples with Oranges?

In 1978, China boldly embarked on a journey from a planned to a market economy, with its pragmatic new leadership turning its focus on pursuing economic success. Fiscal decentralization, the reform of state-owned enterprises (SOEs), and the emergence of alternative economic sectors marked the departure from a command economy (Walder 1995). The urban land reforms and housing reforms ushered in the emergence of real estate markets in the late 1980s when China was enjoying its phenomenal growth rate (Wu 2000). Since then, large-scale inner-city redevelopment programs have prevailed in cities across the country. These programs were started with the objective of improving the living conditions of residents in the older neighborhoods and modernizing the older cores. However, they have quickly been transformed into a large-scale speculative form of development involving massive demolition and ruthless displacement. Localities have seen elevated highways, modernist and postmodernist skyscrapers, and vast shopping malls replacing old neighborhoods at a remarkable pace (Fang 2000; O'Neil 2000). While these projects have helped Chinese cities upgrade their much out-of-date economic and physical infrastructure, the improvement has not come without significant cost: in most of the redevelopment programs, the majority of the local residents have either been forced to relocate to the city outskirts where infrastructure is inadequate or to move to the adjacent slums that have remained untouched. Although largely understudied, these government-run programs involving large-scale clearance remind many scholars, both in China and overseas, of US urban renewal in the 1950s and 1960s.

Readings in Planning Theory, Third Edition. Edited by Susan S. Fainstein and Scott Campbell.
Editorial material and organization © 2012 Blackwell Publishing Ltd.
Published 2012 by Blackwell Publishing Ltd.

The US federal urban renewal (then called urban redevelopment) program was launched under Title 1 of the Housing Act of 1949. Supported by multiple interest groups, the program aimed at revitalizing the nation's declining central cities through large-scale slum clearance. Although the program was intended to "[provide] more and better housing through the spot removal of residential slums" (Keyes 1969, 2–3), the next two decades witnessed the replacement of people and their homes with comprehensively planned structures (mostly office buildings, commercial complexes, and luxury housing) and, all too often, empty tracts. Moreover, urban renewal simply pushed the slum dwellers (mostly African Americans and other minorities) to other parts of the city or to the suburbs, a result that actually exacerbated the ills the program sought to solve (Gans 1968). By the early 1960s, the program came under increasing fire from the Left and the Right alike. Conservatives assailed the program as a costly failure of big government and social engineering (e.g., Anderson 1964). Liberals attacked the program's devastating effects on the diversity and vibrancy of neighborhoods as well as the wellbeing of the poor (Jacobs 1961; Hartman 1966; Gans 1968). These controversies, resonating with many of the public and social movements such as the civil rights and the antiwar movements, led to the demise of urban renewal in 1974.

Is history repeating itself? To what extent is the experience of the urban renewal in the United States relevant to China? This article intends to address the above questions by comparing the similarities and differences between US urban renewal in the 1950s and 1960s and the current inner-city redevelopment in China. In examining their trajectories, this analysis shows that the lofty intentions of providing housing to low-income people were ignored and sometimes even dismissed by governments in both redevelopment programs. Instead, economic growth became the underlying motivation for political alliances between local government and local enterprises. Taking the lens of the "growth machine" concept (Logan and Molotch 1987), this study finds that in both countries, local elites used the programs to acquire land as a commodity for accumulating wealth (exchange value) at the expense of the local communities that view these sites as necessities for everyday life (use value). The two programs, however, are subject to different political, socioeconomic, institutional, and historical contexts, which explain the distinctions in scale, scope, and intensity between two redevelopment activities. Urban renewal in the United States was an ill-fated program in which the federal dollars were misused to facilitate local government and downtwon business interests in a declining inner-city economy. In China, on the contrary, the rapid urban redevelopment results from unfettered local actions taking advantage of the nascent market economy and the booming real estate market fostered by the devolution of the state power.

In contrast to the intensively studied urban renewal in the United States, there has been little thorough analysis of the redevelopment programs in China, even though they have become increasingly controversial over the course of the past decade [2000s]. Moreover, current related research in China merely focuses on physical planning and architectural design but avoids further analysis of the underlying political and socioeconomic forces.[1] Constrained by the dearth of reliable data on this topic,[2] the statistics and narratives of urban redevelopment in this study mostly are drawn from the case of Beijing's Old and Dilapidated Housing Redevelopment (ODHR) program launched in 1990.[3] Studies show that other cities' inner-city housing redevelopment programs, although slightly differing in names, resemble the ODHR program in fundamental ways (see Wu 2000; Zhu 1999; Zhang 2002).

The authors recognize that this study might run the risk of "comparing apples and oranges," considering the remarkable dissimilarities in national contexts between the two countries. There also exists a danger of oversimplifying the complex nature of politics of urban places by overlooking particularities of each city in the United States and China. Moreover, rigorous logic and solid methods of cross-national comparative analysis of urban change have yet to be further developed (Walton 1990). In addition, although such studies have been increasingly available in the literature, the majority of current scholarship is cross-Atlantic and concentrated on advanced industrialized nations (see, e.g., Logan and Swanstrom 1990; Molotch 1990; Fainstein [1994] 2001).

Intrigued by the puzzle of seeing history repeating itself, however, the authors attempt to confront the above difficulties and expand the current efforts by conducting cross-Pacific comparative analysis of urban renewal between China and the United States, a research endeavor that has relatively few precedents. It is worth noting that this study is neither aiming at generalizing a universal account of urban renewal nor advancing the theory of "growth machine" for its own sake. Rather, by highlighting differences and variations of urban redevelopment between cities in China and cities in the United States, the authors strive to identify the relevance of certain factors unique to each society, thus ultimately enriching our understanding of the diversity of urban renewal in both countries from the perspective of the political economy of urban redevelopment.

Similarities

Although China and the United States have different political and socioeconomic systems and the redevelopment of the city took place at different historical periods, the two countries followed markedly similar renewal strategies with similar results. The disturbing similarities lie in the devastation of traditional forms by mass-produced modernity; the elusive and increasing proportion of commercial development; the trick in identifying "slum" areas; the lack of consideration of, and compensation to, local residents; and the fact that the stated beneficiaries of the program became its victims.

Devastation of tradition by mass-produced modernity

In both countries, older inner-city neighborhoods were viewed as obsolete and belonging to the nineteenth century or, in China's case, to feudalism,[4] not to the modern city. The politicians and planners believed that the blighted areas in the

United States required "major surgery" (quoted in Halpern 1995, 67) and that the dilapidated inner-city neighborhoods in Beijing and many other Chinese cities needed to be eliminated by the year 2000 (Fang 2000).

As an integral part of the urban renewal from the onset, the city planning profession in the United States seized the opportunity of redesigning the city according to the "Radiant Garden City Beautiful" planning orthodoxy (Jacobs 1961, 25). Demolishing the urban past and replacing it with Corbusier's towers in the park became the formula for remedying the evils of "slum." Meanwhile, the modernist aesthetic championed by the Congress Internationaux d'Architecture Moderne rendered a modernized city with grand schemes distinct from the context, soon turning international style into a global model for urban development.[5]

Despite the forty-year lapse, interesting parallels exist in the transitional economy in China: overcrowded, deteriorated, and old-fashioned structures in central cities have become targets for demolition in pursuing a new era of modernity, prosperity, and renaissance. For instance, since the 1990s, the historic cityscape of Beijing, including traditional housing forms, street patterns, and close-knit neighborhoods, has been rapidly disappearing to make way for American-style skyscrapers and highways, which are nationally recognized symbols of China's returning as a key player on the world stage. Largely continuing their conventional role as spatial implementers of national economic planning, Chinese planners have resorted to the technical mode of planning and the production of blue-prints to resolve urban problems, enhance efficiency, and achieve economic objectives (Ng and Wu 1995; Leaf 1998; Tang 2000).

Twists, turns, and tricks

Although it is a myth that urban renewal's original spirit was to build more housing for the poor (see Weiss [1985] 1990), many of the earliest Title I projects in the United States did produce a substantial amount of moderate-income housing (Teaford 2000; Biles 2000). As urban renewal went on, however, local governments used this program to rejuvenate the downtown business district and build luxury housing, in hopes of boosting their tax bases and providing a psychological lift for the city. This "twist" was facilitated by the ambiguous wording in the 1949 Housing Act. Title 1 stipulated that urban renewal sites be "predominately residential" either before acquisition or after redevelopment. It neither enforced construction after clearance to be residential nor required that new housing be for low- and moderate-income people, thus leaving an opening for nonresidential projects and abundant room for interpretation by authorities (Teaford 2000; Weiss [1985] 1990). After the 1954 amendments, urban renewal diverged in two directions: one aimed at reviving central business districts and the other concerned with rehabilitating existing housing stock (Keyes 1969). The former goal prevailed in the urban redevelopment scene as the federal government further allowed specific allotments of 10 percent of redevelopment projects for nonresidential construction (increased to 20 percent in

1959 and 30 percent in 1961), giving more latitude to private developers and city agencies (von Hoffman 2000; Teaford 2000). In many cases, the priority areas designated for renewal did not meet the criteria of blight and disrepair to be defined as "slums." Rather, they were located on prime locations ripe for more profitable uses (Hartman 1966). In New York City, for example, the government conveniently used the power of eminent domain to seize and level the Columbus Circle area, only 2 percent of which was taken up by slums (Friedman 1968). In Los Angeles, officials bulldozed Chavez Ravine, a 315-acre tract planned for public housing, but eventually, a stadium was erected there owned by the Los Angeles Dodgers baseball team (Gans 1962).

Similarly, the redevelopment programs in China set off with several successful small-scale pilot housing projects. Without substantial governmental monetary subsidies, these projects were financed by allowing developers to sell commercial properties to pay for infrastructure improvement and residents' relocation (Abramson 1997; Wu 1999; Fang 2000; Fang and Zhang 2003). When localities scaled up these experiments and accelerated the pace of housing redevelopment, however, there was not a provision in the programs to limit market-rate housing and nonresidential uses.[6] Therefore, moderate-and low-income housing quickly lost favor: developers have exploited the loophole to build as many luxury apartments and commercial developments as possible. In some cases, such as the Hubeikou project, none of the original residents could afford to return. In others such as the New Oriental Plaza, no housing units have been built; the largest commercial complex in Asia sprang up there instead. In addition, although the renewal program in Beijing was to start with the sites in the worst condition and proceed incrementally from the edge of the old city toward its core, as with urban renewal in the United States, the local governments have prioritized redevelopment in the vibrant neighborhoods in prime locations instead (Fang 2000).

The careless, if not ruthless, eviction of the poor highlights another commonality between the two programs. In both countries, relocation was (in the United States) and has been (in China) considered by policy makers to be "no more than a hurdle which must be overcome to implement the urban renewal plan."[7] By 1967, the "federal bulldozer" had knocked down 404,000 housing units, most of which had been inhabited by low-income tenants, while only 41,580 replacement units for low-and moderate-income families were built over the course of nearly two decades (Friedman 1968). Although there are no national-level statistics available, even a glance of case studies on individual cities presents a daunting picture: Fang (2000) estimates that by 1993, 221 ODHR projects had been approved by the Beijing municipal government, involving nearly 1 million residents. Between 1990 and 1998, the city of Beijing demolished 4.2 million square meters of housing in the old city. Approximately 32,000 families, comprising about 100,000 people, were not resettled.[8] The city of Shanghai witnessed an even greater scope of relocation and displacement. From 1991 to 1997, 22.5 million square meters of housing were knocked down, leading to the relocation of more than 1.5 million residents – one-seventh of the city population in the early 1990s (Zhang 2002).

Moreover, according to Halpern (1995, 68), during urban renewal in the United States, "only half of all people displaced from their homes and neighborhoods received any relocation payment at all, and for those who did the average payment was $69 per family." Similarly, in the ODHR program in Beijing, compensation has been an elusive and sensitive topic. As the government authorizes developers to act as the agents to deal with relocation and compensation issues, developers often find leeway to interpret the related policies. As a result, the amount of compensation can vary greatly, ranging from more than 6 million yuan ($750,000)[9] for a high-ranking official's home to $10,000–$50,000 for some affected families, to $0 if the resident is not cooperative with the developer in the relocation process.[10]

"Growth Machine in the Making" in China

Why do the urban redevelopment activities in post-reform socialist China bear a striking resemblance to the urban renewal programs of an advanced capitalist nation, the United States, in the 1950s and 1960s? To conceptualize this intriguing puzzle, one should look beyond the debate over capitalism versus socialism, West versus East, free market versus transitional economy, and democracy versus autarchy. Among the numerous theories of urban change and urban politics, the authors find the "growth machine" model, first developed by Harvey Molotch (1976), the most useful in explaining urban renewal past and present in both the United States and China.

In their influential work *Urban Fortunes: The Political Economy of Place*, Logan and Molotch (1987) theorize that in a market economy, the space that we inhabit and use every day is not only a human necessity (use value) but also a commodity that generates revenues (exchange value). Jonas and Wilson (1999, 3) summarize their insight as follows: "Coalitions of land-based elites, tied to the economic possibilities of places, drive urban politics in their quest to expand the local economy and accumulate wealth." By manipulating place-bounded real estate development, progrowth coalitions often produce exchange value at the expense of the local community's use value.

The "growth machine" concept is considered one of the most influential frameworks to analyze urban politics and local economic development in the United States (Jonas and Wilson 1999). Logan and Molotch (1987), Weiss ([1985] 1990), and others give a thorough account of urban renewal in the United States through the lens of progrowth coalition. Title 1 owes its origins to the influential alliance of a variety of interest groups with substantial financial stakes in reviving the real estate value in the city centers.[11] The national urban redevelopment policy as formulated in Title 1, in fact, had been shaped by longtime efforts of the National Association of Real Estate Board and, later, the association's research arm the Urban Land Institute. Well before the passage of the 1949 Housing Act, the Urban Land Institute aggressively worked with local business groups and eventually got their preferred urban redevelopment legislation adopted by the majority of the states, thus successfully setting the stage for central city redevelopment across the country

(Weiss [1985] 1990). The ever-increasing proportion of urban renewal funds for nonresidential use also resulted from the realtor-developer-financer's lobbying for maximum flexibility in controlling and developing central city land.

Although recent attempts to apply the model to other settings have shown mixed outcomes, the growth machine framework has demonstrated wide applicability because it "encompass[es] the accommodation between the realization of private interests and the exercise of state power at the subnational scale" (Wood 1999, 173). Along with other scholars (i.e., Jessop, Peck, and Tickell 1999), Molotch himself has identified several key factors that are important in determining whether local circumstances are conducive to the growth machine in any given context. Building on Molotch's analysis, the section below shows that the transformation of the political economy in China toward localization has enhanced the potential for using this model in describing the reality of urban redevelopment in China.

Land and buildings treated as a commodity

Acknowledging the importance of state and political party arrangements, Molotch (1999) argues that the degree of commodification or exchangeability is a decisive element to identify the level of growth machine capacity – in other words, the possibility of speculation on urban land for the private gain of the growth coalition. This factor turns out to be key in that not until land markets were introduced in 1988 in China did local governments start using land, in concert with local business groups, to convert more resources into local economic development by operating the property-oriented industry (Zhu 1999; Fang 2000; Zhang 2002).

During the pre-reform socialist era, the land was under dominant public ownership and housing was considered a welfare good. Land reform in 1988 changed the forty-year history of administrative land allocation, thus revealing the market potential of land-based development. Paralleling land reforms, the national urban housing reform launched in the midst of the 1980s began the process of "commercialization" and restoring the long-abandoned concept of private property (Wang and Murie 1996). As a result, the property market began to emerge, and land and buildings have been increasingly treated as commodities.

Decentralized land-use powers and a conducive national political system

In the late 1970s, the severe national fiscal deficits triggered the decentralization of the once paramount power of the socialist state. As the central government had little choice but to downplay its role of interlocality fiscal redistribution and ceased allocating its resources for urban development, lower levels of government faced tremendous pressure to finance their local expenditures. On the other hand, localities have been empowered (in de facto terms) to take on primary responsibilities over economic development within their jurisdictions. They have also acquired substantial ' autonomy in designing and implementing policy (Wu 2001; Zhang 2002).

As land reform further granted the land leasing and management power to the local government, local officials have obtained extensive authority for land use and fiscal responsibility for urban services. With locally dependent tax revenues, municipalities have faced strong fiscal incentives to pursue local prosperity and come to light as the key player in urban development (Yeh and Wu 1999; Logan 2002). With land-generated income accounting for as much as 25 percent to 50 percent of local revenue in some cities (Zou 1998), property-led development has been increasingly favored as the instrument for promoting local economic growth. In the city of Shanghai, for instance, from 1992 to 1997, the city and its district governments released 582 parcels for leasing, among which more than half were located in the old city (Wu 2000). In Beijing, almost all the available parcels in the inner city had been allocated to the ODHR developers by 1995.

Concurrent with fiscal decentralization, the nationwide state-owned enterprises (SOE) reform, an ongoing process for SOEs to separate business functions from administrative functions, has given rise to quasi-private, semi-independent enterprises[12] (Wu 2001). To gain a foothold in the emerging real estate industry, many quasi-private development companies have been established by various SOEs. While these companies have continued to undertake projects to fulfill government plans, they have been encouraged to enhance productivity and compete in the ever-expanding property market. Meanwhile, non-state-owned modes of organization for production such as joint ventures and foreign and private enterprises have emerged to participate in China's burgeoning economy.

Substantially high financial stakes in real estate

Facing declining profit rates in the production sphere in the post-socialist era, banks and other financial institutions as well as enterprises in China have been seeking other outlets for higher returns (Wu 2001). Therefore, the potential increase in land value through the change of land use has become an apparent drive for capital flowing into the property market. In 1992, shortly after the late leader Deng Xiaoping called for speeding up reform, the real estate and construction sectors became heatedly sought after and imprudently funded, leading to booming real estate markets across China in the mid-1990s. Moreover, the chronic shortage of buildings of all types in China turned the emergent real estate business into a seller's market in which work units[13] composed the demand side of the new housing market at the time (Zhou and Logan 1996).[14] Taking Beijing as an example, among the major buyers were ministries and agencies of the central government, which were often able to afford whatever market price and distribute the housing to their employees at heavily subsidized prices (Leaf 1995).[15] Therefore, land and housing prices in the inner city skyrocketed,[16] and the number of real estate companies registered in Beijing grew from fewer than twenty to about seven hundred from 1990 to 1995.[17]

Massive profits could be made in real estate, with some ODHR projects enjoying windfall profits of more than 100 percent, fueling many elements of a growth machine system (Wang 1996).

With these necessary preconditions, the place-dependent nature of the interests involved in local economic development has led to the reemergence of long-subdued localism through the formation of local coalitions between local governments and the new business elite of post-Mao China (Zhu 1999). Being gradual, adaptive, and partial in nature, economic reforms have resulted in a dual system of urban land and property development involving both market and administrative mechanisms. In the early stage of the housing redevelopment programs, use value was still emphasized and fulfilled by SOEs and their supervisory departments, which were readjusting themselves to the emerging markets (Zhang 2002). With the discovery of exchange value in the marketplace, however, local SOEs have actively maximized profits as other private sector developers do in the market, and at the same time, they have used their close ties with governments to acquire free land, obtain approval, and secure financing and building materials for their projects (Fang 2000; Zhang 2002). To achieve the "highest and best uses," it is not uncommon for developers to overturn zoning and building codes with skillful arguments and, quite often, bribes, turning inner-city redevelopment into a process of "speculation, private deals and corruption"[18] (O'Neil 2000).

Meanwhile, local authorities, with the sole control of land on the primary market, aggressively manipulate property development, thus making great fortunes out of redeveloping places.[19] It is estimated that by the late 1990s, the municipal government of Beijing generated an average of $361 million per year from land leasing, nearly 20 percent of the city's total revenue of around $2 billion (Deng 2003). Despite the efforts of the central government to strengthen the marketization of land transaction, local authorities continue to assign all the redevelopment projects exclusively to local SOEs in exchange for giving them social responsibilities, which excuse the SOEs from operating under market conditions. As such, enormous subsidies in the form of free land are turned over to these local SOEs under the guise of housing redevelopment (Fang 1999; Fang 2000; Zhang and Fang 2003).[20] Local SOEs therefore literally monopolize the inner-city land and thus can easily mark up the price in the secondary land market, where developers would build and sell properties to individual users. Many ODHR developers in Beijing, for instance, earned $300 to $500 per square meter simply by transferring the allocated land to another developer without any genuine development (Yan 1998). In exchange, SOEs provide the local governments with a substantial share of local revenues and much needed social welfare, including housing, health care, public facilities, and retirement income. These "extra-budgetary revenues" – self-raised funds by local governments that are outside the purview of the central government – constitute another dimension of the burgeoning growth coalition between local governments and developers.[21]

Evidence is ample that the coming of market economies, as Molotch (1999) has shown with the former Soviet Union's case, has turned China into growth "machines-in-the-making" and, in many large cities, full-fledged growth machines that drive policy formation and implementation toward private interests.

Differences

Urban transformation in the United States and China, however, has occurred in strikingly different political, socioeconomic, cultural, institutional, and historical settings. The distinctions range from root causes of problems, metropolitan market dynamics, property rights, and institutional structures to the issue of racial tensions. Three key differences between the two programs are highlighted below.

Economic role of cities

Although urban renewal in the United States has evoked images of destruction and displacement, its impact might have been overstated by observers (Teaford 2000). In fact, it generated more proposals and plans than buildings: many cities refused to participate in the urban renewal program, and a considerable number of renewal projects at the time were not Title 1 programs. Moreover, urban renewal activities were undertaken over long periods, with an average of ten to thirteen years from the date of proposal to completion, with roughly a fourth for planning and the rest for execution (Teaford 2000; Weiss [1985] 1990; Rothenberg 1967). Despite sizable public subsidies,[22] many renewal projects turned out not to be a "pump priming device" (Rothenberg 1967, 210–11). Rather, they often failed to attract much private development, let alone sparking private investment on adjacent tracts. As a result, vacant tracts, "unable to produce anything but a crop of weeds," testified to large-scale urban rebuilding being a poor investment (Teaford 2000, 449).

Although the red tape and poor administration contributed to the lengthy implementation, to view the limited impact from a regional perspective, the efforts of boosting central cities were in the face of the ongoing outflow of population and businesses to suburbs at the time. Indeed, with the unprecedented mobility provided by the automobile and advances in techniques for mass housing construction to meet the pressing need created by population explosion, it was in the suburbs that substantial investments, economic activities, employment opportunities, and growth actually occurred. Meanwhile, a series of federal initiatives, intentionally or unintentionally, promoted suburbanization and sprawl and made "reurbanization" relatively less attractive. The federal interstate highway program, Federal Housing Administration–Veterans Administration mortgage assistance, and tax breaks for home owners, just to name a few, overwhelmingly pulled middle- and upper-income people toward the city's periphery, while private enterprises eagerly seized the virtually "unlimited" capital to invest in mass production of "Levittowns" and suburban shopping malls.[23]

Unlike in the States where long-vacant lots and numerous delays plagued urban renewal despite the infusion of massive federal funding, urban redevelopment in China has been taking place within a rapidly rising economy in which cities have taken the lead.[24] Long thought of simply as production units of national industries, cities have recently been energized by new autonomy and propelled by gradually emerging market powers. Substantial capital has been mobilized and pumped into the built environment, previously regarded as nonproductive areas, leading to accelerated urban (re)development. Furthermore, with a low level of urbanization,[25] cities remain the regional powerhouses that can absorb a massive demographic shift toward cities. The demand for construction has been soaring as a result of rapidly expanding economic activities, a chronic shortage of housing and infrastructure, and the large "floating population" migrating from rural areas. Although some studies show that suburbanization has appeared in several large cities (Zhou and Ma 2000), development pressures remain in central cities throughout China. This concentration has become more acute since 1998, when the central government tightened up control of leasing cultivated land.

Global forces constitute another dimension influencing current urban development in China, which had not gained momentum in the post-World War II days. When Chinese cities were opened up to face the increasingly elusive and mobile capital investment that characterizes internationalized economic competition, local governments adjusted their regulative regimes to pursue foreign capital to provide up-front investments to stimulate and sustain local economic growth[26] (Wu 2001; Logan 2002). Municipalities, land rich but cash poor, have aggressively adopted place-promotion strategies and sought support from the private sector in partnership arrangements in which the upper hand is usually with capital. The real estate sector in coastal cities such as Shanghai, Shenzhen, and Guangzhou has become pivotal to attract direct foreign investment (Wu 2000; Zhu 1999).[27] Not surprisingly, this development strategy resembles the central city redevelopment patterns in the West as responses to globalization by engaging in interregional and interurban competition since the late 1970s (see Logan and Swanstrom 1990; Fainstein [1994] 2001).

The role of the governments in growth coalition

Federal and central governments Generally speaking, urban renewal in the United States was a product of the political liberalism in the wake of the New Deal, when the federal government intervened extensively in the economy. Underlying the Housing Act of 1949 was the belief that the federal government had a responsibility to address social problems. In retrospect, the program was in a directive period when the federal involvement in housing and urban policy reached its peak and when "lawmakers and voters had great faith in the federal government's capacity to work wonders" (Fainstein 1986; Biles 2000; Teaford 2000, 461). The steady growth of federal initiatives brought into being a massive federal administrative structure. As part of President Lyndon B. Johnson's War on Poverty, the Department of Housing and Urban

Development was created to give a more deliberate policy direction to the earlier scattered efforts in housing and urban affairs.[28] Urban renewal, according to Freidman (1968, 171), was "one of the jewels in the crown" of this newest cabinet department.

The essence of federal urban renewal subsidies was to reduce the cost of redevelopment on a piece-by-piece basis, a practice that was believed to be otherwise too expensive to attract investment by private entities. Weiss ([1985] 1990, 257–8) reports that the federal government provided more than a two-thirds share of net project costs to local government of land acquisition, slum clearance, site preparation, infrastructure, and city planning. Local redevelopment agencies were granted the right to use eminent domain powers to assemble large tracts of land and sell them to private developers at heavily discounted prices, in return for a promise to pursue development in the public interest. In reality, however, city governments often took advantage of the federal subsidies to pave the way for private developers without financially burdening their constituencies. With an extraordinary faith in free enterprise, opponents of big government quickly challenged Uncle Sam's intervention in the market and hammered on the chasm between expectations and realities of urban renewal (e.g., Anderson 1964). America's democratic tradition and devotion to individual rights clashed with the "federal bulldozer's negligence of the locality and its people" (Teaford 2000). Urban renewal, however, still left a legacy of creating a legitimate role in which the federal government could grapple with local housing and economic development issues (Sohmer and Lang 2000).

In sharp contrast to the federal government's jumping into the local real estate market in the United States, inner-city redevelopment in Chinese cities has been carried out through locally initiated programs made possible by the central government's retreat from direct involvement in the city building process. By devolving financial and land-use authority to localities, the central government has gradually transformed itself to assume the role of a regulator and an advocate for growth in a transitional economy in which market influences are increasing. In pursuing local prosperity in this transitional system, the central government has adopted a laissez-faire attitude toward urban development. On the other hand, the declining fiscal power and the lack of law enforcement led to the limited role of the central government with regard to local redevelopment programs.

Local government versus local business – driving agents of growth coalition   The internal dynamics of the progrowth coalition further distinguishes the two growth machines across the Pacific. China has seen a much more intertwined and integrated growth machine than that in the United States.[29] In the United States, urban renewal took place in a mature capitalist society in which public and private sectors were well established and defined. The early establishment of private organizations for economic development was attributed to the fact that local business groups often had a privileged role in exercising their interests via the state power (Wood 1999; Zhang 2002). When the developers and local business groups sensed the infeasibility of making a profit, and the bait of federal funds failed to attract other big businesses, the mobilization around government began to fade away or at least became less effective.

By contrast, in China's transitional economy, in which considerable vestiges of its previous form still exist, the distinction between private and public is often ambiguous, if not totally unclear. In fact, local SOEs, or other government spin-off companies that are tightly networked with the governments, largely orchestrate urban redevelopment processes. With public land at their disposal, local governments, instead of the nonpublic sector, took the lead in shaping the urban development agenda (Zhu 1999, Fang 2000, Zhang 2002, Zhang and Fang 2003).[30]

Constrained by indigenous financial resources, local governments in China have chosen to achieve redevelopment with minimal public investment through public and private partnerships in which the government provides the land but lets developers assume the other responsibilities of development. While developers have coveted strategic locations, larger estates, and a prestigious image in pursuit of maximum profit, the authorities have adopted a laissez-faire attitude toward urban redevelopment and turned a blind eye to the resulting negative social and environmental impacts (Broudehoux 1994; Yeh and Wu 1999).[31]

Land-based development has also proved valuable in winning the political favor of the central government (Zhu 1999). Given the centralized personnel appointment system, political conformity to the central government and local economic advancement are the top two most important criteria for measuring local officials' performance. As such, the "politically visible economic growth" frequently has enjoyed popularity among localities (Zhu 1999; Goldman 2003). Consequently, the motivation for promoting growth is not necessarily genuine economic growth, let alone serving the needs of local residents.[32]

Civil society – checks and balances

Another difference between the two growth machines lies in the forces that counteract the driving redevelopment processes. Five years after Title 1 of the 1949 Housing Act was launched in the United States, the 1954 amendments responded to the deficiencies of the bulldozer approach and required local citizen participation in developing and executing the urban renewal program. This change was made possible partly because of community resistance to urban renewal and the rising antagonism between neighborhood groups and development agencies. Although in most cases the participation process wound up being "ritualistic and highly manipulated" and quite passive (Keyes 1969, 7), as Mollenkopf (1983) points out, "neighborhood activism created a new 'political space' which allowed, and sometimes forced, urban politicians and administrators to interact with new contenders of power" (p. 190). Moreover, there were also many successful grassroots efforts to halt the razing of their beloved neighborhoods, ranging from staging mass rallies and taking over redevelopment authority offices to turning out the vote in city elections (Anderson 1964; Jacobs 1961; Gans 1962; Mollenkopf 1983). These popular oppositions built the foundation for a growing movement of community organizing and community development beginning in the late 1960s.

Overall, the public's antagonism and the upsurge of neighborhood movements that have helped stem the tide of large-scale slum clearance in the United States have not yet appeared in China, a society with a long history of autocracy and tight social control. Despite the relevant legislation at the national level, the local governments and redevelopment companies in China can quietly formulate and execute large-scale development plans on their own, without adequately notifying the affected residents.[33] Not surprisingly, citizen participation, a concept derived largely from the notion of democracy, is not common in China. In fact, residents are virtually shut out of the redevelopment decision-making process.[34]

However, evictions, relocation to suburban areas, and irregularities in the redevelopment program have sparked petitions from academia (Husock 1998), resident complaints, court actions, and several mass protests against developers and local governments across China. According to a report from the Xinhua News Agency in mid-1995, "from January to July 1995, a total of 3151 persons registered 163 collective complaints about the ODHR projects with the Beijing Municipal Government" (Wang 1996, 35, authors' translation). Local residents have organized class-action suits with increasing frequency and growing scale (Fang 1999). For example, in early 2000, 10,356 former courtyard residents filed a class-action lawsuit against the Beijing government, charging the government with violating resettlement laws.[35] Nevertheless, to date, most of the lawsuits remain pending, and the residents have won none of the cases.

In recent years, many Chinese cities have also witnessed repeated protests by residents angered by government-forced demolition and eviction for the sake of urban redevelopment. In March 1995, Shanghai residents demonstrated in the city's central shopping district, fighting a plan to relocate them to distant suburbs where schools, shops, and hospitals are in short supply. In April 1997, about fifty middle-aged and elderly residents gathered at city government headquarters near Tiananmen Square, declaring that they did not want their homes demolished to make way for a new subway line (Eckholm 1998). However, these protests were limited in scale; with most of the local job opportunities still tied up with SOEs, residents risk being laid off if they fight for their housing.

These lawsuits and protests have attracted public attention, mostly from overseas.[36] China's major newspapers and TV stations have steered clear of such stories or criticism of problems with the redevelopment programs to avoid being branded as the "opposition to progress." Smaller newspapers have run articles on the rising discontent among displaced residents, although they have been cautious in tone and have not published open criticism of the government or exposure of the redevelopments' abnormal finances or corruption.[37]

Several factors offer some preliminary explanations for the lack of leverage on the part of residents in neighborhood redevelopment in China: first, key local officials do not need to care about or be responsible to the residents, as they are appointed by upper level governments rather than elected. Second, public ownership of land legitimizes the redevelopment activities by local governments and SOEs, even though inner-city neighborhoods have a rather complicated ownership structure in which, on average, one-third of the property is privately owned. Third, traditionally, local communities have the least power in Chinese society (Shi 1997). Currently, the Communist Party still maintains its dominance of civil society, claiming members among the vast majority of the nation's leading intellectuals and institutions (Huang 1996; Shi 1997). Although in rhetoric the governments encourage the formation of civil society organizations, in reality, enormous obstacles exist as to registration and securing access to financial and human resources on the part of nongovernmental, community-based organizations. This situation is particularly true for politically sensitive subjects such as human rights, labor, relocation, or religion.[38] Therefore, despite the steady growth in the number of nongovernmental organizations in China, and despite the growing demand from the residents, it is unlikely that we can expect citizen participation and organized resistance to arise in response to urban redevelopment schemes in China.

Conclusions

Despite their stated intentions, the urban renewal in the United States and urban redevelopment programs in China both used government authority and subsidies to make largescale private or quasi-private investment attractive. Economic growth for the benefit of the local elites, rather than enhancement of the well-being for local residents, has become the real underlying motivation of political alliances between local governments and enterprises. As a result, the inner city has been turned into an engine for the local "growth machines" in the United States and "growth machines-in-the-making" in China to maximize exchange value at the expense of local communities' use value. Physical planning and design professions have played an auxiliary role in constructing images and physical forms to stimulate economic activity, thus reaping profits for powerful elites. Indeed, localities in both countries enjoyed the relative autonomy and the dominance of local property and political elites, which powerfully transcended the seemingly different socioeconomic and political patterns of the two societies.[39]

Nevertheless, urban renewal in the United States was an ill-fated federal program in which the local government and downtown business interests converged to boost a declining inner city that was competing with burgeoning suburbs. In contrast, in China, the unprecedented central city redevelopment has been fueled by emerging local elites taking advantage of the de facto devolution to pursue growth during explosive urbanization in a transitioning economy. Unfortunately, the "growth machine" in China has not only been invigorated by much more intertwined interests of local governments and their offshoots but also less constrained by checks and balances than that of its counterparts in the United States. Despite the growing opposition and organization from the local communities, a strong civil society or effective mechanisms have yet to arise in an authoritarian society in which the state retains its direct control on the political front. Compared to the actual impact of urban renewal in the United States, therefore, China's inner-city redevelopment has progressed and will most likely continue at a much faster speed, on a larger scale, and at a greater magnitude. In the midst of the economic accomplishments, the increasing social tension and stress induced by the forceful growth machine loom large in China.

Although some clear and formidable challenges exist, China's new, fast-paced environment presents some emerging opportunities for urban planners to draw on the experiences of urban renewal in the United States, such as the community movements that challenged the land-based elites and the birth and growth of nonprofit organizations dedicated to the service of inner-city neighborhood revitalization. The paucity of balanced redevelopment policies in the United States, however, makes the US experience a dangerous mold from which China's policy and action would be cast. In fact, although the very term *urban renewal* has rarely been used in current planning practice in the United States, its enduring legacy is evident in central city redevelopments in North American cities during the "new federalism" era: since the 1980s, cities have increasingly relied on the property industry to attract investment and to compete in the emerging "infoedutainment" economy in the context of globalization (Frieden and Sagalyn 1989; Fainstein [1994] 2001). Despite mounting regulations and local resistance, this "urban boosterism" is often reminiscent of seizing profits from the whole community in the service of property owners during urban renewal in the 1950s and 1960s. Indeed, "the growth machine system remains durable, sustained in manifold ways through the mutual reinforcement of political, cultural and economic dynamics" (Molotch 1993, 49).

Planners in China and the United States, although they may not have sufficient resources and political power, must recognize the political nature of their work, take responsibility for mediation among different interests, construct power relations, and link aesthetic imagination with the public interest. Despite the fact that "capital moves faster than the victims of change can organize for reform" (Molotch 1990, 193), urban planners cannot afford not to work diligently to mobilize a civil society at the grassroots level, which should be in tandem with each country's own resources and potentials. A context-sensitive approach to providing growth with the first priority given to the well-being of the citizenry must be informed by an ever-evolving understanding of the political economy of urban change, for which a cross-national comparative framework might be a vantage point.

Notes

1 At least two reasons can explain the phenomenon. First, for scholars inside China, these active governmental programs remain a sensitive topic in that they are related to issues considered as politically taboo, such as massive relocation and corruption in land deals. Second, it is hard for scholars, especially those overseas, to obtain the relevant data from the Chinese government.

2 For a variety of reasons, official data in China are often inflated and distorted.

3 Beijing as a city has a history of more than three thousand years and had functioned as the capital since the Jin dynasty (Wu 1999). The inner city of Beijing, often called Old Beijing, is defined as the area inside the Second Ring Road where the former city wall was.

4 When the Communists came to power in 1949 and chose Beijing as the capital of China, they took a revolutionary view of the "feudal" heritage passed on to them. Soviet experts advised that the new regime follow the model of Moscow and turn Beijing from a consumer city into an industrial city (Wu 1999).

5 The Congress Internationaux d'Architecture Moderne is an international organization of modern architects founded in June 1928 at the château of La Sarraz, Switzerland.

6 Although there has been no specific regulation or legislation, during the Old and Dilapidated Housing Redevelopment program in Beijing, there is a general understanding that governments intended that 30 percent of the new housing stock be reserved for sale or leasing at minimum profit (fixed at 8 percent of development costs) to original residents, while the rest could be sold at market rate (Fang 2000).

7 This is Norman Watson's remark, quoted in Frieden and Kaplan (1975, 25).

8 They stayed in temporary housing provided by the government, lived with friends or relatives, or rented their own accommodations. Some of them had waited more than three years before relocation.

9 One US dollar is equivalent to roughly eight yuan (Yn).

10 For example, two district governments in Beijing invested Yn 1.8 billion ($225 million) to resettle 3,328 families whose homes were demolished in the Ping An Avenue Project in 1997 and 1998. Theoretically, the compensation totaled $67,500 per family. In reality, however, only 14 percent of the affected families received compensation in cash ranging from $12,500 to $50,000, while the remaining 86 percent were given apartments in remote suburbs for which they had to pay rent, even though a third had owned their original houses (Fang 1999).

11 This includes the downtown merchants, banks, large corporations, landlords, newspaper publishers, realtors, and so forth.

12 These former subbranches of governments have gradually been restructured to function like other private or joint-venture companies in the market, although governments still appoint the CEOs for these state-owned enterprises (Steinfeld 1998).

13 Work unit (*donwei*) refers to a variety of state-owned enterprises and institutions in which most urban residents were employed in the Chinese centralized economy. It is also an effective mechanism for party and government officials to control social, political, and economic behavior of residents.

14 Note that the majority of inner-city residents do not work for the powerful work units; therefore, they are still "trapped" in overcrowded places.

15 In 1995, 29 percent of all urban households in China had purchased their homes from their work units since housing reform began. But more than nine-tenths of these households purchased their units at subsidized prices that averaged less than a fourth of the market price (Zhou and Logan 1996).

16 The rent of a class A office soared up from $400 per square meter in 1992 to $3,000 per square meter in 1995, and the housing price of $900 to $1,200 per square meter doubled the amount in 1992 (Fang 2000).

17 Nationwide, the number of real estate companies grew at a staggering pace: from merely 12 in 1981, to 2,200 in 1986, to 7,000 in 1990 (Wu 2001).

18 It was estimated that Yn130 billion has been pocketed by the developers and corrupt officials (Fang 1999).

19 There are two levels of land market in China: the primary market and the secondary market. The primary market has remained monopolized by the state, in which the conveyance of the land-use rights has been dominated by low-priced administrative

allocation, primarily through negotiation, rather than tendering or auction. Developers that obtained the land from the primary market would then build and sell properties to users on the secondary market.

20 During urban renewal in the United States, similarly, city governments often dishonestly reported the displacement activities, hoping to get the federal assistance without living up to their responsibilities (Norman Watson's remark, quoted in Frieden and Kaplan 1975).

21 According to the State Statistics Bureau (1992), from 1978 to 1992, self-raised funds increased from 31.9 percent to 52.3 percent of the total investment in fixed assets.

22 Subsidies were estimated as about 1:1 public dollar to private dollar ratio (Anderson 1964, 138–40).

23 Later, the deindustrialization process accelerated the loss of manufacturing jobs that used to be abundant in central cities (Bluestone and Harrison 1982).

24 It is worth noting, however, the national economy of the United States was growing substantially during the 1960s – although suburbs, rather than central cities, were where the growth occurred.

25 Logan (2002) and Zhang (2002) report that China's urbanization level increased from 12 percent in 1950 to 33 percent in 1998. The number of cities increased from 381 in 1987 to 668 in 1998.

26 Interestingly, the capital flowing into the real estate market mostly comes from overseas Chinese developers, rather than from Europe and North America (Wu 2001).

27 According to Wu (2000), the real estate sector in Shanghai has become the second largest one to absorb foreign direct investment.

28 Starting from 1961, President Kennedy repeatedly urged the establishment of a cabinet department. Congress enacted legislation in 1965 to create the Department of Housing and Urban Development at the request of President Johnson.

29 Thanks for the comments and suggestions of the anonymous reviewer.

30 There has been significant difference as to the relative power of the state and the marketplace. According to Zhang (2002), in northern China, the public sector dominates most resources, whereas in southern China, market forces play a much greater role in formulating development agenda.

31 In pursuing local prosperity in this transitional system, localities have been stimulated to capitalize from a dual market of urban land and property development as well as exploit the holes in the redefined central-local intergovernmental relations (Zhu 1999; Wu 2001).

32 This factor partly explains the ironic situation that luxury apartments as well as shopping and entertainment complexes continue to mushroom, despite the daunting vacancy rates in some cities such as Shanghai and Beijing.

33 It requires that before the clearance, the redevelopment agency informs residents at least three months in advance and reaches agreement with the residents regarding compensation.

34 Citizen participation has recently been introduced into the sphere of urban planning, usually in the form of the exhibition of planning and design schemes for large-scale public projects. This tends to be a one-way flow of information from officials to the citizens, with no real opportunity for two-way dialogue or negotiation. However, establishing participation as a formal channel of political involvement might also be a function of time: for example, the city of Quanzhou in the southern Fujian province has witnessed the first participatory community planning experiment in an established

urban neighborhood setting in China (Tan and Nilsson 2000). This project was funded by the Ford Foundation, which chose a southern city for its first venture of this kind instead of Beijing, even though Beijing was the city the grant applicants proposed.

35 The source of this is interviews with Mr. Luo Qichun, a community activist, formerly displaced from the Financial Street project under the name of the Old and Dilapidated Housing Redevelopment (ODHR) program in Beijing.

36 News coverage includes the *South China Morning Post*, the *Washington Post, New York Times, Boston Globe*, and *Baltimore Sun*.

37 A document titled "Special Revelation" presented at the National People's Congress last March by delegate Hu Yamei stated that Yn138.72 billion in public money disappeared into private accounts of developers and corrupt officials between 1990 and 1998. This includes an amount of Yn58.67 billion that should have been paid in compensation to relocated residents but went instead to developers, Yn36.6 billion that should have been paid in compensation to private owners of demolished homes, and Yn43.45 billion as the difference between the market price of land and what the developers actually paid (Fang 2000; O'Neil 2000).

38 In areas of lesser political sensitivity such as environmental education, health activities, or general education, nongovernmental organizations can enjoy relatively few restrictions and little interference from the governments.

39 In fact, many scholars have suggested that today's world economy shows strong trends of decentering capitalism and shrinking economic and political distance between nations (see Gabriel 2002).

References

Abramson, Daniel B. 1997. Neighborhood redevelopment as a cultural problem: A Western perspective on current plans for the Old City of Beijing. PhD diss., Tsinghua University, Beijing.

Anderson, Martin. 1964. *The federal bulldozer: A critical analysis of urban renewal, 1949–1962*. Cambridge, MA: MIT Press.

Biles, Roger. 2000. Public housing and the postwar urban renaissance. In *From tenements to the Taylor Homes: In search of an urban housing policy in twentieth-century America*, edited by John Bauman, Roger Biles, and Kristin Szylvian, 143–62. University Park: Pennsylvania State University Press.

Bluestone, Barry, and Bennett Harrison. 1982. *The deindustrialization of America: Plan closings, community abandonment, and the dismantling of basic industry*. New York: Basic Books.

Broudehoux, Anne-Marie. 1994. Neighborhood regeneration in Beijing: An overview of projects implemented in the inner city since 1990. Master's thesis, McGill University, Montreal.

Deng, Frederic F. 2003. The political economy of public land leasing in urban China. In *Leasing public land: Policy debates and international experiences*, edited by Steven C. Bourassa and Yu-Hung Hong. Cambridge, MA: Lincoln Institute of Land Policy.

Eckholm, Erik. 1998. A burst of renewal sweeps old Beijing into the dumpsters. *New York Times*, March 1.

Fainstein, Susan S. 1986. *Restructuring the city: The political economy of urban redevelopment*. New York: Longman.

Fainstein, Susan S. [1994] 2001. *The city builders: Property development in New York and London, 1980–2000*. Lawrence: University Press of Kansas.

Fang, Ke. 1999. Housing relocation and housing property in Beijing. *China Lawyers* 17 (5): 33–6.

Fang, Ke. 2000. *Contemporary redevelopment in the inner city of Beijing: Survey, analysis and investigation*. Beijing: China Construction Industry Publishing House.

Fang, Ke, and Yan Zhang. 2003. Plan and market mismatch: Urban redevelopment in Beijing during a period of transition. *Asia Pacific View Point* 44 (2): 149–62

Freidman, Lawrence. 1968. *Government and slum housing: A century of frustration*. Chicago: Rand McNally.

Frieden, Bernard, and Marshall Kaplan, 1975. *The politics of neglect: Urban aid from model cities to revenue sharing*. Cambridge, MA: MIT Press.

Frieden, Bernard J., and Lynne B. Sagalyn. 1989. *Downtown, Inc., how America rebuilds cities*. Cambridge, MA: MIT Press.

Gabriel, Satya. 2002. Transnational cyber-superorganisms, capitalism, and the struggle over political policy in China. Retrieved from http://www.mtholyoke.edu/courses/sgabriel/economics/china-essays/16.htm.

Gans, Herbert J. 1962. *The urban villagers: Group and class in the life of Italian-Americans* New York: Free Press.

Gans, Herbert J. 1968. *People and plans: Essays on urban problems and solutions*. New York: Basic Books.

Goldman, Jasper. 2003. From Hutong to high rise: Explaining the transformation of Old Beijing, 1990–2002. Master's thesis, MIT, Cambridge, MA.

Halpern, Robert. 1995. *Rebuilding the inner city: A history of neighborhood initiatives to address poverty in the United States*. New York: Columbia University Press.

Hartman, Chester. 1966. The housing of relocated families. In *Urban renewal: The record and the controversy*, edited by James Wilson, 293–335. Cambridge, MA: MIT Press.

Huang, Yasheng. 1996. *Inflation and investment controls in China: The political economy of central-local relations during the reform era*. Cambridge, UK: Cambridge University Press.

Husock, Howard. 1998. *The widening of Ping An Avenue: Making decisions about historic preservation*. Cambridge, MA: Kennedy School of Government Case Program, Harvard University.

Jacobs, Jane. 1961. *The death and life of great American cities*. New York: Random House.

Jessop, Bob, Jamie Peck, and Adam Tickell. 1999. Retooling the machine, the urban growth machine. In *The urban growth machine: Critical perspectives, two decades later*, edited by Andrew Jonas and David Wilson. Albany: State University of New York Press.

Jonas, Andrew, and David Wilson, eds. 1999. *The urban growth machine: Critical perspectives, two decades later*. Albany: State University of New York Press.

Keyes, Langley C. 1969. *The rehabilitation planning game: A study in the diversity of neighborhood*. Cambridge, MA: MIT Press.

Leaf, Michael. 1995. Inner city redevelopment in China: Implication for the city of Beijing. *Cities* 12 (3): 149–62.

Leaf, Michael. 1998. Urban planning and urban reality under Chinese economic reforms. *Journal of Planning Education and Research* 18 (2): 145–53.

Logan, John, ed. 2002. *The new Chinese city: Globalization and market reform*. Oxford: Blackwell.

Logan, John R., and Harvey L. Molotch. 1987. *Urban fortunes: The political economy of place*. Berkeley: University of California Press.

Logan, John R., and Todd Swanstrom, eds. 1990. *Beyond the city limits: Urban policy and economic restructuring in comparative perspective*. Philadelphia: Temple University Press.

Mollenkopf, John. 1983. *The contested city*. Princeton, NJ: Princeton University Press.

Molotch, Harvey. 1976. The city as a growth machine. *American Journal of Sociology* 82 (2): 309–32.

Molotch, Harvey. 1990. Urban deals in comparative perspective. In *Beyond the city limits: Urban policy and economic restructuring in comparative perspective*, edited by John Logan and Todd Swanstrom. Philadelphia: Temple University Press.

Molotch, Harvey. 1993. The political economy of growth machines. *Journal of Urban Affairs* 15:19–53.

Molotch, Harvey. 1999. Growth machine links: Up, down, and across. In *The urban growth machine: Critical perspectives, two decades later*, edited by Andrew Jonas and David Wilson. Albany: State University of New York Press.

Ng, Mee-Kam, and Fulong Wu. 1995. A critique of the 1989 City Planning Act of the People's Republic of China: A Western perspective. *Third World Planning Review* 17 (3): 279–94.

O'Neil, Mark. 2000. The city that went under the hammer. *South China Morning Post*, Hong Kong, January 1.

Rothenberg, Jerome. 1967. *Economic evaluation of urban renewal: Conceptual foundation of benefit-cost analysis*. Washington, DC: Brookings Institution.

Shi, Tianjian. 1997. *Political participation in Beijing*. Cambridge, MA: Harvard University Press.

Sohmer, Rebecca R., and Robert E. Lang. 2000. From seaside to southside: New urbanism's quest to save the inner city. *Housing Policy Debate* 11 (4): 751–60

State Statistical Bureau. 1992. *Urban statistical yearbook 1992*. Beijing: China Statistical Publishing House.

Steinfeld, Edward. 1998. *Forging reform in China: The fate of stateowned industry*. Cambridge, UK: Cambridge University Press.

Tan, Ying, and Johan Nilsson. 2000. Advocacy work on conservation and tourism development in the old city of Quanzhou, Fujian Province, China. Paper presented at the International Conference on Anthropology, Chinese Society and Tourism in Kunming, China, September 28 to October 3, 1999.

Tang, Wing-Shing. 2000. Chinese urban planning at fifty: An assessment of the planning theory literature. *Journal of Planning Literature* 14 (2): 347–66.

Teaford, Jon. 2000. Urban renewal and its aftermath. *Housing Policy Debate* 11 (2): 443–65.

von Hoffman, Alexander. 2000. A study in contradictions: The origins and legacy of the Housing Act of 1949. *Housing Policy Debate* 11 (2): 299–326.

Walder, Andrew. 1995. The quiet revolution from within: Economic reform as a source of political decline. In *The waning of the Communist state – Economic origins of political decline in China and Hungary*, edited by Andrew Walder. Berkeley: University of California Press.

Walton, John. 1990. Theoretical methods in comparative urban politics. In *Beyond the city limits: Urban policy and economic restructuring in comparative perspective*, edited by John Logan and Todd Swanstrom. Philadelphia: Temple University Press.

Wang, Jun. 1996. Review of land development in Beijing. *Outlook (Liao Wang)* 1: 35–7. Beijing: Xinhua News Agency.

Wang, Yaping, and Alan Murie. 1996. The process of commercialization of urban housing in China. *Urban Studies* 33 (6): 971–89.

Weiss, Marc. [1985] 1990. The origins and legacy of urban renewal. In *Federal housing policy and programs, past and present*, edited by Paul Mitchell, 253–76. New Brunswick, NJ: Rutgers University Press.

Wood, Andrew. 1999. Organizing for local economic development: The growth coalition as a cross-national comparative framework. In *The urban growth machine: Critical perspectives, two decades later*, edited by Andrew Jonas and David Wilson. Albany: State University of New York Press.

Wu, Fulong. 2000. The global and local dimensions of placemaking: Remaking Shanghai as a world city. *Urban Studies* 37 (8): 1359–77.

Wu, Fulong. 2001. China's recent urban development in the process of land and housing marketisation and economic globalisation. *Habitat International* 25: 273–89.

Wu, Liangyong. 1999. *Rehabilitating the Old City of Beijing – A project in the Ju'er Hutong neighbourhood*. Vancouver: University of British Columbia Press.

Yan, Zhigang. 1998. Land speculation in Beijing. *Economy Daily (Jing Ji Ri Bao)*, June 24.

Yeh, Anthony, and Fulong Wu. 1999. The transformation of the urban planning system in China from a centrally-planned to transitional economy. *Progress in Planning* 51:165–252.

Zhang, Tingwei. 2002. Urban development and a socialist progrowth coalition in Shanghai. *Urban Affairs Review* 37 (4): 475–99.

Zhang, Yan, and Ke Fang. 2003. Politics of housing redevelopment in China –The rise and fall of the Ju'er Hutong Project in inner-city Beijing. *Journal of Housing and Built Environment* 18 (1): 75–87.

Zhou, Min, and John Logan. 1996. Market transition and the commodification of housing in urban China. *International Journal of Urban and Regional Research* 20: 400–21.

Zhou, Yixing, and Laurence J. C. Ma. 2000. Economic restructuring and suburbanization in China. *Urban Geography* 21 (3): 205–36.

Zhu, Jiemin. 1999. Local growth coalition: The context and implications of China's gradualist urban land reforms. *International Journal of Urban and Regional Research* 23 (3): 534–48.

Zou, Deci. 1998. Chinese cities towards the 21st century. *City Planning Review* 22 (1): 7–9.

27

Re-engaging Planning Theory?
Towards "South-Eastern" Perspectives

Oren Yiftachel

Yes, this is what they did to Tallinn … in a city where about 50 percent of the population is Russian, they simply removed all Russian signs, billboards, street names and Russian sounding businesses … Russian is not an official language, so we cannot use it in planning discussions and city government … we are wiped out of our own city, where most of us were born … (we are) now the invisible half of this place which still remains our homeland. (Vadim Polischuk, Russian human rights activist, Tallinn, Estonia, personal interview, May 2005)

Tallinn, Estonia's capital city is seen by ethnic Estonians as the jewel of "their" ethno-national homeland. During the 1990s, following five decades of Soviet rule, they began a process of "Estonization", which systematically disenfranchised and marginalized the large local Russian community. How does this link to planning theory? It does so very directly, as Estonization is a planning policy par excellence, being concerned with the heart of urban and regional planning – the shaping of urban space.

Yet, the example does not "sit" well with current planning theories, which rarely address such a process of ethnically guided spatial change. Where was deliberative or collaborative planning? Where was communicative rationality? Did Tallinn's planners try to reach consensus? The Estonian example does not "respond" to any of these key questions, all framed by the leading discourses of planning theories in recent times. On the other hand, Tallinn is but one of hundreds of similar cases, where people's lives have been profoundly affected by ethno-spatial policies. This illustrates a conspicuous mismatch between the main concerns of planning theory and the actual, material consequences of planning.

Readings in Planning Theory, Third Edition. Edited by Susan S. Fainstein and Scott Campbell.
Editorial material and organization © 2012 Blackwell Publishing Ltd.
Published 2012 by Blackwell Publishing Ltd.

The planning of Tallinn, similar to Sarajevo, Kuala Lumpur, Belfast, Gujarat, Jerusalem and Cape Town, to name just a few, also illustrates one of the main points I advance in this essay – the need to create new conceptualizations, not premised on the material and political settings of the dominant regions of the "North-West", from which most leading theories emerge. Hence, it is high time to conceptualize from the "South East" (the wide range of non-western, non-northern societies), and create meso-level theories which would genuinely engage with the framing realities of various south-eastern regions. Such theories would avoid the pitfalls of false and domineering universalism; reject the postmodernist retreat from substance and values, yet offer meaningful generalizations to guide and inspire students, scholars and practitioners.

I further argue here that the "communicative turn" among planning theorists, while insightful and rich, has also worked to "disengage" the field's centre of gravity from its core task of understanding and critiquing the impact of urban policies, as a platform for transformative intervention. Consequently, the communicative emphasis has resulted in several disciplinary blind spots. Two examples – the concepts of *ethnicity* and *home-land* – will be explored briefly in the essay's final section. Introducing these concepts to the debates of planning theory could re-engage planning scholarship with the material basis of urban planning, and facilitate much needed south-eastern contributions.

Before putting flesh on these arguments, let me clearly qualify that the use of binary categories in this essay is aimed at sharpening the arguments, rather than at describing an "objective reality". Needless to say, there are no clear-cut distinctions between North and South, West and East, discourse and materiality or homeland and diaspora. These categories should be seen as "zones" in a conceptual grid which attempts to draw attention to the main loci of power and identity within an obviously messy, overlapping and dynamic world.

Scholarly Settings

The main debates in planning theory during the last decade and a half have been commonly described as "communicative", "deliberative" or "discursive", focusing on finding analytical and normative frameworks to understand and mobilize planners. These endeavors have been illuminating, drawing on major philosophical sources of inspiration, and debating thorny issues such as power, consensus, communication, empowerment and multi-culturalism.[1]

Yet, the debate appears to have come to a cul-de-sac by increasingly focusing on an important, yet limited, sub-field – the world of professional planners. This search has employed ever-more sophisticated concepts to analyze planners' practices and percep-tions, inspired by the likes of Habermas, Foucault, Rawls, Young, Lacan or Bourdieu, with a touch of remaining Marxist, rationalist and liberal perspectives.[2] The competition between alternative theories – so critical to the development of any field – has thus focused on rivaling approaches to the study of professional planners, who form but one (at times marginal) element in myriad forces shaping the nature of cities and regions.[3]

Most theories emerging from the North-West have therefore concentrated on *planners rather than planning*, the latter standing for the broader arena of publicly guided transformation of space. The emphasis on planners and decision processes has left a particular void for those working in the diverse south-eastern settings where decision-making is generally less transparent and organized, and where public participation and deliberation efforts are often perceived as "lip service" or forms of co-optation, in a more uncompromising development environment characterized by "creating facts on the ground".

From south-eastern perspectives, the credibility of leading communicative theories is challenged by a constant mismatch with a wide range of south-eastern "stubborn realities" (to invoke a useful Gramscian term), where liberalism is not a stable constitutional order, but at best a sectoral and mainly economic agenda; where property systems are fluid; inter-group conflicts over territory inform daily practices and result in the essentialization of "deep" ethnic, caste and racial identities. As perceptively noted by Vanessa Watson (2006), this has resulted in the development of conflicting and often irreconcilable rationalities. Moreover, recent economic policies, coupled with the latest spasms of globalizing capitalism have prised open insurmountable social disparities, deepening fragmentation and social conflict. It is clear, then, that despite major forces of globalization, the urban environment – and hence the practices and possibilities of planning – has remained vastly different in the diverse regions of the world.

Needless to say, discursive and material dimensions – that is, process and substance – are intimately linked, as they ceaselessly constitute one another. The point here is not to deride the many valuable aspects of deliberative planning, and the need to study planning processes, but to critique what appears to be a *distorted balance* between procedural and substantive aspects. This is troubling, not only because knowledge needs to be accumulated and theorized on all aspects of urban planning, but also because approaches to decision-making and planning practices may change or be long forgotten, while the material legacy of these decisions remains for generations.

What is the problem, one may ask? Using simple metaphors, the situation can be likened to medical theorists concentrating on the way doctors communicate with patients (which is, of course, important) in preference to studying the impact of medical treatment on the human body (especially the side-effects); or education theorists focusing on teacher–pupil interactions, while neglecting the analysis of how teaching influences levels of acquired knowledge.

Therefore, a concern with mainstream planning theory has been the *degrees of removal* it has created between theorists, theories and the materiality of planning. As theorists learning from the literature, we know now a great deal about planners' deliberations, methods of consensus building, their values and even psychology. Mainstream planning theory can thus be (somewhat crudely) characterized as "talk about the talk". This has been accompanied by an underlying assumption that the "right kind of talk" can provide answers to most planning conflicts. This literature says little about the spatial impact of *actions* taken by planners and other key agents of spatial change, and about the possibility that in some settings talk may never lead to resolution, and may have the adverse impact of concealing or legitimizing planning oppression suffered by marginalized groups.

In this context, it is revealing that John Forester has recently defined planning as "the organization of hope" (Forester, 2006), overlooking in this definition not only the ubiquitous existence of planning's "dark" and "gray" sides, but also that planning, in most settings, is first and foremost the organizer of space. The main tools at the planner's disposal are designed to shape cities and regions, and theories must be developed through this necessary medium. It is symptomatic, then, that despite repeated calls in the literature to "bring the city back", and some exciting and grounded theoretical work on planning concepts such as "just cities", "network society", "partitioned cities", "mongrel cities", "ethnocratic cities" and urban informality, such effort has remained at the margins of the theoretical debate.[4] Most theorists who write in the leading journals have remained focused on decision-making and planners' interaction with clients and power-brokers, thereby refraining from studying the messy interactions between planning policies, spaces and people.[5]

Positionality

As is clear from recent critical theorization about "ways of knowing", positionality is central to the production of knowledge. Hence, the dominance of discursive approaches is not accidental. While the language of these debates is often universal, implicitly pertaining to global application, they mainly emerge from the dominant liberal North-West and reflect the concerns and intellectual landscapes of these prosperous, liberal societies, where property relations are relatively stable, and where most individuals, even members of minorities, have reasonable (though often less than desirable) personal liberties, existential security and basic welfare provision.

The dominance of the North-West in the production of planning knowledge is somewhat predictable, given the location from which the main journals are published and the global dominance of the English language. Still, it is conspicuous that in the first eight issues of the new *Planning Theory* journal (2002–4), only three of 47 articles were devoted to issues emerging from the South-East, while 40 articles dealt with various aspects of decision-making and communicative processes. Mapping the "gate-keepers" of theoretical knowledge (Table 27.1) reflects a similar picture: 168 of 203 scholars (82.7 percent) serving on the editorial boards of six leading journals hail from the Anglo-American countries (including Australia and Canada); 41 (12.8 percent) are from Europe, and only nine, that is just over four percent, work in South-Eastern countries, including border cases such as Israel, South Africa and Singapore.[6]

Let us pause here for a second, and qualify some of the distinctions made above. Clearly, my use of North-South and East-West dichotomies is over-simplified. The production of space and knowledge in a world as intertwined as ours is so complex, variegated, and contested, as to negate the existence of sharp dichotomies. There exist a multitude of gray areas, hybridities and dynamic "patches" between the "haves" and "have-nots" of the academic and professional worlds, as well as a plethora of differences within each "region". Hence, the differences between North-West and South-East are, of course, just a matter of degree. Further, it is impossible to equate one's place of residence with the nature of scholarship. Some of the most radical and counter-hegemonic texts,

Table 27.1 Mapping the gatekeepers of planning knowledge: Editorial Board members of international planning journals

Journal	Anglo-Americans	Other "North-West"	"South-East"
EPS	7	15	–
JPER	42	1	–
Planning Theory	20	5	4 (2 Israel)
JAPA	46	1	1 (Israel)
Plan. Theor & Prac.	22	13	3 (1 Israel)
TPR	31	6	1 (Israel)
Total	168	41	9

as we all know, have been written from the "belly of the beast", by luminaries such as Karl Marx, Antonio Gramsci, Yuri Sakharov, Edward Said or Herbert Marcuse, who showed that the grids of power imposed over daily experience need not colonize our consciousness.

However, the power of "north-western", and particularly Anglo-American academia has been overwhelming in influencing the curricula, the teaching, and – most profoundly – the thinking, of scholars and practitioners in the South-East. For that reason, and bearing in mind the above reservations, I shall continue to use the awkward North–West–East–South terms, as an unsatisfactory shorthand for the differences between the power of the "metropolitan" centers of academia and professions, and the multitude of "southern" or "eastern" settings.

Given the context in which north-western academia is produced, and the inevitable domination of western concerns on planning knowledge, it may be time for a conceptual change. Rather than wait for "better" theories to emerge from the North-West, serious theorization effort should emerge from the (very diverse) settings of the South-East. But this effort should not be perceived as creating "peripheral theories for peripheral regions", but should constitute the basis for alternative bases of knowledge. New concepts may not only be relevant to their own regional settings, but may also become a source of "reverse flows" of theoretical knowledge, as north-western cities increasingly face "south-eastern" phenomena such as urban informality, "deep" identities, open urban conflicts, and mass poverty. A serious elaboration on "theorizing from the South-East" is clearly beyond the scope of this essay. However, a possible "first taste" may include a brief discussion of two key concepts, currently very marginal in the planning theory discourse, but central to the production of space in most parts of the world – ethnicity and the homeland.

Ethnicity, Homeland and Planning

Ethnicity has been an immensely influential factor in modern politics, fostering powerful links between identities and space, by imbuing a wide range of spatialities, such as territory, homeland, region, city, locality, place and even the body, with potent cultural and political importance. It is therefore astounding how little theorization has taken place on the links between (spatial) planning and ethnicity, in contrast to other social markers such as class, gender and race. However, ethnicity appears to influence, and be influenced by urban and regional planning at least as powerfully as these other categories, if not more.

Ethnicity can be defined as "cultural identity, based on belief in common ancestry associated with a specific place". While obviously constructed through ongoing struggles, power relations and blatant manipulations, ethnic identity – propelled by the "family myth" of common descent – has remained an immense force in the making of collective narratives and the governance of public spaces, even during an era of structural and relatively rapid globalization.

It may be useful to distinguish analytically between two main types of ethnic identity – "immigrant" and "homeland", which should be perceived of as two poles in a continuum of ethnic spatial mobilizations. Homeland ethnicity is held by groups who reside on the territory they believe to be the "cradle" of their identity and history. Immigrant ethnicity, on the other hand, is based on distance from the homeland and long-term association with other societies. The former tends to form the basis for national or regional movements aspiring for statehood, self-determination, or group autonomy; while the latter tends to energize campaigns for minority and civil rights framed by a gradual (though uneven and conflict-riddled) process of incorporation into the "host" society.

Ethnicity has been introduced into theoretical planning discussions mainly through the concepts of "difference" and "multiculturalism", both of which denote broader and "softer", identity markers. Where ethnicity has been directly introduced, it is often confined to immigrant groups or marginalized indigenous peoples, and rarely addresses the immense power of ethno-nationalism and ethno-regionalism to influence planning in "homeland" cities and regions.[7] There were several attempts to theorize the powerful links between ethno-nationalism, the state and urban policies, but these have been few and far between, and have not resulted in a fruitful theoretical conversation.[8]

A critical link here remains the state. Theories of the state abound, and their impact on planning theory has been significant. However, these have centred on discussions of the state's (and planning's) role in facilitating capital accumulation and developing regimes of regulation, surveillance and developmentalism. Little has been said in the planning literature on a most fundamental function of the modern state – imposing ethno-national spatial control, often in conflict with groups holding counter territorial claims.

The ethnicizing and nationalizing dimensions of planning are for all to see, as manifest in land policies, settlement systems, municipal and regional boundaries and cultural landscapes. Elsewhere I have termed this "ethnocratic planning" – being a regime furthering the goals of a dominant ethnic group while using a crude rhetoric of "democratic" majoritarian rule (Yiftachel and Yacobi, 2004). In extreme (but far from rare) cases, ethno-national planning has caused massive destruction, violent colonialism and ethnic cleansing – all in the name of the "ethnic homeland", as described below. Yet, this state–ethnicity–territory axis has been largely taken for granted by theorists – conservative and critical alike. They have simply assumed the ethnicized nature of space as an unproblematic point of departure, or wished it away as a temporary relic of the past. The theoretical literature has thus shifted attention away from a major force of controlling space and shaping social relations. My call is to foreground the never-ending struggle for ethnicizing space as part and parcel of theorizing planning. This requires treating the nation-state as a dynamic force internal to the planning endeavor, and not a "flat" and unexplored platform. This is particularly so in cases of "homeland" ethnic groups.[9]

The homeland can be defined as a territory believed to be the "birthplace" of a group's identity. It is often associated with a state scale, where ethno-nationalism has been translated into a major force of territorial transformation. However, homeland mobilization manifests powerfully on other scales – the neighborhood ("urban turf"), the city, the region and in transstate situations. This is reflected in the multilayered meanings of the word in various languages. The Arabic *balad*, for example, denotes both village and country; *moledet* in Hebrew stands for place of birth and national land; and *rodina* in Russian stems from a word denoting either family origin, tree roots, or a state territory. To be sure, homeland sentiments and mobilization are often "artificially" constructed or invented outright, as in the case of "homelands" in the Soviet Union, or apartheid South Africa. Yet in dozens of states, regions and cities, the homeland "card" is critical for understanding the way space is planned, settled and transformed.

Ethnic attachment to the homeland frequently translates into a program of stamping exclusive ethnic control over contested territory. Here lies its direct relevance to planning scholarship, since the instruments with which ethnicization is practiced are often classical planning tools of development controls, investment incentives, housing programs, land allocation and boundary delimitation. The ethnic homeland is thus not a mere residual force which operates in some remote places as a relic of bygone pasts, but one of the most persistent, structural, and – most importantly – profoundly spatial forces shaping the outcome of planning policies. A cursory look around the globe would immediately illustrate the importance of homeland ethnicity for planning – from Quebec through Ireland, Spain, to virtually all the post-Soviet states, Africa, the Middle East and Asia. In fact, planning across the majority of the globe is deeply steeped in continuous ethnic struggles over space including, of course, major cities.

Yet, somewhat astonishingly, the homeland too has largely remained "untouched" in planning literature, as well as in urban and even geographic scholarship. Here are some indicators: the "homeland" is not even listed as an item in several important reference books and scholarly dictionaries (*Dictionary of Political Thought*, 1992; *Dictionary of Human Geography*, 1994; *Dictionary of Politics*, 1995). It is rarely mentioned in numerous urban, spatial and planning journals, readers and books; for example, in a search of a total of 414 scholarly pieces published by the six major planning journals mentioned earlier during the 2000–4 period, the term was mentioned in the title or abstract in only three articles; "ethnic" or "ethnicity" did not fare better, being mentioned only twice. By contrast, currently popular terms were discussed far more frequently; for example, "globalization" was mentioned in the title of 42 articles, and "communication" by 28.

These numbers, while obviously representing only a broad brush picture, reflect conspicuous blind-spots to major forces shaping spatial policy. These reflect the context, concern and challenges of the north-western societies in which the majority of theorists work. Since in most of the liberal North-West, ethnicity has by and large been privatized and homeland issues have been often appeased during the recent period of "long peace" and economic prosperity.

Given the above, how do we move forward and link planning theory with these issues? A promising option is to conduct "thick" comparable studies as a base for generalization about the origins and impact of policies and urban struggles. This kind of grounded theoretical work could form a necessary foundation for mobilizing both professionals and communities. These theories would be grounded in the actual context of cities and regions, defined both geographically (African, South Asian or Baltic) or thematically (informal, ethnocratic, global cities), with clear possibilities to "cut across" the North-West, South-East regions. Such theorizations are likely to "re-engage" theory with the "coal face" of the planning endeavor, thereby reducing the "degrees of removal" prevalent in current theoretical debates.

In this vein, I offer the concepts of "homeland" and "ethnicity" as possible new focal points for planning studies, based on the vantage point of the Middle East, Africa, Eastern Europe and South Asia. We need to show how ethnicity and homeland, alongside other issues of development and governance, have shaped cities and group relations, and how power has spawned resistance to the darker sides of planning. But we need to be watchful not to romanticize these concepts, while remaining critical of the regimes of planning "truths" in all settings, and the contested and manipulative nature of these very concepts. Nevertheless, homeland and ethnicity can form central components of "meso"-level planning theories, alongside the key concepts of class, capital, gender and governance processes.

Such investigation should also continue to explore the "dark side" of planning, as ethnic identities and "the homeland" are commonly used by dominant groups to create hegemonic and oppressive projects of reshaping space. These are often premised on the dispossession and marginalization of the "Other". But exposing the details of the "dark side" is never an end in itself, as recently implied by some critics of the concept. It is only the beginning of unpacking the distorted "truth" disseminated by power, as a necessary foundation for transformative mobilization, including the generation of innovative planning strategies to transgress oppression and actually improve people's lives and places.[10]

Here planning theorists can be at the forefront of devising resistance, empowerment and liberation strategies, based on their insights into the working of hegemonic (spatial) powers. They can equip planners – in Tallinn, Jerusalem, Gujarat, Colombo or hundreds of other cities – with a range of strategies to contest spatial oppression, developmental inequalities and essentialized ethnicities. They can devise ways to resist and transform the harsh realities of land confiscation, forced removals, home demolitions, pervasive poverty, and endemic urban violence in an urban environment where consensus building and public deliberation are only a distant possibility. They can lead the efforts to recognize and make sustainable multi-group coexistence in the city by putting planning "flesh" on concepts such as "spatial justice", "asymmetrical federalism", "multiple homelands" or new forms of self-determination. These have been articulated in the work of political thinkers John McGarry, Ranabir Samaddar and Iris Marion Young, respectively.

Let us conclude with a poem by Tawfiq Ziyyad, the late Palestinian leader and poet, who encapsulates the power of ethnicity and homeland embedded in the Palestinian strategy of Sumud – hanging on mentally and physically to their localities and lands, and refusing to fold in the face of Israeli expansionist planning strategies. The poem's invocation of spatial and ethnic struggles over Israel/Palestine, its reference to the legacy of past colonization and expulsion, and its linking of identities to specific place, all point to the very materials from which planning is remade daily in many south-eastern settings and through which it should be re-theorized and re-engaged with people's actual life and meanings.

> *We are Staying Here* (Hunna Baqoon)
>
> …We guard the shades of our figs
> We guard the trunks of our olives
> We sow our hopes like the yeast of bread
> With ice in our fingers
> With red hell in our hearts …
> Here we shall stay
> Like a brick wall on your chest
> Like a glass splinter in your throat
> Like a prickly cactus
> And in your eyes
> Like a storm of fire
> If we are thirsty, we shall be quenched by the rocks
> And if we are hungry, we shall be fed by the dust …
> And we shall not move
> Because here we have Past, Present
> And Future.
>
> (Tawfiq Ziyyad, 1978)

Notes

1 Given the polemic nature of this essay, I have refrained from extensive citations from the literature, although the many authors who contributed to the planning theory debate have naturally been my main source of inspiration. Details of the works mentioned here, including full references, are available from the author.

2 See works by Patsy Healey, Jean Hillier, John Forester, James Throgmorton, Seymour Mandelbaum, Tom Sager, Judith Innes, Phil Allmendinger, Michael Gunder, Stan Stein, and Thomas Harper, to name but a few leading theorists.

3 In comparison, my own scholarly and activist approach draws, intra alia, on neo-Gramscian and Lefebvrian inspirations, emphasizing the simultaneous material and discursive construction of hegemony and resistance.

4 See, for example, works by Susan Fainstein, Robert Beauregard, Tim Richardson, Bent Flyvbjerg, Leonie Sandercock, Manuel Castells, Michael Neuman, Margo Huxley, Emily Talen, Oren Yiftachel, Nezar al-Sayyad, Alan Mabin, and Ananya Roy. It is also noteworthy that two stalwarts of procedural planning theory – Andreas Faludi and John Friedmann – have openly re-grounded their recent work in the spatiality of city and region.

5 This kind of "engaged" scholarship does exist, mainly in fields including geography, anthropology, development studies, and political science; but being published in these disciplines it often loses a critical focus on policy implications, and is often unexplored by planning theorists.

6 The journals studied included the *JPER*, *Planning Theory*, *Town Planning Review*, *Planning Theory and Practice*, *JAPA* and *European Planning Studies*. Even on the board of *Third World Planning* (now under a new title – *International Development and Planning Review*), only six of 28 members are from the South-East.

7 See, for example, the groundbreaking works of Leonie Sandercock, Ruth Fincher, Jane Jacobs, and Iris Marion Young.

8 See here, for example, the works of Huw Thomas, Roderick Macdonald, Scott Bollen, Tovi Fenster, and Oren Yiftachel.

9 This is the approach taken by some scholars associated with "postcolonial" studies, including Ella Shohat, Derek Gregory, Don Mitchell, and Timothy Mitchell; recent work by Phil Harrison has attempted to bridge between this school of thought and planning theory.

10 A detailed response to the criticism of the "dark-side" concept and an elaboration of the concept is now in preparation.

References

Dictionary of Human Geography (1994) Oxford: Blackwell.

Dictionary of Political Thought (1992) New York: Pan.

Dictionary of Politics (1995) Cambridge: Polity.

Forester, J. (2006) "Making Participation work when Interests Conflict". Moving from Facilitating Dialogue and Moderating Debate to Mediating Negotiations', *Journal of the American Planning Association* 72(4): 247–56.

Watson, V. (2006) "Deep Difference Diversity Planning and Ethics", *Planning Theory* 5(1): 31–50.

Yiftachel, O. and Yacobi, H. (2004) "Urban Ethnocracy: Ethnicization and the Production of Space in an Israeli "Mixed" City", *Environment and Planning D: Society and Space* 21(3): 322–43.

Credits and Sources

The editors and publisher gratefully acknowledge the permission granted to reproduce the copyright material in this book.

Chapter 1   Robert Fishman, "Urban Utopias in the Twentieth Century: Ebenezer Howard, Frank Lloyd Wright, and Le Corbusier," from *Urban Utopias in the Twentieth Century: Ebenezer Howard, Frank Lloyd Wright, and Le Corbusier*, pp. 3–20, 23–6, 40–51, 226–34. © 1982 Massachusetts Institute of Technology, by permission of The MIT Press.

Chapter 2   James C. Scott, "Authoritarian High Modernism," from *Seeing Like a State: How Certain Schemes to Improve the Human Condition Have Failed*, pp. 87–102, 376–81, Yale University Press, 1998. © Yale University Press.

Chapter 3   Jane Jacobs, "The Death and Life of Great American Cities," from *The Death and Life of Great American Cities*, pp. 3–25. Copyright © 1961, 1989 by Jane Jacobs, published by Jonathan Cape. Reprinted by permission of The Random House Group Ltd.

Chapter 4   John Friedmann, "The Good City: In Defense of Utopian Thinking," *International Journal for Urban and Regional Research*, 24, 2 (2000), pp. 460–72.

Chapter 5   Heather Campbell and Robert Marshall, "Utilitarianism's Bad Breath? A Re-evaluation of the Public Interest Justification for Planning," *Planning Theory*, 1 (2) (2002), pp. 164–86. Copyright © 2002 by Sage Publications. Reprinted by permission of Sage.

Chapter 6   Richard E. Fogelsong, *Planning the Capitalist City*, pp. 18–24. © 1986 Princeton University Press. Reprinted by permission of Princeton University Press.

Chapter 7   Tim Love, "Urban Design after *Battery Park City*: Opportunities for Variety and Vitality in Large-Scale Urban Real Estate Developments" *Harvard Design Magazine*, 25, (Fall 2006/Winter 2007), pp. 60–9. Reproduced by permission of Tim Love.

Index

Note: The letters *f*, *t*, and *n* after page numbers refer respectively to figures, tables, and notes.

Readings in Planning Theory, Third Edition. Edited by Susan S. Fainstein and Scott Campbell.
Editorial material and organization © 2012 Blackwell Publishing Ltd.
Published 2012 by Blackwell Publishing Ltd.